applied
PSYCHOLOGY

Hugh Coolican
Tony Cassidy
Amar Cherchar
Julie Harrower
Gillian Penny
Rob Sharp
Malcolm Walley
Tony Westbury

Hodder & Stoughton

A MEMBER OF THE HODDER HEADLINE GROUP

Dedication

To Ama, my mother-in-law, without whom this book could never have been completed.

Orders: please contact Bookpoint Ltd, 130 Milton Park, Abingdon, Oxon OX 14 4SB. Telephone: (44) 01235 827720, Fax: (44) 01235 400454. Lines are open from 9.00-6.00, Monday to Saturday, with a 24 hour message answering service.

British Library Cataloguing in Publication Data
A catalogue record for this title is available from The British Library

ISBN 0 340 63092 2

First published 1996
Impression number   10   9   8
Year   2004   2003

Papers used in this book are natural, renewable and recyclable products. They are made from wood grown in sustainable forests. The logging and manufacturing processes conform to the environmental regulations of the country of origin.

Typeset by Wearset, Boldon, Tyne and Wear.
Printed in Great Britain for Hodder & Stoughton Educational, a division of Hodder Headline, 338 Euston Road, London NW 1 3BH by J. W. Arrowsmith Ltd., Bristol.

CONTENTS

Working with children: implications of education acts; special educational needs; assessment and testing. Working with schools: consultancy models; theories of learning in education; motivation to learn; teacher behaviour and style; pupil behaviour; problem behaviour in schools; gender differences in education; whole school approaches. Family, school and community: home, early learning and school; compensatory education; parental involvement; community and culture. Unique aspects of the work of the educational psychologist

Interpreting the environment: environmental perception; the carpentered world hypothesis; social influence and attitude; environmental personality. The impact of the environment: behaviour settings; emotion and motivation; environmental stress - noise, weather, cataclysmic events. Living in the environment: proxemics; personal space; territoriality; crowding; privacy. Use of environmental resources. Basic principles revisited

Health behaviour: the health belief model; theory of reasoned action; theory of planned behaviour; primary prevention. Changing health behaviour: attitude change and behavioural approaches. Life stress, coping and illness: approaches to the study of stress; the effects of stressful experiences on health. Type 'A' behaviour and coronary heart disease: measurement of type 'A' behaviour; the relationship between type 'A' behaviour and coronary heart disease; reducing type 'A' behaviour. Medical settings - patient-practitioner communication and adherence to treatment. Pain and pain management

Personnel psychology: personnel selection and assessment; measurement of people and jobs; job analysis; improving the job-person fit; personnel selection in practice. Training and development: training, education and the psychological theory of learning; training models. Motivation: work attitudes and job design; goal setting theory; socio-technical systems approach. Organisational psychology - group processes: group formation and norms and their influence on the individual; group cohesiveness; leadership; intra-group conflict and its reduction; inter-group behaviour; group polarisation; communication in groups and organisations. Organisations as whole units: organisational culture, climate and development

Gender perspectives in sport. Sport and personality. Motivation in sport: drive theory; cognitive perspectives; achievement motivation. Anxiety in sport: anxiety behaviour, feeling and thought; the stress process in sport; conceptual development in sport anxiety. Introducing skill: the information processing model; theories, practice and testing of motor learning; theories of motor control. Exercise psychology: psychological benefits; participation motives; exercise adherence. Aggression in sport: theories and research; reducing aggression in sport

APPENDIX 1: THE MAJOR THEORETICAL APPROACHES WITHIN APPLIED PSYCHOLOGY

Levels of explanation in psychological theories. Philosophical issues - mind, body, freewill and determinism. Psychological approaches and applications: the psychoanalytic approach; the behaviourist approach; the cognitive approach; the biological approach; the humanist approach; the value of different approaches - eclectism

APPENDIX 2: METHODS FOR THE PRODUCTION OF RESEARCH AND PRACTICE DATA

Places for research: laboratory vs field; problems with the laboratory. Types of research: experiments, quasi-experiments and correlation. Sampling, field data and other problems: the quantitative-qualitative debate. Asking questions: questionnaires, scales and tests; interviews. Observation: controlled, naturalistic and participant observation. Case studies. Measurement and statistics: descriptive and inferential statistics; the concept of significance

APPENDIX 3: THE CODE OF CONDUCT AND ETHICAL PRINCIPLES FOR CONDUCTING RESEARCH WITH HUMAN PARTICIPANTS (BRITISH PSYCHOLOGICAL SOCIETY)

PREFACE

There is a lot going on in applied psychology. The television series *Cracker* has popularised a glamorous and distorted image of a police psychologist. I talked today with a new student, interested in a police career and attracted to psychology mainly by this programme. In reality, forensic or criminological psychologists keep out of the public eye but they *do* achieve some success in the profiling of criminals and in the investigation of courtroom behaviour. Educational psychologists are grappling with rapid changes in government thinking on educational policy, dealing with a widening variety of special needs and looking nervously over their shoulders at hints of privatisation. Clinical psychologists, subject to the same economic concerns, are engaging in debate about their special role in the health service, about 'care in the community' and even about authority to prescribe drugs, whilst their qualifying courses are extended and can now provide doctorates. Occupational psychologists may improve the selection and training of employees but they also deal increasingly with problems of stress and unemployment, both apparently permanent effects of a highly technological and competitive world of work. Growing numbers of health and sport psychologists are attempting to contribute towards a healthier population in the 21st century, whilst environmental psychologists may discourage the psychologically unhealthy housing and commercial developments of earlier decades and may help us care for where we live.

A vast majority of psychology undergraduates are attracted to the subject because they are interested in eventual jobs with people, mostly in some sort of caring capacity. Relatively few wish to progress to research in what would, until recently, have been considered the core of the subject – for instance experimental, cognitive or social psychology. Psychology teaching, therefore, must respond to this demand and help students discover that they can indeed do interesting things when they have acquired expertise in the analytic and research skills of academic psychology. Courses in applied psychology are expanding and multiplying. But is applied psychology a breakthrough? Are mainstream psychology research findings suddenly, as never before, being applied to the solution of problems in practical life? Is this a new area or direction? Not really. One of the most intriguing insights I had as I read through the various contributions to this book was just *how much* of what I once learnt as 'mainstream psychology' was, in fact, produced or at least prompted by psychologists tackling practical real-life problems in education, the workplace and even in wartime.

Throughout this book you will discover that applied psychologists do indeed apply psychology to people's problems, but they also *make* psychology, and they make it through the practice of psychology as both a science and an art. This book, then, does not confine itself to describing 'how psychology is applied to real life', as though there were an independent body of psychological knowledge on the shelf waiting to be used. In each chapter it takes a 'what applied psychologists *do*' approach, though it will eventually tell you how research is applied along with tales of how research has been generated through practical investigation of people's problems and challenges.

This book was mainly written by staff at Nene College, Northampton. We were prompted by finding no adequate text to use with our own students. One or two volumes have appeared since we started and we hope ours can take its place alongside these, reflecting our particular perspectives and experience. No book can be perfect and we welcome any advice or comments which might help us promote clearer understanding of the issues and debates in applied psychology – this being the one overriding objective of the book.

I would like to use this preface to thank the members of the author team, my colleagues who have provided material from their specialisms. Alphabetically then... Tony Cassidy teaches environmental and community psychology; Amar Cherchar teaches work psychology; Julie Harrower teaches criminological psychology; Gillian Penny teaches health psychology; Rob Sharp is a practising educational psychologist in Hertfordshire; Malcolm Walley and Tony Westbury teach sport psychology. I have interests in occupational psychology and in the teaching of so-called abnormal psychology, along with general methods and statistics. I very much hope that you can enjoy and benefit from the knowledge and the great effort the team has put into this project.

Hugh Coolican

Working with this book

- To help you break the barrier of psychological jargon, we have included a glossary of terms. All terms that appear in the glossary are indicated in SMALL CAPITALS in the main text. Glossary terms are indicated with a **bold** page entry in the Index at the back of this book.
- At the end of each of the main chapters, there are exercises for you to work on either alone or with your fellow learners.
- For students new to the field of psychology, Appendix 1 offers a summary of the major theoretical approaches, whilst Appendix 2 explores the research methods used in the discipline.

Acknowledgements

The author team would like to thank the following:

Ray Cochrane, University of Birmingham for a very useful article; Adrian Nelson at UMIST for materials; Dawn Leeming at Nene College for some useful advice; Marc Rostock at Nene College for help with error checking; Lynn Mancey for her patience in typing the educational chapter; the BPS for provision of various materials; Louise Tooms, Julie Hill and Tim Gregson-Williams at Hodder and Stoughton for their hard work and endless patience in pulling things together at their end.

1 INTRODUCTION TO APPLIED PSYCHOLOGY

GENERAL INTRODUCTION

When I told family and friends that I was going to university to study psychology, rather than maths and physics in which I had A levels, one of the common replies was, 'Ah, that's all very well, but what can you do with it?' I must admit, at the time, I had no idea what was done with psychology, apart from the popular image of the bearded psychoanalyst at work with his sofa-lying client (yes, the analyst *was* usually male). This book is all about what psychologists actually do with psychology.

If you are contemplating a career in psychology, the time could probably not be better, though, as we shall see, the route may be long and arduous and, in some areas, training is hard to come by. However,

'Demands for the services of professional applied psychologists are increasing and are outstripping the increase in personnel available to meet them.'

(Lindsay and Lunt, 1993)

Until just after the Second World War it would be rare to meet a psychologist who was working independently outside the academic world of university teaching and research. In this book most examples of applied work in the field before that time come from workers in the United States, or from UK researchers based in universities, who largely kept their results within the institution. The situation has changed enormously in the meantime. Box 2 shows the variety of fields in which psychologists now work as psychology professionals. Since the majority of these, the most active and popular areas, are covered by the next seven chapters of this book, each including a section on development, we shall not cover the 'development of applied psychology' in general at this point. There are, however, a few points which are best dealt with here rather than under each specialism.

WHAT IS APPLIED PSYCHOLOGY?

The term 'applied psychology' can summon up an image of psychologists working in a rarefied scientific atmosphere, making grand discoveries about human behaviour, thinking or personality, and then sallying forth to apply these findings, either in the interest of humankind (by 'fixing' personal problems; giving an athlete that ultimate extra 'fizz'; discovering the profile of serial killers) or in the interest of efficiency and (often therefore) profit (by improving worker–manager relations; enhancing management team motivation; manipulating perceptions through advertising). These are indeed among the many sorts of thing that applied psychologists have attempted to achieve. However, the research–application link is by no means a one-way route. Many of the classic findings of psychological research have been the result of problems in the field of application or a direct result of applications themselves. Examples would be:

- the development of intelligence tests, initiated by a French Government attempt to identify children with learning difficulties and give 'remedial' education
- much of the original work on attitude change, developed through the US government's attempts to boost fighting forces' morale in the Far East at the end of World War Two, or through attempts to educate the public on health issues such as regular cleaning of teeth or the beneficial effects of eating offal
- the whole of the psychoanalytic 'school' (or approach to understanding humans), originally founded on the work of a few doctors (especially Freud) working with a relatively small number of psychologically disturbed patients
- Freud's influence on psychoanalysts and psychologists (especially Bowlby) working with delinquent and/or deprived children and their problems, from whom we inherited much of the controversial theory concerning infants' attachment to their main caregiver.

Human problems: understanding and change

What are applied psychologists about? What defines them exactly? A starting point is to talk about problems, about solving them and, therefore, about changing human experience and behaviour. A psychologist who is interested in *pure* or BASIC RESEARCH will want to *understand* human behaviour and experience. The overall aim of most *applied* psychological work is to produce some form of *change* in human behaviour or experience. The usual aim is to solve a problem with some form of *intervention*. To create change one must *understand* first. Hence, applied psychologists are, of necessity, extremely interested in the products of basic research. They may look to research to guide them in any specific intervention with clients. However, they may, at the same time, *create* research findings as a result of their interventions.

Applied psychologists: looking for solutions

The applied psychologists whose practical daily work is described in this book almost invariably began their professional lives *as* applied psychologists having completed an undergraduate degree in psychology, followed (but not necessarily immediately) by a further course of study and training practice, usually lasting not less than two years and often resulting in a higher degree title, such as MSc or PhD. Nevertheless it is hardly the case that applied psychologists encounter a problem in everyday working life and simply consult their mental or physical library of psychological theories, picking a procedure off the shelf to provide *the* correct solution. Imagine a comparable situation involving the 'hard' sciences. The projects manager at Cereal Toys plc is given a problem one morning: 'Look Julia, we've got a great design but we need some scientific input on this one. We need a container for this toy submarine strong enough to hold a spring. The container needs to be made of some non-toxic, edible material which slowly disintegrates on submersion in milk, so that, eventually, it is too weak to withstand the spring and the submarine will pop out of the little kid's cereal bowl! Can you get the boffins downstairs onto this one in a hurry?'

The 'boffins' will work in an entirely systematic and scientific manner, drawing upon a store of known properties of chemicals and, in the case of some projects, theories of why some matter behaves as it does. The theories employed are usually so well and accurately tested that predictions can be made and progress achieved quite rapidly so long as the problems require no breaking of new frontiers. There is no one correct path here either. The scientists may have several possible solutions but each one of them will be effective – it *will* work.

The situation in psychology could never be so clear cut. There is very little theory or factual knowledge within psychology which will *guarantee* that a solution to a problem will 'work' every time it is tried or that it will 'work' on identified individuals. Some psychotherapies are known to be better than others, but none can be absolutely guaranteed to have a positive effect on all those to whom it is administered. Similarly, there are popular ways to motivate a workforce or attempt to change attitudes on health issues. But people just aren't much like those little submarines in the cereal product problem. Each one will *not* behave in the same way as another even though external circumstances are almost identical. Toy submarines vary ever so slightly, but not enough to upset the outcome of well-worked equations. People vary enormously and psychologists' ability to predict performance from a known history and with control over several current variables is exceedingly crude, compared with the control that cereal toy boffins can exert over bits of plastic. Furthermore, there are very few known 'facts' of psychology and there is no one theory that is absolutely 'correct'. Physicists may argue that their theories also always need some revision and are never just neatly *true*. However, it *is* possible,

in physics and chemistry, to use known theory to make precise predictions. The calibre of predictive accuracy in mainstream psychological research is just not in anything like the same category.

A depressing start? A great failure that we can't just employ psychology to solve human problems with great confidence of success and run-of-the-mill accuracy? Not really. It was never imagined, except by some very rare romantics within the subject, and many sci-fi film directors, that psychology would eventually attain such fine-grained power to predict and control *individual* human behaviour. On the other hand, before psychology was born as a research subject, there were plenty of managers and leaders able to control people effectively and make relatively accurate predictions about large numbers of people at a time. Most of the research knowledge in mainstream psychology is based on studies of groups of people rather than individuals. We can't usually predict that a memorising technique will produce improvement in any particular individual but we can be fairly confident that overall performance in a group of say 15 to 20 people will be superior using the technique.

So where do applied psychologists fit in here? What can they add? Non-psychologists can control groups of people and predict their behaviour. Psychologists cannot predict much *individual* behaviour very accurately. Many problems confronting the applied psychologist, particularly in clinical and educational psychology, concern specific individuals. If all the knowledge and theory of psychology do not equip the applied psychologist to do better in predicting the behaviour of one individual than might any thoughtful person simply using 'common sense', then what is it that makes psychologists unique and valuable? Why should anyone employ and pay them to help solve problems?

The special role of the applied psychologist

Applied psychologists *do* have qualities that the thoughtful manager or observant user of common sense do not possess. Let us consider a few.

1. Use of scientific method

In all the categories of application covered by this book, most working psychologists would claim to make use of the SCIENTIFIC METHOD in approaching the problem-solving they are required to carry out in their professional activities. There are several ways in which this might occur, but let's first have a quick *résumé* of what is meant by scientific method. Box 1 gives the generally recognised stages used in the method and a concrete example might make the meaning of the whole process a little clearer.

We might observe that certain classes in several schools do substantially better, on a regular basis, in the A level psychology exam each year. We interview as many students from these classes as we can and find that students with high pre-exam confidence tend to do better in their exams. It could be that the confidence just stems from the students being academically good. We can rule out this factor as a complete explanation of their exam success by comparing them with other A level psychology students who are academically equal but lacking in confidence just prior to the exam. Suppose we find that, in this comparison, the

more confident students again do better. We conduct some interviews and it emerges that two factors could be responsible for the higher confidence levels and consequent exam pass rate: tutors in the successful classes give particularly full and usefully detailed summary notes and exercises in a consistent manner each week; also these tutors include a good deal of group discussion in their teaching approach. We could now set up an EXPERIMENT in which we give one group the discussion method, one group the full notes treatment, and give both methods to a third group.

Let us suppose that the full notes group does significantly better than the discussion-only group and that the group receiving both treatments does no better than the full notes group. ('Significant', roughly meaning non-coincidental, is a term explained in Appendix 2 for those who have not already encountered this social science term.) The two better groups also have higher confidence levels prior to the exam.

We have observed a regularity – more successful classes. We have attempted to relate accompanying variables – including confidence, ability, full notes method and discussion method. We have ruled out ability as the vital factor making one group perform better *as a whole*. We have formu-

BOX 1

Stages in the traditional scientific method

Observation: collect measurements, data, 'facts', collect verbal information, descriptions

Induction: extrapolate 'laws' – assume relationship between X and Y, e.g. more attractive defendants get lighter sentences

Theory production: produce explanation(s) which would predict the relationships found above, e.g. assume that people's judgement of a person's guilt and culpability depend in part on a person's attractiveness; suggested relationships or explanations are often referred to as 'models'

Hypothesis testing: develop specific investi-

gation designed to test the theory, e.g. under controlled conditions give people identical description of crime and criminal but vary *only* the defendant's attractiveness

Data collection and analysis: analyse results – look for significant differences or relationships, e.g. do people give higher sentences to the less attractive criminal, beyond the level of coincidental difference? Do they give quite different descriptions?

Support, rejection or modification of theory: results are fed back into the thinking cycle, e.g. if we get a significant difference between our two conditions we support our theory of discrimination through attractiveness. If we do *not* get a difference, we can either reject the theory or look for improvements in our testing design lated hypotheses that one or other of two further variables (the teaching methods), under well-controlled conditions, will produce improved confidence and consequent higher exam grades. We have tested these hypotheses and found that the full notes method is specifically related to higher confidence and exam performance under controlled conditions. This will *support*, but not *prove*, the notion that the full notes method is an important causal factor in producing confidence and subsequent good exam grades. In Appendix 2 further possible explanations are explored.

An experiment may not have been possible or desirable here. Applied psychologists use interviews, OBSERVATION, SURVEYS, QUESTIONNAIRES and a host of other methods. All are used to gather data and test HYPOTHESES or otherwise develop and test models with which to attempt an understanding of what is important in the production and changing of human experience and behaviour. These methods, and a brief introduction to how social scientists decide whether apparent trends in results can be taken seriously, are briefly described in Appendix 2.

What makes the applied psychologist more rigorous than the user of common sense then, is the application of this structured thinking and investigation process:

- to research within the psychologist's domain of applied psychology
- to practical problems in everyday work situations (schools, hospitals etc.)
- in attempts to tackle individual problems and change behaviour.

The difference between the applied psychologist and journalists (who also investigate human behaviour, in a sense) or the thoughtful manager is that the latter will often not have the training, nor feel they can spare the time, to go back, check and strengthen a hypothesis by ruling out alternatives (as was achieved with the confidence comparison). They may not recognise that the full notes hypothesis, currently, is only *supported*. They may forge ahead assuming they have found the 'magic formula'. The applied psychologist will be alert for CONFOUNDING VARIABLES (explained in Appendix 2), such as particular teacher qualities and other teaching techniques, which occur along with giving full notes and which may, instead, be the effective success factor.

The method of scientific thinking and hypothesis testing can be practised with individual clients (see the example of Keith, the custard pie phobic in the clinical psychology chapter). Freud felt that he was using a fully scientific approach in his psychoanalytic interviews, and he used the information to form psychological ideas which have significantly altered the pattern of twentieth-century models of human thought and behaviour. Most applied psychologists will concur that this is one of the main features which sets them apart from other professional practitioners working within their field.

What sort of science is psychology if at all?

We should state now that there is a strong current debate about what exactly constitutes a true scientific approach in psychology and whether the conventional model, as outlined here, is really appropriate to a human social science rather than a 'hard' physical science. A taste of this debate is encountered in Appendix 2 with the discussion of QUANTITATIVE and QUALITATIVE methods. For a critique of gender bias in psychological science and a feminist view of science as 'masculinised', see Wilkinson (1989), Ussher (1992), Paludi (1992) and Tavris (1993).

Paradigms

A further reservation which should be expressed here about psychology as a science is the fact that, as yet, there has emerged no single, over-arching PARADIGM which unites researchers in their study of human psychology. A *paradigm* is a framework of major principles which guide investigation. Within it, hypotheses are tested and the results can be fitted into an existing near universally agreed structure of explanation. We once had the paradigm of Newtonian physics and, in the 20th century, this was supplanted by Einstein's system. In the biological sciences, most researchers are united by the paradigm of evolution initiated by Darwin. A little later we shall see that there are PSYCHOANALYTIC, BEHAVIOURIST, COGNITIVE and HUMANIST approaches to understanding and explaining human experience and behaviour, but none of these is a near universally accepted paradigm.

2. Membership of a professional learned body

The role of the British Psychological Society (BPS)

The BPS is the national organisation which acts as the professional and academic reference point for all psychologists in the UK. Founded in 1901 and incorporated as a company in 1941, the Society was granted a Royal Charter in 1965 and important amendments to this, concerning the chartering of psychologists, were granted in 1987. Some of the society's principal aims are:

- 'to promote the advancement and diffusion of a knowledge of psychology pure and applied and especially to promote the efficiency and usefulness of Members of the Society by setting up a high standard of professional education and knowledge'
- to maintain a Code of Conduct including 'strict rules of professional conduct' – see Appendix 3
- to maintain a Register of Chartered Psychologists
- to provide resources for 'promoting invention and research in psychological science, or its applications'
- to print, publish and circulate papers, books and other communications on psychology created through work related to the Society.

(BPS, 1994a)

Apart from various boards and standing committees on subjects such as the Scientific Affairs Board and Disciplinary Board, the BPS contains several scientific groups (Sections) and professional groupings (Divisions and Special Groups). Note that some of the applied areas covered by this book are Divisions. Health is a Special Group. Sport appeared as a Section for the first time in 1993. Environmental psychology receives no mention. There are few practising environmental psychologists as such, and, presumably, not yet enough clear separation of the area or interested individuals to form a Section or Special Group, though a grouping is highly likely in the future.

BOX 2

Active fields of applied psychology

Clinical	Environmental
Community	Health
Counselling	Occupational/work/organisational
Criminological/forensic	Sport
Educational	

BOX 3

Divisions, Sections and Special Groups of the BPS

(numbers denote 1997 membership figures)

Sections
Psychotherapy	661
Education	828
Occupational	2398
Social	836
Mathematical, Statistical and Computing	198
Developmental	814
Cognitive	705
Psychobiology	277
Occupational Psychology	1145
History and Philosophy	225
Psychology of Women	548
Sport and Exercise	343
Consciousness/experiential	269
Transpersonal	278

Divisions
Educational and Child Psychology	1153
Educational (Scottish division)	141
Clinical Psychology	3474
Criminological and Legal Psychology	494
Counselling Psychology	1226

Special Groups
Teaching of Psychology	421
Psychologists in Central Government	77
Clinical Neuropsychology	327
Health Psychology	858

The address of the British Psychological Society is:
British Psychological Society
48 Princess Road East
Leicester
LE1 7DR
Tel 0116 254 9568

The stamp of authenticity

In recent years there have been disturbing media accounts of clients abused or taken advantage of by their therapists. There have been media debates concerning the usefulness of forensic psychologists after advice given to police about the highly specific features of an as yet unapprehended attacker was unwisely used. There are a plethora of exotic therapies, allegedly successful psychological treatments for illnesses as serious as cancer, armies of 'training consultants' offering psychological methods to management and even psychological methods to give your child an apparently enormous pre-school boost.

One role of the BPS is to validate any member as someone with sound psychological training. Since 1987 the BPS has maintained a Register of Chartered Psychologists the aim of which is to guarantee that Chartered Psychologists (those on the register) have appropriate practical training and academic achievement, satisfying rigorous standards. This work of the BPS is expanding quite quickly at present, for instance, in terms of qualification to carry out occupational testing and in its provision of training courses in occupational and counselling psychology and in the applied psychology of teaching.

The Register does not have the independent strength of the national register of nurses or doctors where any unregistered person practising and claiming to be a nurse or doctor would be committing a criminal offence. It is perfectly legal to call yourself a 'psychologist' even though you have never taken a course in psychology, let alone obtained a degree or a further course of training. However, it is to be hoped that the Register will become more widely known and that people requiring the services of a psychologist will consult it in the knowledge that members can be 'struck off' for incompetence or unprofessional conduct and that chartered status acts as a 'Kitemark' for professional competence in much

the same way as Kitemarks do for other professions and construction or engineering organisations.

Chartered psychologists use the title 'C. Psychol'. In addition they may describe themselves according to their specialism:

- Chartered Clinical Psychologist
- Chartered Educational Psychologist
- Chartered Occupational Psychologist
- Chartered Forensic Psychologist
- Chartered Counselling Psychologist.

3. *Drawing on a body of knowledge and theory*

Although there is no one correct theory or approach within psychology, or an ability to predict exactly how individuals will react to various conditions, there is, nevertheless, a body of research knowledge, theory and debate upon which the trained psychologist can draw. How is this body drawn upon if not just to obtain the 'facts' or relevant equation? Trained psychologists know how to *evaluate* a theory and research findings. They will know that such and such an approach has produced some good results but they will also attempt to discover its limitations, either through practice or by reading up on research and professional literature. They will know how to extend the findings of other researchers in a careful and well-controlled manner and they will know how to apply the most appropriate assessment techniques available. Trained psychologists use a body of knowledge *and* the skills of assessment, analysis, evaluation, hypothesis development and hypothesis testing. Much of this they have learned from their academic studies, but the practising psychologist has also developed what some consider to be the *art* of applying an appropriate method and theory at a particular time.

4. *Interventions and their evaluation*

A primary aim of applied psychologists is to *help*. By this it is meant, in broader terms, that a major goal is the alleviation of hardship, the development of full human potential and the promotion of people's opportunities within society. To achieve these aims, professional applied psychologists take on real-world problems. That is, they tackle problems in a working organisation or with individual clients with immediate difficulties. The psychologist's role in an INTERVENTION programme can be seen as occurring in several fairly well-defined stages:

Contact with the client (individual or organisation)

The client may come hesitantly to the psychologist as when, for instance, the clinical psychologist acts as therapist. The client may expect a service without question and as a right, as in the relationship between schools and educational psychologists in the none-too-distant past. Again, the client may approach the psychologist on a business consultancy basis, as when a company contacts an occupational psychologist. The psychologist may get involved as a member of a team (say, of health professionals tackling a public health awareness programme), through a branch of their academic research, or because they are already employed by the organisation requiring an intervention.

Assessment

Having discussed and considered with the client(s) the general problem to be tackled the applied psychologist will set about initial ASSESSMENT of the difficulties and issues. This may include:

- discussion of the problem as seen by the client and the consideration of whether there really *is* a problem
- data collection through any of the methods outlined in Appendix 2, in particular, through interviews, observation and the administration of psychological assessment instruments
- analysis of problematic behaviour or systems (for instance, in a prison setting, the initial recording and analysis of occasions on which inmate frustrations rise to a critical level).

Diagnosis or formulation

It is at this point that the applied psychologist's background in scientific method, psychology and research becomes of crucial importance. Previous similar cases will be compared and successful treatments or interventions analysed for their relevance to this case. The *scientific* aspect of the SCIENTIST–PRACTITIONER ROLE includes the application of a *model* (working theory or preferred approach) and the generation of hypotheses. Having formed such hypotheses, predictions might be made and initial tests of confirmation applied. For instance, the criminological psychologist might predict the circumstances provoking prison disturbances and await the next outbreak for confirmation. The health psychologist might look for regions in which certain forms of publicity appear to have worked.

Construction of the intervention programme

Here is where the implications of the analysis already carried out are put into practical terms. The psychologist, other team members and the client (in most cases) draw up a specific course of action to be taken which is intended to resolve a problem or improve a situation. It is very important at this stage to define exactly what will be counted as showing that the intervention 'worked'. This is done by specifying desired or expected outcomes – what it is hoped will be achieved. These must be OPERATIONALLY DEFINED (see Appendix 2) so that the evaluation stage (see below) can have definite measures to work with in assessing the success or otherwise of the intervention. For instance, 'aggression' reduction in a disturbed child might be specified as an 80% drop in the child's hitting rate. Increased athlete motivation might be measured in consistent performances above the current average. Worker satisfaction might be measured by increased positive statements made at weekly appraisal sessions, by a lower frequency of disputes, by increased factory output, and so on.

Implementation of the intervention programme

Implementation may involve a lot of people in quite different roles. It will almost certainly involve consideration of a number of ethical and practical issues too vast to discuss thoroughly here. However, some main features of this stage can be listed for reference and further thought. Here, the 'change-agent' is either the psychologist or a team of professionals implementing change and the 'client group' are those people who are the focus of intended change (say a departmental workforce, or some children whose behaviour is difficult to handle). In this sense the 'client group' could be just one individual as is often the case in clinical psychology.

Information   Decisions must be made as to how much information is dissipated. There will be an extent to which the client group is aware of the nature or existence of the programme. There will also be an extent to which information on progress is made available to the client group and to other people working or associated with it, for instance the family or care staff working with a child with severe learning difficulties.

Ethics   These decisions necessarily involve very detailed consideration of ethical issues. It might be argued that the client group should have been made aware. In some cases a careful watch must be kept on the extent to which the intervention is resisted or rejected. Confidentiality of any information gathered is extremely important (see Code of Conduct and Professional Ethics below). The psychologist may discover a conflict of interest only after the implementation is in progress. For instance, an employer's ulterior motive to fire staff using intervention findings may only be revealed when a programme is already under way and where the *declared* aim was to improve staff morale and efficiency.

Contracts   In part answer to the ethical points, but also to ensure that all are informed, committed and agreed, the change-agents and client group would usually draw up and agree contracts on all important stages, terms and principles of the intervention.

Monitoring and feedback   A constant watch must be kept on progress. It must be clearly agreed in advance at what point certain aspects of the intervention will be brought to an end or at what point new measures will be taken or new stages implemented. This depends very strongly on the agreed outcome measures.

Unexpected outcomes   As a result of close monitoring, any unexpected changes in client group behaviour or other outcome measures will need to be dealt with. Children's behaviour might unexpectedly deteriorate because of an unanticipated

variable – they 'rebel' against a scheme of withdrawing privileges, for instance. Workers may unite to slow down production in protest at the presence of 'alien' observers. Appropriate and previously unplanned responses to these outcomes must be produced quickly, whilst keeping in the spirit of the original model on which the intervention is based.

Evaluation
At some point a decision must be made about whether the intervention has achieved what it was meant to achieve. Did it work? How well did it work? If outcome measures were clearly specified at the start these decisions will be made easier. Further very important questions remain. The answers to these serve as valuable knowledge with which to increase general knowledge in the psychologist's area of expertise and to guide solutions to similar problems in the future. These questions include:

- what were the overall costs and benefits of the intervention?
- were particular individuals helped and/or was the intervention beneficial to the whole client group?
- what implications are there for the model upon which the intervention was based? Do we have further support or contradiction of the background theory? If the latter, how can further research help clarify any conflict in results?
- what was the particular value of the *psychological aspects* of this intervention?
- what is the next step for the client (group)? Should the intervention strategy continue? Is there another step with which to make progress?
- what practical and ethical issues have arisen from which we have learned something? How will this be transmitted to other practitioners and agents of change (e.g. through a journal article)?

5. Code of conduct and professional ethics

Every student of psychology as an academic subject should soon encounter the issue of ethics in the conducting of psychological research with human participants. For a discussion of the major issues, see Coolican (1994). The principles outlined by the British Psychological Society (BPS, 1991) should certainly be stringently observed by all chartered psychologists and other members who make a living from psychology. However, it is the special relationship of applied psychology practitioners with their clients which makes ethical principles particularly significant here. The Code of Conduct and Ethical Principles for Conducting Research with Human Participants are included in full in Appendix 3. A word on several of the principles is appropriate.

'... the investigators may not have sufficient knowledge of the implications of any investigation for the participants.'

This is particularly so where, rather than testing individuals in a psychological laboratory or office, the investigation is carried out in the participants' workplace or home. Here the psychologist cannot be present on every working day to appreciate the subtleties of interactions, pressure from peers, superiors or care staff and the consequent sanctions or discomfort which participants might actually experience but be unable to report or act upon.

'... the best judge of whether an investigation will cause offence may be members of the population from which the participants in the research are to be drawn.'

There could be no more pertinent 'golden rule' applying to all the research cited in this book and to any research which the reader may one day wish to undertake. Nothing should ever be initiated with just an image of the participating population in mind. One should have encountered the people to be studied or, at least, people who are representative of the group(s) to which they belong. It is quite unacceptable, for instance, to enter into research with members of a minority ethnic group without first discovering what their common feelings, customs and thoughts about their social position are. Equally, this would apply to a prison population where it is not an agreed aspect of a criminal's sentence that they can be the subject of research without their permission.

Consent

The applied psychologist has to be especially vigilant that permission has been truly given in a free and unconditional manner. It is not wise simply to accept a manager's word that the workforce has been consulted and has agreed. Where children or adults with learning difficulties are the subjects of research, care must be taken to find the most sympathetic and genuinely understanding people concerned with the case.

Debriefing

The applied psychologist must maintain professionalism by fully explaining the purpose of any intervention carried out on people in their everyday work or home settings, especially where the research design has involved any deception of the participants. Their lives have been altered or at least significantly intruded upon. This is very different from the typical academic research situation (see below) where students or volunteers have participated in the researcher's design which is *extra* to their lives and (usually), at most, fascinating. This kind of research can be walked away from.

Withdrawal, confidentiality and protection

All of these take on special meanings in an applied setting. Can a worker or school pupil genuinely withdraw without some sanction, perhaps well hidden from the researcher, a sanction which could be applied long after that researcher has left the scene? Confidentiality is not just polite but again, could protect participants from serious future discomfort. The researcher is also responsible for the effects of the intervention. This might include discomfort or injury to a participant or client caused by a staff member carrying out an agreed programme of action.

Advice

The applied psychologist is very often in a fast-moving, real-work learning or caring environment. It is far easier here (than in the psychological research establishment) to be seen as an expert and to influence people. The psychologist must be sure that information given, whether intended as advice or not, is always based on the soundest of psychological research findings, theory and practice or is clearly given on an individual lay basis and not as part of professional expertise.

6. Production of practice and research data

As they engage in the application of theory and method, applied psychologists also *develop* theory through their gradually accumulating fund of findings, failures, successes and appropriate techniques. The theories may be termed 'local' in the sense that they do not apply to everyone, everywhere, but are useful in particular working contexts. This body of theory will be drawn upon in the applied psychologist's continuing professional practice. However, practitioners will also contribute important and useful findings to the general knowledge pool. This is accomplished through publication of their own research in journals, bulletins and newsletters, through conferences, meetings of local practitioners and interest networks, and, increasingly, through links with members of other professions.

Fundamental (basic) and applied research

It is worth drawing a distinction here between what is often called FUNDAMENTAL (or *basic*) and APPLIED RESEARCH. The crude notion here is that *applied* research tackles specific practical problems and is not geared to investigating general features of human behaviour, thinking or mental activity. Findings are therefore considered to have relatively 'local' application – they are not findings of universal principles but are largely limited to the applied situation in which they were developed. *Fundamental* research is seen as the type, as in any other science, where researchers are interested in furthering our knowledge of the subject in general for the sake of knowledge in itself, whether or not those findings can be applied to real-world problems. As several writers point out (e.g. Schönpflug, 1992), unlike the situation in 'hard' sciences such as physics, psychology has not experienced a two-step process whereby academic researchers make laboratory discoveries independent of real-life problems which are then applied at a later time ('off the shelf' as it were) by practical psychologists. Much psychological theory and research content has developed out of practical problems in the first place, whilst much

laboratory research has found little application in the real world. The reader who has studied academic psychology already may be surprised to find how much familiar work from their syllabus originated as attempted solutions to practical problems.

Middleton and Edwards (1985) suggest the terms 'theory-driven' and 'need-driven' be applied to various types of research depending upon whether it arose largely from an interest in abstract theory or a genuine interest in the people whose specific problem is being investigated. This division could be relatively independent of whether the investigating psychologists consider themselves as *applied* or *pure* researchers.

Gale (1994) points out that the crude and misleading distinction between pure (theory-oriented) and applied (problem-oriented) psychological research is challenged by the Scientific Affairs Board of the BPS (1988). This group proposed a *multi-dimensional* approach. Each research project or intervention can be described in terms of several dimensions:

- *context of the investigation*
  – laboratory, field or mixture of the two
- *nature of the problem*
  – theory-driven, need- or problem-driven
- *relevance of the outcome*
  – advance of theory; applicability to problems
- *generalisability*
  – across situations
  – across individuals
  – across groups
  – across tasks

Applied psychology as applied science or as psychological science?

In the world of clinical psychology, Shapiro (1985) argues that the idea of clinical psychology as an applied science should be dropped. That is, the notion of applied science implies that a validated set of scientific tests and procedures exists and that a practitioner merely *applies* these to practical problems (as in the practical problem at Cereal

Toys plc). Shapiro argues that a more appropriate model is to see clinical psychologists as engaged in *producing* science in their work, through their use of scientific method in everyday practice. This was outlined more generally under 'Use of scientific method' above. As you progress through this book, I hope it will become obvious that Shapiro's model applies to *all* applied psychological work and that applied psychology is not so much the application of tried and tested theories but a part of psychological science in action and in the making.

Areas of overlap in applied psychology work

As applied psychology grows in importance, as each specialism grows and expands to deal with an ever wider range of problems and issues, it is inevitable that once distinct applied areas will begin to overlap with one another. For instance, educational psychology was once pretty much confined to the testing and assessment of children in a mainstream educational context. Today however, educational psychologists will be engaged in the STATEMENTING of children with special educational needs. For a long time there has been co-operation with therapeutic services such as the Child Guidance Service and its successors. Though this kind of co-operation continues, some educational psychologists today will themselves be engaged in the creation, management and operation of therapy programmes, for instance with children who are difficult to manage in the school setting. Similarly, clinical psychologists can work inside hospitals alongside health psychologists. Occupational psychologists can be involved in counselling employees or in health-related programmes such as the provision of stress reduction programmes within a large company. Forensic psychologists may be involved in prison education programmes or in what amounts to therapy work with offenders and so on.

Challenges to applied psychologists

Changes in the role of professional psychologists and trends in service demands and delivery led to the setting up of a Professional Affairs Board by the BPS in 1990. An interim report of the activities and findings of this board can be found in Lindsay and Lunt (1993). This article raises several aspects of change in applied psychology which are worth mentioning here.

Europe   Training for applied psychologists tends to be quite different in the rest of Europe and the BPS will need to investigate the differences between training routes here and abroad in order to facilitate interchange of psychologists on an equivalent basis.

Transfer   At present to switch from one field of applied psychology to another requires almost complete retraining. With all the time this would involve the switch is in reality extremely rare. Continuing Professional Development (CPD) means organising training so that it is relevant and coherent to professional needs. The BPS currently has a committee involved in accreditation of CPD and it is possible that such training could facilitate easier but valid transfer.

Private–public, independent–central   There is a continuing political contradiction between centralisation (for instance, the National Curriculum) and devolution of power (for instance hospital trusts, local management of schools and their opportunity to 'opt out' of local authority control). In parallel, there is a continual move towards a commercial basis for services previously considered to be welfare provisions (e.g. management of health budgets in terms of provider and purchaser; privatisation of prison services). The climate has created a 'client–user' and 'provider–purchaser' mentality. This has particular relevance for educational and clinical psychologists who may yet find themselves working not for education or health authorities, but in some more independent and commercial manner. If and when this occurs, such practitioners may have something to learn from many of the occupational psychologists who have worked in a commercial manner for quite some time. Lindsay and Lunt argue that there may be one positive result from the lessening of emphasis on the education and health services as areas of employment for psychologists. This is that there could be a concentration on the *competencies* of professional psychologists, skills they share in general, and a lessening of the distinctions between one sort of practitioner and another.

THEORETICAL APPROACHES WITHIN APPLIED PSYCHOLOGY

A defining characteristic of applied psychologists at work, we have said, is their reliance on fundamental research, applied research and background theory in psychological science. Much of the research in psychology has been carried out within a framework of thinking provided by one of a few over-arching 'schools' of thought. These are also often known as 'approaches', 'perspectives' or, at times, just 'theories'.

The reader who has tackled no psychology at all before reading this book might like to consult a general textbook in order to become familiar with the major schools of thought in the history of psychology's 100 years or so of development as a theoretical and scientific research discipline. Space will not permit a thorough grounding here. However, as with research methods (see Appendix 2), to appreciate the general outline of the approaches and to refresh those psychology students who don't wish to consult old notes or other texts (and to save our authors repeating themselves in each chapter!), Appendix 1 provides a brief outline of major approaches and general theoretical issues in psychology.

2 CLINICAL PSYCHOLOGY

WHAT IS CLINICAL PSYCHOLOGY?

Dealing with psychological problems

Clinical psychology deals primarily with the alleviation of people's psychological problems. There are a bewildering variety of practitioners who claim to be able to help those people unfortunate enough to be termed as 'suffering from a psychological problem'. We have PSYCHIATRISTS, (community) psychiatric nurses, psychotherapists, priests, counsellors, hypnotherapists, aromatherapists, primal therapists, and any number of others. Many professionals who do not have therapy as their essential occupational role nevertheless deal with individual psychological problems as part of their work. These include social workers, nurses, probation officers, teachers, managers and personnel officers.

What unique qualities or roles mark out the clinical psychologist from all these others?

The first major distinction to make is between the psychiatrist and all others. Only the psychiatrist needs to have qualified in medicine (is a doctor) and has the authority to prescribe drugs (although

there is a debate in the USA at present in which clinical psychologists are arguing for authority to write drug prescriptions; see also Wardle and Jackson (1995) for a UK argument). A second major distinction is between the clinical psychologist, as *therapist*, and all other therapists. Any person may put up a plaque outside their house claiming to be a 'psychotherapist'. There is no legal definition of this term. A *clinical psychologist*, however, will have the qualifications and training described in Box 3. Counsellors are a specialist group, usually with psychological qualifications but again with no legal status. They offer help, support and advice of a specialised psychological type and this will be discussed later on.

What are the principles of clinical psychology?

We shall see what clinical psychologists actually do in a short while, but let's now look at the defining features of the specialism.

First In common with all other applications included in this book, the clinical psychologist will usually operate on a relatively *scientific* basis. Although there is and always has been a vigorous debate about the extent to which the traditional

BOX 1

Definitions of clinical psychology

Most clinical psychologists:

'... see their task as using their scientific knowledge and expertise in the application of their professional and clinical skills, in order to develop and provide services for people in a wide range of health and social service settings.' (West and Spinks, 1988)

'... a clinical psychologist applies psychology within a clinical context, usually a hospital, medical or community setting, with people (patients or staff) who consider themselves to be in need of a psychological perspective on their lives.' (Llewelyn, 1994)

'Clinical psychology ... embodies a scientific approach to clinically related psychological phenomena and entails a close and disciplined acquaintance with those phenomena – an approach informed by immersion in a long and not always specifiable tradition of scientific enquiry.' (Nottingham NHS Psychologists, 1988)

SCIENTIFIC MODEL is applicable within psychology, very few clinical psychologists would disagree on the following principles:

- reliance on thoroughly verified research findings
- open publication of results
- objectivity and precision in description and investigation
- careful evaluation of models of abnormality through public debate and communication
- use of hypothesis creation and testing with individual clients.

The last point, in particular, will distinguish the clinical psychologist from counsellors, who are skilled in listening and helping clients to focus their ideas and conflicts more clearly. It will also exclude those many specialist therapists, such as 'Primal' or 'Gestalt', who concentrate on one approach or one type of psychological problem, and tend not to engage in general mainstream research and debate about interventions and outcomes.

Second Clinical psychologists are also applied psychologists. They therefore provide a service to others, not always directly to those with psychological problems, through the *application* of knowledge, theory and principles developed within mainstream psychological research. To the extent that clinicians *do* apply the findings of research in their practice, or contribute to research *from* their practice, they are said to represent the SCIENTIST–PRACTITIONER MODEL in clinical psychology[1].

Third Clinical psychologists are professionals. In part this means that there is an agreed code of practice which, if violated or dishonoured, would result in the withdrawal of the title from the practitioner. Clinical psychologists form their own division of the British Psychological Society with over 2500 members. The one-time newsletter of this division is now known as the *Clinical Psychology Forum* and contains topical research and debate. The main research knowledge vehicle for British clinical psychologists is *The British Journal of Clinical Psychology*. Clinical psychologists were leaders in the movement towards the CHARTERING of psychologists within the BPS (see chapter 1). They have long desired a legally recognised professional status, on a par with that of doctors or nurses, which would guarantee to potential clients their intense training background and their belief in placing therapeutic service above, say, profit. However, unlike other 'true' professions, there is no exclusivity. A clinical psychologist need not appear in the Register of Chartered Psychologists in order to be employed (though it might now be unwise not to and there

---

[1]Roth (1990) uses a more subtle definition – the use of hypothesis generation and testing in the field with individual cases, *guided by* psychological knowledge, rather than the application of psychological knowledge to clients. Roth sees the former as an alternative model for aplying science in clinical work with an emphasis on the saturation of clinical work with scientific thinking.

are new restrictions within the NHS – see below). They do not have a monopoly of their discipline as do, for instance, doctors, architects or lawyers.

A hesitant definition of clinical psychology might be:

a clinical psychologist is primarily concerned, directly or indirectly, with the assessment and alleviation of people's psychological difficulties and applies the findings and skills of psychological research in achieving this aim, as well as conducting research into the social and psychological origins of such difficulties and into the evaluation of different approaches to intervention and therapy.

WHAT DO CLINICAL PSYCHOLOGISTS DO?

Box 2 lists some examples of projects or work situations in which clinical psychologists might be found. The range is large yet still can't cover every conceivable circumstance, since new ones emerge all the time. Relevant developments in recent years include:

- the implementation of the government initiative of CARE IN THE COMMUNITY
- increasing work with children and adults with various levels of learning difficulties
- the growth in demand for individual therapy and personal help
- the growing awareness by companies of the benefits of in-house schemes, such as those involved in stress management and teambuilding.

The ASSESSMENT/DIAGNOSTICIAN ROLE Well into the 1960s a large part of the clinical psychologist's role was that of assessment and diagnosis, using conventional standardised psychometric measurement instruments, with the psychiatrist carrying out any remedial treatment. Today clinical psychologists conduct therapy but still make use of assessment tests. These might include the Present State Examination (Wing et al, 1974) in suspected schizophrenia, the Beck Depression Inventory (Beck et al, 1961 and 1988) or the Symptom Check List – SCL-90 (Derogatis et al, 1973), among many others.

The researcher role The clinical psychologist, as a scientist applying the methods of mainstream psychology, also developed a research role, mainly centred around assessment of *therapeutic interventions* and attempts to answer questions like, 'Does it work?', 'Are patients/clients made better by it?', 'Is one therapy or intervention better than another?' 'What kinds of problem can this approach manage?'

The therapist role Many clinical psychologists plan therapy with the client and implement a programme of remedial work intended to alleviate their difficulty or help them learn appropriate ways of living with it. A broader focus occurs where the clinical psychologist includes the client's family in the therapeutic process. It may be felt that a young person's problems are made worse by a lack of family support. It may be suspected that the family rejects the person as 'bad', or 'scapegoats' them as responsible for all the family's difficulties. This focus on one 'bad' person in the family may serve to avoid other conflicts which, if allowed to surface, would threaten the family unit. In this case individual therapy will require some work also being carried out with family members, so that they do not maintain the destructive home situation. Again, family members might be brought in to help an individual keep to a programme of change in the absence of the clinical psychologist. Clinical psychologists also practise as team members in the support of whole groups within the community (such as those with alcohol problems or those with learning difficulties).

BOX 2

Examples of work situations for clinical psychologists

Individual therapy – with a wide range of psychological problems, including most of those shown in Table 2.

CONJOINT THERAPY – with couples or family members where, as is often the case, one person comes forward with the problem but treatment requires support, understanding, behaviour and attitude change on the part of significant others in relationship with the client. Clinical psychologists also work with couples who are trying to salvage their relationship together, i.e. marital therapy.

Work with children – school refusal; persistent offending; solvent abuse; bed-wetting; specific anti-social behaviours.

Work with people with learning difficulties – encouraging life skills; reducing behaviour which interferes with normal interaction or treatment by others; planning and implementing appropriate sex education.

Work with sick clients or those with disabilities – those with cardiovascular and respiratory problems; terminal or life threatening illness;

extreme pain; neurological problems; extreme tension; stress-related problems; those adjusting to injury, loss of limb or paralysis.

Work with care staff – in the last two cases the clinical psychologist might be involved, not directly with clients but with the care staff who may need support in working effectively and coping with the behaviour of residents; the work also often includes helping staff run more effective training programmes for residents.

Counselling – after bereavement; more recently, after disasters (air crashes, sea accidents, terrorist attacks).

Forensic – work with adult offenders; sex abuse; dealing with violence; appearing as an 'expert witness' in court; assessment of the potential danger posed by certain individuals.

Organisational change – involvement in a process of radical and complete change, including staff retraining. Occurs when a service, such as psychiatric care, provision for the elderly or a children's' home, is modernised to become 'customer-friendly'.

Planning – of new schemes such as a new health authority centre for the care of people with moderate or severe learning difficulties or a rationalisation programme for the merging of psychiatric care over several districts.

The consultative/organisational development role
A clinical psychologist may work at an overall planning level or with overall institutional change – see examples in Box 2.

How do clinical psychologists divide their time?

According to the survey below conducted by O'Sullivan and Dryden (1990) on 81 clinical psychologists in the South East Thames Regional Health Authority, only 56% of practitioners spent time in research and, for these alone, the average working time on research was 10% (5.8% for the

whole sample). The most common activity was therapy, with 96% of clinical psychologists involved, taking 40% of their time, rising to 47% when associated assessment is included. When asked how many papers they had published, 49% said none and only 23.5% had published 3 or more. Pilgrim and Treacher (1992) argue that the widely advertised model of the clinical psychologist as both therapist–practitioner and scientific researcher is unrealistic. The division of activity, they argue, is lopsided, in that the researchers probably practice little therapy and are associated with academic institutions, whereas the practitioners get little time or resources for research.

Milne et al (1990), however, argue that this view is somewhat pessimistic. In their survey, when 'local' research activity was included (such as presenting a paper at a local meeting of profes-

TABLE 1
Percentage time spent per week in various activities from
O'Sullivan, K. and Dryden, W. (1990)

% time p/w 40.0	Activity therapy
14.0	consultancy and administration
6.9	assessment
6.6	supervision
5.9	teaching
5.8	research

sionals) they found more like 74% had been involved. They end on an optimistic note that research is 'alive and well' and that the scientist–practitioner model is 'after all … an appropriate model of good and realistic practice, particularly given a more flexible and work-centred definition of research.'

THE DEVELOPMENT OF CLINICAL PSYCHOLOGY

The term 'clinical psychologist' was introduced by Witmer in 1896 who set up the first recognised clinic for psychological testing in an abnormal context, mainly for children who were failing to learn. More than 20 clinics existed before 1920. However, more than 50 years elapsed between the establishment of Witmer's clinic in the USA and the emergence of the first practitioners in the UK. As with other practical applications, war played a crucial role in the foundation of clinical psychology as a professional domain of applied psychology. Although there were no clinical psychologists in the UK in 1939, the onset of war found psychologists prepared to investigate and treat war-shocked victims. The most important base was the Mill Hill centre which dealt with regular and war-created psychiatric patients during the Second World War whilst the regulars' usual base, the Maudsley Hospital in Camberwell, was used for non-psychiatric civilian casualties. In 1942 Hans Eysenck was appointed as Research Psychologist and prospered as Chief Psychologist after the Institute of Psychiatry came into being in 1948, becoming Professor of its psychology department in 1955. 1948 is also the birthdate of the National Health Service within which clinical psychology has largely evolved.

Although Eysenck was a researcher and not a 'hands-on' clinician or therapist, he acted as a colourful spokesperson, first for the new profes-

sion of clinical psychology, and soon after, for the emerging 'practical and scientific' conduct of

Hans J. Eysenck pioneered *behaviour therapy* in the UK.

BOX 3

How would I become a clinical psychologist?

The first requirement would be a BPS recognised psychology first degree. In 1994 14 UK clinical psychology courses led to a Masters level higher degree. The other 11 led to a Diploma and/or the BPS qualification in clinical psychology. Several of these courses had been of two years duration. However, by 1995 all courses will offer an integrated three-year programme, because of a new training requirement that all applicants for employment at the basic A grade in the National Health Service will be required to have completed three years of pre-registration training. A majority of courses are adopting a 'doctoral' degree title (Psy D, D Clin Psy or Clin Psy D), making the holder a 'Doctor' without the presentation of the traditional doctoral thesis – for a review of developments, see Turpin (1995).

In all cases you would need at least a 2.1 final psychology degree classification to be accepted for clinical training, though a 2.2 might just be enough with other exceptionally good evidence of potential. In addition, most courses require

you to possess some work experience in an area relevant to clinical psychology, such as assistant psychologist, research assistant, nursing, social work, care work and so on. Some courses make it clear that candidates are highly unlikely to be selected without such experience, whilst others ask you not to rule out the possibility of acceptance without it.

For application there is a clearing house scheme, information about which is swiftly available from the BPS. The address of the clearing house is **The Clearing House for Postgraduate Courses in Clinical Psychology, University of Leeds, 15 Hyde Terrace, Leeds, LS2 9LT**. Telephone calls are not accepted. Competition for places is fairly stiff, since trainees are virtually all supported by salary or bursary from a Regional Health Authority. About one person in every five applicants is accepted for a place overall. Expect a pretty gruelling interview, or series of them, delving fairly deeply and carefully into your motivation, reasons for application, personal strengths and suitability for dealing with people requiring the last reserves of your professional ability to help them without prejudice and without expecting any favours in return.

BEHAVIOUR THERAPY and BEHAVIOUR MODIFICATION, which posed a serious threat to both the medical psychiatrists and the then single most accepted psychological approach of PSYCHOANALYSIS. Eysenck saw the role of a clinical psychologist as purely and simply that of a scientist–technician applying scientific principles to the assessment of patients and to the evaluation of their improvement under therapy. At that time he tended to accept uncritically the MEDICAL MODEL of mental illnesses and conditions. The clinical psychologist's job was to allocate patients to the appropriate category so that they could then be treated by a specialist (doctor) using the 'correct' procedures in much the same way as conventional medical practice deals with physical illness. In the world of psychological 'illness', Eysenck was, at first, vehemently opposed to the idea of clinical psychologists ever

dealing with therapy or being required to undergo what is now known as 'personal work' (some form of self-examination or analysis) to qualify as clinical psychologists. This was not necessary, he argued, since they were objective scientists, free of the inevitable bias of a therapist in regular contact with distressed persons. For quite some time, the psychoanalytically-oriented Tavistock Clinic, along with the Crichton Royal Hospital in Dumfries, provided the only sources of trained clinical psychologists in the UK, other than the course initiated by Eysenck at the Maudsley.

The switch into therapy

Behaviour therapy and modification (or 'BT/BM' – methods of changing behaviour established from behaviourist learning theory – see Appendix 1) became very influential from the early 1960s onwards. This provided clinical psychologists with an apparently scientific set of BEHAVIOURAL ENGINEERING techniques with which to modify clients' behaviour in a manner allegedly more reliable and certainly far quicker than traditional (Freudian) psychoanalysis. Eysenck is notorious for an onslaught upon the psychoanalytic techniques in use at the end of the 1940s claiming that psychoanalysis made people worse not better. He championed the use of BT/BM, contrary to his earlier rejection of the therapist role for clinical psychologists. Why the sudden U-turn? Well, here was a technique which could be used by those who were not doctors, yet it was also light years away from (and very much distrusted and disliked by) those practising psychoanalysis. It appeared 'scientific', based as it was on mainstream (BEHAVIOURIST) psychology research which formed the backbone of academic psychology at that time. The psychologist could assess patients and devise a technical-sounding and technical-looking programme of REINFORCEMENT or association exercises, even involving quite technical apparatus at times, with no need for the therapist to become too emotionally or personally involved with the 'patient'.

Behaviour therapy did not remain so clinically detached. Later uses are coupled with sensitive interviews to understand the client's position, and, very often, some other therapeutic methods as well as behaviour-oriented techniques. This mixed or ECLECTIC approach is far more likely to be the approach taken nowadays than any slavish adherence to a single model. Unswerving allegiance to one explanation of human behaviour occurs when such a model is new, entirely radical and has the potential to sweep aside ailing, ineffective old models. This was certainly the atmosphere with behavioural methods in the early 1960s which rapidly established clinical psychologists as therapists. In clinical practice, as the 1960s wore on, behavioural methods were applied in the psychiatric hospital, in the classroom and even in the home.

The shift towards more cognitive approaches

At just about the time that applied behaviour therapy was in its ascendancy, mainstream psychology itself was turning sharply towards what is now seen as the COGNITIVE REVOLUTION – see Appendix 1. The first step away from a purely behavioural approach occurred when the work of Bandura and his colleagues (1963, 1969, 1986) on SOCIAL LEARNING THEORY was used in therapy. Rather than concentrating entirely on behaviour, one could claim that a person's repetitive and highly negative thoughts were 'conditioned' and therapists could concentrate on reinforcing these. In addition social learning theorists emphasised imitation or MODELLING in learning and concentrated on important human models which influence a person. The purely COGNITIVE APPROACHES which emerged in the 1970s have flourished, especially that of Beck (Beck et al, 1979). Their common thread is to deal with thoughts *directly*. Each approach tends to deal with the client's set of irrational beliefs since these are seen as having a direct and possibly detrimental effect on the individual's behaviour.

Changes in status since 1980

In the 1980s and into the 1990s, there has been growth in areas complementary to clinical psychology, in particular, in COUNSELLING PSYCHOLOGY but also in a plethora of individual therapies. The approach used in counselling is usually very close to the CLIENT-CENTRED methods espoused by Carl Rogers, described later. Clinical psychology has been a separate 'Division' within the British Psychological Society since 1966. Counselling psychology, having sought divisional status since 1979, acquired this position in 1994.

It was partly because counselling and therapy developments were seen as something of a threat that the Division of Clinical Psychologists decided in 1979 to seek government approval for legal recognition. In the full version, through official statute, clinical psychologists would have been entered on an independent register, as are doctors and nurses. Negotiations through the 1980s, however, resulted in the weaker version of registration described in chapter 1. For clinical psychology, this means, in effect, that people advertising their skills as a psychologist or psychotherapist still need *not* be registered or authorised in any official manner. However, CHARTERED status gives clients confidence that a clinical psychologist has been exhaustively trained and vetted, though other psychotherapeutic workers also have organisations with stringent membership criteria.

The Manpower Planning Advisory Group (MPAG) Review (1990)

Contrary to the fears of many clinical psychologists towards the end of the 1980s, the profession received a flattering boost from a government-sponsored, full-scale report on the role of clinical psychologists. The report was requested by the MPAG and carried out by a management consultant instructed to report on exactly what clinical psychologists do. Many had felt that, in the 1980s Thatcherite atmosphere of value-for-money, it would be hard to present a case for the special role of clinical psychology over and above the work of doctors, psychiatrists and mental health nurses in the NHS. In fact, though the report was surrounded by controversy, it favoured expansion of the clinical psychology service (since clinical psychology is now, in general, chronically understaffed) and an improvement in its status. It argued that clinical psychologists had a unique contribution to make to psychological issues in health care settings. They alone, of all those using psychology in the health service, have a training in psychological research and the academic skill to apply research findings and methods to new problems (MPAG, 1990). The BPS (1992) has responded to this with a statement on the core purpose and philosophy of clinical psychology.

In the end, the favourable report was largely shelved by the Department of Health since the NHS was about to undergo dramatic changes on a much larger scale. Currently, NHS services have been divided into those of 'purchaser' and 'provider'. Some clinical psychologists now enjoy larger salaries as 'directors of services' but clinical psychology as a whole is seen as a provision with a cost, to be 'purchased' by hospitals and clinics as part of their overall budget strategy. A further difficulty for clinical psychology in the 1991 NHS reforms was the change which caused training to be regionally rather than nationally planned. The numbers of new clinical psychologists will now be a decision of local (e.g. regional health authority) employers rather than being based on national need.

These serious problems of funding and staffing put a focus on efficiency and, in turn, on OUTCOME STUDIES (to be outlined later). They also emphasise that third skill which the report identified as the unique contribution of clinical psychologists – the ability to think through problems from a research perspective. Ironically, the research area was identified by O'Sullivan and Dryden's survey as a relatively low priority for many clinical psychologists. *Without* research-based skills, clinical psychologists share their abilities and contribution with other health professionals. It is not unreasonable to imagine a group of community psychiatric nurses forming a consortium to 'bid' to provide psychological therapy at a cheaper price than that of clinical psychologists.

THEORY, RESEARCH AND APPLICATIONS

What sort of psychological problems do clinical psychologists deal with?

It is not the role of this chapter to introduce the reader to the whole range of 'abnormal behaviour' as studied by psychologists. The interested reader might consult either of the two very popular (North American) texts by Davison and Neale (1994) and Rosenhan and Seligman (1989). However, it is useful to get some idea of all the possible syndromes, to clear up some confusions and to stress some important points about aspects of the range of psychological and behaviour problems.

Miller and Morley (1986) provide a useful crude category system and that shown below in Table 2 is an extension of theirs. No category system will ever be satisfactory because people vary around categories and the person conducting diagnosis is required to force the individual into one of them. On the other hand, it is impossible to start dealing with people's problems, and learning from the exercise, without producing some sort of basic category system to aid comparisons. Although British and other European psychologists tend to work with the ICD10[1], which does use categories like those in Table 2, the United States' system of DSM-IV[2] requires individuals to be assessed along five 'axes'. These are:

I   Clinical syndromes
II   Personality disorders
III General medical conditions
IV   Psychosocial and environmental problems
V   General level of adaptive functioning (from very disturbed or dangerous to self/others through to superior control and coping).

[1]International Statistical Classification of Diseases, Injuries and Causes of Death, 10th revision, 1993, World Health Organisation.
[2]Diagnostic and Statistical Manual, 4th revision, 1993, American Psychiatric Association.

Even with this system, the person conducting diagnosis, being human, is likely to operate with a limited number of categories, though the emphasis in the DSM system is on withholding judgement on a type of disorder until all relevant data have been gathered and summarised. One major intention here is to get diagnosticians to concentrate on individual symptoms, rather than a whole type of disorder, and to assess these symptoms, along with the likelihood of changing them, in relation to the person's surrounding environment and individual circumstances. Also, the idea is to consider short-term problems (such as addiction) along with longer-term ones (such as a general personality disorder or likely permanent unemployment). Although DSM-IV is USA-based, it is used quite often in UK training programmes (Macaskill et al, 1991).

Neuroses and psychoses

Although the DSM-IV, and modern diagnostic practice in general try to dissuade clinicians from settling on one specific category of disorder, there are some broad headings still in general use which require some clarification.

What are broadly termed 'psychoses' generally differ from 'neuroses' both in severity and in nature. PSYCHOSES, of which *schizophrenia* is the most notorious, tend to include a 'splitting' (the meaning of 'schiz') of cognitive functions from reality. The person, when in a serious state, is relatively irrational in thinking and subject to delusion and fantasy. A very common trait is that of paranoia, where the person believes, for instance, that the local water system has been spiked with heroin. It is important to note that schizophrenia does *not* refer to 'split personality' in the popular sense of *multiple personality* which is a NEUROSIS.

In neurotic conditions the person generally keeps hold of reality, and can operate efficiently within prescribed limits, e.g. within the home, if agoraphobic. Neurotic disorders are almost always associated with some heightening of anxiety even

TABLE 2 Some categories of psychiatric classification

Functional (no known mainly physical cause)

Psychoses	Neuroses	Personality disorders	ORGANIC DISORDERS (known physical main cause)
Schizophrenia	Phobia	Psychopathy	Senile dementia
Manic depression	Anxiety state, panic attacks, post-traumatic stress	Addiction, substance disorders	Arteriosclerotic dementia
Depression (psychotic type)	depression (neurotic)	Sexual deviation (e.g. pedophilia),	Toxic confusional states
	Obsessions Hysteria	Sex/gender identity, Impulse control problems like gambling, kleptomania, etc	Huntington's chorea
	Dissociative, e.g. fugue, amnesia, multiple personality		

Childhood disorders e.g. retardation, tics, Tourette's disorder, autism, feeding disorders, reading, writing or mathematics disorders, communication disorders, elimination disorders, e.g. enuresis (from DSM-IV)

if, as in the case of depression, this is not always obvious or currently displayed. *Hysteria* does not have its normal language meaning but refers to any symptom (such as blindness, a tic, cough or even phantom pregnancy) which has no physical cause yet is not a sham.

Having separated these two broad categories it should be said that there is great debate about such a clear-cut division. Depression can appear either psychotic or neurotic at different times. A person can be very unhappily neurotic, whereas another person can have a psychotic condition yet, in 'good' phases, operate quite clearly. Overall though, the psychotic conditions, especially schizophrenia, are most resistant to change.

The physical and the psychological

Physical and psychological factors can be inextricably linked in any individual case and the clinical psychologist may often be dealing with problems at the interface of the two. For instance, the clinician may be dealing with the psychological effects of a physical condition, such as the organic ones

mentioned above, or with a physical condition which is *not* classified as a psychological problem, such as learning to cope with the loss of a limb or a serious illness. Work most often occurs with those FUNCTIONAL DISORDERS shown in Table 2, but here it must also be recognised that the psychological condition may well have physical and social effects, such as illness from anxiety, loss of friends and job, physical difficulties associated with poverty, all of which are interdependent.

Is there such a thing as 'mental illness'?

So far this chapter has been wary of terms such as 'mental illness', 'mental disorder', 'patient', and so on. There are several reasons for arguing that the term 'mental illness' is less than useful.

■ Most importantly, there is a tremendously aggressive debate about the issue of whether *any* psychological condition or disturbance can usefully be compared with, or classified as, an illness. This is the great MEDICAL MODEL debate.

- A very large number of clients seen by clinical psychologists are a long way from being 'sick' in any reasonable use of that term as we saw in the description above of what clinical psychologists do.
- The speech of the 'sick' person may well be taken as just deranged and irrational whereas psychologists might consider it to be genuine (if obscure) communication.
- If we are sick we expect doctors to cure us. There is no equivalent of a quick cure in psychological therapy. Many therapists believe that the client's reliance on another to cure them will be a most unhelpful starting position. The client, it is felt, must be *actively engaged* in the process of personal change. They need to take responsibility for their 'faulty thinking' or damaging and distorted ideas of themselves or others.
- In the world of medical (physical) disease and sickness, doctors make diagnoses based on *symptoms* but they then check for *signs* to make certain that the underlying disease is present. There is no sense in which clinical psychologists can diagnose a neurotic as 'obsessional', or a schizophrenic as 'paranoid', and then make some independent test in order to be fairly sure they are correct. The symptoms are the *only* evidence and seem to constitute the 'disease'.

Diseases, symptoms and current ideology

To underline this hesitation about the reality of diseases, consider how much they can depend on the current ideological social climate. For instance, Cartwright (1851) outlined the 'disease' of 'drapetomania', diagnosed as that which caused slaves to run away. Even at the time this category was derided, with other practitioners claiming that *not* to wish to run away would be more a sign of imbecility or dementia. However, it can be noted that it was only from 1973 onwards that the American Psychiatric Association decided *not* to call homosexuality a disease. Again, the syndrome of 'cannabis psychosis', diagnosed 95 times more frequently among Afro-Caribbean males than white males in the mid-1980s in the UK, disappeared within two years of a study which exposed this anomaly (Littlewood, 1989). Caplan (1991, as

described in Gross, 1995) reports on a 'proposed diagnostic category needing further study', included in an earlier DSM system which was a sub-category of *masochism*. It included playing the martyr, putting others' needs before one's own, sacrificing pleasure and so on. Caplan argued that these behaviour patterns would describe many women living up to the traditional feminine ideal. Hence, this 'feminine' behaviour could start to be treated as pathological. To stress the point, Caplan proposed a new category of 'delusional dominating personality disorder', designed to include stereotypical 'macho' characteristics and to be included in DSM-1V. This was rejected because there was 'no clinical tradition' for this disorder. One can see then that categories of 'mental illness' can be very much influenced by prevailing social norms rather than being tied objectively to agreed signs of disorder.

Arguments *for* the 'medical model' are that:

- realising they are 'ill' may be what prompts some people finally to seek help
- seeing themselves as sick makes some people feel less guilty (and therefore less anxious) than if they think their bizarre behaviour is entirely their own responsibility
- treating disturbances as illnesses, and *initially* prescribing drugs, may start a 'bootstrap' process in which the client finally gets taken seriously and commences on the road to self-correction and discovery.

Race, gender and sexuality issues in clinical psychology and diagnosis

Race and ethnicity

It is unfortunate that a long story must be cut short in a chapter this size and a fuller story will be obtained from the texts by Littlewood and Lipsedge (1982), Rack (1991) and Fernando (1991) from which most of the following points are drawn. Race issues here, as elsewhere, are not a simple matter of (relatively few) openly prejudiced individuals, but cannot be extricated from Britain's history as a colonial power over several hundred years. Early psychiatric writing on so-called 'primitive cultures' saw many non-Westerners as either mentally degenerate or free from mental illness because they were generally free of Western responsibility. Even in the 1950s, Carothers (1953, cited in Fernando, 1991), echoed a popular colonial view, still sometimes heard today, that the (Kenyan) African was 'hardly an individual ... but a series of reactions', so lacking in worry about the future that 'the resemblance to the European leucotomized patient ... is, in many cases, complete.'

It is hard now to fully appreciate this colonial atmosphere, but not too many eyebrows would have been raised at such a claim, nor to that of Jung, a highly influential psychoanalyst, that:

> 'The inferior (African) man exercises a tremendous pull upon civilised beings who are forced to live with him, because he fascinates the inferior layers of our psyche ...'
>   (Jung, 1930)

There is, however, evidence that health professionals are still affected in their judgements by social stereotypes. Lewis et al (1990) asked 139 psychiatrists to judge a written case history where only the race (black/white) and sex of the patient were varied. Afro-Caribbeans were seen as more likely to require drug treatment and as potentially more violent with the psychiatrists more likely to see criminal proceedings as an appropriate consequence of the patient's behaviour.

Cochrane and Sashidharan, in a recent review (1995) of mental health service use by members of minority ethnic groups, report several well-founded, statistically significant differences between black ethnic minorities and the white ethnic majority for in-patient admissions. Since 'race' is very much a socially defined concept and there is so much biological overlap, it is not possible to explain these differences as results of 'racial' (i.e. biological) difference – see the recommended reading for a full argument. It is also not possible to explain all the differences as a result of immigration. Some of the differences are not declining among the British-born offspring of immigrants which is usually the case for immigration mental health effects. It is important to note that the majority of black people in Britain today are *not* immigrants and the majority of immigrants (about 70%) are *not* black. A further explanation of the black–white differences could be the experi-

ence of racism. Though black groups certainly experience serious levels of racist abuse in the UK, this will not fully explain marked differences in mental health statistics *between* various black groups.

Littlewood and the other authors cited above centre their argument on the EUROCENTRIC or Western nature of psychiatric classification and practice. They argue that we have not, as a society, shaken off the view of black people as somehow less civilised. They do not rule out individual prejudices as having an effect but concentrate on the overall tendency to see the Western (white) pattern of illness as a 'norm'. Negative variations from this norm, among other ethnic groupings, are seen as a problem. Cochrane and Sashidharan point out that there is a tendency to conduct research only into 'problems'. For instance, there are dozens of studies on high rates of schizophrenia among Caribbean-born males, yet only one on their low rate of alcohol-related problems. The low rate of neurotic conditions among Asian women is sometimes turned into a problem with the explanation that their culture inhibits them from coming forward to admit or seek treatment for psychological disturbance. Assessment measures are seen as ETHNOCENTRIC in that they are STANDARDISED (see Appendix 2) on Western expressions of emotion yet used with other groups. Western therapy is based on INDIVIDUALISM. It emphasises the independence and ACTUALISATION (see below) of the *self*, whereas other cultures emphasise relationships with *others* as the main focus for creating mental health (e.g. in Japan – see Noone and Lewis, 1992).

It has been known for some time that clients from black communities are far more likely to receive medication and far less likely to receive psychological therapy. Lorion and Felner (1986) show that race, age and socio-economic status can affect whether psychotherapeutic service is offered. Parry (1992) argues that indirect exclusion can occur where a therapeutic service fails with members of certain groups and, in the end, patients are referred to that service only for those things it offers, thus failing to meet the needs of the whole community. There are very few clinical psychologists from black communities (Bender and Richardson, 1990) so it is unlikely that every client can be seen by a practitioner from even a similar culture to their own. The solution of developing separate services specifically for individual ethnic communities has been attempted to some extent in the USA but is, according to Cochrane and Sashidharan, 'fraught with dangers', both political and clinical. The clinical psychologist, then, is likely to be involved in the development of services sensitive to ethnic background. They will need to examine closely their often unconscious assumptions about race or their behaviour towards members of certain groups, and question any variation, however subtle this might be. The service has a duty to investigate and respond to the needs of clients from specific ethnic groups, not just those people who walk through the door.

Gender issues

As white is the unwritten norm for race, so male has been the assumed gender norm to which problems have been referred in mental health issues. Broverman and Broverman (1970) showed that psychiatrists' descriptions of the healthy adult were very similar to their descriptions of the healthy male and quite different from those for the healthy female. We saw earlier that those women behaving in accordance with the stereotypical, traditional home-oriented wife and mother, could have been assessed as pathological, had the original proposal to include the extended definition of masochism in the DSM III-R been successful. Tavris (1993) demonstrates that much psychological research on sex differences emphasises female *deficit* (such as lower self-esteem) rather than male deficit (such as overestimating their abilities – see Beloff, 1992). In a sense, abnormal to start with on this view, if women strive for the male characteristics, which include assertiveness and aggression, their behaviour risks being assessed as pathological in departing from the female norm (Gross, 1995).

These contradictions may have played a part in the fact that women are significantly greater users of the mental health system than are men. In 1986 total admissions to mental hospitals in the UK were more than 25% higher for women, and two large contributing categories were neuroses and depression, where female admissions were double

the male figure (Burns, 1992). Female applications to clinical psychology courses vastly outnumber those for males at around 5 to 1, though the ratio of successful applications is more like 2.5 to 1. There are about double the number of female to male clinical psychologists employed at basic grades, though, predictably, at the higher professional and academic levels of clinical psychology, males well outnumber females, especially at the most senior levels (Nicolson, 1992).

Specific mention of gender and race issues has the danger of appearing a 'token' gesture in a book of this size and range. However, given the statistics just mentioned, it is important to stress the relevance of contemporary feminism within psychology and its effects on changing what has been an overwhelmingly male-oriented view of psychiatric clients, their disturbances and what are considered successful outcomes. Freud (1971) refers several times to evidence of psychological improvement in a woman patient being a return to husbandly devotion and support, running the family and so on. There is rarely a hint that a valid outcome *might* be the starting of a new life or a renegotiation of the relationship with her partner in terms of her career or of his responsibilities with the home and children. These ideas would be common-place today. Rather than see a female client as somehow deficient in certain behaviour, a feminist-oriented therapist (and, it is to be hoped, most others) might urge her to engage in a reassessment of her perception of female roles. It may be necessary to analyse the socialised role of thinking of others first, or of blaming oneself, rather than others, for failure (see Dweck, 1975, below). It may be necessary to work towards a recognition of the unrealistic demands of career and motherhood. An analysis may be required of the contradictions involved in media images of being pure yet adventurous, or in attempting to obtain the svelte figure of some contemporary media models.

There is a growing FEMINIST PSYCHOLOGY literature tackling gender issues, including the male-dominated nature of science which mainstream psychology has traditionally adopted. It brings into focus the effect of gender on the relationship between therapist and client, a matter often ignored or treated as a neutral variable by male

Analysis may involve reassessment of unrealistic, media-inspired images of femininity and appropriate roles for women.

therapists. FEMINIST PSYCHOANALYSIS (described later) is prominent as is general analysis of the ways in which men and women differ in their approach to language and relationships, differences which inevitably affect understanding of disturbance and routes to personal growth.

Influential readings on women and psychology are Wilkinson (1986), Ussher (1991) and Ussher and Nicolson (1992), particularly the latter which concentrates on clinical psychology, sexism and gender issues, including males' concepts of their own gender in mental health work. *Clinical Psychology Forum* (Volume 22, 1989) discusses poor provision for women in mental health services.

There is at least evidence of shifts in stereotyping. Later attempts to replicate the Broverman effect have largely failed (e.g. Oyster-Nelson and Cohen, 1981). Phillips (1985) found that mental health professionals rated feminine traits favourably and as appropriate for adults in general, though they suspected that clinicians' assessed attitudes may not match their behaviour in practice. Silvern and Ryan (1983) found that participants as a whole group, with the exception of 'traditional males', rated the 'ideal person' as more feminine than masculine. 'Traditional males' still saw the ideal person in masculine terms. 'Traditional females', as a group, distinguished between the 'ideal woman' and the 'ideal person', whereas the rest of the participants, taken as whole, did not make this distinction. However, males as a whole group, rated the 'ideal' person significantly differently from *both* the 'ideal man' and the 'ideal woman'. It is to be hoped that therapists do not tend to belong to the 'traditional female' or 'traditional male' categories.

Sexual orientation

The category of 'sexual deviation' or sexual identity can create serious dilemmas for the clinical psychologist involved in assessment and diagnosis. In the early days of clinical psychology there was not such a public awareness of sexual orientation issues. People presenting themselves as deeply unhappy about their homosexual orientation were often treated without question. It was assumed that they wished to change and that the homosexuality was a behavioural deviation which might be successfully 'reversed'. Apart from the naïve ambition of this suggestion, to move straight towards treatment would be seen nowadays as ethically reprehensible. The argument that one's orientation is a matter of personal choice, not 'illness', is now well accepted. Many have argued that people suffering extreme guilt about their orientation may wish to change mainly because of external social pressure. They might first be made thoroughly aware of the view that homosexuality or lesbianism are acceptable lifestyles and that other peoples' reactions to sexuality are the problem of those other people. Some clinicians would proceed with help only after exhaustive discussion of these issues. Others might not take on the case.

Stages in a case history

1 Reaching the clinical psychologist

There are several ways in which an individual might arrive as a client of a clinical psychologist. Figure 2.1 below shows that person X might have originally consulted a doctor, though, more often than not, this will be after some discussion with, and perhaps pressure from, relatives, colleagues and/or friends. To consult a doctor directly about an apparently 'mental' problem is a step which is highly threatening to one's self-image. No one likes to think they are somehow 'mad' or 'insane'. Of course, very many problems do not start out as obviously psychological ones. The initial visit may have been about sleeplessness, breathlessness or a rash or infection which is slow to clear up. Some parents may consult the doctor or health visitor about a specific child problem, such as weight loss, related to eating difficulties, which then leads to a more thorough examination of general behaviour problems. Figure 2.1 also indicates that a person may first approach a helping organisation (such as the Samaritans or a helpline), who might direct the individual to one of the specialists, including the clinical psychologist, or initially to a doctor. On occasions, the person simply needs to be reassured that their problem is not just 'silly' but one for which a doctor is the first appropriate step. An example might be that of depression where the individual concerned feels bound to 'pull himself/ herself together'.

2 Initial assessment

Obviously then, the clinical psychologist will require excellent interpersonal skills in first reassuring the person seeking help that they will be treated seriously with respect and with sensitivity. Having attempted to reduce these extra anxieties with as comfortable a professional relationship as is possible, the clinician will commence assessment.

Is there a problem? – the ethical issue of sexuality above is an example of redefining a 'problem' as a case of differing personal values. A further case might occur when a parent presents a four-year-old child as having a serious behaviour disturbance. Instances might be wilful disobedience at the meal table (playing with toys whilst eating, leaving the table, etc.) and constant destructive behaviour. A clinician, after a short interview with the parents, might suspect that the problem is not the child, who may only 'suffer' from extreme energy and normal childish curiosity. The problem may lie with perhaps over-rigid parents who run a neat, tidy but child-unfriendly house. As any parent of an energetic, 'difficult', but normal young child will know, engaging in battles over what the child must do before leaving the table can create an energy-wasting and ultimately destructive situation.

Analysis of behaviour and thinking – the more behaviourally-oriented clinical psychologists would now probably conduct some form of FUNC-TIONAL ANALYSIS as described later on. Others would

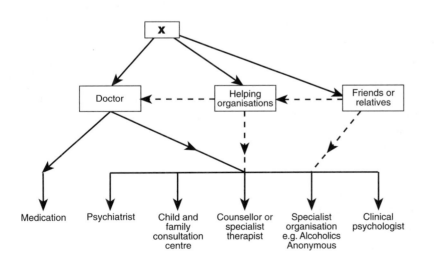

FIGURE 2.1

Routes for person X to reach a clinical psychologist

concentrate on patterns of thought and a case history of the client's overall background and relationships. Relatively simple cases may be assessed using an assessment instrument such as the Spielberger Trait Anxiety Inventory (1983).

3. Formulation of the overall problem

Further assessment will tend to merge into an overall FORMULATION of the client's problem. Genuine problem behaviour will have been identified and separated from that which is now seen as associated, but not necessarily problematic. Triggers, consequences (which tend to maintain behaviour), problem situations and accompanying thoughts are all listed and organised where possible. The reactions of others are important since family members may, for their own purposes and not necessarily consciously, find it convenient to reinforce the client's problem behaviour or to see it as problematic when it need not be.

The clinician's training in scientific method and hypothesis testing is now valuable. Even though the clinician mostly works with single cases, the logic of hypothesis testing will still be important. (See Morley, 1989, for a review of single case research in mental health work and Canavan, 1994, for specific detail of research design.) A prediction might be made that, if a particular behaviour or stimulus (trigger) is removed, or if the client is taught to respond differently (e.g. by using a breathing exercise to calm anxiety) the result will be an improvement in their symptoms. The 'treatment' is then applied and results monitored. Success supports the approach taken, failure indicates a flaw in the overall explanation or procedures used. Clinical psychologists will not often be hoping to support any 'global' theory. Their approach is practical and 'local'.

4. Construction of and implementation of the intervention programme

Each clinical psychologist will have a personal preference for this or that type of therapeutic treatment. However, the largest proportion today are ECLECTIC in approach (O'Sullivan and Dryden, 1990) and each case will suggest a different subtle blend of behavioural programme, education, cognitively-oriented discussion, deeper analysis and 'homework' for the client. Implementation may involve not just the therapist, but also the client's family, friends, and other professionals (social worker, nurse, care staff) where appropriate. All these people must stick carefully to whatever plan has been implemented. Often this is difficult to monitor and failures are sometimes attributed to this factor.

5. Completion of programme

The clinical psychologist has to be pragmatic about when the programme should stop. This is not always when a complete 'cure' has been achieved but may be simply when the client feels able to cope with life again, however tentatively. Keith (see Box 6) was not taken to the originally planned end of his desensitisation programme but only to a point where he could rejoin an active, normally progressive life for a young boy. In general, however, therapy programmes need to be completed. Luborsky (1984) argues that in eclectic therapy where several approaches may be tried, each programme should be fully completed to plan before another is started, otherwise difficult problems can just be avoided by both therapist and client.

6. Evaluation, review, reformulation

Not all cases end simply. If the intervention is not working, or is stalled, or if the client makes little progress, then the psychologist needs to think again. There is no magic formula in any approach. If the client *has* made progress in some areas it may be time to approach other areas that had been left to one side because originally they were too threatening. The client and therapist may decide that it's time to move on to tackle more complex problems if the initial stages have been largely successful. If the intervention has been on a larger scale, and has produced important findings and consequences, now is the time to *evaluate* the method, review and perhaps publish the results so that other practitioners can use the additional knowledge provided by the study.

BOX 4

A fictitious case

Natascha is 27 years old and gave birth to her second boy, Lawrence, just over three months ago. Her first son, Jason, is now nearly 3 years old. 18 months after the birth of her first son Natascha plucked up courage and started an Access course at her local college. Natascha had always held a very low opinion of her academic abilities (but in fact sets herself *very* high standards). She liked the early part of the course. Her tutors gave her much encouragement and told her she had good potential. She made friends and thoroughly enjoyed both the social relationships which evolved and the knowledge she was acquiring about possible routes into higher education or training when the course finished. The discovery that she was pregnant for a second time came as a complete surprise. Natascha carried on with the course, though the last few months were difficult. This was when most of the important assessment occurred, including one or two end of course tests. Her tutors felt she did very well indeed to obtain a C+ grade, considering her condition. She and her husband could not afford the child-minding which Natascha would need in order to take up one or two offers from higher education colleges. A few weeks after the birth, Natascha became severely depressed and was prescribed anti-depressant drugs for post-natal depression. Unfortunately, the depression has lasted quite a while. Natascha sees no point in reapplying to colleges since, in her mind, she 'failed' her Access course and would never cope with the advanced work she believes would be required in higher education. Anyway, she argues, some calamity or other would mess things up. She has started to blame herself for being a poor mother since she was 'enticed' away by the college course and failed in her duty which has resulted in her older son currently wetting his bed. She has also come to believe that her parents and in-laws disapprove of her mothering and her college experience. Hence, she will not see them or allow them to visit the family home.

MAJOR THERAPEUTIC APPROACHES IN CLINICAL PSYCHOLOGY

We will now look at each of the major approaches to therapy likely to be employed currently by clinical psychologists. At various points we will refer back to the fictitious case of Natascha outlined above.

The psychoanalytic (or psychodynamic approach)

In the 1950s and 1960s clinical psychology established itself via a sometimes openly hostile, three-cornered fight against traditional medical psychiatry on the one hand and psychoanalytic thought and therapy. The Tavistock Clinic in London, however, started producing clinical psychologists early on who had more of a psychoanalytically-oriented training than did those at the Maudsley. Although practitioners using behaviour therapy provided the impetus towards clinical psychologists using therapy, clinical psychology's hostility to psychoanalysis has waned a lot since its 1960s peak. O'Sullivan and Dryden (1990) report that 21% of clinical psychologists gave their first choice of theoretical orientation as psychodynamic whilst a further 35% of eclectic practitioners gave psychodynamic as their preferred type of eclecticism. This gives around one third of the sample with a majority interest in a psychodynamic approach to therapy. Nevertheless, most clinical psychologists are not trained psychoanalysts and are only influenced by the principles, especially the briefer versions discussed below.

Who gives psychoanalytic treatment?

People rarely receive full psychoanalytic treatment under the NHS, though the Child Guidance Service, now the Child and Family Consultation Clinics, has been very much influenced, employing, for instance, 'play therapy' techniques with children. Llewelyn (1994) argues that the situation is changing and that psychoanalysis is available, in theory, to anyone within the NHS. Nevertheless, private practice would be the easier route but full psychoanalytic treatment is very expensive and time-consuming. The traditional method requires at least five sessions per week, each of 50 minutes, possibly over more than a year. The 'brief' courses described below are less intense. Psychoanalysts themselves must experience deep analysis as part of their training and this would usually be in the form of at least five 50 minute sessions per week for several years.

Psychoanalytic thought and principles

Psychoanalysis is *the* classic therapy. It was born with the twentieth century and all others can be traced from it as derivations. It is not possible to give a detailed and therefore fair account of Freud's psychoanalytic thinking in the space permitted here. Freud himself altered his major theoretical beliefs several times during his life and there have been many splits into a variety of 'schools' since the original formulation. Some of the major principles of psychoanalytic thinking are given in Appendix 1. For now it is important to recall that humans, according to this theory, strive to present a rational 'front'. The psychoanalytic explanation of our frequent *irrational* behaviour is that we are struggling with inadequate defences against hidden conflicts which we do not wish to expose to others or even ourselves – see Figure 2.2. Hence, the causes of at least *some* of our behaviour are beyond our conscious awareness or control. The principles were not drawn up through armchair abstract thinking but through Freud's interactions with his patients.

In the UK

The UK psychoanalytic scene has been much influenced by the work of Fairbairn (1952), Winnicott (1953) and Bowlby (1969) who all belonged to what is called the OBJECT-RELATIONS school of psychoanalytic thought. The emphasis is on the early development of the infant, its sense of self and its social relationships, especially with its main caregivers – its 'objects'. These theorists considered the ways in which we 'internalise' an image of the objects to which we are strongly attached, especially mothers, and how the quali-

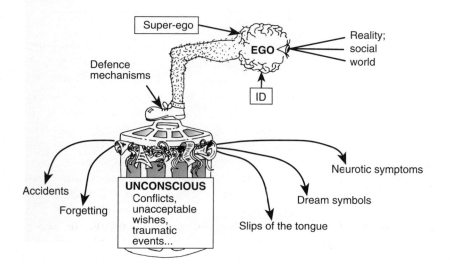

FIGURE 2.2
The Ego's defence mechanisms being only partially successful in repressing serious conflicts

ties of these images affect our self-assessment and sense of security in the future. Winnicott is largely responsible for the introduction of *play therapy* in which it is believed that children's deeper feelings and hidden thoughts are exposed through play. Bowlby is generally well-known for his theory that children who do not make one special bond with their main caregiver (usually the mother) are highly likely to exhibit disturbed and even criminal behaviour. For a thorough critique of this view, see Rutter (1981).

Feminist psychoanalysis

The theorists just mentioned have worked with an emphasis on the mother as most influential in our development of self-identity, and as a symbol of security, growth and giving, rather than on women's lack of a penis which figures so strongly in Freud's original work. For instance, he argued (1932) that boys generally acquire a strong SUPER-EGO through, among other events, a fear of losing their penis and that girls, who did not have one to start with, therefore developed a weaker super-ego, resulting in a poorer sense of justice and 'social interests'. As mentioned earlier, *feminist psychology*, once marginalised, has begun to have substantial influence on psychological thinking and practice, particularly in the area of clinical psychology. In psychoanalysis, however, there has been a longer tradition of effective challenge to 'masculinist' thinking. Sayers (1992) considers the women pioneers of psychoanalytic thought to be Helene Deutsch, Anna Freud, Karen Horney and Melanie Klein, the latter being a tutor of Winnicott. Although we can only present the basic and original approach to therapy here, in the space given, the reader can obtain thorough accounts of feminist psychoanalysis from Wilkinson (1986) and Sayers' article in Ussher and Nicolson (1992). Though methods and principles will be somewhat similar to those outlined below, the underlying theory will be less oriented towards the father, emphasising instead the nurturant qualities of the mother as did Winnicott and Bowlby. Modern feminist psychoanalysts might, however, challenge the masculinist assumptions of these writers, especially the latter, since Bowlby's theory led to the overall conclusion that children are probably psychologically dam-

aged if their mothers do not rear them at home for several years.

Psychoanalytic therapy

Although there are variations, most psychoanalysts practising today would largely agree that therapy has the goal of:

■ achieving new insight by clients into their underlying personality make-up and their previously puzzling behaviour

■ recovering lost memories (initially attempted by Freud through hypnosis)

■ pushing back defences and unravelling the underlying conflicts and associations which gave rise to them, partly by decoding symbols

Anna Freud was a pioneer of *feminist psychoanalysis*.

present in behaviour and thought; symptoms of conflict, especially those found in neurotic conditions, are very often SYMBOLIC in nature. They require interpretation so that the analyst and client together can uncover the hidden links they represent

- dealing with the 'untrapped' emotions which will pour forth when hidden barriers to feeling are discovered and destroyed
- analysing in depth the client's closest relationships, especially parental ones.

Therapists work with a preferred selection of the following possible tools or techniques:

- detection, challenging and interpretation of the client's defences
- suggestion of meanings for symbolic content. A client resisting all forms of responsibility might be seen as attempting to hang on (hopelessly) to childhood which a lack of responsibility symbolically represents. SYMBOLIC CONTENT occurs in hysterical symptoms (see below), avoidance behaviour, unusual forgetting, meaningful 'accidents' and so on, along with the famous case of dreams. *Suggesting* meaning is controversial. Some therapists would claim meanings can only be found by the client. Nevertheless, most therapists would give 'hints' and leads
- analysis of the symbolic content of dreams, since here is where our unconscious 'censor', defending our conscious mind from threatening ideas, is most likely to be 'caught off guard'; symbols from dreams are thought, in traditional versions, to represent suppressed and unfulfilled sexual wishes
- analysis of any resistance on the part of the client. This might be resistance to particular interpretations or suggestions or it might be symbolised in the client's late arrival for, or missing of, crucial sessions, or even in the late payment of fees
- exploitation of the TRANSFERENCE which often occurs in therapy where the client starts to treat the therapist as a displaced symbol of a hated or loved parent or other figure
- FREE ASSOCIATION of dream content or other verbal material, in which the client is encouraged to state the first thing that comes

to mind in association with each item mentioned. Again, our 'censor' will be unable to prevent some clue to hidden emotions 'seeping' out. Of particular interest will be odd, 'peculiar' associations, or even the client's 'unwanted' remarks, about which they feel embarrassed and which they find strange and puzzling.

The role of the psychotherapist

Freud saw symptoms as symbolic of the suppressed traumatic conflicts 'buried' by the ego in the UNCONSCIOUS mind. For instance, a person with hysterical *anaesthesia*, where the skin is insensitive even to unexpected pin pricks, might be (unconsciously) deeply ashamed of some act performed with the hand concerned. The client/patient could not retrieve this association unaided. Only a trained psychoanalyst, thought Freud, could assist in unearthing the web of conflicts eventually surfacing as neurotic symptoms. Patients needed to be helped to self-discovery through the detective work of the analyst who could guess at connections, suggest these to the patient and discuss their reactions.

An example of symptom interpretation

Freud (1917) recounts an example of a young female patient with an obsessive bedtime ritual which took time and tormented her parents. The ritual involved stopping and removing clocks and watches ('to reduce noise'), placing all vases and flower pots in one place ('in case they fell over and made a noise'), keeping the door ajar, placing the pillows away from the bed-head, arranging the duvet so that feathers were shaken to the bottom and many other details. In such cases, Freud explained, the patient's 'rational' explanation for each detail is soon seen as a shallow excuse – keeping the door open, for instance, conflicts with the stated aim of noise reduction, and how are heavy vases to fall over all by themselves? In one session of probing questions and investigation by Freud his patient revealed a vivid memory, as a small child, of falling and cutting herself on a vase she had been carrying. This was then associated with bleeding on first sexual intercourse and her fear that this would not happen on her wedding night. In the Western world this association of virginity and wedding nights would now be mostly viewed as quaint. But here we can perhaps appre-

BOX 5

Depression – the psychoanalytic model

There are several psychoanalytic explanations for depression. One of the earliest, coming from Freud himself, argues that depressive people turn anger upon themselves, an anger which originally had its cause and direction elsewhere. Early in life the depressed person directed an intense love towards someone (usually a parent, very often the mother) who could not return the emotion at the same strength. The disappointed child identified with the 'lost' love object and incorporated that person as a part of themselves. Later the anger becomes turned in towards that part of oneself which 'is' the loved one/parent. In Natascha's case, dislike of and dissatisfaction with herself might be seen as a symbolic form of the dislike and disappointment, actually but never consciously, felt towards her mother. A version of this, emanating from the work of Fairbairn and Winnicott, argues that, very early on in childhood, we need to *internalise* an image of our mother which then serves, in the future, as a source of love, care and support in our self-esteem. Depressed people, in this theory, have failed to develop the appropriate image. A third explanation is that the depressed person feels helpless when considering the extremely high goals set by their super-ego.

Whichever of these explanations is appropriate, therapy would involve attempting to bring obscured and conflicting emotions to the surface. Natascha might be helped, especially through the transference process, to recognise the self-direction of her anger and its origins in her early frustrated feelings towards her mother. She might try to *redirect* the energy of the anger (through a process known as *sublimation*) towards new goals, such as her possible higher education course. She may need to recognise why she can't boost her own self-esteem and feel warm about herself, but she may also need to learn to set or accept realistic goals and to value those she achieves.

ciate the kind of culture in which Freud worked and perhaps why he placed so much emphasis on sexual issues as the main source of neurotic but hidden conflict. Notice the patient's difficult conflict between the fear of bleeding and the fear of *not* doing so.

Hypnosis (and recovered memory)

Freud came to distrust the method of hypnosis because it proved too easy for patients to invent or exaggerate their experiences. He came to rely far more on the methods of *free association* described above. Nowadays, clinical psychologists would not often use hypnosis for deep investigation of childhood memories or well-hidden, unconscious conflicts. However, there is currently an aggressive debate concerning RECOVERED MEMORIES – accounts of early abuse 'discovered' by clients, sometimes after hypnotic techniques have been used. Critics have argued that the therapists concerned have been over-enthusiastic in the help and support given in order for these 'memories' to be 'recovered'. At least one client in the USA has now sued a therapist for helping her 'recover' a memory, which she has now rejected as false, but which led to accusations and trauma within the family. See BPS (1995) for a review of the issue.

Hypnosis is used today by a small number of therapists dealing with relatively specific problems such as alcohol abuse or even with someone who wishes to give up smoking, perhaps because they are hopelessly addicted yet know it is a serious threat to health.

Brief psychodynamic psychotherapy

Nowadays it is possible to receive BRIEF PSYCHOANALYTIC or DYNAMIC PSYCHOTHERAPY. There are very early precedents to brief psychodynamic therapy (Ferenczi, 1960; Alexander and French, 1946). However, in the modern era therapists have used the approaches promoted by Malan (1976) working from the Tavistock Clinic. Even more recent interpersonal-based approaches include that of Klerman et al (1984) in which the client focuses on their current social context and 'blocks' to progress. This type of therapy need only be received once or twice a week for, say, six months. The therapy focuses on specific conflicts, emotional difficulties and current modes of interacting with others. The therapist might *provoke*, not wait for, the common TRANSFERENCE process.

Evaluations of this approach are generally favourable. Beutler (1991) reviews the brief dynamic psychotherapy scene and finds, among the 300 odd versions now identifiable, a variety of effective results for stress, bereavement, types of depression and anxiety disorder. Howard et al (1986) showed that after 26 sessions of brief therapy, 75% of patients had improved. Howard et al (1991) show that the stronger the WORKING ALLIANCE – the strength of the therapist–client relationship in terms of mutual respect, trust and co-operation – the better the outcome.

Difficulties in assessing psychotherapeutic effectiveness

Ambiguous evidence One of the major problems with the psychoanalytic approach is the possibility that events can be taken as evidence for proposed explanations whichever way they turn out. For instance, an analyst who suggests that a client's repressions may be related to dormant homosexuality *may* receive agreement but is also quite likely to receive a very hostile reply and denial from the client. This energetic denial may be an honest one, and may be based on truth, but it might in turn be interpreted as a REACTION FORMATION – a hostile denial of an unacceptable notion, somehow recognised at an unconscious level as having some validity.

Submitting psychotherapy to measurement Traditionally psychoanalysts have seen their work as a mix of scientific deduction and highly developed interpersonal skills used to investigate, extremely carefully and sensitively, the mental paths that even the client fears to tread. This emphasis on the unique nature of individuals and the intense client–therapist relationship has generated an atmosphere of resistance to assessing in any QUANTITATIVE fashion the 'improvement' in

their clients. It has therefore been relatively rare for psychoanalytically treated clients to be compared with those experiencing other forms of therapy, though examples are given below in the *outcome research* section.

Behaviour therapy and modification

This was the therapy which helped clinical psychologists make the transition from the research and assessment role to that of therapist with individual clients. The main principles of behaviourism are outlined in Appendix 1, where the technical terms used below (e.g. 'unconditioned stimulus') are explained. Here we should emphasise the following points which follow from that approach concerning abnormal behaviour:

- there is no 'mental illness'; there are sets of responses which are MALADAPTIVE – i.e. learned, yet not wanted by the individual (for instance, a phobia) or by others upon whom the behaviour has an adverse effect (for instance, a sex offender's behaviour)
- LEARNING THEORY PRINCIPLES derived from the study of animals may be generalised to learning in humans and therefore to the treatment of abnormal behaviour patterns
- the goal of therapy is to change responses from 'maladaptive' to 'adaptive' ones.

According to this system of explanation, a maladaptive response, for instance, petty shoplifting, may be maintained by the succession of reinforcements (admiration of friends, goods obtained, thrill) in the face of the odd aversive consequence, such as being told off and banned from a shop, or even a court appearance with warning, especially where this, too, makes one important with peers.

On this explanation, the excessive rituals of the compulsive or obsessive person are seen as shaped responses linked in a chain which have, in the past resulted in some form of REINFORCEMENT. Often, the reinforcement has been assumed to be reduction of anxiety. The reader might like to refer to an explanation of phobia given under 'The

Behaviourist Approach' in Appendix 1. Behavioural therapists tend not to search back, probably fruitlessly, looking for the original source of a problem. They argue instead that if a compulsive or phobic individual can be 'weaned off' reinforcement, or taught to obtain reinforcement for *not* engaging in ritualistic or avoiding responses, then the altered behaviour largely represents the solution of the problem.

Methods of behaviour therapy and behaviour modification

Classical conditioning-based methods

AVERSIVE THERAPY   The theoretical notion here is that a naturally aversive UNCONDITIONED STIMULUS (UCS), often an electric shock or a drug which creates nausea, can be paired with a problematic, triggering stimulus (e.g. alcohol, cigarettes, object of sexual desire) which can be considered a CONDITIONED STIMULUS or CS. In future, the CS alone will produce nausea or apprehension (now the CONDITIONED RESPONSE or CR) instead of the undesired, problematic behaviour. In the treatment of alcoholism, for instance, alcohol will be paired with nausea so that drinking alcohol, or even thinking about it or entering a public house, will produce uncomfortable nausea. Smoking and sexual deviance are among behaviour patterns treated in this way, where a cigarette or picture of the illicit sex object serve as the CS. When these stimuli are approached or thought about in future the conditioned aversive responses should occur, perhaps at a reduced level. A problem is that, without continuous association, aversive effects wear off. The answer to this criticism is that other, more adaptive and rewarding behaviour patterns will occur in the meantime. Hence, the person conditioned against alcohol should feel uncomfortable when contemplating a drink but happy with the increased money, lack of sickness and increased warmth from friends which are a consequence of abstention. This approach then relies on OPERANT processes occurring *with* the aversive therapy.

Aversion techniques are not often used alone but with other methods which teach an alternative pattern of behaviour. Aversive conditioning has attracted strong ethical criticism, especially in its application to altering homosexual behaviour.

Rosen and Beck (1988) report a large decrease in this sort of use since 1975 and the issue of 'treating' homosexual behaviour *at all* was discussed in the section on 'sexual orientation' above. In addition, although its defenders see it as *association*, not punishment, it can nevertheless represent punishment to clients, and perhaps also to care staff and other personnel.

Bed-wetting   A less controversial use of the classical conditioning model has been in the attempt to control bed-wetting or 'enuresis'. A pad beneath the sleeper is connected so that, when wetting commences, an alarm bell sounds. The muscle movements preparatory to urinating are a neutral set of stimuli which become associated with the UCS represented by the alarm so that, after several pairings, the initial muscle movements produce waking and the nasty accident can hopefully be avoided.

Systematic desensitisation or COUNTER-CONDITIONING   This is an exceedingly popular set of techniques where the basic goal is to associate a feared object, spiders for instance, with the responses involved in some form of relaxation. New conditioning is intended to overcome older conditioning. As with aversive therapy this method has the appearance of a 'common sense' technique, probably tried and tested by many people who had no idea about psychology. The important point, however, is that clinical psychologists have attempted to underpin the seemingly obvious technique with conditioning theory so that the approach is not haphazard.

The first recorded formal use of this kind of technique is ascribed to Jones (1924) who gave a young boy, 'Little Peter', his favourite food whilst bringing gradually closer a rabbit of which he was seriously afraid. After only a few trials Peter began fondling the rabbit and eventually lost his fear of it entirely. In fact, Peter's changes in behaviour were often quite sudden and this highlights an early criticism of therapies which are supposedly supported by experimental research. If Peter was being conditioned by the same processes demonstrated with laboratory animals, the changes should have been gradual. In many behaviour therapy cases change is sudden and a qualitative leap is made, suggesting that a more thought-based, internal insight has been achieved. Contrary to popular mythology still appearing in some texts, another little boy, known as 'Little Albert', was never counter-conditioned out of his phobia of white furry objects. This had been created artificially by producing a loud clang on an iron bar whenever Albert played with a white rat (Watson and Rayner, 1920).

SYSTEMATIC DESENSITISATION in clinical use is first accredited to Wolpe (1958). Here the client first lists, in a 'hierarchy', typical events which produce anxiety, graded according to how much fear they provoke (see Box 6). The person is then taught how to relax through deep breathing or other similar exercises. Starting with the least frightening situations, the person now starts experiencing each of them. Each event may be imagined by the person, or acted out *in vivo*, that is, in reality, for instance by a spider phobic having a spider walk on their arm. As anxiety rises for each event the person starts their relaxation exercise. Either the anxiety level becomes acceptable or the person takes a break, then restarts at an acceptable level in their hierarchy. The theory here is that relaxation replaces fear as a conditioned response to the once feared object and the things associated with it.

Some therapists on some occasions reverse the hierarchy and employ FLOODING, in which the person encounters, right at the outset, the most feared and possible situation, such as the spider walking on one's body as described above. (IMPLOSION is much the same but here the person is asked only to imagine the feared stimuli, or else the stimuli used are not real but lifelike – a plastic spider, for instance.) The notion here is that the person cannot sustain an extreme level of anxiety for too long. Gradually, through sheer exhaustion of autonomic responses (such as adrenaline secretion), the anxiety subsides a little and this reduction in anxiety becomes associated with the spider. Eventually the fear response will extinguish, that is, if the client has not, by now, fled the clinic!

'Impure' behaviourism in behaviour therapy To support the argument that most therapy is eclectic and that behaviour therapists certainly engage in behaviour quite uncharacteristic of the stereotyped cool, scientific and mechanical behaviour

'engineer', consider the business of establishing a client's personal and appropriate hierarchy. A case reported by Lazarus (1971, in Phares, 1992) includes a conversation between therapist and client which is certainly as interpretive and probing as a psychoanalytic session might be. A female client is presented as being specifically frightened of eating in a restaurant with her husband's business associates. The therapist, through a quite leading and energetic series of questions, eventually establishes that this is not the case. It eventually transpires that she actually resents her husband usurping her father's position, after his death, and sees her husband as less of a man than her father was. The desensitisation was then directed towards her feelings about her father's death. Here, the assessment interview was virtually psychoanalytic in form, yet the treatment was behavioural.

Operant conditioning-based methods

Operant and extinction therapy A simple example of OPERANT THERAPY might be rewarding one's child with sweets or TV watching for saying 'please'; an example of EXTINCTION is ceasing to pick up a crying baby in order to remove the reinforcement it keeps receiving for its crying responses. In most cases the exact reinforcement to tamper with, and when, will not be so obvious. FUNCTIONAL ANALYSIS of a case of 'problem behaviour' at school would include the clinician taking careful measures over several days or even weeks in order to pinpoint incidents which trigger disruptive behaviour and those events which tend to maintain (reinforce) it. A programme would be worked out involving gradual removal of reinforcement for unwanted acts, and introduction of reinforcement for desired acts. Often it is the professional in closest daily contact with the client who has to administer the programme – the teacher, psychiatric nurse, residential care worker or simply a child's immediate family. The failure of many cases of behavioural programmes has often been attributed to misapplication by the staff or family involved. Staff, for instance, might fail to reinforce or remove reinforcement. In one (unpublished) case, a mother was asked to reward her child with a coloured star for each day when he didn't fight or jump down from the furniture.

BOX 6

Keith, the custard pie phobic

West and Spinks (1988) report work with an 11-year-old boy, Keith, who was so seriously afraid of custard pies and circuses (but also masks, make-up, slapstick with shaving cream, crazy foam and so on) that he avoided children's television, parties, pantomimes and the like. The build-up of fears was serious enough to create extreme anxiety for him on entering secondary school with the worry that he would be taunted. He could not tolerate even the use of the words 'foam' or 'snow'. He frequently got upset when he encountered a picture, on television or in a paper, of someone with something on their face. Here is a case of fear which warrants intervention because the person's life is so seriously restricted from what could be expected in a normal, healthy young boy. In fact, the early stages of his therapy using systematic desensitisation were very difficult, simply because Keith would scarcely talk about the objects of his fears, such was the anxiety even this created. Hence, it was hard to get him to produce a graded hierarchy of feared situations in the initial evaluation stage.

A hierarchy *was* finally produced and here is a sample from it, worst fear at the top:

1. Someone throwing a custard pie at Keith's face and it hitting him ...

4. Someone throwing crazy foam at Keith's shoulder and it hitting him
5. Squirting crazy foam at the cat
6. Seeing a custard pie being thrown at someone else ...
13. Sitting in a circus tent where there will be no clowns ...
19. Squirting a fly spray can
20. Squirting some Pledge™ on the table
21. Sitting at home and reading

Notice that the lowest item is an easy base line to start with. Within six one-hour sessions Keith had moved from item 21 to item 8 in his imagination, visualising the scene only. The *in vivo* work started with the psychologist squirting a can of air freshener and moved to a stage where Keith could, with the psychologist, handle crazy foam freely and pile it up like custard pies ready for throwing. Since Keith was anyway a meticulously clean type, he was never going to *enjoy* slapstick or willingly engage in it. Hence, the psychologist, Keith and his mother decided to stop when Keith had achieved a standard of coping which meant he could continue with a normal full life. They didn't require him to have a custard pie on his face. A four-month follow-up showed that he was indeed enjoying such a life though still avoiding some possible slapstick situations.

Unfortunately the mother generalised the idea and withheld stars for all 'naughty' behaviour. Since most children do not refrain from all 'naughty' behaviour in any one day, the child was getting no stars! After re-explanation it was then found that the mother was giving stars almost indiscriminately, partly to 'make up' for stars lost earlier and also because she enjoyed it! Eventually the system was operated as planned and the targeted behaviour did finally change.

Token economies The principle of rewarding with tokens (stars are an example) has been applied in institutional settings where the tokens obtained are used somewhat like money in the outside world. Each patient in a psychiatric ward programme is assessed for types of behaviour which are desirable and which are attainable goals. For instance, a patient might have on their desirable behaviour list: combing hair, staying at table throughout meals, giving verbal greeting in the morning to staff, staying out of the bedroom and on the ward for five minutes. For each goal achieved tokens are awarded which can later be exchanged for sweets, cigarettes, hours of television, time in a favoured activity and so on. The tokens act as SECONDARY REINFORCEMENT in behaviourist terminology.

In a now classic study (Paul and Lentz,1977) the patients treated were '... the most severely debilitated institutionalised adults ever studied systematically. Some of these patients screamed for long periods, some were mute; many were incontinent, a few assaultive ... and some buried their faces in their food.' Three groups were used, one receiving a social learning programme (mainly token economy), one a 'milieu therapy' (treated as normal adults, given responsibility, praised) and one routine ward management. The treatment period lasted four and a half years and the follow-up period one and a half years. Staff were thoroughly trained in the various approaches. Results were impressive with 10% of social learning, 7% of milieu and none of the routine patients leaving to live independently. Prescribed drug usage fell to 18% in the milieu group and 11% in the social learning group, whilst it rose from the overall pre-treatment average of 90% to 100% in the routine care group. Patients were not 'cured' but could live outside the total institution in which they had been living for an average of 17 years.

Davison and Neil (1994) report that Paul realised the token economy did not hold the central role in the success of the programme. The token system initially grabbed patients' attention and gave them the opportunity to 'get good things into their heads' (Paul, 1981), i.e. pay attention to new information. Nevertheless, Davison and Neil decry the fact that, following a survey by Boudewyns et al (1986) in the US, '... only 1.01 per cent (of 46,360 patients) were being exposed to the best-validated therapy program available for them'. Paul and Mendito reported little improvement in 1992. They blame a combination of bureaucratic inertia, staff resistance (the approach seems rather controlling and patronising), conservatism in the medical establishment and cutbacks.

The system can, of course, be criticised for establishing rather mercenary reasons for producing behaviour. Its supporters argue that better this, to get chronic schizophrenic patients back to some level of dignity, than simply leaving them where no other therapy can touch them. In addition, once positive behaviour is produced, no matter that this is originally contrived with 'bribes',

social reinforcement takes over and the behaviour may become self-sustaining, as most parents of 'bribed' children, at least privately, admit. Critics argue that the system has often been used more to satisfy staff in keeping an orderly, neat ward than in the service of the patient. One anecdote might support the mercenary argument. A friend was working at the Tavistock Institute where a minor form of token rewarding was in operation. One child received a new goal, which was to come in for lunch and not stay out in the garden. Another child was heard to say: 'Well blow that! (or similar). *I'm* gonna stay out in the garden if he's gonna get rewarded for that!'

Cognitive behaviour therapy

Natascha has received medication as part of National Health Service treatment. A weakness of this approach occurs if no other service is provided for her to come to terms with, and attempt to alter, her negative self-image and her poor expectations of any success in life, if these are at least part of the cause of her depression. Psychoanalysis might provide this form of support but it is time-consuming, costly and rarely available, in practice, in the public health service. The shortcomings of purely behavioural approaches to depression are raised in Box 7.

When a depressed person keeps repeating 'I'm useless', rather than just ignore these responses (to extinguish them), it is very tempting to ask the client to consider contradictions of this statement by pointing out what the client *can*, in fact, do quite successfully. It is a short step from here to COGNITIVE THERAPY or COGNITIVE BEHAVIOUR THERAPY – the latter being a mixture of both cognitive and behavioural techniques. Traditional behaviour therapists saw thoughts as ineffective in affecting behaviour directly. If thoughts can control behaviour directly, why would a person continue to indulge in behaviour they *know* to be undesirable and/or destructive? SOCIAL LEARNING THEORY introduced the concept of applying conditioning principles to thoughts or 'cognitions' as well as observable behaviour. In particular, Bandura

BOX 7

Depression – the behavioural model

An early behavioural explanation of depression was that patients had acquired LEARNED HELP-LESSNESS (Seligman, 1975), because their actions always seemed futile. It was argued that depressed people learn that they cannot control what happens to them and give up trying to exert influence over their lives. Further explanations (see Miller and Morley, 1986) concern the role of reinforcement. Perhaps depressed people reduce their responses because they get little reinforcement or because reinforcement has lost its strength for them or it might even have become aversive – as when music one shared with one's departed partner now serves only to strengthen feelings of loss. Until the marriage of behaviour therapy with cognitive approaches, treatment for depression did not tend to tackle depressive thoughts directly but concentrated on:

> extinction *of depressive responses (such as a helpless response of saying one is 'useless')*
> reinforcement *of adaptive responses which would conflict with depressive behaviour.*

For example, Natascha might have received treatment similar to that of 'Sarah Jane' reported in Liberman and Roberts (1976). Sarah Jane attended a day clinic which operated on a form of token economy principle. Positive 'behaviours' were taught including grooming, conver-sation skills, recreational activities and assertiveness training using behaviour rehearsal, modelling, coaching and social feed-back ('reinforcement'). An example of the mental health nurse's approach with Sarah Jane during daily review sessions is illustrated in the following extract:

> *'During these sessions Sarah Jane repeatedly tried to provoke a response in Johnie (the nurse) by complaining about how difficult it was for her to complete housework duties, how inadequate she felt as a mother and wife, and how she felt like a "blob". These remarks were ignored and instead Johnie inquired further about the details of Sarah Jane's adaptive strivings and small accomplishments.' (p.213)*

Here, 'depressive responses' are simply not reinforced and it is assumed they will eventually extinguish if there are enough *adaptive* responses to nurture and reinforce in their place. In cognitive therapy the content of these responses (what Sarah Jane wanted to say) is taken on and challenged for its contradictions or falsity. In fairness it should be pointed out that, in this case, the therapists went on to initiate marital therapy by attempting to get Sarah Jane and her husband to rekindle their virtually dead relationship. This consisted of coaching the pair in interpersonal skills, again using modelling (of the therapists 'appropriate' conversational skills) and rehearsal of affectionate responses and non-verbal elements (posture, eye contact etc.).

(1977) believed that *expectations* could be learnt through observing others (i.e. MODELLED) in the same way as he had already shown that behaviour could be acquired VICARIOUSLY – through noting the rewards to others for behaving in certain ways. 'Expectations' referred both to what we think will be the outcome of a certain behaviour, and our SELF-EFFICACY – our assessment of whether we can successfully perform that behaviour. Hence it was important to get depressed clients to observe how other people, especially those the client respected, managed their lives and believed in themselves. Bandura's work is still influential today but it also serves as a stepping stone from behavioural to cognitive approaches.

Although there are 'pure' versions of cognitive therapy, most practitioners today use a combination of cognitive and behavioural principles. It is possible to argue that behavioural techniques always included some reliance on affecting people's thoughts and that cognitive therapists may not recognise when some of their procedures rely on basic principles of reinforcement. Bandura (1986) has certainly argued this latter position very forcibly.

Most cognitive practitioners would probably agree on the following major principles:

1. Thoughts play a strong role in *maintaining* unwanted 'maladaptive' behaviour.
2. Many aspects of disturbed behaviour are caused by FAULTY THINKING.
3. A person's thoughts can be trained in order to create effective behaviour change.
4. Proven aspects of behaviour therapy are worth keeping.

The mixture of cognitive and behavioural approaches

A good example of the mixture of principles occurs with Meichenbaum's SELF-INSTRUCTIONAL TRAINING. Meichenbaum and Goodman (1971), for instance, used self-instruction with impulsive young schoolchildren. The children observed an adult talking to himself whilst doing a simple drawing task. They then did the task themselves, copying instructions from the adult, then producing the instructions themselves, first out loud, then silently. The approach has been useful in helping those with acute anxiety concerning specific situations, such as public speaking. Here clients might be asked to:

- identify situations which precipitate anxiety
- keep a diary – record thoughts which accompany anxiety onset
- accept that our emotions very much depend upon interpretation of what surrounds us. A 'maladaptive' thought is to think one is boring because people leave one's lecture. The constructive approach is to think it a shame they'll miss your best bit
- learn to see anxiety-related 'automatic' thoughts as badly developed 'cues for coping' (e.g. 'I'm going to make a mess of this anyway so why bother?')
- develop new, positive coping thoughts, e.g. 'I can do this. I've done it before. I must start

Meichenbaum's self-instructional training techniques have been used to help presenters overcome debilitating fear in circumstances like these.

breathing more slowly. I must maintain eye contact'
- observe these techniques being modelled by the therapist or assistant
- do graded exercises in a secure setting (e.g. a clinic).

Here we see the use of graded exercises with short-term goals ('rewards') as used in systematic desensitisation, the use of modelling and the cognitive emphasis on altering 'maladaptive' and 'automatic' thoughts to influence behaviour directly. Purely cognitive approaches (e.g. Beck et al, 1979) would criticise this tackling of merely 'superficial cognitions' which leaves the underlying 'faulty' structure of beliefs intact.

Purely cognitive approaches – Ellis and Beck

Ellis (1962) argues that such tampering with superficial, individual thoughts will not be as effective as getting at clients' deep-seated and enduring beliefs about themselves and the world around them. Ellis' view was that clients should not only be brought to recognise that their thoughts are harmful barriers to effective change, they should also be made to realise that these thoughts are illogical and irrational. The therapist's role is to argue with the client, demonstrating the contradictions and unnecessary links in their systems of logical belief. For instance, the therapist might argue with Natascha that she has no evidence that her son's bed-wetting is linked to her absence at college but that there is plenty of evidence linking this behaviour with the arrival of another child in many families. She clearly did *not* fail her college course. She thought she would never pass this course but she did. Still she claims to know, in advance, that she would fail a course at a higher level.

Ellis believed that the depressed or anxious person is oppressed by a 'tyranny of shoulds' and that their thinking can be 'mustabatory' – they *must* be loved, or they *must* be an absolute success (Natascha would have given in even if she had received a B). However, people can be very capable at arguing against rationality. Confronted with contradictions in their thinking, or evidence which conflicts with their beliefs, people find ways to explain this away if they are committed to their present state of being. For instance, Natascha might argue that, to her, 'failure' is not getting the grade she set herself. Also she need only find one example of a mature student quitting a higher education course to support her prediction that she will almost certainly fail.

Beck's TRIAD OF DEPRESSION

Beck has had a strong influence on cognitive therapy developments, particularly in the area of depression. Although Beck published work based on client case notes, parallel experimental research work also supports his position. A starting point was the explanation of depression in terms of the LEARNED HELPLESSNESS demonstrated in laboratory studies. A problem with this view was that it didn't account for the observation that depressed people often feel responsible for all the negative outcomes which appear to surround them – 'It's rotten and it's all my fault'. Abramson et al (1978) revised this view by relating it to the theory of individual ATTRIBUTIONAL STYLE. Depressed people, it seemed, had a tendency to attribute the causes of any negative outcomes to themselves. Generally, people tend to follow the SELF-SERVING BIAS principle and attribute *successes* to themselves (ATTRIBUTION, INTERNAL) and *failures or problems* to outside circumstances (ATTRIBUTION, EXTERNAL). With many depressed people the opposite occurs – 'It's my fault if it's wrong and if it's right it's luck'. Dweck (1975) and others have found that women are more likely to attribute success to luck and failure to more global, stable features of their personality. This might go some way towards explaining the higher number of women in treatment for depression.

Beck's central belief was that his clients had the habit of using illogical and negative thinking about their position in their world, their self-image and their prospects for success. This is the so-called Beck 'triad' of self, world and future. Depressed people, according to Beck, tend to use the following EXPLANATORY STYLE:

- *selective abstraction* – e.g. only seeing negative outcomes
- *polarising* – seeing things as only one extreme or the other
- *over-generalising* – one failure means I always fail – 'I never get *anything* right'
- *global attribution* – assuming 'I'm not attractive' rather than '*That* person doesn't find me attractive'
- *arbitrary inference* – ambiguity in speech seen as personal criticism, e.g. a relative saying 'He didn't wet the bed *before*' is taken to mean '*before* you went to college' rather than '*before* the new baby arrived'
- *maximising and minimising* – emphasising failures, trivialising successes; this is close to the reversal of 'self-serving bias' emphasised by Abramson.

The explanatory style (or set of habitual thought

patterns) also includes a belief that the (distorted) self-image is permanent – 'I'm like this. There's no way I'm going to change.' Of course, many people who are not depressed use these thinking modes quite frequently. Students often say, 'I didn't understand a single word' and are corrected by a tutor who might say, 'Well let's see which ones you didn't understand'. According to Beck's approach, though, the 'healthy' student would tend to blame the book or the tutor and this *is* a relatively common occurrence! The depressed person, however, uses the patterns of thought on themselves relentlessly and mercilessly, though they don't necessarily think this way about the rest of the world unconnected with themselves. For instance, they might not think that *most* people's failures are their own fault. If they did, perhaps the world would be a little easier to bear.

Support for the use of the first thought pattern listed above has been produced by Finkel et al (1982) who showed that depressed people reading a variety of statements assessed less of them as positive compared with non-depressed people. There have been some successful attempts to show that people with a certain type of thinking style are more likely to become depressed but there have also been well-controlled studies which failed to show this (Lewinsohn et al, 1981). Golin et al (1981) found a significant link between thinking and depression but only where the period between prediction and occurrence of depression was short (1 month ahead). Unfortunately, it could be argued here that the cognitive style was simply an early *symptom* of oncoming depression, not a *cause* of it. This is always the chicken–egg problem in this area. It is difficult to establish that thinking *causes* depression. Perhaps people just get irrational, morbid, distorted and rigid in their thinking *as a result of* whatever does cause depression.

Beck's therapy

Like the behaviour therapies, Beck's work is testable and has had an important influence in shifting therapists' focus of attention to their client's thinking patterns as a direct route to changes in behaviour and feelings. The therapy session involves the therapist and client devising an agenda and the therapist ensuring this is kept to. The therapist leads with a questioning style, summarising periodically and engaging the client in reaction to the summaries. The client also summarises main points at the end of the session. The therapeutic process consists of:

- full assessment and formulation as in other therapies
- client gathering data, often using a diary, about their repetitive and obstructive, depression-related thoughts
- REALITY TESTING in which the therapist encourages the client to test their often distorted ideas against actual facts or others' perceptions of them
- therapist offering alternative interpretations and outlooks on clients' beliefs about themselves
- client being urged to find contradictory alternatives to their beliefs, for instance, 'think of when you *did* succeed in a task or when you *didn't* mess up a date'
- client being encouraged to analyse habitual thoughts in order to recognise how they get in the way of positive self-appraisal (e.g. Natascha might say 'I'm bound to fail')
- therapist sets 'homework exercises', for example, by getting the client to 'experiment' in testing out reappraisals. For instance, Natascha might be persuaded to agree to short visits with her parents or in-laws and to note down only positive comments which they make about her life and her children. She might also be asked to check whether she *did* fail on each occasion she thought she would

In addition depressed clients are taught not to:

- expect themselves to be perfect
- expect more of themselves than they would of others; Natascha might be asked why she is so happy for, and admiring of, two of her friends who also obtained C grades and have taken up teacher training
- expect one bad event to automatically be followed by others; why *should* some calamity occur in another college course?
- exaggerate the likelihood or importance of failure or error; Natascha must accept that some of her early college work might well not be perfect

- ask questions with no answers like 'Why aren't I different?'; Natascha tends to say, repetitively, 'Why *am* I so thick?'
- assume there is no solution or possibility of change
- misinterpret others' reactions (as in the arbitrary inference example given above).

Is the therapy effective?

Several studies have shown cognitive therapy to produce superior treatment results compared with drugs (Rush et al, 1977) or social skills training (Shaw, 1977). Elkin et al (1986) conducted a very thorough study on patients randomly assigned to one of four groups: cognitive therapy; interpersonal therapy; tricyclic drugs; or placebo. The placebo condition also included clinical management and advice where this was thought necessary. All three treatment groups produced improvement over the placebo group after 16 weeks. The drugs worked more quickly, but there was evidence that cognitive therapy produced longer-acting effects – less relapse and less depression on follow-up. The reason for this could be that drugs apparently do not affect thinking skills. Hollon et al (1989), in an experiment randomly assigning clients to cognitive therapy, drug treatment or both, showed that better explanatory style was related to cognitive therapy *and* correlated with improvement from depression. Those clients not improving in explanatory style tended to relapse later. Hollon et al (1992), amongst several others, argue that Beck's therapy is effective in preventing further bouts of depression. Beck himself (1986) has argued that cognitive therapy would be a clear advantage *in addition to* drug prescription, whereas it is not obvious that drugs need to be taken in addition to cognitive therapy except for the most extreme cases.

Other practical applications for cognitive (behaviour) therapy

Cognitive therapists are expanding the application of their approach beyond the original focus on depression (Scott et al, 1989). They are keen to argue that distorted beliefs and faulty interpretation of surrounding events can explain many disturbances in behaviour and, if fundamentally altered, can lead to elimination of that behaviour

B O X   8

Why aren't we all depressed? – a weakness for cognitive theory

According to Beck, depressed clients have distorted images of themselves and their capabilities. However, Lewinsohn et al (1980) found depressive clients to be *more* in accord with judges about their interpersonal skills than were a control group. The latter seemed to hold a 'warm glow' of confidence and their self-assessments differed markedly from those of observing judges. Also, contrary to Seligman's prediction, it emerged that depressed people did *not* have a particular tendency towards 'external locus of control' (that is, feeling that one's life is directed by external forces beyond one's control).

Alloy and Abramson (1979) showed that depressed people were significantly *more* realistic about the control they could exert in an experimental situation than students who were not depressed. In their assessments of real-life experiences, they were all too painfully aware of the amount of control they *could* exert over their outcomes, but didn't! Rosenhan and Seligman (1989) argue that what needs explaining here is how 'normal people' produce such a strong defence against 'grim reality'. Overall, this amounts to some weakness in the 'faulty thinking' view of disturbed clients. A further weak point is that successful treatment appears to require clients who are good talkers, who can argue coherently and recognise illogical arguments when they are produced.

or, at least, a much enhanced quality of life (see Boxes 9 and 10). Cognitive therapy has been extended with some success to obsessions, compulsions, hypochondria, drug abuse, suicide attempts, conjoint or family therapy, social skills training, cancer patients, people who are terminally ill, violent criminal behaviour, sex offenders and child abusers. In the latter case we see a clear example of the need for some clients to alter their attributions *towards* themselves (rather than making them external, as is the need for some depressed clients). For abusing clients an important goal is to achieve the recognition that it was *not* 'all the child's fault'. Here it is also necessary to alter perceptions so that the child is seen *as* a child and not as a person with seductive ability – a view commonly held by pedophiles.

BOX 9

Recent cognitive therapy applications – BULIMIA *and* ANOREXIA NERVOSA

Cognitive approaches are particularly appropriate in these cases since so much of the problem concerns mental distortions of body image. However, cases are often so dangerous that quick, effective action must be taken and a behavioural programme is also often employed. West and Spinks (1988) and Marzillier and Hall (1992) discuss a case study of 'Susan', a 24-year-old who followed binge eating with self-induced vomiting. She was obsessed with food and body weight and was also depressed. Her treatment included elements of both cognitive and behavioural therapy. She was encouraged to engage in more threatening behaviour, such as wearing more revealing clothes; to swap thoughts like, 'Everyone will notice if I put on 3 pounds' to 'It's unlikely that anyone will notice a weight change of that amount'; and to use information about food intake, the harmful effects of vomiting and the cultural and unrealistic pressures on slenderness. Her course was 12 weekly sessions and, at the end of this period, she had regained an acceptable weight and all but ceased bingeing and vomiting. A little over a year later she wrote to tell the clinicians that she was married and pregnant. This is not to say that marriage and babies are to be seen as universal signs of good health but, in this case, at its worst, Susan's self esteem was low, she was depressed, menstruation had ceased, her relationship with her boyfriend was poor and she tried to hide her problem from him.

It is tempting to ask, if Susan was keen to change (as she was), why she might not have sought all this information on her own and changed her thinking patterns as advised. However, it is not hard to think of instances in your own life where you know just what you would like to change, and how to do it, yet you don't or won't. Smoking, lack of exercise or a difficult-to-end relationship might be good examples. One might feel that clients like Susan simply need the attention and the formality of professional treatment in order to change. This may be so but this then underlines the role of applied professionals in such cases and it does not detract from the strength of the approach as a theoretical explanation. It may be that the attention and formality were effective in getting Susan to take note of the relevant factors which then were available for change.

Cognitive therapists might attempt to alter beliefs about body image and female roles as part of their treatment of anorexia nervosa.

BOX 10

Recent cognitive therapy applications –
AGORAPHOBIA

This is rarely the simple 'fear of open spaces' it is popularly considered to be. Usually entwined is some extreme aversion to crowds and travel with a sense of panic that, should the client need help, they will not be able to obtain it. Hence, home is a secure haven and cannot be left without great anxiety and fear of social failure. Cognitive therapists acknowledge the role of early experience but, rather than engage in the emotional upheaval of analysis, would normally attempt to disentangle clients' obstructive thinking pretty much in their present and recent conscious worlds. The case of 'John' (Greenberg, 1989) gives us a good example of

the therapist engaging with deep, emotional and long-standing personal relationship problems whilst avoiding the back-to-childhood-feelings path that analysts might take.

John was 30 years old and often needed to drive substantial distances in his job. However, he was terrified of driving long distances, feared being alone, did not like restaurants or theatres or riding in a car with others, worrying that each instance would lead to a heart attack. The therapist had been unsuccessful in using hyper-ventilation to get John to see that it produces feelings similar to a panic attack but that these can be dealt with by certain breathing techniques. Behaviour therapy had also been ineffective. It emerged that the therapist needed to work on the client's extreme emotional loneliness, feelings of inadequacy and incompetence, marital problems, fear of expressing emotion, especially anger, and general dissatisfaction with those he depended upon (noted earlier in psychoanalytic explanations of depression). Here are some extracts from the tenth session where 'Ruth' (Greenberg) is the therapist; dots represent missing sections:

John   ... I was reading about the Oedipus complex. I realised that I really had some angry feelings towards my mother. I didn't think she cared about me enough the times I needed her.

Ruth   You had this angry thought about your mother?

John   Yeah. I feel real bad about it. You have these ill feelings, yet you are not supposed to have ill feelings against your mother.

Ruth   What kind of a person would have those feelings about his mother?

John   I don't know. I just have this feeling that society would think something must be wrong with a person who had bad feelings about his mother.

Ruth   So that is an assumption that you have ...

John   Well, what I have been doing is putting distance between my parents and myself. If I don't have to be in their company, then I feel like maybe I can resolve it.

Ruth   ... you have just been staying away from them. But there's a thought that if you *are* close to them, they will take away your problems. And at the same time you have a sense of resentment against your mother for not having been there in the past.

John   Yeah there is.

Ruth   So, that's contradictory. What do you make of that?

John   When I see her I want her to be real affectionate, give me a hug or something ...

Ruth   And does she make up for it?

John   Not like I want her to.

Ruth   What is it that you want?

John   That she would be very warm, and hug me ... All the things that I never really got ...

Ruth   Was she warmer to your sister?

John   I don't really think I can say that. No ...

Ruth   Has she ever been warm to anybody that you know?

John   Not especially. I think she is warmer to my wife than she is to me ... She will kiss my wife but she won't kiss me.

Ruth   Did you ask her why not?

John   No.

Ruth   Well, does she kiss other men? Does she kiss your father?

John   Definitely not.

Ruth   Is it possible that that is just her nature? She is generally not very warm ...

Notice how the therapist attempts to work with the client in exposing contradictions in thinking. To solve some of these there is an attempt to alter attributions – for instance, to get John to accept that his feelings about his mother might *not* be all his own fault. His mother need not be perfect. It is normal not to like what people do but this doesn't entail rejection of them. Note how the therapist *could* have led the discussion back to childhood emotions as might a traditional analyst. Here, however, the immediate strategy is to defuse the guilt and blame with rational argument about the normality of such feelings. Although the investigation of jealousies and forgotten feelings is not ruled out, this therapist bides time and lets such reflection emerge later, even then using the opportunity to adjust John's egocentric perception of his mother's attitude towards him – his mother *doesn't* just act cold towards him, this is perhaps her nature. Of course, the therapist doesn't *tell* John this. She allows him to reason it through as a result of her questions.

Client-centred (humanistic) therapy

The practice of counselling has been very heavily influenced by the thinking and practice of Carl Rogers who, along with Abraham Maslow, counts as a founding figure of the HUMANISTIC movement in psychology. Sometimes known as the 'third force' (between overly scientific and coldly technical behaviourism and overly interpretive psychoanalysis), humanistic psychology has its focus on the whole 'self'. It is not happy with behaviourism's concentration on very specific aspects of behaviour or the idea that a few 'responses' can be dealt with in isolation from how the person interprets that behaviour in terms of their overall self-image. Equally it is unhappy with a Freudian emphasis on interpretation of an individual's behaviour in terms of its symbolic content if the individual concerned does not reach those conclusions independently.

Although only 2.5% of clinical psychologists surveyed by O'Sullivan and Dryden (1990) gave 'person-centred' therapies as their first choice of theoretical orientation, nearly 30% of those using an eclectic approach (themselves over 30% of the total) named person-centred as their type of eclecticism. Rogers' influence on general therapy cannot be dismissed but his greatest influence has been on the counselling movement and in associated caring professions such as social work, an area where Rogerian terms, like 'non-judgemental', 'client', and 'non-directive' are commonly used.

The explanation of anxiety-related disorders

Rogers (1961) started with a fundamental belief in the human quality of goodness. In the absence of adverse childhood experiences, in a comfortable home with sensitive parents, a child will naturally orient towards the positive things and attitudes in life. A further natural human quality is the drive towards ACTUALISATION – the tendency to strive to grow, experience new events and to incorporate these into our developing understanding of the world. A need which accompanies development is that for POSITIVE REGARD, that is, WARMTH for want of a better term. A few people, including our parents, give this UNCONDITIONALLY, but even parents can be driven to withhold this love, making it CONDITIONAL – 'Mummy doesn't love you when you scream like that'. As one begins to rely more on one's own resources, so there develops a need for SELF-ACTUALISATION. Some literature, confusingly, fails to distinguish between actualisation and self-actualisation. The latter includes developing a positive image of oneself as successful at coping with life, understanding oneself and developing a sense of SELF-WORTH or POSITIVE SELF-REGARD. Trouble can occur when the need to see oneself as having integrity conflicts with overall actualisation. For instance, a normal actualising desire may be to leave home and travel around the world but, if your parents start accusing you of deserting them after all they've done for you, and you accept their criticisms, your self-image as a loving and grateful child may be threatened. You now have a dilemma. Actualisation may be compromised in favour of self-actualisation, that is, satisfying the need for conditional positive self-regard. We all have CONDITIONS OF WORTH which are criteria we must satisfy in order to feel comfortable with ourselves.

Rogers emphasised the notions of ACTUAL SELF (how I am) and IDEAL SELF (how I'd like to be), and of the relationship between these two and actual experience – that is, what actually happens to you and what you see in the world. INCONGRUENCE occurs when there is a sizeable distance between one's actual self-image and one's ideal self (as in the example just given), or between self-image and experience (e.g. I *am* generous but get called mean in the pub). We may develop (Freudian-type) DEFENCE MECHANISMS to protect ourselves form these threatening incongruences. Too much of this protection, too much incongruence, leads to a development of anxiety which, in turn, leads to unnatural and unwanted, disturbing behaviour – disturbing for ourselves or for others. One effect will be a further lessening of positive regard, especially unconditional, and the individual may have to work hard for any positive regard at all, since fewer people will spend a decreasing amount of time with the person who is difficult or uncomfortable to be with. The individual cannot be happy with their self-image because their conditions of worth are far too severe. This is when therapy may be sought or offered.

Notice that Natascha has cut herself off from possible sources of positive regard. Even if it were given by her in-laws when she saw them, it is possible that she might misinterpret the respect they do show her as subtle criticism. For instance, a relative might say 'I do admire you. I just don't know how you coped with Jason, being pregnant *and* did so well on your course'. Natascha sees this as implicit criticism of her duty as a mother to Jason, having 'abandoned' him whilst at college during the day. It is also possible that Natascha's relatives *are* spiteful and destructive in their comments, in which case her means of coping is to shut them out. However, this defence may not be adequate for long, especially if her partner is strongly attached to them. Sooner or later she may need to alter her strategy and confront the issues with the family. It might even be that the therapist will have to step out of the purely non-directive role (see below), become 'eclectic' and teach Natascha some assertiveness skills. Using these she will firmly, but not aggressively, declare and live by her own beliefs, values and norms of behaviour in contrast with those of her in-laws, no matter what comments and judgements they might make.

Client-centred (non-directive) therapy

Rogers' therapy is called NON-DIRECTIVE and CLIENT-CENTRED. The therapist offers unconditional positive regard and *listens* – something which the individual has usually rarely experienced in recent times. The therapist reflects back the client's confusions and contradictions in a way which should help the client to restructure them. The client is not argued with as in cognitive therapy. The non-directive principle arrived out of Rogers' dissatisfaction with the extreme interpretations of psychoanalysis. He argued that analysts could exert too much power and influence over clients for it to be valid to say that clients had acquired self-enlightenment. A further argument for client independence was in reaction to one of the major criticisms of the medical model – that if a person

believes their mind is 'sick' then, as with physical illness, they will assume that an 'expert' can cure it. Rogers, however, believed that change can only come from within the person, using their own inner resources. The therapist can only support this process.

In Rogerian therapy no deep interpretations are made. Nothing can happen without the client's agreement and co-operation in sorting out their own entanglements. The client is free to reintegrate and self-actualise. It is important that the client is, and feels, autonomous, responsible, confident and secure. They find previously rejected experiences valued by the therapist. These are examined by the client through the therapist's reflection of them as *valid* experiences. Strict rules of therapeutic procedure cannot be laid down because the client-centred therapist has to be ready to go where the client goes. Although Rogers' original position was one of complete non-directiveness, Davison and Neale (1994) describe the later incorporation of 'advanced EMPATHY' as follows:

> '. . . the therapist generates a view that takes the client's world into account but conceptualises things, it is hoped, in a more constructive way. The therapist presents to the client a way of considering himself or herself that may be quite different from the client's accustomed perspective.' (p.543)

The therapy must go at the client's pace, but lead towards acceptance of the client's conflicts as impossible clashes between self needs, overly strict internal standards and external demands. These are then dealt with by an increasingly more rational restructuring of the client's attitudes and beliefs – parents need not be so possessive; everyone does things which displease parents; one cannot be perfect in one's parents' eyes and so on. This overlaps with cognitive therapy. The difference here is that the emphasis is on the whole self and more on the notion of PERSONAL GROWTH – the client is helped to realise what they really want to achieve, not just to get rid of what troubles them.

Part of the attraction of this approach to counsellors and those working in social services, for instance, is that the former do not see their clients as 'ill' and the latter are usually delivering a service to people who have usually not been deemed 'ill' by anyone. Such workers usually reject the 'expert' image of the other types of therapist. They see themselves as facilitators of personal change rather than curers of the sick.

A major criticism of the approach has been that, since it relies on the client leading the process of change, with the therapist listening carefully and reflecting back progress, the system is only likely to work with people who are articulate, rational and willing to talk about their problems and conflicts with little prompting.

Validation of client-centred therapy

Rogers, as a trained natural scientist, was eager to subject his therapy and those who practised it to empirical test. Early studies of the effective therapist (e.g. Truax and Mitchell, 1971) drew the conclusion that three major qualities were possessed by those therapists who produced the most positive results in their clients. These were:

- WARMTH – assumed to be related to unconditional positive regard
- GENUINENESS – the ability to be oneself; if a therapist feels they cannot maintain this, and give warmth, because they are, for instance, disgusted by the client's offences, they should declare this and give up the case
- EMPATHY – the ability to see and appreciate the world from another's point of view.

Later studies were not so supportive of these qualities as effective in facilitating positive change. Mitchell et al (1977) found that more than half the studies they reviewed didn't produce the expected correlations between therapist qualities and client outcomes. There has also been much debate about whether the three skills can be trained. Egan (1982) devised programmes to train helping skills, whereas Plum (1981) argued that the qualities are unique to the developed individual therapist and therefore can't be artificially acquired. Mitchell et al argued that poor measurement issues were largely to blame for their lack of positive findings but Beutler et al (1986) and Lambert et al (1986) have also produced evidence against these qualities as important in producing positive outcomes.

Qualities of the therapist

If studies on the effectiveness of these therapist qualities produce ambiguous results, why bother with the qualities? Well, there is plenty of evidence that therapist qualities make a significant difference to outcomes. McConnaughty (1987) reviews much of this and argues that there is more variability among therapists within one technique than there is among the techniques themselves. Hence, it appears to be the therapist, not the technique, that is important for improvement. However, it does not seem to be the specific three Rogerian qualities which matter. For instance, Garfield and Bergin (1971) found that therapists low in emotional disturbance themselves were more effective in lowering depression and defensiveness in clients. Beutler et al (1986) found that therapist well-being had significant effects on client improvement. Similar effects were found by LaCrosse (1980) for characteristics of interpersonal influence such as attractiveness, expertness and trustworthiness. Beck et al (1979) argue that the three Rogerian qualities are essential to a good working relationship in which the client feels secure, trusting and comfortable in divulging what are pretty threatening and extremely intimate thoughts and feelings. However, relying *only* on these qualities appears insufficient for improvement in clients.

Pilgrim and Treacher (1992) argue that clinical psychology training, especially the more behavioural programmes, has consistently underplayed the importance of the therapist's relationship with the client in securing positive change. Early research on Rogers himself as therapist showed he did not respond impartially and identically to clients with different qualities and interpersonal styles. Truax (1966) suggested that he was, in fact, delivering 'reinforcement' rather than working on the client's self-image through discussion.

Outcome research

The vast amount of research in clinical psychology concerns EFFICACY. This is the question of whether a certain type of therapy 'works' or not. By 'works' is meant a number of issues concerning client improvement. A research study which investigates the results of one or more types of therapy is known as an OUTCOME STUDY. Several have been described in the course of covering the various approaches so far outlined.

A major difficulty in producing outcome studies which follow the pattern of strict scientific comparison studies is the unique nature of each case treated. Whatever the general approach taken, in each case the exact reinforcer or pattern of cognitive contradictions will be different for each client. For instance, Keith, whose case was described earlier, had to be *asked* how he relaxed and his favourite method was brought into the relaxation process. Some types of client do better with certain types of therapy. For instance, those whose personality is 'integrated' (self-reflective, self-controlled, etc) do better with 'exploratory' therapies (e.g. psychoanalysis) whereas more structured techniques (e.g. behavioural techniques) favour the less well-integrated personality (Jones et al, 1988). We must also keep in mind that the character of the therapist affects clients' progress within any one particular therapeutic approach, according to McConnaughty's findings, described above.

Where one therapist looks for overall personal growth another is satisfied with removal of symptoms. In the same time period then, one may appear more successful than the other who, nevertheless, is achieving more substantial and long-lasting personal change. We said earlier that psychoanalytically-oriented therapists were traditionally rather shy of publishing quantitative results. Eysenck (1952) claimed that 'person-centred' therapies produced results no better than the rate of spontaneous recovery (66%) with psychoanalysis, in particular, producing inferior results (44%), with the clear implication that psychotherapy makes people worse, not better. Bergin (1971) rebutted many of Eysenck's claims, showing that with altered criteria for 'success', psychoanalysis was effective.

An additional problem with outcome studies is the fact that therapists can and do choose which clients they will take on. Malan (1979) lists criteria for excluding certain potential clients from short-term therapy since they are in danger of suffering negative effects from it. Some studies take a more rigorous path and randomly allocate clients to therapy types to avoid such SAMPLING BIAS. One

problem with this solution is, however, that clients often have a clear preference for a certain type of therapeutic technique. Therefore the outcomes may be CONFOUNDED by the interaction between what the client prefers and the type of therapy they are, in fact, allocated to. Brewin and Bradley (1989) recommend greater use of designs permitting patient choice.

A well-controlled experimental study of therapies

In Appendix 2, it is explained that in a true experiment participants are RANDOMLY ALLOCATED to groups and then an INDEPENDENT VARIABLE is manipulated. Hollon's study, mentioned earlier, did this as did a thorough experimental study conducted by Sloane et al (1975). Here, 90 patients at a US hospital psychiatric clinic were randomly divided into three groups, one receiving behaviour therapy, one receiving psychoanalytically-oriented treatment and the remainder acting as a CONTROL GROUP (ethical, since none of the patients was in a serious condition). They were assessed by a psychiatrist, 'blind' to the patient's type of treatment, at initial diagnosis, at four months (when treatment ended) and after one year. Both treatment groups significantly improved over their starting position (compared with controls) but there was no difference between them. 74% of behaviour therapy clients thought they had improved, as did 81% of the psychotherapy group, compared with 44% of the control group. Similar numbers thought they had gained overall benefit from the treatment. One sobering point however, is that the assessed difference in improvement between the therapy groups and the control group had entirely disappeared at eight months. The control group had caught up, though at least it can be said that the therapies appeared to hasten improvement and therefore to help clients to go further sooner.

A UK experiment at the doctor's

Research by Robson et al (1984) in the UK, on clinical psychology in the primary care sector, used drug prescription cost, consultation and hospital appointments as improvement measures, in addition to psychological assessment scales. They randomly allocated patients to one of four clinical psychologists or to (control) treatment by the GP with whom they were associated. Just as in the Sloane et al study, the control group eventually caught up with the other groups on most measures (except cost of psychotropic drugs) having been significantly higher, up to 24 weeks, on GP visits, assessment scales and receiving medication. The researchers used this as part of an argument for the cost-effectiveness of clinical psychologists since it appeared that psychological treatment speeds up natural improvement. Marzillier and Hall (1992), commenting on the Robson study, point out that natural improvement may occur for milder conditions but cite evidence (Milne and Souter, 1988) to support the view that, for more chronic problems, waiting list patients did *not* improve until they had received sessions of cognitive behaviour therapy.

Comparing therapies in the UK

One of the results of outcome studies has been an argument that it is difficult to compare disorders. Even those as clearly related and well-defined as phobias can rarely, if ever, be seen as equivalent. There has been growing acceptance that it makes sense to investigate specific procedures for clearly-defined problems rather than try to compare this or that overall therapeutic approach across a wide range of disorder.

In line with this thinking, Shapiro and Firth (1987) conducted a strictly controlled study at the University of Sheffield. Only professional and managerial workers suffering depression and/or anxiety were seen, limited to those who complained that the condition affected their work, had no other symptoms, and who had not recently changed drug regimes or had similar psychological therapy. The patients experienced two forms of therapy in a 'cross-over' design – half received 'prescriptive' therapy, then 'exploratory', while the other half experienced these in the opposite order. To avoid therapist effects, each therapist stayed with the same patient throughout. There were stringent checks on the therapists' maintenance of the appropriate therapy style. 'Prescriptive' therapy was a mix of cognitive and behavioural techniques including diary keeping, relaxation,

SELF-MANAGEMENT tasks, assertion training and rational restructuring. The 'exploratory' (humanistic/analytic) method used Hobson's (1985) Conversational Model where the client's interpersonal relationships are seen as a root cause and are investigated through the relationship between therapist and client. Results favoured prescriptive therapy, which showed particular improvement on the Beck Depression Inventory and the SCL-90 (referred to earlier).

Combining outcome studies – meta-analysis

Outcome studies sometimes support one therapy but others may not. META-ANALYSIS is a method of combining the results of many studies and is described in Appendix 2. In one of the most rigorous and early meta-analytic studies, Smith and Glass (1977) included about 400 studies of the efficacy of psychotherapy. The main findings were that the average therapy patient showed improvement superior to 75% of non-therapy patients and that behavioural and non-behavioural therapies were not significantly different in their effects.

Shapiro and Shapiro (1982) reviewed 143 published studies from a five-year period. Overall they found that therapies were largely effective in bringing benefit as compared with 'minimal' approaches, including placebo treatment. However, there was a clear advantage for behavioural and cognitive approaches as compared with psychodynamic and humanistic methods. The authors recognised that the number of these latter approaches represented among the studies was low by comparison with the former approaches.

Schulberg and Rush (1994) report the findings of the 'Depression Guideline Panel of the United States Agency for Health Care and Policy Research' – a multi-disciplinary panel conducting a wide-ranging review of the diagnosis, treatment and follow-up of depression. The work included a meta-analysis of 12 cognitive therapy studies, 10 behavioural studies, one interpersonal (client-centred) therapy study and six brief dynamic psychotherapy studies. Using a complex 'efficacy rate' they found the following effectiveness for the therapies: cognitive 47%; behavioural 55%; interpersonal 52%; psychotherapy 35%.

THE FUTURE OF CLINICAL PSYCHOLOGY

Care in the community

Figure 2.1 (page 28) shows the traditional 'filters' in operation through which a prospective client has had to pass before meeting a clinical psychologist. There have been two recent major influences which have had the effect of putting the clinical psychologist and the client together outside of the traditional hospital meeting place. One is the move towards CARE IN THE COMMUNITY for many patients who would once have been confined within large psychiatric hospitals. Radical thinkers in the 1960s and 1970s spent a good deal of energy arguing that the last place that would be beneficial for a psychologically disturbed person would be a large, gloomy hospital run on strict routines, where the patient is regarded and treated as 'sick' and sessions with the specialist psychiatrist are extremely brief and formal, if they occur at all. Ironically, under the monetarist political regimes of the 1980s, continuing into the 1990s, this 'radi-

Large institutions can create problems in human behaviour but 'care in the community' can only work if adequate resources are made available.

cal' philosophy has been used by governments looking hard for public spending cuts wherever possible. Closure of an institution as large and expensive as were the grey, Victorian 'mental hospitals' makes a significant financial difference to health authorities strapped for cash under repeated cuts in their spending budgets.

The radicals had assumed that adequate compensating resources would be necessary in the community – day centres, adequately staffed hostels, plenty of respite care[1], training, effective communication between professionals and so on – in order for ex-patients to be supported and to improve, and in order that disasters would be avoided. However, although this is indeed what successive health ministers have claimed to be providing, it would be hard to find community care providers who feel that anything like adequate funding has been available. Clinical psychologists have found themselves increasingly involved in the community care trend, mainly through their increasing involvement in the 'primary care' field – the system of health care operating outside of large institutions and the system a person is likely to encounter first on their way to their most appropriate treatment. Clinical psychologists, then, have become attached to General Practitioner surgeries (as in the Robson study), health centres, and specialist groups such as day centres for drug rehabilitation and the newer community mental health centres. Pilgrim and Treacher (1992) express a concern that this trend has the danger of blurring the role of the clinical psychologist with other health professionals and of weakening their specialist status.

The influence of consumerism and financial constraint

The second factor stimulating work by clinical psychologists outside of hospitals, is a by-product of consumerism. In traditional health care the doctor is God, unquestioned and obeyed for the good of one's body and life prospects. In the climate of consumerism even gods are questioned. Unheard of queries such as, 'Is this really the best approach for me?' or 'Am I getting the best service possible from my doctor(s)?' suddenly become commonplace. An unexpected and beneficial spin-off from this, perhaps, has been people's greater interest in the health care process, in leading healthier lifestyles, and in organising their environment to promote greater health, even though this last initiative is somewhat patchy and often ill-informed (see the health and environmental psychology chapters). An important new direction has been the involvement of clinical psychologists in the planning of new health care systems and in creating 'customer-friendly' approaches, even at the level of the reception desk at your local doctor's surgery and certainly in terms of the various special clinics run by most large practices.

In addition, the public now expects counselling for most major disasters and many other crises. One recent 'disaster' requiring counselling appears to be the winning of a few million pounds on the National Lottery! On a more serious note, regular sufferers of psychological disturbance and problems can themselves criticise the treatments they receive and may well start to cast around in a wider area for appropriate treatment from professionals.

Changes in the role of the clinical psychologist

Challenges to the clinical psychologist's role and influence will continue to flow from changes within the National Health Service, as health employers attempt to balance ever more sensitive budgets. Parry (1992) argues for a greater effort at evaluation of psycho-therapeutic services. She notes the worry of Strupp (1986) that policy-makers and health insurers tend to use a drug metaphor in evaluation of therapies, looking for the quickest and 'safest' treatment, thereby misrepresenting the nature and aims of psychothera-

---

[1]'Respite' is the technical term for time given to, for instance, parents of a child with severe learning difficulties or the partner of a person with schizophrenia, so that they can get some relief from their 24-hour caring responsibilities.

pies. She uses Maxwell's (1984) six criteria by which a service can be evaluated: 1. *relevance* – do services meet clients' needs? 2. *equity* – do assessment methods, for instance, exclude some who need treatment? 3. *accessibility* – can clients get to the service? 4. *acceptability* – relevant research here would be that of Llewelyn et al (1988) on patients' perception of 'helpful events' in therapy. Parry recommends not just looking for 'satisfied' clients via questionnaire, for instance, but using a panel of users and ex-users to investigate why clients are dissatisfied 5. *effectiveness* – an assessment of outcome studies 6. *efficiency* – clinical psychologists would be hostile to improving service at the cost of quality (see Seager and Jacobson, 1993, for a typical argument), hence Parry argues that the focus should rather be on cost-effectiveness which is achieving the same outcomes for lower cost or better outcomes for the same cost. The relevance of this debate is unlikely to lessen in the current economic and political climate.

Dooley (1994), in a review of current trends in clinical psychology, raises two issues concerned with the traditional one-to-one relationship between clinical psychologist and client. First of all we must ask who *is* the client? This can be seen as, not just the client, but those intimately concerned with the client – family, carers and so on. Another interpretation of 'client', however, includes the 'purchaser' of the service which the psychologist offers – for instance the hospital trust or even the local doctor. Clinical psychologists might also need to use their specialist psychological skills to ask, 'who are the potential clients and which of these is not in fact getting any access to psychological services?' This issue has already been raised in connection with members of minority ethnic groups but there is a far wider range of the population who might require help but do not seek it – those over-stressed at work, those depressed through unemployment and so on. The second and connected point is that there are already far too many clients for clinical psychologists to deal with realistically on a one-to-one basis. Some clinicians therefore talk only of 'improving life quality', given their limited resources, or they leave the service because they are disillusioned. Dooley argues that clinical psychologists might redefine their role and concentrate on their specialist psychological abilities – dealing with basic theoretical principles and research problems. The suggestion is that clinical psychologists might abandon the one-to-one role and concentrate on consultancy, training other professionals to run face-to-face and group therapy and so on. Their future role then might become that of educators, therapy planners, therapy programme managers and evaluators of outcome in the interest of efficiency and effectiveness.

FURTHER RECOMMENDED READING

Davison, G. C. and Neale, J. M. (1994) *Abnormal Psychology*. New York: Wiley.

Lindsay, S. J. E. and Powell, G. E. (eds.) (1994) *The Handbook of Clinical Adult Psychology*, 2nd edn. London: Routledge.

Marzillier, J. and Hall, J. (1992) *What is Clinical Psychology?* Oxford: Oxford University Press.

Rack, P. (1991) *Race, Culture and Mental Disorder*. London: Routledge.

Ussher, J. M. and Nicolson, P. (1992) *Gender Issues in Clinical Psychology*. London: Routledge.

exercises

1. Using a grid like that below fill in what you see to be the main features, and then the advantages and disadvantages, or strengths and weakness, of each of the therapeutic techniques which might be employed by clinical psychologists.

	Psychodynamic	Behavioural	Cognitive/ cognitive– behavioural	Humanistic
Role of therapist Role of client Main causes of condition Route to improvement How therapy helps along the route to improvement Signs or measures of improvement Strengths Weaknesses				

2. Imagine you are producing an advertisement for a clinical psychologist to join your working team which takes a particular approach to therapy. Without consulting a textbook as you write, try to describe in brief terms the main principles of the approach your team uses and then describe the qualities you would therefore expect any applicants to possess. Describe any other qualities required in working with a team of clinical psychologists who engage in research, teaching and consultancy work, as well as therapy.

3. Create a mini-survey to be used on ordinary members of the public designed to demonstrate how ignorant many people are of the distinctions between psychiatrist, psychologist and psychotherapist. Also include questions on the true sense of 'schizophrenia', types of therapy (e.g. 'psychoanalysis would involve' followed by some multiple responses to choose from) and assumed causes of psychological problems (e.g. genes or environment). Discuss your findings with your class or other co-learners.

4. Imagine that a hospital or health centre is reconsidering its decision to employ a clinical psychologist. Design an argument which gives convincing reasons why the clinical psychologist can make a unique contribution to patient care and the areas in which they would be most useful and effective.

5. Together with a trusted partner, choose an issue which has been bothering you (such as fear of speaking in class, worry over not getting an assignment done, weakness at taking things back to shops to complain, etc). Using the thought mechanisms listed on p. 42, present the worst possible view of the situation. Then, helped by your partner, try to alter each thought or typical behaviour into the best possible way of coping or dealing with the situation. Then swap roles with your partner and repeat the exercise.

HEALTH WARNING! Treat this as a fairly light-hearted learning experience, NOT a genuine therapy session. Do not use this exercise on a problem which is *very* serious for you. If you really feel you need help, then seek this professionally.

3 CRIMINOLOGICAL PSYCHOLOGY

WHAT IS CRIMINOLOGICAL PSYCHOLOGY?

Criminological psychology, or FORENSIC PSYCHOLOGY as it is also increasingly known, is a branch of psychology which attempts to apply psychological principles to an important real-life setting, the criminal justice system. CRIMINOLOGICAL PSYCHOLOGY is very much rooted in empirical research and draws on the areas of COGNITIVE PSYCHOLOGY, developmental psychology, social psychology and CLINICAL PSYCHOLOGY. One of its main areas of focus is the study of criminal behaviour and its management, but in recent years criminological psychologists have expanded their research interests to a number of other areas, most notably those with a high media profile, such as:

- jury selection
- the presentation of evidence in court
- eyewitness testimony
- improving the recall of child witnesses
- false memory syndrome and recovered memory
- offender profiling
- crime prevention
- devising treatment programmes
- assessing the risk of releasing prisoners.

Criminological psychologists are suddenly becoming media celebrities, experts who are wheeled on to offer definitive solutions to the 'problem' of crime. Inevitably there tends to be a backlash to this sort of overnight success, and so, whilst offender profiling has been called 'a new enterprise zone for the British Psychological Society' (Hughes, 1994) with TV series like *Cracker* highlighting the glamour of expert knowledge in the form of Robbie Coltrane, there has also been a downside with the contribution of a criminological psychologist being seen as one of the main reasons why the case against a suspect in the Rachel Nickell murder case was dropped when it went to court in September 1994. It is in this context that the massive growth of interest in criminological psychology, and the number of new courses emerging, should be understood. The British Psychological Society is already concerned that the title of Chartered Forensic Psychologist should only be conferred on members who are able to demonstrate the following:

1. A sound conceptual basis of the context within which he or she practises in terms of:
   a) psychology and criminal behaviour
   b) the legal framework – the law and the criminal justice system

2. A sound understanding of the contribution – actual and potential – of applied psychology to the criminal justice system in terms of:

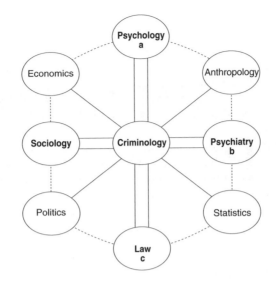

Notes to Figure 3.1
Double lines indicate close
subject links.
Single lines indicate less
close association.
Broken lines indicate overall
subject association.
a. is abnormal psychology.
b. is forensic psychiatry.
c. is criminal law, law
enforcement, and police
science.

FIGURE 3.1
Criminology relies heavily on its
affiliations with other disciplines.

a) psychology and the processes of criminal investigation
b) psychology and the legal process
c) psychology and the custodial process
d) psychology and the treatment process (offenders and victims)

3. An appropriately detailed understanding of psychology in relation to the following key individuals:
   a) offenders (adults and children; non-disordered and mentally-disordered)
   b) victims (adults and children)
   c) witnesses (adults and children)
   d) investigators (e.g. police officers, and allied professionals)

4. A sound understanding of forensic psychology in practice in terms of:
   a) the different demands for assessment of offenders

b) the processes of investigation, prosecution and defence
c) decision-making in respect of innocence, guilt, sentencing, custody, treatment and rehabilitation
d) approaches to assessment of offenders
e) professional criteria for report production and giving of testimony
f) extensive practical experience in engaging in at least one area of forensic psychology

(from the Division of Criminological and Legal Psychology (DCLP) Training Committee, BPS, 1994.)

Crombag (1994) neatly reverses this emphasis on psychologists as 'experts' when he suggests that lawyers occasionally make 'pretty good applied psychologists', and it is well worth remembering the potential contribution of other disciplines such as law, sociology, psychiatry, politics and anthropology to a full and coherent understanding of criminal behaviour (see Fig 3.1).

WHAT DO CRIMINOLOGICAL PSYCHOLOGISTS DO?

Criminological psychologists can be found working within a wide range of contexts. Those with clinical or forensic training tend to work in psy-chiatric hospitals and special hospitals, whilst psychologists working for the prison psychological service are situated in young offender institutions and prisons. These individuals will often be involved in risk assessment, establishing on the basis of a range of evidence what the degree of risk might be if certain offenders are to be considered for release. They will also be involved in devising treatment programmes for specific groups of offenders, for instance, anger management. A crucial part of this work involves research and evaluation in order to determine what constitutes successful treatment. Success may be evaluated in terms of a reduction in subsequent offending, or in terms of personal growth and increased self-knowledge which may allow the offender more choice in the decision to reoffend and the ability to reflect on alternatives.

There are many professionals working in both health and offender contexts who also have some psychological training, for example, forensic nurses, prison officers, and police officers. They too may be involved in the processes of assessment and treatment. Criminological psychologists also work within an academic context, teaching on both undergraduate and postgraduate courses. All of these professionals may offer consultative advice to a variety of agencies, including social services departments, probation and after-care departments and the police, and may also be asked to appear as expert witnesses in court cases. Criminological psychologists also engage in research activity, and may be employed to do this by specific agencies such as the Home Office Research Unit, or the police, or they may conduct independent research. The significant feature of research within criminological psychology is that it is almost exclusively of an applied nature. Thus examples of research in which criminological psychologists might be engaged are:

- analysis of official criminal statistics
- conducting a longitudinal study of children in order to determine which of them become offenders
- setting up experimental studies whereby an attempt is made to discern the association between screen violence and AGGRESSIVE behaviour.

Whilst the potential range of issues to explore is enormous there is a need to observe the ethical guidelines of the psychological profession (see Appendix 3) very strictly when such sensitive matters are involved.

THE DEVELOPMENT OF CRIMINOLOGICAL PSYCHOLOGY

Garland (1994) states that, 'As with most "human sciences", criminology has a long past but a short history' (p.27), and the same can be said of criminological psychology. Discourse about the causes of crime and the link with human nature has existed for centuries, but it is only during the latter half of this century that the discipline of criminological psychology can be said to have emerged in its own right, and indeed only in the last 20 years that an established body of knowledge based on empirical research has been recognised.

At the beginning of the twentieth century, a debate ensued about the relevance of psychology to law. Psychologists were eager to demonstrate how their research findings could be applied to the practice of law, and in 1908 Hugo Münsterberg published *On the Witness Stand* in which he called upon lawyers to appreciate the relevance of experimental psychology to their profession. Münsterberg was particularly interested in improving the performance of witnesses in terms of recall. His pleas remained unheeded however, and lawyers appeared to close ranks, dismissing the findings of psychologists as imprecise. A fallow period then occurred where work in the field of psychology as applied to law was rather irregular, though with some notable exceptions, e.g. Burt's *The Young Delinquent* (1925), and several psycho-

BOX 1

How would I become a criminological psychologist?

If you would like to become a criminological psychologist you should first complete an undergraduate course in psychology which is acceptable to the British Psychological Society. You might want to combine your studies in psychology with other relevant subjects such as sociology or law. There are also an increasing number of courses which specifically link criminology with psychology offering joint honours in these two subjects. If there is a dissertation requirement in your degree course, you would be well advised to choose an empirical and part-quantitative study in the area of criminology and psychology, and tackling a topic which allows reasonable collation of data might be advisable, i.e. not an in-depth case study of a serial killer!

As a graduate you must then complete a Masters degree in criminological psychology, investigative psychology, or forensic psychology. It is often an entry requirement for these courses that you have relevant work experience, and if you decide to join the prison psychological service you will be sent on one of these courses as part of your professional training. Alternatively you might decide you would like to follow the clinical psychology route (see

chapter 2), and choose forensic psychology as your specialism within that context. You might then obtain a diploma in clinical criminology. Again you will need relevant work experience before you can join a clinical psychology course. The academic path can be joined by registering for a PhD in an area of criminological psychology which will sustain your interest for at least three years. Most teaching posts will require a doctorate in a relevant area, and may also require some evidence of teaching experience.

It must be said that the career opportunities for criminological psychologists probably do not as yet match the expectations and enthusiasm of those undergraduates who have developed an interest in this field. You will have to enter stiff competition for a place on any professional Masters course, and there is still the old 'Catch 22' situation in relation to securing relevant work experience without any qualifications – you may find it difficult to obtain work without qualification, yet qualification requires work experience! Those interested in a career in clinical psychology experience the same kind of problems, so any relevant work, either in a paid or voluntary capacity, will improve your chances of success. There are relevant career alternatives in many areas, such as social work, mental health, youth work, victim support, probation and the police force, which are well worth considering.

analytic studies of young delinquents, e.g. Aichorn (1925). There was also the work of John Bowlby (1944), whose study of juvenile delinquents led to a theory of maternal deprivation as a key causal factor in offending behaviour. The criticisms of this work are legion, e.g. Morgan (1975) and Rutter (1981).

In the 1960s, however, the picture changed and a new demand for applied psychology emerged, particularly in the area of understanding criminal behaviour. Attempts to find the 'criminal personality', or the elusive 'criminal gene', were made.

Chief amongst researchers in this area was Hans Eysenck (1964), who suggested that neurotic extroverts were more likely to become offenders because they are less easily conditionable to social and other stimuli and will therefore be less likely than other personality types to learn social control via the process of socialisation. Their personality characteristics of neuroticism and extroversion, as measured by Eysenck's scales, were held to be biologically determined. Eysenck's theories generated considerable interest and research, which is well documented by Bartol (1980), but the findings have not been wholly consistent, and many writers have distanced themselves from its pessimistic principle that criminal behaviour is largely determined by our biology and by conditioning processes in early life well beyond our personal control (Trasler, 1987).

Increasing concern about the apparent increase in crime rates, violent crime in particular, and an increasing recognition of the need to provide rehabilitation programmes which actually reduce *recidivism* (return to crime) prompted the next wave of research. As a result, there was a dramatic increase in the application of psychological principles to criminological issues, and the potentially positive role of psychologists within various systems was increasingly recognised, as the following examples demonstrate:

- *in the legal system* – assisting with trial strategy, jury selection, police training, interviewing witnesses, and offering expert testimony
- *in the prison system* – assessing offenders' needs, their likelihood of reoffending, and devising treatment programmes

- *in the political system* – offering advice on policy changes in relation to the treatment of offenders and victims.

The Home Office set up a research unit to explore these areas, a Division of Criminological and Legal Psychology was recognised by the British Psychological Society in 1977, and a wide range of relevant journals specifically looking at these areas began to appear. Examples include: *Psychology, Crime and Law*; *Legal and Criminological Psychology*; *Forensic Update*; and *Behavioural Sciences and the Law*. Criminological psychology now looks set to become one of the most popular areas of applied psychology.

In order to demonstrate how psychology can be applied to the criminal justice system, four areas have been selected to give a flavour of what is a much bigger cake! The selected areas are:

- attitudes to crime and victims
- offender profiling
- eyewitness testimony
- juries.

THEORY, RESEARCH AND APPLICATIONS

Attitudes to crime and victims

The 'rise' and recording of crime

There is increasing concern about the growth in crime rates, particularly offences involving violence, and it has been suggested that this increase is only the tip of the iceberg, i.e. that the crimes which are reported to the police are very few compared with the 'dark figure' of unreported crime. Examples of crimes which are often unreported include rape and domestic violence.

In contrast to this view, some writers suggest that the growth in crimes of violence is only

apparent, and that public fears about it are a result of media panic. A historical review of crime rates, it is argued, demonstrates that society has always suffered from the consequences of violence. Whatever the interpretation of criminal statistics, there can be little doubt that the *fear* of crime is a reality which seriously affects many people's lives, though often those who are most fearful, women and the elderly, are statistically least likely to be victims of crime.

Many crimes are simply not recorded. Official statistics bear little relation to the true extent of crime, whilst self-report studies (Belson, 1975) indicate that a surprisingly large number of adolescents are involved in crime and yet are not apprehended. Crime is not, therefore, confined to a deviant minority, but seems to be a normal feature of adolescence in large segments of Western society. Furnham and Thompson (1991) asked 100 undergraduates at the University of London, none of whom had a criminal record, to complete a self-report delinquency questionnaire. An average of 12 offences each was recorded, though many of these were minor. More worryingly, Groth et al (1982) asked 137 sex offenders in confidence about their true history of offending. They admitted to an average of about 5 undetected sexual offences, and some individuals had carried out 250 undetected offences.

Belief in a just world

An interesting area of research into attitudes to crime has begun to explore how we view victims and how our perceptions are influenced. The concept of a BELIEF IN A JUST WORLD locates the degree of sympathy felt towards a victim in the psychological attitudes of the observer, and can help us to understand why some often very deserving victims appear to receive very little sympathy. It is an unusual concept, because it is almost counter-intuitive – surely seeing a suffering victim will arouse nothing but sympathy and a desire to help, but very often this is followed by a cognitive process which determines that we differentiate ourselves from the victim in a significant way. We would all like to believe that the world is a fair place, and that people by and large get what they deserve. If this were not true it would increase our sense of vulnerability, and make our attempts to introduce order and predictability rather pointless. When we see someone suffer who has not done anything to deserve that suffering it calls into question our belief in a just world. In order to make sense of the suffering we may convince ourselves that the victim in some way did deserve their fate. How many innocent victims of rape have been described as having 'asked for it'? How many mothers of abducted children have been considered careless for having allowed their children to play unattended? There seems to be a need to consider victims as in some way different from the rest of us in order to protect our own fragile hold on a view that the world is a safe place.

Victims of the Nazi SS Concentration Camp on the outskirts of Uhrdruf. How can these victims be blamed in order to see the world as just?

In COGNITIVE DISSONANCE terms (Festinger, 1957), the unbalanced fraction:

Fred's little boy got assaulted
Fred's a good parent

produces *dissonance*. To reduce this dissonance we can:

- lose our belief in a just world (that people only ever get what they deserve)
- alter the belief in the bottom half of the fraction, e.g. by considering possibilities such as, 'Well, they don't always keep a watch on him when he's in the front garden,' and '... there was that accident his daughter had,' and so on. This partially balances the bottom of the fraction with the top.

Lerner and Simmons (1966) first established the 'belief in a just world' hypothesis. They asked female participants to take part in a laboratory experiment about emotion. When the participants arrived they met a stooge posing as another participant who was taking part in an experiment about learning. Before the study began all participants rated themselves in relation to social attractiveness. Next, the participants were asked to observe through a one-way screen the person they had met earlier. She appeared to be participating in a learning task, and each time she got the answer wrong she received an electric shock. They were asked to observe closely so that they could pinpoint the cues of emotional distress. After ten minutes of observation during which the stooge appeared to receive several electric shocks, one group of participants were told they would need to observe another ten minutes, whilst another group were asked if the stooge should continue to receive shocks or be rewarded for getting the correct answer. Most responded sympathetically and wanted the stooge to be rewarded. All participants were then asked to rate the stooge in terms of social attractiveness.

In line with the belief in a just world hypothesis, those who thought the stooge was going to continue getting shocked rated her as less attractive than they had rated themselves, and less attractive than did those who thought she was going to be rewarded. Lerner and Simmons suggest that seeing the victim suffer, and knowing that she would continue to do so, led the participants to devalue her, whereas seeing her rewarded resulted in less of a need to engage in VICTIM DEROGATION.

Since this experiment, there have been many studies of the belief in a just world and its effects. Jones and Aronson (1973) gave participants an account of a rape in which there was no evidence that the victim was in any way at fault. They were then asked to estimate the degree to which they thought the victim might have been at fault, and they were also asked to assign a hypothetical prison sentence to the rapist. Some participants were told the victim was a virgin, others that she was married, and others that she was divorced. The results were rather surprising in that the participants assigned less blame to the divorcee and most to the virgin whose attacker they awarded the heaviest sentence. Thus for the crime they found most horrifying, they blamed the victim the most, as if she was more responsible for what happened and had in some way brought the offence upon herself.

Rubin and Peplau (1975) developed a scale to measure individuals' degree of belief in a just world, and Furnham and Proctor (1989) provide an extensive review of the literature which attempts to correlate belief in a just world using this measure, with other characteristics, e.g. religious beliefs, personality traits, attitudes to feminism, and locus of control, etc. It would be interesting to determine whether there is a difference in the degree of belief in a just world demonstrated by different groups within the criminal justice system, e.g. judges, lawyers, offenders, police officers, etc.

Offender profiling

What is offender profiling?

The psychological profiling of offenders involves:

'the preparation of a biographical 'sketch' gathered from information taken at a crime scene, from the personal history and habits of a victim, and integrating this with known psychological theory.'

(Turco, 1993, p. 147).

The resulting sketch can be used by police officers to reduce their list of suspects or to offer a new line of enquiry. Traditionally the only clues noted at crime scenes tended to be hard evidence, such as bloodstains, saliva, or semen, but with the advent of OFFENDER PROFILING there is a recognition that there may be less visible clues at the crime scene too. These could include, for instance:

- the choice of victim
- the location
- the time
- the nature of the assault
- what is and is not said to the victim.

All of these clues define the offender, and psychologists can assist the police in interpreting these clues. Caution needs to be used, however, in the application of profiling, and it should not be used to specifically target a suspected offender, or indeed to totally eliminate a suspect. The status of profiling is currently uncertain though it has undoubted potential if used properly by trained professionals. The uncertainty has not been lessened in the light of Colin Stagg's acquittal in September 1994 for the suspected murder of Rachel Nickell, and the likelihood of one criminological psychologist appearing for the defence, and another for the prosecution, both professing quite different views of the adequacy of profiling. Geberth (1983) has described profiling as 'little better than information one could get from the neighbourhood bartender', and he was anxious to point out the danger of over-reliance on so-called 'expert' profiling without acknowledging the invaluable contribution of experienced police officers.

The development of offender profiling

Offender profiling as a process is not new although the term was only introduced during the early 1970s by FBI officers in the USA. During World War II, a psychiatrist, William Langer, was asked to compile a profile of Adolph Hitler by the Office of Strategic Services. Langer (1972) accurately diagnosed Hitler's psychiatric state, and was able to predict, accurately as it turned out, his likely response to defeat, that of suicide. Politicians became interested in the idea of psychological profiling as a means of assisting them in negotiating with foreign Heads of State. For example, Wedge (1968) advised President Kennedy how to interpret the behaviour of President Kruschev of the then Soviet Union.

Not surprisingly, the potential of profiling as a means of identifying criminals and developing appropriate interviewing strategies for them soon became apparent. There were successes and failures though. In the mid-1950s James Brussel, a psychiatrist, was asked by the New York police to help them find the 'Mad Bomber of New York'. This person had carried out a series of bombings

over several years, and Brussel was able to build a picture of him by examining the crime scenes and the letters written by the bomber. He provided such a detailed account of his likely personality, lifestyle, and place of residence, and even dress sense, that the police were able to arrest the bomber by a traditional process of elimination. A less successful attempt at profiling concerned the 'Boston Strangler' whose crimes were thought by a group of psychologists and psychiatrists to have been committed by two male school teachers living alone, one of whom was probably homosexual. When Albert DeSalvo was finally arrested, he was revealed as a heterosexual construction worker living with his family (both cases cited in Boon and Davies, 1992).

The contemporary scene

Contemporary offender profiling tends to follow one of two approaches, the first developed by the Behavioural Sciences Unit of the American Federal Bureau of Investigation primarily in response to serial murder, and the second pioneered by David Canter in the United Kingdom. It should be noted, however, that although the bulk of the literature on profiling focuses on serious crimes, e.g. serial murder and rape, there is also valuable work being carried out using profiling in relation to other areas of crime, e.g. burglary. In 1979 FBI investigators began to interview the growing number of incarcerated serial killers and sex murderers. As a result of their in-depth interviews with criminals such as Charles Manson, Sirhan Sirhan and Ted Bundy, amongst others, they began developing theoretical models which would allow the compilation of accurate profiles based on meticulous examination of crime scenes. Ressler (1993) was one of the interview team, and he concluded that sex killers tended to be white, unmarried males who were either unemployed or in unskilled jobs. They tended to have previous psychiatric or alcohol histories, and had a sexual interest in voyeurism, fetishism, and pornography. The FBI now train profilers world-wide, though their view is that profiles are not suitable in all crime investigations and are most useful in cases where there is some indication of psychopathology. The basis of their approach is that the crime scene and the offender's *modus operandi* will reveal indicators of individual pathology, which may fit into a pattern already observed from case studies of incarcerated offenders. According to Holmes (1989) the aims of profiling within this framework are:

- to reduce the scope of an investigation by providing basic information in relation to the social and psychological core variables of the offender's personality, e.g. race, age range, employment status and type, educational background, marital status, etc
- to allow some prediction of future offences and their location
- to provide a psychological evaluation of belongings found in the offender's possession, e.g. souvenirs from previous offences
- to provide strategies for interviewing offenders which can take account of individual differences, but profit from experience with offenders who have displayed a common pattern of offending.

The major theoretical contribution made by the FBI team is their division of serial killers into two categories – *organised* and *disorganised*. An *organised* offender is identified if the crime scene reveals evidence of planning, the victim was targeted, and the element of control has been important. The offender might then be presumed to have the following characteristics – average intelligence, social and sexual competence, and an intimate partner. In contrast, the *disorganised* offender is described as socially inadequate, and someone who may know the crime scene and/or the victim, and who lives alone. His crime scene will reveal evidence of an impulsive and unplanned attack using minimal restraint with no attempt to conceal the victim's body.

Offender profiling in the UK

In the United Kingdom offender profiling has been dominated by the work of David Canter, currently Professor of Psychology at Liverpool University. Professor Canter's psychological expertise is wide-ranging, but he had not focused on crime until he was approached by the Metropolitan Police in 1985 to advise whether the behavioural science of psychology could contribute to criminal investigations. The following year he was to become centrally involved in what was initially a serial rape investigation and which subsequently became a notorious serial murder case. With the help of Professor Canter the police were able to arrest John Duffy, who was subsequently convicted in 1988 for two murders and five rapes and given seven life sentences. The profile which Professor Canter provided described Duffy and where he lived so accurately that the response of the police and the media was one of astonishment.

Canter's approach to profiling is much more rooted in psychological principles than is the approach of the FBI, and he describes profiling which is merely based on crime scene analysis as 'more of an art than a science' (1989, p.12). He believes that criminals, like all other people, act consistently, i.e. their actions have some coherence whatever the setting, and that an analysis of their behaviour will reveal a pattern which can offer clues to their lifestyle during the non-offending part of their lives. In addition, Canter suggests that we all operate within a social context, so there is an implicit social relationship between the offender and his/her victim which again will offer major clues to the pattern of the offender's life. Sensitive and detailed examination of the victim's testimony can reveal speech patterns, interests, obsessions, and ways of behaving which will have also occurred outside of the criminal act. For example, rapists may treat their victims in the way they treat most of the women in their lives, and some may be hesitant and apologetic after the offence, thus revealing their characteristic difficulty in relating to women in an appropriate way.

Canter (1994) has demonstrated that his approach to profiling is far removed from the processes described in films such as *Manhunter* (1986) and *The Silence of the Lambs* (1991). He suggests that interviews with serial killers who are known to be manipulative, disturbed and sensation-seeking, are unlikely to be helpful. His own approach to criminal investigation involves advising experienced police officers on the basis of correlations between banks of data (for instance, time

In *Silence of the Lambs* (1991) Jodie Foster played the part of an FBI agent wanting assistance from a convicted serial killer, played by Anthony Hopkins.

and location of offences, or choice of victim) and content analysis of speech, in an attempt to develop patterns and identify trends. Canter feels this is likely to be of more practical use than sensational interviews whose validity is suspect. Interestingly, Gresswell and Hollin (1994) suggest that 'functional analyses of a large number of multiple murder perpetrators to facilitate the development of appropriate, testable, cognitive–behavioural models' is the logical next step in British research. Their approach should not be seen as a repetition of the FBI in-depth interviews of the 1980s, however, but as a challenging way to use profiling for clinical rehabilitation purposes. The knowledge gained in this way could be used to plan appropriate treatment programmes which would be geared to the needs of particular groups of offenders.

Boon and Davies (1992) have borrowed terminology from cognitive psychology to draw out the differences between the American and British approaches to profiling. They suggest that the British approach is based on 'bottom-up' type data processing. The profiling depends on an analysis of existing evidence which aims to identify specific associations between offences and offender characteristics. That is, the picture is constructed from specific items of information. In contrast, the American approach is described as more 'top-down' in its reliance on potentially subjective conclusions drawn from investigative experience of crimes and interviews with criminals. The picture is constructed more from comparison with other criminals and crime sequences. Boon and Davies (1992) suggest that in the American approach the concern is 'principally in what the serious offender does and when, rather than in psychological questions as to why' (p.6). However, the aim of both approaches is to predict when further offending is likely to occur, and to identify the crucial details which will help pinpoint the offender.

The potential of offender profiling is extremely challenging, but it needs to be thoroughly evaluated before it is hailed as the solution to criminal investigation. Pinizzotto and Finkel (1990) attempted to discover whether professional profilers would be more accurate than informed laypersons, and so they asked groups of profilers, detectives, psychologists and students to examine closed police cases and to draw up profiles. What they found was that the profilers did indeed produce richer and more detailed profiles, and they correctly identified the characteristics of the convicted offenders. Pinizzotto and Finkel concluded, however, that this was the result of both confidence and experience rather than the use of an exclusive technique. The implications would therefore be that both training and practical experience are vital in developing profiling expertise, and that productive liaison between the police and psychologists is the way forward in order to achieve both investigative and clinical objectives.

Eyewitness testimony

Juries tend to attach considerable importance to the evidence of eyewitnesses despite research which suggests it should not be considered foolproof. In 1980 Buckhout showed a 13-second film of a mugging on prime-time TV, then showed an identity parade of six men, and asked viewers to phone in and identify the offender. Over 2000 viewers responded, but picked the mugger correctly only 14% of the time, a rate close to random guesswork (with six possibilities, around 17% would be right by chance guessing alone).

Mistaken identity and the law

There are many famous cases of mistaken identity – one of the most notable was that of James Hanratty who was hanged in 1962. Another was Peter Hain, a prominent anti-apartheid activist (now an MP) wrongly accused of robbery. A recommendation in a 1976 report by Lord Devlin that trials based solely on identification evidence should not proceed has still to be implemented. The report was prepared after a miscarriage of justice in 1969, when Laso Virag was wrongly convicted of the attempted murder of a policeman on the basis of witness identification. He was subsequently pardoned in 1974 and received substantial compensation. Graham Davies (1994), Professor of Psychology at Leicester University, and an expert in eyewitness testimony, has argued strongly for a change in the law to prevent people from being convicted on the basis of identification without corroborating evidence. He argues that research clearly shows that most people remember faces poorly and recall details not from memory but from STEREOTYPES of what they think criminals should look like. Yarmey (1983) found that elderly people were more likely than younger people to identify an innocent bystander as an observed offender if that bystander 'looked like a criminal'; and Bull and Rumsey (1988) found that people were quite prepared to identify criminals by their appearance alone, presumably on the basis of quite firmly-held stereotypes.

One potential explanation for mistaken convictions seems to be the importance attached to eye-witness identification by jurors who seem prepared to believe this sort of testimony above all others. This may be because, intuitively, we think of memory and perception as passive copying processes, rather like a camera or a tape recorder which provide a permanent record of events. Most modern psychological research in fact shows both memory and perception to be *active* and *constructive* processes. Perception does not produce an accurate record, but an *interpretation* of events. This is found when someone takes a snapshot of a beautiful scene only to find, when the film is developed, that the view is traversed by several telegraph wires! These were ignored by the human perceptual system at the time. The camera, however, is faithful to reality. Our memory processes, too, are susceptible to both deterioration over time and reconstruction. Our memories of childhood tend to reflect these processes, where we may nostalgically remember 'positive' events and conveniently 'forget' how many times we were told off!

Research evidence

Elizabeth Loftus (1974) has conducted a series of experimental studies to explore the impact of eyewitness testimony. In one study she asked people to play the role of jurors by listening to evidence in a criminal case of robbery and murder in a grocery store. The mock jurors had to decide whether or not the defendant was guilty. The following circumstantial evidence was presented to a group of 50 mock jurors:

- the fact that the robber ran into the defendant's apartment block
- money was found in the defendant's room
- tests revealed there was a slight chance the defendant had fired a gun on the day of the offence.

Only 18% of participants hearing just this information said the defendant was guilty. Another group of 50 participants was given the circumstantial evidence plus another piece of evidence – the store clerk's eyewitness identification of the defendant. Of these, 72% were prepared to convict the defendant, demonstrating the powerful effect of eyewitness testimony. Nothing that surprising? Rather more striking were the results of a third condition in Loftus' study in which 50 participants received the circumstantial evidence, plus the eyewitness testimony, plus information *discrediting* the witness, i.e. that he was short-sighted, was not wearing his glasses, and that he could not have seen the robber's face from where he was standing. Nevertheless, 60% of the mock jurors *still* convicted.

The constructive nature of perception and memory

Traditional beliefs about eyewitness testimony tend to overestimate its accuracy and fail to take into account developments in the field of perception and memory. Contemporary research highlights the dynamic and fluid quality of both processes especially over time. Researchers find it useful to view memory as a three-stage process involving:

- acquisition   – the witness's perception at the time of the event
- storage   – the witness stores the information in order to prevent forgetting
- retrieval   – when the information is needed, e.g. in court, the witness has to retrieve it from storage

This model suggests that errors can occur at three different points. During the original event an individual perceives it and encodes it in memory but many factors influence this process. For instance, people almost always overestimate the amount of time events take (time seems to stand still, or events take place in slow motion). Buckhout et al (1974) staged an assault on a professor in front of 141 students. The attack only lasted 34 seconds, but the average estimate of the event's duration was 81 seconds.

Stress, perception and memory

There also seems to be a relationship between stress and perception, namely the YERKES-DODSON LAW, which states that perception, learning and performance are best at moderate levels of arousal and worst at very high or low levels of arousal. This is the curvilinear (or 'inverted-U') relationship between arousal and performance which is referred to in the chapter on sport psychology. The principle may well seem counter-intuitive, in that subjective recall of personal events indicates that high emotion often produces very clear and vivid memories. In fact psychologists have lent credence to this – Brown and Kulik (1977) investigated people's memories of the assassination of President Kennedy in 1963, and found that a phenomenon called FLASHBULB MEMORY existed. Their participants could remember – as if a camera flash had gone off and preserved the details – where they were and what they were doing when they had heard the news. The trouble with this is that, although recall may be vivid, there is no guarantee that it is accurate, and current research would indicate that stress can impair the recall of a witness in a variety of ways.

Weapon focus

Clifford and Scott (1978) demonstrated that people's recollection of non-violent events was superior to their memory of violent events. Violence, in particular, seems to interfere with recall, causing witnesses to focus on one aspect of the situation to the detriment of more general observation. This is known as WEAPON FOCUS which allows the witness to provide lots of details about the weapon used, but virtually nothing about the user of the weapon. Loftus et al (1987) showed that people viewing a film will focus on a gun held by a customer in a restaurant, rather than (in an alternative version of the film) on a cheque in his hand. Identification of the suspect in an identity parade and the answers to more specific questions were more accurate in the 'cheque' condition than in the 'gun' condition. Maass and Kohnken (1989) demonstrated a version of the weapon focus effect. Participants approached by a white-coated female experimenter with a syringe in her hand were less accurate at subsequently identifying her than those who saw her with a pen in her hand.

Post-event information

Experiences which occur *after* the event can also

When J. F. Kennedy was assassinated there were many eyewitnesses but their testimonies differed quite radically. Some said they saw one gunman, others said two or three, some said the shots came from a tall building, whilst others said the shots were fired from the ground.

affect recall. They appear to affect the memory trace itself. Loftus (1979) has vividly demonstrated this. In one study participants watched a film of a car accident and afterwards filled in a questionnaire. There were two conditions in the experiment. In one condition, participants were asked:

About how fast were the cars going when they hit *each other?*

In the second condition, participants were asked:

About how fast were the cars going when they smashed *into each other?*

The second group of participants made significantly higher estimates of the speed of the cars. One week later they were all brought back and asked:

Did you see any broken glass?

There was no broken glass, but those who had received the question with 'smashed' in it were more likely to say they had seen glass (32% versus 14%).

The cognitive interview

The most notable development in research involving eyewitness testimony has been that which examines the use of a technique called the COGNITIVE INTERVIEW which is used to assist witnesses' recall of events. Traditionally police officers and lawyers use the Standard Interview Procedure which involves a period of free recall about the event, followed by specific questions on the information which is revealed during the free recall stage. Gieselman et al (1984) suggested that using the cognitive interview would result in a 40 – 70% improvement in recall. The technique involves:

- mentally reinstating the context of the event, i.e. the sounds, smells, feelings experienced during the event
- asking witnesses to recall the event in various orders, or in reverse order
- asking witnesses to report absolutely everything, regardless of the perceived importance of the information
- recalling the event from a variety of perspectives, e.g. imagining what the scene must have looked like from the point of view of several characters there at the time.

Each of these retrieval strategies serves the purpose of allowing the witness to review the event without the interference of leading questions but forces them to scrutinise their memory record.

The cognitive interview procedure may have special benefits for those interviewing child witnesses, especially those who may have been the victims of physical or sexual abuse (Westcott, 1992). Children have traditionally been viewed as unreliable witnesses (Goodman et al, 1987), but Gieselman et al (1990) found that children produced more accurate recall of a road accident when interviewed with the cognitive interview procedure than when a standard interviewing procedure was used. It is clear that this is an area which should yield useful applications of psychological research.

Juries

The very dramatic nature of jury deliberations will be apparent to anyone who has seen the film *Twelve Angry Men* (1957) in which Henry Fonda managed to persuade the other members of the jury to acquit the defendant after they had already decided he was guilty, or to those who have followed the media coverage of two recent trials, the one relating to the assault of Rodney King in Los Angeles and the trial of OJ Simpson for the alleged murder of his wife and her companion.

In England no qualifications are required other than age and the right to vote in order to sit on a jury. Juries deliberate in secret, and are therefore accountable to no one, though they may seek advice, and it is becoming a matter of increasing concern that some jury members find themselves under considerable pressure to reach a decision which is favourable to the defendant – a process termed 'jury nobbling'. The verdicts which juries reach can often appear to the public or to the police as irrational, and yet the jury system is admired and emulated throughout the world.

It has been suggested that the processes which occur when juries deliberate to reach their decisions are similar to the small group dynamics which are well documented by social psychologists (see also Chapter 7, p. 227 onwards). However, since it is illegal in this country to question jurors about their experiences, one of the only ways to explore this possibility is to study mock juries and their deliberations. Whilst this can be informative, particulary if the reconstruction is as realistic as possible, the jurors will always be aware that the defendant's fate is not actually going to be determined by their decisions. However, other countries have more liberal laws, and one of the largest and most influential studies of juries was conducted in 1966 by Kalven and Zeisel in America. They compared jury verdicts with the trial judges' views in 3,576 criminal cases, and found agreement in 78% of cases, though following the publication of their study, many states passed laws forbidding jurors to participate in such studies in future.

Electing a leader

If juries are essentially small groups of decision-makers, what can social psychologists tell us about their decision-making? In theory all the jurors are equal, but in practice they have to elect a foreperson who will relay their decision back to the court. This person may or may not be the actual leader of the group, however, and dominance hierarchies soon develop with a handful of individuals tending to control the discussion. Others participate at a much lower rate, and others merely watch from the sidelines. This phenomenon – allowing some people to do all the work – has been dubbed SOCIAL LOAFING (Latané et al, 1979). How is the foreperson elected? It is usually by vote within a few minutes of the jury beginning their deliberations, but the outcome tends to follow a predictable pattern (Stasser et al, 1982). People of a higher occupational status or with previous experience on a jury are often chosen. Similarly, men tend to be chosen more often than women. Kerr et al (1982) examined the records of 179 trials in San Diego, and found that 50% of jurors were female, but 90% of the forepersons were male. The first person who speaks is often chosen as foreperson (Strodbeck et al, 1957), and when jurors debate around a rectangular table those who sit at the head of the table are more likely to be chosen than those seated in the middle (Bray et al, 1978). Since men are more likely to speak first, and to take the prominent seats (Nemeth et al, 1976), this may explain the sex difference in the selection of a foreperson. Gender differences in communication patterns, however, would seem to be a prime area for further research in exploring the dynamics of jury deliberation.

Stages of decision-making

The decision-making process passes through three stages (Hastie et al, 1983). In common with other problem-solving groups, juries begin in a relaxed, open-ended ORIENTATION PERIOD during which they set an agenda, raise questions, and explore the facts. Differences of opinion then start to become apparent, usually when the first vote is taken, and factions may develop. The group then slips quite into a period of OPEN CONFLICT where the debate may become fierce and focus on quite detailed aspects of the case and the different interpretations possible. There is still a common objective, however, and the jurors look together at the facts before them and discuss the judge's instructions. If all the jurors agree, they can return a verdict, but if they do not agree the majority may try to convert the others through social pressure. At that point the group enters a period of RECONCILIATION, during which an attempt is made to smooth over previous conflicts.

Kalven and Zeisel (1966) interviewed the members of 225 criminal juries in order to compare their first votes with the eventual outcomes. Out of 215 juries who opened with an initial majority, 209 reached a final verdict which was consistent with this vote. So, in the main, the majority tends to get its way, and the heroics of Henry Fonda begin to look a bit unrealistic, but there is one reliable exception to the 'majority wins' rule. Deliberation tends to produce a LENIENCY BIAS which favours the defendant. Individual jurors are more likely to vote guilty on their own than in a group. If juries are initially split, they are more likely to return a 'not guilty' verdict – it seems to be easier to raise a reasonable doubt in people's minds than it is to remove such a doubt.

The effects of social pressure or 'conformity'

The process of resolving disagreements has merited special attention. From social psychologists' research on CONFORMITY it would seem that there are two possibilities – sometimes people conform because, through a process of INFORMATIONAL SOCIAL INFLUENCE, they are genuinely persuaded by what others say. They listen to other people's opinions and use that information as the basis on which to reach their own judgement. At other times, however, people seem to yield to the pressures of NORMATIVE SOCIAL INFLUENCE by changing their stated view in the majority's direction even though they may privately disagree. They go along with the group norms because they do not want to appear deviant. Within social psychology the RISKY SHIFT (Stoner, 1961) or GROUP POLARISATION phenomenon is well documented – individuals in a group tend to modify their views so that the overall group decision is riskier than that of individual members – and research by Kaplan and Scherching (1981) would indicate that this phenomenon can occur in juries too. Other studies indicate that consensus is usually achieved by a vigorous exhange of views and information, but occasionally heavy-handed social pressure can be brought to bear, and, as Asch (1956) showed, it can be very difficult to resist intense pressure publicly. His studies demonstrated that participants were inclined to go along with a majority view (the estimate of a line's length) even though they could see that the estimate was obviously incorrect. Gender differences in conformity and compliance would be worth exploring in the area of juror decision-making.

Does the size of the jury make a difference? In keeping with the British tradition, 12 has tended to be the ideal number, but in America there have been a number of initiatives which have varied jury size. In 1985 a defendant 'fearing the mob mentality of 12 people' successfully argued for a one-person jury, but this was overturned on appeal. Since 1970, however, American courts are allowed to use six-person juries except in cases which involve the possibility of the death penalty. In fact the Supreme Court cited the work of Asch to conclude that reducing the number of jury members would not affect a minority's ability to resist normative pressure. Asch had shown that, when an individual is alone in their dissent, their resistance does not depend upon the size of the agreement group and majorities from 4 to 12 were equallly effective in producing much the same level of conformity. The Supreme Court felt that a lone dissenting juror in a 5:1 situation was in an identical position to the minority in a 10:2 split. In fact, Asch's research demonstrated that these situations are very different – the presence of just one ally, as occurs in the 10:2 split, can enable a dissenter to maintain their independence quite fiercely. The presence of an ally in Asch's studies tended to reduce the conformity rate by up to 75% of what it would be when individuals were alone.

The size of a jury can also make a difference in other ways too – the smaller the jury the less likely it is to represent minority groups in society and the more likely it is to begin deliberating at a near

unaninimity position. Smaller juries spend less time deliberating, and are less likely to declare themselves undecided (Saks, 1977). This may save the courts time and money, but may not always be in the best interests of justice.

Unanimous or majority verdict?

Should jury verdicts always be unanimous? Common sense would indicate that if a majority verdict is acceptable (say, agreement by at least 10 individuals) discussion time will be reduced. Research tends to support this – Hastie et al (1983) recruited 800 people to take part in mock juries, and, after watching a re-enactment of a murder trial, the groups were instructed to reach a verdict by a 12:0, 10:2, or 8:4 margin. The differences were quite marked. Compared with juries needing unanimous decisions, the others spent less time discussing the case and more time voting. After reaching the required margin they often ended the discussion abruptly and returned a verdict. When Hastie et al watched tapes of the juries reaching their decisions they observed that 'majority rules' juries tended to adopt 'a more forceful, bullying, persuasive style.'

Attractiveness of the defendant

There are some factors which seem to influence jurors quite markedly in their decision-making. Two which have been revealed by research include the *attractiveness of defendants*, and *pre-trial publicity*. A range of studies indicate that when defendants are physically attractive they tend to be sentenced less harshly (Sigall and Ostrove, 1975), unless they are deemed to have used their attractiveness to secure their ends, e.g. fraud. Similarly, Dane and Wrightsman (1982) suggest that in the courtroom, stereotypes are imported which predict that villains are unattractive, of low socio-economic status, of dubious moral character, and from a powerless minority group. Thus when attractive, high status, majority group members of previously good character appear in the dock, the temptation to find reasons for acquittal are strong.

Race or ethnicitiy of the defendant

Many studies ask people to give a sentence to a fictitous character who has committed a crime. The race of the defendant and victim can both be varied for different groups of participants and the researcher looks for any significant difference in sentencing. The general trend of studies in the literature is that racial bias is prevalent and, for instance, white participants tend to give harsher sentences to black defendants (see Sweeney and Haney, 1992). In line with this trend, Pfeifer and Ogloff (1991) showed that a group of white university students overwhelmingly rated black defendants guiltier than white defendants, especially when the victim was white. When, however, a group was given specific jury instructions noting that each separate element of the crime had to be proven beyond reasonable doubt, the differences disappeared.

Gordon et al (1988) showed that the effect of race can be complicated by the type of crime. They varied both the race of the defendant (black or white) and the type of crime supposedly committed (embezzlement or burglary). The white embezzler received a significantly longer sentence than the black embezzler but this situation was reversed for the burglary crime. In a later study (1990) they showed that people saw the black burglar and the white embezzler as more internally responsible for their crimes. That is, the 'juries' tended to react according to race stereotypes for particular crimes.

Pre-trial publicity

Pre-trial publicity can be very influential too and difficult for juries to ignore. An example of this would be the media attention granted to the Rodney King beating by the Los Angeles Police Department, and more recently the glare of publicity which O. J. Simpson received after being charged with the murder of his ex-wife. In Britain the press attention given to Frederick West, the alleged serial killer, particularly since his suicide in 1995, seems likely to have prejudiced the case against his wife, Rosemary West. The chances of selecting a jury whose members were not exposed to media speculation about these crimes are remote. In these circumstances it is almost impossible for jurors to remain neutral and only consider the information presented to them at trial when attempting to reach a verdict. Pre-trial publicity can also influence the fate of the victim as well as the accused. Victims of rape, prior to the ruling of no publicity, often suffered from negative media coverage, and a good example is provided by Benedict (1993), who analyses the way the media covers sex crimes and focuses on the adverse publicity suffered by the victim of a New Bedford (USA) gang rape – her story was subsequently made into a film, *The Accused* (1987).

O. J. Simpson was eventually acquitted after his murder trial in 1995, but the trial, televised in the US and the UK contained all the elements of pre-trial publicity, juror selection, jury dynamics, the examination of specialist forensic evidence, eyewitness testimony and racial prejudice.

THE FUTURE OF CRIMINOLOGICAL PSYCHOLOGY

Whilst the future of criminological psychology looks extremely bright, with undergraduate and postgraduate courses flourishing at several colleges and universities, and a very credible range of academic journals in this area being introduced, it must be said that there are some areas of concern. Firstly, debate continues about the very name which should be allocated to this area of psychology. Thus, whilst the Division of the British Psychological Society is called Criminological and Legal, the label attached to Chartered Psychologists in this area is 'forensic', and the latest journal affiliated to the Division is *Legal and Criminological Psychology*! In many ways the debate over nomenclature accurately reflects the broad interests of psychologists who work with offenders in prisons and special hospitals and others who work more directly with the courts, some with the police service, and some in a purely research role. Similarly, the background of criminological psychologists is varied, with expertise and knowledge emanating from academic specialisms in clinical psychology, educational psychology, social, cognitive and biological psychology, and also specific practitioner experience.

Secondly, although the gulf between the disciplines of law and psychology has significantly narrowed since the early part of the century, and there are now productive links between the two, there is still unresolved debate about the role of the 'expert witness' in British courts. In the USA criminological psychologists from the academic sphere, but also from within the ranks of the police force, are routinely called upon to provide expert witness testimony in legal cases. In this country there is still suspicion that introducing academics into the criminal justice system will be a challenge to the rights of defendants and that the evidence introduced will not be subject to sufficient scrutiny. It goes without saying that the rights of defendants need to be protected, but the rights of alleged victims also need to be defended,

particularly in cases of child sexual abuse. This would seem to be an area where further work is needed in order to disseminate appropriate knowledge to key members of the legal profession, including the judiciary.

There would appear to be several important directions in which criminological psychology can proceed. Traditionally psychological knowledge has been used *post hoc*, to understand why offenders have committed their offences, to predict degrees of dangerousness in order to ascertain whether certain offenders should be released into the community, and importantly, to develop appropriate treatment programmes which will help to rehabilitate convicted offenders. An important area where research needs to be directed in order to make full use of psychological expertise and to demonstrate its utility is that of *prevention*. If crime and violence can be prevented or reduced then the benefits for society will be considerable. This need not necessarily involve the dubious use of early screening to detect potential offenders, but could be in the form of environmental shaping which reduces the opportunity for crime, or increasing use of parental training and recognition of the importance of early childhood.

Another fruitful direction would be a move towards assisting the police service, not necessarily in the dramatic form of offender profiling or crime scene analysis. This is well established and will hopefully grow but in a less public way and supported by rigorous empirical studies. The areas for co-operative work would be in relation to police training and the interrogation of suspects leading to the collection of sound and untainted evidence which will secure convictions.

The future for criminological psychology looks exciting, particularly in view of the number of young graduates who want to enter the field. Their enthusiasm, and the value they place on empirical research, should ensure that criminological psychology grows in a systematic way and is recognised as a truly applied science.

FURTHER RECOMMENDED READING

Blackburn, R. (1993) *The Psychology of Criminal Conduct: Theory, Research and Practice*. Chichester: John Wiley.
Bull, R. and Carson, D. (1995) *Handbook of Psychology in Legal Contexts*. Chichester: John Wiley.
Eysenck, H. and Gudgonsson, G. (1989) *The Causes and Cures of Criminality*. New York: Plenum Press.
Hollin, C. (1992) *Criminal Behaviour: A Psychological Approach to Explanation and Prevention*. London: Falmer Press.
Stephenson, G. (1992) *The Psychology of Criminal Justice*. Oxford: Blackwell.

exercises

1. 'BELIEF IN A JUST WORLD' EXERCISE

This workshop involves students answering a questionnaire to determine their belief in a just world. This questionnaire is taken from Rubin, Z. and Peplau, R. (1975), Who Believes in a Just World? *Journal of Social Issues*, 31, No. 3, 65 – 89.

Questionnaire
Answer the following questions on a scale of 1 – 6, when 1 indicates total agreement with the statement, and 6 indicates total disagreement with the statement:

1. I've found that a person rarely deserves the reputation she or he has.
2. Basically the world is a just place.
3. People who get 'lucky breaks' have usually earned their good fortune.
4. Careful drivers are just as likely to get hurt in traffic accidents as careless ones.
5. It is a common occurrence for a guilty person to get off free in court.
6. Students almost always deserve the marks they get in college.
7. Men who keep in shape have little chance of suffering a heart attack.
8. The political candidate who sticks up for his principles rarely gets elected.
9. It is rare for an innocent person to be wrongly sent to jail.
10. In professional sports, many fouls and infractions never get noticed by the referee.
11. By and large, people deserve what they get.
12. When parents punish their children, it is almost always for good reasons.
13. Good deeds often go unnoticed and unrewarded.
14. Although evil people may hold political power for a while, in the general course of history good wins out.
15. In almost any business or profession, people who do their job well rise to the top.
16. Parents tend to overlook the things most to be admired in their children.
17. It is often impossible for a person to receive a fair trial.
18. People who meet with misfortune have often brought it on themselves.
19. Crime doesn't pay.
20. Many people suffer through absolutely no fault of their own.

We want *stronger* belief in a just world to receive a *higher* score. Agreement with items 2, 3, 6, 7, 9, 11, 12, 14, 15, 18, 19 indicates a belief in a just world. Therefore, on these items *reverse* the score you obtained. If you scored 1 give yourself 6, if your score was 2, you get 5, 3 gets 4, 4 gets 3, 5 gets 2 and 6 gets 1. Agreement with the remaining items indicates low belief in a just world, so these scores should be left as they are. Finally, add up all your scores. Scoring should allow you to identify those who do believe in a just world, and also how much they do!

Prior to administering the questionnaire you could have a class discussion on various contemporary court cases, e.g. rape trials, and ascertain how responsible the victim is held to be in the different cases by small groups within the class. You can then compare this with the scores on the 'belief in a just world' questionnaire. You might also like to compare these scores across male and female students.

2. EYEWITNESS TESTIMONY EXERCISE

This is an interesting exercise, but requires diplomacy and maturity. Make sure you get permission to carry out this study – it may be that you have to conduct the observations within your college campus rather than out in the real world!

Ask a confederate to approach members of the public (or fellow students if you are restricted to campus) and ask for directions to the hospital (or medical centre) under one of two conditions:

i) no stress factor
ii) stress factor – a 'cut' finger wrapped in a bandage.

Then approach each subject and ask very politely if they will complete a short questionnaire about the person who just asked for directions. You will need to fully debrief all subjects who agree to participate, and you may also need to provide evidence of your identity.

If stress does affect recall there should be a difference in the accuracy of recall under the two conditions. You will have to design a short questionnaire to test their recall which will provide you with an accuracy score under both conditions, and you would be advised to pilot this in order to exclude irrelevant questions. Items for inclusion might be the age of the confederate, the colour of their hair, their clothes, eye colour, accent, etc. Be careful not to include any leading questions!

3. JURY SIZE EXERCISE

Divide the class into mock juries, some containing three members and some containing six members. Allocate an observer to each of the groups. Each of the 'juries' should read the extract from a murder trial (below) which is taken from a study by Pennington, N. and Hastie, R. (1986) Evidence evaluation in complex decision-making. *Journal of Personality and Social Psychology*, 51, 2, 242-258.

After reading the evidence they must come to a unanimous decision as to the guilt or innocence of the accused. Set a maximum time for decision-making, and advise the observers how to record proceedings.

The observer should take notes of the following:

a) how long it takes to reach a unanimous decision
b) how often votes are called for and the result of each vote
c) the leadership style of the foreperson.

Ask the observers to report back, and there can then be a discussion of:

a) the processes involved in the decision-making
b) how the foreperson was elected
c) whether jury size makes a difference – in theory smaller juries should be able to reach their decision sooner and with fewer votes.

Extract
Indictment
The defendant, Frank Johnson, is charged with killing Alan Caldwell with deliberate premeditation and malice aforethought.

The defendant's plea
The defendant, Frank Johnson, pleads NOT GUILTY.

Officer Richard Harris
On May 21st, at about 11pm, I was on my usual foot patrol when I heard shouts from the direction of Gleason's Bar and Grill and hurried in that direction. From across the street I saw Caldwell (the victim) hit the defendant Johnson in the face. Johnson staggered back against the wall, then came forward and raised a knife above his head with his right hand. I yelled, 'Frank, don't do it', but he plunged the knife downward into Caldwell's chest. Caldwell had fallen to the ground by the time I reached the scene. I apprehended Johnson and phoned for a police cruiser and an ambulance.

Cross-examination I had a clear view of the fight from across the street approximately 75 feet away. I did not see anything in Caldwell's hand although I could not see Caldwell's right hand which was down by the side away from me. Johnson did not resist arrest, but he did say, 'Caldwell pulled a razor on me so I stuck him'. (This last statement was declared inadmissable by the trial judge.) The knife Harris retrieved from the ground near Caldwell is introduced as evidence. It measures 11" end to end.

State pathologist, Dr Robert Katz

I found the following items on the body of Alan Caldwell – a ring, a watch, and small change in the right front pocket, and a straight razor in the left rear pocket. Caldwell was killed by a stab wound to the heart between the third and fourth ribs. I was unable to determine the angle at which the knife entered Caldwell's chest. His blood alcohol level was .032. This is enough alcohol that Caldwell may have been drunk. Caldwell had numerous surgical scars on his body. There were other scars of undetermined origin. The straight razor is introduced as evidence.

Patrick Gleason

I am the owner of Gleason's Bar and Grill. That night I had occasion to run to the window because there were some shouts outside. Actually I expected it because I had watched Caldwell and Johnson leave the bar together a few minutes before. Through the window I saw Johnson raise his hand up and stab Caldwell. I didn't see anything in Caldwell's hand. Caldwell and Johnson didn't come to the bar together. First, Johnson and his friend Dennis Clemens arrived at about 9 pm and later Caldwell arrived. Then later, Caldwell and Johnson were talking at the bar and then they walked outside together. On the way out Caldwell put his watch in his pocket. Earlier in the day Johnson and Caldwell had both been in the bar. At that time they were arguing. Caldwell pulled out a razor and threatened to kill Johnson. A couple of patrons said something to Johnson and he left. That was earlier in the afternoon – before the fight in the evening.

Cross-examination There was a neon light in the window which partially obstructed my view and I could only see Johnson and Caldwell at an angle. Frank Johnson had a reputation for peacefulness and has never caused trouble in the bar. (The judge does not allow Gleason to testify about Alan Caldwell's reputation.)

Dennis Clemens

I stopped at Frank Johnson's home on the evening of May 21st and asked Johnson to join me for a drink at Gleason's, which is where we usually go. Before we went in the bar, we looked around. We didn't see anything. At about 9.30 pm Caldwell entered, and after a while motioned Johnson to come and talk. In a few minutes Johnson and Caldwell left the bar. I could not hear what they said, but went near the front door which was open. I heard a few shouts, saw Caldwell punch Johnson to the ground, and begin to attack him with a razor. Johnson tried to hold Caldwell off but Caldwell attacked, there was a scuffle, Caldwell staggered back, and after about twenty seconds fell to the ground. I didn't go outside to stop the fight because it happened so quickly.

Cross-examination Johnson and I did not go to Gleason's looking for Caldwell, and Johnson was reluctant to go into Gleason's until we had assured ourselves that Caldwell was not there. I saw the razor clearly in Caldwell's right hand. I didn't see the knife in Johnson's hand because of the angle of the two men.

Janet Stewart

I am a waitress at Gleason's Grill, and on the night of the fight I noticed both Caldwell and Johnson in the grill before the fight. There was shouting outside. When I ran outside I saw Caldwell on the ground. I also noticed that Caldwell's car, which I recognised, was parked illegally in front of the grill and would have obstructed a view of the fight from across the street.

Frank Johnson

I was in Gleason's Grill on the afternoon of May 21st. A woman asked me to give her a ride somewhere the next day. Alan Caldwell immediately came over screaming at me and threatening me – he pulled a razor and threatened to kill me. I was quite upset and frightened and I went home and spent the day with my wife and six children until 9 pm when Dennis Clemens came by and suggested we go out for a drink. When we got to Gleason's Grill I was afraid to go in but was finally convinced when we could find no evidence that Caldwell was

WHAT DO EDUCATIONAL PSYCHOLOGISTS DO?

Describing what educational psychologists do is likely to lead to a clearer picture of what educational psychology is. Others have also found this approach useful, e.g. as Wolfendale et al have stated, 'our definitions of what educational psychology *is* lie in our descriptions of what educational psychologists do' (Wolfendale et al, 1992, p1).

Working as an educational psychologist encompasses a wide range of activities and a variety of roles implied in the following description:

'Educational psychologists are essentially applied psychologists whose work is concerned primarily with the psychological and educational development (and problems which may be associated with these) of children and young people within the context of home, school and community. The work involves psychological investigation and treatment as well as advisory and research activities relevant to educational provision and policies.'

(Association of Educational Psychologists, 1993)

Most educational psychologists work for local education authorities (LEAs) where their main duties would include:

- working directly with children and young people
- consulting with parents, teachers and other education staff, such as advisory teachers or administrative personnel
- working with other professionals in the health authority or in social services.

Working with others can encompass a wide range of experiences and responsibilities. These could include:

- being part of a paediatric (child health) assessment team
- being part of a child and family centre team (what was 'child guidance')
- working with a social worker in relation to a child's domestic difficulties, behaviour

problems at home, or suspected or actual child abuse
- liaison with, or working in a team with, speech therapists and specialist teachers in the local speech and language unit
- being part of an audiological team and working with technicians, specialist teachers and speech therapists in a unit for the partially hearing
- being part of a SPECIAL EDUCATIONAL NEEDS (SEN) panel including teachers, community clinicians and others concerned with the assessment of SEN and statementing (see below)
- working with schools to find solutions to problems, e.g. teaching strategies in relation to effective management of pupil attention and behaviour
- working with schools on whole school issues such as organisation and communication, effective use of resources or whole school policies on SEN or 'problem' behaviour; this might involve joint work with other professionals, e.g. working with the education welfare officer on truancy
- carrying out in-service work with teachers, parents and other professionals, e.g. on bullying or identifying specific learning difficulties
- carrying out research:
  - at a *local* level, e.g. ACTION RESEARCH in investigating a solution to a problem in a particular school, such as a high incidence of reading failure or school phobia
  - at a *service* level, e.g. the whole educational psychology service may be involved in research of value to the LEA, such as evaluating the success of its policy of integration of children with SEN into mainstream schools
  - at an *organisational* level, e.g. senior management of the educational psychology service may be expected to keep the LEA informed of advances in educational psychology of relevance to the authority, such as the likely effectiveness of particular models of educational psychology service delivery to schools.

The above information has been adapted from the Association of Educational Psychologists Careers Information Sheet, 1993. Readers can obtain further information directly from the AEP (see Box 1).

The main areas of work of the educational psychologist are discussed in more detail below.

Clearly, educational psychologists need communication skills of a high order and need to be skilled in a wide variety of techniques of psychological assessment (AEP, 1993). It is not surprising, therefore, that educational psychologists undergo a lengthy period of training.

BOX 1

How would I become an educational psychologist?

(Adapted from the Association of Educational Psychologists Careers Information Sheet, August, 1993.)
You may take the following routes:

EITHER

1. A BPS recognised honours degree in psychology – 3 years
2. Teacher training – Postgraduate Certificate of Education (PGCE) – 1 year
3. Professional experience as a qualified teacher – 2 years minimum
4. Postgraduate professional training – usually a Masters degree or a postgraduate diploma at a university – 1 or 2 years

OR

1. Initial training as a teacher – 3 years
2. Teaching experience – 2 years minimum
3. Honours degree in psychology (BPS recognised) – full-time 3 years; part-time 4 years, which may be concurrent with the teaching experience
4. Postgraduate professional training as an educational psychologist

Grants may be available for some stages.
Further information may be obtained from:

The Association of Educational Psychologists (AEP), Sunderland Road, Durham DH1 2LH. Telephone: 0191 384 9512.

The training of educational psychologists

Initial training for educational psychologists is outlined in Boxes 1 and 2. The 15 training courses have an agreed core curriculum, last reviewed in 1990. This consists of:

- personal skills and communication
- collecting information and assessment
- intervention approaches
- disabling conditions and special educational needs
- professional practice
- research and evaluation
- issues in child development
          (from Wolfendale et al, 1992, p10)

Wolfendale et al add 'equal opportunities perspectives are expected to inform each curriculum area' (p10). The consensus seems to be that training should provide educational psychologists with basic skills which can be adapted to changing circumstances with a particular emphasis on problem-solving interventions (e.g. Cameron and Stratford, 1987).

Qualified educational psychologists are eligible to become chartered and subject to the BPS Code of Practice (see chapter 1). Hopefully, they will continue their professional development during the course of their careers through post-professional training.

BOX 2

Training courses for educational psychologists

Approved courses of professional training for educational psychologists are run at the following universities:

London	University of London, Institute of Education
	University of London, University College*
	University of East London
	Tavistock Clinic*

Birmingham	**Exeter**	**Nottingham***	**Strathclyde**
Belfast	**Manchester**	**Sheffield**	**Swansea**
Dundee	**Newcastle**	**Southampton**	

* People taking these courses are also eligible to work with children in the National Health Service. Further information is available from the AEP or BPS.

(Adapted from AEP, 1993.)

BOX 3

Professional journals

Both the BPS and the AEP produce journals relevant to educational psychologists, e.g.

1. *Journal of Educational and Child Psychology* (BPS)
2. *Educational Psychology in Practice* (AEP)

Post-professional training

Educational Psychology Services recognise the importance of professional development for practising educational psychologists and have collaborated with training course tutors to expand training opportunities (Wolfendale, 1992, p10).

THE DEVELOPMENT OF EDUCATIONAL PSYCHOLOGY

In England the educational needs of the blind and deaf were recognised by legislation in 1839. From the 1880s onwards several developments in psychology and educational philosophy combined to contribute to the development of educational psychology and subsequently 'school psychologists'. In 1889 the Elementary Education (Defective and Epileptic Children) Act created a new category of handicap, i.e. 'educable mental defectives' (see Gillham, 1978). Education authorities were then expected to ascertain the number of 'defective' children in their area and provide for them. Identification and selection initially fell to the medical profession, though eventually such decisions became the responsibility of people more directly involved in education.

BOX 4

Career opportunities for educational psychologists

1. Local Education Authorities

Educational psychology is a relatively small profession. Most educational psychologists work for LEAs. In December 1992 there were 1583 educational psychologists working for LEAs in England, Wales and Northern Ireland (AEP, 1993). Most of these will work within an Educational Psychology Service (EPS) which provides a service to young children, their families and schools. The Educational Psychology Service may itself be part of a larger structure of LEA support services, e.g. incorporating the Educational Psychology Service, the Advisory Teacher Service, other specialist teachers and other professionals such as the Education Welfare Service (EWS). The career structure within the Educational Psychology Service is normally as follows:

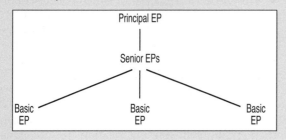

Basic grade educational psychologists will normally be responsible for a patch of schools to which they pay regular visits. Senior educational psychologist posts may be 'specialist', e.g. may carry special responsibility for an area such as speech and language. Alternatively, they may be 'management' posts in line with a particular Educational Psychology Service structure or model of service delivery (see below).

2. Assessment units

Some educational psychologists work for the health authorities in assessment units which may be multi-disciplinary, or which may be hospital-based paediatric assessment units, or child psychiatric units.

3. Teaching, training and research

Some educational psychologists teach in university departments and may be involved in training courses for educational psychologists. Some such tutors often work part-time as practising educational psychologists. Others may be involved in research. Educational psychologists may be concerned with teacher training. It is also not unknown for educational psychologists to return to class teaching in schools.

Such developments necessitated the development of more objective methods for the assessment of children. At around the same period, the beginnings of PSYCHOMETRIC TESTING or 'mental measurement' were taking root (see Appendix 2). Working for the Paris authorities, Alfred Binet (1857–1911) had the task of identifying 'dull' children who would not benefit from the state school system and, hence, would need special schools. He developed the Binet Scale which consisted of a group of different tasks which were considered to tap a broad range of a child's abilities. This was adapted in the USA for use in English as the STANFORD-BINET TEST and became popular there. In addition, the outbreak of the First World War led to the development of tests of specific skill in order to allocate conscripts to different tasks.

The concept of intelligence and mental measurement had important implications for both mainstream and educational psychology as well as other areas of applied psychology. The debate over the extent to which intelligence was considered to be genetic or related to environmental factors is well documented and is outlined in Appendix 1. Modern developments in intelligence testing and their use in educational psychology are discussed below (Assessment and Testing).

Educational psychology was influenced by the BEHAVIOURISTS, in particular William James at Harvard, who started a laboratory for the scientific study of psychology and in 1899 published his classic book *Talks to Teachers on Psychology*. In 1903 Thorndike published the first book with the title *Educational Psychology*, emphasising 'scientific approaches to the study of educational programmes'. In 1910 a journal of educational psychology was founded and the first article was written by Thorndike (see Pettibone and Jernigan, 1989, for a summary).

In England Sir Cyril Burt became the first school psychologist in the UK in 1913 when he was appointed to the London County Council. His work on identical twins was influential in the nature–nurture debate on intelligence although his results in this area, as mentioned in Appendix 1, are now considered to be unreliable. In addition Burt influenced the role of the psychologist in education which he saw primarily as that of a 'scientific researcher'. He used teacher reports and medical officer reports but the educational psychologist's role was to investigate the educational, emotional and motivational characteristics of children, using mostly STANDARDISED tests and observations and DIAGNOSTIC TEACHING (Dessent, 1978). This approach was influential.

The second 'school psychologist' in the UK was not appointed until 1931, this time in the city of Leicester. At about this time, the child guidance movement was growing with its emphasis on a multi-disciplinary approach to guidance for children with problems. The first child guidance team established in the UK was in Birmingham in 1932, consisting of a psychologist, a psychiatrist and a psychiatric social worker (Dessent, 1978).

By 1944 there were 70 child guidance clinics in the UK. Teams usually had a medical director (psychiatrist) who had the major diagnostic role. Educational psychologists worked mainly with children in schools or administered tests to aid the psychiatrist's diagnosis. Psychiatric social workers interviewed parents. Psychologists, therefore, were identified with what became known as the 'traditional' or even 'medical' model:

> '... the identification, diagnosis and treatment of individual children with learning and adjustment problems'
>
> *(Dessent, 1978, p31)*

The causes of problems were seen to be primarily within the individual and the educational psychologist was seen to be heavily involved in:

- psychometric assessment
- allocation of children to special education.

This led to expectations by schools and other professionals of what the educational psychologist's role involved (Dessent, 1978), a role to some extent reinforced by the following pieces of legislation (a pattern repeated in the history of educational psychology – see below):

- *the Education Act 1944*, which created the concept EDUCATIONALLY SUB-NORMAL (ESN) and confirmed the central role of educational psychologists in advising local authorities on special educational needs
- *the Education (Handicapped) Act 1970*, which brought responsibility for severely handicapped children under the local education authority, thus increasing the involvement of school psychological services with this group of children
- *Circular 2/75 (DES 1975)*, which ended school placement decision-making by the medical profession. It was considered more appropriate for the educational psychologist or adviser in special needs to be involved in this.

Further legislation (Education Act 1993, see below) was going to make it even more difficult for educational psychologists to break away from their traditional role in relation to individual children. Recently, Wolfendale et al (1992) have said:

> 'Ever since the first school psychologists functioned in the United Kingdom, the expectation was that they would be concerned with "damage limitation, remedial and curative approaches to identified deviant and pathological conditions". That legacy, while diffused into a positive, benevolent conception of "special educational needs", has never been shaken off successfully by educational psychologists themselves.'
>
> *(Wolfendale, 1992, p12).*

The Summerfield Report (1968) provided further evidence of the activities of the school psychologists. This report investigated the work of educational psychologists, their numbers and their training. It reported that, by 1968, there were 368 in local authorities. Over half of these authorities had only one, and only 15% had more than four (Summerfield, 1968). The report emphasised the diagnostic and therapeutic work of the educational psychologist but not advisory, preventative or in-service work (Dessent, 1978, p31). Given the relatively small numbers of educational psychologists available, this is probably not too surprising.

According to Summerfield, there was also little evidence of the 'scientific research role' considered by Burt to be central to the role of the school psychologist. Summerfield reported educational psychologists' concern then about the lack of research time and, nearly 30 years on, this situation appears little changed. Summerfield also challenged the usefulness of teaching experience for educational psychologists. However, this remains a condition of training today and remains an area of continuing debate in the profession.

The economic boom of the 1960s contributed to growth in the late 70s and 80s of support services. However, the profession remains relatively small, with 1583 educational psychologists in LEA work in England, Wales and Northern Ireland in December 1992 (AEP, 1993).

Nevertheless, expansion led to the development of school psychological services, at first closely linked with child guidance clinics and with some educational psychologists working for both. However, a number of influences served to separate the services and now most school psychological services operate completely separately. These influences coincided with a continued and growing 'unease' within the profession in relation to the traditional model and included:

- concern about the effectiveness of the child guidance movement (e.g. Tizard, 1973),
- concern about intelligence testing and its links with educational programmes. Within the profession there was and remains concern about labelling effects and teacher expectations (see below and Quicke, 1982)
- the increasing influence of *social/ecological* approaches to learning, i.e. that the child needs

to be assessed in the context in which learning is taking place
- the influences of SYSTEMS APPROACHES and studies of organisational structure on the development of CONSULTANCY MODELS and Educational Psychology Service delivery (see below)
- concern that the Burt influence had tended to ignore remedial approaches and strategies for intervention, i.e. programmes designed to remove blocks or delays in learning progress (Dessent, 1978).

New directions were urged by the RECONSTRUCTION-ISTS (see Gillham, 1978). This was a movement away from individual casework and the use of normative assessment towards systems approaches. These involved looking at organisations like schools as a whole in order to be *proactive* (to *prevent* learning or behavioural difficulties) rather than *reactive* (i.e. to come in with the *treatment* after the problem had been identified). The new directions were to include:

- an emphasis on in-service training, particularly for teachers and schools
- consultancy models of working, particularly 'helping schools to help themselves.' This might involve:

- 'giving psychology away', for example teaching teachers how to use methods of TASK ANALYSIS (see below), possibly helping to reduce the number of individual referrals to educational psychologists
- project work, for example helping the school to adopt a WHOLE SCHOOL APPROACH to bullying (see below)
- systems approaches/policy involvement. This might include, for example, examining the role of the Educational Psychology Service within the LEA support services or the LEA organisation itself.

However, these approaches did not stem the flood of individual referrals to educational psychologists, nor were they particularly effective in directing change, i.e. the 'reconstructing' was not as successful as had been hoped (see Dessent, 1992). Some of the reasons for this were again new legislation, particularly the 1981 Education Act and the 1993 Education Act, which clarify the concept of special educational needs and again confirm the central role of the educational psychologist in the identification and assessment of the special educational needs of individual children (this is dealt with in more detail below). The effects were an increased emphasis on individual casework to such an extent that Wolfendale et al (1992) have estimated that as much as 60 per cent of current workload is still individual casework.

In addition to a statutory (parliament-governed) emphasis in the direction of individual casework, there were also a number of other concerns about de-emphasising individual assessment:

■ concerns about the reliability of teacher reports and observations
■ difficulties with 'new assessments', such as the National Curriculum levels, i.e. that these may not be 'fine tuned' enough to indicate clearly specific areas of concern
■ concern that decisions about a child's levels of cognitive ability should not be made on the basis of their levels of attainment. Quicke (1982) has suggested that the use of IQ assessment has been useful in preventing some children being segregated into special schools or classes. That is, there are instances where a child's IQ indicates a higher level of ability than

is reflected in the child's attainments or teachers' perceptions of that child. In addition such points have particular relevance to areas of learning difficulty which, almost by definition, relate to a discrepancy between a child's actual cognitive ability and their (more limited) specific attainments (see specific learning difficulties below).

■ indications from research that the usually accepted negative effects of 'labelling' and 'teacher expectations' did not in fact occur (i.e. that children's learning and development were not, as one thought, affected by these). This issue is also discussed later.

The development of educational psychology can, therefore, be seen to encompass two rather conflicting strands:

■ on the one hand, the dissatisfaction of many educational psychologists with the 'narrow' perspective of individual case work and, therefore, the necessity for high levels of expertise in assessment and diagnosis of the child's difficulties
■ on the other hand continued legislation reinforcing the focus on individual case work.

The main issues in relation to these conflicts will be discussed here and the future of educational psychology is returned to at the end of the chapter.

THEORY, RESEARCH AND APPLICATIONS

Working as an educational psychologist encompasses a variety of different functions and roles. Cameron and Stratford (1987) have indicated the need to operate at on at least three different levels: that of the individual child, the school level and the policy level.

For most educational psychologists, regardless of how they might wish to work, statutory requirements have generally meant that the greater part of their workload is with the assessment of individual children which is therefore a high priority.

Working with children

A number of factors have combined to influence the necessity for educational psychologists to work with individual children but have also influenced the *way* in which they should work with children. Principal among these has been the requirements of legislation in relation to children and education.

Education Acts and the educational psychologist

The past fifteen years have seen fundamental changes in education within this country, with numerous white papers, government circulars and Education Acts affecting these changes. Principal among these have been the 1981 Education Act, the 1988 Education Reform Act and the 1993 Education Act. In addition, the Children Act, 1989, had far-reaching implications for children's rights in relation to their own education.

The 1981 Education Act

This followed from the Warnock Report, which was concerned with the concept of 'special educational need' and with the necessity to integrate children with special educational needs into mainstream school settings. The 1981 Act enshrined these principles in law and confirmed the educational psychologist as one of the key agents in the identification of children with special educational needs. Children were to undergo a staged process of needs assessment. If necessary, children with exceptional needs would require a STATEMENT. Once such a statement of special educational needs had been made by a local education authority, the LEA was bound by law to make provision for those needs. The educational psychologist's role was to assess the child and give the LEA advice on the child's special educational needs; advice would also be requested from the child's school (educational advice) and a medical officer of the local health authority (medical advice). In the case of a pre-school child, the educational advice may be requested from, say, the pre-school advisory teacher.

The 1988 Education Reform Act (ERA)

This act changed the whole nature of schools' relationships with their LEA. Under the principle of Local Management of Schools, individual schools were given 'delegated budgets', so that they, rather than the LEA as previously, could now deal with much of their own financing. Schools were then free to deal with their own finances and, if required, buy in support services as they wished, possibly including educational psychologists (previously a free resource) as private consultants.

Between the publication of this act and the 1993 Education Act, it was a possibility that funding for educational psychology services would become part of the delegated budget system. The implications were that schools could then buy in an educational psychologist if and when needed and the LEA Educational Psychology Services would no longer exist in their current form. This led to considerable evaluation of Educational Psychology Service delivery and consideration of alternative models of service delivery (see Wolfendale et al, 1992 for a pre-1993 discussion of these alternatives).

In addition, the act introduced the requirements of a National Curriculum, with children to be assessed on a variety of STANDARD ASSESSMENT TASKS (SATs) at the ages of 7, 11, 14 and 16 and for the school results to be published. Where appropriate, statements of educational needs were to reflect the child's abilities in relation to attained levels in the National Curriculum. This clearly had implications for educational psychologists writing advice for statements and, in particular, for types of assessment (see below).

The 1993 Education Act

This act clarified and extended the process of assessment of children's special educational needs. Children were to undergo a 4 – 5 stage assessment process, with schools having the responsibility for initial identification of SEN and the necessity to utilise their own resources to try to meet the SEN of individual children. The stages of assessment, any necessary statementing and any review of the statement were to be carried out according to a new code of practice. The act also reconfirmed the educational psychologist as a principal agent in the assessment of SEN. It also confirmed that Educational Psychology Services should remain funded as a central (LEA) resource and, hence, should remain a free service to schools.

The Children Act, 1989

Conn (1992) states that this act 'represents the most fundamental change in child law for 100 years' (p155). The main principle of the act is that the child's welfare should be the overriding consideration in matters relating to care and upbringing. The implication for educational psychologists, in assessment and in preparation of psychological advice, is the duty to ascertain the child's wishes and feelings. They are also expected to play a significant role in the assessment of children's physical, emotional and educational needs and the likely effect on them of any change in circumstances.

Special educational needs

In general, the statutory duties of educational psychologists focus on the identification and assessment of children with special educational needs, a concept requiring some definition. Children's difficulties have been categorised in a number of different ways over time. Examples in education are the terms 'mental handicap' and 'educationally sub-normal'. The 1981 Education Act developed the concept of special educational needs and the 1993 Education Act further refined this. The spirit of the Warnock Report, 1978, which formed the basis for the 1981 Education Act, was to move away from labels of 'handicap' which tended to emphasise segregation and towards assessment of the needs of the whole child with emphasis on integration within mainstream settings. Terms such as 'educationally sub-normal' were replaced by 'learning difficulties.'

Under the 1981 and 1993 Education Acts, a child is considered to have special educational needs if he or she has a 'learning difficulty' which requires 'special educational provision'. Such provision is in addition to, or different from, that which is normally available. For example, this could be additional teaching support within the child's mainstream school. Definition of learning difficulty under the acts is that the child has either:

- a significantly greater difficulty in learning than the majority of children of the same age and/or
- a 'disability' which prevents the child from making effective use of the facilities of the local school (Education Act 1993).

For children under five years, the LEA has a duty to consider whether either condition would apply if special provision was not made. If this is the case, the LEA must make a formal statement to this effect (known as 'statementing'). For younger children, early identification may come via health authority personnel, e.g. a problem could be picked up by a family's health visitor and referred to the GP and then on to a paediatrician or consultant. The health authority has a legal obligation under the act to notify the education authority of a child's likely special educational needs.

It has been estimated that about 2% of children will have difficulties severe enough to warrant statementing, while a further 18% are likely to experience difficulties at school at some stage in their educational careers (Warnock, 1978). In practice, LEAs have varied in the percentage of children they have statemented, ranging in a recent survey from 0.8% to 3.9% between authorities (Tyerman, 1993).

Within the group of children identified as having special educational needs will be a range of difficulties and impairments. The educational psychologist will need to have some understanding of how to assess difficulties in these areas, how such difficulties are likely to affect a child's ability to cope with his or her learning environment and how to adapt or modify the learning environment to facilitate the child's difficulties. This may well mean working with schools on appropriate intervention strategies (see p. 95).

Major categories of special educational need
1. Sensory impairment – visual and hearing impairment
One in ten children enter school with some degree of visual impairment (Tyerman, 1993). Most impairments can be corrected and have little or no effect on the child's social or educational development, though there may be a reluctance on the part of some children to wear newly prescribed glasses. One in one thousand children suffer from visual impairment severe enough to affect educational progress, on a continuum from 'low vision' to 'blindness'. Some syndromes, e.g. Usher's syndrome, have blindness associated with them.

Hearing loss interferes with the reception and production of language and consequently can be crucial to a child's educational development. Hearing losses can be categorised as slight, moderate, severe or profound. The loss can be pre-lingual (before spoken language has developed) or

Integrating the hearing-impaired child –
signing as an alternative language.

post-lingual. It can be conductive in nature, i.e. there is a reduction in the intensity of the sound reaching the inner ear, or sensori-neural, i.e. a defect of the inner ear or auditory nerve. There has long been a debate within education as to the most appropriate method of teaching children with hearing difficulties to communicate. These methods have traditionally been the auditory–oral versus manual (signing) approaches though, more recently, TOTAL COMMUNICATION approaches have combined elements of both. Evaluation of the success of methods is difficult, since such evaluations need to take into account both educational achievement and the social/emotional adjustment of the child.

2. Physical/medical difficulties

Physical impairment can result from cerebral palsy or spinal cord injury. A number of children also appear clumsy and uncoordinated with often no known cause (no clear aetiology). The extent of the physical impairment will depend on the number of limbs affected, i.e. gross and fine motor difficulties can be expected, though there is not necessarily any cognitive impairment. A number of medical conditions, such as cystic fibrosis, diabetes and epilepsy, as well as a number of syndromes, e.g. Asperger's, can cause problems requiring special educational provision.

3. Communication, speech and language disorders

There are a wide range of speech and language disorders. A child can have difficulties with the physical processes required to produce sounds (e.g. articulation, resonation) or difficulties in one or more of the language dimensions, i.e.

- *phonology* (sound)
- *morphology* (word structure)
- *syntax* (sentence structure)
- *semantics* (word meaning)
- *pragmatics* (language function)

Educational psychologists are, therefore, concerned with the assessment and identification of disordered and delayed speech and with difficulties such as DYSPRAXIA (a motor condition which may affect the production of speech sounds).

4. Learning difficulties

The definition of these under the 1981 and 1993 Education Acts has been given above. In practice, learning difficulties identified by schools range across a whole continuum through those that schools can cope with (e.g. by adapting the curriculum) to those requiring additional support or specialist teaching in mainstream classes (MODERATE LEARNING DIFFICULTIES). In addition, there are a group of children requiring an extremely modified and differentiated curriculum (SEVERE LEARNING DIFFICULTIES).

Although the 1981 and 1993 Acts emphasise integration as far as possible (that is, teaching all children in the same class, whether they have learning difficulties or not), some LEAs still segregate children with moderate learning difficulties for a part of the time (e.g. special units attached to a mainstream school) or all of the time (a separate system of segregated special schools). The aetiology of moderate learning difficulties is often unknown. Many children in this category will have post-16 educational provision or join appropriate college link courses. Most will be fully independent as adults.

The aetiology of severe learning difficulties may be known and may include genetic disorders, infectious diseases or brain damage at any stage of development. These children will require post-16 educational provision and are unlikely to be able to lead independent lives as adults.

There is also considerable debate within education concerning a further group of children who may be identified as having SPECIFIC LEARNING DIFFICULTIES. This term has generally replaced the more umbrella label of DYSLEXIA. Typically a child appears of at least average cognitive ability but has specific difficulty in one or more areas of attainment, e.g. reading or spelling, and/or a particular difficulty in expressing himself or herself in writing. A child may also have a specific number problem (DYSCALCULA).

5. Emotional and behavioural difficulties (EBD)

The likelihood of a child becoming included in this category will depend on the level of difficulty of the child's behaviour (intensity), how long disruptive behaviour lasts (duration) and how often it happens (frequency), as well as how inappropriate the behaviours are in the context in which they appear (Tyerman, 1993).

Mann (1993) lists four major classifications of problem behaviour:

- conduct disorders
- anxiety and withdrawal
- immaturity
- socialised AGGRESSION.

The category of EBD can include children with phobias, neurotic children and autistic children. Assessment in this area is difficult and requires a wide range of approaches, e.g. observations, ratings and STANDARDISED TESTS – see assessment and testing below.

6. ATTENTION DEFICIT (HYPERACTIVITY) DISORDER (ADD and ADHD)

ADD is gaining recognition as a particular difficulty category and is characterised by high distractibility, fleeting attention and an inability to focus attention on relevant detail at an age when such control is expected. ADHD includes children who cannot maintain attention because they cannot remain still for long enough. Clearly, inability to maintain attention creates a considerable barrier to learning. In addition, such a disorder creates considerable difficulty in assessing a child's underlying cognitive ability.

7. Multi-handicapping conditions

Naturally the categories above are not mutually exclusive and children may have combinations of difficulties. Conditions such as AUTISM may mean severe learning difficulties with severe behaviour problems. Some children may be deaf and blind; some of these may have severe learning difficulties with behaviour difficulties. Some children with severe learning difficulties may have hearing impairments. Teaching strategies are often based on breaking down tasks into target behaviour (known as TASK ANALYSIS) and *operant conditioning* (as described in Appendix 1).

8. Gifted and talented children

There has long been a debate about the extent to which gifted children have special educational needs. Some educationalists make a distinction between gifted (implying superior ability over a wide range) and talented (implying having a specific area of expertise, e.g. musical aptitude – see Short, 1993). In addition, any such definitions are relative to culture. Arguments hinge on the necessity to avoid 'under-achievement' for these children, i.e. the necessity for an educational environment that can maximise the child's academic as well as social-emotional developments.

Such children have traditionally been recognised by high scores on intelligence tests but now broader concepts are used, e.g. creativity, specific academic ability, leadership and visual and performing arts (Short, 1993).

The educational psychologist may well be faced with having to give advice in relation to a gifted child. Approaches tend to involve one of the following:

- ACCELERATION – the child may be moved up a year in the school. The educational psychologist would need to consider, in particular, the likely social-emotional effects
- SEGREGATION – some educationalists may feel the need for such a child to have a specialised curriculum in an environment where the child would meet other high ability pupils
- ENRICHMENT – the classroom curriculum is adapted in such a way to develop and extend the child's particular abilities (see Short, 1993).

The main categories of special education need have been outlined here. It would be appropriate at this stage to consider ways in which educational psychologists would approach the assessment of such difficulties.

Assessment and testing

The evaluation of learning has long been an issue in psychology and education. In the course of their school careers, children will undergo a number of formal and informal assessments. The Education Reform Act, 1988, has introduced new procedures for testing children at ages 7, 11, 14 and 16. Records of achievement are to be used to record progress and attainment within the National Curriculum assessment system. However, this type of assessment indicates a shift on the part of educators (and psychologists, see below) away from standardised tests towards more flexible types of assessment '... which are directly related to the individual's needs in a particular context' (Smith and Cowie, 1994, p394).

In general, tests can be divided into NORM-REF-ERENCED or CRITERION-REFERENCED tests:

- *norm-referenced* tests are standardised on a given population and measures taken of their

RELIABILITY and VALIDITY (see Appendix 2). A score, therefore, will enable the psychologist to compare a child's score with the typical score of a child that age from a large sample of the population. If a child is said to be on the '80th percentile' for reading this means that, compared with the relevant group of children (usually those the same age), only 20% of children would get a higher score on that specific reading test. A typical example of a norm-referenced test is the traditional intelligence or IQ test (see below)
- *criterion-referenced* tests indicate whether a child has successfully achieved a given objective or not, irrespective of whether this is appropriate for its age, e.g. a pupil passes or fails regardless of the percentage of individuals of the same age who perform at that level. An example might be being able to tie your shoe laces. This could also be broken down into a number of sub-skills and the number of these a child has achieved could be ascertained, giving an idea of progress towards the overall objective.

Assessment under the National Curriculum is criterion-referenced. Standard Assessment Tasks are carried out by the child's individual class teacher. Such assessments, whilst clearly assessing the child within the normal learning context, raise some methodological problems, for instance:

- the competence and expectations of the assessors (teachers)
- bias in measurements, i.e in observations and checklists; this is related to the reliability and validity of the measures and other measurement issues discussed in Appendix 2.

An important current issue, then, is the extent to which teachers have training and experience in administering the tasks and the extent to which the scoring by such large numbers of individuals is STANDARDISED – see Appendix 2.

In addition to school-based assessment, educational psychologists may need to carry out further assessments in given areas of difficulty. They will vary in the methods they use and in the choice of tests (if any) that they carry out, employing a wide

TABLE 1 Methods of assessment used by educational psychologists

Rating scales	Tests of ability
Direct observation	Tests of attainment
Observation checklists	Questionnaires
Interviews with pupils, staff and parents	

variety of assessment techniques, several of which are shown in Table 1. Choices of approach will vary and will depend on the nature of the child's difficulties.

Of the many tests available, some are 'open' and can be used by any individual (e.g. most reading tests); others are 'closed' and available only to those who have particular qualifications and/or training (e.g. intelligence tests). Given the sheer volume and variety of tests available, those outlined in the following sections are only a small sample to illustrate areas in which tests might aid the assessment of children.

The assessment of school-based learning difficulties

In assessing learning difficulties the first step is some definition of what constitutes a learning difficulty. Criteria in terms of the 1993 Education Act have already been mentioned (see above). In addition, there will be a further group of children with some degree of learning difficulty which has been recognised by the school. The educational psychologist would usually become involved in individual work with the child at the stage where the school has used its resources (e.g. additional small group teaching) but feels the child has failed to make enough progress. The educational psychologist would begin with the teacher's assessment but also view the child's work relative to his or her peers and then make decisions about the need for further assessment. There are basically two types of test:

■ ABILITY TESTS – what a person can do in general – an example is a test of general intelligence
■ ATTAINMENT TESTS or *verbal reasoning* – what a person has achieved after learning or training – an example is a reading or geography test.

Attainment tests

Both educational psychologists and school staff may be concerned with a child's level of attainment in reading, spelling and numeracy, as well as handwriting skills. Such assessments can range from informal assessment, e.g. a noticeable improvement in the number of words spelt correctly in a weekly test, to standardised tests. The following are examples of some of the widely used standardised tests of attainment.

Oral reading tests can be used to assess word recognition and a child's WORD ATTACK SKILLS (e.g. sounding out) with unfamiliar words. Examples would be the Schonell Word Reading Test (Schonell, 1974) or the British Ability Scales Word Reading Test (Elliott, Murray and Pearson, 1979). The child is presented with words arranged in rows of increasing difficulty. The number of words read correctly is then related to age norms, giving a WORD READING AGE.

Diagnostic investigation of reading errors and tests of comprehension. Some reading tests combine story reading with comprehension questions to yield an accuracy score and a comprehension score which are both age-related. The type of errors made by the child can also be recorded, e.g. substitutions and omissions. Examples of such tests would be the Neale Analysis of Reading Ability (Neale, 1989) and the Macmillan New Reading Analysis (Macmillan Education Ltd, 1989).

Spelling tests A number of tests require individual words to be read out to the child who then has to write these down. This continues to a specified criterion (e.g. ten consecutive incorrect responses). The number of words spelt correctly can be translated to a SPELLING AGE using appropriate norms. Examples of such tests would be the Schonell Spelling Test (Schonell and Goodacre, 1974) and the BAS (British Ability Scales) Spelling Scale (Elliott, 1992). The Wechsler Objective Reading Dimensions (WORD, 1993) combines basic reading skills, reading comprehension and spelling to give a composite reading score.

Numeracy tests A number of tests assess a child's understanding of the basic arithmetical functions. For example the BAS Basic Number Skills Test presents children with a printed sheet of problems beginning with simple addition and subtraction and continuing to complex fractions and decimals. Again, raw scores can be converted to a NUMBER AGE.

Handwriting Assessment of handwriting is difficult to quantify and is generally not appropriate for norm referencing. Assessment might include grip and finger control, fluency, legibility, excesses of pressure and evenness of size. The LDA Aston Index (1976) contains a graphomotor test where the child is required to copy a directional pattern to test motor fluency with both right and left hands. Scoring is related to fluency and overall motor control and to comparisons between hands.

Ability tests

Ability tests have been developed to measure underlying constructs which are not a direct result of training, e.g. intelligence. Intelligence is clearly an important construct in education and intelligence tests have been used to make predictions about future academic achievement (e.g. see Davenport's summary, 1994).

The measurement of intelligence Since intelligence defies exact definition a relevant question has always been, 'what do intelligence tests measure?' and also, 'what do intelligence quotients (IQs) tell us?' These issues will only be dealt with here in relation to test scores. The interested reader is referred to Davenport (1994) or Gross (1992) for discussion of issues in this section. An important issue in the intelligence testing debate is whether it is sensible to think of intelligence as a single main 'factor', a view held by Spearman (1904), or as composed of several or even many abilities, as supported by Thurstone (1938) or Guilford (1959).

Modern intelligence tests tend to sample a wide range of verbal and non-verbal abilities, such as general knowledge, vocabulary and visual spatial ability. IQs are no longer computed as ratios (mental age/chronological age $\times$ 100) but as *devi-*ation IQs indicating how far a score is from the overall (mean) average. For example, the Wechsler tests, developed by David Wechsler and widely used, relate a child's score to the distribution of scores of other children of the same age.

Clearly tests are not valid for groups on which they are not standardised (see Appendix 2). In order to assess intelligence irrespective of particular populations, attempts have been made to produce CULTURE-FREE intelligence tests which have proved difficult because:

- it is difficult to evaluate their validity (see Appendix 2)
- a realistic concept of intelligence must be based in a cultural context (e.g. see Davenport, 1994).

However, some non-verbal tests, such as Raven's Matrices (see below), may approximate to culture-free tests. There have also been attempts to develop CULTURE-SPECIFIC TESTS, i.e. tests that are relevant to a particular ethnic background. In addition, there have been new approaches to the concept of intelligence which include:

- Gardner's (1983) Multiple Intelligences, including spatial and musical abilities which must be defined within a particular cultural context
- Sternberg's (1984) Triarchic Theory of Human Intelligence which he feels consists of three components:

  - the ability to take in information
  - the ability to store information
  - the ability to build on information stored.

Intelligence tests The Wechsler tests were initially standardised on American populations and then restandardised on British populations. The Wechsler Intelligence Scale for Children – Revised (WISC-R) – was initially standardised on 22,000 children in eleven age groups and represented minority ethnic groups in the same ratio as in the USA 1970 census. This test has been through several revisions, the latest of which is the WISC-III UK (Wechsler, 1992) and is standardised on the UK population. The WISC contains verbal tests, e.g. vocabulary, verbal concepts (similarities) and non-verbal tests such as block design and picture completion. There is evidence that verbal and non-verbal scores on the WISC correlate with academic achievement.

The British Ability Scales (Elliott et al, first published 1979, revised 1983) also include a battery of verbal and non-verbal tests as well as a number of visual perceptual tests and also cognitive tests, some of which are based on learning principles or stages proposed in Piaget's theory of children's cognitive development. BAS introduced a new statistical procedure which essentially meant that the test could be used either as criterion-referenced assessment, using pass/fail criteria on individual items, or as norm-referenced assessment in relation to an age-stratified UK population.

Raven's Matrices (Raven, 1965) are intended to be non-verbal tests of intelligence. They present a series of visual symbols of increasing complexity. The child has to choose the next symbol in the series from a range of options given.

There are many tests of intelligence and the above represent only a small sample of those available. The interested reader is referred to Sattler (1982) for a full discussion of the assessment of children's intelligence.

Assessment of speech and language difficulties

In this common and important area of assessment, educational psychologists would generally work closely with speech therapists. Generally what is looked at is the child's ability to communicate (EXPRESSIVE LANGUAGE) and to understand what is said (RECEPTIVE LANGUAGE). Assessment would, therefore, involve information from those who know and work with the child (parents, teachers, speech therapists) and direct observation and assessment. Tests used in this area may include:

■ the British Picture Vocabulary Scale (BPVS – Dunn et al, 1982) which assesses the child's comprehension of the meaning of single words. Each page of the test has four pictures. The child is asked, for example, to indicate the picture that represents the word given

■ the Illinois Test of Psycholinguistic Abilities (ITPA) which yields a LANGUAGE AGE of three to ten years. The language profile is based on three phases of the linguistic process (i.e. reception, organisation and expression or production)

■ the Reynell Developmental Language Scales (Reynell, 1977) aimed at children from six months to six years. This test assesses the child's understanding of connected speech (comprehension), e.g. 'put the doll on the chair' and of communication skills. The test is standardised on children who hear normally, though it may be adapted for use with hearing-impaired children. Reynell makes some very relevant points about the difficulty of producing 'norms' for groups such as children with sensory impairment. In relation to hearing impairment:

– language development in hearing-impaired children is very variable, depending largely on the degree of impairment

– hearing-impaired children often have additional problems so it is difficult to achieve a 'standard' deaf population of children sufficiently homogenous with the same degree of hearing impairment to establish DEAF NORMS

– language development in hearing-impaired children follows a different pattern from hearing children (Reynell, 1977). In particular verbal expressions proceed faster than verbal comprehension and expressive vocabulary proceeds faster than sentence construction (structure) and content (connected ideas). Reynell makes the point that teaching methods could take these points into consideration and also raises the question as to whether they should do. Reynell considers that in using the hearing norms with hearing-impaired children, each child can be used as their own control i.e. compared with their *own* development rather than be compared with hearing peers.

Assessment of emotional and behavioural difficulties (EBD)

This further important area for educational psychologists is a particularly difficult area to assess. In a study by McCall and Farrell (1993) of how educational psychologists would assess a particular EMOTIONAL AND BEHAVIOURAL DIFFICULTY, they found that, out of 57, 44% used some tests while over half used no tests. Of those using tests, 22 different personality tests and procedures were mentioned.

Assessment would often begin with teacher reports of the frequency and intensity of the behaviour of concern, e.g. temper tantrums, fights, victimisation. The extent to which the child's behaviour and/or self-perceptions were maladaptive to his or her educational environment would need to be ascertained. Observation would often be a further step, followed by an individual interview with the child. Rating scales might be used to establish the child's self-perception.

Children often show immature and attention-seeking behaviour. In cases where these have become disruptive, the educational psychologist may use a test such as the *Bristol Social Adjustment Guides* (Stott and Marston, 1971) to indicate, for example, the degree of maladjustment. There are three guides – *The Child in School*, *The Child in Residential Care* and *The Child in the Family*. Each guide consists of a number of statements about a child's behaviour in a variety of situations and the person completing the guide underlines for each situation the statement that best describes the child's behaviour, e.g. how the child greets the teacher. Sometimes behavioural problems result from frustration in the learning situation, in which case some additional assessment of possible learning difficulties might be undertaken. Further discussion of emotional and behavioural difficulties in school are given in the 'working with schools' section.

Assessment of early developmental delay

Educational psychologists are not only concerned with school-based assessment. They will often be involved in the assessment of pre-school children and especially in the assessment of early developmental difficulties which are likely to affect educational progress and future school placement. Such difficulties might include sensory impairment, motor (movement) difficulties and general COGNITIVE DELAY.

There are a number of developmental scales that could be used in pre-school assessment, for example, the *Griffiths Mental Development Scales* (Griffiths, 1970, 1984) covering the age range of 0

– 8 years. Children are assessed on a number of scales (locomotor, personal/social, hearing and speech, hand and eye co-ordination, performance, reasoning) and performance is age-referenced.

The *Bayley Scales of Infant Development* (Bayley, 1969) are another example of some widely used pre-school tests aimed at measuring infants from two months to thirty months of age on three scales, i.e. a mental scale looking at perception and learning ability, a motor scale looking at co-ordination skills, and an infant behaviour record looking at social and personal development as well as attention span.

Educational psychologists may also be involved in local PORTAGE SYSTEMS, an intervention approach involving parents and professionals working with, say, gross motor development – p. 121.

Working with schools

In addition to individual (statutory) assessments, psychologists will spend some considerable time working in conjunction with their patch or group of schools to help them to develop strategies to cope with learning, emotional and behavioural difficulties. The local Educational Psychology Service will offer a particular service to these schools, which may involve an agreed number of visits to the school. The nature of work with schools has been a subject of much debate within the profession since educational psychologists became increasingly disillusioned with child-centred approaches focusing on the individual child, a model representing the 'medical model' – see Figure 4.1, Gillham, 1978 and Wolfendale et al, 1992. This disillusionment developed for a number of reasons:

- ever increasing referral lists
- a perceived lack of influence of such approaches on changes within education
- the increasing influence of studies of organisations and of systems theories on educational practice (Labram, 1992)
- increasing recognition of environmental and social influences on behaviour and learning.

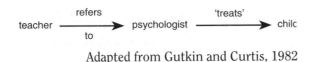

Adapted from Gutkin and Curtis, 1982

FIGURE 4.1
The direct 'treatment' (medical) model – educational psychologist as expert

However, there was continued recognition that the educational psychologist brings to the school certain unique qualities in addition to those concerning assessment and diagnosis:

- detailed knowledge of local and county resources
- information concerning the implementation of LEA policies and procedures
- knowledge of LEA personnel
- knowledge of other support services
- knowledge of interventions and approaches to similar problems.

The question then became how best to combine these qualities with more effective methods of working with schools.

The educational psychologist as consultant

One simple extension of the individual child-focused approach was what Labram (1992) terms *technical involvement*. This represents a simplified CONSULTANCY MODEL where the consultant draws upon expert knowledge and skills to resolve clearly defined problems, i.e. the consultant supplies the solution (Figure 4.2) though 'treatment' is carried out by the 'consultee', i.e. the school and its teachers.

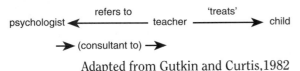

Adapted from Gutkin and Curtis, 1982

FIGURE 4.2
The educational psychologist as consultant

This relies on careful diagnosis of the problem presented. An example might be training teachers in the use of time out procedures in behaviour management programmes (see pp. 97–99).

A more sophisticated consultancy model is gen-erally known as PROCESS CONSULTANCY (e.g. see Labram, 1992; Gutkin and Curtis, 1982). This depends on members of organisations themselves diagnosing problems and arriving at possible solutions. They then implement and evaluate these themselves. The consultant's role is to help the organisation acknowledge and use its own resources to arrive at solutions to problems. The approach is borrowed from the psychiatric model developed by Caplan (1970) for mental health services which had a psychodynamic basis.

Consultancy models have been debated for many reasons, one of the recent ones being the Education Reform Act, which introduced the possibility of educational psychology services in some local authorities becoming independent and operating on a business or 'market' level. Though the 1993 Act lessened this likelihood, the debate had focused attention on who was the 'client' for educational psychologists – e.g. child, school – and who was the consultant and the consultee. (See Wolfendale et al, 1992, Labram, 1992, or Gutkin and Curtis, 1982 for a similar debate some years earlier in the US). The experience, in some authorities, of almost losing central funding and becoming a market commodity, was one influence on managers of these services considering possible advantages in adopting consultancy approaches to educational psychology service delivery. This included greater flexibility in making changes in organisational structure.

Advantages of the consultation model

Gutkin and Curtis (1982), in a summary of research findings, list the advantages of consultancy models:

- teachers and other school personnel often indicate preference for consultative approaches over traditional models where they have a generally more passive role
- teachers exposed to consultation services believe that their professional skills have improved as a result
- teachers in schools which had consultations found problems to be less serious than teachers in matched schools without consultants when presented with an identical list of child problems

- referral rates dropped dramatically after four to five years of exposure to consultation services
- client gains following consultation services may generalise to other children in the same class as a result of increased teacher effectiveness.

Teachers who work with consultants rated as highly effective demonstrate significant improvements in their perceptions and understanding of children's problems (Curtis and Watson, 1980). Other comments made have been that consultation may be less time-consuming than individual assessment and there may be less time between referral of a problem to a psychological specialist and consequent action.

Difficulties with consultation

However, a number of difficulties with consultation have also been noted:

- the quality of consultative services depends on the skill level and motivation of the consultee. (In the case of teachers this has to involve teacher perceptions of where the problems lie and also the demand on teacher time)
- educational psychologists retain statutory duties in the identification and assessment of children with special educational needs, which may limit consultancy time and potential
- there is a need, initially, for a larger amount of consultee time
- there are difficulties with 'newness' and acceptance of these models
- some methods used to assess the effects of consultation have been inadequate, e.g. the use of questionnaire and self-report approaches which can suffer from subjectivity and individual impressions
- there are inadequate descriptions of the specific techniques used by consultants in published research (Gutkin and Curtis, 1982, p828)
- there is a lack of clarity about the influence of feelings and attitudes in consultant/consultee relationships, i.e. on the consultancy process.

Factors affecting learning and behaviour in schools

In the following sections the emphasis will be less on educational problems or specific learning difficulty and more on *general* psychological research applied to the full range of learners within practical educational settings.

Applications of theories of learning to educational practice

Understanding the processes by which children are able to take in information, retain it and use it appropriately are clearly fundamental issues in education. Many theories of learning have been developed, some dealing with the more 'observable' aspects of changes in student behaviour (BEHAVIOURIST theories) and others more related to thinking processes and memory (COGNITIVE theories). One difficulty is in defining learning. It would probably be accepted by most as a *change (of behaviour or thinking) in an individual which is a result of experience*. This would distinguish it from, say, genetic/biological factors in interaction with the environment which produce changes such as those of height or body shape.

Behaviourist theories of learning

Behaviourist theories are described in Appendix 1. Out of this work came attempts to apply behaviourist principles to education including:

- *the use of reinforcement to decrease problem behaviour in the classroom.* One problem with disruptive behaviour is that often, for pupils who achieve little academically, the behaviour is a way of obtaining attention. Teachers may well be rewarding inappropriate behaviour if misbehaviour is the only way in which the child receives attention. Studies by Wheldall and Merrett (1983) have indicated approaches which can help to improve classroom behaviour and hence improve learning and the quantity and quality of work produced. In one study, two children who spent an inordinate amount of time out of their seats were shown scores of how often they were out of their seats and were told they would gain a team point if these scores dropped. The children were shown charts of their progress and praised and encouraged for a decrease in the amount of time out of their seats. Being out of their seats declined rapidly for both children.

Many teachers use adaptations of the TOKEN ECONOMY principle (see the clinical psychology chapter) in behaviour management such as star charts or the use of computer time. In a typical arrangement to increase on-task behaviour, a buzzer is sounded at particular time intervals. Children on task when the buzzer sounds are rewarded. In one variation (Wheldall and Merrett, 1983), pupils themselves ticked if they were working at the time of the buzzer and their scores were then tallied and rewarded. A typical reward might be extra time on the computer and free choice of activity. Target scores increased weekly. Teaching staff reported improvement in noise levels and the amount and quality of work completed. The children felt that the quieter atmosphere helped them to concentrate.

- *the PREMACK PRINCIPLE* (Premack, 1965). Involves linking less desired behaviours to more desired activities. A teacher might offer free choice after pupils have completed some mathematical sums
- *extinction*. For example, in dealing with attention-seeking behaviour, teachers would ignore attention seeking and reward alternative, desired behaviour
- *shaping and chaining*. This involves starting with approximations to the desired final behaviour and gradually building up to the required outcome
- *schedules of reinforcement*. This means not rewarding *every* response and, in particular, the gradual removal of reinforcement until behaviour becomes *self-sustaining* or INTRINSICALLY MOTIVATED – see p. 105
- *the development of TIME OUT procedures*. This means withdrawing children from a situation when behaviour becomes unacceptable. This is justified, *not* as punishment, but as removal from *association* with undesired activities and

also removal from REINFORCEMENT. Where a child must do something (e.g. apologise) before being allowed back into the normal classroom environment, the principle is that of NEGATIVE REINFORCEMENT, since a desired behaviour is strengthened by the *removal* of adverse conditions for the child

- *immediacy of consequences*. This highlights the importance of not delaying reinforcement (e.g. stars in a token system, or work marked immediately)
- *developing 'task analysis' skills*. This is relevant to changing inappropriate behaviour or to developing learning skills. Also covered in the occupational psychology chapter, this involves breaking down an overall task into sub-components and teaching each of these before building up to the whole task. This can be a considerable skill for teachers and of great use in making more complex learning manageable
- *developing objectivity*. This has particular relevance to emotional and behavioural difficulties, e.g. being aware of the antecedents of difficult behaviour, the behaviour itself and the consequences for those involved. It is more useful to engage in such FUNCTIONAL ANALYSIS of behaviour (see the clinical psychology chapter) than to label a child 'unmanageable' or plain 'bad'
- *discrimination and generalisation*. Involves an understanding of the importance of developing discrimination skills, e.g. a child recognising the difference between the letters *d* and *b* and the importance of generalisation, e.g. a child recognising the same letters in different size print or colours or lower and upper cases
- *programmed learning*. This is mentioned in the occupational chapter and was promoted by Skinner (1961), although it never developed as fully as he would have liked. The Skinner dream was to have each child at a machine which delivered a carefully stepped programme of instruction with test and answer (reinforcement) at regular intervals and a 'loop' system whereby the child (or adult learner) went back over unsuccessful steps. Elements of the individually paced learning idea remain in the self-test exercises included in many

textbooks and in more recent computer instruction systems.

Weaknesses of the behavioural approach

In general stimulus–response behavioural approaches were not able to deal effectively with 'thinking', since, in the original versions, mental concepts were ruled out as objects of scientific study. In particular, they dealt poorly with the way language develops in children. Parents reward quite ungrammatical statements. Indeed, they are found to reward truth rather than grammatical correctness most of the time (Slobin, 1975). Since children often produce a combination of words that they could not have heard and use grammatical structures that adults would not use, they cannot be imitating – a point against social learning theory – see below. However, children acquire language rules very quickly from a mass of often 'incorrect' grammar used by adults (Chomsky, 1959). In fact, it is hard to stop children acquiring their local language, hard to suppress the *intrinsic motivation* to learn – see p. 105.

Behaviourist approaches have, therefore, been generally confined to the more 'observable' aspects of behaviour and hence are more relevant to classroom behaviour and its management than to the internal processes involved in the retention of information and how that information may be subsequently used.

Cognitive theories of learning

As described in Appendix 1, Bandura's SOCIAL LEARNING THEORY (1969) was a bridge between classic behaviourism and cognitive approaches within psychology. Bandura considers that four factors are central in observational learning:

- *attention* – looking at the relevant aspects of others' behaviour
- *retaining* information
- *reproducing* information or behaviour
- being *motivated* to reproduce information or behaviour.

Clearly teachers can model desired behaviour and can reinforce those learners who display desired behaviour, ensuring that other students' attention is drawn to these outcomes. There will be fairly clear messages in a classroom where giggles at 'foreign' names or racist comments are reprimanded or directly questioned by the teacher rather than simply ignored, leaving perpetrators to be rewarded by social approval from peers.

Bandura's later theories include the processes of SELF-MANAGEMENT and SELF-EFFICACY. The latter concept is dealt with in the motivation section below. Self-management includes training and encouraging students to set their own goals, self-evaluate their progress and reinforce themselves for work successfully completed. In addition, Meichenbaum's SELF-INSTRUCTIONAL TRAINING has been used in helping learners (e.g. of reading) to internalise steps of instruction (by repeating them as private speech) modelled from competent trainers (see the clinical psychology chapter).

Piaget's theory

Purely cognitive theories are concerned with the internal processes involved in thinking and remembering. A particularly influential theory has been that of Jean Piaget (1954; 1963), who was concerned with the way children's thinking developed over time. He was interested in the processes involved, i.e. how a child arrived at a conclusion rather than content – what the child knew. Piaget believed that children's thinking goes through distinct stages where thought is radically restructured. Thinking is based on internal representations of the world called SCHEMAS or *schemata*, e.g. when a child consistently and accurately reaches out for a favourite toy placed in different positions, the child may be said to have a schema of how to obtain the toy. Recognising any dog is evidence of a general schema for dogs.

Early learning, according to Piaget, consists of incorporating new information, either by ASSIMILATING it into existing schemas or by ACCOMMODATING schemas as a result of information which doesn't fit the existing set of schemas. For instance, a child may have learned that banging two bricks together makes a noise. It may then bang two pieces of cloth together (assimilation) which make no noise. Its internal schemata might then adapt as it learns to differentiate objects which make a noise when banged together from those that do not (accommodation). Piaget considered that schemata change with new informa-

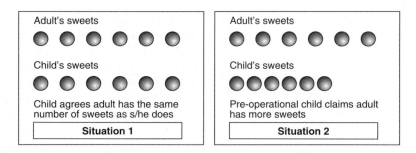

FIGURE 4.3
Conservation and centration – child centres on length of line of sweets and fails to recognise that, in both situations, both lines have the same number. Hence the child fails to *conserve* number.

tion in order to maintain a state of EQUILIBRATION, or balance, whereby problems encountered in the environment are solved at the current stage of development, sometimes creating odd 'solutions' from an adult's point of view.

The first of the four stages is the *sensory–motor* stage (0 – 2 years). Information from the senses is linked with motor development, for example, learning to reach and hold objects or learning where to find the cat. During this stage babies develop the idea that objects do not cease to exist when not looked at (OBJECT PERMANENCE). This stage is also characterised by the development of language and social skills.

The second stage is the *pre-operational* stage (2 – 7 years), characterised by lack of CONSERVATION (of number, size, weight, volume, area etc). For example, a four year old in situation 1 of Figure 4.3 will readily agree that there are the same number of items in each row but if the length of one row changes (situation 2), the child may say the longer row now has more counters. The child has CENTRED on one attribute (length) and has failed to *conserve* number. If the shortened row is then returned to its original state, the child will again agree there are equal numbers in each row.

Similarly, if they agree that two identical beakers contain the same amount of orange juice, but see one beaker's contents poured into a taller, thinner beaker, they seem to see the taller beaker as containing more juice.

This stage is also characterised by the child's EGOCENTRICITY (for example, a child saying 'you

can't see me', when only their own eyes are covered). Piaget showed children a model of a village and three mountains. The child was placed on one side and the child was asked to describe the mountain as a doll placed on the opposite side would see it or to pick a picture showing the doll's view. Children in this stage typically could not describe or choose the doll's view, only their own.

During the third *concrete operational* stage (7 – 11 years) children develop concepts of conservation, can DECENTRE and become less egocentric. They learn SERIATION (ordering lengths, weights etc.) and TRANSITIVITY, e.g. if A is greater than B and B is greater than C, A must be greater than C. Children at this time also develop concepts of CLASS INCLUSION, categories and sub-categories, e.g. animals, animals with fur, and so on.

In the fourth *formal operational* stage (11 years onwards) thinking becomes more abstract and children can handle general ideas and concepts such as those of justice and equality. They are also able to test hypotheses and to hold one variable constant while systematically varying another, as in scientific experimentation – see Appendix 2.

Weaknesses in Piaget's theory Research has shown that it is possible under some conditions to ACCELERATE children through the stages (Meadows, 1988). According to Piaget a child needed to be in a state of READINESS for stage change and he dismissed United States' educators keenness on acceleration as the 'American question'. Acceleration research has led to debate about the supposed radical 'restructuring' at each stage, the need for the child's thinking to be 'ready', and about the existence of clearly-defined stages at all, as opposed to a smooth continuum of development. In particular, studies have shown children *are* able to be non-egocentric in the pre-operational stage (e.g. Hughes, 1975). Explanations for different findings have been related to the type and complexity of language used by Piaget in his tasks. The interested reader is referred to Donaldson (1978) and Siegler (1991) for a review of some of the difficulties with Piaget's work and to Slavin (1994) for further discussion of Piaget's theory and neo-Piagetian ideas.

Educational implications of Piaget's theory
Despite the criticisms and a general lack of recommendations for educators from Piaget, the theory has had strong influence in education, particularly in relation to pre-school development, nursery and early school years. Piaget's theory emphasises the need for:

- developmentally appropriate education, with material and approaches at different ages linked to a child's stage of cognitive development; material should be pitched just at and slightly beyond the child's current level of understanding; the teacher may gently introduce *disequilibrium* in order to promote further exploration
- attention to the way a child *thinks* rather than just what a child can *do*, which in turn should lead to the provision of appropriate learning experiences
- an emphasis on the importance of a child's own *active* involvement in learning situations; children should be encouraged to discover for themselves; teachers should tap their *intrinsic motivation* to learn; teachers need to provide a variety of activities that allow the child to interact with its environment; through this, the child is considered to develop true understanding rather than 'right answers'
- recognition of individual differences in going through the stages of development; with this recognition comes the need to teach individuals in small groups rather than the whole class; in addition, each child should be

Jean Piaget, whose early theory of cognitive development influenced educational thinking, especially for the early years.

assessed according to that child's own performance rather than to any general 'norms'
- physical representation of ideas, i.e. giving concrete activities to develop abstract notions.

Discovery learning and scaffolding Piaget's ideas were influential in the development of DIS-COVERY LEARNING approaches. He said, for instance:

> 'Remember also that each time one prematurely teaches a child something he could have discovered for himself, that child is kept from inventing it and consequently from understanding it completely.'
> *(Piaget, 1970, p715)*

Discovery learning approaches were developed particularly by Bruner (1966). They emphasised the need:

- for students to learn from their own active explorations
- to start with 'real' problems and to help students develop appropriate problem-solving techniques to help to break down those problems, using the teacher as a resource
- for co-operative learning, i.e. with children working in pairs or groups (see p. 113).

The aim is to arouse curiosity, increase (intrinsic) motivation and help children to become more independent learners. Teachers do not instruct directly but provide resources with which children explore relationships (e.g. scales and weights). Difficulties may arise if the information is too far beyond a child's cognitive level. In addition, it may not be easy for children to generalise from a specific real-life incident to other similar situations. It might also be difficult to defend the strong Piagetian position that *all* concepts, taught rather than discovered, must necessarily remain incompletely understood.

The Vygotsky alternative to Piaget   It is odd that an author who died over 50 years ago, at 38 years old, and whose work was only translated from the Russian language in the 1970s, should start to influence Western child psychology, particularly form the 1980s onwards. This has happened with Vygotsky's work (1978; 1986) on language and social interaction.

Piaget believed that children's habit of talking out loud when no one is there to hear what they say demonstrated further evidence of egocentrism. The child took no account of the listener's position, or that there was no listener, and simply went on talking. Piaget also believed that this quirk of children served little, if any, purpose and died out at around 7 years old. Vygotsky, however, saw that such speech served an absolutely central and enormously powerful role in the development of thinking. Whereas Piaget believed that speech simply followed thought (that is, only when we have certain mental concepts can we develop language to express them), Vygotsky believed that thought was very much dependent on the existence of social speech – we could not start to think internally without speaking and interacting with other people. Where Piaget sees the child as alone

with his or her thoughts and only gradually coming into social interactions as thinking develops, Vygotsky argued that social interactions *themselves* are the root of our higher thinking processes. For Vygotsky, then, thinking is social and we develop it through interacting with others. For example, consider a conversation between yourself and a child about a clock:

'Is it quarter past four or quarter past five?'
'Quarter past five.'
'But look where the little hand is. Where is it, just after four or just after five?'
'Four, just after four, it's a long way from five.'
'Right! We say quarter past, then ask where the little hand is. What number is it past?'
'Four. It's a quarter past four.'

From this social interaction the child learns to *internalise* some rules. Developing internal speech, for Vygotsky, is the way we learn strategies. Piaget's *egocentric speech* is actually the child learning to self-instruct. Gradually the skill becomes fluid, developing audible speech into silent thought. Evidence comes from the fact that, under pressure (say when our car keys have gone missing), we return to talking out loud. Meichenbaum's SELF-INSTRUCTIONAL TRAINING is an attempt to harness the power of internal SELF-REGULATORY SPEECH to train children to stick to a strategy in situations they would otherwise find too complex and overwhelming.

Zone of proximal development and scaffolding Vygotsky's ZONE OF PROXIMAL DEVELOPMENT (ZPD) is the area in which a child can solve problems but not unaided, in other words, the area in which they are ripe for learning and discovery. This explains why another learner, who has not long ago gone through the same learning experience, is often a good tutor – still in a similar ZPD, they understand the difficulties.

A strong implication from Vygotsky's view is that simply providing children with materials, then leaving them to discover, will not be successful. The child needs this *plus* support. The teacher needs to identify problems in the child's ZPD and to provide a scaffold of the useful speech, nudges, demonstrations and explanations which will help the child get the point. As this produces greater competence in the child, so the teacher withdraws the scaffolding until the learner can comfortably solve this level of problem on their own. The term SCAFFOLDING has become commonly used for this approach to the design of classroom learning. Wood (1988) gives specific detail on scaffolding and describes the most effective instructional method as CONTINGENT TEACHING, demonstrated by mothers and children working with wooden blocks. Here, the adult provides information where necessary, to meet exactly the child's level of misunderstanding or difficulty, then withdraws and gives more responsibility at stages where the child shows competence. The child is neither defeated by lack of help nor swamped by too much verbal or visual information, and is able to exercise initiative when comfortable with the current demands of the task.

Information processing approaches to learning

The COGNITIVE REVOLUTION in psychology was largely promoted by advances in experimental research on attention and memory processes (see Appendix 1) and has, in its turn, produced implications for educational practice. The emphasis is on a model of humans as processors of incoming information which requires identification, categorisation and analysis. In common with Piaget's approach, we are seen as perpetually (not just at school) solving problems and making decisions. The essential questions which represent the core of academic learning are, how is information absorbed, how is it retained and how do students learn how to learn?

Stages in the process of memory, for example, have been identified. An early model (Atkinson and Shiffrin, 1968) held that humans use three information stores:

- SENSORY MEMORY – where sense data are initially held very briefly in 'raw' form, e.g. sounds or patches of light
- SHORT-TERM MEMORY (STM) – which appeared to have a limited capacity (7 plus/minus 2 letters or numbers) and which was considered to be a temporary store where information needed to be rehearsed if it was to be passed into . . .

- LONG-TERM MEMORY (LTM) – apparently limitless.

Research has indicated at least three types of LTM:

- EPISODIC MEMORY of events that have happened to us as individuals, seemingly stored as images
- SEMANTIC MEMORY of rules, language, other symbolic material and how to use these
- PROCEDURAL MEMORY, for example changing gear in a car, stored as stimulus–response connections.

These last two processes correspond to those of DECLARATIVE KNOWLEDGE and PROCEDURAL KNOWLEDGE discussed in Anderson's model of learning in the occupational psychology chapter where, eventually, the knowledge of rules develops into relatively smooth application of skill to the point of AUTOMATICITY, examples of which would be the ability to add up a column of figures with no hesitation, read fluently or draw a house whilst talking to a friend. In addition to declarative and procedural knowledge, Woolfolk (1993) discusses CONDITIONAL KNOWLEDGE – the knowledge of where and when to *apply* our rules and procedures. Students often know *what* and they know *how*. The big problem is developing smooth strategies for applying this knowledge at appropriate times. For instance, one may know what a correlation *is* and one may know *how* it is calculated. The difficulty is in knowing *when* particular sets of data or research designs require the use of a correlation.

Later versions of STM/LTM theory transformed the STM notion into that of WORKING MEMORY which is considered to be just that of which we are immediately conscious at any moment. It would be the facility we use when adding numbers and we hold the number we wish to carry over. A different development was Craik and Lockhart's (1972) emphasis, not on stores of memory, but on the LEVEL OF PROCESSING used on incoming information. In typical research, people are asked to process at a *physical* level (e.g. state the ink colour of words), at an *acoustic* level (e.g. give a rhyme for a word), or at a *semantic* level (e.g. give a meaning for each word). They are far more likely to recall words processed at the semantic level.

Meaning and construction in memory
Whatever memory model is closest to the truth,

this last research finding has great implications. Much other research shows that the more meaning is given to materials to be learned the more likely we are to recall them. Bower et al (1969) showed that organised items will be better recalled and Bower (1972) showed that making and linking images of items improves recall dramatically. An early view of memory by Bartlett (1932) was that we do not recall ideas precisely, like a camera or tape recorder. We reconstruct what we have seen or learnt from *cues*. This view is important in understanding the problems of eyewitness testimony (see the criminological psychology chapter). For teachers, the use has been in realising that material needs to be made meaningful for students and that rote memory is rarely as efficient as memory with meaning. MNEMONICS are an example of making unlinked material meaningful, for instance the use of *Richard Of York Gave Battle In Vain* to generate the first letter of each colour of the rainbow. Teachers can usefully instruct students in the use of such methods, making them as unusual, personal and even as funny or rude as possible in order to enhance the recall of otherwise unconnected items. We rarely have to store unconnected material but where we do (times tables, formulae, countries and capitals) the following principles have been found to be important. Some are from 'classic' behavioural rather than cognitive research.

PRIMACY and RECENCY effects Information which comes at the beginning or end of a list is more likely to be remembered. The same appears to be true of any sequence of events, including the school day.

RETROACTIVE and PROACTIVE INHIBITION New information can interfere *retroactively* with information stored a little earlier. Information which is already stored in long-term memory can interfere *proactively* with *new* information. This has implications for school time-tabling – it is preferable for PE rather than Spanish to follow a French lesson.

MASSED versus DISTRIBUTIVE PRACTICE In general material learned over a long period of time and frequently rehearsed is retained better than one single lengthy attempt to take in information. For instance, periods of learning and rehearsal over the academic year appear to be more effective than cramming just before exams.

PART and WHOLE LEARNING One can learn a poem in its entirety or a single verse at a time, eventually linking all of them. The effectiveness of the approach generally depends on the type of material or the learning experience. The question is relevant to debates about reading – whether children should learn to build component parts of words

A traditional model – learning through rote.

(letters and letter sounds) up to the whole, or whether they should start with whole word patterns.

Overlearning There is a considerable body of knowledge indicating the necessity for active rehearsal and OVERLEARNING of material to increase the amount of material retained. How much overlearning is necessary depends particularly on the meaningfulness of the material to the person attempting to retain it and also upon avoiding disruptive fatigue.

Metacognition

Cognitive learning theorists have, relatively recently, turned their attention towards the issue of how learners learn how to learn – the processes of METACOGNITION. The emphasis here is on how learners monitor their progress (Flavell, 1985) and think about their thinking. Learners need to recognise what is important, plan their next moves in problem-solving, balance their time, predict outcomes and evaluate their progress by checking the results of strategies used, discarding them if unsuccessful. Learners who use information given, and attempt to understand *why* the information is given, tend to do better in learning. Bransford et al (1981) gave children certain information about robots that cleaned two-storey houses and robots that cleaned high-rise buildings. The information was relevant to either function. For instance, high-rise cleaners had suction feet and a parachute which opened if the robot fell. Low-achieving learners tended just to rote-memorise the information whereas high-achievers made connections between function and details and recalled these far better. They were better able to use *conditional knowledge* described earlier.

Case (1985) argues that the qualitative changes noted by Piaget in children of five or six years old are partly explained by their *conscious* discovery of learning strategies such as rehearsal. Young children need to use relatively more of their available memory space in storing rules for procedures, therefore their capacity is limited. One reason why children fail to conserve liquid volume (Case argues) is that they use a memory-saving strategy of noting only the height and not the

diameter of the two jars in the classic demonstration.

For further detail on memory theory and research, see Eysenck and Keane (1995). For the many applications of cognitive research to classroom teaching, and the training of adults or those with certain learning difficulties the reader could refer to Slavin (1994). In summary, Pressley and McCormick (1995), applying a strong cognitive information processing approach to educational learning, and providing research evidence, argue that GOOD INFORMATION PROCESSORS (i.e. good learners):

- have a rich repertoire of strategies and possess extensive metacognition
- are able to self-monitor and have extensive knowledge linked to their experiences
- live in (perceptually) rich, stimulating environments
- have well-developed language
- are appropriately confident with well-controlled emotions
- maintain good attention, can inhibit inappropriate, impulsive responses
- are reflective
- contribute to their own education and development
- do not rote-learn but sift important from unimportant information, focusing on the latter
- are highly motivated (a discussion of motivation now follows).

Motivation to learn

Extrinsic and intrinsic motivation

Generally speaking, parents and teachers would rather that their children wanted to learn for learning's sake (INTRINSIC MOTIVATION) rather than wanting to learn for some external reward (EXTRINSIC MOTIVATION). It is true that A level study in the UK can be rewarded with university education and that university success can ultimately be rewarded with a higher-grade job. However, it is to be hoped that most A level and university students find at least *some* aspects of their course rewarding solely for the interest generated. Certainly, children learn many things with little external reward and for the love of discovery. The joy for many primary teachers is that their pupils love to discover things and are not yet disillusioned by school or distracted by temptations which make school work dull by comparison. The 'great' teacher is one who can motivate children by sparking interest rather than controlling with threats or rewarding with stars. Even casual observation will soon confirm that infants' interest in discovering how the world works is internally driven, not requiring external reward. Further, many children in the world learn not just one, but two or even three, languages at once, but, as we mentioned above, it is rarely necessary to reward children in order for them to acquire grammar. They appear intrinsically motivated to acquire the rules of language.

Achievement motivation

This section is concerned with a specific type of motivation, that of motivation to achieve. Research into ACHIEVEMENT MOTIVATION was stimulated by McClelland et al (1953) who saw it as a personality factor responsible for enabling some children to escape the CYCLE OF DISADVANTAGE which normally operates between home background, education and final occupation. That is, they were exceptions to the usual link between being relatively poor, receiving inferior education and ending up in a low-paid job, if any. Cassidy and Lynn (1989) have argued that many of the inconsistent research results concerning achievement motivation have been caused by researchers treating motivation as a *single* (or *unitary*) factor, whereas they believe it to be *multi-factorial*, comprising at least seven separable factors. Cassidy and Lynn (1991) present evidence that there is at least some significant influence on overall achievement motivation from a child's type of home background and type of school attended. In particular, they believe that important factors explaining achievement motivation in educational attainment are:

- *acquisitiveness* – one's desire for material rewards (negatively related to attainment)
- *dominance* – a desire or ability to lead (positively related to attainment)
- *work ethic* – a belief in the value of hard work (negatively related to attainment).

The last relationship is odd in that people with lower work ethic tended to have higher educational attainment, but this is possibly because hard work is seen as physical work. Acquisitiveness was also negatively correlated (see Appendix 2) with educational attainment whereas dominance correlated positively.

Theoretical perspectives on motivation to learn

The behavioural approach

As Appendix 1 explains, behaviourist approaches largely rely on the concept of association and reinforcement to explain and promote learning. The behaviourist approach is often referred to as LEARNING THEORY, signifying that this approach once dominated psychological thinking, but, of course, there are and always have been cognitive approaches (e.g. Tolman, 1932). These have grown in importance since the 1970s.

We have seen that rewards can be useful in controlling pupils' behaviour so that they are at least in a position to benefit from learning in school. However, research supports the common sense hunch that rewarding children for learning itself may create less robust retention and interest than internally motivated learning. Lepper et al (1973) found that children drew enthusiastically but, after rewarding one group for drawing, they spent only half as much time drawing as groups given either an unconnected reward or no reward at all. Lepper and Hodell (1989) found rewards to be undermining if children's initial interest in a task is high and the reward could easily be interpreted as a bribe. The undermining effect of rewards has been much replicated (e.g. Deci and Ryan, 1985) but it cannot be the whole story. Athletes work hard, at first, for the sheer joy of winning, but (and perhaps this is sad to say), once successful, they may refuse to perform for fees most of us would consider to be a good salary. Lepper used the term OVER-JUSTIFICATION EFFECT to describe the situation where we find it hard to justify doing something for no reward in the knowledge that it *could* be rewarded. Tang and Hall (1993) produced a meta-analysis (see Appendix 2) of relevant studies and concluded that this effect is inconsistent. What is required is to recognise when rewards *do* help to start or retain learning interest and *do not* undermine it. Slavin (1994) cites research to support the use of rewards in the following circumstances:

- when rewards are based on quality of performance (not just *any* performance)
- when rewards are seen as a recognition of competence
- when the task involved is uninteresting
- when rewards are social rather than physical
- when rewards are seen as an extra (unanticipated) consequence (Lepper and Hodell, 1989)
- when rewards are used as a 'bootstrap' – to initiate learning or involvement in a task which may then become intrinsically motivating. Parents often reward (or 'bribe') their children to try out an activity and are pleased to see that the need for reward is soon eliminated by the child's immediate or growing enthusiasm.

As we have just seen, external reinforcements can have limited or even demotivating effects. Behaviourists would, however, point to the rewarding value of intrinsic motivation, for instance, rewards of solely personal interest or satisfaction in a task completed. A strategy used in BEHAVIOUR MODIFICATION (see the clinical psychology chapter) is to gradually remove extrinsic rewards, as internal ones, such as increased self-esteem and personal pride, take over.

The social learning approach – EXPECTANCY × VALUE THEORY

An implication from the behavioural emphasis on reinforcement is that rewards need to be valued by the recipient. It is no use rewarding with a star, or an A grade, a pupil who thinks all stars or As received in school are useless. Values may easily become relative. For instance, if you offer me £10 to complete a task, then give me £50, I shall find this sum far more rewarding than if you gave me the same amount after offering £100! In addition, it is no use offering a valued reward to someone who thinks they have no chance of succeeding and therefore acquiring that reward. Later versions of Bandura's (1986) social learning theory emphasised this factor of *expectancy* (what I think will be the outcome of my behaviour on this occasion)

and it is clear that expectancy is linked strongly to SELF-EFFICACY – our general sense of likely success with a particular skill or task (see Appendix 1). There are some important classroom principles which can be extracted from expectancy and reinforcement principles:

- it would be pointless lavishing praise on a student for achieving something they found easy; the implication is that they had to work hard for their result
- it is important to reward relative success – the weaker student in a class can never expect rewards if these are given on the basis of absolute achievement (i.e. the higher levels achieved in the class). More effective is to reward change from a student's original to their present position
- there may be benefit in increasing students' *self-efficacy.*

Increasing students' self-efficacy: feedback from the actions of self and others   One effect on self-efficacy, according to Bandura's general theory, is that of seeing others who are like us doing well. Our peers may act as models and our observation of these models may make us feel, 'Well, I can do that!' Far more important than praise (social reinforcement) *or* modelling, however, is the information provided to us by FEEDBACK from our own actions (Schunk, 1991). Pressley and McCormick (1995) present evidence that our knowledge of what we can and can't do is highly specific and generally quite accurate. They argue that this is why it is very important to provide students with tasks with a level of difficulty just a little *beyond* their present capability (as did Vygotsky). Success at easy tasks provides us with no information about how we might get on with harder tasks. Failure, because the task was too difficult, may well diminish our self-efficacy and, in turn, our motivation to pursue that sort of task further. Continued success at calculating percentages tells us nothing about our likely success with algebra but being launched straight into complicated algebra may well put us off maths forever! In addition, if we believe that only certain people have 'mathematical minds', we are assuming that abilities are fixed and unalterable – a further barrier to progress which we shall now consider.

Intelligence as a thing or a process – entity versus incremental theorists

Dweck and her colleagues (e.g. Henderson and Dweck, 1990) have produced a hypothesis that people tend to vary in the way they view the concept of intelligence, including their own. ENTITY theorists believe it is fixed and consequently tend to view failure as a sign of their (permanent) inadequacy. INCREMENTAL theorists believe one's intelligence can be changed and added to by gradual learning. Failure is seen as a natural part of this learning process, usefully indicating where one has gone wrong, as in the Piagetian discovery-based model of learning. Ames has conducted research in support of this view (Ames and Archer, 1988) and has shown that students believing themselves to be in classrooms operating on an *incremental* view of intelligence use more effective strategies, are open to challenge and believe improvement is a result of effort. They are less likely to view their abilities negatively and to assume that low ability causes classroom problems, compared with those believing themselves to be in *entity-oriented* classrooms. Pressley and McCormick (1995) believe there is plenty of evidence in support of both Ames' and Dweck's views which they see as new and crucially important information about classroom processes. They believe that students are better off in classrooms where the messages are:

1. trying hard fosters achievement and intelligence
2. failure is an important part of learning
3. being best is not what school is about; getting better is. (p.129)

If this classroom practice is maintained it is likely that students will *not* lower their sense of self-efficacy even when they encounter failure, difficulty or apparently superior peers.

Cognitive explanations of motivation – attribution theory

Cognitive theories emphasise the problem-solving nature of human thinking and consequent behaviour – see Appendix 1. We constantly ask *why* we (and others) succeed or fail – 'how does she do so well?', 'why did I do so badly on that essay?' In answering these questions to our own satisfaction we employ ATTRIBUTIONS (either INTERNAL or EXTERNAL). An *internal* attribution occurs where I explain behaviour in terms of enduring personality characteristics ('she's like that') or motives ('he meant to do that'). *External* attributions blame circumstances outside the individual such as luck, provocation or physical cause ('he isn't clumsy – that floor is very uneven'). In addition, people tend to view events as more or less controllable and as more or less stable (Weiner, 1979). Woolfolk (1993) discusses how these three dimensions of attribution of causes of events can be applied to understanding students' responses to learning experiences and resulting motivation. For instance, a helpful way to explain failure is to make *internal, controllable* attributions. If we blame our lack of preparation rather than the teacher's lack of help (internal vs external), and if we blame insufficient knowledge rather than lack of natural ability (controllable vs uncontrollable), we are more likely to produce and follow strategies to make success more likely next time. Focusing on a perceived inadequacy and/or poor teaching/ luck /a cold will not lead us to produce useful adjustments to our learning plans – see Table 4.2.

These dimensions help explain why giving praise for easy work may be unhelpful. If a child is offered help, without requesting it, for a relatively simple task, observers tend to see the child as having lower ability than an unhelped child (Graham and Barker, 1990). Graham (1991) argues that this has implications for teachers who are genuinely sympathetic towards students from minority groups with a history of under-average achievement – see p. 121. Where teachers lower requirements, in order for students to experience some success, the unintended message can be that the teacher is overlooking the student's failure because of their lack of ability (rather than attempting to produce greater motivation to progress through small successes). On the other hand, teachers, in general, should not make steps in the learning programme too large, otherwise failure of all but a few class members will generate an overall impression of learning being uncontrollable and permanently beyond students' capability.

The entity–incremental view of ability (above) is pretty much an attributional factor. If we add it

TABLE 4.2
Attributional styles and views of intelligence as factors in motivation to learn

	Attributional style		View of intelligence
Causes of people's behaviour are generally ...	Events are generally ...	Events are generally ...	
Internal	**Controllable**	**Unstable**	**Incremental**
'Results have a lot to do with the kind of effort I put in'	'I can control events around me'	'My ability is not fixed; it can change and grow'	'I can gradually improve in ability'
External	**Uncontrollable**	**Stable**	**Entity**
'Results are largely down to bad teachers, bad exams and luck'	'I can't do much about things that happen to me'	'One's ability doesn't change much'	'You can only use what you're born with'

to the attributional dimensions just discussed we can see that entity theorists would see intellectual ability as stable and uncontrollable whereas incremental theorists view it as controllable but unstable to the extent that it changes as we concentrate on improving it through problem-solving.

Goal setting   The work largely inspired by Locke (see the occupational psychology chapter) has shown that workers or students usually perform better under the following circumstances:

- where goals are *specific, clear* and a *clear strategy* for attaining them is provided
- where *moderately difficult* goals are set but, for *complex* tasks, relatively *simple* goals
- where learners *accept* the goals set as valid for them
- where learners *set their own goals*, under certain circumstances
- where goals are likely to be reached *in the near future*, especially for younger learners (Schunk,1991)
- where LEARNING GOALS rather than PERFORMANCE GOALS are set.

What does not work is setting a learner a generalised goal of just 'doing well' or 'improving'. In

circumstances where goals are not easy to reach (for instance, learning statistics), the teacher (rather than the learner) needs to set easy, clear, accepted goals with an obvious route to completion.

Acceptable goals   How can a teacher make statistics goals acceptable? This is one of the arts, rather than scientific principles, of teaching. If a tutor can make the *need* for statistics (or any other 'boring' topic) real and valuable to learners, then interest becomes intrinsic. One can make statistics real by relating it to the lottery or to media distortions of facts (such as the real proportion of unwanted teenage pregnancies compared with a politician's gross over-estimate). This leads on to the value of a topic such as statistics. They are useful in countering arguments or in protecting oneself from advertising hype. Generating this value is sometimes known as stimulating COGNI-TIVE CONFLICT. We have seen that Piaget's theory depends on the idea that discrepancy (i.e. conflict between 'facts' of the world) motivates investigation and problem solution. In relatively adult classrooms, for instance, UK students are often very surprised to find that, contrary to the exaggerations of many politicians or media writers, the black (including Asian) population of Britain is just 5% and over 70% of immigrants are white. This often stimulates an intrinsic interest in the source of derogatory myths about black people and a consequent increasing awareness of race issues as well as a respect for statistics.

Learning and performance goals　Where learners are simply motivated only to 'look good' and not appear incompetent, irrespective of any learning content, they are said to set PERFORMANCE GOALS. LEARNING GOALS have the aim of improvement, of gaining knowledge or ability, no matter what impressions or how many mistakes are made.

Putting it all together – mastery orientation versus failure avoidance

Covington (1984, described in Woolfolk, 1993) refers to two extreme types of student – *mastery-oriented* and *failure-avoiding* students.

MASTERY-ORIENTED students see ability as incremental and therefore improvable. They set themselves, or are motivated by, moderately difficult and challenging learning goals. They generally set about energetically discovering the 'rules' of any new problem situation. They attribute learning outcomes to their own effort but they are not threatened by failure, seeing it as useful information to correct future attempts. Such correction involves constructive strategies such as confidently asking a tutor for help or engaging in further practise, taking smaller steps and so on.

FAILURE-AVOIDING students see ability as fixed. They set only performance goals, wishing to avoid damage to their self-image. They see themselves as only as clever as their marks or grades so far. They may set easy goals or stay with material and strategies that they already know well as relatively safe and with which they have been generally successful so far. They do not risk embarrassment and dents in their self-image by striking out into unknown 'risky' areas. If they fail too much or too often, they may employ 'externalising' defences (e.g. 'studying is a waste of time, anyway'; 'this won't get me a job, so why not have fun?'; 'I could never get a good grade with *that* teacher anyway – she hates me'; 'I just don't have a mathematical brain').

Failure-avoiding strategies, by their very nature, do not lead to further learning. They lead to just the sorts of failure which the learner intended to avoid. When this occurs failure-avoiders become one of a third category described by Covington – FAILURE ACCEPTERS, who operate in a depressed, helpless, lethargic, negative and apathetic mode, at least in their learning environment (they may well be vitalised in learning anti-social activities outside school or be motivated by sports activities). They believe their learning failures to be entirely the result of poor, unchangeable ability. Without some form of minimal success they are likely to accept this gloomy view from which they may earlier have been protected by their psychological defences to some extent.

Teacher behaviour

One major area of research has been into those factors and qualities which make for effective teaching and happy classrooms. Interest is in the factors which influence the ways in which teachers generally affect the social and economic development of their pupils. Some studies are focused on teacher style and teacher expectations.

Teacher style

Research into the effects of teacher/trainer/leadership style has a long history and includes an early study by Lewin et al (1939) described in the occupational psychology chapter in which it was found that democratic, informal trainers produced better morale, though lower production, than authoritarian formal trainers. Research indicates various style categories but a general distinction can be made between the:

■ *formal*, teacher-centred or traditional style in which teachers tend to control, dominate and direct their pupils; they tend to emphasise academic attainment and the development of skills

and the

■ *informal*, child-centred, progressive style in which teachers tend to promote the child's development of responsibility for their own learning; they encourage questioning (even of the teacher) and enquiry; they are likely to emphasise self-expression and creativity.

A study in British schools by Bennett (1979) on the link between these styles and pupils' attainment showed that 'formal' teachers were associated with low noise levels whereas 'informal' teachers had classes characterised by greater interaction and communication. Children with formal teachers demonstrated better reading and maths skills, whereas, contrary to popular expectations, children in informal classes did not do better on imaginative writing tasks. Generally anxious or insecure children seemed threatened by the looseness of an informal setting and Bennett concluded there was a complex interaction between personality and teaching style. The extremes of each style had general effects (such as general anxiety where exam classes were taught informally – students *expect* more formality here), but in other circumstances there were interaction effects. For instance, anxious students sought the help of peers in formal classes whereas more conforming students were happy to work alone. Something like the opposite occurred in the informal classes.

Later research suggests that encouraging students' self-responsibility for learning *does* appear to show benefits for the students' overall approach to learning and problem-solving (e.g. the Johnson study, see p. 113). Such encouragement still needs to be structured and carefully planned, probably far more than were the 'informal' approaches studied in the 1960s and 1970s. There have been considerable difficulties with looking at teacher styles since there is evidence suggesting that teachers may change their style in different teaching situations. Also, not surprisingly, pupils rate friendly teachers more highly. As follows from the motivation section, they rate more highly those teachers who give appropriate feedback rather than teachers who praise everything.

Physical arrangements of the classroom

The Plowden Report (1967), influenced by followers of Piaget and Bruner, emphasised the importance of learning through discovery. Such an approach requires informal teaching and, as a result, classrooms are often arranged with pupils seated in groups.

Wheldall et al (1981) compared 'on-task' versus 'off-task' behaviour for two classes of ten to eleven year pupils in the same school. 'On-task' behaviour was defined as carrying out teacher instructions, eye contact with the teacher, reading text books and materials when asked to get on with set work. 'Off-task' behaviour was defined as calling out, interrupting or talking, pupil being out of

The interactive approach – the teacher as a guide to discovery learning.

his/her seat without permission, not carrying out teacher instructions and not getting on with set work. For both classes the usual arrangements were for groups of four or more pupils to be seated at a table. Children were initially observed in this seating arrangement for the first two weeks of observation followed by two weeks in which they were seated in rows and then for a further two weeks when they were seated in tables again.

The results indicated that, for children rated more able in both classes, seating arrangements made little difference to their behaviour. However, for the children rated less able, their on-task behaviour increased when seated in rows. Axelrod et al (1979), in the USA, showed similar results. Wheldall et al considered that seating at tables encourages social interaction but may also cover up peer aggression and teasing. However, the authors recognised that there would be times when classroom discussion is important to learning and suggested that flexible seating arrangements would be the optimum arrangement. They also recognised that increasing on-task behaviour does not necessarily increase quality and quantity of work accomplished. However, a further study by Merrett and Wheldall (1978) did increase the amount of written work produced with no increase in spelling errors.

Teacher attitudes and expectations

Appendix 2 discusses the effects of expectancy on the part of trainers. The classic 'Pygmalion' study, described below, prompted much research into and debate about the extent to which teachers' attitudes, values, prejudices and consequent expectancies might affect children's academic attainment and even their development of social values. Good and Brophy (1991) present evidence from many studies that expectancies alter judgements about and behaviour towards pupils or trainees and that pupil behaviour may alter as a result.

Rosenthal and Jacobson (1968) conducted the classic and influential PYGMALION study in which IQ tests apparently identified 'academic spurters' among classes of 5–10-year-old disadvantaged children. Teachers were given the names of the 'spurters', expected to gain in achievement over the academic year, though actually they were cho-

sen at random. After eight months, Rosenthal and Jacobson reported that the IQs of the 'spurters' were significantly higher than the remaining 'control group'. They were described in more positive terms (more eager, happy, interesting etc) by their teachers. This study stimulated considerable reaction whilst also raising some ethical questions. Smith and Cowie (1994) report serious flaws in the experimental design:

- tests were administered by both teachers and researchers; test procedure was therefore not standardised – see Appendix 2
- norms used were not suitable for the younger and low social/economic status children in the sample
- Elashoff et al (1971) repeated the data analysis and found no effect on the 8–11-year-old children in the study
- many teachers could not later recall the names of the 'spurters'; it would therefore be difficult for them to have discriminated in their favour.

Although later studies have often failed to replicate the expectancy effect (e.g. Wilkins and Glock, 1973), research continues, perhaps because intuitively there is a feeling that teacher values and interactions *must* influence children. Brophy and Good (1974) found it was difficult to get expectancy effects if they were 'induced', i.e. given by the experimenter. However, where teachers had already developed their perceptions of pupil ability independently, these *did* appear to affect the quality of teacher/pupil interaction and levels of achievement. Eden (1990), in Appendix 2, demonstrates a fairly recent research effect supporting the original hypothesis that the expectancies of a tutor can affect the later performance of tutees. It may be that children sometimes start off the cycle of expectancy, followed by different teacher behaviour and different responses from the child. Jamieson et al (1987) found that 11 year olds, told that their teacher was highly capable, performed better than control pupils not so informed.

Teachers inevitably have different expectations based on experience and prejudice. Egglestone et al (1986) found that many UK teachers held partly negative stereotypes about Afro-Caribbean and Asian pupils. In the US, 'impressive' black law school applicants were judged more positively than white applicants with identical background information, possibly because the black candidates exceeded expectations (Linville and Jones, 1980). Some teacher expectations may be valid. Poorer children in their classes may well do worse overall. Expectations then affect behaviour. Kehle (1974) found that the amount of verbal contact by teachers was related to the physical attractiveness of children. In a carefully controlled study, Harari and McDavid (1973) showed that simply possessing an 'attractive' name (according to other teachers' assessment) caused teachers to mark essays a whole grade higher than those written by children with 'unattractive' names. Green (1985) found black pupils receiving less time and attention from teachers, whilst Cooper et al (1991) demonstrated black pupils' greater likelihood of disadvantage through teachers' misinterpretation of their academic skills and performance. Tizard and Hughes (1984) showed that even at nursery school, teachers lowered their standards for working-class children.

Children expected to do well may be given more questions or longer to talk in class. More questions means a probability of more correct answers. Expected results may appear to be confirmed and teachers respond accordingly. Brophy and Good (1970) found that high-achieving, first-grade pupils received more praise than low-achieving pupils, whereas the latter received more criticism and discouragement. Children recognise the amount of attention and approval they receive. Nash (1976) gives evidence that primary school pupils judged less favourably by teachers tended to have lower opinions of their ability to succeed. In the UK, however, Ferri (1972) showed that low ability children did not necessarily retain their low self-esteem in secondary schooling and Smith and Cowie (1994) argue that older children may well not respond to teacher expectations as younger children do.

The fact that teachers respond differently to various categories of pupil has often been seen as part of the HIDDEN CURRICULUM of any school (the unwritten rather than official expectations for behaviour and success in the establishment). Sadly, some teachers' preferences may not always be so hidden and children quickly learn who is expected to do well, even if they have the integrity to succeed despite such inhibiting factors.

Pupil behaviour

Pupil interactions and co-operative learning

The emphasis on 'learning through discovery' approaches has led to many classrooms being organised with children sitting in groups. This naturally encourages pupil interactions. Some of the difficulties associated with this have been discussed above and not everyone agrees about the benefits of children working in groups. However, back in 1949, Deutsch showed that students working co-operatively in groups and all awarded the same grade for their assignments were more productive, participative and co-operative than students expected to compete against each other in the standard manner. They also liked each other more. There were design faults, but Johnson et al (1981), reviewing more than 100 studies comparing co-operative with competitive working, found only eight where competition was superior. Doise and Mugny (1984) claimed that children handle problem-solving activities better and produce high-quality outcomes when they work together. Bennett and Dunne (1989) found that children working in small co-operative groups showed less concern for status, were less competitive and more likely to show they could think logically. Johnson and Johnson (1985) in the USA found that, so long as group work demands interdependence (the task is too complex for one child), is face to face, requires children to be individually accountable and children are taught social skills where necessary, then group work serves to: increase children's intrinsic motivation and expectations of success; improve willingness to learn; and, in general, improve their attitudes about school.

On a cautionary note, Bennett and Dunne argue that much 'group work' in schools is in fact children working alone but seated with others at one table, where the chance to discover something about group work and interaction is not exploited by the teacher. This view is echoed by Topping (1992) who concluded that children often work *in groups* rather than *as groups*. It appears that different types of learning skills and social skills are

BOX 5

Interaction of classroom design and teacher management skills

Effective classroom teaching will depend on factors of *classroom design* **interacting** with the teacher's *classroom management skills*. It is little use having good interpersonal skills in a poorly constructed environment, nor having a good environment but poor pupil/student management.

Classroom design

Primary school classrooms are generally arranged with small groups of tables and chairs around the room to enable children to work in groups of 4 to 6. This reflects an emphasis on discovery learning and the importance of pupil interactions. It is important that the teacher can see all pupils from her/his desk and that they can see the teacher when necessary. Various other factors appear to minimise disruptions and maximise learning:

■ ensuring easy access to all parts of the classroom with no congestion
■ ensuring that materials and tools needed are readily available e.g. paper, pencils
■ having displays which stimulate relevant interest and ensuring that they are at the right academic level and can be readily seen by pupils.

Adapted from Slavin (1994)

A number of studies have illustrated how seating arrangements can affect both the behaviour of pupils in class and their learning in terms of

time on task and the amount of written material produced, e.g. Wheldall et al (1981) as described in this text.

In addition the use of appropriate 'calming' colours is considered important in approaches to the control of 'challenging behaviour' such as that shown by autistic children or those with severe communication disorders.

For both primary and secondary classrooms it is important that the physical layout minimises the inevitable disruption of fairly large groups of pupils entering and leaving.

Classroom management skills

■ *Beginning a lesson* –
skills in greeting pupils, getting them seated and starting to learn
■ *Effective pacing* –
skills in presentation of material at the right level with an understanding of the different needs of individual pupils. This may involve some 'differentiation' of the curriculum – altering the approach and the content for a particular pupil or pupils. Skill in providing hints, prompts and in holding back and allowing students to discover ideas for themselves
■ *Positive interaction* –
skills in training the group, being able to anticipate and control problems and being seen to be fair; particular attention to the effects of *expectancy* and *stereotype* predictions
■ *Ending a lesson* –
skills in effective instruction on concluding work, or how to continue, and in controlling the physical exit of students.

necessary in group work situations. The attention control necessary may well be beyond children below a particular developmental level and further research in this area is needed. However, Smith and Cowie (1994) comment that group work may have positive implications for the acceptance and social integration of some members of minority ethnic groups. Aronson et al's (1978) JIGSAW

METHOD gave one essential feature of a problem solution to each member of a small multi-racial group of children. Only co-operation could produce success and these children significantly lowered their negative attitudes, at least for class members (see also Singh, 1991, p. 122). There is also some evidence that co-operative work may help to combat bullying (Herbert, 1989).

Peer tutoring

A further example of co-operative working can be found in the use of peers to help children less able than themselves in the given area, e.g. reading. This involves communication skills and instruction from the more capable peer and demonstrates the value of social interaction in promoting fuller understanding. This again would be in line with the Piagetian model of development where *disequilibrium* is caused by discovering other ways of viewing the same problem and thus motivation to solve the problems raised is produced. Foot, Morgan and Shute (1990) argue that the instruction is effective when it is slightly ahead of the tutee's actual level since the 'expert' will not be far ahead of the 'novice' therefore being better able to see what problems the tutee experiences. The expert will also be more likely to work within the tutee's 'zone of proximal development' – see Vygotsky above. In fact, some studies show a greater benefit for the tutor – nothing promotes more thorough understanding than having to explain something to someone else. Top and Osguthorpe (1987) argue that a main aim of PEER TUTORING has often been to improve the attainment of low-achieving older learners. Some schools have incorporated peer tutoring in their reading schemes where a more advanced reader is paired with a less advanced pupil and time is set aside for each pair to work quietly together on a reading book.

Problem behaviour in schools

Educational psychologists will be involved in a range of behaviour problems in school. These are likely to include:

- distracting, attention-seeking behaviour, e.g. calling out, wandering round the class
- withdrawn, anxious behaviour – this may be related to a number of factors, such as domestic difficulties, abuse or bullying (see below)
- anti-social behaviour – on a continuum from verbal insults to extreme physical aggression
- bullying – this may be directed towards one or two individuals for a variety of reasons (see below) or may be pervasive within a given school culture
- patterns of violent and aggressive behaviour

towards peers and adults which are not necessarily related to individual victimisation or bullying. Some of these children may be identified as having social and emotional problems requiring special help or even a special school. More boys than girls are referred as having such problems (McCall and Farrell, 1993), although assessment in this area is a difficult issue (see the earlier assessment and testing section).

Many aspects of negative problem behaviour can be dealt with using some form of behaviour modification programme as described in the clinical psychology chapter. Forms of cognitive behaviour modification may also be used where at least part of the problem is anxiety, unrealistic fears, depression or where aggressive behaviour is a defence against threatened changes to the child's life, imagined or real.

Explanations for problem behaviour

Behavioural Problem behaviour is seen as the result of inappropriate reinforcement and associative learning experiences. Social learning theorists would emphasise learning from other wayward peers. The behaviour is seen as modifiable using similar processes, that is, behaviour modification and/or provision of positive models.

Cognitive Using Piaget's ideas, 'difficult' children are seen as simply problem-solving and testing the world in the usual manner except that they are investigating areas which lead them into trouble. A child may want to know what happens if he or she disobeys, hits or sets fire to things. The home discipline system may not be adapted to foresee or prevent this behaviour. Once it occurs, if the school reacts negatively and without sensitivity, the child experiences further problems of alienation from school life and norms and the problem gets worse. Such a child, according to cognitivists needs reeducating, not just sanction, in order to *understand* why change will be beneficial.

Social explanations A further set of explanations, which need not contradict those above, is that the child comes from a cultural or sub-cultural background where norms and values differ widely from the school's. Consider the child who responds to 'Jason, we *don't* run in the corridors' with a shrug and, *'I* do'. The teacher is using middle-class language which *implies* children are not allowed to run but she doesn't make this *explicit*. The child may not be disobeying, just not getting the message. LABELLING THEORY argues that if such a child then gets known as 'problematic' or 'difficult', and responds to this as in the teacher expectation work covered above, then we have an extra set of factors contributing to a possible self-fulfilling prophecy of problem behaviour.

Bullying

A number of studies have looked at the problem of difficult behaviour in schools, e.g. the Elton Report (1989). In particular, there have also been a number of more recent studies of bullying in both primary and secondary schools in the UK as well as studies abroad. The reasons for bullying appear to be multi-factorial with family factors as well as physical, personality and school factors all apparently contributing.

Mitchel and O'Moore (1988) found that 77% of bullies and victims were experiencing family problems. Victims have been found to have more coordination problems (Olweus, 1978), to be younger (Elliott, 1989) and less attractive (Lowenstein, 1978) than bullies. Victims tend to be more anxious, have a more negative self-image and have a negative attitude to aggression compared with bullies (Olweus, 1978). Bullies show an anti-social and destructive profile (Byrne, 1987). Victims generally have a more positive attitude to school (Lagenspitz et al, 1982, in Besag, 1989). Both victims and bullies have a negative view of peer relationships (for bullies, outside their own circle), but bullies are able to elicit more support.

Comparing studies of bullying again presents some methodological problems, particularly with respect to how bullying has been defined in terms of the study and what measures were taken. Most such studies rely on questionnaires and interviews with some attempt to rate the seriousness of incidents. Two large-scale studies in this country have been the Sheffield Bullying Project (Sharp and Smith, 1991) and a series of studies by Michele Elliott between 1984 and 1986 (Elliott, 1991) In Elliott's studies bullying was generally taken to be

the 'wilful, conscious desire to hurt, threaten or frighten someone.' The result suggested that something in the region of 25% of primary school children experience bullying more than once. The ratio of male to female victims was 2:1 and they were likely to be younger than the bullies. Male bullies out-numbered female bullies 3 to 1. In general, boys have shown more anti-social and disruptive behaviour and a higher incidence of bullying. However, more recent evidence indicates a more aggressive trend in secondary age girls.

Elliott's studies involved a large number of children. Of 4000 children aged 5 – 16, 68% complained of being bullied at some time. 38% had been bullied more than once or had experienced a particularly terrifying incident. 38% had been bullied more seriously and, of these, 68% were boys, 32% girls. 8% of the boy victims and 4% of the girls were so severely affected as to be truanting, terrified of school or even attempting suicide. The true incidence of bullying is difficult to ascertain since pupils often keep quiet about it. In the Elliott studies, parental involvement was minimal. When asked, most parents expressed a preference for the children to sort it out for themselves rather than with parental help. However, the following study provides evidence that parental involvement can be effective in bullying prevention programmes.

Olweus (1989) published results of a nationwide campaign – The Norwegian Campaign Against Bullying – which began in Norway in 1983. Research had indicated that about 9% of the school population were regular victims and 7 – 8% were regular bullies. In particular, there had been two suicides in Norway in 1982 as a result of bullying. An intervention programme was devised for students, teachers and parents and included:

- a booklet for school personnel, giving information on what can be done to counteract bullying
- a folder with information and advice for parents
- a video showing two bullied children to be used as a basis for class discussion
- a survey of pupils themselves concerning the incidence of bullying behaviour and victimisation.

The effects of the programme were evaluated over

Bullying in the playground – a fact of life for too many children?

three years (1983, 1984, 1985). Results were encouraging and showed a reduction of incidents of bullying and being bullied in both girls and boys. This type of programme provides a clear example of a WHOLE SCHOOL APPROACH to a problem, i.e. the involvement of pupils, teachers and parents in a controlled way to tackle a common problem. The development of 'whole school' approaches and policies is currently an important issue (see below).

School factors/whole school approaches

A number of studies have attempted to investigate the effects that schools have on pupils' success, i.e. how effective are schools and what makes some schools more effective than others? Early studies indicated that schools were singularly ineffective in changing early learning patterns, i.e. 'poor' pupils identified at, say, seven years remained 'poor' pupils throughout their schooling, regardless of school size, class size and methods of teaching (e.g. Jencks

et al, 1975). The main predictors of academic success were socio-economic status and intelligence tests or IQ scores. These have been discussed above. However, it is possible to view the school as an organisation or 'system' and to look at factors within that system which facilitate or inhibit learning and achievement. Factors such as the previous success rate of the school, expectations of success, type of leadership, channels of communication within the school as well as parental involvement (particularly following the Elton Report – see below) have all been indicated as important factors. However, in studying processes within an organisation it is difficult to test hypotheses, and studies in this area have tended to indicate 'good practice' rather than provide empirical support for particular structures within the organisation of the school. Rutter et al (1979) stressed the influence of school values and norms. Mortimore et al (1988) stressed the importance of teacher involvement in school policy- and decision-making.

In fact 'whole school approaches' have developed with particular relevance to special educational needs as part of the 1993 Education Act Code of Practice. However, the management of pupil behaviour, including bullying, provides a good example of an area that necessitates a 'whole school approach'. This might involve staff, both teaching and non-teaching, agreeing on definitions of inappropriate behaviour, on what action to take following an incident, on what should be recorded and by whom and who should be involved (e.g. parents), and at what stage.

Gender differences in education

A number of gender differences, apart from the bullying figures above, are apparent in education. Research indicates that IQ scores and school progress are positively correlated, although there are no overall differences in average IQ between boys and girls (Davenport 1994, p204). Up to six years of age, girls are ahead in arithmetic and then boys, until very recently, have tended to take over. Girls develop language skills ahead of boys and stay ahead. In adolescence boys appear better at thinking about abstract shapes (visual-spatial) and girls better at verbal reasoning (solving word problems). There is evidence that girls increasingly underestimate their abilities while boys increasingly overestimate theirs. Certainly, late teenage females estimate their own IQ scores significantly lower than do males (Beloff, 1992). Parsons (1994, cited in Davenport 1994, p205) looked at parents' perceptions of their children's performance in secondary schools in the USA. Parents thought that maths and science were more important for boys than girls and that maths was more enjoyable and easier for boys than girls. The children themselves had similar perceptions, i.e. girls who had similar ability to boys did not think they had the same ability as the boys thought they had. When girls did well at maths, parents said it was because they worked hard and when boys did well, parents said it was because they had the ability. This expectation follows a familiar research finding that women, more than men, have tended to attribute success to luck and failure to their own perceived deficits in ability – see Dweck (1975) in the clinical psychology chapter.

TABLE 4.3
Summer 1994 A level and GCSE results in traditionally 'male' subjects – by sex (Statistics, Summer 1994, AEB; Statistics, Summer 1994, SEG)

Examining board	Subject	Girls	Boys
Southern (GCSE)			
(A to C grades)			
	Maths*	49.2%	49.3%
	Single science**	26.5%	21.6%
	Double science**	56.3%	55.1%
AEB			
(A to E grades)	Physics	75.6%	73.7%
	Maths	74.7%	71%

* The most popular version of this subject
** These are the combined figures for all versions. In the *main* versions of these subjects girls out-perform boys by some 7% and 4% respectively.

However, recent examination results in the UK are likely to alter these perceptions. In 1992 girls achieved more A to C grades in GCSE physics, a traditionally boy-dominated area, and outperformed boys in general with 46% obtaining five or more A to C grades, compared with 37% for boys. The results for 1994 in Table 4.3 speak for themselves. Far fewer girls than boys actually take A level maths, yet more girls take GCSE and are now performing equally well. Hence the lower number of girls in more advanced maths cannot now be explained by lack of ability at GCSE level. It may be based purely on dislike of the subject or (perhaps unfounded) expectations of failure, but certainly is in need of research.

Family, school and community

Previous sections have dealt with the areas of knowledge relevant to assessment and intervention in working with children in schools. The educational psychologist's brief extends beyond the school to the family and the wider community and, again, a body of knowledge exists which, hopefully, informs this area of the educational psychologist's work. The focus here is on how the home situation and family attitudes to education influence a child's academic and social progress at school.

Home, early learning and school

The child's early learning and development of attitudes and values naturally begin in the home. A number of studies over time have consistently indicated the importance of parental attitude and involvement in the child's likely achievement in school. Douglas (1964) found that parental attitude to education was the single most important factor in predicting academic success. In addition, there is no doubt that pre-school education has beneficial effects in the area of social development (and therefore 'readiness' for school and its disciplines) even if the evidence of benefit to cognitive development is less clear (see Tizard, 1978, for an early review).

The Plowden Report (1967) noted a correlation between poor school performance and poverty. The National Child Development Study (Davie et al, 1972; Wedge and Essen, 1982) recorded the link between poverty and poor reading, as well as the link between family birth order and achievement. Children from big families were found to do less well at school. In general, there is a recognised link between IQ and school progress.

In the late 1960s such findings led to the development of a CULTURAL DEPRIVATION model to explain educational disadvantage and the perceived under-achievement of children from lower social classes and from minority ethnic groups (see below). Some studies looked at language in the home, as well as resources such as books and toys. Achievement was seen to be related to the use of language and opportunities for learning and socialisation in the home as possible factors affecting early stimulation and development (e.g. the Newsom Report, 1963). The emphasis on language deprivation was partly prompted by the work of Bernstein (e.g. 1965) who, at that time, was developing his classic work on RESTRICTED and ELABORATED LANGUAGE CODES. He suggested that the middle class language environment of schools left chil-

dren from lower socio-economic classes at a disadvantage.

As a result of the deprivation model, COMPENSATORY EDUCATION PROGRAMMES were introduced initially in the USA and later in the UK for pre-school children. The aim was to make up for disadvantage by providing an early 'boost' for children considered to be at risk. The programmes focused particularly on language, since this was where much of the deficit was thought to be located. Principle amongst these programmes was Project Headstart, which began in the summer of 1965 in the USA. It ran for several years, still has some offshoots and has involved millions of children. It assumed that:

- disadvantaged children were often language-deficient
- disadvantaged children lacked appropriate cognitive strategies for school learning
- parents of disadvantaged children used ineffective modes of control.

However, there was no detailed syllabus and the nature and length of programmes varied widely in different areas (e.g. see Smith and Cowie, 1994, pp428–430).

In 1969, the first national evaluation of Headstart showed little effects of these intervention programmes. Benefits were short-lived and disappeared after a year or so at school. However, later longer-term follow-up studies of some projects showed better performance at age 15 on reading, arithmetic and language tests and significantly fewer such pupils in remedial classes by the end of High School (Lazar and Darlington, 1982). There was also evidence that pupils in such programmes were less likely to become delinquent compared with a control group. Weikart, in several publications (e.g. Weikart and Schweinhart, 1992), has consistently argued that money spent by the state on pre-school educational experience will repay itself and more, in terms of lowered delinquency, less unwanted teenage births, more positive attitudes towards school and work and, in general, a lowered drain on welfare services. In particular, Weikart has championed the use of the HIGH SCOPE approach in early education, which is structured, but encourages children to plan their class activities and reflect upon these and what they might have learnt or experienced.

Although follow-up studies did show some benefit from these programmes, at least socially, many researchers began to question the blatant assumption of 'deficiency' in children from lower-class and minority ethnic backgrounds. Baratz and Baratz (1970) were concerned that the approach threatened to destroy valuable aspects of cultures other than that of the white middle classes. A later argument was for a DIFFERENCE MODEL, in which it was seen that communities differed in their parental style, language and values but all these were equally valuable. A range of differences among children was recognised rather than the acceptance of a norm or standard in which just some children were deficient for some areas. Tizard et al (1988) suggested that 'language deprivation' was a myth and that the home is a richer source of language than school, irrespective of social class differences, and therefore that deficiencies of working-class language do not cause working-class school failure. However socio-economic status *has* been linked to differences in child rearing and family values, and to serious material disadvantages which may in turn affect educational attainments – see Rutter and Madge (1976) for an early review.

Compensatory education in the UK
In the UK the Plowden Report (1967) called for the recognition of 'Educational Priority Areas' in extremely deprived communities. These were to be given more resources, more teachers and better school buildings. The response to Plowden was co-ordinated by Halsey (1972) who co-ordinated the Educational Priority Area (EPA) Project. This included the setting up and evaluation of a variety of compensatory education programmes in various parts of the country, including nursery and playgroup projects and home visits (*interventions*) by researchers bringing toys, books and equipment to help mothers play and develop language with their children. Halsey (1972) published evidence that specific language interventions had some effect where existing nursery provision was poor or non-existent. Smith (1975a), evaluating a large intervention programme in Denaby in the West Riding of Yorkshire, found that special pro-

grammes had some effect on aspects of language and that nursery education had the typical effect of promoting cognitive gains which declined three years into main school.

Home and school – parents as partners

Parental involvement and home intervention
An important finding by Smith (1975b) was that, where programmes included home visits, with children being given stimulating toys and activities and parents becoming involved in the process, distinct gains of an average four months of mental age were maintained. Donachy (1976), working in a Renfrewshire project, showed that nursery education *and* home-based intervention produced gains over a nursery-only group who, in turn, gained over a non-nursery group. Many such studies have demonstrated a change in behaviour and involvement by parents as a consequence and Klaus and Gray (1968) showed that younger siblings of children in home intervention studies also benefited, probably because of these parental changes. An argument against the 'difference model' mentioned above has been that parents in the target families (e.g. relatively poor) do not possess the necessary skills and knowledge to promote cognitive development through language. However, Leach and Siddall (1990) show that where parents are specifically trained the effects can be highly positive and significant.

Recommendations from the EPA project included the development of COMMUNITY SCHOOLS as a means of bridging the gap between home and school, stressing the central role of education and parental involvement in children's cognitive and language development. A number of education reports have recognised the importance of parental attitude and involvement in education. The Plowden Report has been mentioned. The Bullock Report (1975) recommended that schools involve parents in early reading and language activities. The concept of 'parents as partners', first developed in the Warnock Report, has important implications for new developments in education, particularly in relation to special educational needs following the 1981 and 1993 Education Acts. The importance of parents' influence on pupil behaviour in school has long been recog-

Helping your child at home – parents as partners in education.

nised. The Elton Report on disruption in schools stressed the importance of parents in promoting good behaviour in school (the effectiveness of parents in preventing bullying has already been mentioned).

Wheldall and Merrett (1988) conducted a survey of 900 secondary pupils in the West Midlands. Pupils were asked which rewards and sanctions were effective. The most effective reward was considered to be a letter of praise to parents while the most effective sanction was a letter home or for parents to be called into the school. This is interesting, since sending positive letters home to parents is probably a rarely used device by schools, yet in pupils' perceptions it is likely to be highly motivating.

Parents and special educational needs

Educational psychologists are likely to be closely involved with parents in the area of special educational needs and will meet them directly in the process of informal or formal (i.e. statutory) assessment of their children. During this process,

parents are usually keen to know what they can do to help their children at home. Active involvement of parents is clearly to be encouraged and a pre-school scheme set up for this very purpose is the PORTAGE SYSTEM. This developmental programme involves working with young children in the areas of motor development, cognitive development, speech and language and is both a preventative and interventionist strategy. It involves parents, educational psychologists, pre-school advisory teachers and other specially trained personnel working in the home on specific areas of special need. Wolfendale et al (1992) say 'it operates at all levels in a community and empowers the parents'. This is a particularly noteworthy area of work with pre-school children. However, educational psychologists will of course work with parents of children of all ages and all areas of special need.

Community and culture

A number of studies have indicated the poorer performance of children from some minority ethnic groups in the education system. Eggleston

(1985) studied examination performances and experiences of a large sample of white, South Asian and Afro-Caribbean teenagers. Though the Afro-Caribbean girls did as well as the white boys, and Asians and white groups did not differ, Afro-Caribbean boys had significantly lower results. Tomlinson (1983) found similar results.

Cooper et al's findings (1991) may partly explain the group differences (see p. 113). Egglestone et al (1986) found the strong stereotypes already mentioned and we have discussed the subtle influence of teacher expectations. A study by Wright (1985) produced evidence that children from minority ethnic groups of equal ability to white children were put in lower bands at school for reasons other than ability, in some cases clearly because of their attitude. The Campaign for Racial Equality (1985) reported that Afro-Caribbean pupils were four times more likely to be suspended from school than white children for comparable behaviours. In addition, theorists take into account the effects of attitudes to education and the influence of the family, as well as socio-economic status, housing and unemployment – far more Afro-Caribbean adults are unemployed (Taylor, 1987). It is likely that a combination of these is responsible for the poorer performance of some minority group children, rather than any 'natural' group difference.

The Swann Report (1985) expressed concern about the performance of British Afro-Caribbean pupils within the education system and the treatment of minorities in general. Swann argued that the racial prejudice existing within the system, for which there appeared to be evidence (some reviewed here) had direct effects on minority pupils' achievement and motivation. He proposed that educational professionals should recognise Britain as multi-racial and should project, *throughout the school curriculum*, a positive image of all communities. This policy of reflecting, in all books, lessons and other messages, a picture of a 'plural' society, consisting of many equal cultures, has since been taken up in the many educational attempts to promote MULTI-CUL-TURAL EDUCATION throughout most education authorities.

It has been suggested that recent developments in education, particularly in relation to the National Curriculum, may inhibit rather than facilitate cultural exchange. For instance, changes are occurring in the religious education component, opportunities for school selection may create greater polarisation of cultural groups and there is less flexibility in how to teach some subjects, possibly meaning less opportunity for multicultural approaches. Cowie and Rudduck (1991) found evidence that co-operative learning strategies (described earlier) can help to create equal opportunities for all pupils and foster a social climate more conducive to learning. Singh (1991), using Aronson's 'jigsaw' method (described earlier) in Sunderland, increased cross-race friendships equally for students of different ethnic backgrounds, sex and achievement levels.

The studies suggesting extreme differences may also need attention. It is important to be aware of the tremendous methodological problems in comparing studies of groups, in relation to the fair comparison of samples and measures taken. Different studies use rating scales, questionnaires or exam results. The difficulties of eliminating cultural bias in assessment, both in relation to tests and the assessor, have been well documented (e.g. Hegarty and Lucas, 1979). Nevertheless, some newer trends can be identified from such studies and careful data analysis has suggested more encouraging movements. Afro-Caribbean and Asian pupils are increasingly likely to stay on in full-time education, (Griffin, 1986) and children from some minority ethnic groups, such as African, Asian and Chinese, have comparable performance to white children (ILEA, 1987). Black pupils do better the longer they are in the education system, though some groups do consistently poorly, for instance, Bangladeshi children.

In working with children from minority ethnic groups and their families, the educational psychologist will need to work at both the individual and the school level. At the individual level, the psychologist will need to ensure:

- effective communication with parents if the home language is not primarily English
- that developmental and learning difficulties can be distinguished from English as a second language difficulty in some families
- that there is awareness of factors likely to be

Multi-ethnic education – preventing
barriers through learning together.

affecting the child's motivation and achievement at school.

At the school level, the psychologist will need to encourage the development of a whole school policy in relation to equal opportunities and cultural difference.

Unique aspects of the work of the educational psychologist

The work of educational psychologists is unique in a number of ways:

- educational psychologists are dual professionals, i.e. both psychologists as well as qualified and experienced teachers. Educational psychologists, therefore, have a combination of theory and knowledge about children's learning and development, as well as experience of the practical application of these theories to the instruction of children in classrooms and schools
- educational psychologists work directly with children over the whole age and ability range, i.e. from 0 – 19 years. They work in all areas of

special educational need which involves special training in assessment and testing. They therefore have a unique developmental perspective on children's problems
- educational psychologists can compare difficulties at an individual child level and at a whole school level across a range of schools.

As a result of these aspects of their work, combined with their direct work with children, parents and schools, as well as their detailed knowledge of the LEA and its services, it has been suggested that educational psychologists have

'... a potential contribution to organisational problem-solving that is unmatched by any professional group working in the educational field.'

(Fox and Sigston, 1992, p114)

Wolfendale et al (1992) also refer to the:

'... privileged and unique perspective available to Educational Psychologists on organisational functioning gained through their work with teachers, parents and children about the needs of individuals ...' (pxiii)

Future directions in educational psychology will need to bring together some of these unique qualities in ways which so far have not been accomplished successfully.

THE FUTURE OF EDUCATIONAL PSYCHOLOGY

Clearly individual case work remains central to the role of educational psychologists as some of the early 'reconstructionists' have now acknowledged, for instance Dessent (1992), who argues that somehow their unique knowledge gained through case work needs to be combined with knowledge of organisational structure to effect change.

It is likely also that educational psychologists will continue the most 'objective' testing of young children as is possible in order to reduce or avoid the difficulties of bias in measures such as teacher reports, teacher ratings and questionnaires. Large-scale studies (e.g. Quicke, 1982) indicate that norm-referenced testing is likely to continue as part of the assessment of the child in his or her learning environment. There may, therefore, be a need to integrate normative approaches and consultancy models.

Educational psychology needs firmer theoretical and practical underpinning. Wolfendale et al (1992) advocate '. . . the foundation of a set of core principles that inform policy and practice' (p4).

Now that the 1993 Education Act has (it is hoped) clarified the debate about delegation, perhaps such issues can be addressed more coherently. Movements in this direction are being made in educational psychology training and there appears to be more general agreement on the most appropriate model of practice – a 'problem-solving alliance' but including the *ecological* viewpoint (Wolfendale et al, 1992, pxii). In relation to training, there may be some other changes. As our links with the rest of Europe become increasingly stronger, it is likely that the UK's unique insistence for educational psychologists to be trained and experienced teachers will be reviewed.

The way forward would, therefore, appear to be through empirical evaluation of models of working in real educational settings, prior to the adoption of models that appear to offer solutions. Wittrock and Farley (1989) claim:

'Lasting improvements in practice will continue to come from advances in theory and models that are applied, evaluated and revised in empirical research conducted in realistic educational settings.' (p75).

The application of business models to service delivery is one area that needs to be properly evaluated. As part of this approach has come an emphasis on 'quality', which is laudable but extremely difficult to define. It is clear throughout the history of educational psychology that the full expertise of educational psychologists developed in training and practice is not being utilised in their everyday work (e.g. Summerfield Report, 1968; Quicke, 1982; Wolfendale et al, 1992). An important aspect of this expertise is research at the individual, group and 'systems' levels. A 'quality' service needs to ensure maximum use of the potential within it. Some recognition of this is possibly apparent in the growth of post-professional development courses.

Educational psychology remains an exciting and challenging field of applied theory and practice. Clearly the balance between 'professional' and 'business' models of service needs to be addressed. What is fundamental, however, and what must continue to underlie all aspects of this work, is the focus on 'the best interest of the child'.

FURTHER RECOMMENDED READING

Pressley, M. and McCormick, C. B. (1995) *Advanced Educational Psychology for Educators, Researchers and Policy Makers*. New York: HarperCollins.

Slavin, R. E. (1994) *Educational Psychology: Theory and Practice*. Boston, MA: Allyn and Bacon.

Smith, P. R. and Cowie, H. (1994) *Understanding Children's Development*, 2nd edn. Oxford: Blackwell.

Wolfendale, S., Bryans, T., Fox, M., Labram, A. and Sigston, A. (1992) *The Profession and Practice of Educational Psychology: future directions*. London: Cassell Education Limited.

Woolfolk, E. (1993) *Educational Psychology*, 5th edn. Needham Heights, MA: Allyn and Bacon.

exercises

1. Indicate some of the difficulties that might be encountered when conducting research in schools as, for instance, in the Rosenthal and Jacobson (1968) 'Pygmalion' study.

2. Discuss with a colleague the advantages and disadvantages of educational psychologists working as consultants to schools rather than directly with individual children. Have one of you produce arguments for and the other produce arguments against. Consider what sorts of problem might be better handled with a consultancy approach, which are better dealt with by an educational psychologist directly, and outline the reasons in each case.

3. List some ways in which *behaviourist* approaches to learning have been adopted in schools. Consulting the clinical psychology chapter, devise a programme of behaviour modification to help a child with school phobia (terrified of going to school). Outline other methods which might also be required in work with this child.

4. What characteristics might you expect to find in a child who bullies others at school? Outline in detail a programme which parents, teachers and pupils might have drawn up at any school you once attended in order to combat bullying. Make sure that your programme helps frightened children speak out.

5. Define 'norm-referenced' and 'criterion-referenced' in relation to testing. List the ways in which you think tests might not give an accurate picture of a child's current ability. Try to get hold of an actual test in order to make this assessment. How might psychologists assess children fairly *other than* by using tests?

6. Make a list of situational and personality factors which are associated with effective learning. In each case, in a second column, explain why you think there is such an association and, in a third column, cite relevant research.

5 ENVIRONMENTAL PSYCHOLOGY

If you read the national press in Britain during the summer of 1994 you might have noticed several stories on the effects of noisy neighbours. A number of court cases dealt with serious complaints concerning psychological distress caused by living next door to high levels of noise. In one case an individual who complained was assaulted and at least one suicide was attributed to the effects of noise in the neighbourhood. This is a good example of an area that is the domain of ENVIRONMENTAL PSYCHOLOGY. During the same period rail services in Britain were disrupted by industrial disputes. Again the national press were the source of some discussion regarding the psychological consequences of this disruption for commuters – another example of an area that has been addressed by environmental psychologists. These are only two examples of the ways in which the environment affects our behaviour.

WHAT IS ENVIRONMENTAL PSYCHOLOGY?

Problems with definitions

In order to introduce any field of psychology it is common practice to begin with some sort of defin-

ition, and indeed, definitions are useful summaries of the basic principles of an approach. However, it is also important to recognise definitions for what they are, i.e. over-simplified summaries. This poses a serious problem in a diverse area like environmental psychology and can lead to the imposition of limitations on subject matter by setting rigid boundaries of the field. One of the lessons that applied psychologists have learned is that a narrow focus which draws only on knowledge and method in one field of psychology is likely to be ineffective. As a result you have the development of approaches which combine several fields such as the area of clinical health psychology, an amalgam of clinical psychology and health psychology. A second problem with definitions is that psychology is a living discipline which is continuously growing and changing as new research is produced. It therefore follows that definitions are likely to become outdated and need to be changed to reflect new developments. This is indeed the case with environmental psychology.

Towards a definition

Burroughs (1989) provides the following definition of environmental psychology as 'the study of the interrelationships between the physical environment and human behaviour'. Gifford (1987) provides a similar definition: 'environmental psychology is the study of transactions between individuals and their physical settings'. An important aspect of both definitions is that they define the process as *reciprocal between the person and the environment*. In other words, not only does the environment influence the individual, the individual impacts on the environment. Both definitions are based on Lewin's (1951) famous equation

$$B = f(P,E)$$

where B is behaviour, P is the person and E is the environment. The equation states that *behaviour is a function of the person, the environment and the interaction between the two* and is referred to as a PERSON-IN-CONTEXT approach to understanding behaviour. The basic perspectives in psychology tend to focus on one or other side of this equation in seeking causes for behaviour either in the per-

son or in the environment. It is important to recognise that for Lewin it was not simply a matter of combining these perspectives. He argued that research should take account of the *interaction*, something that was advocated by many psychologists in the 1970s but which was often actually ignored in practice. An *interactional* perspective is a central principle of environmental psychology.

Both definitions above limit the area of environmental psychology to the *physical* environment and this reflects the evolution of the field from what was called *architectural psychology* in the early 1960s. It is a good example of the ways in which definitions can be limiting and misleading. First of all it is perfectly clear from a brief glance at the areas listed as the domain of environmental psychology that the definition is actually contradicted by the subject area. Research into:

crowding	clearly include
personal space	both the **social**
territoriality	and **physical**
urbanisation	environment

In addition, as we shall see later, understanding the influence of *physical* settings on behaviour is inextricably bound up with *social* aspects of the setting. In many cases the main effect of a physical setting on behaviour is through the meaning it has acquired from social interaction. A lecture theatre in physical terms is just another room. However, people tend to behave in a particular way in a lecture theatre because its function has been defined in social terms. One of the most prominent American environmental psychologists, Harold Proshansky, in the introduction to a text on environmental psychology (Proshansky, Ittelson and Rivlin, 1976), concludes:

> *'The physical environment that we construct is as much a social phenomenon as it is a physical one.' (p. 5)*

The French psychologist, Claude Levy-Leboyer (1982), echoes this:

'The physical environment simultaneously symbolises, makes concrete, and conditions the social environment'. (p. 15)

It would therefore seem appropriate to suggest that environmental psychology is also concerned with the social environment and while it may not be the major focus, it is unavoidably part of its subject matter. If we were to summarise the discussion so far we could postulate a definition of environmental psychology as the 'study of the transactions between individuals and their physical and social environments'.

The principles of environmental psychology

An alternative way in which we might define environmental psychology is to list its basic principles and provide a list of topics or issues to which it has directed attention. We will first turn our attention to the basic principles and in later sections we will sample a selection of areas which have been researched by environmental psychologists. The basic principles of a field outline the *basic assumptions* or *philosophy of behaviour* of psychologists who work in the field and which determine the way in which they operate. This includes their *methodology*.

B O X   2

The basic principles of environmental psychology

1. An *interactional* (or *person-in-context*) perspective – behaviour is a function of the person, the environment, and the interaction between the two. B = f (P, E).
2. An *applied* research focus in which there is an integration of *theory* and *practice*.
3. *Multiple levels of analysis* – all levels of analysis from individual to societal/ organisational (MICRO/MOLECULAR to MOLAR) are used, with a particular emphasis on the molar level.
4. A research base in the *field*, or *natural environment*. This is based on a recognition of the poor ECOLOGICAL VALIDITY or *generalisability* of laboratory research on human behaviour (see Appendix 2).
5. A MULTI-METHOD approach – QUALITATIVE and QUANTITATIVE methods are used and in particular the usefulness of the FULL CYCLE MODEL (see p. 133) where basic and applied research can be used to complement and validate each other.

6. A model of the person as *active* rather than *passive* in interacting with the environment. This raises the issue of DETERMINISM versus FREEWILL/*autonomy*. The person in environmental psychology is given some degree of autonomy.
7. An interdisciplinary perspective.
8. A HOLISTIC rather than a REDUCTIONIST approach (see Appendix 1). To some extent this is contained within the societal level of analysis but goes further in recognising the limitations of breaking the environment or the person into small parts without reference to each other. A reductionist approach in this area is analogous to trying to complete a jigsaw from the individual pieces with no idea of what the complete picture looks like.
9. A SYSTEMS MODEL of the relationship between different aspects of the environment and behaviour. In other words, the dynamic interrelationship between aspects of the environment is recognised and an awareness of how change in one part will affect others is part of the process.

We will return to these basic principles later in the chapter but let us first have a look at what environmental psychologists do and some examples of theory.

WHAT DO ENVIRONMENTAL PSYCHOLOGISTS DO?

The critical mass of environmental psychologists tend to be academics, teaching, carrying out research and building a knowledge base. This is because there is no currently recognised profession of environmental psychologist in the way there is for other fields such as clinical or occupational psychology. There are postgraduate courses in environmental psychology leading to both masters and doctoral qualifications, but these are relatively few in comparison with some other fields. The most common route to a career in environmental psychology is through a postgraduate research degree (PhD or DPhil). On completion individuals go into teaching, research or a combination of the two.

Individuals who work as applied environmental psychologists tend to concentrate on consultancy, advising on the behavioural aspects of building and other physical environmental structure design. Thus they might be consulted on any aspect of the process beginning with working out what the building is supposed to do (e.g. enhancing interaction in a home for the elderly), how the building might be designed to meet its aims, and assessing how effectively it does its job once it has been built and occupied. The opportunities for consultancy would appear to be increasing with the development of community psychology and the recognition of the social or 'people' element in environmental psychology.

BOX 3

Focus on practice – post-occupancy evaluation

In any area of applied psychology the job is not complete until the effectiveness of the intervention has been assessed. Evaluation of the intervention will indicate its success and allow the psychologist to modify the process if it is not successful. Ultimately the information gained will feed into the process of designing future interventions. In environmental psychology, one example of this is the evaluation of a building after it has been occupied. What the psychologist is interested in is:

- does the building effectively serve the purpose for which it was designed?
- how does the building affect the behaviour and experience of the people who occupy it?

- what lessons can be learned for future designs?

In one such evaluation, Becker and Poe (1980) looked at the outcome of their recommended changes to a hospital building and targeted three categories of variables:

- organisational climate (attitudes and feelings of staff and patients)
- ratings of the changes in terms of a range of dimensions
- changes in behaviour.

The first two items were assessed using questionnaires, while the third was assessed by OBSERVATION. (ORGANISATIONAL CLIMATE is covered in more detail in the occupational psychology chapter.) They found that the organisational climate had improved for all, but most noticeably for staff. Ratings of changes were favourable, again most noticeably for staff. In terms of behaviours they found that facilities, such as the solarium, were used more frequently and that there was a general increase in verbal interaction among the users. The only negative feedback was the initial reaction of visitors. Becker and Poe had been involved in the design process from the beginning and the post-occupancy evaluation allowed useful feedback on the success of their work.

B O X   4

How would I become an environmental psychologist?

Having obtained a first degree in psychology, becoming an environmental psychologist involves either completing one of the few MSc courses in Environmental Psychology offered at universities in the UK, or completing a research degree (PhD/DPhil) in an area of environmental research. It is then usual to go into either teaching or full-time research and to become involved in consultancy on a part-time basis. Many of those with a background in environmental psychology use it in other areas such as community psychology or criminological psychology. The most famous example is David Canter who has moved from being one of the leading British environmental psychologists to his current position as the leading British criminological or investigative psychologist.

THE DEVELOPMENT OF ENVIRONMENTAL PSYCHOLOGY

Psychologists have always been interested in the ways in which the environment influences behaviour and in this sense the history of environmental psychology is as long as the history of psychology itself. For a variety of reasons, however, there has been a tendency to acknowledge that environmental factors play a causal role in behaviour, but not to follow this acknowledgement with serious research. It is generally accepted that a turning point occurred with the ideas of Kurt Lewin (1890–1947) who developed some of the main principles upon which environmental psychology is based. Lewin's work is generally claimed within the field of social psychology and it is within this field that we find the first serious stirrings of what was to become the separate field of environmental psychology. It is from the work of social psychologists in the 1940s and 50s that the knowledge base of environmental psychology has developed. Lewin introduced the term *psycho-logical ecology* to describe his field of study. This was later changed to ECOLOGICAL PSYCHOLOGY by Roger Barker and Herbert Wright. The term *architectural psychology* was used for two conferences in 1961 and 1966 and it would appear that it was only around 1969 that the field began to be called *environmental psychology*. During the 1970s the ZEITGEIST (spirit of the age) favoured environmental psychology and it flourished. During this period, environmental psychology, which had traditionally been taught as part of courses on social psychology, began to appear as a separate course within undergraduate psychology programmes. This potted history of environmental psychology largely reflects what happened in the USA and it would appear that changes in political attitudes during the 1980s have not been so favourable to the field. Growth has slowed down somewhat.

The vast bulk of the research in environmental

psychology has occurred in the USA, encouraged by political attitudes during the 1960s and 70s. However one must acknowledge the European influence on the field made by psychologists such as Lewin who moved to the USA in advance of the First World War. It is arguably the integration of these European ideas with American pragmatism which has produced the most radical developments in applied psychology. In Britain many undergraduate degree courses in psychology in the 1970s offered environmental psychology as an optional course but this practice seems to have diminished. This does not mean that environmental psychology has disappeared. Currently many of its areas are presented within courses on social psychology.

The development of any discipline is a function of a combination of many influences. The current knowledge base is only one of these factors, and perhaps one of the least influential. More impor-tant are social and political attitudes which deter-mine the popularity of the discipline and, as a con-sequence, the human effort which will be exerted in its advancement. Part of this process is the funding of research and the employment of practi-tioners in the area. At the moment it would appear that funding for environmental research is not a priority. In the USA the principles and methods of environmental psychology have been utilised in the development of COMMUNITY PSYCHOLOGY, an area of practice that has been around since the mid-1960s. Community psychology is currently begin-ning to take off in Britain. It may be that environmental psychology as a field will be sub-sumed by this new field. Whatever happens, there is no doubt that the work of environmental psy-chologists over the relatively short history of the field has made a major contribution to knowledge and practice in applied psychology.

THEORY, RESEARCH AND APPLICATIONS

Theory, research and application in environmental psychology are inextricably bound together since research always has an applied focus and theory is the result of research. In this section we will look at a representative sample of the areas covered by environmental psychology. Given the limited amount of research and practice in environmental psychology in Europe, the bulk of what follows relies heavily on the American literature. However, some very good work has been done by researchers such as David Cantor and Terence Lee in the UK and Claude Levy-Leboyer in France and this will be included.

Given enough space, we could explore all the topic areas covered by environmental psychology devoting a chapter to each one. Within the con-straints of a single chapter we can only sample these areas and it must be stated at the outset that there are a variety of ways in which the subject matter could be categorised. I have chosen to use three categories:

1. *interpreting the environment* (or environmental perception), which includes the model of the person in environmental psychology
2. *the impact of the environment*, which covers environmental stress and the environment as a setting for behaviour
3. *living within the environment*, which covers the areas of PROXEMICS, and using the environment.

Interpreting the environment or environmental perception

Given that a person-in-context model is funda-mental to environmental psychology, a good place to start a discussion of theory and practice is by looking at how the person sees their context, i.e. their environment. Through this we can build up a model of the person in environmental psycho-logy. This is important because the basic assumptions that psychologists hold regarding the person in any field of psychology will set the boundaries for their theoretical perspectives and the research method they use. In turn these will determine how the knowledge is applied.

How the person comes to understand and deal with the environment can be understood in terms of perception. The study of perception in cognitive psychology attempts to explain how we become aware of information in our environment, how we process that information and how we give meaning to that information which eventually leads us to respond to it in one way or another. A vast amount of research has been carried out and a number of influential theories have been developed by people such as J. J. Gibson (1979), R. L. Gregory (1966) and U. Neisser (1976). Initially theories tended to be one or other of two types:

- ■ BOTTOM-UP THEORIES, which focus on how the information itself and ultimately the environment determines our interpretation
- ■ TOP-DOWN THEORIES, which focus on how our stored previous experiences influence our interpretation of new information.

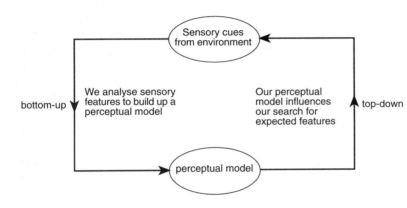

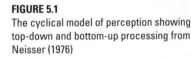

FIGURE 5.1
The cyclical model of perception showing top-down and bottom-up processing from Neisser (1976)

It is generally accepted these days that any universal theory of perception must include *both* bottom-up *and* top-down processes (see Figure 5.1 from Neisser, 1976, for an illustration). It is difficult to conceive of a situation where the information itself and its context (the external or bottom-up aspects) will not be important in providing cues to aid our interpretation. For example let us look at the most under-researched sense modality – smell. If we were to become aware of a mix of exotic aromas while standing outside a Thai restaurant we would know the source was the Thai food being cooked inside. However we might be confused to pick up the same smell in the middle of a deserted island. We required both the aroma and the context (the restaurant) in order to begin to give some meaning to the smell. But that is not the complete story. If we had never previously encountered this particular aroma we would be unable to give meaning to it. The memory of this aroma from the past is located internally and its use in helping to give meaning to the smell is the top-down aspect. Thus we can see both bottom-up and top-down processes interacting to give some sense of meaning to the experience. Previous experience will also be important in determining our emotional reaction to the smell. The area of smell has not been extensively researched though it is recognised as a potential AMBIENT STRESSOR (explained later) and as a source of pollution. Recently an American organisation has introduced rules governing body odour in the workplace. They have made it a disciplinary offence both to exude excessive natural body odour and to use too much artificial perfume!

Another example of the interaction of bottom-up and top-down processing can be seen in the area of vision. Although the light reflections that hit our retina are essential to seeing, it is true that ultimately we see with our mind. We can demonstrate this very simply by the visual illusion shown in Figure 5.2. In this illusion, we see an overlaid triangle which in fact is not there because we add the information from our experience which leads

FIGURE 5.2
Seeing things that aren't there – the KANIZSA illusion

us to expect a complete picture. This principle of *closure* (completing the picture) is central to GESTALT approaches to psychology. The Gestalt approach is discussed later in relation to the environmental psychology position on reductionism and is based on the assumption that 'the whole is greater than the sum of its parts'. What makes the whole greater than the sum of its parts in psychology is generally the *meaning* given to the experience by the individual. From the vast store of research in the area, it can be generally concluded that as we grow and develop, we encounter a wide range of information which increases in complexity with the complexity of encountered environments. We develop *cognitive schemata* (singular: SCHEMA) *blueprints,* or COGNITIVE MAPS of our world, which guide our perceptual processes (see Appendix 1). The essential aspects of this guidance are the *filtering of*, and *giving meaning to* incoming information from the environment. Filtering occurs at all stages in the process and determines what aspects we attend to, what aspects we store in memory, and ultimately the aspects to which we respond. Bottom-up aspects are also active in this filtering process, for example, attention will be influenced by aspects of the stimulus such as novelty, intensity and movement. Any consistency over time within an individual's behaviour can be

partly explained in terms of similarity or continuity between situations (the *environment* factor) and partly in terms of the development of particular COGNITIVE STYLES reflecting stability in cognitive schemata – in other words, an enduring cognitive map of the world (the *individual* factor).

Environmental perception

The process of research in cognitive psychology tends to be experimental, REDUCTIONIST and focused on individual level explanations. *Environmental perception* (a central area of environmental psychology), on the other hand, adopts a HOLISTIC approach which focuses on perception as a total process in the natural environment. The aim is to bring together the pieces gleaned from the reductionist, laboratory-based research in order to understand how we perceive the real world and from this understanding to devise ways in which we can improve it. It uses a multi-method approach with the ideal being the FULL CYCLE MODEL proposed by Cialdini (1980), where research begins with an initial analysis of the behaviour in its natural setting. The model devised from this initial analysis is then tested experimentally, and the results from the experimentation are then tested again in the natural setting. Modification of the model occurs at all stages as appropriate, particularly in adapting experimental explanations to the real world. Since the meaning given by the individual to experiences is central to the process of perception, any analysis must pay particular attention to personal meaning. All too often research ignores the very simple principle embodied in the statement by George Kelly (1955), 'If you really want to find out what is wrong with a client, ask them, they may tell you'.

The carpentered world hypothesis

Environmental perception has tended to focus on how the physical environment shapes our cognitive schemata. A proposed explanation of how different environmental experiences can lead to differences in perception between cultures is the CARPENTERED WORLD HYPOTHESIS demonstrated by Turnbull (1961). Turnbull was a social anthropologist who worked with the pygmies who inhabit the rain forest of central Africa. These people live most, if not all their life, in a forest environment and hence never fully develop *distance perception*, i.e. the ability to relate size to distance over longer distances and to understand that objects appear smaller the further away they are in the natural environment. Our reliance on a variety of learned cues in distance perception is demonstrated by a currently popular advertisement for a particular beer. In the advertisement a man appears to walk off into the distance across a desert, leaving a beer bottle in the foreground. However after walking for some time, the man turns to his left and walks into a giant beer bottle. The illusion is based on our expectations about the relationship between distance and size. Meanwhile, back in Africa, Turnbull took his pygmy guide onto the plains and showed him the plains buffalo. As they walked towards the buffalo, the guide grew fearful and wanted to run away in terror. He couldn't understand how objects (the buffalo), which appeared as tiny insects at a distance, grew larger as they approached. The phenomenon is explained in terms of our cognitive schemata becoming shaped to fit the physical environment within which we live – for most Westerners, a 'carpentered' one with very many cues to distance (corners of buildings, telephone wires disappearing into the distance, and so on). We live within not only a physical environment but also a social environment. Thus our cognitive styles are also shaped by our social and interpersonal experiences.

Each of us will see the environment we look at in different ways. For example a developer, a farmer and a tourist looking at the same piece of countryside will have quite different perceptions of it. Though they receive much the same physical stimuli, the tourist might have an overall view (a *Gestalt*) of 'a pretty scene', the farmer may see the fields in terms of current crops, who they belong to and so on, whereas the developer may superimpose a new by-pass or superstore complex.

Social influence and attitude

The social equivalent of the carpentered world hypothesis is the area of social influence and the social psychological cognitive schemata or cognitive style is our system of attitudes. We develop complex systems of interrelated attitudes which help us to simplify, categorise and react to the social world. These attitudes will vary in terms of their importance (central or peripheral) and the functions they fulfil. They lead to STEREOTYPES and expectations about the social world which determine our reactions to it. A good example of this is the way in which prejudice affects our memory of events, something that is important in terms of eyewitness testimony (see the criminological psychology chapter). As with the physical environment, attitudes will be influenced by forces which range from interpersonal up to the level of culture and similarly such influences will be reflected in individual and cultural differences.

The interrelated nature of social and physical environments

This very simplistic summary of the social psychology of attitudes highlights the fact that in psychology it has traditionally been the accepted procedure to treat the physical and social environments as two separate areas of influence for study. This is evidenced by the two separate literatures, one located mainly within cognitive psychology and the other within social psychology. The integration of the two is essential since it is clear that our understanding of behaviour in the physical environment cannot be divorced from interaction with the people who occupy it, while social interaction always has a physical context. For example, how we feel about and react to an empty physical place is often influenced by its association with people who have previously occupied and may in the future occupy it. The farmer, above, has a view of the fields which is influenced by his/her attitude to the tourists or developer, either of whom may ruin them. Barker's (1968) *Ecological Psychology* – to which we will return later – demonstrates clearly how social behaviour is shaped by its physical context. A very good example of the importance of attitudes in environmental psychology is in the area of environmental appreciation or preference. The work of Kaplan and Kaplan (1982) is the most prolific in the area and they have conducted a great deal of research into the factors that influence our likes and dislikes and hence preferences for different types of environment. Some good British work on environmental evaluation and meaning was carried out by David Canter (1968; 1969; 1983).

This work demonstrates the ways in which our evaluation of the environment and meaning we give to it influence our behaviour in that environment, and this can be usefully applied in the planning of physical environments such as new housing projects (Canter and Thorne, 1972). David Canter is currently one of the leading British criminological or forensic psychologists although he prefers the term 'investigative'. This demonstrates the interrelationship between applied areas of psychology and the transferability of psychological skills across different fields of application.

Just as our perceptual processes can be demonstrated to be vulnerable to deception in the form of visual illusions in the laboratory, so also can we be deceived (like Turnbull's pygmy) by the physical environment. An example of this is the *terrestrial saucer effect* discussed by Gifford (1987). This is an illusion created by the juxtaposition of mountains in a natural landscape which can lead to rivers appearing to run uphill or to roads which actually incline upwards, appearing to be sloped downwards. I know of a road (in the North of Ireland), where, if you stop your car with the handbrake off, it will appear to roll uphill. You may have experienced the phenomenon whilst driving, when your car engine indicates that you are travelling uphill while what you see seems to be a level or downward-sloping road. If you are a cyclist you will have perhaps experienced this even more closely (and more emotionally!)

The empirical evidence from perception and social cognition research raises important questions about our definition of reality. It would appear that, in fact, the real world of our experience is more of a subjective than objective reality – the notion that 'beauty' really does, at least partially, 'lie in the eye of the beholder'.

Environmental personality

Before leaving this section we will have a brief look at a personality approach to understanding the person aspect of the person-in-context model. In essence this involves categorising people in terms of their typical reaction to the environment. In a broad sense we are probably all aware of individual differences in this area. For example, some people like cities, while some prefer rural life. Some people enjoy sandy beaches, while others prefer rugged mountain terrain. In considering these examples we have identified one of the problems with personality approaches, i.e. they provide a *description* of behaviour or experience, not an *explanation*. We describe a person as being a 'city lover' as opposed to a 'country lover', but doing this does not provide us with an explanation as to why this is the case. In order to explain their preference, we would need to consider their life experiences or their particular biological or psychological needs and motivations. On the other hand, it can be argued that any scientific approach begins with some sort of classification or description of subject matter. There is a strong case to be made that personality theory has always been based on the environment, since the traits that have been produced are based on the person's reaction to their environment. From observing how people behave, we infer a level of need for stimulation from the environment which is the basis of Jung's *extroversion–introversion* concept. Indeed many of the early personality theorists did adopt a person-in-context model. Henry Murray's *needs–press* theory of personality explained behaviour in terms of the interaction between the needs of the person and the influence of the environment which he called 'press' (Murray, 1938). A number of environmental psychologists have attempted to describe the environmental personality using traditional questionnaire methods. An example is the work of McKechnie (1974) who developed the Environmental Response Inventory (ERI). This 184-item questionnaire measures eight dispositions towards the environment which are outlined in Box 5.

The personality approach has obvious utility in environmental design and trying to fit people to places, for example in designing rehousing projects where people are being moved from their original homes for some reason (Lee, 1976). The traditional personality perspective which assumes stable traits is, however, questionable in the light of work showing that *situations* produce similar behaviour patterns irrespective of any individual personality differences (see Appendix 1). For example, see Barker and Wright's work (1955) on behaviour settings which is discussed from p. 136.

BOX 5

The eight environmental personality traits from the ERI

Pastoralism The tendency to oppose land development, preserve open space, accept natural forces as influences and prefer self-sufficiency.

Urbanism The tendency to enjoy high-density living, and appreciate the varied interpersonal and cultural stimulation found in city life.

Environmental adaptation The tendency to favour the alteration of the environment to suit human needs and desires, oppose developmental controls, and prefer highly-refined settings and objects.

Stimulus seeking The tendency to be interested in travel and exploration, enjoy complex or intense physical sensations, and have very broad interests.

Environmental trust The tendency to be secure in the environment, be competent in finding your way around, and be unafraid of new places or of being alone.

Antiquarianism The tendency to enjoy historical places and things, prefer traditional designs, collect more treasured possessions than most other people, and appreciate the products of earlier eras.

Need for privacy The tendency to need isolation, not appreciate neighbours, avoid distraction and seek solitude.

Mechanical orientation The tendency to enjoy technological and mechanical processes, enjoy working with your hands, and care about how things work.

(From Gifford, 1987, p85)

The impact of the environment

With some basic ideas about the person in the environment in mind, we now turn to the other half of the equation, i.e. the environment, to see if we can find some general conclusions from the research and practice of environmental psychology.

In very basic terms, our encounters with both physical and social aspects of the environment will impact on us in a number of ways. This may be in terms of restricting or facilitating our behaviour, providing resources which improve the quality of our life, or making demands which overstretch our coping resources and lead to negative health consequences. In other words, the environment is a source of either reward or punishment. In many cases, in fact for the greater part of our lives, our encounters with the environment will appear to be neutral, but appearances are deceptive. It will be the case that strength of reward or punishment present is low, or that some aspects are rewarding and some punishing. In any situation, the variety of stimuli impinging on us is numerically great, interrelated and complex. However, as we know from perception research, only some of these stimuli will actually be attended to or come to have any significant meaning for us. It will be those with greater reward or punishment strength that become most significant. Research on how the environment impacts on the person has focused on a number of areas.

Behaviour settings – the external perspective

One focus has been to recognise that in any interaction the environment provides a BEHAVIOUR SETTING. This particular approach has been termed ECOLOGICAL PSYCHOLOGY by Barker (1968). It is perhaps the closest to a pure interactional approach in the literature and the work of Barker and his colleagues provides a useful model for environmental psychology research. For example, in a series of studies carried out in the 1950s, Barker and Wright (1955) set up a psychological field station in a small town in America referred to as Midwest. Barker and his colleagues carried out intense observational study of the 800 inhabitants of Midwest. They tried to identify discrete behaviour settings and then to record behaviour patterns which occurred in these settings. For example, the main street was one behaviour set ting while the post office was another. Barker concluded that behaviour cannot be separated from its setting and there tends to be a fit between the behaviour and the characteristics of the setting. In essence, the setting provides clues as to the roles to be played by the person in the setting and determines the range of behaviours that are possible in that setting. A micro-analysis might lead us to the behavioural concepts of DISCRIMINATIVE STIMULI (Skinner, 1953) – see Box 6.

BOX 6

From Skinner box to the real world – the case of behaviour settings

Skinner's (1953) concept of a *discriminative stimulus* (see Appendix 1) can be used to explain why we behave in different ways in different situations. We have learned to associate certain cues in the environment with particular types of behaviour and consequent reinforcements. The extreme example is a church where a wide range of cues such as an alter, pews, and stained-glass windows immediately indicate what type of behaviour is expected (and will be socially rewarded). The process operates at a much more subtle level than this very obvious example, and is inextricably bound up with social and cultural factors. Buildings and other environmental objects cue different types of behaviour as a function of our culture and our social experience. In another study, Skinner (1938) demonstrated how SUPERSTITIOUS BEHAVIOUR develops. Whilst training pigeons to peck a disc for food, he noticed that the birds often associated food delivery with whatever they were doing *just before* REINFORCEMENT was delivered. This eventually produced some quite bizarre and irrelevant behaviour which Skinner termed superstitious behaviours. For example, one bird turned around three times before pecking, while another moved its head up and down vigorously. The explanation was that it was not only the pecking which was being reinforced, but a sequence of behaviours which all became associated with the acquisition of food. Do you ever knock on wood, or press the button for a pedestrian crossing even if someone else has just pressed it? If you do, you are behaving just like Skinner's pigeon. These are all unnecessary behaviours and have no connection with outcomes, but they are controlled, according to Skinner, by association with other behaviours or experiences. You can probably think of a large number of places in your everyday experience which exert a control over your behaviour. These are what Barker and Wright call behaviour settings.

In a behavioural setting, the discriminative stimuli will include aspects of the physical environment and aspects of the social environment, but will also extend to non-visible aspects in terms of the BEHAVIOURAL RULES which we have learned through our socialisation. We can all recognise how rearranging the physical objects in a setting can change the behaviour in that setting. For example, if we are at a party where the tables are arranged around the room and laid out with buffet food, we feel reasonably comfortable about moving around the room and talking to lots of different people. Now picture the same room set up for a sit-down meal. We no longer feel comfortable about walking around the room and moving from group to group. However, the restriction on our behaviour is not simply a function of the physical structure of the setting, but is a relationship between the structure and the social NORMS which prevail. One of the most important conclusions from the ecological psychology of Barker was that knowledge about the behaviour setting is more useful in predicting behaviour than knowledge about the characteristics of the individuals in the setting. In other words, there is much more consistency *between* individuals in the same behaviour setting than there is *within* the same individual in different behaviour settings. For example there is often very little variation in the behaviour of a large group of students in a lecture theatre. The same group of students in the university bar would again tend to behave in fairly similar ways. However, if we were to take any one student and compare their behaviour in the lecture theatre to their behaviour in the bar we would probably find quite a difference. Of course if we were to know about both the person and the situation we could predict behaviour with an even greater degree of accuracy. It is clear that behaviour in the real world cannot be understood from one or other perspective alone, but requires a person-in-context or interactionist approach.

The work on behaviour settings provides us with a great deal of insight into the impact of the environment and indicates the need to incorporate this approach in environmental planning and design. However, the research tends to take an *external* perspective in assessing the relationship between the setting and externally observable behaviour. The environment also impacts on the emotional and motivational life of the person and we need to take an *internal* perspective to complete our understanding.

Emotion and motivation – the internal perspective

Threat and challenge – environmental stress

This perspective looks at how the environment impacts on our emotional life. In understanding the role of the physical and social environment in the development of problem behaviour, it is useful to use the approach of stress research which looks at the impact of the environment in terms of threat or challenge. Research on stress has generated a vast literature which can be categorised under three main areas of focus:

- stress as stimulus
- stress as response
- stress as a process.

The consequences of stress include:

- the whole range of AFFECTIVE DISORDERS
- the range of problems that can be grouped under *substance abuse*, or *addictive disorders*
- a wide range of DYSFUNCTIONAL BEHAVIOURS,

including sexual and negative health behaviours
- an ever growing list of *physical illnesses*.
(Fisher and Reason, 1988).

In fact in November of 1994, as I write this chapter, the national press carries stories of the first worker to win a legal case against his employer for stress induced through work overload. Stress is covered in more detail in the chapter on health psychology and for a brief review, see Cassidy (1994). In this chapter we shall focus more on the effects of the environment which tend to be contained under the *stimulus approach* to stress.

The focus of the stimulus approach has been to identify potential sources of stress for the individual in the physical and social environment. A vast literature has accumulated providing evidence of the stressful effects of a vast range of stimuli which at first seems to provide the reader with an impossible task in trying to produce any general conclusions. However, some general statements can be made. First of all, a system which allows categorisation is useful, and the one used by Rotton (1990) seems to be appropriate. This gives us four categories:

- AMBIENT STRESSORS
- CATACLYSMIC STRESSORS
- LIFE STRESSORS
- MICROSTRESSORS.

It is important to be aware from the outset that any categorisation such as this is a working tool which does not preclude alternative categorisations, and acknowledges the overlap and interaction between categories and the co-existence of events in the life experience of the individual which appear under different categories. In order to place events in particular categories, one must have dimensions, which allow evaluation of events, and for this system the dimensions are:

- severity
- scope
- duration.

The *severity* of an event is assessed on a dimension from high to low, the *scope* in terms of the numbers of people affected ranging from individual to community, and the *duration* in terms of how long it lasts, which can range from *acute* (of temporary duration) to *chronic* (always present).

Ambient stressors, such as noise, temperature, climate, pollution and crowding, are low to moderate severity, affect a range of people from large groups to whole communities in scope and are chronic in duration.

Cataclysmic stressors, such as war and major disasters are high in severity, affect whole communities and are generally acute in duration. It is important to point out the changing nature of stressful events at this point in noting that the immediate impact of war or disaster is severe, widespread and acute, but that effects of disaster or war for survivors and families become less severe, more individual and chronic in the long term. Thus the immediate impact fits the cataclysmic label, but the long-term effect fits the life stressor category.

Life stressors are those generally listed under the label 'major life events', such as bereavement, divorce, unemployment and moving house. They tend to be high in severity, individually focused and towards the acute end on the duration dimension. The classic studies of life events are those of Holmes and Rahe (1967), which produced the well-known Social Readjustment Scale listing 43 major life events with their stress weightings (see the health psychology chapter), and Brown and Harris (1978), which produced the Life Events Directory, a structured interview technique for assessing life events.

Microstressors   It is not always the major events which cause most stress, however, and it is often said that the accumulation of little irritations can be much more stressful. These little irritations, such as losing your keys, sleeping in and being late for work, dealing with an awkward or pushy salesperson and concerns about weight, are everyday events which have a cumulative effect. While writing this chapter this morning, there was a brief power cut which resulted in my losing about three pages of text which I had not saved. I was also expecting something in the post this morning which didn't arrive. Neither of these were major life events, but together they did have an emotional effect. These type of events tend to be low in severity, mainly affecting the individual, but

This photograph of a plane crash on a motorway is an example of a human-made disaster involving transportation. Think of all the people who might be affected in some way by this disaster. These will range from passengers and crew, through the rescue services, to the relatives of passengers and crew and the people living in the local area.

chronic in that they are always around. Kanner et al (1981) label these *daily hassles* and their alternative *daily uplifts* (see the health psychology chapter). It is the accumulation of daily hassles and the lack of daily uplifts which can have a detrimental effect.

Stress or challenge? – Warr's vitamin model These four categories of stressors each covering a very large number of events give us some idea of the vast number of events that have been empirically linked with the experience of stress. In fact research supports the conclusion that any event in the physical or social environment has the potential to be a stressor. Alternatively, the same events have the potential to be *challenges* which stimulate individuals to greater efforts in problem-solving and coping, and ultimately produce a sense of growth and development as a person. Even the most distressing events can have a positive side if dealt with successfully. Peter Warr's (1987) VITAMIN MODEL of the relationship between the work environment and mental health can help in understanding the notion of threat and challenge. Warr's model was derived from research on the positive and negative effects of work and unemployment. Warr suggests that the analogy of the effect of vitamins on physical health can be applied. Some vitamins such as C and E have a detrimental effect if we don't have them in sufficient quantities, but more than the required amount has no ill effect. This type of influence Warr calls CUMULATIVE EFFECT. On the other hand, vitamins such as A and D have a negative effect if we have too little or too much, and need to be sustained at an optimal level for good health. This effect is referred to as ADDITIONAL DECREMENT. Events which are positive such as good health, or daily uplifts, tend to operate in terms of cumulative effect, in other words, we cannot really have too much good health. However, events that have the potential to be stressful operate within the additional decrement model in that an optimal level of stress acts as a motivator while too much becomes detrimental. Stress that motivates is a challenge, while stress which has negative consequences is a threat.

Characteristics of stressful events In trying to understand the role of the environment in the stress process, one useful approach is to try to identify aspects or characteristics of events or stimuli which increase their probability of being perceived as stressful. We know that any event has the potential to be stressful but what are the distinguishing features of the event where stress occurs? Four dimensions have been identified in the literature and these are:

- *controllability* – this dimension is central. It is both an aspect of the environment and part of the person's appraisal process. The classic studies are the LEARNED HELPLESSNESS studies of Seligman and his colleagues carried out in 1966–67 and reported in Seligman (1975). Using animals, they demonstrated the stressful consequences of being in an environment where escape was blocked while being given electric shocks. These studies were later modified to demonstrate that when the animals were given an escape route and therefore some control over the environment, the stressful consequences were modified. The evidence for the central role of controllability in the stress process is very strong
- *predictability* – if an event is unpredictable, it will also present problems of control in that we can never be totally sure of our effectiveness in coping with the unpredictable. On the other hand, events that are totally predictable may also be stressful. It is not surprising that studies have shown that stressful events tend to rate on one or other of the extremes of predictability
- *threat* and *loss* – the literature shows that stressful events contain elements of threat or loss. For example, being told one is to become unemployed involves both a loss of job and a threat to social identity (Branthwaite and Trueman, 1989).

In essence, if one looks at the range of events that have been shown to be stressful, one can see elements of threat and loss and of predictability. Threat, loss and predictability influence control and it is likely that it is through their effect on control that they determine *appraisal* – the assessment of the event, by the individual, as stressful. What is suggested is that where an event removes or reduces the opportunity for control, it is more likely to be perceived and experienced as stressful.

In summary, we can say that any event has the potential to be stressful, but will only be experienced as stressful if so perceived by the person. Events are more likely to be perceived as stressful if they involve threat, loss or are unpredictable, therefore reducing or removing opportunities to exercise power or control over them.

Social support Another aspect of the social environment which has been clearly identified as important in the stress process and in the development of problems is the quantity and quality of SOCIAL SUPPORT available. One way to conceptualise the environmental influence is to see the environment as the base of resources for the person in dealing with life. Where resources are lacking or inadequate, problems are more likely to develop. The major resources suggested are provision of social support (e.g. friends, colleagues, family) and opportunities for power and control.

In the following sections we will focus on ambient stressors and cataclysmic events in terms of disasters, since life events and daily hassles and uplifts are covered in detail in the chapter on health psychology.

Ambient stressors

As described above, ambient stressors are sources of stress that are a constant part of our environment and tend to have low severity, affect large numbers of people and are chronic in duration. There are many examples – noise, temperature, chemical pollution, wind, humidity and also things like crowding, queuing and traffic jams, which are becoming more part of the daily life of those who live in cities and large towns. We will focus on two categories – noise and weather/climate.

Noise Our environment is subject to permanent and continuous noise pollution. It is impossible to find places even in the most isolated rural areas of Britain where our peace is not broken by the distant hum of traffic, the sound of passing aeroplanes or the sound of farm or building machinery. We are often unaware of the noise that fills our world and we do habituate to it to some

extent. Have you ever been to a dance club where the music has been so loud you are unable to talk above it? Have you ever been disturbed by the sound of a low-flying aircraft, or next door's lawnmower early on a Saturday morning? What is common to both these situations is the high level of sound. In fact the level of sound in the dance club is probably much the highest. However, you probably enjoyed the sound in the night club, but the other noises caused some annoyance as you tried to roll over and go back to sleep. In fact the latter was unwanted sound, which provides us with a useful and simple definition of noise.

Sound is generally described on three dimensions, the most obvious of which is *loudness*. This is technically defined in terms of the amplitude of the sound waves. In addition there is *timbre*, or *tonal quality* and *pitch*, which describes the frequency of wavelengths but is experienced as 'high' or 'low' sound, as in musical scales. The human ear can only detect sounds within a range of pitch and above a minimum level of loudness. In addition the combined effect of loudness, timbre and pitch vary in the way they are perceived.

Sound may be unwanted for two main reasons. It may be of a loudness, timbre or pitch which causes us *physical discomfort* or it may be unwanted because of the *situation*. For example, a lawnmower is not normally uncomfortable but is unwanted outside the window while you are in the middle of an examination!

The physical damage to hearing caused by noise in the workplace has attracted both extensive research and legislation. Research has shown that large numbers of workers develop hearing problems because of noise. One estimate suggests that three million Americans suffered noise-induced hearing loss in 1972 and that this figure had grown to nearly ten million by 1991 (Veitch and Arkkelin, 1995). This is despite extensive Health and Safety legislation which both controls noise levels at work and makes it a legal necessity to wear protective ear devices.

In addition to physical damage, it is also clear that, as a stressor, noise contributes to many mental health effects (Dubos, 1965) and to both acute and chronic physical illness (Cameron, Robertson and Zaks, 1972). A link between noise at work and reduced performance has also been suggested, though the evidence is not conclusive (Kovrigin and Mikheyev, 1965; Kryter, 1970). One explanation for this lack of agreement in results may lie in the fact that humans adapt to sound, a process known as *habituation* (see Box 7).

BOX 7

Things that go bump in the night

In a residential area of New York during the early 1970s the overhead tram system which had been part of the environment for many years was removed. While it had been running it had passed quite close to many blocks of flats at periodic intervals throughout the day and night. After it ceased to run there was a massive increase in the number of residents reporting to their local medical centres complaining of sleep disturbances. It took the medics some time to make the connection, but eventually the only plausible explanation was in terms of habituation. The residents had become habituated to the sound of the trams over the years and now that they were no longer there, they were aware of something missing. They were being disturbed by the sound of silence, to quote the Simon and Garfunkel song.

While the potential to habituate to ambient stressors, such as noise, means that people may not be aware of these stressors, the question that psychologists need to address is whether habituation removes the harmful effects. The correlational evidence would suggest that whether or not we are aware of noise, over long periods it is still a chronic stressor (Levy-Leboyer, 1982). Noise is part of our general environment and has effects other than those observed at work. For example, noise in the home has been shown to have a detrimental effect on child development in areas such as language acquisition and attention (Wachs et al, 1971) and reading ability (Cohen et al, 1973). Given the evidence for recent massive increases in

noise levels in all areas of life, this developmental effect is rather worrying.

Noise levels have also been shown to correlate with admission rates to psychiatric hospitals. For example, Herridge (1974) and Abey-Wickerama et al (1969) compared admission rates between high- and low-noise areas around Heathrow Airport in London and found significantly higher rates of admission in higher-noise areas. This effect remains after other contributory factors have been controlled. Kryter (1970) identifies aircraft noise as a significant contributing factor in health disorders requiring psychiatric attention.

Noise has also been linked with miscarriages and birth defects (Veitch and Arkkelin, 1995). It is important to recognise the wide range of environmental variables which may contribute to these sorts of problems and the difficulty in isolating the effect of any one variable. Hence the best that can be said is that noise is one of the possible contributory factors.

Other studies have looked at the relationship between noise and social behaviours such as aggression, attraction and altruism. The evidence suggests that noise can facilitate aggressive behaviour (Geen and O'Neal, 1969; Konecni, 1975), and can reduce altruism or helping behaviour (Page, 1977). The findings for attraction are ambiguous and tend to suggest a gender effect with noise reducing attraction for males but not for females (Bull et al, 1972). The best conclusion from the research on noise and social behaviour seems to be that noise disrupts the harmony of interpersonal relations and under particular conditions may have negative consequences. These conditions are not well understood and require more investigation.

In summary, research supports the conclusion that noise in the environment is associated with negative consequences in terms of both physical and mental health. However, not everyone suffers these negative consequences. On the other hand, the evidence has been sufficient to lead to legislation. It would seem appropriate that environmental psychologists should be involved in preventing these negative consequences. The question is what can be suggested from the evidence. One problem with this area is that much of the noise in our environment has been the result of developments in industry and technology. With the major economic contribution involved it is not surprising that the attempt to reduce noise levels is a somewhat uphill struggle. The most obvious intervention must be through changing the attitudes of governments and those who wield the reins of power. However, one alternative is to utilise the potential positive side of sound . . .

BOX 8

If music be the food of love . . .

While unwanted sound in the form of noise can be both physically and psychologically damaging, sound that is desired (e.g. music) can have a healing effect. It is widely recognised that music, and other sounds such as the sound of the sea, birdsong or whale communication, can be relaxing and can be used effectively in stress reduction. Research on memory and recall in cognitive psychology has shown that noise interferes with the ability to recall in serial recall tasks (Salame and Baddeley, 1989). Initially it was thought that any type of noise had a disruptive effect on attention and rehearsal. However recent research has begun to distinguish between background music and other forms of noise and there is some evidence that background music can enhance performance on some types of tasks (Davies, Lang and Shackleton, 1973). It is worth speculating that the subjective distinction between unwanted sound (noise) and wanted sound plays an important role in the process. Given the potential positive effects of some forms of sound on both emotions and performance, it may be worth looking at the possibility of modifying noise in situations where it cannot be eliminated. No doubt the idea of ten-ton trucks with exhausts blasting out the 1812 overture, the current number one, or sounding like a nightingale singing in Berkeley Square, are pipe dreams. However, a basis for future research might be the notion that if we cannot eliminate noise we *could* make it more pleasant.

Weather and climate Weather is somewhat of a preoccupation for many people in our society and is often used as a non-controversial topic when making polite conversation. When I was growing up in a farming community I remember how boring it was to listen to the many predictions and speculations about current and future weather. Of course weather is of particular concern for the farming community since their livelihood depends on the predictability of seasons. Weather and climate cover a wide range of atmospheric conditions, including wind, rainfall, sunshine, heat, humidity and storms. Like it or not, much of our behaviour is controlled by these aspects of our environment, determining things like the clothes we wear, whether we can go outside or are confined indoors, the types of leisure activities we can pursue and how comfortable or uncomfortable we feel physically. These are the obvious effects. Research in psychology has shown that there are many more subtle and far-reaching effects of weather and climate. As with many other areas of real-life research there are many problems involved. One major problem is that weather and climate co-exist with a wide range of other environmental factors and hence it is difficult to distinguish between the direct causal effects of weather and the effects of CONFOUNDING VARIABLES. An example will illustrate this. One effect of weather and climate that has been widely researched is the effect of heat on aggression. The best-known work on this is the work of Baron (1972; 1978). Baron used his theory of the causal relationship between heat and aggression to explain the American university campus riots of 1976. He suggested that the most intense rioting took place after the hottest periods. However, there are a lot of other possible confounding variables. For example, there were a range of student issues which were being opposed at the time. There is also the fact that the warm dry weather facilitated large open-air meetings. Consumption of beer and lager tend to increase during periods of hot weather in an obvious response to heat-induced thirst. These are only three from a range of possible factors which could have contributed to the violence. You can begin to see the difficulty in identifying which factor was most influential. In fact some would argue that this type of thinking is essentially the problem because it leads to attempts to establish simple explanations based on single variables. Real life does not operate like this and perhaps a more fruitful approach would be to try to identify the combination of factors which contribute to behaviours such as aggression. This MULTIVARIATE approach reflects many of the principles of environmental psychology outlined in Box 2 and discussed in more detail later.

Another effect of weather and climate which has attracted attention is the relationship between sunlight and health. Recently, with the recognition of the deterioration of our upper atmosphere as a result of pollution, and the fact that this has led to people being exposed to more harmful rays, there has been an increase in concern for a number of environmental issues. It is recognised that while sunlight is necessary for the survival of our planet, direct exposure to some forms of ultraviolet radiation can cause illnesses such as skin cancer. This has impinged on the field of environmental psychology in terms of attempting to understand environmental behaviour and how it might be changed to reduce pollution. This is discussed in a later section.

It has also been recognised that the absence of sunlight may have a negative effect on mental health. This has led to the recognition of a form of depression called SEASONAL AFFECTIVE DISORDER (SAD) – see Box 9.

As you can see from the above examples, attempts to establish a direct causal link between any one type of weather or climatic phenomenon and a particular behaviour are unlikely to be successful and are indeed rather short-sighted. Variables which occur together are likely to have a combined effect and their combination needs to be included in any analysis. There is clear evidence that weather and climate are implicated in a wide range of effects. For example, Rosen (1985) suggests that there are correlations between weather factors and 44 conditions, including blood pressure, migraine headaches and mood shifts. Some of the claims seem a little premature given the research problems. For example, Rim (1975) found increases in neuroticism and extroversion and decreases in IQ during periods of hot desert wind in Israel. A wide range of factors has been

BOX 9

Do you feel SAD in the winter?

A small number of individuals exhibit behaviours such as social withdrawal, loss of motivation and general unhappiness during winter months to such a degree that they are considered clinically depressed. In the summer they tend to move to the other extreme and appear almost manic. This effect has been linked to the amount of sunlight available and is recognised as a clinical disorder called Seasonal Affective Disorder (SAD). The use of 'light therapy', exposure to bright light for about two hours per day, appears to alleviate SAD (Byerley et al, 1987). This has led to the postulation of a direct link between sunlight and the physiological process underpinning emotions. Most people, however, experience some depressing of mood during winter and some elevation of mood during summer which raises questions about the best explanation. While biological processes are undoubtedly involved there are alternative possibilities. One such alternative explanation is based on the observation that there are more positive experiences associated with summer in most people's lives. Summer is associated with holidays, more freedom to engage in outdoor leisure activities and the opportunity to wear a greater variety of bright, comfortable and attractive clothing. Again this identifies the difficulties and dangers of single and simple explanations for real-life behaviour.

looked at. Heat, sunshine and wind are examples. Attempts to explain the effects of these variables on the psychology and physiology of humans have drawn mainly on biological factors. An example of a recent development is the focus on ion concentration which affects the amount of electricity in the atmosphere. It has been demonstrated that this air electricity has an effect on plant growth (Soyka and Edmonds, 1978). The effect of ion concentration has been studied on rats (Lambert and Olivereau, 1980) and has recently been transferred to humans (Baron, 1987). The research so far is inconclusive.

In essence the research on the effects of weather and climate has identified a range of variables as being implicated in the development of both physical and psychological disorders. However, because of the complexity of the relationships involved, the conclusions are still rather general. In fact there is room for a great deal of development of research in this area. In addition, the ever-changing nature of our weather and climate as a process of both the natural evolution of the planet and the damage being done by pollution has hardly been recognised. It would appear that there may be support born out of necessity in the future for taking this issue more seriously. In the meantime it is a worthwhile area for research.

Cataclysmic events

We have considered some aspects of ambient stressors and now turn to the area of cataclysmic events which are described as high severity events, affecting large numbers of people and generally of limited duration. These type of events are generally divided into the two categories, war and disasters. We will consider the latter. Disasters are defined as:

> 'any event that stresses a society, a portion of that society, or even an individual family, beyond the limits of daily living.'
>
> (Gist and Lubin, 1989)

The history of the world we live in contains many reports of large-scale natural disasters, perhaps the first of which was the (biblical) flood. Volcanic eruptions, earthquakes, floods and wind storms have claimed thousands of lives and are evidenced on the physical canvas of our world. One such example is the Giant's Causeway in Northern Ireland which is the result of a volcanic eruption. North Western Europe has not experienced the natural disasters which have hit other parts of the world in the recent past. However, it has not escaped the tragedy of more recent artificially-created disasters (see Box 10).

This brief look at how the environment impinges on the individual gives a flavour of the rich source of information and the complexity of that information which is available to the environmental psychologist. It is clear that if we are to live in harmony with our environment we need to understand the consequences of the many aspects of it that we so often take for granted. While environmental psychology has gone some way towards trying to improve our understanding there is a lot still to be done.

Living in the environment

Proxemics

PROXEMICS refers to the relationship between people and space in the environment and covers the topic areas of PERSONAL SPACE, TERRITORIALITY, CROWDING and privacy. The field was founded by E. T. Hall (1966).

Personal space

Personal space refers to that invisible bubble we all carry around with us which defines how close we will approach to other people and how close we will allow other people to approach us. To a very large extent it is a function of our relationship with the people involved and the society or culture to which we are accustomed. To some extent the terminology is misleading since in fact what we are considering is *interpersonal* space. It only becomes important when we interact with others. In addition we need to be aware that the bubble can expand or shrink. Hall (1966) identified four categories of personal space, each of which can be divided in two, near and far.

Intimate distance   Ranges from 0 – 45 cm. This closest distance is generally the domain of those who have an intimate relationship with each other, but also includes situations where the social rules allow contact, for example in a wrestling match. Hall distinguishes between near situations requiring body contact (lovemaking) and those which require being very close but not in contact (whispering). It is quite clear that the distinction is rather artificial since whether or not contact occurs will depend on a variety of things such as the social setting.

BOX 10

Disasters

This morning there was a news broadcast about two petrol pipelines in Texas which burst as a result of a flood, and subsequently ignited, spreading a wall of flame across the water. The igniting petrol caused a serious of explosions and currently 69 people have been injured. Over the past 15 years there have been a series of disasters in and around Britain which have brought the issue firmly into public consciousness. We can all probably remember Zeebrugge, Piper Alpha, Hungerford, Locherbie, the M1 plane crash, King's Cross, and many more. The list goes on. Such cataclysmic events have consequences for a wide range of people, from the survivors to the bereaved and those workers who are directly and indirectly involved in rescue services. These are all artificially-created disasters in that they are generally the result of human error or technological breakdown. In places like the USA and Japan, natural disasters such as floods, earthquakes and volcanoes have a similar effect. While the psychology of disasters has become more the domain of COMMUNITY PSYCHOLOGY, it is relevant here for two main reasons. First of all, environmental psychology has provided the inspiration and much of the knowledge base for community psychology, and, secondly, environmental psychology has a lot to contribute both in determining how and why these disasters occur – see the Challenger disaster on p. 241 – and in dealing with the consequences. It is one of those areas where the boundaries of fields become blurred in practice.

Personal space   Ranges from 45 – 120 cm. This is the zone generally reserved for good friends or intimate partners in a social setting. Again Hall defines two aspects of this based on the level of friendship. The near aspect is reserved for couples or very close friends whereas the far phase is used by acquaintances or friends.

Social distance   This varies between 1.2 – 3.5 m. This is the zone where those who are not acquainted interact or where business transactions occur. The near distance would be used by those being introduced or for informal business transactions whereas the far phase would be reserved for formal business processes.

Public distance   This is described as 3.5 m or greater. It is subdivided into near phase such as the distance between a speaker and an audience, and the far phase being the distance for example between the public and an important public figure.

These categories help to illustrate the different functions of personal space but on the face of it appear to be rather artificial. In fact it is likely that personal space spans a vast continuum which is determined by a number of factors including relationship with the person, cultural or societal norms and the immediate environment. The important contribution of these categories lies in identifying the ways in which they influence behaviour and experience. We do tend to maintain distances between ourselves and others and to reserve various distances for different people. If a stranger invades our intimate distance we feel angry or frightened. A serious aspect of this is the invasion of intimate space in the workplace (see Box 11).

The situations shown illustrate two of the categories of personal space, i.e. public distance (in a lecture situation) and social distance (at work). The distance between the individuals involved is determined by their relationship to each other, their role and task requirements, social and personal norms and the physical setting.

Different cultures tend to have different sizes of personal space bubbles. For example Middle Eastern peoples tend to tolerate closer distances than people from Britain. The caricature is the British and the middle eastern person who meet for the first time and end up going round and round the room as the British person keeps moving backwards to avoid what is seen as an invasion of personal space.

Research also suggests that the personal space bubble is not circular, but elliptical, in that it is bigger in front and behind us than at the sides. This means that we will tolerate people coming closer to us at the side than in front or behind. It

BOX 11

Sexual harassment and the invasion of personal space

Over the weekend I read in the national press about a court case between a woman and her male boss. The woman (Jenny, for the purposes of this chapter) worked in a restaurant. Jenny was British and her male boss was Italian. Over a period of time Jenny felt she had been the object of unacceptable sexual behaviour. This initially involved her boss touching and rubbing against her when they worked in the kitchen. Over a period of time the touching became more and more of a sexual nature, and during the touching her boss would revert to speaking in Italian. Jenny couldn't speak Italian, but she memorised some of what he said and later looked it up in a dictionary. She was very distressed to discover that he had been making lewd and inappropriate remarks. She complained and was sacked. She took her boss to court for wrongful dismissal and sexual harassment. In court her boss argued that Jenny had misinterpreted his touching which was only meant as a friendly gesture and would have been perfectly appropriate in Italy. Jenny won her case, but only because of the lewd language that had been used. This highlights the problem of cultural differences in personal space when people from different cultural backgrounds interact.

is perhaps not surprising that violent criminals tend to prefer very large areas of personal space behind them!

Territoriality

Related to personal space is the concept of territoriality, which originated in work on animals. The acquisition, marking and defence of territory is essential to the survival of animals in the wild in terms of both provision of food and drink and in enabling the continuity of the species through mating. Very often animal territoriality involves *group* territory rather than *individual* territory and watching any of the wide range of nature programmes on television will give you an idea of the processes involved. Territoriality can be observed in domesticated animals as well. A cat will mark out the boundaries of its territory by urinating around the borders and will defend that territory against invasion by other cats. In human societies territorial behaviour can be observed at its most horrific in wars. However it occurs on many less obvious levels as well. We build houses, erect fences or other markers and defend this claimed territory against invasion. In many places a great deal of anger is generated over parking places in a street. People tend to regard the space outside their house as theirs and will resent another driver parking there. The strength of resentment will vary from person to person. People leave towels on sun beds at the beach to mark their territory and in libraries students place books and other belongings on desks to mark the spot which they intend to occupy. Territoriality on this level is closely related to personal space in that markers serve to indicate territory and to reduce the likelihood of an invasion of personal space. We have probably all experienced irritation when someone takes our seat and observed others being irritated when we have encroached on their territory.

Again psychologists have tried to measure and define territoriality and the most commonly used categorisation is that produced by Altman and Chemers (1980) which identifies three types – *primary, secondary* and *public* territory.

PRIMARY TERRITORY refers to space that is felt to be owned by an individual or an interdependent group on a relatively permanent basis and is central to their daily lives. One's home is a primary territory and so also could be one's nation. It is not the size that matters, but the psychological importance which will be indicated by the strength of feeling aroused when the territory is encroached upon and the strength of the defence response.

SECONDARY TERRITORIES are generally less important to the person and are likely to be only owned on a temporary basis, for example a locker in a changing room. The distinction between a primary and a secondary territory is not an objective one, but rather depends on the individual's perception of its importance to them. Hence in order to distinguish between what was primary and secondary territory for one person, we would need to know how the person felt about it.

PUBLIC TERRITORIES are more distinct in that they don't belong to any person and are generally accessible to anyone, for example a beach.

Objects and ideas also come into the arena of territoriality. We mark objects and go to great lengths to ensure that they remain with us. Similarly we defend our ideas through copyrighting, patenting and rules about plagiarism. The latter raises the issue of the legal system and indeed many aspects of territoriality are subject to laws in many societies. Invasion of another's home is trespass or burglary.

There is some debate about why we behave in territorial ways and part of the debate hinges on the nature–nurture controversy (see Appendix 1). Some theorists from the socio-biological perspective argue that territorial behaviour is *inherited* and is a carry over from our evolutionary past. Others argue that it serves an organising function and is *learned*. The latter explanation is based on the basic notion from cognitive psychology that our cognitive processes operate to simplify the world and do this through categorising information. These cognitive processes are based on the biological processes in the brain and central nervous system which provide the 'hardware' for psychological functioning. In this explanation what is inherited is a brain which is physically designed to categorise. The types of categories, hence the types of territorial behaviour, are a function of our experience in the world, that is, the content is not programmed in at birth. Territorial behaviour is very much dependent on social and cultural factors.

What benefit can we derive from a knowledge of territoriality in humans? Again, since it

Fences around houses are clear territory markers. However, even if no one else is present, when we encounter an area like the one in the picture we have a sense that it has been marked out as the territory of those who produced the graffiti. This illustrates one of the many ways in which territorial behaviour is exhibited.

impinges on the emotions and behaviours of people, it helps in environmental design. However, a more specific application is suggested in the area of crime reduction in Box 12.

BOX 12

Using territoriality to fight crime

A concept that has attracted a lot of attention in regard to crime prevention is the notion of DEFENSIBLE SPACE. The idea is that space which was originally public space is organised so that residents feel some sense of ownership of it. It is based on the observation that much crime in the community is centred around public space. While offenders are unlikely to congregate in someone's front garden they are likely to occupy public spaces such as street corners or pathways. Newman (1972) studied crime rates in two housing projects in New York. While both projects housed the same number of people, one (Brownsville) was organised in smaller blocks catering for 5 – 6 families while the other (Van Dyke) was high-rise. In Brownsville, the buildings were built around courtyards while the large Van Dyke blocks were separated by large parks. In essence, the area around the Brownsville blocks was defensible, while the Van Dyke parks were public and became a base for juvenile gangs. In Brownsville, people knew their neighbours and a sense of community developed, whereas families in Van Dyke kept to themselves. The difference in crime rate was such that the rate in Van Dyke was 50% greater than that in Brownsville. While it is difficult to be exact about the causes for such a difference in the natural environment because of the number of possible variables, it has been suggested that four factors are important (Newman, 1972):

■ *zone of territorial influence* – this refers to markers which indicate to outsiders that an area is private rather than public
■ *opportunities for surveillance* – this involves two aspects. First of all a physical arrangement of the environment so that intruders can be easily spotted, and secondly knowing who is and who isn't an intruder. The latter is enhanced by smaller groupings and a sense of community
■ *image* – this refers to the identity portrayed by the design of the building. High-rise blocks tend to be similar wherever they appear and don't portray a sense of individuality. In fact there is often little difference externally between them and multi-story car parks! Individuality also suggests privacy and is linked to the zone of territorial influence
■ *milieu* – this refers to the surroundings of the buildings or the setting. Buildings that are set in the middle of open public spaces are more likely to attract vandalism than those organised around more personalised space such as the courtyards in Brownsville.

Central to the effect of the environment on crime is the facilitative effect of the environment in generating a sense of community in inhabitants. People must be able to feel some sense of ownership of the environment and hence a sense of responsibility for it. Terence Lee (1984) described a new development where a new motorway was built through a town, effectively dividing it in two. A subway was built to allow access between the two parts of town. Crime rates in the town escalated with much of it being based around the subway which became a haven for street gangs and a source of many violent crimes. A survey revealed that people felt they had lost a sense of community. People who had once visited each other regularly and were now separated by the motorway ceased to visit and rarely saw each other. It was as if there were now two separate towns with a sort of no-man's-land between them. This serves to illustrate the consequences of change in the physical environment and the need to consider the effect on human behaviour in planning environments.

Crowding

Crowding is closely related to previous topics since it is suggested that the effect of crowding on behaviour and experience is largely through its effect on personal space and territoriality. In other words people feel crowded because their territory or personal space is being invaded by others. Crowding is at once a fairly simplistic concept, in that we all have some experience and personal view of crowding, and a complex concept when we come to consider its impact on us. Imagine several different situations, for example, an airport lounge when several flights have been delayed, a London underground train, a Greek bus in the rush hour, an office party, a discothèque, or a live concert. We could envisage all of these situations having a very great deal of similarity from the outside observer's point of view, yet differing greatly in terms of the experience of an individual in the middle of it all. We can imagine a lot of anger and distress being experienced in the airport, the bus and on the underground, but a great deal of enjoyment and pleasant experiences occurring at the party, the discothèque or the concert.

The difference just outlined leads to a major distinction which has been drawn by environmental psychologists between *crowding* and *density* as a result of their research findings (Stokols, 1972). Density refers to the number of people in a prescribed space, for example, the number of people per square kilometre in a city and is an objective measure. Crowding refers to our experience of the number of people in a given setting, and is a subjective, psychological concept. The importance of the distinction lies in how useful each concept is in predicting behaviour and experience. From the examples outlined, a measure of density would predict a similar experience in all six situations and would therefore be of very limited use. To measure crowding we would need to ask people about their experience. There are a great many variables that will influence our experience of crowding. These will include our relationship with the people involved, the duration of the experience, the physical context of the experience and the meaning of the experience. We are likely to feel less crowded in a group of friends than a group of strangers if we have chosen to be there. However, there may also be situations where the

While both these situations would be described as high density, the people in the bottom picture are not experiencing crowding because of the relaxed and happy context. The people in the top picture, however, experience crowding as stressful on their journey to work. This illustrates the subjective nature of crowding.

opposite is true. For example, it may feel more uncomfortable to be crowded by a work colleague who we know but with whom we are not intimate than by a total stranger on a train. Again we tend to be more tolerant of crowding if we know it is short-term and will soon end.

Privacy

Privacy is something we are very much aware of these days as we observe the ongoing debate about invasion of privacy by the media. The concept of privacy is something that impinges on each of us daily. People talk about being given 'space' to grow and develop. In research on relationships it is recognised that even intimate partners need time away from each other. In essence privacy is about seeking respite from the direct influence of others. Altman (1975) defines privacy as:

BOX 13

The behavioural sink

While there are many problems with animal studies in terms of both the ethics involved and the generalisation of findings to humans, a series of studies by Calhoun (1962) is pertinent to the effects of crowding on behaviour and experience. Calhoun built an environment for rats where they were provided with abundant food, water and nesting material and allowed to live and breed freely. As the population of rats grew in size Calhoun was able to observe the effects of increased crowding. In fact the behaviour of the rats under crowded conditions deteriorated so much that Calhoun coined the phrase BEHAVIOURAL SINK to describe the effect. Despite a quarter of an acre of space with no predators the population levelled off at 150 while such a space might have been predicted to accommodate several thousand. The reason for this was the very high level of infant mortality caused by the aggressive attacks from adult males on pregnant females and often cannibalism in eating the newborn. The females lost their maternal instinct and often abandoned their young. In general there appeared to be a vast increase in psychopathology. Aggression was rampant, and aberrant sexual behaviour was common. Some animals became hyperactive while others became withdrawn and appeared depressed. There have been many criticisms of Calhoun's research not least because of the distress caused to the animals. Critics have suggested that the environment was not natural even for rats and ultimately that findings from animal studies cannot be generalised to humans. However this study inspired much of the work on crowding in humans that followed and there is nothing to contradict the suggested relationship between extreme crowding and psychopathology. One would expect that a human replication of such extreme conditions would not be allowed to occur.

'selective control of access to the self or to one's group.' (p. 18)

As with most areas of psychology the concept of control is important, and identifies the psychological aspect of privacy. It is not necessarily the case that the person desires to isolate themselves; simply having the option to do so may be sufficient. It is when this option is removed that psychological distress ensues. As with crowding therefore, we need to be aware that measurement is not an objective estimate but involves how it is appraised by the person. This includes the level of privacy preferred by the person. The flow model shown in Figure 5.3 from Altman (1975) illustrates this interactional perspective on privacy and also provides a model of the relationship between personal space, territoriality, crowding and privacy.

The discrepancy between *achieved privacy* and *desired privacy* will be a good predictor of the emotion experienced by the individual. This discrepancy will be a function of the individual's experience and personality in interaction with the environmental constraints imposed. In terms of desired levels of privacy we can easily observe how individuals differ. Some students study better alone and isolated, while others prefer more open space in a library. Some people work better in their own individual office; some quite like sharing office space. It should be fairly clear that this will relate to the strength of the territorial motive and the size of the personal space bubble.

What can we learn from research on privacy in terms of applying environmental psychology? Again it can contribute to environmental design (see Box 14).

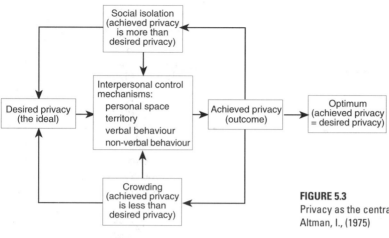

FIGURE 5.3
Privacy as the central process in the regulation of space from
Altman, I., (1975)

BOX 14

Open plan or secluded offices?

We spend up to a third of our life at work and the work environment is perhaps the one which individuals have least control over in terms of its design or layout. For those who are involved in designing work buildings all the factors relating to proxemics and many more are important. One question that is often addressed is whether it is better to provide one large open office for staff in a department or if the best design is to provide everyone with their own office. These questions are generally driven by considerations of the effects of different types of office design on performance and productivity. However, these days it is widely recognised that performance is only one part of a dynamic system of human behaviours and experiences. In other words, performance is related to levels of motivation, job satisfaction, absenteeism, job turnover, stress levels and even physical health. Hence factors that influence one will influence others as well. This is demonstrated by the experience of British Gas at their head office in the UK. They opted for the open plan office design based on economic factors. Basically, it is cheaper to build one large office, space can be more effectively utilised without obstructing walls, less supervi-

sion is required since people can be easily observed and there was some belief that communication between individuals and groups could be facilitated. However, occupation of the new office was followed by an increase in levels of symptoms of illness, absenteeism and in turn a general reduction in motivation and performance. The conclusion drawn from the experience was that the building itself was the source of the problems – something that has been labelled SICK BUILDING SYNDROME. This is a relatively recently identified phenomenon which recognises that particular buildings, because of their design, can cause physical illness in workers. Currently a debate is in progress as to what factors are most important (Ryan and Morrow, 1992). Some theorists focus on psychological factors (Bauer et al, 1992), others explore the physical aspects such as air quality (Skov et al, 1990; Norback, Michel and Widstrom, 1990), while other studies indicate interactions between job-related factors and personality (Skov, Valbjorn and Pedersen, 1989). It is unlikely that any one factor will emerge triumphant and that a number of interdependent factors are involved. However, the identification of sick building syndrome is strong support for the need to plan work environments with a range of possible influences on people in mind.

Sick building syndrome is not necessarily

associated with open plan offices. The example above just serves to show how a change of office design can have a major effect on people at work and the fact that the effects of work environments on behaviour are not likely to be in terms of any *single* dimension or aspect of the design. In terms of the debate about open plan or individual offices, research seems to point to privacy as a major factor (Sundstrom, Burt and Kamp, 1980). These researchers found that regardless of job type, workers gen- erally preferred individual offices and identified privacy as a major concern. In fact privacy cor- related positively with job satisfaction, satisfac- tion with the workplace and job performance. While correlational studies do not allow any definitive conclusions about causality they do indicate factors that planners need to consider in their work. The evidence is that open plan offices have more disadvantages than advan- tages mainly because they impinge on workers' need for privacy.

Use of environmental resources

There are a number of different aspects to our use of the resources in our physical environment. First of all, the physical world in which we live provides us with a vast range of resources, but these resources are not limitless. Hence we are faced with the need to consider seriously how we use these resources in the long term. On the other hand, we live in a physical environment which is often largely of human construction and we share that environment with others. How we use facili- ties therefore impinges on their experience.

The natural world and behaviour

The natural environment provides us with life, but we often take much more than we give back, lead- ing to concerns about the future of our natural resources. In Stephen King's *Children of the Corn,* the horror theme presented involves the earth taking revenge for the way humans have exploited it without restoring the balance that is assumed to exist in nature. While this is an extreme example, to some extent the outcome of our exploitation of natural resources could have even more horrific results. Understanding the relationship between the natural environment and behaviour can contribute to this issue. There is clearly a need to conserve our natural resources and as I write this I am reminded of a very recent news item concerning the possible closure of one of Britain's most advanced recycling centres. The argument is that the centre is not making a profit and is actually costing money to run. One cannot but be disappointed at the short-sighted argu- ments from politicians which ignore the conse- quences for the future of our planet, something which is very difficult to put into economic terms. When Adam Smith wrote his *Wealth of Nations* in 1776, he presupposed that individual capitalism would automatically lead to a promotion of public interest and the good of all. As the example above and our general experience indicates, Smith was wrong.

Recycling material is one way of reducing the depletion of resources. In recent years we have been made aware of the ways in which the use of various substances affect the ozone layer around our planet and therefore make it more vulnerable to harmful rays from the sun. The combined effect of depletion of natural resources and factors that damage our physical world is to shorten the life expectancy of our planet. Because it is such a very recent awareness, little psychological research has been carried out on the subject. However, some suggestions can be made from current psychologi- cal knowledge. The most obvious area is that of attitude change, since it is generally accepted that attitudes to conservation and use of resources underpin their actual use. To this end, the lessons learned from attempts to change attitudes in health psychology can be used. Education pro- grammes aimed at communities generally tend to be less successful than hoped for and one reason may be the problem of the *social trap* (see Box 15).

BOX 15

Escaping from the social trap: Beyond freedom and dignity

Platt (1973) identifies what is called the SOCIAL TRAP phenomenon which works against changes in attitudes and behaviour under certain circumstances. The social trap occurs when the behaviour in question has immediate reinforcing consequences, while the costs are in the distant future and to some extent hidden from immediate view. Such is the case with depletion of natural resources and the use of polluting and harmful materials. A fast and sporty car provides immediate gratification to the owner, while its exorbitant consumption of fuel will probably not directly effect the owner in his lifetime. This difference between short- and long-term consequences is a major factor according to Platt. Other factors are ignorance of the long-term consequences (which, until recently, was the case for most people) and the notion that a behaviour has positive consequences unless repeated too often. An example of the latter case is that my car isn't likely to do any real damage if only all those millions of other users would buy bicycles and leave their cars at home! It is this tendency for individuals to opt more often for the selfish choice that is the problem. Platt (1973) suggests four ways in which we might escape the social trap.

1) *Moving the future negative consequences closer to the present* – it is the same principle as keeping a picture of an overweight person on the refrigerator or a picture of a damaged lung on a packet of cigarettes. A suggestion provided by Seamon and Kendrick (1992) is to have a bright red indicator which flashes when energy is being wasted either at home or in the car.

2) *Reinforcing more desirable behaviours* – an example might be making it more rewarding for people to use buses rather than cars, or using car pools where a number of people travel in one car. Providing more peak-hour buses and special bus lanes have been shown to be effective in encouraging more people to use

them (Rose and Hinds, 1976).

3) *Changing the nature of the long-term consequences* – this involves a larger-scale intervention where for example cars are designed to run on a less endangered fuel and to be more economical. Other examples are the use of alternative energy sources and the building of homes that are more efficient in terms of energy consumption. The important thing here is to consider the possible consequences of change. For example, there is a debate about whether nuclear energy is really a safer alternative.

4) *Use of social pressure* – one of the reasons put forward to explain why people opt for the selfish choice is the DIFFUSION OF RESPONSIBILITY hypothesis (Latane and Darley, 1968) or the process of DEINDIVIDUATION (Zimbardo, 1969). Both these processes involve individuals not taking responsibility for their own actions because they are in a situation which allows them to assume that others can be blamed and that the finger won't point at them. Use of social pressure tackles just this issue by ensuring that the finger will point at specific individuals if people don't respond. An example might be where people are encouraged to make a public commitment, for example, at a community meeting. It is much more difficult for people not to meet commitments if others know about them and are likely to be aware if the commitment was honoured.

To some extent the suggestions put forward by Platt reflect the ideas expressed by Skinner (1972) in his book *Beyond Freedom and Dignity*. In essence what Skinner proposed was that society should be designed around behavioural principles so that reinforcements operated to produce and maintain behaviours that would ultimately be for the good of all. Because it would involve control over people, even if the motivation was positive, the idea is controversial. It is useful to consider for yourself the ethics of behavioural control in all areas of psychological application.

An interesting approach to large-scale social issues such as depletion of natural resources is the analogy of the *social dilemma* (Dawes, 1980). This stems from laboratory research into co-operation and competition (Coombs, Dawes and Tversky, 1970). This research involved a game called the *Prisoner's Dilemma,* where players have to choose between benefiting themselves or the group. Players are competing for a resource, and can each gain in the short term from a selfish choice. However if there are too many selfish choices the resource runs out and everyone loses. Rather like our planet's resources! While simulations like this cannot totally reflect real-life behaviour, they do allow psychologists some insight into the processes involved in light of the fact that field studies for these issues are almost impossible to set up and control. By varying the conditions, researchers may identify some of the contingencies which make co-operation more likely. Such research may help to identify ways in which physical and social environments might be manipulated to increase co-operation over scarce resources in the real world.

Sharing the world with others

When the M25 circular motorway around London had been in operation for just a short while it became apparent that it was totally inadequate to meet the demand in terms of traffic volume. The horrendous congestion that ensued led Chris Rea to write a song called *The Road to Hell* in its honour. Comedians referred to it as the largest car park in the world. This is just one example of problems that occur in sharing the world with others. Have you ever gone to a school or college coffee bar on a very busy day and found the tables covered with litter despite the fact that bins and return points for trays are provided? This, though on a different scale, is another example of sharing the world. On an even more familiar level, consider your home environment. Have you ever had to wait while someone else hogged the bathroom, or had to engage in a particular activity when you would have preferred to do something else just because someone else assumed control? These types of situation lead environmental psychologists to attempt to work out why the problems occur and to attempt to produce possible solutions.

The stress of travel The problem identified by the M25 example has been researched under two main interrelated areas – driver stress and the experience of commuting. To some extent this is an area where it is easier to identify the need for psychological input than to produce evidence of its effectiveness. In the UK it would appear that psychologists have not played an active role in the design of transport systems, though the evidence would suggest that they have a lot to contribute. Travel to and from work is certainly a source of psychological distress and would appear to present a threat to both work and family life (Cassidy, 1994). There is a need to identify the specific sources of stress and to incorporate this knowledge into design. Some very good work has been done on driver stress which could be used to inform those who design transport systems (Matthews, Dorn and Glendon, 1991; Dorn and Matthews, 1992; Gulian et al, 1990).

In the USA psychologists have been involved in the design of transport systems, the most famous being the San Francisco Bay Area Rapid Transit system commonly known as BART. This system has been in operation since 1972 and has had a psychological input both in its design and in more recent evaluation of its effectiveness. On the whole, BART has not been a resounding success. It has been attacked on a number of fronts, including its failure to reduce road traffic congestion, its lack of financial viability and the fact that it exposes the backs of houses, invading people's privacy. It is probably best considered as the source of learning about how *not* to design a transport system.

An example of an innovative approach to the problems of traffic congestion and commuter stress is the *neighbourhood work centre* (NWC) approach in Sweden (Becker, 1984). The aim here is to bring the worksite to the people rather than have people commute long distances. This does not work for every employer but many can benefit from having small work centres in the community thereby reducing the need to travel and enhancing family and community life by giving back the time normally taken to commute. This looks like a growth area for environmental psychologists.

BOX 16

Keeping it tidy: using litter bays

When I was an undergraduate student, one of the second-year practical assignments was to identify a problem around the university and to design an intervention. We were given a list of possible problems, and my group chose the issue of usage of litter bays in the university refectory. The problem was that students didn't generally return cutlery, etc. to the bays provided which meant that tables often became cluttered with rubbish and unwashed dishes. We came up with many possible solutions such as giving people a token every time they used the bays, with a condition that a specified number of tokens earned free food items. Whether such schemes would have worked we will never know since we didn't have the power to implement them. In the end we had to settle for notices to remind people. Why do people not use return bays and how might we get them to use them? There are no simple answers. We can probably use the social trap explanation in that the immediate costs are not always obvious. If you have found a clear space for yourself it is the next person who will be disadvantaged. On a large scale, the problem of litter is a serious one and costs tax payers in terms of cleaning services. There is also the issue of recycling in that much of what becomes litter could be recycled therefore contributing to the preservation of the planet.

This section has attempted a very brief overview of research on the experience of living in the environment and the implications for those involved in environmental design. On a grand scale, the objective is to design environments which maintain behaviours beneficial to everyone.

We have now sampled some areas of environmental psychology and got a flavour of the vast area which has been and needs to be researched. As with any area the initial exploratory research needs to be improved upon and there is a need to learn from past experience. Research in psychology often tends to generate more questions than it answers which is not necessarily a bad thing. Environmental psychology attempts to provide some understanding of the transaction between humans and their environment and provides us with suggestions which may be used to improve the human condition. We now turn again to the basic principles of the approach which help us to understand how it differs from other applied fields.

THE BASIC PRINCIPLES REVISITED

An interactional perspective

The interactional or person-in-context perspective is discussed above and it reflects a very basic assumption in environmental psychology that reciprocal relations of causality exist between the person and the environment.

Application and research – a reciprocal relationship

The applied orientation is also based on the philosophy of Kurt Lewin that academic and applied psychology should go hand in hand and that the best approach is that of ACTION RESEARCH (see also Appendix 2) whereby research is a problem-solving exercise focusing on real-world problems, and where results inform both knowledge and practice. Lewin was particularly concerned by the separation that existed between academic psychology which took place in the universities, and the practice of psychology which took place in the real world. The following quote from a book published in 1951 exemplifies his position:

> 'The greatest handicap of applied psychology has been the fact that, without proper theoretical help, it had to follow the costly, inefficient, and limited method of trial and error. Many psychologists working today in an applied field are keenly aware of the need for close co-operation between theoretical and applied psychology. This can be accomplished in psychology, as it has been accomplished in physics, if the theorist does not look toward applied problems with highbrow aversion or with a fear of social problems, and if the applied psychologist realises that there is nothing so practical as a good theory.'
>
> *(Lewin, 1951, p. 169)*

Environmental psychology adopts the approach outlined in chapter 1 that theory and practice are necessarily interrelated. Psychology has traditionally sought individual level explanations for behaviour and tended to ignore the larger-scale environment. For example, the five traditional perspectives in psychology, BEHAVIOURISM, COGNI-

TIVE PSYCHOLOGY, HUMANISTIC PSYCHOLOGY, BIOLOGICAL PSYCHOLOGY and PSYCHODYNAMICS, all focus on the individual in seeking causes for behaviour. Thus studies generally involved oversimplified environments and used a MICRO-LEVEL analysis. While these perspectives all contribute to an understanding of behaviour and experience, it is clear that no one perspective provides a complete explanation. In addition they tend to ignore factors at a more MOLAR level, such as the influence of groups and social and cultural factors. Environmental psychology moves towards a molar-level analysis by trying to understand the individual in her/his natural habitat. It is clear, for example, that an analysis of the experience of commuting must include consideration of economic and political factors that influence current transport policy and systems, especially at the level of trying to improve those systems.

The problem of ECOLOGICAL VALIDITY (see Appendix 2) has led environmental psychologists to locate their research in real-world settings. A good example was the work of Barker and Wright (1955) on behaviour settings, discussed on pages 136–138. However, because of the difficulties in controlling variables in the field, environmental psychology research sometimes doesn't reach an ideal level of ecological validity. This can to some extent be overcome by the use of a *multi-method* approach or a *full cycle model* of research as discussed below.

BOX 17

Spotlight on research methods in environmental psychology

Methodological issues are central to applied psychology because it is through the choice of method that the range of application will be limited or enhanced. In environmental psychology a multi-method approach is used. In essence this reflects a philosophy of problem-centred research where the problem being investigated determines the method rather than the other way round. In experimental psy-

chology it is often the case that topics which are not accessible by experimental methods are ignored. For example, the study of mental processes was rejected by early behaviourists. A wide range of methods are available in psychology and are covered in introductory texts on research methods in psychology such as Coolican (1994). For the purposes of introducing students to the different methods, they tend to be presented separately in introductory texts. However, in applied psychology methods often have to be combined or modified. It is useful to think of the methods as a set of tools and just like any other tools they can be used in combination with each other and often for purposes other than that for which they were designed. As long as we all know and follow ethical guidelines and are aware of the reliability and validity of our methods we can be inventive in their application to applied problems. In this brief introduction to environmental psychology we have encountered a range of different methods which are covered in more detail in Appendix 2.

The ideal model of research in environmental psychology is one which employs multiple methods and allows analysis at multiple levels. However, this is not often the case in practice and often knowledge in an area is accumulated by integrating research carried out by different researchers, each using a single method. For example in this chapter, in the section on environmental perception, we drew on experimental work (Gibson, 1979), participant observation (Turnbull, 1961), attitude research using questionnaire and survey methods, and the work of Kelly (1955) which was based on clinical interviews and the Role Construct Repertory Grid. It should be fairly obvious why not many researchers actually use a multi-method approach. It is mainly because of the time and expense of such a large-scale project. However, one can see at the same time that a more complete understanding is achieved when data from all sorts of sources and methods are collated.

A good example of multiple method use, albeit not by the same researchers, is in the area of crowding. In Box 13 there is a description of a study by Calhoun (1962) which used rats in a study of crowding. A study by Galle, Gove and McPherson (1972) used a survey method to investigate the correlation between crowding and social pathology in Chicago.

In applied social psychology in general, researchers are increasingly adopting a multi-method approach. To some extent this is a reversal of thinking in regard to psychological research, from one where many topics were avoided by researchers because they could not be accessed by the researchers' favoured method, to one where the main focus is the topic, and methods are adapted accordingly. Not only does this mean a willingness to incorporate any of the traditional methods that shed light on the issue, but also a willingness to modify traditional methods or even invent new ones. Related to this is what has already been referred to as the full cycle model of research where a variety of laboratory and field studies are combined to validate each other and provide a more complete understanding. In this approach a problem would be identified in the real world in the first instance. This might lead to a field study using either observational methods, surveys, interviews, diary methods or a combination of the above. Because of the complexity of the data generated from a field study, it might be appropriate to design a laboratory study to test some of the initial conclusions. The outcome of the laboratory studies would then be re-tested in the real world. This cyclical process helps to clarify the problem and identify possible interventions for the applied psychologist and reflects a very healthy approach to research. Environmental psychology was the first applied approach to advocate both a multi-method approach and a full cycle model.

The whole process of research and application in any area of psychology is dependent on the assumptions which the researcher holds about people and these assumptions are inextricably bound up with the researcher's position on major philosophical questions. In some areas, it is easier to avoid philosophical issues such as FREEWILL. The issue of whether or not an individual has autonomy or freewill in determining their own actions is a source of some tension in psychology. Traditional perspectives have assumed that individuals have no autonomy and the only perspective that clearly acknowledges the person as having a role to play in determining their own actions is the humanistic perspective. The cognitive approach presents a model of the person as being active in the process of learning (for example Piaget's theory of development). However, although by implication an active role appears to involve some exercise of autonomy, the issue is not really explicitly dealt with in cognitive psychology. The issue becomes more pressing when we come to apply psychology. Related to the freewill issue is the question of whether the person plays an active or a passive role in behaviour. A basic assumption of environmental psychology is that the person is engaged in reciprocal relations of causality with the environment, so that as well as being influenced by the environment they play an active role in modifying it. In doing so they exercise some degree of autonomy. Part of the process involves the person *constructing* their own view of the world so that reality is not so much what exists out there, but what exists within the person. Thus the model of the person in environmental psychology is one of an active person who exercises a degree of autonomy in their interactions with their environment and who constructs their own internal reality through giving meaning to their experience.

An interdisciplinary approach

Related to the issue of levels of analysis and the advocacy of research and practice based in the real world is the need for an interdisciplinary approach. The traditional compartmentalising of disciplines in the academic world often leads to situations where several disciplines are covering some common areas. The most obvious examples are psychology and sociology. In understanding and modifying behaviour in the environment several disciplines make a contribution. For example, those with backgrounds in architecture, environmental studies, social geography, urban studies and anthropology will all have a contribution to make. In addition, to be effective in practice, environmental psychologists will need to take account of factors that fall within the domains of the other specialists just listed and more, since this is not an exhaustive list. This may be done through working with other specialists, or in some cases the environmental psychologist may have had training in some of the other disciplines. Interdisciplinary

work is necessary in all areas of applied psychology and how well the interdisciplinary principle is put into practice is a determinant of the effectiveness of the approach.

A holistic approach

Environmental psychology reflects a holistic rather than a reductionist philosophy in which it is recognised that reductionism is often necessary because of the complexity of the subject matter but where it can only be useful within a holistic framework (see REDUCTIONISM and LEVELS OF ANALYSIS in Appendix 1). However, since the issue is an important one in both research and practice and has far-reaching implications for the philosophy of science applied to psychology, it is important to highlight it here. Science has traditionally assumed that anything can be understood by breaking it down to its basic components. The objection to this comes from those who argue that 'the whole is more than the sum of its parts', and in psychology is represented by the Gestalt theorists (Wertheimer, 1944). The ultimate in reductionism is the assumption that everything in the universe will eventually be explained in terms of physics. However, even in physics, reductionism is being challenged as a sound basis for science. As Stephen Hawkings (1992) says in his book *A Brief History of Time*:

> *'If everything in the universe depends on everything else in a fundamental way, it might be impossible to get close to a full solution by investigating parts of the problem in isolation.' (p. 11)*

Certainly in psychology it is widely accepted that events and experiences are interrelated in fundamental ways which should make us wary of what can be gleaned from partial analysis. In environmental psychology, reductionist approaches are seen as limited and would only be used in the context of a holistic model.

Multivariate methods

To meet the requirements of a holistic approach, methods used need to be MULTIVARIATE (i.e. using a large number of independent and dependent variables – see Appendix 2) rather than the more limited traditional UNIVARIATE approach (one independent variable, one dependent variable). For example, in a study of commuter stress, Novaco et al (1990) produced an ecological model which located the person within their total environment and considered a wide range of both person and environmental variables. The model is presented in Figure 5.4. This type of model allows for univariate research on aspects of the model which can then be related to the overall perspective. For example, research on the sources of stress in the work domain may be carried out as a separate activity, but can only be fully interpreted with regard to the effects of other domains such as home, commuting, and leisure. It is easy to see, once such a model is used, how limited a reductionist, univariate approach is in the real world.

Systems models

Finally, a principle which is becoming more a part of applied psychology is the adoption of a SYSTEMS MODEL of the person and their world. The concept originated in biology where it describes not only the interrelatedness, but also the interdependence of biological processes. In environmental psychology it is recognised that the person and their world operate in a similar fashion. The importance of a model like this becomes most obvious in application where change is being made in some aspect of the person – environment relationship. Instigating change in this way without recognising the possible unintended consequences can be disastrous. For instance, at present there is a new debate in the press and in government about the ill-effects of high-rise housing. Here, as Box 12 tells us, a simple, economical solution to housing may ignore very serious effects of that environment on individual and group behaviour. Now even government ministers are recognising that deteriorating mental health, family breakdown and serious crimes are all likely results of not clearly considering the whole system in making a person- or environment-oriented intervention. Adopting a systems model allows the practitioner or the researcher to recognise important links and

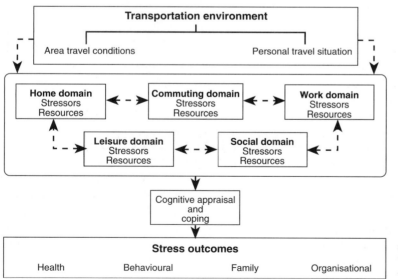

FIGURE 5.4

The ecology of commuting stress adapted from Novaco et al (1990)

to avoid as far as possible the negative consequences of an intervention. The concept is inextricably bound up with the issues of reductionism

and levels of analysis. Using a reductionist approach or a micro level of analysis is likely to ignore the interdependence of parts.

BOX 18

Spotlight on theory in environmental psychology

In any area of applied psychology there is no single or unified theory. Rather, applied psychologists have access to the total range of theoretical perspectives in psychology generally. Indeed this is as it should be because it allows greater scope and flexibility in application, and there is little reason to expect that the complex subject matter of psychology, human experience and behaviour should lend itself to a simple or single theoretical explanation. However, some general themes are identifiable which help in explicating a field, as long as it is clear that this does not preclude other perspectives which might be of use in a specific area. It is because psychology is a living discipline where

new research is being produced continually that we can never presume to have said the last word. Indeed this is the exciting and optimistic aspect of the discipline.

In environmental psychology explanations incorporate all the psychological perspectives and since it is an applied area it is not a matter of any one theory being the correct one, rather it is a case of which provides the most useful explanation allowing a practical intervention. One of the themes which runs through explanations in environmental psychology is that of HOMEOSTASIS, or OPTIMUM LEVELS. This approach in psychology originated in the work of Yerkes and Dodson (1908) on the relationship between anxiety and performance, from which they produced what is known as the YERKES–DODSON LAW. The Yerkes–Dodson law is covered in more detail in the chapter on sport psychology.

These basic principles reflect the ways in which environmental psychologists currently approach research and practice. They are all logically interrelated. For example, a systems model implies a molar level of analysis and a holistic philosophy. Not all text books will present the principles in the

same format, but the basic ideas covered will generally be the same. An understanding of the principles enables us to better understand how environmental psychology relates to psychology in general and gives an insight into the approach adopted by the environmental psychologist.

THE FUTURE OF ENVIRONMENTAL PSYCHOLOGY

Throughout the chapter I have indicated areas for future research and application, but it is perhaps useful to make a few further comments before we close. It seems clear that with the growing demand for conservation of resources and concern with the future of the planet that the area of envi-

ronmental behaviour will become increasingly important. Understanding why people continue to exploit the physical world in ways which permanently damage it looks like a major area for future research. Devising strategies for overcoming this resistance to change are clearly related future developments in application. Similarly with areas of environmental design, and ambient stressors such as noise, there is a growing need to draw on the knowledge base and methods of psychology to help improve the quality of life. In this area new and under-researched areas such as smell would seem to be likely growth areas for research. Recently some work organisations in the USA have drawn up legislation on levels of smell which apply not only to 'nasty' odours but also to the excessive use of cosmetic smells such as perfume and aftershave! Environmental psychology has also made a major contribution to the development of community psychology in the USA and with the recent emergence of community psychology in Britain one might expect an increased focus on the physical and social environment in both research and practice.

Summary

With this brief look at environmental psychology it is hoped you will have gained some sense of the immediate relevance of psychology to understanding and improving the quality of everyday life. In addition you may have recognised the living quality of psychology in the fact that as a discipline it is continuously developing. Much has been done, but much is yet to do. A simple definition of the field would be

'the application of psychological knowledge and method to understanding the process and implications of the human–environment transaction and applying the insight attained to improving the quality of the experience.'

All behaviour and experience occurs within the environment, which suggests that the subject matter of environmental psychology is very broad indeed. In many ways it has generated a wealth of data about the effects of the environment on behaviour, yet much of this only provides us with a broad general knowledge of the process. Just as relationships with people begin at a very general level but must proceed to much greater depths before we really know them, so too must we move from this broad acquaintance with our environment to deeper levels of friendship.

FURTHER RECOMMENDED READING

Bonnes, M. and Secchiaroli, G. (1995) *Environmental Psychology: A Psycho-social Introduction*. London: Sage.

Gifford, R. (1987) *Environmental Psychology: Principles and Practice*. Boston: Allyn and Bacon.

Levy-Leboyer, C. (1982) *Psychology and Environment*. London: Sage.

Veitch, R. and Arkkelin, D. (1995) *Environmental Psychology: an interdisciplinary perspective*. Englewood Cliffs, NJ: Prentice-Hall.

exercises

The following exercises are designed to give you a more practical understanding of environmental psychology and to encourage you to engage with some of the issues involved. They attempt to give you some insight into the use of multiple methods and the use of multiple levels of analysis in environmental psychology. In addition they may be useful in raising your awareness of your own relationship with the environment.

1. EVALUATION OF THE PHYSICAL ENVIRONMENT

This exercise can be carried out in a small group or on your own. It can be considered as one large exercise or you may want to just take one or two of the stages.

The aim will be to consider your college building in terms of how effectively it fulfils its functions. You might want to focus on just one room (such as your classroom, sports hall, or refectory) or on several rooms or even the total building.

Stage 1

Start by rating the overall response to the place for yourself and a sample of your peers. You can use the dimensions below and add your own dimensions if you wish.

When I am in this building/room, I generally feel:

Pleasant	Unpleasant
Happy	Sad
Comfortable	Uncomfortable
Relaxed	Tense
Motivated	Unmotivated
Angry	Calm
Frustrated	Encouraged

Stage 2

Now consider how the physical environment might influence these responses. You could take a sub-sample from those who carried out stage 1 and interview them. Focus on what aspects of the environment contribute to their ratings of the place. Distinguish between physical aspects and social (people) aspects.

Stage 3

This stage involves an observational method. Start by carrying out a general observation of how people interact with their environment in selected parts of the building. Try to identify negative and positive aspects. Are there particular aspects of the physical environment that seem to cause problems, to frustrate people etc? Are there aspects which seem to be conducive to effective functioning?

Stage 4

Drawing on your information from the above and your knowledge of environmental psychology, make recommendations about changes which could improve the effectiveness of the building. Remember to consider all aspects of the environment including things like noise levels, temperature, lighting as well as positioning of entrances and exits, furniture, etc.

2. Design and carry out a simple survey among your peers to assess their environmental personality. Use the dimensions outlined in Box 5 to guide your work. Is there a common profile?

3. Using the work of Barker and Wright (1955) – see pages 136–138 – as a model, investigate the effect of behaviour settings in your environment. You could focus on your college or on the wider community. Identify a range of behaviour settings (such as the library desk). Try to observe a small number of the same individuals in these settings. Do your observations confirm the findings of Barker and Wright?

4. Identify an issue in your environment which involves damage to the environment, for example the pollution of the atmosphere from car exhausts. When you have chosen the issue, use the social trap model presented in Box 15 to consider how you might reduce or eliminate the problem. In particular, consider the different levels of analysis. Divide targets for change into three categories:

- societal level factors, such as political attitudes, economic factors, media, etc.
- group level factors, such as family influences, peer-group pressure, etc.
- individual level factors, such as personality, individual needs, etc.

Using this 'multiple levels of analysis' approach, produce a plan for change.

5. Keep a diary for two weeks of your relationship with the environment. At the end of each day record significant events of the day in terms of how your environment has provided positive or negative experiences for you. Distinguish between physical and social aspects of the environment. At the end of the two weeks consider how the information from your diary relates to what you know about environmental psychology. Has the exercise made you more aware of your environment?

CHAPTER

6 HEALTH PSYCHOLOGY

WHAT IS HEALTH PSYCHOLOGY?

Health psychology is the field of psychology which focuses on understanding psychological processes which are relevant to HEALTH and illness. Health psychologists study why people stay healthy, why they get ill, and how they respond to illness. They try both to understand these issues and to apply their knowledge to help people to stay well or to recover from or cope with illness. HEALTH PSYCHOLOGY includes the study of people who are healthy as well as those who are ill. It is distinguished from other fields in psychology by the methodology it uses, the theoretical models it employs and the findings it obtains. It draws upon knowledge from a range of other areas of psychology, including cognitive, physiological, social, and developmental psychology, and from several other disciplines such as medicine, physiology, epidemiology and public health.

Topics and issues addressed by health psychology can be encompassed within three main headings of health, illness and health care (after Johnston, 1994):

■ *the theme of health* focuses on the psychological processes and behaviours which influence people's health and well-being. Concerns include people's concepts of health, differences in people's health-related behaviour and ways of promoting healthier lifestyles

■ *the theme of illness* focuses on the psychological and social ('psychosocial') factors that contribute to the onset and development of illness. Issues include the role of personality factors in DISEASE, the ways people make sense of their illness and the methods by which people cope with pain or physical limitations resulting from illness

■ *the theme of health care* focuses on what happens to people within the health care setting. Topics include the ways in which people respond to and make use of medical services; the nature of the patient–practitioner relationship and its influence on treatment and pathology; the development and application of measures to assess illness and associated experiences such as pain; the management of chronic illness and disability; and psychological issues involved in terminal illness. Health psychology is also concerned with the analysis and improvement of the health care system and with the formulation of health policy.

These various facets of health psychology are reflected in the definitions of health psychology proposed by people working within the field. One of the earliest, most influential definitions but probably the most complex was that of Matarazzo, one of the founders of health psychology:

'Health psychology is the aggregate of the specific educational, scientific, and professional contributions of the discipline of psychology to the promotion and maintenance of health, the prevention and treatment of illness, the identification of etiologic and diagnostic correlates of health, illness, and related dysfunction and the improvement of the health care system and health policy formation.'

(Matarazzo, 1980, p. 815)

A more recent and simpler definition is that of Marks (1994):

'the application of psychology to health, health problems and health care.' (p. 113)

WHAT DO HEALTH PSYCHOLOGISTS DO?

Health psychologists carry out a variety of activities in a range of contexts. Their work encompasses the four main domains of education, research, health promotion, and clinical practice.

Education

Health psychologists may be employed in a variety of educational establishments and may be responsible for educating doctors, nurses, other health professionals and psychologists. They will provide courses on the relevance of psychological and social factors to the disease process.

Research

They may devise and carry out research programmes to determine factors relevant to the maintenance of health and the development of disease. They may be based in academic institutions, the community or in hospital settings depending on the nature of the research topic. Thus health psychologists can be found researching:

- in laboratories examining the effects of stress on the immune system
- within schools trying to establish young people's attitudes towards health-related

behaviours such as smoking, exercise and diet
- within the lay community or medical services exploring factors that might explain people's differential use of health services or why individuals differ in the extent to which they follow medical advice
- in hospitals researching the effects of different psychological interventions on health outcomes, such as the impact of stress management programmes on recovery from coronary heart disease.

Health promotion

Health psychologists may develop interventions to improve the health or health behaviour of particular populations. They may be employed within particular health promotion organisations to devise health education programmes for schools to use in their attempts to discourage pupils from using cigarettes, alcohol and/or drugs. Or they may be involved in the development of programmes which are targeted at a whole community. These may involve a range of techniques including:

- the use of mass-media campaigns via newspapers, television and radio to alert people to health issues
- interventions in the workplace to change company policy on, for example, smoking

within the organisation or to alter the menu of the company canteen to promote better eating habits

- interventions to influence patterns of consumption through, for example, approaches to supermarkets to change the range of foods they carry
- direct interventions through local community health services using programmes to lose weight or stress reduction sessions run by health professionals.

Clinical practice

Health psychologists may do clinical work within a hospital or other treatment setting relating to patients, usually individually but sometimes in groups, who require help with particular health problems. They may be involved in:

- psychotherapeutic activities to alleviate depression arising from physical illness
- BIOFEEDBACK programmes to control pain
- stress reduction interventions to improve the recovery of patients with heart disease
- sessions with family members to establish a home-care treatment programme for a chronically ill family member.

THE DEVELOPMENT OF HEALTH PSYCHOLOGY

Health psychology is one of the fastest developing sub-branches of psychology. However, its historical roots can be located in early attempts to understand and treat illness and considerations of the relationship between disease processes and the mind.

The mind–body relationship

The question of the relationship between body and mind has occupied philosophers through the centuries. In Appendix 1 there is a brief introduction to some of the issues and you might wish to consult that section. We tend to refer to the body and the mind as though they are separate entities – the body reflecting our physical being, the mind reflecting more abstract processes of thoughts, beliefs and emotions. Although we can distinguish conceptually between the body and mind, a major issue is whether they function independently.

The early Greek philosophers, between 500 and 200 BC, were the first to propose that the body and mind were separate. They considered that illness was caused by an imbalance in bodily fluids; the mind had little or no influence on the body and its health status. In the Middle Ages the influence of the Church was considerable and sickness came to be regarded as God's punishment for wrongdoing. The Renaissance saw the birth of a more rational, scientific approach to the problem which has continued to the present day.

During the eighteenth and nineteenth centuries, knowledge of science and medicine grew rapidly. Developments in science and technology, advances in surgery and an understanding of the role of bacteria in the development of disease led to an emphasis on the importance of biological processes and a rejection of the notion that the mind or mental processes could influence the body. The BIOMEDICAL MODEL OF DISEASE became established. This model explains illness solely in terms of biological processes. It assumes that biological processes are separate from psychological and social ones and that illness and disease can be fully explained at the biological level, either through the malfunctioning of physiological processes or through the invasion of the body by PATHOGENIC (disease-producing) agents such as bacteria. The model has several implications:

How would I become a health psychologist?

At present in this country there is no designated professional training route to a career in health psychology. This is partly a result of the immaturity of this branch of psychology. It is also partly a reflection of the difficulties encountered when trying to decide on one professional training which will address the needs of people working within the range of contexts in which health psychology can be practised. At the moment there is considerable debate within the BPS Special Group of Health Psychology about the appropriate form that any professional training in the country should take. A number of alternative models have been proposed which are under consideration. By the time you read this, further discussion might have produced a more definitive stance but currently the jury is still out. Those models have been described as the *academic–researcher* approach, the *professional* and the *clinical*. Until the model has been established then a specific form of professional training cannot be devised, much less implemented. In the meantime, people are still working as health psychologists but the route they have taken has depended on the type of health psychology they were interested in and the context in which they wanted to work.

In Britain, the most usual route is through the acquisition of an undergraduate qualification in psychology or the behavioural sciences. You will first of all need to obtain a degree which is recognised by the British Psychological Society as providing the Graduate Basis of Registration. Only those who study psychology on a BPS-recognised degree course or who take the Society's qualifying examination or who take a conversion course to raise the amount of psychology studied to this recognised level will be eligible to go on to further training in one of the applied areas of psychology. It is unusual to have a degree course dedicated especially to health psychology at undergraduate level, although there is at least one undergraduate degree in health psychology in the country. An increasing number of psychology degree courses are now offering at least some health psychology courses within the curriculum and you should try to take one of these.

The second stage in the path to becoming a health psychologist is through studying for a postgraduate qualification, such as a taught Masters degree in health psychology or a research degree at either Masters or Doctoral level where the focus of the research study is in an area of health psychology. There are currently a small number of taught Masters courses in health psychology and the indications are that they are increasing. Obtaining one of these qualifications would allow you to teach health psychology in higher education or to carry out research in an academic or an applied setting which could be in a hospital or the community. The BPS has a list of courses which you could attend and they will send this to you if you contact them. If you wished to implement therapies and work directly with patients within the National Health Service you would need currently to train as a clinical psychologist. The relevant section in the chapter on clinical psychology will tell you how to go about becoming a clinical psychologist.

- it is based on an assumption that the mind and body are two separate entities
- it is a REDUCTIONIST model (see Appendix 1) meaning that it reduces illness to the lowest level processes such as cellular activity
- it is a uni-causal model explaining illness in terms of *one* factor rather than recognising that a *number* of factors may be involved in the development of disease
- its main focus is on illness rather than health

in that it attempts to explain the conditions which lead to ill health rather than those which promote or maintain health.

The model has been very useful and has been responsible for many of the medical achievements of the Western world. It has predominated well into the second half of the twentieth century. However, there is now increasing recognition that such a model does not fully describe or explain illness. Throughout this century there has been an increasing unease with the model as a result of a rising appreciation of the importance of psychological and social factors in disease. These factors are closely related to the growing recognition of psychology's role in health and the development of different sub-fields including those of PSYCHOSOMATIC MEDICINE, BEHAVIOURAL MEDICINE and HEALTH PSYCHOLOGY.

The emerging role of psychology in health

One of the first to throw doubt on purely biological explanations of disease was Freud. Freud was responsible for the psychoanalytic model described in Appendix 1 and his approach to mental 'illness' or psychological disturbance is covered in the clinical psychology chapter. Freud noticed that some of his patients appeared to have symptoms of physical illness but without any underlying organic disorder. For example, patients experienced paralysis, deafness, blindness and loss of sensation which could not be explained through bodily dysfunction. Freud considered that such illnesses were the result of the conversion of unconscious emotional conflicts and proposed the condition of 'conversion hysteria'. Such disorders were often cured by psychological treatments.

Psychosomatic medicine

In the 1930s some researchers were developing interests in the relationship between emotional experiences and physiological processes. The psychoanalyst, Franz Alexander, and the psychiatrist, Elizabeth Flanders-Dunbar, were leaders in the

field of psychosomatic medicine which resulted in the production of the journal *Psychosomatic Medicine* in 1939. The American Psychosomatic Society was founded four years later. Initially, the focus of research in psychosomatic medicine was on PSYCHOANALYTIC explanations for various disorders, notably ulcers, high blood pressure, asthma and migraine headaches. Asthma, for example, was interpreted as a 'cry for help'. Later developments resulted in a broader concern with the interrelationships between psychological and social factors and physiological processes and the development and progression of illness. Lipowski (1986) argues for a very broad interpretation of the field.

Behavioural medicine

This field developed in the 1970s as a direct result of the rise of BEHAVIOURISM in psychology. The clinical psychology chapter describes how CLASSICAL and OPERANT CONDITIONING techniques were applied successfully to the modification of problem behaviours such as alcohol abuse and excessive anxiety. Researchers demonstrated first in animals and then in humans how physiological processes such as heart rate could be controlled, providing feedback is given (Miller, 1978). This led to the development of the highly useful therapeutic technique of BIOFEEDBACK in which people gain voluntary control over physiological processes such as blood pressure, through the monitoring of such processes. The technique has applicability to a range of disorders including headaches and hypertension (Rimm and Masters, 1979).

In the United States, the Academy of Behavioral Medicine Research was formed in the late 1970s and the *Journal of Behavioral Medicine* was established. A separate Society of Behavioral Medicine was also formed. Members are drawn from a range of disciplines, not just psychology, and include colleagues from sociology and the medical professions.

The emergence of health psychology

These two fields of psychosomatic medicine and of behavioural medicine are the historical predecessors of health psychology. A number of recent trends within psychology and medicine has influenced the emergence of the third field of health psychology. They reflect the changing patterns of disease and the changing role and status of psychologists working within the medical field.

Patterns of illness across the Western, technologically advanced nations have changed considerably. Until the twentieth century, the main causes of MORBIDITY and MORTALITY were acute disorders particularly tuberculosis, pneumonia, and other infectious diseases. However, now the major causes of illness and death are chronic systemic disorders such as heart disease, cancer and diabetes. These are diseases in which psychological and social factors are more clearly evident in their development and treatment. In addition, the very fact that these are chronic rather than acute disorders means that people may experience them for many years and so psychological issues occur with them. As the number of psychological questions concerning disorders has increased, so the field of health psychology has prospered.

There is also increasing recognition of the contribution that psychologists can make to the health field. Initially psychologists working within medicine focused on assessment – the administration and interpretation of tests on people who were thought to be psychologically disturbed. Their function was similar to that of psychiatrists in that they dealt largely with patients whose problems were thought to be psychological in origin or whose behaviour was difficult for staff to manage. Patients with problems viewed as legitimately medical by the professionals were seldom seen by psychologists. Progressively however, psychological and social factors were seen to be important in health and illness generally. The contribution of the psychologist in modifying patients' health habits and managing treatment was increasingly demonstrated. The work of Janis (1958) provides an early example of the contribution of psychologists. Janis showed that if patients were prepared for unpleasant medical procedures such as surgery then their adjustment improved and their recovery was accelerated. Without substantial evidence of a contribution to health and health care the field of health psychology would not have thrived.

Health psychology formally began with the founding of the Division of Health Psychology within the American Psychological Association in 1978. The first major textbook (Stone, Cohen and Adler, 1979) was published shortly afterwards and a few years later in 1982, the journal *Health Psychology* was established. Europe was somewhat behind the USA. A number of countries have developed separate organisations for health psychologists. In 1984 a Health Psychology Group was established within the British Psychological Society. By 1987, this had developed into the Health Psychology Section and by 1992 into the Special Group of Health Psychology. The seminal British-based publication, *Psychology and Health*, was founded in 1987. The first European Conference on Health Psychology was held in 1986 in Tilburg in the Netherlands and this was followed by the development of the European Health Psychology Society.

At this point you may well be wondering about the differences between the three fields just described. They appear to be very similar. The aims of the three fields are substantially the same and there is considerable overlap in their knowledge base. Sarafino (1993) proposes that perhaps the feature which most distinguishes them is the degree of interdisciplinarity – the extent to which they draw from a broad range of disciplines. Behavioural medicine is based on knowledge from a broad range of disciplines; psychosomatic medicine is closely connected with medical disciplines; and health psychology draws on a range of subfields of psychology. However, all three approaches recognise the importance of psychological and social processes in health and illness.

The biopsychosocial model

The bases on which the three fields described above developed have provided the impetus for an alternative model of disease – the BIOPSYCHOSOCIAL MODEL (Engel 1977; 1980). Engel maintained that the biomedical model had proven inadequate to explain the disease process and proposed the biopsychosocial model of health and illness as a more inclusive alternative. It maintains that *psychological*, *social* and *biological* processes are all involved in determining health and illness. It proposes that:

- both 'macro-level' processes (large-scale causes, such as the extent of social support available to an individual) and 'micro-level' processes (small-scale causes such as chemical imbalances) interrelate to determine health status – HOLISTIC approach
- illness is *multi-causal* in origin (several causes might often work together)
- because both mind (or mental processes) *and* body influence the development of health and illness they cannot be considered as separate entities
- one needs to consider the person as a whole if one is to fully understand his or her health status – a HOLISTIC approach
- health is something the person achieves through a consideration of biological, psychological and social needs.

To illustrate this, let's take the hypothetical example of Richard who, at 45 years of age has just experienced a first, relatively minor heart attack. His father had a history of heart problems and indeed died of a heart attack at 56 suggesting that Richard may have inherited some factor which could have contributed to his heart trouble. However, Richard also has a weight problem. This began in childhood. His mother showed her care for the family by providing an abundance of food at mealtimes and his father insisted the family appreciate her efforts and eat everything on their plate. Because of his weight as a child Richard tended to prefer low-energy activities rather than sport, and this lack of exercise has continued into his adult life. It has been exacerbated because Richard is now struggling to maintain the family business which is going through a very difficult patch. Richard has always been aware that his father never seemed to have much faith in his ability to manage the business and his current economic problems seem to be proving him right.

Richard has been working seven days a week and frequently late into the night in order to turn the business round. Often he has missed eating regular meals, making do with snacks or takeaways instead, and his consumption of alcohol has gone up considerably. His family has noticed that he is becoming increasingly irritable and impatient. The heart attack came soon after a particularly distressing argument with his teenage son. This example shows how different biological, social and psychological factors may contribute to a person's health problem.

THEORY, RESEARCH AND APPLICATIONS

In order to demonstrate the nature of health psychology five broad areas have been selected which illustrate the scope and range of the field. In the following sections we will examine:

- the issue of health behaviour and health promotion
- the influence of stressful experiences on health
- type 'A' behaviour as a risk factor for coronary heart disease
- the use of medical services, patient–practitioner communication and adherence to treatment advice
- the topic of pain and pain management.

Health behaviour

The onset and progression of the major causes of disease and death in the Western world today, such as CORONARY HEART DISEASE, lung cancer and diabetes, have been linked to behavioural factors. For example, deaths from cancer are partly due to our lifestyles and personal habits. Doll and Peto (1981) estimated that approximately 30% of all cancer deaths were linked to tobacco smoking and 35% to dietary factors. Risk factors for coronary heart disease include smoking, diet, alcohol use and lack of exercise. It has been estimated that

50% of all deaths in this country may be due to lifestyle factors. In addition, the most common disorders today are CHRONIC DISEASES which mean that people suffering from them need continuing health care for the rest of their lives. Thus, if people changed their lifestyles and stopped indulging in those behaviours which are risk factors for illness, the number of deaths and the high demands on health services could be reduced.

The results of an early study examining the influence of HEALTH BEHAVIOUR on illness illustrates the positive benefits which health practices can have on maintaining health. American researchers Belloc and Breslow (1972) asked more than 6,000 residents in Alamedo County in California to indicate which of the following seven health behaviours they practised:

- sleeping seven to eight hours per night
- not smoking
- eating breakfast almost every day
- having no more than one or two alcoholic drinks each day
- taking regular physical exercise
- not eating between meals
- being at or near their prescribed weight.

The respondents were also asked about their health status during the previous six to twelve months. For example, they were asked to indicate the number of illnesses which they had had, and how many days they had missed work because of illness during the previous six to twelve months. The researchers found that the more health behaviours the respondents practised the fewer illnesses they had. Follow-up studies showed that people who practised positive health behaviours were less likely to die.

In one follow-up study nine and a half years later the researchers examined the health practices of those respondents who had died in that period. They found that the fewer health behaviours they practised the more likely the respondents were to die (Breslow and Enstrom, 1980). The MORTALITY RATE of men who practised all seven health behaviours was only 28% that of men who practised three or less than three of the behaviours. The death rate for women who practised all seven behaviours was 43% of those who practised three behaviours or less. The practice of positive

health behaviours would appear to delay death and reduce the level of illness and infirmity experienced. Thus, the practice of health behaviours may delay the onset of chronic disease and improve the quality of life in later years.

What are health behaviours?

We can define health behaviours as 'those behaviours which people undertake to maintain their current level of health or to improve it'. Kasl and Cobb (1966) define health behaviour as 'any activity undertaken by a person believing himself to be healthy, for the purpose of preventing disease or detecting it in an asymptomatic stage' (p. 246). Thus when you go for your six monthly check-up at the dentists you are indulging in health behaviour – you are going to try to prevent the development of tooth decay.

People vary in the activities which they undertake to protect their health. Harris and Guten (1979) conducted a survey of adults in the Cleveland area of the United States and asked them to indicate which of 30 behaviours they 'always or almost always' carry out to protect their health. The 30 behaviours are listed in Box 2.

Nearly two thirds of the people interviewed reported eating sensibly and getting enough sleep in order to protect their health. Most of the respondents reported carrying out at least one behaviour regularly.

People differ in the importance they attach to certain health behaviours. Turk, Rudy and Salovey (1984) compared the attitudes and the health behaviour of three groups of people – licensed practical nurses, high school teachers and college students. Respondents were given the list of 30 health protective behaviours used by Harris and Guten and asked to rate the importance and the frequency with which they practised each of the behaviours. Overall, the three behaviours considered to be the most important were eating sensibly, getting enough exercise and getting enough sleep. However, the three groups differed in the frequency with which they carried out the various health behaviours. The three most frequent behaviours practised by the nurses were keeping emergency numbers by the phone, destroying old

BOX 2

Percentage of respondents who said they always or almost always performed the protective health behaviours listed

BEHAVIOUR	%
Eat sensibly	66.0
Get enough sleep	66.0
Keep emergency phone numbers near the phone	65.9
Get enough relaxation	56.4
Have a first aid kit at home	53.1
Destroy old or unused medicines	52.3
See a doctor for a regular check-up	51.1
Pray or live by the principles of religion	47.5
Avoid getting chilled	47.4
Watch one's weight	47.0
Do things in moderation	46.4
Get enough exercise	46.0
Avoid parts of the city with a lot of crime	41.2
Don't smoke	41.1
Check the condition of electrical appliances, the car, etc.	40.0
Don't let things 'get me down'	39.3
Fix broken things around the home right away	39.2
See a dentist for a regular check-up	36.6
Avoid contact with doctors when feeling okay	35.3
Spend free time out-of-doors	33.7
Avoid overworking	33.0
Limit foods like sugar, coffee, fats, etc.	31.9
Avoid over-the-counter medicines	30.2
Ignore health advice from lay friends, neighbours, relatives	29.0
Take vitamins	24.1
Wear a seat belt when in a car	22.8
Avoid parts of the city with a lot of pollution	21.5
Don't drink	20.0
Discuss health with lay friends, neighbours, relatives	17.1
Use dental floss	15.9

From Harris and Guten (1979, Table 1)

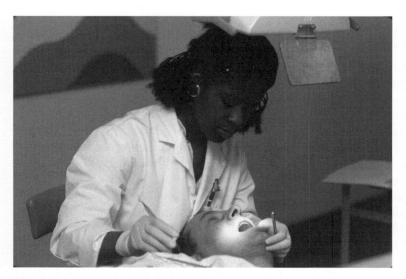

Virtually everyone practises some health behaviours. Many, like eating balanced meals or getting enough sleep, are carried out individually within an everyday context. Others, like having a check-up at the dentist, involve access to health care services.

or unused medicines and having a first aid kit in the home. Those practised by the teachers were watching one's weight, seeing a dentist for a check-up and eating sensibly. Those practised by the students were getting enough exercise, not smoking and spending free time outdoors. The results of these studies suggest that whilst people do carry out activities to protect their health they vary in the degree to which they practise them. Indeed, they do not always carry out health protecting behaviours which they themselves consider the most important.

Why do people adopt or not adopt health behaviours?

The health belief model

The most widely used theory of why people do or do not practise health behaviours is the HEALTH BELIEF MODEL which was originally developed to try to explain why people did not make use of disease prevention or screening tests to detect diseases in their early stages (for a review, see Janz and Becker, 1984). The model assumes that the likelihood that a person will engage in a particular health behaviour is a function of two factors:

- the extent to which they believe that they are susceptible to the associated disorder
- their perception of the severity of the consequences of getting the disease.

Together these determine the perceived threat of the disease. Given the threat of a disease, the likelihood that the person will adopt a health behaviour depends on the extent to which the person considers that the action will result in benefits that outweigh the costs associated with the action. Thus, if a middle-aged man who is overweight, smokes and has high blood pressure believes he is at risk of heart disease, and he also believes that heart disease could result in his death or severe disability, then he is likely to consider taking action. Whether he changes his behaviour and gives up smoking, takes more exercise and changes his diet will depend on whether he believes that the benefits of such actions in terms of reducing his risk of heart disease would outweigh the costs of discomfort, loss of pleasure

and effort of giving up smoking and taking more exercise.

The model also proposes that people who are reminded of the potential health problem are more likely to act than those who are not. Cues to action may take a variety of forms. For example, they might include advice from others, a health problem, or a mass media campaign. Thus in our example of the middle-aged man, he might decide to take action if a friend of his has a heart attack.

The health belief model has generated a considerable amount of research, most of which would seem to support its predictions. However, the model also has some shortcomings. It does not account for habitual behaviours such as cleaning one's teeth and there are methodological problems associated with a lack of STANDARDISATION (see Appendix 2) in the measurement of its various components. Thus several different types of questionnaire have been devised to assess perceived susceptibility or vulnerabilty. It also assumes that people's behaviour is governed by rational decision-making processes and does not take into account emotional factors such as fear and anxiety.

The theory of reasoned action

The second theory which has been applied extensively to the area of health is the THEORY OF REASONED ACTION (Fishbein and Ajzen, 1975), which is a more general theory than the health belief model. This theory assumes that behaviour is a function of the intention to perform that behaviour. A behavioural intention is determined by the person's attitude to the behaviour and by subjective norms. Thus a person's intention to stop smoking will depend on their attitude to smoking which in turn is determined by their beliefs about the consequences of stopping smoking. If they believe that stopping smoking will reduce the risk of lung cancer and if they believe that they are likely to get lung cancer if they continue to smoke, then they are likely to form the intention to give up. Subjective norms are based on our beliefs about how others important to us expect us to behave and how willing we are to behave as they would wish. Thus if the person believed that their family and friends would like them to stop

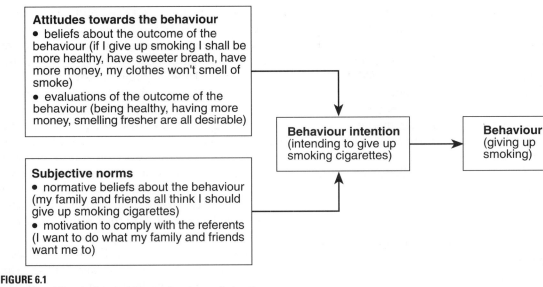

FIGURE 6.1
Fishbein and Ajzen's theory of reasoned action applied to the intention to give up smoking

smoking and they wanted to please these people, then they would be more likely to form the intention to give up.

If the behavioural intention is effectively a function of the person's beliefs, then what forms the beliefs? The theory proposes that beliefs are influenced by a range of variables including age, sex, social class, educational level, religion and personality traits. Such variables influence the beliefs which in turn give rise to the behavioural intention.

The model has been successful in predicting a wide range of behaviours including blood donation, smoking marijuana, dental hygiene behaviour and family planning (for a review, see Eagly and Chaiken, 1993). However, the model has also been criticised on a number of grounds. The criticisms include the fact that attitudes and behaviour are only moderately related in that people do not always do what they say they intend doing. It does not take into consideration people's past behaviour despite evidence suggesting that past behaviour is a good predictor of the occurrence of that behaviour in the future. Like the health belief model, it also does not account for the irrational decisions which people make.

The theory of planned behaviour

The theory of reasoned action has been modified by Ajzen (1988, 1991) to produce the THEORY OF PLANNED BEHAVIOUR. This revision includes the element of perceived control over the behaviour. It assumes that perceived control – the extent to which people think the behaviour is under their control – influences behaviour through intentions. For example, if a person does not feel that they have the will-power to give up smoking then they are likely to modify their intentions to give up. Thus someone who has already tried several times to give up smoking is less likely to believe that they can do so successfully in the future and therefore they are less likely to intend to try giving up. The theory of planned behaviour has been applied to a range of behaviours (for a review, see Ajzen, 1991) and the findings tend to be supportive. Predictions of behaviour from this model tend to be better than those for the theory of reasoned action.

Primary prevention

Developing good health habits and changing behaviours which carry risks for health are the goals of PRIMARY PREVENTION. It may take one of two forms:

- encouraging people to change behaviours which compromise their health – thus intervention programmes might be designed to help people to lose weight or to give up smoking cigarettes
- preventing people from adopting health risk behaviours in the first place – intervention programmes developed to discourage adolescents from starting to smoke would fall into this category.

It would obviously be better if we could prevent people taking up harmful habits rather than having to help them change those habits. However, the emphasis of many primary prevention programmes has been on encouraging people to change health risk behaviours. Taylor (1991) points to a number of reasons for this:

- there is a lack of knowledge as to why and how faulty habits develop. Often they arise slowly and it is difficult to determine the point at which one should or could intervene. Thus a reduction in the amount of exercise a child takes may occur gradually as the child grows older
- most health behaviours develop within a family context through the modelling of parental or sibling behaviour. For example, children whose parents smoke cigarettes are more likely to take up the habit themselves (Leventhal and Cleary, 1980). If parents do not actively encourage good health practices then it can be difficult for others to do so
- often there is little apparent reason for practising good health behaviour. Health habits are largely developed in childhood and adolescence when most people are in good health. The damage from poor health habits, such as an inadequate diet, lack of exercise, or smoking, does not become obvious until middle age. Most children and adolescents find it difficult to think so far ahead
- people are not very good at assessing health risk and they are normally over-optimistic about the risk of developing health problems. They tend to underestimate their risk compared with that of other people (Weinstein, 1987).

In addition health habits tend to be largely inde-

pendent of one another. Harris and Guten's (1979) study to which we referred earlier is one of several which show that knowing that a person practises one health behaviour does not enable you to predict another. Someone might be very careful with their diet and take regular exercise but could still drink too much alcohol.

Research also shows that health habits change over time. Being physically active in their teens doesn't guarantee that a person will be active in their forties. Someone may give up smoking cigarettes and yet revert back some years later. Thus people not only have to be encouraged to change their risk behaviours but they also have to be helped to maintain that change.

Furthermore, certain health risk behaviours are pleasurable and may even be addictive. This means that, once developed, health risk behaviours can be highly resistant to change. The variability in the reasons why particular behaviours are adopted and maintained also makes effective intervention programmes difficult to devise.

Changing health behaviours

Intervention programmes devised to encourage people to practise positive health behaviours are largely based on one of two approaches – that of attitude change which attempts to change people's behaviours by changing their beliefs and that of changing the incentives associated with the behaviours.

Attitude change approaches

Attitude change approaches assume that if a person can be persuaded that their behaviour is harmful then they will be motivated to change it. Research has tended to focus on *fear appeals* and on *informational appeals* or a combination of both. The early research examined whether fear was a good motivator of change. It assumed that if people became fearful that a given behaviour would harm their health then they would change it and that the more fearful they were the more likely they would be to act in order to reduce that fear. A review of 35 laboratory-based studies of fear-arousing communications by Sutton (1982) showed that increases in fear were consistently associated with increases in change in intentions or behaviour in the direction of the message.

Mass-media campaigns often use fear-arousing messages to motivate people into changing their behaviour.

Sutton and Hallett (1988) found further evidence of the effectiveness of fear in persuading people to adopt more health-promoting behaviours. However, it may not be sensible to create very high levels of fear through, for example, unpleasant visual images, as there is some evidence that it interferes with people's processing of the information and it may stop them attending to the message. Jepson and Chaiken (1990) found that emotional tension interfered with systematic processing of information. We do not want our intended audience to be so frightened that they do not take in what we want to tell them.

One of the difficulties of using fear-arousing messages is that whilst they provoke changes in attitude these attitude changes do not always lead to behavioural change. Sutton's (1982) review showed that people were more likely to carry out a recommended behaviour if specific instructions were given for performing it. He also found that the more effective the recommended action was perceived to be, the stronger was the intention to adopt the behaviour.

Whilst laboratory studies can enable researchers to establish what factors are important in the development of persuasive messages, they may lack ecological validity and are limited in showing the effectiveness of messages in a real-life context. A real audience can choose to listen or to avoid listening. However, there is evidence that mass-media campaigns can produce changes in intentions and behaviour, although the strength of the change may only be modest (for a review, see McGuire 1985). Stroebe and Stroebe (1995) highlight a number of reasons why it is difficult to persuade people to change their behaviour:

- people may not be interested in health issues. For example, adolescents do not appear very concerned about their health. They will therefore be less motivated to attend to messages about health issues
- there is evidence that socio-economic status is an important factor in the effectiveness of health communications. Kittel et al (1993) analysed studies occurring over a period of 20 years in Belgium and noted that the programmes were less effective for those of lower socio-economic status
- programmes often do not address the issues which are important for the audience. Abraham et al (1992) showed that young people's intentions to use condoms were related to barriers to condom use such as not knowing how to obtain them or difficulties in negotiating their use with partners
- Stroebe and Stroebe's final point relates to the difficulties people have in estimating their level of risk of developing disorders or diseases. Campaigns often focus upon level of risk of the

given disease in the population. This relative figure may be quite high but the absolute risk to any one individual may be quite low. Thus, whilst smokers run a much greater risk of developing lung cancer than non-smokers, the 10-year absolute risk of a 35-year-old heavy smoker dying from lung cancer is only about 0.3% (Jeffery, 1989).

However, as Taylor (1991) points out, mass-media campaigns can introduce people to the health risks of particular behaviours which they may not have found out about from other sources. In addition consistent messages from the mass media may gradually change the culture. For example, considerable changes in attitudes towards smoking have taken place over recent decades so that non-smoking is now viewed as the preferred behaviour (Lau et al, 1980).

Behavioural approaches

We have already mentioned that persuasive and informational communications often succeed in changing intentions or attitudes but have limited success in changing behaviour. The second approach to health promotion focuses on behavioural techniques which provide people with the skills needed for changing and maintaining the behaviour. The principles of LEARNING THEORY (see Appendix 1) have been employed in the modification of health behaviour. Methods employed include altering the consequences of the health-related behaviour by providing reinforcers for the required behaviour. Thus, for example, financial incentives are often used as a way of reinforcing and maintaining the decision to stop smoking. However, the effectiveness of such a method depends on a variety of factors and there is evidence that providing tangible rewards for behaviours can reduce rather than enhance motivation. More recent recognition of the role played by people's thoughts and beliefs has led to the development of COGNITIVE–BEHAVIOURAL strategies. Programmes using such techniques tend to be limited to clinical settings, and delivered on a one-to-one or small group basis. As such, they are more intensive and expensive compared with attitudinal change approaches. They are sometimes used in a variety of settings – medical, work, community – to supplement the larger mass-media campaigns.

We will illustrate how both attitude change and behavioural change approaches can be used successfully in health promotion programmes by describing the Three Communities Study. In the 1970s, J. W. Farquhar and his colleagues (Farquhar et al, 1977) devised a public health programme to reduce the risk of CARDIOVASCULAR disease. As the primary risk factors of smoking, inappropriate diet and high blood pressure were common across large sectors of the population, they needed to use mass communication techniques. They selected three comparable communities in northern California – two experimental and one control:

- Tracy, the control community, did not receive any health education
- Gilroy received an education campaign using the mass media of television, radio and newspapers
- Watsonville received the same education campaign via the mass media but it also included face-to-face instruction with a sample of people at high risk of cardiovascular disease.

The mass-media campaign was designed to teach behavioural skills as well as to provide information and attempt to change attitudes and motivation. The face-to-face instruction employed self-control training principles. The goal was to effect changes in smoking, exercise and diet and to evaluate those changes. Baseline data and yearly follow-up data over three years on a representative sample of 35 to 59-year-old men and women were obtained. Variables assessed included knowledge of risk factors, eating habits, smoking behaviour and physiological indicators such as cholesterol levels, etc. The results indicated that all three communities showed an increase in knowledge of risk factors for heart disease over the period of the study, but the two communities which experienced the campaigns showed greater improvements. Some reduction in smoking occurred in Gilroy but most reduction occurred in Watsonville primarily amongst those with the intensive face-to-face instruction. The mass-media programme on its own was not very effective. Both of the campaign communities showed a significant decrease in dietary cholesterol, especially amongst those receiving intensive instruction in

Watsonville. Overall, the mass-media campaign was effective but it was particularly effective when supplementary face-to-face instruction was used. Behavioural changes were more long-lasting amongst those receiving intensive instruction in Watsonville.

Life stress, coping and illness

STRESS is a word which you have probably heard used quite frequently. You may hear someone say 'she's under a lot of stress' to explain a friend's forgetfulness or short temper. Someone else may explain their feelings of tiredness and lack of energy by saying that they are 'stressed out' and need to take time out to relax. Another may refer rather proudly to their 'high-stress' occupation, perhaps flagging up their ability to cope with all the pressure entailed. You may well have used the word yourself to explain your feelings when taking an examination or going for a job interview or when

things just seem to be getting on top of you. Such differing usages have in common the notion that stress involves some form of demand which people may have difficulty coping with. However, sometimes the term is used to signify the pressure exerted upon us whilst at other times it is used to signify our responses to the demand. It is this ambiguity in the use of the word stress that is sometimes confusing. Indeed, the specialist literature provides many examples of attempts to define stress.

Studies on stress can be divided into one of three categories reflecting the ways in which stress has been defined for the purposes of studying it (Cox, 1978). The first approach treats stress as an independent variable where stress is described in terms of pressures or threats in the environment; the second treats stress as a dependent variable where stress is described in terms of the individual's response to a threatening or demanding environment; the third treats stress as an intervening variable where stress is viewed as the result of an imbalance between the demands of the environment and the individual's ability to cope with those demands. Box 3 illustrates these different approaches to stress:

BOX 3

Approaches to the study of stress

STRESS AS A STIMULUS

Here the focus is on the event or circumstances which produce discomfort:
– *cataclysmic events* e.g. earthquakes
– *stressful life events* e.g. bereavement
– *chronic minor circumstances* e.g. work overload.

STRESS AS A RESPONSE

Here the focus is on the physiological or psychological reactions to external demands. Examples of reactions studied include hormonal changes, heart rate responses, levels of morbidity and mortality, anxiety and anger, task performance, etc.

STRESS AS AN INTERVENING VARIABLE

Here the focus is on the nature of the relationship between the demands of a situation and the actual or perceived resources the person can draw on to cope with the demands. Resources include *biological factors*, *psychological factors* (such as self-esteem or locus of control), and *social factors* (such as the amount of support available from family and friends).

The idea that stress contributes to ill health is not a recent one. W.B. Cannon (1914, 1929) was one of the first to assess systematically the physiological response to stressful stimuli. He studied the way in which animals and people respond to environmental threats such as cold or lack of oxygen. In particular he examined the 'fight or flight' reaction – the way in which, under situations of danger, people undergo physiological changes which prepare their bodies to react to the threat. He considered that these changes have both positive and negative effects – they are adaptive because they help the organism to respond more quickly to the threat but they can also be harmful to health if they are prolonged.

Perhaps the most important early contributor to the attempt to explain stress-related illness was Selye (1950; 1956; 1976; 1985). Selye carried out research investigating the effects on animals of a range of stressors, such as heat, cold, injections of organic substances and surgery. He found that, irrespective of the nature of the stressor, the animals displayed a similar pattern of responses. These included the enlargement of the outer layer of the adrenal cortex, shrinkage of the thymus, spleen and other lymphatic structures, and the development of gastrointestinal ulcers. It was from these observations that Selye developed his GENERAL ADAPTATION SYNDROME which consists of a three stage response to stressful situations:

- the ALARM REACTION in which initially there is a phase of lowered resistance which is followed by the activation of the body's physiological defence mechanisms

- the STAGE OF RESISTANCE in which the body begins to adjust to the stressor and begins to show signs of adaptation or resistance to it. However, if the stressor continues resistance is lost and the individual moves on to the third stage

- the STAGE OF EXHAUSTION when adaptation is lost, symptoms reappear and, if stress continues, death occurs.

Selye proposed that our ability to adapt is not infinite. Whilst sleep and rest may restore resistance close to normal levels there will be inevitable signs of wear and tear. If stressors are prolonged, they may cause damage through the very processes which are evoked to defend the body. Selye refers to the diseases which arise as a consequence of the stress response as DISEASES OF ADAPTATION. Examples of such diseases of adaptation include ulcers, high blood pressure and heart problems.

Although Selye's model has been criticised on a number of points it has been very influential in the field of stress research. Systematic study of *psycho-social stress* (that related to psychological or social factors) has in large part been based on the assumption that it produces the same sort of bodily reactions as those Selye observed in relation to biological stressors.

One of the main difficulties in assessing the importance of social and psychological stressors on health was the lack of an objective measure of stress. The major advance in this area was the development of the life event scales, most notably the *Schedule of Recent Experiences* (SRE) of

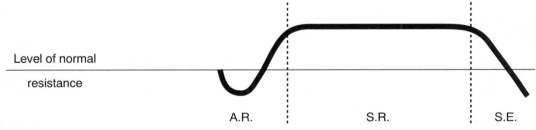

FIGURE 6.2
Selye's General Adaptation Syndrome
As the organism is exposed to the stressor the alarm reaction (AR) occurs and the level of general resistance to the stressor falls below normal. In stage 2 – the stage of resistance (SR) – the organism adapts to the stressor and the ability to resist increases above the normal level. However, if the stressor continues, the stage of exhaustion (SE) is reached when the organism's ability to resist falls below normal again (after Seyle, H. 1957, p. 87).

Hawkins, Davies and Holmes (1957) and the *Social Readjustment Rating Scale* (SRRS) of Holmes and Rahe in 1967. These scales, and those developed from them, enabled researchers to calculate the amount and rate of change experienced by a person.

The Schedule of Recent Experiences consisted of 43 LIFE EVENTS which appeared to be most relevant to the onset of disease when life histories of patients had been examined. The questionnaire allowed people to indicate which of the changes listed they had experienced within a specified period of time. This work was extended by Holmes and Rahe with the development of the SRRS which enabled them to quantify the amount of stress associated with changes experienced in everyday life. Using the same 43 events they asked a sample of 394 people to rate each of the events in terms of the amount of social readjustment the average person would have to make in order to accommodate them. In line with Selye's concept of stress, which assumes that any change necessitates adjustment, the events listed included both pleasurable ones (e.g. marriage, going on holiday) and unpleasant ones (e.g. death of a spouse, divorce). The resulting scores were labelled *Life Change Units* (LCU) and the events were ranked in terms of their LCU scores. The scores of the items checked could be summed in order to obtain a total measure of the intensity of life change experienced. The scale can be seen in Box 4. Thus a measure of the amount of change and the intensity of change was now available which could be related to the amount of illness experienced.

A large number of studies used these scales to examine the relationship between life events and illness. Many of the studies were retrospective ones. People who were ill were asked to complete the checklists for a previous set period, usually 12 months, and the resulting scores were compared with those of a healthy control group. These showed positive relationships between life change and sudden death from cardiac arrest (heart failure) and also with the onset of MYOCARDIAL INFARCTION (a form of heart attack in which heart tissue dies because of a lack of oxygen and other essential nutrients caused by a blockage in the blood supply to the heart). In prospective studies of naval personnel, Rahe (1974) found that illness

episodes reflected the life change levels experienced prior to sailors' embarkation. Many other investigators used these scales or similar ones based on a wide variety of different populations to study the relationship between life change and both psychological and physical illnesses. High levels of life change have been implicated in, for example, the development of coronary heart disease, diabetes, tuberculosis, cancer, pregnancy complications, psychiatric impairment and depression (for a review, see Dohrenwend and Dohrenwend, 1974; 1981).

However, some researchers have not obtained positive results and typically the degree of association between life change and illness has been slight. The correlations between life stress and illness are usually around or under 0.30. Stressful life events thus account for less than 10% of the variance in illness (Rabkin and Struening, 1976). This suggests that people become ill for many other reasons apart from life change. In addition, one can make a number of criticisms of the SRRS:

- some of the items listed could have a number of different meanings – e.g. change in responsibilities at work could refer to either an increase or a decrease. There is nothing to indicate the extent of the change, and the person whose responsibilities have increased gets the same score as the person whose responsibilities have decreased
- some of the items could be linked so if a person experiences one of the events there is an increased likelihood of them experiencing others. Thus someone fired from work is quite likely to experience financial difficulties, have problems with their mortgage, a change in their living conditions and may have an increase in the number of arguments with their spouse. It is even possible that all these events may reflect illness rather than be the cause of it, especially if that illness is psychological in nature
- some of the items, such as 'personal injury or illness' or 'pregnancy' reflect states of health so that the total life change score is already contaminated with the individual's current state of health
- the scale does not allow for individual

BOX 4

The Social Readjustment Rating Scale

RANK	LIFE EVENT	MEAN VALUE	RANK	LIFE EVENT	MEAN VALUE
1	Death of spouse	100	23	Son or daughter leaving home	29
2	Divorce	73	24	Trouble with in-laws	29
3	Marital separation	65	25	Outstanding personal achievement	28
4	Jail term	63	26	Wife begins or stops work	26
5	Death of close family member	63	27	Begin or end school	26
6	Personal injury or illness	53	28	Change in living conditions	25
7	Marriage	50	29	Revision of personal habits	24
8	Fired at work	47	30	Trouble with boss	23
9	Marital reconciliation	45	31	Change in work hours or conditions	20
10	Retirement	45	32	Change in residence	20
11	Change in health of family member	44	33	Change in schools	19
12	Pregnancy	40	34	Change in recreation	19
13	Sex difficulties	39	35	Change in church activities	19
14	Gain of new family member	39	36	Change in social activities	18
15	Business readjustment	39	37	Mortgage or loan less than US$10,000	17
16	Change in financial state	38	38	Change in sleeping habits	16
17	Death of close friend	37	39	Change in number of family get-togethers	15
18	Change to different line of work	36	40	Change in eating habits	15
19	Change in number of arguments with spouse	35	41	Vacation	13
20	Mortgage of US $10,000	31	42	Christmas	12
21	Foreclosure of mortgage or loan	30	43	Minor violations of the law	11
22	Change in responsibilities at work	29			

Source: Holmes and Rahe (1967)

differences in response to the events – it assumes that all people will experience similar degrees of stress in relation to each event. However, death of a spouse could mean very different things depending on the length of the marriage, the happiness of the relationship, and the person's dependence on the partner. Whilst the original contention was that individuals would be equally susceptible to life change, the results do not appear to support this

■ the scale is based on the assumption that all

change is aversive, irrespective of whether it was desirable or undesirable. Thus in assessing degree of life change, the scale does not distinguish between the number of desirable or undesirable events that respondents have experienced. However, researchers have found that undesirable events appear to be more clearly associated with illness but desirable events are not.

Despite its various weaknesses, however, the scale has been extremely useful in guiding research in this area and providing reasonable evidence for the existence of an association between life change and illness. A number of other scales have been devised in an attempt to improve on the shortcomings of the SRRS and some researchers have taken a more intensive and individual approach to the assessment of psychological and social stress.

Not all of the stress we experience results from major life events – more minor everyday happenings can be stressful. For example, having to get an essay in on time, or finding your bicycle has a puncture when you are already running late may create stress. Kanner et al (1981) developed a scale that reflected these minor events or HASSLES. They defined hassles as 'irritating, frustrating, distressing demands that to some degree characterise everyday transactions with the environment' (Kanner et al, 1981, p. 3) and developed a *Hassles Scale* which lists 117 potential hassles. Respondents are asked to mark how many times they have experienced each item during a given period of time and then to indicate the severity of

each hassle – 'somewhat severe', 'moderately severe' or 'extremely severe'. Two scores are therefore obtained. One is the *number* of hassles they have experienced and the other is the *severity* of the hassles they have experienced. Examples from the Hassles Scale can be found in Box 5.

The researchers tested 100 middle-aged adults each month over a nine-month period. They found that the items most frequently reported were:

- concerns about weight
- health of a family member
- rising prices of common goods
- home maintenance
- too many things to do
- misplacing or losing things.

The researchers also wondered whether desirable experiences lessened the impact of hassles. They therefore developed another scale, the *Uplifts Scale*, which consists of 135 positive events that bring peace, satisfaction or joy. This scale was also given to the 100 middle-aged adults along with the Hassles Scale. Respondents had to indicate

BOX 5

Examples from the Hassles Scale

1 Misplacing or losing things	16 Smoking too much
2 Troublesome neighbours	17 Use of alcohol
3 Social obligations	18 Personal use of drugs
4 Inconsiderate smokers	19 Too many responsibilities
5 Troubling thoughts about your future	20 Decisions about having children
6 Thoughts about death	21 Non-family members living in your house
7 Health of a family member	22 Care for pets
8 Not enough money for clothing	23 Planning meals
9 Not enough money for housing	24 Concerned about the meaning of life
10 Concerns about owing money	25 Trouble relaxing
11 Concerns about getting credit	26 Trouble making decisions
12 Concerns about money for emergencies	27 Problems getting along with fellow workers
13 Someone owes you money	28 Customers or clients giving you a hard time
14 Financial responsibility for someone who doesn't live with you	29 Home maintenance (inside)
15 Cutting down on electricity, water, etc.	30 Concerns about job security

Source: Kanner et al (1981)

how many of the positive experiences they had had during the past month and whether they had been somewhat, moderately or extremely strong. The most frequently occurring UPLIFTS were:

- relating well to your spouse or lover
- relating well with your friends
- completing a task
- feeling healthy
- getting enough sleep
- eating out.

A number of studies have explored the relationship between hassles, uplifts and health. In addition, researchers have also measured major life events in an attempt to compare the relative strength of the relationship between everyday stress and more acute major stressors. DeLongis et al (1982) gave middle-aged adults the Hassles Scale, the Uplifts Scale, a life events scale which did not include any desirable items and the *Health Status Questionnaire* which assesses a range of bodily symptoms and general health. Hassles and undesirable events scores were weakly associated with ill health. There was virtually no relationship between uplifts and health status. Other studies have shown similar results (e.g. Weinberger et al, 1987)

However, research using the Hassles Scale has been subjected to many of the criticisms directed at research using the major life events scales. The Dohrenwends (Dohrenwend et al, 1984; Dohrenwend and Shrout, 1985) argued that many of the items could reflect *symptoms*, especially psychological ones (e.g. you have had a fear of rejection), or that the response format meant that only individuals who had difficulties coping would check the items in the first place. As the lowest level of intensity of response permitted on the scale is 'somewhat severe', then it is possible that only those respondents who had experienced problems dealing with the item would report it as a hassle. Watson and Pennebaker (1989) also showed that hassles scores were associated with a measure of *negative affectivity* – a stable tendency to experience negative mood or have negative feelings – suggesting that the Hassles Scale was not an objective measure of potential sources of stress.

However, there is sufficient evidence from a wide range of studies to suggest that an accumulation of stressful experiences is related to illness. The major debating point though is the extent to which life events cause illness directly. Illness may arise from the physiological processes which are involved in the response to stressful events, or it may arise indirectly through changes in health-related behaviour which occur as people try to cope with the stressors – e.g. in the amount of smoking or alcohol use, lack of exercise, poor eat-

Pleasant events such as eating out with a friend may help buffer against the potentially harmful effects of stress.

ing habits, etc. In addition, lifestyle factors may be important in the level of people's exposure to stressful experiences in the first place.

Moderating variables on the stress–illness relationship

One of the reasons put forward to explain why the stress–illness relationship was not found to be as strong as expected by researchers is that people may respond differently to the stress events. Lazarus (1976) proposed that stress can only be understood in terms of both the environmental stimuli and the individual reacting to it. He argues that it is the nature of that interaction which is important and that the reaction to events is dependent on the individual's APPRAISAL or inter- pretation of the significance of the events. Thus, events are not themselves inherently stressful; their effect depends on how they are interpreted. Where an individual does not judge the situation as stressful then the stress response will not emerge. Lazarus maintains that people initially review the situation and decide whether it is harmless or whether it presents a challenge or a threat to them. Where a situation is appraised as threatening, then secondary appraisal occurs as we search for COPING responses that will reduce the threat. Thus, if we find that the car won't start on a morning when we have a mid-term test beginning at 9 o'clock, we might initially be extremely worried. One alternative might be to telephone the local garage or the Automobile Association and ask them to come out. We know that they might take some time to arrive and there would be no guarantee that they would make the car mobile in time to get to college to take the test. However, if we remembered that a neighbour worked at the college and, on looking, we saw that her car was still outside her house we might feel less worried, thinking that we would be able to obtain a lift from her and thus not miss the test. By exploring the alternatives and weighing up the costs and benefits of possible choices we decide on a coping strategy.

Factors which affect the way in which we inter- pret potential stressors include psychological, social and environmental variables. To illustrate some of these effects we shall focus upon the way

in which individual characteristics and SOCIAL SUP- PORT influence the experience of stress.

Some people seem more able to cope with stressors than others. Kobasa (1979) was interest- ed in finding out which individual characteristics were important in resisting stress. She studied executives in an American company which was preparing for a reorganisation – a time of uncer- tainty and potential stress for the workforce. She found that those who coped best and had the fewest physical and psychological problems were people who had:

- a strong sense of commitment – a strong sense of purpose and involvement with work, family, friends and activities in their lives
- a high sense of control, a belief that they could influence events in their lives
- a sense of challenge, in which they approached change positively as something which provided them with opportunities for growth.

Kobasa coined the term a HARDY PERSONALITY to describe those people with this set of characteris- tics. Kobasa and her colleagues have carried out a number of studies to investigate the buffering effect of hardiness. They have found significant relationships between stressful events, hardiness and illness. Rhodewalt and Zone (1989) found that hardiness provided a protective effect. Women who displayed hardy characteristics were less like- ly to experience physical illness or depression compared with those who did not. They also found that level of hardiness affected the degree of stress the women perceived, in that women with hardy characteristics judged fewer events to be negative and reported that the negative events did not require as much adjustment. This suggests that the buffering effect of hardiness operates at least partly through the appraisal process.

Research has also shown that social support is an important factor in the response to stressors. Social support refers to the feeling that one is loved and cared for and that there are others who can provide emotional and material help should it be needed. Empirical work indicates that social support is beneficial in a wide range of situations including pregnancy, job loss and bereavement and that those who lack support are more vulnera- ble to ill health (Schwarzer and Leppin, 1989). It is not clear how social support affects health and well-being. It could have a direct effect on health irrespective of the amount of stress a person experiences. This may arise because individuals with high levels of support may have more positive experiences. An alternative explanation is the BUFFERING HYPOTHESIS – that social support influences health by providing protection during high levels of stressful experiences. People with high levels of support may appraise a situation as less threatening because they know that there are people available to provide help. Alternatively high levels of social support may directly affect people's ability to cope with adverse situations because they provide direct help or give advice on how to manage the situation.

How do stressful experiences affect health?

Stress may contribute to ill health directly through the physiological responses to stressful events. It may also exert an indirect effect through behavioural changes arising in response to stressors. Behaviour associated with health risks includes increased levels of smoking, excessive use of alcohol, lack of exercise and poor dietary habits.

Let us look more closely at the physiological response to stressors. Our adaptation through the process of evolution seems to have provided us with physiological reactions which prepare the organism for either fight or flight. The stress response comprises largely CATABOLIC PROCESSES which are those involved in the release of energy from reserves stored in the body. Where survival depended on one's ability to fight or to run away then such a response is sensible. Two major neuroendocrine systems, the pituitary-adrenocortical and the sympathetic-adrenal medullary, are responsible for many of the changes associated with stress. Such changes include an increase in the heart rate and blood pressure, redirection of blood to the muscles and brain, improved blood coagulation, an increase in the depth and rate of breathing, increased production of glucose from the liver and the release of fats from the liver which provide energy for the heart and muscles. Such changes prepare the organism for fast and strong movement.

However, whilst such a reaction is highly useful when an organism needs to respond with physical activity to threat, it is not so adaptive today when many of the stressful experiences we have to cope with do not require a physical response. For example, when your work is criticised, striking your boss would not be an appropriate way of dealing with the problem. Indeed, such a response is likely to create more stress. In addition, many stressful situations today are quite long term and so the stress response is prolonged. Prolongation of the response may adversely affect the functioning of many of the organ systems and thus increase the vulnerability of the organism to disease and illness.

Type 'A' behaviour and coronary heart disease

We have already noted that there seems to be considerable variation in people's vulnerability to illness. Many of the people who smoke cigarettes will not develop lung cancer or coronary heart disease. These differences may result from genetic variation in that we know some people have a genetic predisposition to develop a particular disease. For example, you are more likely to develop heart disease if your parents or grandparents did. However, not everybody with a genetic predisposition to a particular disease goes on to experience it. It would seem that a range of other individual factors affect the body's reactions and influence the development of disease. This section explores the link between individual differences and the onset of illness through an examination of the relationship between TYPE 'A' BEHAVIOUR (TAB) and CORONARY HEART DISEASE (CHD).

The belief that personality plays a role in the onset of heart disease is not recent. Osler, a physician practising at the beginning of this century, noted that certain characteristics were likely to be evident in patients who experienced heart disease. He considered that the type of person likely to develop ANGINA PECTORIS was:

> '... robust, the vigorous in mind and body,
> the keen and ambitious man, the indicator of

whose engines is always at "full speed ahead"'

(cited in Harvey, 1988)

Little systematic study of the relationship between personality characteristics and heart disease was carried out however, and it was not until the 1950s when two American cardiologists – Friedman and Rosenman – noted similar patterns in their patients and began to research the issue, that interest in the subject was rekindled. Now, the study of the link between behaviour and heart disease is a major topic within health psychology.

Let's begin by looking at heart disease itself.

What is heart disease?

The heart is a muscular pump. Its function is to ensure that oxygenated blood is circulated around the body and that deoxygenated blood is returned to the lungs for it to take up more oxygen. The pumping action varies according to the body's needs so that when at rest the heart may only beat once every second, but when activity increases and the tissues require more oxygen then the rate increases. The heart itself requires blood to fulfil its task. It obtains this through the coronary arteries. Sometimes these arteries become less effective, less able to expand to cope with increased demands for blood. The walls of the arteries can become narrowed and harder through the development of fatty deposits called *plaque*. The medical term for this process is ATHEROSCLERO-SIS. As the coronary arteries become less responsive the flow of blood to the heart is impaired. If the reduction in the blood supply is considerable then the tissues can become deprived of oxygen, a condition known as ISCHAEMIA, and the result is the death of the tissue thus reducing the effectiveness of the heart. If the oxygen deficiency is extreme then the heart may stop beating completely resulting in a myocardial infarction or heart attack. When there is rather less severe depletion in the amount of oxygen, the condition of angina pectoris may occur. Here the person experiences chest pains especially when the heart has to meet increased demands caused by physical or emotional exertion.

What is type 'A' behaviour?

Let us now look more closely at what we mean by type 'A' behaviour (TAB). TAB is quite a complex concept. It refers to a set of behavioural characteristics which appear under particular conditions. As originally conceptualised, TAB is not a personality trait, that is, a quality that is stable across situations and over time. Rather it is a set of observable behaviours which are exhibited by individuals in specific situations. TAB is characterised by three main dimensions:

- *competitiveness and achievement orientation* – type 'A's are more likely to be involved in many activities and to be highly committed to succeeding in them. They tend to ignore feelings of fatigue or other needs such as the need to eat. Type 'A's are also likely to try harder to achieve control in circumstances where control is threatened

- *aggressiveness and hostility* – type 'A's may not be generally more aggressive and hostile but they are more likely to display hostility and AGGRESSION when, for example, they are criticised or they are under pressure

- *a sense of time urgency* – type 'A's tend to be more aware of time passing and indeed they estimate that time passes more quickly than do TYPE 'B's. They show more impatience and irritability when delayed. They also tend to try to struggle to achieve more in less and less time.

Rosenman (1978a) described individuals with TAB as evidencing:

> *'an action–emotion complex in response to their chronic and excessive struggle to achieve more and more from their own environment in too short a period of time, and against the opposing efforts of other persons or things in the same environment.'*

People who do not display type 'A' behaviour are referred to as type 'B'.

Measurement of Type 'A'

Type 'A' has been assessed by interview and by self-completion questionnaires. The original measure was that of the Structured Interview (SI) developed by Friedman and Rosenman (Rosenman, 1978b). The SI comprises 25 questions which explore the individual's reactions to a variety of everyday events which are likely to produce hostility, impatience or competitiveness. Assessment focuses both on people's non-verbal reactions to the questions as well as on their verbal responses. Interviewers ask questions in a provocative manner so as to increase the possibility of TAB being displayed. Non-verbal aspects of speech, such as speed of speaking or tendency to interrupt the interviewer, and overall behavioural style are assessed, as are visible displays of hostile or aggressive behaviour. On the basis of their results the respondent is placed into one of four categories which reflect the amount of type 'A' behaviours displayed. A1 and A2 categories reflect different degrees of type 'A' behaviour with those in A1 showing more than those in A2. Often these two categories are collapsed together. Where none of the type 'A' behaviours are present the individual is placed in category type 'B'. Where there is a balance of type 'A' and type 'B' behaviours, the individual is placed in category X. The interview is normally taped and rated by two people. Inter-rater agreement is usually quite high but agreement is better at the extremes, that is in categories A1 and B.

The SI depends on carefully trained interviewers and is a time-consuming and costly process and not appropriate for all types of research, especially epidemiological studies – those surveying large numbers of people within the community. A number of paper and pencil measures have therefore been developed. They include the *Jenkins Activity Survey* (JAS) (Jenkins et al, 1967; 1978), the *Framingham Scales* (FTAS) (Haynes et al, 1978) and the *Bortner Rating Scale* (Price, 1979). The most commonly used of these measures has been the JAS. It asks respondents to indicate how they behave in particular situations by selecting one of a number of predetermined answers. For example, one question asks respondents whether they are likely to try to hurry someone who speaks slowly by finishing their sentences for them. Another asks whether they try to do two things at once.

The *Framingham Type 'A' Scale* (FTAS) (Haynes, Feinleib and Kannel, 1980) was derived from participants' responses to a number of psycho-social questions included in the Framingham research study. The scale consists of ten items representing type 'A' behaviours and related to aspects such as pressure at work and home, and hard-driving and impatient behaviour.

The *Bortner Rating Scale* comprises 14 pairs of bi-polar descriptors separated by a 1.5 inch line. One pole represents TAB, the other reflects TBB. Respondents place themselves somewhere along the continuum between the two extremes. Their overall score is obtained through measuring the distance of their response from the Type 'B' pole on each set of pairs and then summing the scores across all 14 responses.

Whilst all three measures have supposedly been designed to measure the same construct there is less agreement between them than we would expect there to be. Agreement between the JAS and the SI is little more than 60% and, although that between the SI and the FTAS is somewhat better, agreement between all three is only modest at best. The SI and the self-report measures are very different types of instruments and this may account for some of the disagreement.

The relationship between Type 'A' behaviour and coronary heart disease

What is the evidence which supports a link between TAB and CHD? Early research findings showed a clear relationship between the two variables. Strong evidence came from the Western Collaborative Group Study (WCGS) (Rosenman et al, 1964), which was a prospective long-term study using the SI to assess TAB in more than 3,000 white middle-class males in non-manual occupations. When recruited into the study, none of the participants showed any signs of CHD. The participants were then followed up for eight and a half years during which time men who were classified as type 'A' were found to be twice as likely to develop CHD than those categorised as type 'B'.

2,750 WCGS participants free of CHD in 1965 were also assessed using the JAS. Four years later, the type 'A' scores for those people who had developed heart disease were contrasted with the scores of a matched group of participants who did not develop heart disease. Those who had developed heart disease had significantly higher type 'A' scores than those in the control group (Jenkins et al, 1979).

Further support for TAB being a risk factor for CHD was obtained from another large-scale study in Framingham in the USA which also included women in the survey. TAB was assessed through the FTAS. Some eight to nine years after their initial assessment, men between the ages of 55 and 65 who had been categorised initially as TAB were found to have twice the level of heart disease compared with those men considered to be type 'B'. A similar pattern was found for women. Prediction was better for angina than for myocardial infarction.

Findings from these and a range of similar studies show support for an association between TAB and CHD. Indeed the Review Panel on Coronary Prone Behaviour and CHD in 1981 concluded that TAB could be considered as significant a risk for CHD as that associated with smoking, high cholesterol levels and HYPERTENSION. However, results from more recent studies have not been so consistent or supportive.

The Multiple Risk Factor Intervention Trial (Shekelle et al, 1985) focused on subjects at 'high risk' from CHD by virtue of their smoking, serum cholesterol and blood pressure levels. After being assessed, the men aged between 35 and 57 years were allocated to one of two interventions – usual care or counselling. When the men were followed up an average of seven years later it was found that TAB was not associated with heart disease in either of the treatment groups. Mann and Brennan (1987) obtained similar negative findings with a group of British participants showing evidence of mild hypertension.

With some exceptions the majority of studies of patients who have experienced a heart attack have also found that TAB as assessed after the attack does not predict future heart attacks. Such findings indicate that TAB does not present an additional risk for heart disease in those people who are already at a high risk of the disorder. They suggest that factors which affect the recurrence of heart disease are not necessarily the same as those involved in the development of the disease. Indeed, some authors (e.g. Evans, 1990) have

argued that type 'A's who experience heart disease may be in a better position to modify their lifestyle and change their behaviour, both because they have more scope to do so than type 'B's, but also because the very nature of being type 'A' makes them more likely to do so.

An additional issue concerns the nature of TAB itself. The behaviour consists of a number of dimensions and investigators have tried to determine which of these is the most 'pathogenic' – the one most likely to bring about CHD. The issue has been explored both because of its intrinsic interest and because researchers have thought that it might explain different results in the various studies, especially where different measures had been used to assess TAB. There is evidence that hostility may be the most significant factor in the TAB–CHD relationship. Several studies have specifically addressed this problem. Barefoot et al (1983) followed up 255 physicians who had been assessed for their levels of hostility 25 years earlier. They found that those whose scores were in the top half of the range had five times the incidence of CHD than those in the bottom half of the range. Barefoot et al (1987) reported similar findings in another study with lawyers. In further analysis of the WCGS data, Chesney, Hecker et al (1988) also showed that anger and hostility were the major predictors of CHD. Whilst not all studies have obtained this result, there is sufficient evidence to support the claim that hostility is a major pathogenic element of TAB in the development of CHD.

How does type 'A' behaviour lead to coronary heart disease?

The mechanisms by which TAB contributes to heart disease are not fully understood. One suggestion is that people with TAB may react more strongly at the physiological level to stress. Evidence is available from laboratory studies with animals and research with people. Manuch has carried out a number of studies with monkeys which illustrate this phenomenon. Manuch et al (1989) measured the heart rates of monkeys who had been fed a high-cholesterol diet when they were at rest and when they were stressed by the threat of capture with a large glove. Monkeys who showed high heart rate responses to the stress were more likely to develop atherosclerosis (see page 187) later compared with those monkeys with lower heart rate responses.

Dembroski et al (1978) found that in the early stages of exposure to stress people with TAB show heightened physiological responsiveness compared with type 'B's. If the stress continues then type 'A's show a reduced responsiveness, and sympathetic nervous activity dramatically decreases. Thus type 'A's show a pattern of extreme responses which may lead to damage to the blood vessels and the development of heart disease.

Other research has suggested that TAB may be a *result*, rather than a *cause* of exaggerated neuroendocrine responses (e.g. high blood pressure) to external stressors. For example, Kahn et al (1980) found that type 'A's experienced greater increases in BLOOD PRESSURE when unconscious and undergoing by-pass surgery than did type 'B's. Type 'A's may therefore be more aroused by events generally and their behaviour may be a way of coping with this heightened level of arousal rather than being a factor in its development.

There have also been other studies which have not shown that type 'A's are more reactive to stress than type 'B's (Carroll, 1992). However, there is another possibility. There is some evidence which suggests that type 'A's experience more stressful life events than type 'B's (Byrne, 1981). It is possible that those with a tendency towards TAB may be more likely to put themselves in stressful environments and are therefore more likely to experience stressors. Rather than reacting more strongly, type 'A's may actually experience more stress and challenge and it is this increased level of stress which makes them vulnerable to heart disease.

Reducing type 'A' behaviour

A number of different strategies have been devised to reduce the level of TAB in people with, or at risk of, heart disease. Some programmes focus on training in relaxation and deep breathing in order to reduce the level of arousal that type 'A's experience. Other techniques include the use of guided imagery to alter people's perceptions of stress. A third approach is to change the individual's concept of success and the hard-driving and competitive methods which they use to achieve it. People can also be trained to change specific type 'A' behaviours such as the explosive speech styles or the tendency to react with hostility and impatience to frustrating situations. They can be encouraged to focus on the environment and their reactions to it and then substitute different, less harmful responses.

However, we should also consider the wider context in which TAB occurs. Western culture seems to encourage the development of TAB and to value it. In the business world, people who display ambition, are willing to take on jobs and to get them done under time pressure tend to be rewarded. We must not forget that TAB arises within a social context and is encouraged by a capitalist society. If we wish to modify this behaviour pattern we therefore need to ensure that institutional and cultural factors are taken into account rather than assuming that the issue can be dealt with at the individual level only.

Medical settings – patient–practitioner communication and adherence to treatment

The question as to why we use health services would seem to be a straightforward one. We seek medical help and go to the doctor when we are ill. However, how do we decide when we are ill? When do we think a symptom is serious and when do we decide that it is not important? When do we decide that all we need is a day or so in bed and when do we consider we need advice and treatment from professionals? Psychological factors are therefore important in the decision to use health services for the following reasons:

- they affect the way in which we recognise and interpret symptoms
- they influence whether we label those symptoms as illness
- they influence whether we think the health care service is the best place in which to obtain treatment.

Let's look at each of these three topics in turn.

Recognition of symptoms

The notion that we view our bodies in terms of specific signs and symptoms is not supported by the literature. Research shows that we only view our body in terms of gross physiological responses and that interpretations of these sensations are affected by the context in which they occur. For example, Anderson and Pennebaker (1980) report differences in participants' experience of touching a vibrating board depending on whether they had been told to expect the experience to be a pleasurable one or a painful one. Pennebaker (1982) has conducted a lot of research into people's perception and interpretation of symptoms. He observed that awareness varies considerably from one person to another and that people are less likely to notice symptoms when they are fully involved in a task than when they are bored.

Why consult?

Virtually everyone in the UK visits the doctor with individuals making an average of five consultations a year (Williams, 1970). However, there is considerable variation around this average and much of the illness experienced is never taken to the doctor. Scambler and Scambler (1984) investigated symptom perception in healthy women and found that they visited the doctor once for every 18 symptoms they experienced. They also reported that they consulted family and friends 11 times more often than they consulted the doctor. This difference between the experience of illness and asking for medical advice is referred to as the *illness iceberg* (Last, 1963). There is a lot of illness submerged within the population which never reaches the attention of the medical profession.

What makes people go to the doctor on some occasions and not others? Researchers have established a number of possible reasons. Mechanic (1978) proposed that if individuals cannot explain the symptoms they are experiencing and they think the symptoms may be indicative of some future harm then they will consult a professional. Scambler and Scambler (1984) reported that it was often the result of a 'lay' consultation with

family or friends. If other people considered that the symptoms were serious then the person was more likely to seek medical advice. If there was a change in the nature of the symptom then this was likely to act as a trigger for getting professional help. Ingham and Miller (1986) tried to assess the influence of social and demographic factors on a person's use of the primary care service. They observed that these played a minor role compared with actual experience of symptoms. They concluded that people were more likely to consult if they couldn't say what was causing the problem and if they thought the problem was internally rather than externally caused. People who consult frequently have somewhat different characteristics to those who don't. Robinson and Granfield (1986) found that frequent consulters had a lot of symptoms that tended to recur. However, they were the type of symptoms that are not usually suggestive of major illness and indeed are ones that the majority of people often ignore. In addition, they also take a greater quantity of self-prescribed medication, vitamins and health foods.

The medical consultation

The medical consultation is an interaction with clearly defined expectations. Patients expect to have to describe the problem, to have their problem diagnosed and to be given some form of treatment advice. Patients spend some time working out the best way of presenting their problem to the doctor. Stimson and Webb (1975) carried out an empirical study in which they asked 150 teenagers to write essays on 'going to the doctors'. They found that 55% of the essay consisted of anticipatory work in which they rehearsed what they were going to say to the doctor, either to themselves or to other people, and only 36% of the essay referred to the consultation itself. This rehearsal may help people to present their worries in a coherent way but it may also distort their illness experience and mislead the doctor. Most patients seem very aware of the limited time the doctor has available to deal with them and so this influences the number of problems they feel able to present at any one time.

Doctors are expected to diagnose the problem. Diagnosis is a complex process and it is subject to a range of influences. The doctor generates hypotheses about the possible causes of the symptoms and then tests out these hypotheses, either with further questions, direct examination or other tests. Weinman (1981) proposed that the production and choice of hypotheses within the consultation is influenced by:

- the doctor's own concepts about health problems – whether they consider social or biological factors to be more or less important. The doctor who considers psycho-social factors to be important will be more likely to diagnose stress-related illness and advise behavioural changes than a doctor who is more biologically oriented
- their estimation of the risks of particular diseases occurring and this may be influenced by their direct experience of particular disorders. A mother is more likely to obtain a diagnosis of measles when her child comes out in a rash if there is an epidemic of measles in the community at the time
- the degree of seriousness and treatability of the disease. Doctors tend to carry out a risk analysis of the costs and benefits involved in the choice of a particular diagnosis. Thus the doctor may consider a diagnosis of appendicitis if a child complains of abdominal pain because it is a serious disorder but one which can be easily treated. Not treating it, however, could have very serious consequences
- the doctor's personal knowledge of the patient. The patient's general past medical history and their previous pattern of consulting will be taken into account. A patient who has a history of frequently consulting the doctor is probably taken less seriously than a patient who seldom attends the surgery.

Issues of communication

Effective communication is essential to good care. Often patients assess the competence of the doctor on criteria based on interpersonal factors rather than on the accuracy of their diagnosis and treatment advice. This may be because we do not really have the knowledge to make an informed judgement on the doctor's advice. We are therefore more likely to judge the quality of care according to whether our symptoms have disappeared, which may not always be directly related to treatment, or by whether we liked the doctor. If doctors are seen as warm and caring, patients are more likely to express satisfaction with the technical aspects of care (Ben-Sira, 1976; 1980). Good communication between patient and practitioner is therefore critical to patient satisfaction.

Empirical findings suggest that a number of factors are important in the communication process (see Taylor, 1991):

- the setting is important. The nature of the medical interview itself may affect the communication process. Patients consulting the doctor are often highly anxious. Anxiety however, interferes with the ability to learn. It makes it more difficult to concentrate and to process the information. Thus patients may be less likely to take in information and to retain it
- the practitioner's use of jargon and technical language may distance the doctor from the patient. Patients may experience depersonalisation where they do not feel they are being treated as an individual. There is some evidence that patients are not very knowledgeable about their anatomy whilst doctors often do not realise the extent to which they use words which are unfamiliar to the lay person
- patients have a different agenda from that of the doctor. They are more concerned with their experience and are more likely to focus on factors such as the pain, discomfort and limitations in their activities associated with their symptoms. However, doctors are more concerned with the underlying illness and its severity. Thus patients may not consider important aspects that the doctor concentrates on and may therefore not listen, or assume that the doctor has made an incorrect diagnosis
- patients may fear that they have a serious illness and therefore unconsciously withhold relevant information or give faulty clues to the nature of the problem. The response of the doctor may therefore support their belief that if there was anything seriously wrong the doctor

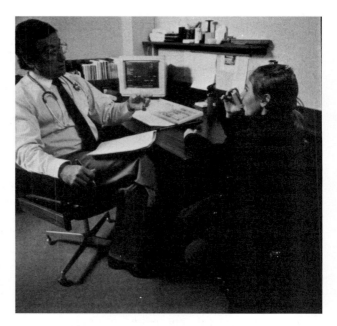

Good doctor-patient communication is essential. Taking time to make sure that the patient understands how to administer the drug is crucial if the treatment is to be effective.

would not tell them anyway. Doctors may assume that if the patient does not ask they do not want the information and therefore they don't give it to them

■ patients' knowledge or prior experience of the disorder is also important. Those who have had the illness before or who don't think that it is serious are less likely to misunderstand and more likely to retain the information.

The consequences of faulty communication between practitioner and patient can be considerable. Patients are less likely to use the health service in future which could pose a threat for their health and well-being. They may also change doctors or even make a formal complaint. Perhaps the most well-known and investigated consequence is that of patient non-compliance or non-adherence to medical advice. It is to this issue of not following doctors' instructions which we now turn.

The issue of non-adherence/non-compliance

The problem of NON-ADHERENCE or non-compliance to treatment advice is a genuine concern. At the least non-adherence can be costly in terms of wasted time, wasted medication and use of hospital facilities. It can also be life-threatening and have adverse consequences for the health of the patient. Non-compliance may happen at any stage of the consultation process. It may include a failure to keep surgery or hospital appointments; a failure to obtain the medication prescribed or to take or complete the course; or a failure to follow prescribed treatment regimes like changes in diet or exercise behaviour.

Non-adherence is a significant problem in all areas of therapeutic practice. For example, Stanton (1987) found that up to 46% of patients with hypertension took less than 80% of their prescribed medicine. Hoelscher et al (1986) reported that only 32% of the 50 patients who were instructed in a stress management programme practised relaxation daily as they had been advised.

There are a number of difficulties in assessing the degree of non-compliance. SELF-REPORT MEASURES are unreliable. Often patients will not admit that they have not followed advice and doctors may overestimate the degree to which patients carry out their instructions because they do not wish to admit to a lack of authority. Often the patient does not return so the doctor assumes that they have got better because of the treatment they prescribed. More objective measures also have associated problems. Counting the number of pills only tells you that the pills have gone. It doesn't say where they went or whether they were taken at the appropriate times. Urine tests can be carried out to assess the amount of the drug in the system but this only tells you that the patient took the drug before the test, not whether they have been taking the medication appropriately in the long term. This is also a very costly and intrusive check and is not appropriate for all drugs.

We tend to assume that the issue is the same for all patients. However, Harvey (1988) suggests that the problem is quite complex. He proposes that there are three types of non-adherence:

- *deliberate* or *volitional* non-adherence where patients choose not to follow advice perhaps because the psychological or financial cost is too great
- *accidental* non-adherence where the patient forgets or perhaps does not understand what is expected. The treatment regime may be so complex that they cannot follow it accurately
- *circumstantial* non-adherence where the nature of the treatment itself may discourage patients from continuing – i.e. there may be unpleasant or severe side-effects.

What determines non-adherence and how can adherence be improved?

Taylor (1991) proposes that several factors are relevant to non-adherence. They include whether or not the person has made a decision to comply, the patient's understanding of the treatment, the nature of the treatment regime itself and a range of individual, social and demographic factors:

- Doctors tend to assume that patients will follow their advice. However, patients are not passive and take active decisions to follow such advice. The application of the health belief model (Rosenstock, 1974 and see page 174) to the problem of non-adherence would suggest that a patient's readiness to follow the treatment regime would be determined by:
  - their perceived severity of the disease and their perceived susceptibility to the disease. Thus if patients do not consider the disease to be serious, the model would predict that they will be less likely to comply than if they considered the problem to be severe
  - whether the costs, including disruption to routine, side-effects, unpleasantness of the treatment, are high compared with the benefits – if this is the case the model would then propose that patients will be less likely to adhere to the treatment.
- Patients' understanding of the treatment regime. If a patient does not understand the treatment then they will not follow it appropriately. Ley (1988) argues that adherence is highest when the patient acquires a jargon-free account of the diagnosis, the causes and the treatment regime. Studies show that patients regularly misunderstand or forget 50% of the information given to them. Ley summarised many studies on patient memory and forgetting and found that 44% of what is told to patients in general practice is forgotten and 50% of what was told to in-patients and out-patients at hospital was not remembered.
- Patient satisfaction appears to be important, but Ley cautions that there are insufficient studies to warrant gross generalisations. However, the evidence available suggests that adherence is more likely when satisfaction is high. Patients are more likely to adhere when their expectations are being met, when the doctor is warm and caring, willing to allow them to ask questions and displays little impatience with them.
- Qualities of the treatment regime. Adherence is less likely when treatment is lengthy, complex and interferes with the patient's lifestyle. Advice is less likely to be followed if the patient is asked to change behavioural factors such as diet, level of exercise, smoking, etc.
- Social and psychological factors. Some demographic characteristics are relevant to adherence. Thus women and older people are more compliant in following the details of the prescribed treatments. The presence of social stressors is likely to reduce adherence. Whilst many doctors refer to individual characteristics as a most important factor in adherence there is very little empirical evidence to support this contention.

There are a number of ways in which the problem of non-compliance can be reduced. Improving the health service at the point of delivery, such as reducing waiting times and giving people specific times for their appointments, has increased attendance rates. Improvements in practitioner–patient communication can be helped by providing practitioners with opportunities to attend courses on how to communicate more effectively. Involving the family can help to support the treatment programme – family members can remind patients to carry out their treatment and they can help to integrate changes or activities associated with the treatment regime into family life so that patients find it easier to carry out the regime. External self-help groups are especially effective in promoting adherence as they involve a public commitment to change, members can learn from each other and they can provide each other with emotional support (for a review, see Taylor, 1991).

Pain and pain management

The relationship between injury and PAIN does not appear to be a direct one. Pain can occur in the absence of any noxious stimuli or tissue (bodily) damage and people's experience of pain in relation to similar levels of damage may also differ. Thus we must also consider factors other than direct physiological ones in pain perception.

Evidence for pain without obvious injury can be found in the syndromes of *neuralgia*, *causalgia* and *phantom limb pain*.

- *Neuralgia* comprises spontaneous stabbing or shooting pains along a nerve pathway without any obvious cause. Light touches such as a breeze may set it off.
- *Causalgia* comprises recurring episodes of severe, burning pains which may initially originate at the site of an old wound. However, the pain continues long after the wound has healed and indeed the pain may get worse and spread away from the initial area. It too may be set off by slight stimuli.
- *Phantom limb pain* offers a third example of pain without apparent damage. People who have had limbs amputated report feeling sensations as though the limb was still there and many report feeling pain in the amputated limb. Bakal (1979) observed that 5–10% of amputees have pain that persists and even becomes worse over time.

It is possible that pain could arise from damage to the neural pathways prior to amputation. Similar explanations could be made for neuralgia and causalgia. However, still unexplained is the question of why patients who suffer from obvious

Rugby players seldom notice pain associated with tackles such as this one until the excitement of the game is over.

neural damage do not develop such pain syndromes.

There is also evidence that social and psychological factors may be important in the perception
of pain. The context or the meaning that one
ascribes to the situation in which pain occurs may
affect the amount of pain experienced or at least
reported. For example, many people playing sports
have not realised that they have been injured until
the game is over. It is only then that they begin to
experience pain.

An early study by Beecher in 1956 reported differences in the use of medication for similar types
of injury for two different groups of patients. In
the Second World War Beecher treated soldiers
who had been severely wounded in a field hospital.
Only 49% of the soldiers claimed to be in severe or
moderate pain and only 32% requested medication when it was offered. He later carried out a
similar study with civilians with similar though
somewhat less severe types of injuries. He found
that 75% of the civilians reported experiencing
severe or moderate pain and 83% of them requested medication when it was offered to them.
Beecher explained these different findings in
terms of the meaning that the situation had for
the two groups. For the soldiers, the injuries
meant that they could legitimately leave an
unpleasant situation, they had survived and could
now look forward to going home. For the civilians
the injury was the beginning of their problems
and was a major disruption in their lives. It was
also possible that the soldiers were expected to 'act
tough' suggesting that cognitive factors influence
the experience of pain.

There is also evidence that cultural factors are
involved in the experience of pain. For example, a
very early study by Zborowski (1958) tested the
pain threshold of members of four different cultural groups – old Americans, Jews, Irish and
Italians – living in the USA. He first of all established their pain threshold, the level of intensity of
an electric shock which they considered to be
painful. He noted that Jews and Italians reported a
lower pain threshold than the old Americans or
Irish. The old Americans were quite accepting and
matter-of-fact about their pain, the Irish were
quite stoical whilst the Jews and the Italians reacted more emotionally. Zborowski concluded that

cultural norms must be taken into account if one
was to fully understand the experience of pain.

Such studies support the notion that factors
other than simply sensory ones are involved in the
perception of pain and that cognitive and emotional factors modify the experience of pain.

How can we explain pain?

A number of theories have been proposed to
explain pain. Early theories, such as *specificity
theory* and *pattern theory* could not account for
the role of psychological factors which had been
seen to influence the perception of pain. They
could not explain PLACEBO EFFECTS, such as occur
when patients show improvement when they are
only given inert substances not active drug therapy (see Appendix 2). Neither could they account
for hypnosis or for the effects of distraction on
pain perception. Such phenomena led to the
development of the GATE CONTROL THEORY (Melzack
and Wall, 1965). The experience of pain requires
both stimulation from the pain receptors on the
skin and the activation of a 'neural gate' which
can be opened or closed to a greater or lesser
extent and which controls the degree to which
incoming pain signals are transmitted to the
brain. The gate must be open for the person to
experience pain. Certain fibres carry messages
such as temperature and pressure from the skin,
and other fibres carry pain information. When
stimulation is largely from the skin senses, then
the gate is closed and pain information is not
transmitted onwards. When stimulation is largely
by the pain fibres, then the gate remains open and
pain messages are transmitted to the brain. This
explains why rubbing the affected area when we
have hurt ourselves reduces the amount of pain
we experience. The gate can also be influenced by
messages sent down from the brain so that mental
states, such as excitement or anxiety, can affect
the intensity of the sensation.

Assessment of pain

Because pain is a very subjective experience, not
directly accessible to the clinician or researcher, it
is quite difficult to measure. Patients find open-
ended questions such as 'what is the pain like?' or
'how bad is it?' very difficult to respond to. They

very often lack a language in which to express their pain. A number of methods have therefore been devised to assess pain systematically. These include rating scales using a five-point scale from 'not at all' to 'a great deal' to describe how much pain patients are under. However, pain is a multi-dimensional experience. It may vary in intensity or have different qualities. Melzack and Torgerson (1971) asked people to sort words which described types of pain into different piles that reflected different aspects of the pain experience. Three types of categories emerged. One set of words described the sensory aspects of the pain such as 'burning', 'shooting', 'sharp'. A second group of words referred to the emotional dimension of pain and included words such as 'terrifying', 'annoying', 'sickening', and 'tiring'. The third dimension reflected the evaluative experience of pain and related to its intensity. Words in this category included 'mild', 'distressing', 'unbearable'. This formed the basis for the development of the *McGill Pain Questionnaire* (Melzack, 1975). It comprises 78 adjectives arranged into 20 groups which reflect different aspects of the pain experience. The scale enables the clinician to obtain an objective measure of the patient's pain.

Assessment of pain behaviour

We can distinguish between the experience of pain and the public evidence of pain. Pain behaviour may vary from one person to another and it can be assessed in a number of different ways. Thus behaviours such as the amount of time the patient spends lying down, grimacing, sighing, talking about their pain can be measured and provide an indication of the degree of pain the individual is experiencing. Turk, Wack and Kerns (1985) distinguished four different types of PAIN BEHAVIOURS. They include:

- facial or audible expressions of distress or discomfort such as moaning, grimacing, clenching one's teeth
- distorted movement or posture such as when one moves in a way which protects part of the body – limping, etc
- displaying negative emotions or feelings such as irritability
- avoiding activity such as when people sit down

frequently or lie down during the day or stop doing normal activities.

Pain behaviours may not reflect the actual degree of pain experienced. Pain behaviours may be strengthened or reinforced by family members or others. People may exaggerate their expressions of pain because they do not feel that others take their pain seriously. Such behaviour can rapidly become part of the person's lifestyle.

Pain behaviours can be reinforced when they are associated with benefits or secondary gain. The person in pain may be excused certain activities such as tasks around the house or even going to work. When the person did not enjoy doing these things originally then pain behaviour is reinforced. In addition, people who suffer from pain receive attention and care from family and friends. This provides social reinforcement for the expression of pain behaviour. Flor, Kerns and Turk (1987) examined the relationship between the degree of solicitousness shown by spouses and the expression of pain behaviours. They found that the more solicitous the spouse was the more pain behaviour the patient showed and the less active he or she was. Showing care and concern is an important part of family life but this evidence suggests that when family members are solicitous without encouraging well behaviours there is a risk that the patient will be encouraged to remain sick. Reduced levels of activity may result in reduced levels of physical ability as muscles atrophy or waste away. In turn this may lead to more pain and even less activity.

The management of pain

Acute, short episodes of pain usually present us with few problems. We take a couple of aspirins or stoically wait until it goes. However, chronic pain or severe pain which keeps recurring is a different matter. Historically pain has been managed by medication and surgery, but increasing recognition of the part played by psychological factors in pain and pain relief has led to a greater involvement of health (and clinical) psychologists in pain management. Techniques with a high psychological element include biofeedback, relaxation, distraction, guided imagery, hypnosis and acupuncture. The placebo also has a recognised place in pain management.

Biofeedback techniques

BIOFEEDBACK is a method of obtaining control over bodily processes. It consists of a number of techniques which provide information or feedback to the patient of some bodily process of which the patient is usually unaware. It uses the principle of OPERANT CONDITIONING (see Appendix 1) to gain control over a particular body function. Thus in the initial stage a specific function such as blood pressure is targeted. The pressure may be converted into a tone so that the patient may monitor it more easily. The patient then has to change the bodily process and through trial and error begins to understand what factors will modify the blood pressure. The patient may become quite effective at controlling a previously automatic physiological function. It is assumed that once they have learned what processes are effective they will no longer need to rely on the technology.

Biofeedback has been used successfully with pain conditions, especially tension headaches and migraines. However, in their review, Turk, Meichenbaum and Berman (1979) concluded that whilst biofeedback reduces the muscle tension headaches and reduces the severity of migraines, alternative methods such as muscle relaxation produce similar results. As muscle relaxation is a more cost-effective method and one more easily implemented, and as the active component in biofeedback has yet to be firmly established, it can be argued that other techniques should be used first.

Relaxation techniques

A variety of relaxation techniques are employed with pain patients. Initially such techniques were developed for use with anxiety patients (Wolpe, 1958), as discussed in the clinical psychology chapter. Thus one rationale for using relaxation in pain management is to reduce patients' level of anxiety which can be a factor in the experience of pain. In addition, relaxation may directly affect a physiological process, such as muscle tension, which is responsible for the pain. Relaxation strategies focus on moving the individual into a lower state of arousal and can be achieved through instructions which guide the individual towards

relaxing each part of the body. Controlling the breathing through encouraging the patient to take longer and deeper breaths is another way of reducing arousal levels and inducing relaxation. Studies have indicated that relaxation training can achieve modest effects with some acute pains (see review by Turk et al, 1979) but that it may not be sufficient by itself to control all types of pain, especially chronic pain.

Cognitive techniques

COGNITIVE THERAPIES (see the clinical psychology chapter) address the thoughts which people experience with pain. When researchers have asked people what they think about when experiencing pain, some, but not all, focus on the pain and the discomfort (Turk and Rudy, 1986). However, many people use cognitive strategies to alter their experience. Brown, O'Keefe, Sanders and Baker (1986) found that by the age of ten, some children were using cognitive strategies such as trying to think of something else or telling themselves to 'be brave' to reduce dental pain. A range of cognitive strategies is available. It includes SOMATIZATION or focusing on the pain. Here the person is told to focus on the part of the body which is in pain but to try to analyse the sensations rationally and objectively. Also included are ATTENTION DIVERSION STRATEGIES which involve attending to other factors in the environment such as looking at pictures or out of the window, or concentrating on activities such as singing a song or doing maths problems. Such strategies are particularly useful in coping with acute pain, and distraction may be useful for chronic pain patients in specific situations, such as when they need to move.

Imagery

IMAGERY is another strategy which involves attempting to reduce discomfort by imagining a mental scene which is unconnected to and incompatible with the pain. Usually people think of a scene which is pleasant or which means something special to them. The patient is encouraged to use all of his or her senses – to smell the flowers, hear the birds singing, feel the sunshine, etc. As with attention diversion techniques, imagery appears to be more successful when it fully engages the person and when the pain is mild or moderate (Turk, Meichenbaum and Genest, 1983).

Pain redefinition

A further strategy of pain control is that of pain redefinition. Here patients are asked to control their emotive thoughts about the pain and the implications of the pain and substitute more realistic and constructive thoughts. The provision of realistic information for medical or surgical pro-cedures can also help to reduce the patient's pain and discomfort through addressing their misconceptions and exaggerated concerns.

In summary a number of behavioural and cognitive methods are available to help people to manage acute and chronic pain. Such strategies seem most effective when used in combination.

THE FUTURE OF HEALTH PSYCHOLOGY

The contribution of health psychology is still in its infancy and its role is still developing. Health psychologists throughout Europe and the United States envisage a much more extended role for their expertise in the development and provision of health care in the future. Health psychologists have much to offer at a variety of levels including those of the individual, the group, the community and that of regional and national health policy-making, and it is anticipated that their contribution will increase markedly over the next few years.

Weinman (1990) argues that in order to meet the World Health Organisation challenge of providing 'health for all' in the year 2000 (WHO, 1981), health psychologists will need to produce high-quality research which clearly identifies those individual behaviours and social conditions which present risks to health. In addition, they will need to contribute to the creation of a social and cultural climate in which individuals find it easier to make positive health choices. By acting indirectly through politicians, local communities, food manufacturers and suppliers, health psychologists could contribute to a change which supports health-promoting decisions. Through, for example, attention to research demonstrating environmental risk factors to health, psychologists may be able to effect changes in government and business organisations resulting in decreased risks to health.

Weinman also points out that recent trends in medicine have implications for the developing role of health psychology. Taking the salient issue of HIV/AIDS, he shows how health psychologists can contribute to raising public awareness of the disease and promoting change in risk behaviours associated with the spread of the disease. In addition, there is evidence of the importance of psychosocial factors in the progression of the disease. By carrying out research assessing the extent to which psychosocial variables are relevant, and developing psychological interventions, health psychologists may contribute to a reduction in the physical and emotional distress of those with the disease. Other areas of medicine present similar opportunities for contributions from health psychologists; the implications of developments in genetic screening create a need to help people make sense of and cope with the information provided. Developments in medical technology which enable people to survive for longer bring into focus the need to consider quality rather than quantity of life issues. Health psychologists have a contribution to make here in the attempt to identify those features which constitute life quality and the means by which they can be assessed.

All such developments have implications for the training of health psychologists. Those currently working within health psychology have had little specialist training. However, to effect those changes and developments outlined above it will be necessary to provide a professional base for psychologists. Such training and resulting qualifications will also serve to enhance the credibility of health psychologists working with other professionals within the health field. As we noted earlier, the beginnings of such training can be seen in the introduction of health psychology courses in undergraduate psychology degrees and in the development of health psychology degrees at Masters level. The establishment of training courses for a professional qualification for health psychologists is on the agenda in many countries in Europe and elsewhere. In addition, the provision of training for other health professionals is also of importance and health psychology must become a part of a core curriculum for these groups.

Whilst this chapter hopefully has given you an indication of the importance and relevance of health psychology to health we must perhaps finish it with a note of caution. Health psychology is a new discipline. As such its knowledge base is still relatively limited and it is important that high-quality research is produced to extend our understanding of the relevance of psychological and social factors in health and illness. In addition, the aims and methods of health psychology are still poorly understood by other health professionals, and increasing that understanding is highly important to the development of the discipline. So too is effective professional training. As Weinman (1990) says, these are the key tasks for health psychology in the 1990s.

FURTHER RECOMMENDED READING

Carroll, D. (1992) *Health Psychology: Stress, Behaviour and Disease*. London: Falmer Press.

Sarafino, E. P. (1993) *Health Psychology: Biopsychosocial Interactions*. New York: John Wiley.

Stroebe, W. and Stroebe, M. S. (1995) *Social Psychology and Health*. Buckingham: Open University Press.

exercises

1. Devise an attitude scale which measures either adolescent or adult views on smoking. Themes which you might consider including in the measure could reflect health risks, pleasure obtained, discomfort or pollution, cost, etc. Then administer the scale to a group of smokers and a group of non-smokers. You will need to consider how to define a smoker – especially if you are using an adolescent population – and ensure that the group of smokers and non-smokers are comparable in other ways, such as age, sex, social class, education, etc. Discuss your findings with your class or other co-learners. Did you observe a difference in the attitudes of smokers to non-smokers? How can you explain your findings?

2. There are many examples of health promotion messages available either in written form such as leaflets or in a visual medium such as film or TV. Try to obtain some examples. Good places to start are your local health centre or doctors, local dentist's surgery, the schools health education service, even television adverts, and, further afield, the Health Education Authority or the national charities involved with cancer and/or heart disease. Try to get a range of examples and then analyse them to determine the basis of their appeals for behavioural change. Are they based on fear or social factors such as resisting peer-pressure, etc. Which do think would be more effective and why? How do they relate to the psychological models introduced in the chapter?

3. Lazarus (1984) defines 'hassles' as 'experiences and conditions of daily living that have been appraised as salient and harmful or threatening to the endorser's well-being' (p. 376) and 'uplifts' as 'experiences and conditions of daily living that have

been appraised as salient and positive or favourable to the endorser's well-being' (p. 376). Create a list of 'hassles' and 'uplifts' relevant to you and your peers. How does your list compare with those of your class or other co-learners? Do the hassles fall into different domains – e.g. school and work, family, financial issues, physical health, etc. What others have you found? Is this the case for uplifts? How do your combined hassles and uplifts compare with those included in respective scales by Kanner et al (1981)? What reasons might there be for any differences or similarities observed?

4. Imagine that you have a particular health complaint and you have made an appointment to see your doctor. You may wish to draw on your own experience by recalling a previous illness which involved a visit to the doctor's surgery or you may prefer to create an imaginary illness episode. Write an essay describing 'going to the doctors'. Compare your essay with those of others in your class or learning group. What themes can you detect? How do your findings compare with those of Stimson and Webb (1975)?

5. Recall an episode of pain which you have experienced. It may have been a headache, a toothache, a result of a fall or a more serious injury or illness. Try to describe the phenomenon – its nature, intensity, location, etc – to another member of your group. What type of words did you use? What difficulties did you encounter? What implications does this have for patient care? Then pool your findings with those of others in your group. Can you distinguish different dimensions of pain as reflected in the range of words used to describe it? You might also like to compare your findings with those of Melzack (1975) and examine the McGill Pain Questionnaire which resulted from his research.

7 OCCUPATIONAL PSYCHOLOGY

Whenever we meet new people, especially at parties, one almost inevitable question we are asked is about what we do for a living. If you try giving different answers to this question, such as unemployed, student, teacher, salesperson, etc., watch carefully how people react. The different reactions will perhaps make you wonder why we attach so much importance to what people do and who they work for. Should we be surprised by the fact that our work plays an important role in how others see us? Not really. The reason our work influences how people see us is partly because work plays an important part in our lives. Whether we like it or not, for most people, work occupies the largest proportion of waking time. It determines part of our social circle as well as the social status we have within it. A lot of the people we know, for example, are likely to be in the same line of work as ourselves. Furthermore, because of the central role work plays in our lives, it should not be surprising that an independent branch of psychology devoted to the study of how people behave at work has developed.

WHAT IS OCCUPATIONAL PSYCHOLOGY?

This area can be known as WORK PSYCHOLOGY, ORGANISATIONAL PSYCHOLOGY or OCCUPATIONAL PSYCHOLOGY. We shall generally use the term 'occupational psychologist' when referring to psychologists working in this area since this is the title of the British Psychological Society's division. The subject may be referred to by any of the three terms depending on the topic. It is concerned with the study of behaviour in work settings and aims to discover the capabilities, the needs, the attitudes and any other factors which affect people's work behaviour. It investigates:

- why people behave differently at work (e.g. some work hard and some will try to do as little work as possible)
- how people affect and are affected by the behaviour of other people around them (their co-workers, their managers etc.)
- how people are affected by the type of work they do (simple and boring work, complex and challenging work etc.)
- how people are affected by conditions in which they have to do their work (temperature, noise, management policies, supervision and so on).

We might look at a couple of definitions given in other texts. Riggio (1990) defines work or organisational psychology as:

> 'the branch of psychology that is concerned with the study of behaviour in work settings and the application of psychological principles to changing work behaviour'.

The 'application of psychological principles ...' emphasises that it is practical. Occupational psychologists study work behaviour not only for the sake of knowledge, but also to manage real-life, work-related problems. Other authors would stress that occupational psychology is a *scientific study*. Gregory and Burroughs (1989) define it as 'the scientific study of work behaviour in work organisations'. They explain further that work organisations 'include both goods-producing industries ... and service organisations'. It is unclear whether non-profit-making organisations are included in these categories but the study of work behaviour in voluntary organisations is just as important as it is in non-voluntary ones.

Growth and change in occupational psychology

Occupational psychology has experienced very rapid growth. The technological revolution which is sweeping the world of work in offices and in factories is reshaping the nature of jobs. In contrast with manual jobs of the first half of the century, today's jobs are becoming increasingly complex in nature, whilst simple jobs become computerised. Many of today's jobs are computer-based and require, not strength, but people with an ability to process large amounts of information and who are capable of making effective decisions. Hence the need to understand cognitive processes such as perception, cognition and decision-making is stronger than it has ever been. In addition, new technology brings social changes. Where once a job was for life, a worker might now be retrained several times, but technology can also produce unemployment and the disappearance of once valuable skills. The occupational psychologist might work with problems caused by any of these changes.

Principle characteristics of occupational psychology

Occupational psychology could be said to possess the following principle characteristics:

- it recognises the importance of *individual differences*; people are different and have different occupational needs and abilities
- it recognises that the factors which affect work behaviour are numerous and often *complex* and *interdependent*
- its approach to understanding and resolving work-related problems is *scientific*, i.e., based on the collection, analysis and interpretation of empirical data (see Appendix 2)
- it looks at problems from a variety of angles or *theoretical viewpoints*; it uses a *combination* of approaches to problem-solving as opposed to simplistic solutions
- research, theory and practice are closely related; apart from the application of mainstream theory to work problems, practice results also feed back into theory in the same way as in other applied areas and as described in chapter 1.

Sub-divisions of work and organisational psychology

Like many other writers, Riggio (1990) subdivides occupational psychology into three main sub-areas:

- PERSONNEL PSYCHOLOGY
- ORGANISATIONAL PSYCHOLOGY
- HUMAN FACTORS PSYCHOLOGY (also known as *human engineering* or *engineering psychology* in the US and ERGONOMICS in the UK).

For some writers the list would also include *vocational* and *career counselling, organisational*

The development of efficient, computerised human imitators has had enormous impact on the nature of work for humans.

development, and *industrial relations* (Muchinsky, 1993).

Personnel psychology

One can very easily identify the issues that this sub-area deals with and arrive at a definition by scanning one of the volumes of *Personnel Psychology*, a leading specialist journal. The area focuses on the individual in the organisation and includes: recruitment, selection, appraisal of work performance, training, promotion, and (more recently) career guidance and counselling. The activities of recruitment and selection of employees are considered the cornerstone of personnel psychology, though training is now almost equal in importance. Most of the work undertaken in personnel selection is based on *psychological testing* and JOB ANALYSIS which we shall look at in some detail further on. Over the last two decades personnel selection has regained some of its popularity. Recent advances in research and theory have enabled the development of better recruitment practices and more accurate selection methods. The effects these advances have had on other areas such as career guidance/counselling and training have been similarly positive.

Organisational psychology

The fact that organisations are primarily social entities means that organisational psychology has a social orientation. This area concerns the interaction between the individual and the work organisation. Here, attention is focused on how the individual is affected by the social and the physical work environments of the employing organisations. This area addresses two major questions:

■ how do people adapt to, and influence, their work and organisation; how do organisations socialise their new members, i.e. what do they do to ensure that new members accept organisational values and work to achieve organisational goals?
■ what combination of organisational characteristics is most likely to lead to high levels of employee satisfaction, motivation, commitment and innovation?

Human factors psychology

This sub-area evolved partly from experimental psychology and partly from industrial engineering. Many of the principles used today to design jobs that suit human capabilities have emerged from experimental psychologists' laboratory experiments. It was firmly established as a distinct area of study during the Second World War and concerned itself with the study of *human behaviour*, *technology* and *the interaction between the two*. Occupational psychologists specialising in these areas seek to understand human capabilities and limitations by conducting experiments on cognitive and physiological processes such as perception, memory and decision-making. Physiological experiments can be carried out to study the effects of noise, temperature, drugs, meals, night-shift work and other similar factors on work performance. Psychologists also seek to understand the working and behaviour of technological products such as computers and robots by carrying out experiments and surveys, or by observing how human operators interact with different technological systems and how they perform their work on such systems. One example of this would be to assess under experimental conditions how well a group of students perform the same task on two different computers and with different software. Results can then be used to design better computers and better software. The disciplines on which human factors draws are:

- human anatomy
- human physiology
- anthropometry – the study of the size and proportions of the human body
- biological psychology
- experimental psychology.

They also work in close collaboration with industrial, electronic, mechanical and computer software engineers. Human factors specialists advise new technology manufacturers on the design of products that will not exceed the physical and mental capabilities of human operators. They also advise work organisations on the reduction of error and accident rates, and on increasing work efficiency which, besides improving productivity, will improve the quality of working life of the workforce through a better match between person, job and environment. Positive work experiences, as will be seen later, lead to job satisfaction, work motivation and commitment to the organisation.

Interdependence of the three areas

It should be clear from the above descriptions that the three main areas cannot be separated in practice. Selecting the best qualified people may not solve every problem within an organisation because even these people can perform poorly if morale, satisfaction and motivation are low, or if work equipment breaks too often despite regular and careful maintenance. Organisational problems are usually complex and their causes are *interdependent* so that it is hardly likely that a solution can be found within a single area of occupational psychology. Any step to remedy a problem, if taken without consideration of other effects, can make a bad situation worse. Organisations are becoming aware that simple, quickly thought out changes can be ineffective. Many organisations are opting for a company-wide change programme, for instance by changing the whole *value and belief system* (the ORGANISATIONAL CULTURE – see below). The organisational culture change programmes at ICL (Mayo, 1990) and at Nissan UK (Drennan, 1989) are examples.

WHAT DO OCCUPATIONAL PSYCHOLOGISTS DO?

Occupational psychologists are by definition concerned with the human side of work. They seek to understand the factors which may affect the performance both of individuals and organisations.

They apply their scientific knowledge and methods to improve organisational effectiveness and promote well-being at work. Occupational psychologists tackle issues of importance to individuals, groups, organisations and to society in general. They can therefore be found working in business and government organisations, in academic institutions, in consulting firms or as independent consultants. The list of services which might be offered is long and examples grouped by the main areas are given in Box 1.

As can be seen from Box 1, the work of individual occupational psychologists can differ in terms of what it focuses on, the type of activity involved or both. The focus can be on the *individual*, as in career guidance or stress management, or on the *organisation*, as in industrial relations or organi-

sational development. The type of work carried out is determined primarily by the *expertise* and *competence* of the occupational psychologist. The BPS Code of Conduct states that psychologists shall 'recognise the boundaries of their own competence and not attempt to practise any form of psychology for which they do not have an appropriate preparation or, where applicable, specialist qualification' (see Appendix 3).

Not all occupational psychologists are involved directly in the application of psychology at work. They all contribute to the achievement of the overall goals described earlier but their contributions come in different forms and under different roles. Only brief descriptions of the main roles which occupational psychologists assume will be given here. For further information contact the

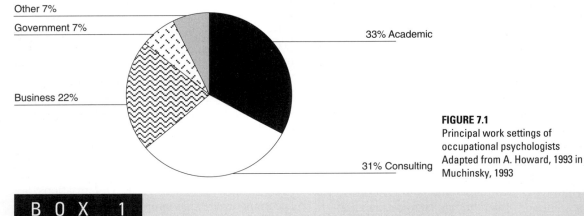

Other 7%
Government 7%
Business 22%
33% Academic
31% Consulting

FIGURE 7.1
Principal work settings of occupational psychologists
Adapted from A. Howard, 1993 in Muchinsky, 1993

BOX 1

Services offered by occupational psychologists

PERSONNEL PSYCHOLOGY	ORGANISATIONAL PSYCHOLOGY	HUMAN FACTORS PSYCHOLOGY
Personnel selection and assessment	Group and inter-group processes	Job design/re-design
Vocational guidance and counselling	Attitude and opinion surveys	Ergonomics and equipment design
Training design and evaluation	Industrial relations	Occupational health and safety
Career choice and development	Organisational change, development and culture	Design and management of new technology
Equal opportunity at work	QUALITY OF WORKING LIFE (QWL)	
Performance appraisal	Leadership and management	

British Psychological Society whose address is given in chapter 1.

The occupational psychologist as an academic or researcher

A number of occupational psychologists work in academic institutions and business or management schools. Their main role within these institutions is to train future occupational psychologists or managers especially those specialising in 'human resources' (people). They teach on courses in applied psychology, organisational behaviour and human resource management offered at undergraduate and post-graduate levels or on short courses for managers. Using their expertise in matters such as training, assessment and evaluation, some may play an active role in planning, developing, assessing and evaluating vocational courses such as those which lead to a National Vocational Qualification (NVQ). The amount of time spent on research varies from one institution to another but most, if not all, occupational psychologists devote a proportion of their time to it. They may also act as supervisors for research students training in occupational psychology.

The occupational psychologist as a company employee

In the UK, occupational psychologists are employed by large organisations such as the Post Office, British Telecom, the Civil Service and the army. Their role is to assess and evaluate the effects of work practices and policies on employees and on their organisation. Work of this kind is carried out as a preventative measure (preventing organisational problems from occurring) or as a 'treatment' (identifying the causes of an unpredicted problem and finding an effective solution). Psychologists working in business and govern-

ment organisations devise selection procedures, design and run training programmes, in-company attitude/stress surveys and so on. They are likely to occupy posts as 'human resources director', 'head of training', or 'head of personnel'.

The occupational psychologist as a consultant

The role of the occupational psychologist as consultant is, in some respects, more complex than the other roles. The psychologist works as an independent adviser charging a fee for specific projects. In addition to being competent in what they do, consultants have to establish the expectations that client organisations have of them. This requires consultants to have highly developed interpersonal skills, avoiding possible conflicts which may arise from differences in perceptions and attitudes between them and their client. The relevance and acceptability of the services offered to the client will depend heavily on the quality of the information exchange between the two parties. The client must be willing to disclose any information relevant to the issues being addressed. Without a complete picture of the problem the consultant is unlikely to achieve a thorough understanding of the problem at hand, its context or its possible causes and the consultation process is unlikely to succeed.

Understanding of, and adherence to ethical principles are critically important. In order to maintain integrity and impartiality occupational psychologists must think very carefully about the possible impact of their actions on people other than those paying for the services being offered. It is possible that a client or some interest groups may seek to manipulate and use the consultant to achieve some hidden agenda, such as a report on individual workers to aid decisions about who should be made redundant. This is why the most complex stage of the consultation process is the *contracting stage* where expectations about objectives and the manner in which these are to be achieved must be clearly laid down. Among other things, it is at this stage that issues regarding confidentiality must be addressed. Where a consultant has been approached to survey the attitudes of the workforce towards management, the consultant's report to management *must not* convey information about, or detrimental to, individual workers.

BOX 2

How would I become an occupational psychologist?

The BPS is the professional body responsible for regulating and overseeing the practice of occupational psychology through its occupational psychology division. Only those recognised by the training committee of this division may use the Chartered Occupational Psychologist title. To qualify for this title you would need a first qualification in psychology that is recognised for graduate membership of the BPS and eligibility for membership of the Division of Occupational Psychology. This is obtained by:

- obtaining a BPS recognised postgraduate qualification in occupational psychology
- acquiring at least two years of successful practice under the supervision of a Chartered Occupational Psychologist.

There are four-year degrees at Hull, Nottingham and Wales (Cardiff) which include training equivalent to a (BPS approved) postgraduate course. A further route is successful completion of five years supervised practice. Those with supervised practice in a range narrower than that approved by the BPS can be awarded the title 'Chartered Psychologist' but not 'Chartered Occupational Psychologist'. In either of these two latter cases the individual would need to approach the BPS to discuss their eligibility and other requirements.

DEVELOPMENT OF OCCUPATIONAL PSYCHOLOGY

Occupational psychology was the first psychological field to be recognised as an applied field. Münsterberg, the first recognised applied psychologist in the USA, declared in 1908 that the time had come for psychology to evolve into an applied science. W. D. Scott's book, *The Psychology of Advertising*, published the same year, was a landmark in applied psychology. The work of these pioneers not only precipitated the emergence of occupational psychology, it also contributed to the development of many current applied psychology fields.

Over the years occupational psychology has been given a variety of names, serving to reflect the splintering which has taken place as it has developed as a scientific discipline. At the turn of the century there was no one agreed name but a variety. Münsterberg referred to it as *economic psychology* reflecting the prevailing concern with work efficiency and industrial productivity.

Münsterberg's 1913 book was entitled *Psychology of Industrial Efficiency*. The term INDUSTRIAL PSYCHOLOGY also appeared around this time and remained popular until 1973, when Division 14 of the American Psychological Association (akin to the BPS Occupational Psychology Division) changed its name from *Industrial* to *Industrial and Organisational Psychology*.

In the United Kingdom Charles Myers founded the National Institute of Industrial Psychology (NIIP) in 1921. The term *industrial psychology* was in use for a few decades but, over the years, *occupational psychology* became a more general term for the area and is still the most popular, preferred because it appears less restrictive, referring not just to the study of work behaviour in industry but also in the service sector and other areas like housework.

In the rest of Europe, the terms *psychology of work* and *psychology of work and organisations* are more popular. This variety of labels should not be taken to mean that there are major differences between industrial, organisational, occupational and work psychology (Arnold et al, 1995). What is useful to remember is that in the UK occupational psychology tends to focus on the study of work behaviour at the individual level. Organisational psychology, on the other hand, tends to be more concerned with the study of work behaviour at the group or organisational levels (Blackler, 1982).

The early years of work psychology

The contribution of scientific management

The need to improve work efficiency and increase productivity at the turn of the 20th century was becoming stronger among industrial engineers than it had ever been before (Taylor, 1911; Gilbreth, 1911). They were concerned with discovering how existing work procedures could be improved to increase productivity. They gave little or no attention to how these new work methods might affect the welfare of the workers. F. W. Taylor (1911) was one of this group but his approach was radically different from the then popular machine-focused approach which sought to improve work efficiency through designing better work machinery. He believed that efficiency and productivity could be improved by changing the way people do their jobs, mainly by breaking them down into smaller tasks or operations which were then analysed as performed by the best workers. The human movements involved in performing every single task could be carefully observed and studied to determine the one best way (fastest and most efficient) of performing each task and, eventually, the whole job.

Taylor conducted the analysis using a worker whom he thought was physically suited for the job. His studies involved measuring the time it took to perform each small task movement. He was thus able to instruct the worker to eliminate useless and unnecessary movements. In TIME AND MOTION STUDIES, Taylor managed to double and sometimes even triple productivity. The applica-

tion of Taylor's scientific principles to increase work efficiency and enhance productivity became known as SCIENTIFIC MANAGEMENT. Note here that Taylor did not use *any* worker in his experiments; he selected one particularly well-suited worker. Secondly, he trained the worker to perform the job tasks more efficiently. However, Taylor did not stop at trying to FIT THE WORKER TO THE JOB – see below. In another series of experiments with employees working as shovelers in a steel plant, he went beyond training them to execute the movements involved in shovelling. He increased productivity by designing shovels so that taller workers used longer handles. The shovelers also complained less of back pain. Redesigning work tools means that Taylor also used the FITTING THE JOB TO THE WORKER (job design) approach.

Scientific management, then, was based on the major principle that:

> *reducing unnecessary movement and redesigning work equipment and the work environment would increase work output and at the same time reduce worker fatigue and injury.*

It left a legacy of:

- *scientific measurement* of job and person aspects
- a 'hard-nosed' *reduction* of any job to its simple elements
- the combination of these two principles in the sole interest of *greater efficiency*
- the value and use of INCENTIVES.

This last principle held that *monetary incentives* were the most effective system of producing and maintaining worker motivation. Many people still argue that monetary incentives remain a prime motivator – more money equals harder work. We shall question this assumption later when we address the issue of WORK SATISFACTION. (At present there is a public debate about high executive salary increases and a defence of these is often in terms of *keeping* the employee rather than obtaining harder work from them.)

Scientific management in the UK

The introduction of scientific management to

British industry was either troublesome or in modified form. Cadbury (1914), head of the famous chocolate company, was pleased with some aspects but found others far too rigid and unsympathetic to the position of his workers. His concerns with worker welfare paralleled the general rise of British industrial psychology in close association with the welfare movement in Britain. At the time, British trades unions were beginning to exercise some power in the industrial arena and resisted crude attempts to speed up production far more successfully than was the case in the USA (Hollway, 1991).

The first British industrial psychologist was employed at the Rowntree Cocoa factory in 1922 where its head, Seebohm Rowntree, held a view, radically liberal for the times, that worker satisfaction could be improved by consulting them on all matters which affected them. To this end he set up a 'works council' comprising representatives from the various workers' groups within the factory. He also set up a factory psychological department and worked closely with Charles Myers of the NIIP who reported on workers' views of industrial psychology:

> 'By improvement in efficiency they feared speeding-up and the dismissal of their less competent comrades. The mention of scientific management made them suspect that all their craft knowledge would pass from them into the hands of their employers and that they would be degraded to the position of servile mechanisms.'
>
> (Myers, 1926, in Hollway, 1991)

Rowntree took it for granted that employers should consider their workers' physical and spiritual condition, internal feelings and job satisfaction. To him, owners and managers performed a public service and were therefore publicly accountable. Other not so humane employers eventually started to recognise the feelings and attitudes of their workforce, partly as a result of the HUMAN RELATIONS MOVEMENT to which we now turn.

The contribution of the human relations movement

In the period from 1924 to 1939 a series of experiments known as the HAWTHORNE STUDIES were carried out at the Hawthorne electric plant in Chicago (Mayo, 1933; Roethlisberger and Dickson, 1939). These studies investigated the effects of the physical work environment (e.g. illumination, the number and length of rest pauses) on productivity. Eventually, they showed that people were not machine-like. Instead they have feelings and attitudes which are affected by what they experience, feel and think about their work. The effects of work on people are not simply physiological such as tiredness or illness. Nowadays, this is regarded as common sense, hardly requiring research to discover such a simple fact. However, at that time workers were seen as simple extensions to their machine. The findings of the Hawthorne Studies, which contradicted the beliefs of most managers at that time, resulted in much research being carried out to find out how attitudes affected work behaviour.

One of the most talked about of the studies is one carried out by Elton Mayo and his associates in 1927. The study involved a group of female workers who assembled telephone relays. The workers were moved from the large department in which they worked into a separate test room where their work output could be measured under controlled conditions. Over a certain period, the working conditions (e.g. illumination levels, rest pauses etc.) were frequently changed and the effects of these changes on workers' productivity were monitored. The researchers found that expected fluctuations in productivity did not follow from changes in working conditions. For instance, one would expect poorer light to reduce performance. In fact, productivity tended to increase whatever the change made. The most surprising result obtained from the study was that productivity increased even when the working conditions were put back to their initial level or made worse. The research team concluded that factors more *social* in nature were responsible for the increases in productivity and the very high morale among employees.

Examples of the social factors said to affect

employee morale and productivity levels are given by several writers.

> 'The employees were enjoying the attention they were receiving from management, the relaxed, self-imposed discipline and supervision and the opportunity to interact with one another.'
>
> (Tajfel and Fraser, 1978)

It can also be added that the way the employees interpreted what was happening to them may have played an important role in how they felt. Being moved from the large department to a separate assembly room may have been interpreted as recognition that they were special.

> 'The women . . . had considerable freedom to develop their own pace of work and divide the work among themselves in a manner most comfortable to them.'
>
> (Schein, 1988)

> '. . . production rates were affected by the guidelines of the informal work groups as well as the goals of the organisation and the behaviour of the immediate supervisor.'
>
> (Landy, 1985)

'The guidelines of the informal work groups' refers to the rules and NORMS (unknown to the management) which other groups in the factory complex developed among themselves, such as setting their own production targets which group members should not exceed.

> 'It was generally considered that the increase was due to social factors within the group, although it could be accounted for by the change in group piece-work which was shared among a group of five instead of a larger group, the smaller variety of work done, the replacement of two of the girls by faster ones, the enthusiasm of the penurious operative number two, and the general expectation throughout the works that the experiment would be a "success."'
>
> (Gregory, 1987)

A notorious legacy of these studies is the so-called *Hawthorne effect* which refers to changes in behaviour caused by people knowing they are under observation or in an experiment – factors not purposely manipulated by the experimenter – see Appendix 2.

It is ironic that the Hawthorne investigations, designed to study the effects of physical conditions on work performance, led to conclusions concerned primarily with social effects on worker morale and productivity. The Hawthorne Studies can be considered as an unintended social experiment in group dynamics. In summarising the various conclusions drawn from the Hawthorne Studies, Riggio (1990) states that social factors 'are the most important determinants of productivity'. The Hawthorne Studies set in motion the human relations school of thought (and organisational psychology) which developed in the 1930s, and strengthened through the 1940s, later giving rise to the Quality of Working Life (QWL) movement. In summary, the human relations movement generated the following set of principles:

- social relations and the psychology of the informal small group are important factors in work productivity
- mechanical features of the job and the individual are not enough to explain worker performance and motivation; workers' feelings, emotions and attitudes are equal, if not more important variables
- workers are not solely motivated by immediate financial gain
- interviews, as a method of investigation, have great power and can even be used by employers to obtain more useful information than by other techniques.

This last point was a radical step away from the cool and distant measurement techniques of scientific management. It had been found at Hawthorne that workers responded far more positively to an interview in which their own thoughts and ideas were valued and given full freedom of expression. This appeared to improve workers' attitudes to their work situation as well as providing very valuable information for those involved in organisational change.

The Hawthorne Studies suffered from a number of methodological weaknesses, one being that the effect of high unemployment in the late 1920s/1930s depression was not fully taken into account. Job insecurity might well lead to harder work. Indeed, this probably explained the finding of very strict yet informal norms among the Bank Wiring Room staff who ensured that production was kept down to an informally agreed rate. In times of unemployment, faster production spells earlier termination of jobs.

A conclusion from the studies, and from Mayo's thinking, was that employers and workers would benefit from emphasising the small group, its solidarity, loyalty and consequent co-operativeness. As Hollway (1991) points out, however, this was not the eventual emphasis of the human relations movement. Employers did not generally see great value in promoting warm and communicative relations between workers. The emphasis became that of worker satisfaction – how to encourage

management and personnel staff to ensure, through training and work organisation, that workers' attitudes to work were at their best. The emphasis did not become the *group* so much as the *individual in the group*.

Both scientific management and human relations approaches have limitations and the explanations they offer about work behaviour are simplistic. The first approach ignores the importance of social factors and the second does not seem to fully recognise the importance of technological factors – see Figure 7.2. Nevertheless, the two sets of conclusions and subsequent research findings have alerted occupational psychologists to the importance of both social and technological factors in explaining work behaviour.

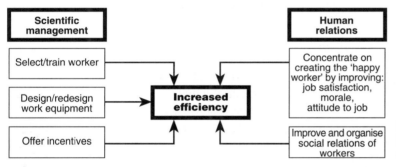

FIGURE 7.2
Main principles of scientific management and human relations approaches

The influence of war on work psychology

Unfortunate though it might be, the development of work psychology was largely shaped by the demands of the two world wars of the twentieth century. The First World War played a major role in the development of personnel psychology. The first large-scale project by occupational psychologists to assess work-related abilities came in the form of two major psychological tests of general mental ability (the Army Alpha and the Army Beta) which were developed to select United States army recruits. In just over a year, it is reported that over one million men were tested. This extensive use of psychological testing for the selection and placement of military recruits generated a lot

of enthusiasm and public approval for personnel psychology applications. After the First World War this enthusiasm was weakening but the type of research initiated by Taylor and Mayo continued.

In Britain, the Health of Munitions Workers Committee (which developed into the Industrial Fatigue Research Board after the end of the First World War) gave psychologists much credit for being involved in programmes which managed to increase war weapons production whilst reducing hours and improving conditions (Hollway, 1991). When the Second World War started psychological assessment techniques were advanced enough to enable occupational psychologists to play a more important role in the assessment and placement of army recruits than they did during the First World War. The assessment techniques were used to classify recruits on the basis of their abilities to learn new tasks, and to work in, and cope with, difficult and stressful situations. More advanced techniques were used to identify recruits who would make good spies.

The impetus for human factors psychology development also came from the Second World War. The increase in air accidents during the war, with some planes crashing before reaching their target, created a greater need for improvements in aircraft design. Human factors psychologists, or *engineering psychologists*, were called upon to advise army manufacturers on how the displays and controls of war planes should be designed to fit the capabilities of their operators thus making them easier or safer to operate. Even after the war ended, the demand for engineering psychologists did not decrease. The Cold War (against the then Soviet Union) which followed it, and the associat-

ed arms race, created a stronger need for more sophisticated weapon systems.

In parallel to these developments in personnel psychology and human factors psychology, organisational psychologists (and some sociologists) were busy researching into human behaviour in work organisations. Research on leadership styles (e.g. Fleishman, 1967; Fiedler, 1967) had made interesting advances. Research on job satisfaction and work motivation concluded that work behaviour is determined not only by individual characteristics but also by the characteristics of organisations. Considerable developments in research were also made in the area of organisational change and development, leading to a better understanding of factors which help or hinder change and growth in organisations, and even their survival (e.g. Lewin, 1951).

THEORY RESEARCH AND APPLICATIONS

Occupational psychology is a vast area and to introduce some form of order we have divided the work into that focusing on the *individual* – personnel psychology – and that focusing on organisations – organisational psychology. To some extent this division is arbitrary and involves much overlap – people make up organisations after all.

Personnel psychology – focus on the individual

This section will focus on psychological research, theory and applications which assume that in order to improve work performance and well-being at work it is necessary to intervene at the individual level. Mainstream psychology already provides a wealth of information about human behaviour, and the factors which direct and sustain a wide range of human activity, which occupational psychologists use in their applications. A large part of the work in this area has involved the

assumption that psychological knowledge can be harnessed in the cause of producing the most productive and satisfactory 'fit' between worker and job.

The job–worker fit

Two major views of the job-worker fit have been referred to in the past (when gender-specific language went unnoticed) as 'Fitting the Man to the Job' (FMJ) and 'Fitting the Job to the Man' (FJM). For obvious reasons we shall refer to FWJ and FJW, 'W' being 'worker'.

Fitting the worker to the job
As the name suggests, this approach is based on the assumption that different jobs will require specific knowledge, skills and abilities (KSAs) which not every individual will possess. This implies that if people are placed into jobs randomly it would be unlikely that they would end up doing jobs for which they are best suited. Therefore, to find 'the right person for the right job' or the best *person–job fit* we need to find some non-random method of allocating people to

jobs. The FWJ approach assumes that:

- both job requirements and individual qualities such as personality traits, abilities, skills, knowledge, attitudes and interests can be adequately measured
- jobs are fixed entities and not the target for change.

What is needed to achieve the best person–job fit is to determine what a job requires in terms of human qualities and then choose from among a number of people the one person who has all or most of the qualities required by the job in question. Where a person does not have *all* the necessary qualities, training is required to reduce the gap between what the job requires and what the person can do successfully. The approach aims to accomplish the best person–job fit by choosing or training the *person* not altering the job. Many current personnel psychology areas, such as selection, vocational *guidance* and training are based on FWJ thinking.

Fitting the job to the worker

By contrast, this approach focuses on the *job* as a target for change. Supporters of this approach argue that a best match between people and jobs can be attained by also changing jobs to suit people. A better person–job match can be obtained by designing jobs so that the majority of people can do them and by designing work environments in which most people feel comfortable. These efforts are the basis of ergonomics, engineering or human factors psychology.

A combination of both approaches is probably most useful and this is what occurs in most cases, depending upon the relative costs of either training or job redesign. Each model is too simplistic, assuming that either the job, or just people's KSAs are simple factors. In fact people have values, interests and needs which change over time as a result of many factors. There is no evidence that people with the same KSAs in similar jobs will do their jobs equally well. This is the importance of studies of work attitudes and motivation which we shall discuss later.

Personnel selection and assessment

If you have ever attended a job interview or been surprised by a friend or relative jumping up and down before telling you that they have just been promoted or that they were one of ten people who received a pay rise or a desirable performance-related bonus, then you have witnessed the results of selection. Even though not all organisations employ occupational psychologists there is a chance that you have indirectly experienced the outcome of the kind of practical decisions that occupational psychologists are sometimes called upon to make or recommend be taken.

PERSONNEL SELECTION refers to the systematic process used by organisations to recruit new staff into specific jobs. Valid selection methods, when carefully administered and when their results are cautiously interpreted by an occupational psychologist or a competent assessor, will, it is hoped, most often result in an appropriate hiring/rejection decision. Ideally they are free from bias and will guard against possible employment discrimination. Assessment is not only used for selection purposes, it can provide objective information which would help human resource managers make decisions on promotion, demotion, training, career guidance, salaries etc. We shall now consider three major assumptions upon which personnel selection tends to be based. To the two FWJ assumptions given above is added a third:

- individual differences are the main source of variance in behaviour (TRAIT APPROACH).

Measurement of people and jobs

DIFFERENTIAL PSYCHOLOGY (see Appendix 1) has had a big influence on the psychology of personnel selection. In the main, occupational psychologists tend to have taken a NOMOTHETIC approach to personality differences (see Appendix 1) and to assume that personality and abilities are measurable. Without the vast amount of psychological research into the nature of intelligence and human abilities (Spearman, 1927; Thurstone, 1938; Burt, 1940; Vernon, 1961, 1969; Guilford, 1967) and the effort to identify and explain the causes of human individual differences at work, including personality characteristics (Cattel, 1965) and attitudes such as satisfaction and commitment (Wicker, 1969; Ajzen and Fishbein, 1980; Ajzen, 1991; Mottaz, 1988; Meyer, Allen and Smith, 1993), much of the personnel function today would not be possible. Equally, occupational psychologists would not have got too far without the sophisticated methods of JOB ANALYSIS which will now be briefly described.

Job analysis

Assuming that jobs are static entities, places to be filled, it is argued that any given job is made up of a number of *tasks* or *activities* which can be performed very successfully if the job holder has the right KSAs. A variety of methods and techniques have been developed to enable psychologists to measure with some accuracy the physical and mental demands of jobs. The systematic study of jobs generates information about job requirements which is then analysed and translated into a JOB SPECIFICATION. A job specification is that section of the *job advertisement* which outlines the human characteristics required to perform the job such as 'must have excellent verbal and written communication skills and be able to work under pressure'. The tests which are developed to measure these job-relevant qualities are called *selection methods*, *tools* or *instruments*. Interviews, ability and personality tests are all examples of selection tools. Techniques of job analysis fall into two broad categories, each with certain advantages:

- TASK-ORIENTED JOB ANALYSIS *methods* – the emphasis is on the *result* of tasks involved in the job. It focuses on whether each task was completed successfully, rather than on the specific behaviour displayed. For a customer service job we may get tasks such as dealing with customer complaints, analysis of the nature of complaints, writing reports and so on

- WORKER-ORIENTED JOB ANALYSIS *methods* – these focus on the specific behaviour carried out by a job holder (it is sometimes termed FUNCTIONAL ANALYSIS). Instead of listing the tasks as whole units the analysis will describe on-job behaviour at a MOLECULAR level (see Appendix 1). We may end up with a list such as 'communicates orally with customers, reads and writes to customers, speaks to and calms down angry customers', and so on.

An advantage of functional analysis is that it is easier to move from the analysis to specifying what kinds of characteristics are required in the individual to be appointed. Many tasks, on the other hand, can be carried out in several different ways by people with quite widely differing characteristics. The advantage of analysis by tasks is that these can be 'sampled' (see below) and applicants asked to perform them during the selection process. Typically, well-defined jobs (like post delivery) can be broken down into tasks, whereas customer service or management posts tend to be analysed in terms of qualities required. Further details and evaluation of these two methods can be found in Prien (1977).

Ultimately either type of method will produce a JOB DESCRIPTION including details such as: job title; job location; the person or persons the job holder deals with and in what form; objectives of the job; working conditions and environment; pay; overtime; safety hazards; training and promotion prospects, and so on. The PERSON SPECIFICATION should specify the qualities required in the prospective employees (especially KSAs) in order that they can perform the job to the standard required. Depending on the type of job these might include: academic and professional qualifications; special abilities; general aptitudes; personality characteristics; interests; physical characteristics and so on. Only in rare circumstances may employers in the UK legally specify sex or ethnic background.

Individual differences – personality traits

The TRAIT APPROACH has probably had the greatest influence on the practice of assessment and selection. It argues that differences between people's behaviour are largely determined by forces within the individual (PERSONALITY TRAITS), which keep behaviour relatively consistent across situations in that individual (see Appendix 1). Clearly, this argument suggests that, if external factors do not have a great effect on how we behave, then most of what we do comes from within us and there is little point changing a person's environment in order to alter their behaviour. Of course, the person–situation interaction view also sees traits as important (see Appendix 1) since we should be able to predict how people with certain traits behave under certain environmental conditions. The practice of personnel assessment and selection is based on and reflects the widespread belief that 'personality traits are alive and well' (Deary and Matthews, 1993). Some of the most widely used tools in personnel assessment of traits are the 16 Personality Factor Questionnaire (16PF) (Cattell et al, 1970) and the Occupational Personality Questionnaire (OPQ) (Saville and Holdsworth, 1990).

The assumption that people differ in terms of ability and personality largely as a result of internal factors explains, at least partially, why attempts to improve work performance usually involve interventions at the individual level, though other variables are sometimes taken into account. Other approaches would concentrate more on job redesign or other environmental alterations designed to accommodate the worker and we shall meet some of these later on. Although occupational psychologists make use of the assessment methods developed in mainstream psychological research they have also developed a number of ability and personality tests (e.g. the OPQ) and interest inventories (e.g. Rothwell-Miller, 1968) designed specifically for use in work settings and which are RELIABLE and VALID (see Appendix 2). Nevertheless, there are serious and sometimes hostile debates about the validity of personality measures and, indeed, the usefulness of the concept of personality traits at all (see Deary and Matthews, 1993; Blinkhorn and Johnson, 1990).

Improving the person-job fit

Occupational psychologists have tended to see many work-related problems as the product of mismatches between people and jobs. Solutions involve selecting people into jobs through systematic methods of personality assessment and job analysis so as to improve the PERSON–JOB FIT. With accurate job specification on the one hand, and appropriate selection measures on the other, the recruiter sets out to assess and select the best person for the job, the outcome expected to be an increase in work efficiency. Today, more than ever, occupational psychologists see systematic selection as an important determinant of effective human resources use and this, in turn, is considered a factor critical to organisational survival, health and growth (Peters and Waterman, 1982).

Efforts to develop better and more accurate methods of selection have resulted in two main approaches to assessment and selection, namely, SIGNS and SAMPLES (Vernimont and Campbell, 1968).

The signs approach

If you apply, say, for a part-time job in your local pub and the manager presents you with a test of numerical ability or a personality test then your prospective employer is using the *signs* approach to selection. The tests would be used, *providing they are both valid and reliable*, because your scores on them will indicate the extent to which you possess numerical ability and certain personality traits deemed necessary for good performance in bar work. According to this approach the personality test is a 'sign' which will indicate whether you have the qualities which most successful bar staff possess, *as established from prior research*.

The samples approach

A bar manager who adopts the samples approach might ask if you don't mind getting behind the bar so you can be observed at work for half an hour. Proponents of this approach argue that selection methods should reflect successful work behaviour *directly*. For example, secretarial applicants might be given a typing test. If they perform successfully they are likely to be successful in the job, at least this part of it. Notice that a *task-oriented* job analysis will more neatly produce *samples* for prospective employees to perform. The samples approach is less prone to error since it does not involve speculation about what human qualities must be measured in order to predict successful job performance. Rather than give a personality inventory to applicants for a secretary job we simply present them with a carefully selected subset of tasks from the job itself and see whether the applicants complete these. The emphasis here is on how *well* a person completes a task, not on *how* they do it. The approach is also easier to defend since tasks have *face validity* – the applicant can straightaway see the relevance of the task whereas the same cannot be said for a personality test.

Supporters of the signs approach have their own arguments in defence, mainly concerning

VALIDITY GENERALISATION. If a test of personality characteristics or general ability can predict performance on a job with some accuracy then the same test can be used to predict performance on other similar jobs. The ability to generalise validity from one job to other similar jobs means that the need to develop a test for every different job is reduced.

Whichever approach is adopted, valid selection methods which can predict with some accuracy how successful the applicant will be if hired can lead to human and financial gains (known as the UTILITY of the selection method). An organisation which used a valid selection test, at a cost of $10 per applicant, to recruit 600 computer programmers was estimated to have made a financial gain of more than $97 million within a year (Schmidt, Hunter, McKenzie and Muldrow, 1979).

When do organisations benefit most from systematic personnel selection?
It is important to note that predictive validity is not the only important factor in determining how much and when selection is most beneficial. Robertson and Cooper (1986) describe two other factors which partly determine the SELECTION UTILITY:

■ the SELECTION RATIO – imagine you apply for a job and find out that you are one of twenty people who have applied (*selection ratio* of 1 to 20 or .05). Assume that on this occasion you have been unsuccessful so you decide to go around the world which takes you two years. On your return, you are pleasantly surprised because the unemployment rate has dropped to 1 per cent. You reapply for a job and this time you dicover that you are the only applicant (selection ratio of 1 to 1). In which of these two scenarios does an organisation stand to benefit more from using a valid method of selection? Obviously, in times of low unemployment it is possible that in some occupations there would be more jobs than there are applicants (selection ratio is greater than 1). In situations like these it would not make sense to use even the most valid of selection methods if an organisation has no choice but to accept the one applicant. When unemployment is high and the average number of applicants

competing for a single vacancy can be up to 100 (a ratio of 0.01) an organisation will benefit a great deal from using a valid method of selection

■ the BASE RATE OF SUCCESS – this refers to the proportion of employees, selected *without* a valid selection test, who are successful in the job. If 80 per cent of an organisation's workforce perform to the required standards the organisation will not benefit a great deal from introducing a new method of selection even if it is highly valid.

Hence, the benefits of selection are not determined solely by the validity of the selection method(s). Maximum benefits are achieved when the methods have acceptable validity *and* both the selection ratio and the base rate of success are low – see Table 1.

TABLE 1
Relative utility depending on selection ratio and success rate

	high utility	moderate utility	no utility
Selection ratio	low	moderate	high
Base rate of success	low	moderate	high

Personnel selection in practice
A company developing an efficient selection scheme needs to go through three main stages:

1. Conduct a job analysis
This is done in order to make clear exactly what it is the job entails. Smith and Robertson (1993) outline a six-stage process which can usefully be reduced to three major phases:

■ Immediate   – collect all information such as job descriptions and training manuals
■ Intermediate – interview any person who should know about the job's aims and objectives (such as managers, engineers, related job holders)
                – interview/give questionnaires to job holders

– observe job holders at work
– the analyst might attempt to perform the job; this last approach may not always be possible. How would you feel if you were an air passenger and were told that an inexperienced job analyst was going to try flying the plane in order to appreciate aspects of the job?

■ Final   – analyse, weight and categorise all gathered data and detail all job aspects.

2. Develop predictors

From the detailed job analysis it should be possible to generate samples or signs to be used in later selection of staff and which are intended to serve as PREDICTORS of a person's future efficiency or value to the organisation. If the job is found to require verbal and numerical abilities there would be no need to develop new tests since a variety of reliable and valid measures already exist. On the other hand, if currently available tests are inadequate, new ones will be needed. Predictors might take the form of tests, sample tasks, ratings from interviews and so on. ASSESSMENT CENTRES, used by several large companies, use a range of such predictors and include, for example, in-tray exercises and leaderless group discussion.

3. Validate predictors – the use of criterion validity

The aim here is to see how well people's *predictor scores* correlate (see Appendix 2) with their performance (their CRITERION SCORE). There are two ways to do this and both are examples of CRITERION VALIDITY:

■ PREDICTIVE VALIDITY. Correlate measures of staff *at selection* with their *later* performance on the job. In this case we must store all initial predictor scores away from anyone involved in the assessment of an individual's later job performance in order to avoid CRITERION CONTAMINATION – the effect that knowing a person's selection test score might have on an assessor (e.g. supervisor) who is rating that employee's performance at a later date

■ CONCURRENT VALIDITY. Correlate measures of current staff on the predictors with their current job performance.

It is important that predictors are not used to make selection decisions until they have been fully validated. Using either type of validity test we would expect correlations of *at least* 0.4 or 0.5 to consider our predictors to be good. We can also establish the point at which predictor scores are too low to risk employing the applicant, allowing for possible improvement through training. This point will be known as the CUT-OFF SCORE.

Training and development

This chapter cannot really hope to cover the essential factors to be taken into account when planning any form of training. A list of some of these is given below:

Individual differences	External factors
knowledge	practice
skills	media for training
abilities	organised sequence of steps
motivation/attitude/ self-efficacy	trainer qualities
present state	transfer of training

However, we can point the way in certain areas and simply emphasise how important it is that the psychologist engaged in training has a good knowledge of these factors and their effects on training, when attempting to develop behaviour change in the work situation.

Training, education and learning

Landy (1985) defines training as:

'A set of planned activities on the part of an organisation to increase the job knowledge and the skills or to modify the attitudes and social behaviour of its members in ways consistent with the goals of the organisation and the requirements of the job.'

On the difference between education and training, Warr (1987) says:

'Training tends to minimise individual differences whereas education sometimes tries to maximise them.'

Training, as compared with more general education, aims to equip trainees with a set of capabilities which enable them to perform certain activities to the same uniform standard. The last decade in this country, however, has seen a shift towards more vocationally oriented education courses in the form of BTEC and GNVQ, thus blurring the traditional separation between education and training.

Training and psychological theory of learning

Clearly there is an important role for psychological theories of learning when occupational psychologists are involved in attempts to alter human behaviour through training. Early theories were behaviourally oriented and applied the principles of classical and operant conditioning (Appendix 1). However, the use of incentives ('reinforcements') to alter behaviour must be as old as human society and certainly the scientific management practitioners were advocating their use a couple of years before the 'school' of behaviourism was officially born. What the psychologist would have added though, would be the scientifically investigated factors of SHAPING (building up behaviour through graded steps), effective use of *practice*, similarity of training and real work environments (to enable TRANSFER OF TRAINING) and so on. Operant theory gave rise to the techniques of PROGRAMMED LEARNING, a system of self-learning using self-paced materials in a strict and graded sequence. The learner usually may not progress until certain stages have been successfully completed and has to return to earlier steps using feedback (usually the correct answer) given as a consequence of failure at that stage. The original 'teaching machines' which presented these materials have evolved into book form self-learning materials and into computer programmes.

By far the greater influence on training over the last few decades, however, has come from the cognitive schools of psychology, partly from social learning theory, but largely from the area of 'pure' experimental cognitive psychology research.

Social learning theory

As described in Appendix 1, Bandura's social learning theory (1969) broke the hold of strict behaviourism which did not include the scientific study of cognitive processes. Bandura's early work demonstrated that people could learn by simple observation, without the necessity for obvious or direct reward (reinforcement). Again, psychological theories were not required to stimulate observational learning. A traditional training technique in factories was that of SITTING BY NELLIE – watching how a job was done. Social learning theory, however, investigated several features of observational modelling, for instance that learning could be VICARIOUS – observing the rewards and punishments delivered to others could have an effect on the extent to which the observer would, in turn, exhibit the same behaviour. Modern training methods such as role-play, demonstrations and audio-visual presentation are based on the assumption that people can learn by observing others perform behaviours which they will be required to perform in future. In general, reviews of the power and utility of behavioural modelling continue to be positive.

Bandura's later work has concentrated on several factors, in particular the *interaction* between learners and trainers, the role of SELF-MONITORING – the extent to which we *check* our behaviour as it occurs and *alter* as a consequence of the feedback we receive, and the role of SELF-EFFICACY – the extent to which a person *believes* they are capable of learning or performing a new task. Bouffard-Bouchard (1990) showed that trainees high in self-efficacy prior to training out-performed those who were lower.

Cognitive learning theory

The nature of the 'cognitive revolution' in psychological research is described in Appendix 1. It has serious implications for training and has had a substantial effect on training theory. Cognitive psychologists concentrate on mental processes which, they argue, are critical to our understanding of learning. They do not concentrate on overt behaviour but on the *information processing* which occurs (perception, memorising, decision-making, problem-solving) within our system and which guides our behaviour to a particular goal.

Work-shadowing can be seen as a form of observational learning.

Humans are active problem-solvers and seekers of information and therefore require guided steps and relevant data by which they can adjust behaviour appropriately to match their desired goals. This analysis applies as much to the baby picking up an awkward object as to an operative balancing processes safely at a nuclear electric plant. A useful model for analysing the various stages involved in acquiring a new skill comes from Anderson (1983).

Declarative stage DECLARATIVE KNOWLEDGE of a task is knowledge of facts concerning it. Many people know *that* we depress the clutch in order to change gear in a car but far less are able to do this smoothly, for instance. The early stages of skill learning at this level involve learning the 'rules' , often in verbal form, and are therefore quite demanding on attention and memory.

Knowledge compilation stage – PROCEDURAL KNOWLEDGE This concerns knowing *how* to do something. Anderson's main interest was in how declarative knowledge becomes transformed into procedural knowledge. After some experience of driving, you would find it quite hard to *tell* someone exactly how you change gear so smoothly. Compare holding a pencil and drawing a letter 'R' with telling a child how to do this. At this stage the learner may still utilise declarative knowledge to string sub-groups of well-learned routines together into one overall performance. One may be able to change gear well *and* steer round corners smoothly, but not both together.

Tuning stage (stage of AUTOMACITY) Finally, all sub-routines are strung together smoothly and the learner now attends to fine tuning various components. Underlying rules are refined and the overall skilled performance becomes increasingly more smooth and AUTONOMOUS.

In general it can be said that, whereas behavioural theories concerning reinforcement concentrated on *why* an individual performs certain tasks, and how to encourage them to perform more or less or in different circumstances, the cognitive approaches have concentrated far more on *how* skilled behaviour is acquired.

The role of training at work

Many organisations will spend more time, money and effort in purchasing computers than they will on the type of training required by the individual to *operate* the computer. Decisions on training are at least equally as important as purchasing decisions. After all, what the computer produces can be only as good as the skills acquired and utilised by the operator. On the other hand, managements are also known to see training as a global cure or to just *suspect* that training will be useful. It is very easy to blame poor performance or other organisation problems on the inadequate training of workers rather than, as is often true, on a more general organisational weakness in structure or morale, or even on poor management decisions. If training is seen as an answer then those proposing a programme must be quite clear

about what they want the training to achieve. It is no use saying to a dog trainer, 'Just train this dog; it doesn't really matter what for.' Vagueness of training objectives will render evaluation of training very difficult, if not impossible. If you want to judge a trainer's level of competence you might try asking them the following:

- what will the trainees be able to do at the end of the training?
- in what conditions and with what equipment will they be able to do it?
- how will you measure whether they are able to do it to the required standard?

Training in practice – models for training programmes

A number of training models have been developed to support good practice. For illustration we can work through Goldstein's (1974) model which outlines the different steps involved in developing a training programme. Note that Patrick's more recent model (Figure 7.3) incorporates similar stages but in a more elaborate manner.

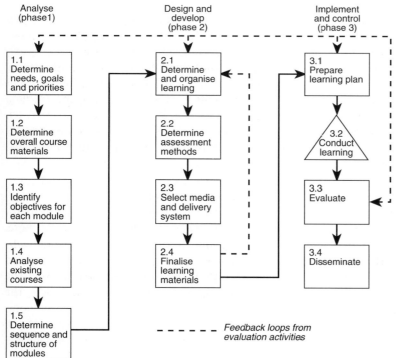

FIGURE 7.3
Learning Systems Development model
(from Patrick, 1992)

Step 1 – Assess training needs and specify train-ing needs and objectives
Both models begin with a TRAINING NEEDS ANALYSIS (TNA). This is traditionally considered at three lev-els – the *organisation*, the *task* and the *person*. Latham (1988) has argued for a further *demo-graphic* level of analysis where the needs of vari-ous sub-groups of personnel are considered (females, minorities, people with disabilities, age groups, etc.).

The organisation Whatever training employees *feel* they might need, it is often the case that it won't be received unless the organisation recog-nises the need as part of its overall development plan – long-term improvement of efficiency, cli-mate (see below), growth and so on.

The task There are many models for the analysis of tasks and a good guide to these is contained in Patrick (1992). A popular method is HIERARCHICAL TASK ANALYSIS in which an overall task is broken down into its constituent parts in a 'family tree' pattern. Hence, fixing a flat tyre requires the sub-task of jacking up the car, removing the wheel which, in turn, has its own sub-tasks to complete (e.g. removing bolts) and so on.

The person Analysis of the person incorporates all the methods of assessment mentioned earlier on. It should also include employees' own appraisal of their needs and the views of any supervisor involved. However, there can be virtu-ally no relationship between employees' assess-ments of their own training needs and supervisors' assessments, especially where the employee is female and the supervisor is male (Staley and Shockley-Zalabak, 1986).

Demographic analysis This forms part of a con-sideration of *equal opportunities* at work on the part of occupational psychologists and others. The use of objective and careful methods of training needs assessment, rather than the opinions of managers, should go quite a way towards prevent-ing discrimination in training against any individ-ual, minority or sub-group. Decisions on who should be trained and what kind of training is given should not be based solely on subjective

judgements made by organisational decision-mak-ers. In Britain, employed women have received fewer training opportunities than men (Elias and Main, 1982), particularly where they are in tradi-tionally non-female jobs (Davidson and Cooper, 1983). The situation is likely to have improved slightly since that time but Aitkenhead and Liff (1991), surveying 20 top UK companies, found that the majority of staff responsible for equal opportunities felt little needed to be done, did not see these matters as organisational issues and had only vague, if any, criteria for evaluation of needs. Berryman-Finck (1985) found that senior man-agement (male and female) viewed the training needs of managers differently by gender. Women required training in assertiveness, confidence, and dealing with males, whereas men needed training in listening, verbal skills, empathy and sensitivity.

Step 2 – Select training methods and content
From the assessment of training needs, the barri-ers which prevent employees from achieving their own or the organisation's objectives will have been identified. The training might be aimed at altering *knowledge* (updating a legal expert on European law), *skills* (introduction to new com-puter software), *abilities* (improvement of man-agement decision-making) or *attitudes* (improvement of attitude to customers). Only when all training objectives have been clearly defined is it possible to start considering training content and methods of delivery. The methods should be those best suited to facilitate *training transfer* – see below. It is at this stage too that cri-teria are devised which will be used in final *evalu-ation* to demonstrate that the programme was successful.

Step 3 – Conduct training
Trainers can choose from a huge variety of meth-ods too wide to be dealt with in any detail here. Methods include: *lecture, seminar, role-play, sim-ulation, audio-visual presentation, programmed learning, observation, modelling* and so on. The training may well occur 'on-the-job' where the trainee may be supervised by a mentor. JOB ROTA-TION involves experiencing various types of job and, if well-structured, might result in flexible, adaptable employees.

Transfer of training Where training is off-the-job an important issue will be the extent to which newly acquired changes can be *transferred* from the learning situation to the workplace. Imagine you are a professional snooker player and have been asked by friends to teach their children to play snooker. You might decide to teach them trigonometry and physics because this is what snooker is really all about. But you probably wouldn't. You might, advisedly, choose to teach them to play pool on a junior table. If they learn well here it should be fairly easy for them to transfer their skills from pool to snooker, whereas knowledge of trigonometry and physics is unlikely to transfer from paper to either of the ball games.

Step 4 – Evaluate training

A friend, working for a government organisation, recently went on a two-day word processing training programme. At the end of her training she reported she and all her colleagues felt the training was a waste of time. What is surprising about this is that the organisation did not even ask the trainees about their impressions of the training. Even more surprising is the fact that in two weeks' time another group of employees will be put through the same experience. The evaluation stage is as important as the first. As this abridged story shows, absence of any training evaluation can lead to a waste of time and money since we will not know whether the training has achieved its intended objectives. Training evaluation can take many forms. Table 2 gives a description of some of the methods used and the frequency of their use. Good training evaluation texts to consult would be Phillips (1990) or Patrick (1992).

A difficulty with training evaluation can be the nature of the research design employed. If a group of employees is compared both before and after their training it is difficult to exclude a CONFOUNDING VARIABLE (see Appendix 2) which might be responsible for any changes observed. A programme reported by Jack (1992), where staff voluntarily worked for NVQs, apparently demonstrated a decrease in staff turnover from 50% to 24% between 1990 and 1991. However, success was rewarded with a pay increase. In addition, the programme coincided with a very sharp increase in unemployment throughout the country. Either of these factors, rather than the training itself, might have been responsible for the improvement in turnover. In the past, evaluation has consisted of simply asking trainees for their impressions. There is no doubt that large numbers used to say the training was good simply because it felt nice to be away from work for a day or two! The best designs will be true EXPERIMENTS (see Appendix 2) with random allocation of trainees to control and experimental groups. Most training programmes using a trained group and a comparison group are QUASI-EXPERIMENTS – see Appendix 2. Cook and Campbell (1979) discuss a variety of complex experimental methods for evaluating training effectiveness.

TABLE 2
Forms of training evaluation

(Frequency is % of 333 personnel managers who do and don't use the method; from Dudgill, *Personnel Today*, June 1994)

Level	Type of evaluation	Description	Frequency
one	trainee reaction	how they felt about their training	99 versus 1
two	amount of learning	the amount of learning which has taken place	90 versus 9
three	change in behaviour	actual changes in behaviour, e.g. newly acquired skills	79 versus 19
four	results	outcome measure, e.g. increase in productivity	68 versus 30

Motivation – work attitudes and job design

Suppose you are a highly qualified and highly skilled worker; will you exercise yourself at work to your maximum capability at all times and regardless of the conditions in which you are expected to work? If you are not an exception, you would be thinking 'of course not'. Research has shown that work performance is affected by a host of factors unrelated to the knowledge, the skills and the abilities of the worker. WORK ATTITUDES, the way people see, think and feel about their jobs and organisation, constitute a factor which will have considerable effects on satisfaction, motivation and performance. Negative attitudes are often associated with high levels of lateness, absenteeism, turnover, grievance and low productivity.

Work satisfaction

Work satisfaction can be defined as the psychological state experienced at work as a result of how people feel and think about (a) their jobs, its rewards and its physical conditions, (b) the people they work with, both co-workers and superiors and (c) management policies and practices. These attitudes will predispose the individual to behave in particular ways towards the job, other people and the organisation.

Causes of work satisfaction

One of the theories which had important implications for job design was Herzberg's (1966) two-factor theory, so-called because it proposed that satisfaction and dissatisfaction are determined by two *different* categories of factors.

MOTIVATORS include achievement, recognition, the intrinsic characteristics of work, responsibility and advancement. These factors, especially the last three, Herzberg argues, are responsible for determining *work satisfaction*.

HYGIENE FACTORS include company policy and administration, supervision, salary, interpersonal relations at work and working conditions. These factors which he called 'dissatisfiers' are responsible for producing *dissatisfaction* with work.

Herzberg argued that the factors which produce satisfaction are not the same factors as those which produce dissatisfaction. The *presence* of motivators produces satisfaction. When absent, they do not necessarily produce dissatisfaction. Conversely, hygiene factors produce dissatisfaction when *absent*. In other words, contrary to past research, Herzberg argued that satisfaction and dissatisfaction are separately caused. The factors were developed through research by Herzberg, Mausner and Snydermam (1959) with a sample of 200 engineers and accountants in Pittsburg using interviews in which respondents were asked to:

- think of a time when they felt exceptionally good or bad about their work
- say what special event about this time made them feel good or bad
- state whether this feeling of satisfaction affected their work performance, their relationships at work and their well-being.

According to Herzberg (1966) this research was carried out 'to test the concept that man has two sets of needs: his need as an animal to avoid pain and his need as a human to grow psychologically'. The theory can be criticised on several grounds. First, it ignored attribution effects; people are known to attribute good things (e.g. exam success) to the self and poor things (exam failure) to external factors. Second, the use of 'good' and 'bad' might be partly responsible for producing two sets of factors. Third, similar results might not occur with a sample of shop-floor workers. It is not surprising that highly paid professionals might claim that responsibility and achievement, not wages, are responsible for satisfaction.

Despite being flawed, the theory's implications for job design led to the idea of JOB ENRICHMENT where jobs are made more interesting and stimulating by increasing motivator factors. The idea is that jobs that are more challenging, give people greater opportunity to develop their skills, and give more responsibility and recognition, will be associated with higher levels of satisfaction and motivation. Making hygiene factors adequate will prevent dissatisfaction. Herzberg's theory has been followed by many attempts to specify how to improve jobs by redesigning old ones and designing new ones in ways that make them more appealing. Turner and Lawrence (1965) and Cooper (1973) are examples.

The job characteristics model

Influenced by Herzberg's theory, Hackman and Oldham's (1976) JOB CHARACTERISTICS MODEL has contributed a great deal to job design theory. The model describes five well-defined job characteristics, readily applicable to job design programmes – see Figure 7.4.

1. *Skill variety* – the extent to which a job is made up of a variety of tasks which require the use of a diverse range of skills and abilities.
2. *Task identity* – a job is high on identity if it allows the job incumbent to carry out a complete and clearly identifiable piece of work.
3. *Task significance* – the extent to which a job can affect people's lives (e.g. surgeon) or work of other people (e.g. anaesthetist) in a critical way.
4. *Autonomy* – refers to the degree of freedom a worker has over how the job is done. Note that autonomy and responsibility are positively correlated; more autonomy means more responsibility.
5. *Feedback* – refers to the degree to which the job provides information on work performance which enables the worker to know how well she or he is doing the job. A computer designed to sense typing errors and blip every time one is made would be providing clear feedback.

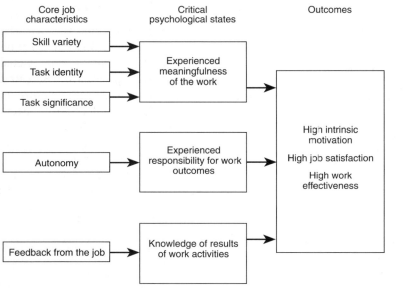

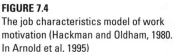

FIGURE 7.4
The job characteristics model of work motivation (Hackman and Oldham, 1980. In Arnold et al, 1995)

These characteristics are of critical importance; they affect both workers' attitudes and work behaviour. The model goes on to identify the psychological experiences and states associated with the five 'core characteristics'. It also identifies the positive psychological states and outcomes that jobs have both for the individual worker and for the organisation. Hackman and Oldham (1975) have also produced an instrument (the JOB DIAGNOSTIC SURVEY – JDS) by means of which the different job characteristics can be measured. This enables any organisation to attempt to create or redesign jobs to be more satisfying and motivating.

The theories and models of work satisfaction and motivation have not escaped criticism. The most important relates to the fact that very often the same people are asked to describe the characteristics of their jobs, their attitudes and their motivation. Some (e.g. Algera, 1983) argue that people will try to give compatible answers out of fear of appearing inconsistent, otherwise known as COGNITIVE DISSONANCE (see the criminological psychology chapter). Another criticism concerns the narrow focus on jobs and individuals, rather than on groups and wider organisational characteristics. The SOCIO-TECHNICAL SYSTEMS approach (below) has sought to address some of these criticisms.

Goal-setting theory

Associated with Edwin Locke, this theory of motivation argues that workers need *clear, specific* goals to work towards and that telling people 'to do their best' without setting clear targets will be unlikely to have any effect (see Locke and Latham, 1984 and a more recent thorough review in Locke and Latham, 1990). So long as goals are reachable, then setting *harder* goals produces greater performance, but these goals must be initially accepted by workers. Hollenbeck et al (1989), however, found no difference in students' performance between those whose goals were set for them and those who set their own, except for high-achieving students who performed better after setting their own goals. In addition, performance is *not* increased after clear goal-setting where a clear strategy to achieve the goals is not obvious (Earley et al, 1989). Similarly, Earley et al (1990) found no help from goal-setting where tasks were complex and where participants started out with few of the necessary skills developed. In other words, if you want a team to perform well, set clear attainable goals and ensure the team can see how to reach them and that they accept them before starting out. Check that they have adequate preparation and skills, and, if possible, break tasks into sets of less complex routines. If people are new to a difficult task set very easy goals, if any.

Austin and Bobko (1985) argue that the theory has weaknesses because real work (unlike the experimental situation) produces *conflicting* goals. *Individuals* were tested in these studies but work goals are *group* goals and the quality of goals in the studies was nothing like the quality or richness of real work goals.

The socio-technical systems approach

This approach has a psychoanalytic root and emanated from the Tavistock Centre in London. A brief description of Trist and Bamforth's (1951) classic study in the Durham coalfields will introduce the approach. Traditionally minework was carried out by small, self-managed and self-supervised work teams, known as 'marrow groups', usually consisting of three miners per shift, with three shifts altogether. As the mining task required high co-operation between work team members, close and stable relationships developed

between them. Trist and Bamforth reported that 'In circumstances where a man was injured or killed, it was not uncommon for his mates to care for his family.' The groups negotiated a price for their coal with the managers. To avoid favouritism work places on the coal seam were 'cavilled' each quarter, that is, places were allocated by drawing lots. When new technology (fast coal-cutting machines) was introduced it led to the breaking down of the small work teams and the forming of larger work groups of 40–50 miners to operate what was known as the 'longwall' method. Existing social structures were disrupted. Each large group carried out just one major task per shift, with groups on the next shift carrying out a different task, perhaps carrying a lower status and less well paid. Each group was under the supervision of one person rather than self-supervised. The new technology, intended simply as a production improvement, led to the following unpredicted negative consequences, because the implications for the existing social networks, the nature of work and the management and control system had not been considered:

- the variety in the tasks which the miners were used to had been reduced as the new technology led to further specialisation which the miners resented
- the increase in specialisation, coupled with the need to co-ordinate work efforts, also meant a greater need for close supervision to check that miners were effectively carrying out the tasks to which they were assigned.
- these changes produced low satisfaction, higher absenteeism and lower productivity.

When the causes of these effects became obvious it was decided that the new technology should be managed in a way that would reintroduce some of the earlier working practices. When both social *and* technological factors were taken into account, productivity increased, absenteeism decreased and the production system was estimated at 95 per cent of its potential compared to only 75 per cent previously. Since then, advocates of the socio-technical approach have stressed the importance of work groups that are *self-managed* or *semi-autonomous*, giving workers a degree of independence and responsibility in their jobs (Emery,

1959; Taylor, 1975).

Jackson et al's (1984) intervention (see p. 248) demonstrates the kind of benefits that self-managed groups can bring. One of the major characteristics of the socio-technical approach to job design is its stress on the complex interactions between all social and technical aspects of work. In addition to the individual and the mechanical aspects of the job, the approach also considers group relations, the units of an organisation and the organisation as a whole. The evidence concerning the complex interdependence of the different factors affecting work behaviour serves to remind organisations that technical innovation and restructuring may affect the nature of the existing social systems.

Organisational psychology– focus on groups

Group processes – towards organisational psychology

So far in this chapter we have concentrated on factors at the individual level. We have looked at the psychology of the individual which is relevant in a work setting. The socio-technical approach, however, emphasised the fundamental aspect of humans' *social* nature. An organisation is not merely a collectivity of individuals. It cannot exist without them but it also cannot have goals or make decisions which are not acceptable to them *as groups*. Schein (1988) offers the following definition:

'An organisation is the planned co-ordination of the activities of a number of people for the achievement of some common, explicit purpose or goal, through division of labour and function, and through a hierarchy of authority and responsibility.'

An organisation consists of several or many formal groups. However, all organisations also produce *informal* groups. These may result from work friendships and common social interests. They

may also occur because individuals may need to operate and communicate in ways other than those formally provided for, even to oppose some aspects of the formal system. Doing so on an individual basis would be running a risk but this is reduced within an informal group and norm structure. Group formation in organisations is interesting in its own right. It is also central to understanding organisations and how they function. In the following sections we will look first at the process of GROUP FORMATION and SOCIALISATION. Then we shall explore the mechanisms which guide behaviour within groups (*intra-group behaviour*) and between groups (*inter-group behaviour*), followed by the psychology of *decision-making* in groups and, finally, move to a study of organisations as whole units with a *culture*.

Group formation and norms of behaviour

Work groups consist of two or more people co-operating together to achieve a common goal, for instance the delivery of a psychology course to first-year students. The formation of work groups is not that different from the formation of any other social groups and usually proceeds in stages possessing certain characteristics. Four stages of group formation were suggested by Tuckman (1965):

Forming This involves establishing a common goal and going beyond individual differences for the sake of the group. Group members will need to compromise so as to arrive at a set of rules and norms which will enable them to work as a cohesive group.

Storming Here conflicts start to emerge. Decisions regarding how to proceed, who should do what and when, who will take overall responsibility, and the process of reaching some consensus on the best approach will produce dissenting voices. Some may feel that their opinions have not been considered. The stage is therefore characterised by refusal to compromise, contest over leadership (if this is open to change), resistance to certain proposals, etc. These are all conflicts which the group will seek to resolve in the next stage.

Norming As the name suggests, here the group will focus on overcoming the differences which arose at the previous stage. By this time, some of the group members have come to terms with each other, differences are partially reconciled, dissenting voices are brought into line with the majority. This is indicative of a more cohesive group which can develop a set of norms according to which the group members will behave.

NORMS are formal or informal rules of behaviour (usually the latter and usually unwritten) which indicate appropriate and unacceptable behaviour for group members. We saw that the Hawthorne Plant workers had developed unofficial norms to restrict output. These workers also delivered SANCTIONS to those who did not conform, including 'binging' – a sharp, painful blow on the upper arm.

Typically, if all goes well, co-operation, mutual trust and understanding, sacrifice of personal interest to safeguard the group, and 'we' as opposed to 'I' feelings are characteristics of groups at this stage. Having overcome most differences and resolved conflict the group can now focus on clearly stated and agreed goals.

Performing The energy previously used to resolve interpersonal and sub-group conflicts becomes freed. It is now directed at completing the different tasks to achieve the goals of the group. The group will have established norms and procedures which every group member is expected to comply with.

Organisational socialisation

Most work groups are already formed when individuals join them. They do not form spontaneously and unofficially, as do, for instance, protest or neighbourhood groups, and it is relatively rare for *all* the members of a work group to be put together at once for the first time (though this happens regularly in some occupations. House building teams might be an example). Most employees are *socialised* into their work group. Feldman (1976) has outlined three stages of employee socialisation into a work group, to some extent mirroring those of Tuckman for whole group development.

Anticipatory The newcomer is developing realis-

tic expectations about the job and the organisation's potential to satisfy his or her needs.

Accommodation As newcomers develop their relationships with individual group members they learn the norms of the group, the roles played by others and the roles expected of themselves.

A ROLE is a position within a group with an accompanying set of expectations for fulfilling that role. Most work roles are *formal* (e.g. head of department, drilling supervisor), but others are *informal* (e.g. the 'office clown', the 'carer'). ROLE CONFLICT may occur when a person occupies two roles with conflicting attached expectations. For instance, a health and safety representative's meeting might conflict with an important sales conference (INTER-ROLE CONFLICT). Conflict within *one* role (INTRA-ROLE CONFLICT) might occur when a manager, effective because her team respect her, has to announce a redundancy.

Role management The new employee takes on role expectations and tasks with increasing ease and develops wide enough knowledge to count as a regular member.

Intra-group behaviour (behaviour within groups)

The influence of groups on the individual

We have assumed, above, that where group norms exist these are effectively transmitted by the majority of the group to new members in a fairly comprehensive way. Psychologists have produced ample evidence concerning the strength of group pressure on an individual. The work of Asch is almost too famous to require description (a full account can be found in Gross, 1992). Asch (1956) demonstrated the 'emperor's clothing' effect that unwitting participants could be persuaded to agree that two obviously unequal lines were in fact equal when six or seven other 'students' (actually confederates of the experimenter) publicly agreed that they were. Although some critics argue that the effect was a product of the 1950s, Nicholson et al (1985) give evidence that it is still observable in UK and US participants. In addition, the important point in the work context is not so much how many people *conform* but the fact that most peo-

Within organisations, new workers are socialised into normative patterns of behaviour through many informal processes, including canteen conversation.

ple who do *not* conform in these circumstances feel *very* uncomfortable.

Of special importance to the occupational psychologist would be the findings of Crutchfield (1955) because these studies were carried out on a management training course for US military personnel. Officers were given false information that four other peers agreed with wrong or inappropriate answers. Unexpectedly strong conformity to the group view was demonstrated when, for instance, 37% agreed with the statement, 'I doubt whether I would make a good leader'. No officers in a control group (answering alone) agreed with this.

Also important here, for the work situation, is the fact that members of minority groups were more likely to conform to the group answer when their minority status was emphasised by the nature of the rest of the group. A similar effect was found for female participants. This has particular relevance to the phenomenon of 'groupthink', described below, where wrong and damaging decisions are taken because group members are wary of speaking out. It has of course *general* relevance to the issue of creating conditions where people feel comfortable about disagreeing in public. This is made dramatically clear by an example from Brown (1988) of a section of cockpit conversation between three crew members bringing a passenger plane in to land:

Co-pilot: (*cautiously*) Isn't this a little faster than you normally fly this John?

Captain: (*confidently*) Oh yeah, but it's nice and smooth. We're going to get in right on time. Maybe a little ahead of time. We've got it made.

Co-pilot: (*uncertainly*) I sure hope so.

Engineer: You know, John, do you know the difference between a duck and a co-pilot?

Captain: What's the difference?

Engineer: Well, a duck can fly!

Captain: Well said!

This was in the last few minutes before the plane crashed. Here a majority of just two, including some seniority of rank, managed to silence a very wise minority.

What sort of group influence?

Two main mechanisms have been put forward as explanations for influence processes: NORMATIVE SOCIAL INFLUENCE (NSI) and INFORMATIONAL SOCIAL INFLUENCE (ISI). *Normative influence* is defined by Deutsch and Gerard (1955) as 'the influence to conform with the positive expectations of another', that is, we conform to group norms because it is comfortable and we receive support from others. This seems plausible. In everyday social interactions people are constantly attempting to discover the expectations of others in order to decide what forms of behaviours would be most appropriate. In their first few weeks, new employees will usually limit themselves to observing what is happening around them. 'Learning the ropes' in the social sense refers to discovering organisational culture and the norms which govern behaviour within work groups.

Informational influence is defined by Deutsch and Gerard as 'influence to accept information obtained from another as evidence about reality', that is, we may alter our opinion because we receive information from others and *not* because we are worried about deviating from group norms. Some of Asch's participants reported that they changed their minds because, since everyone else was in agreement, there must be something wrong with their eyes. This is a rational decision based on information (assuming the participant is being honest) rather than an attempt to look good. In social interactions, shifts or changes in a person's ideas, beliefs or attitudes are associated with greater psychological discomfort when they result from NSI than from ISI. NSI agreement tends to be 'all the way' whereas ISI is often a compromise position, since ISI is based on reason rather than social pressure. Burnstein and Vinokur (1977) suggest that ISI depends on the ratio of pro and con arguments accessible to individuals who are formulating their views or making decisions.

Innovation: minority influence

Despite the power of majority influence, MINORITY INFLUENCE cannot be ignored for if it did not exist little innovation would be possible. Many studies have attempted to discover how minority views come to influence a majority. Moscovici (1985) proposes that minorities who are *confident* and *consistent* in presenting their view *can* succeed in their attempts at influence, especially where the minority view is realistic and in accord with changing times against an outmoded majority view. Nemeth (1986) argues that minority views which deviate from majority views have positive effects on group decision-making. Such challenges force the majority to look at problems from new perspectives. Without minority views narrow-mindedness may develop. Nemeth concludes that majorities exposed to minority views make better decisions even if the views of the latter are incorrect. In terms of leadership, this suggests that leaders should encourage minorities to state their views and foster group norms which encourage minority participation.

There are some reservations about the minority influence model. Maas et al (1982) use the term *single minority* for groups who simply differ in opinion and argue that DOUBLE MINORITIES, those who, in addition, clearly belong to an out-group (e.g. defined by race or gender), are less effective since they can be dismissed as different anyway. The research also doesn't account for minorities with power, such as two managers attending a general staff meeting. Brown (1985) argues that minority groups do not only use argument but use organised actions, such as meeting as a caucus before a large group meeting, and, in general, create a power base. This has occurred recently where small shareholders have produced a strategy to protest at shareholders' meetings about large pay rises for executives in recently privatised UK companies. Brown also argues that a minority might be successful for a short while but that the majority, once it realises it is under attack, may well fight back as has the 'moral majority' in the USA and, to some extent, in the UK.

Group cohesiveness

GROUP COHESIVENESS refers to the extent to which members interact positively and adhere to norms without conflict. A cohesive group is not necessarily productive nor need it be forward-thinking or inventive. As we have seen, a *lack* of difference or small-scale conflict, or the presence of strong peer pressures may well lead to narrow-mindedness and an inflexible group. Nevertheless, psychologists would obviously be interested in analysing the processes which lead to healthy cohesiveness, which in turn produces productive and satisfied work groups. There is much research in this area so here we can only summarise (in Table 3) some of the main factors found to be associated with cohesive groups (for supportive research, see Riggio, 1990).

Field research has produced support for the view that external threat produces cohesiveness. Stagner and Eflal (1982) were able to compare USA Ford car workers who went on strike in 1976 with Chrysler and General Motor Company workers who did not. The Ford workers showed greater militancy, more support for their leaders and

For industrial action to be effective, workers need to be involved in highly *cohesive* groups.

TABLE 3

Factors associated with group cohesiveness

Goals	groups with a clear set of goals, which are perceived as valid and shared by most group members, tend to be more cohesive
Similarity	the more similar the members, the more cohesive the group
Size	larger groups tend to lose their cohesiveness, a clear example occurring in the Trist and Bamforth (1951) study described earlier
Status	where workers are of more equal status, cohesiveness is likely to be higher
Stability	new members, with new, unfamiliar or unpredictable qualities, can disrupt cohesiveness; the less turnover, the greater the cohesiveness, though familiarity might also breed contempt and disharmony in some cases
Threat	nothing brings people together like an external threat; this can generate an us–them mentality which can also be obstructive in organisations as a whole where, for instance, it is caused by an aggressive management style. Some studies show, however, that cohesiveness only improves where people have some hope of success against the threat – see Rabbie et al (1974) below

greater union participation. Myers (1962) showed that only those army cadet rifle teams who *won* their events tended to increase in cohesiveness after competition, whereas losers tended to be *less* satisfied than before with their group members. Rabbie et al (1974) used a union–management simulation to show that *anticipation* of conflict enhanced cohesiveness but only for those groups who were informed that they were in a strong bargaining position, presumably because they expected success, thus echoing the Myers finding.

Leadership and its effects on group cohesion

The concept of leadership

Why is leadership so fascinating? Political leaders, social leaders, religious or business leaders – we like some and hate others. Moreover, we often think we can distinguish between effective and less effective leaders. However, this is often far from the truth. In the present context we shall be interested in what style of leadership can best create and maintain group cohesiveness and the extent to which this ability, or any others, can make groups productive, satisfied, or, better still, both. We might also want to distinguish between:

APPOINTED LEADERS – for instance, a manager appointed by management rather than chosen by the workers
and
EMERGENT LEADERS – for instance, a popular staff social group leader.

Fiedler (1967) defines a leader as:

> '*the individual in the group given the task of directing and co-ordinating task-relevant group activities, or who, in the absence of a designated leader, carries the primary responsibility for performing these functions in the group.*'

Trait theories

Trait theories (see Appendix 1) argue that effective leaders are people who possess certain characteristics such as intelligence, dominance, self-confidence and so on which others do not. Training, according to *biologically* based trait theories, is generally irrelevant since leadership and follower qualities would be determined from conception. Research on trait theories has often shown that there is little relationship between people's personality characteristics and their effectiveness as leaders (Stogdill, 1974; Yetton, 1984). However, recent tests of trait explanations have reported higher correlations than those reported by earlier studies. For instance, Lord et al (1986), using meta-analysis (see Appendix 2), estimated the correlation between intelligence and leadership to be around 0.52 compared with earlier estimates of 0.25. Nonetheless, high correlations do not indicate that intelligence or any other correlates of leadership are inborn (or that they *cause* good leadership).

Behaviour theories

According to these theories, leadership effectiveness is a function of leader *behaviour*. Whether leaders are effective or not in achieving organisational goals, or improving employee satisfaction and motivation, depends on what they *do* and how they treat those under their supervision. This approach to the study of leadership *style* is illustrated by the work of Lewin et al (1939) who trained leaders of boys' club groups to run activities (such as making papiermâché masks) as follows:

- *democratic* – chatted with the boys; included them in decisions about what to do
- *autocratic* – issued orders; *told* boys what to do (they did what the first group had chosen)
- *laissez-faire* – left boys to themselves (after instructing them to do the same as others).

Leaders were rotated and used varying styles. Against trait theory, effects observed were dependent on the *styles* not on the individual leaders producing them. Contrary to widespread belief, no one style was consistently superior in all aspects. While the democratic style was found to foster higher morale, the autocratic style was found to

be more effective in producing results from the tasks. The third group displayed low morale *and* little productivity. As we shall see below, 'open' leadership also seems to lead to superior group decisions. There is also some indication that these leadership styles do not have the same effects across cultures. Meade (1967) reported that in India the autocratic style seemed to produce superior results.

The Ohio studies

A later set of studies which prompted a great deal of research was the leadership research programme at the Ohio State University (Stogdill and Coons, 1957; Fleishman and Harris, 1962). This research identified two dimensions of leadership:

- *initiating structure* – leaders tend to attach more importance to defining group tasks and roles as well as the pattern and type of relations within the groups which they believe will achieve the desired work outcomes. Deadlines and production goals are stressed
- *consideration* – leaders are more concerned with establishing a good rapport with the group and its members, and in promoting mutual trust and respect. They encourage communication from and between staff and bolster workers' self-confidence.

These two dimensions were confirmed by a number of follow-up studies and were replicated by research in Germany (Tscheulin, 1971). In the workplace these two dimensions have been found to correlate with a number of work behaviours. Among other things, the study by Fleishman and Harris (1962) found that high levels of consideration were associated with low employee grievance rate and labour turnover but also with lower productivity – reminiscent of the Lewin study results. High levels of structure on the other hand, tended to be associated with opposite effects.

Blake and Mouton's MANAGERIAL GRID®

Blake and Mouton (1985) have applied the task-oriented vs person-oriented leader concept just described to business training. They ask managers to rate themselves on the two dimensions using a 1 to 9 point scale. They assume that the best management style is a 9:9 scoring manager (high on both dimensions), and they offer training which moves the manager in that direction. A manager scoring 1 on *task* and 9 on *person* orientation is known as a 'Country Club' manager, producing a comfortable team who presumably do not produce much in a day. Others have criticised the model since it emphasises just one type whereas it may well be that a *moderate* combination of *both* dimensions is effective or that one style is better for some tasks or situations and not for others. This is, in fact, the position taken by CONTINGENCY THEORIES.

Contingency theories

Supporters of the contingency model of leadership argue that neither trait nor behaviour theories provide adequate explanations for leadership. While these theorists accept the general task-person oriented distinction, they add that the effectiveness of leadership behaviour also depends on *situational demands*.

Fiedler's model – the LEAST PREFERRED CO-WORKER *measure*   This theory evolved from the analyses of research data collected over a decade in the 1960s, though Fiedler is still adding to his overall database and still adjusting his theory. His most prominent proposition was based on an observation that good therapists tended to see their patients as much like themselves. This was extended to leadership positions in general and Fiedler (1967) developed a measure of the Least Preferred Co-worker (LPC), a scale which measures a person's view of the person they have least liked working with. Leaders who obtain high LPC scores assess even poor co-workers quite positively and are equivalent to leaders high on consideration. Low scorers tend to be high on structure. High LPC leaders are able to distinguish between work competence and personal qualities. A poor worker may still be accepted as a pleasant person.

Low LPC leaders are less likely to make such distinctions; they find it hard to like poorer workers. Fiedler identified three key factors of any situation which can influence leadership effectiveness in addition to a leader's personality and style:

- *leader–member relations* – the quality of interpersonal relations between leaders and their subordinates. Leader–member relations are high when the members like and trust their leader and when the leader has confidence in the group
- TASK STRUCTURE – the clarity of tasks, the number of decisions and solutions possible and the objectives associated with task execution. Where structure is poorly defined, the leader must rely more on motivation and not on established rules and procedures
- POSITION POWER – the amount of power vested in the leader's role, the rewards and punishments which can be administered and the degree of background organisation support. For example, motorists are more likely to listen to, and act on, instructions from a traffic warden than a passer-by with no equivalent legitimate power.

The combination of high and low values of the three situational variables just described gives a possible eight different situations seen in Table 4.

These eight combinations determine SITUATION FAVOURABILITY as being high or low. Leader effectiveness, according to this theory, depends on the quality of match between leadership style and situation favourability. The theory contends, for example, that where situations are either highly favourable or highly unfavourable, a *low* LPC leader will be more effective. This is because when the situation is highly favourable there is little need to focus on improving interpersonal relations as these are already good and low LPC lead-

TABLE 4
Aspects of situation favourability

	High	←		Situation favourability		→	Low	
L-M relations	Good	Good	Good	Good	Poor	Poor	Poor	Poor
Task structure	High	High	Low	Low	High	High	Low	Low
Position power	Strong	Weak	Strong	Weak	Strong	Weak	Strong	Weak

ers concentrate on getting the job done. In highly unfavourable situations it is probably not *worth* trying to improve relations and the leader may as well concentrate on the task. When the situation is moderately favourable, group effectiveness will be better under high LPC leaders who, being people oriented, will be better able to improve group performance by fostering good relations with the members.

The other important point to remember about this theory is the suggestion that leaders should be assigned to situations which are favourable to their styles, a version of *fitting the worker to the job*. The original theory suggested that leadership styles are stable. Thus, instead of training leaders to adapt their styles to the situation we should assess the situation first, especially its level of favourability, and then choose leaders with the most suitable characteristics (Fiedler and Chemers, 1984). Despite the complexity of Fiedler's theory and the fact that it does not seem to give enough attention to possible changes in situation favourability over time, it has received some support. Meta-analyses of past studies (e.g. Strube and Garcia, 1981; Peters, Hartke and Pohlmann, 1985) have been supportive of the theory. Fiedler's later COGNITIVE RESOURCE THEORY (Fiedler and Garcia, 1987) takes into account other leader characteristics, such as the combination of intelligence and experience which they employ in different situations. Although he originally argued that leadership styles were largely stable, he has accepted for some time that leaders can vary their typical style depending on the combination of task features and group relationships they encounter. This is the emphasis of the following model.

THE VROOM AND YETTON DECISION MODEL This contingency model, centring on leader decision-making, was first proposed by Vroom and Yetton (1973) and developed around the *decision-making style* favoured by leaders. The styles are determined by the extent to which leaders involve or do not involve their subordinates in the decision-making process. The theory identifies five different styles:

| AI | *autocratic style* | leader makes a decision with information unavailable to others |
| CI | *individual consultation* | leader informs the subordinates about the problem *individually*, asks their opinions, then makes the decision alone |

AI *autocratic style* — leader makes a decision with information unavailable to others

AII *minimal consultation* — leader collects information relevant to the problem from subordinates and then makes the decision alone

CI *individual consultation* — leader informs the subordinates about the problem *individually*, asks their opinions, then makes the decision alone

CII *group consultation* — leader shares the problem with the subordinates *as a group*, listens to their ideas, then makes the decision alone

GII *full participation* — leader shares the problem with subordinates and accepts whatever decision is reached by collective group agreement. In this style the leader considers himself or herself more as a member of the group.

The model also takes into account situational variables concerning the *quality* of the decision required and the importance of gaining the subordinates' *acceptance* of the decision. In deciding on a course of action for problem-solving a leader needs to ask questions such as:

- is there enough information for a quality decision?
- are subordinates committed to the goals of the organisation?
- will subordinates conflict with each other over the decision?

Answering these questions and using a decision chart provided by Vroom and Yetton, a leader could progress towards one or several strategies (AI to GII, above) which would suit the problem. For instance, a manager introducing new working conditions might choose a more consultative strategy than when the problem concerns redundancy.

Vroom and Jago (1978) asked 96 managers to think back and identify both successful and unsuccessful decisions they had made. These were analysed and it was discovered that when the managers made their decisions in ways similar to that suggested by the model, 68 per cent of decisions were successful, whereas only 22 per cent of decisions not conforming to the model were successful. Later, Vroom and Jago (1988) revised the

model and identified some additional situational characteristics such as *time constraint* and *physical proximity*. The first involves considering whether enough time is available for consultation and the second considers the cost of bringing together all the subordinates. Vroom and Jago have now developed computer software for selecting the best decision style for any given problem. The early theory has been strengthened by much supportive research (e.g. Field, 1982; Heilmann et al, 1984; Crouch and Yetton, 1987).

BOX 3

McGregor's theory y

Theory X	Theory Y
Workers are lazy; they shun responsibility and challenge; they work only because they have to, for money; they are not to be trusted; they are apathetic, irrational, unreliable and respond mainly to reward and punishment. Management therefore involves controlling individuals by external means.	Workers enjoy work in itself; they are self-motivated and take pride in their work; they are trustworthy and accept responsibility and challenge; being rational, they will appreciate the need for greater efforts at times; negative attitudes are the result of bad experience within the organisation. Management therefore involves facilitating workers to achieve and to appreciate that satisfaction of organisational goals can lead to personal satisfaction and well-being.

Leaders' beliefs and expectancies – McGregor's THEORY X AND Y

Work by McGregor (1960) focused on the *attitudes* or *expectancies* of managers concerning their subordinates and their control. There is no doubt a strong link between leaders' attitudes, their LPC position and all the other variables we have considered so far. McGregor outlined two possible BELIEF SYSTEMS (sets of attitudes) which are extremes – see Box 3. 'Theory' is not intended in the usual academic sense here, but refers to the individual manager's belief system. Unfortunately, McGregor's notion is much misunderstood. The two alternatives are very widely interpreted as the *only* two possibilities, whereas McGregor firmly stated (1967, a publication after his death in 1964)

that there could be *many* different belief systems in existence. An example (one which Landy, 1985, describes as a 'recent fad') is Ouchi's 'theory Z', described later.

Leadership research today – transactional and transformational leaders

The leadership theories reviewed so far fall into a category referred to as TRANSACTIONAL theories of leadership and effectiveness. Typically, they focus on what leaders *do* or *think* and how they vary (if they do) their leadership styles to suit the requirements of both the task and the subordinates. Recently, however, there are signs that leadership

Margaret Thatcher: a recent *charismatic* leader in British politics.

research has gone full circle. Since the late 1970s studies have focused more again on the personal qualities of leaders which were the focus of research interest at the turn of the twentieth century. CHARISMATIC LEADERSHIP (House et al, 1991) and leaders' intellectual characteristics (Bass, 1985) are becoming the focus of research which concerns TRANSFORMATIONAL LEADERSHIP. This emphasises the leader's role as one who promotes a set of assumptions within an organisation. If an organisation requires change, it is the transformational leader's role to shift values and assumptions which will help move the organisation to its new position and shape. In short, transformational leaders manage an 'organisational culture' – see below. The research on transformational leaders focuses on how they manage to gain subordinates' trust and how they manage their team's values, motivation and self-esteem in such ways that staff performance may surpass required levels. Transformational leaders have been found to receive higher ratings for performance, they are more likely to be promoted and have higher management abilities (Hater and Bass, 1986). Their subordinates are happier and their work efforts are superior (Pereira, 1986).

Intra-group conflict – conflict within groups

We have seen that conflict can occur *within* groups as a result of role conflicts, minority and

majority views or poor leadership style. Kabanoff (1985) suggests that most conflicts can be understood as the interaction of any two of six possible sources of influence on work teams. These sources are:

- *informal*   factors not part of the official organisational structure
- *ability/knowledge*   what an individual group member knows or can do
- *assignment*   a person's or job's position in the communication framework
- *authority*   the power attached to a role or person
- *allocation*   tasks, time or resources officially allocated to positions, jobs
- *precedence*   position or status of tasks or people in the work flow

Examples of conflict between any two of these sources might be:

- *ability/authority*   incompetent person is given a supervisory or management position
- *assignment/ allocation*   person with few links to others is given too many tasks

- *informal/
  precedence*   people believe their tasks are more crucial than they are

Resolving intra-group conflict

Kabanoff produces resolutions for the different forms of conflict which usually involve balancing up one of the deficient sources of influence. For instance, the incompetent person can be retrained or their supervision can be limited to new staff only. The person with few links can be put in formal touch with others, can delegate or can be given fewer tasks. The third case requires better communication.

Other resolutions of intra-group conflict can be developed from Table 3. Conflict is likely to reduce where groups are given a common goal to pursue which deals with an external threat (as we shall see). A method for promoting group cohesion and aimed specifically at reducing racial hostility within school groups was the JIGSAW METHOD used by Aronson et al (1978), described in the educational psychology chapter. The technique is often used at teambuilding workshops and consists of presenting a group with a problem and giving one part of the solution to each group member. Only co-operation and sharing can produce a result for the group as a whole. Deutsch's (1949) success with student co-operative group working is also described in that chapter but the relevance here is that his students not only worked harder and were more productive, they also liked each other more than those in competitive groups. Johnson et al's (1981) review of more than 100 studies gave strong support to co-operative working compared with competitive groups, making Brown (1988) wonder why our society relies so heavily on competition in education and the workplace.

Groups may conflict internally because members are dissimilar, in which case some attempt at attitude change is in order (e.g. race awareness training). We shall look further at issues of internal group conflict and its resolution when we consider decision-making and communication within groups. Also, some of the factors affecting intra-group conflict are in common with those concerned with inter-group conflict – the clashes *between* definable groups.

Inter-group behaviour – conflict and co-operation between groups

MINIMAL GROUPS – from in-group cohesion to inter-group conflict

A series of studies, initiated by Rabbie and Horowitz (1969) and extended by Tajfel et al (1971), serve as a useful bridge between the notion of in-group cohesion and inter-group competition. Tajfel showed that simply being allocated to a group on a completely arbitrary basis (e.g. the toss of a coin) led individuals to allocate more to their own group than to another, even though they had not been introduced to the rest of the group. Important here was the concept of *differential*. Participants awarded amounts to their own group which would not advantage the other group even where this meant that, overall, they obtained less than they could have received. For instance, they would prefer a them (13) – us (13) split to a them (25) – us (19) split! At work, it is often the *difference* between what others get (especially those close to us) and what we get, or between their conditions and ours, that matters to us, rather than any absolute assessment of hard work or pay levels.

Tajfel's work stresses the formation of 'group identities' *prior to and independent of any competition*. This somewhat challenged earlier views which held that group competition *created* cohesiveness, as is predicted in Table 3 with reference to external threats. The earlier view was supported by now classic studies by Sherif et al (1961) who showed that competition temporarily destroyed previously existing ties between boys at a summer camp and increased inter-group hostility to a serious level. The only strategy found to *undo* this rivalry was the introduction of a goal important to the whole camp (fixing a broken water tank and a broken down bus taking them all to a movie). This would support the earlier notion that external threats *produce* cohesion.

Tajfel, however, argues that the behaviour of individuals towards members of other groups is largely determined, not by threat, but by GROUP IDENTITY and membership, where group identity is emphasised. Brown (1985) holds that in a union–management negotiation, interaction will be determined far more by the *position* each person will take because of their group membership (identity) and 'mandate' than by their personality characteristics. The interaction might be quite different, and more personality-based, in a chance meeting at the golf club. Minard (1952), in a study of West Virginian coal miners, found that their group identities and norms *above* ground still largely determined typical group behaviour of non-integration (white miners lived and socialised separately from black miners), even though some 60% of white miners integrated *below* ground, partly because union and management sanctioned prejudiced behaviour. The group identity argument makes it easier to see why 'double minorities' should find it harder to shift majority opinion (see p. 230). They do not just present an alternative view from that of the majority but also require majority members to identify with an 'out-group'.

The positive side of inter-group conflict

Although there are obvious negative effects of conflict in terms of reduced communication and lower efficiency, especially where members concentrate more on the in-fighting than the original goals, there are several *positive* benefits to the organisation from a non-destructive level of conflict between groups (Riggio, 1990). Conflict can:

- motivate and energise group members; lack of competition can produce complacency
- stimulate creativity and innovation as members seek efficient solutions
- improve the quality of decisions, since members must consider opposing views
- relieve underlying tensions by bringing conflicts to the surface for discussion
- improve worker satisfaction where conflict is permitted through participation in decisions.

Reducing inter-group conflict

Thomas (1976) lists several possible resolutions of group conflict which appear to be exhaustive:

- *competition* one group wins, hence the other must lose (*win–lose*)
- *accommodation* giving in, hence the other side gains something (*lose–win*)
- *compromise* each side gives up something (*lose–lose*)
- *collaboration* sides co-operate (*win–win*); not possible where conflict is over limited resources
- *avoidance* conflict is suppressed; differences likely to continue affecting work efficiency and disharmony in relations.

Can't we just get the workers all together? – the CONTACT HYPOTHESIS

Some conflict in work organisations occurs simply because work groups do not meet. Stereotypes are allowed to strengthen because they are not disconfirmed. The original hostility may well be based on perception of differentials in that, for instance, the shop-floor workers note that the office staff receive slightly better pay yet arrive an hour later each day; the engineering tutors ridicule the social science staff for their sloppy administration and dress. It can be an enlightening experience to sit amongst the group which your group members constantly deride, only to find that this group do the same thing and are convinced of the validity of their own (unrealistic) perceptions of *your* group! Social psychologists have therefore spent much energy in researching the effects of bringing people together in order to reduce the stereotypes which are strengthened by lack of social contact. As we saw above, one method employed by the Sherifs to reduce group conflict was to introduce a SUPERORDINATE GOAL whose achievement was of mutual benefit. Managers might naïvely believe that simply bringing together members of two conflicting teams in, say, a formal discussion, a sporting event or an informal party, might reduce hostility through the destruction of inter-group myths. Research has shown, especially that of Cook (1978), that the party is likely to be successful, rather than competition or formality, but only if the following conditions are met:

- members do not behave in ways which confirm the existing stereotype
- members are seen as typical of their group (otherwise they can be rationalised away by the argument 'I don't mean you; you're different!')
- meetings are informal so personal relationships are possible

- members can engage in tasks requiring mutual co-operation
- the environment *supports* co-operative behaviour and stereotype reduction; the effort will be unsuccessful where meetings are arranged by staff who tacitly support the stereotypes or are obviously performing a token gesture
- members have equal status – this will be the hardest criterion to meet in the real world of work, though some efforts can be made to reduce obvious signs of status difference, such as use of first names, neutral territory, lack of uniform, and so on.

Of course, attempts at reduction of conflict through increased contact may fail miserably if group members discover that they are indeed far apart in values and attitude, as was discovered by Trew (1986) in Northern Ireland.

Group decision-making – conflict and cohesiveness effects

Individual versus group decision-making

Kurt Lewin, a highly influential early researcher on group decision processes, believed that human reason was a social value. He was involved in attempts to get people to use cheaper meat during the Second World War and conducted applied psychology experiments to demonstrate that if people were permitted to arrive at conclusions by themselves, through the self-discovery of facts in group discussion, genuine changes of attitude would be more easily obtained than through efforts at *persuasion*. As we shall see, later research has shown that individuals are not always rational decision-makers; decision errors have been attributed to many psychological factors, both motivational and emotional.

Group polarisation

This refers to a process affecting groups in such a way that their decisions are more extreme than decisions that would have made by group members individually. This was originally known as the RISKY SHIFT phenomenon after Stoner's work (1961, in a famous, yet unpublished experiment on business students), which shows that groups tended to move towards a more *risky* decision

than did the individual members of those groups when asked alone. The results were soon confirmed (Wallach et al, 1962) along with the existence of a complementary shift to caution where, initially, the individual group members are cautious in their attitudes (Fraser, Gouge and Billig, 1971). Hence it appears that the shift which occurs when individuals discuss a decision as a group is to a more extreme position in the same direction as the average group member stood *before* discussion.

Group polarisation has several viable explanations. One explanation is that of REDUCED RESPONSIBILITY (at least psychological responsibility). When decisions are taken in groups the individual members feel that the burden of responsibility does not fall entirely on them; it is shared. Another explanation is that of SOCIAL COMPARISONS (Brown, 1965). Here it is argued that if risk-taking is positively valued then, in the presence of others, individuals would seek to appear as risk-takers, perhaps more so in order to appear socially desirable. The opposite would be expected in cultures that place no value or negative value on risk-taking behaviour. The PERSUASIVE ARGUMENTATION explanation argues that each group member will be exposed more frequently to the dominant view. Hence, so long as correct and new information is persuasive, more influence will occur for the majority view.

Groupthink

Group cohesiveness has so far been considered necessary for group maintenance, but, like everything else, too much of it may have negative effects. Asch's studies showed the strength of group pressure in producing unwise agreement with others. A danger of over-cohesiveness is the GROUPTHINK phenomenon which can lead to very poor decisions. Recall the cockpit conversation which preceded an airplane crash described earlier. The first two lines of Brown's (1988) extract run:

Captain: Well, we know where we are; we're all right.

Engineer: The boss has got it wired.

The captain's opening confidence, followed immediately by support, makes it highly unlikely that the three-person crew will engage in a full, open discussion consequent upon the co-pilot's ensuing expression of unease about their position.

Janis (1972) coined the term 'groupthink' to denote the kinds of calamitous political decision-making seen in the 1960s, especially the Bay of Pigs episode where President Kennedy's government *in retrospect* made a ludicrous decision to send 1400 poorly trained, unfit and doomed Cuban exiles to retake Cuba against 20 000 Cuban troops. Apparently, the Argentinian invasion of the Falkland Islands should not have been a surprise (Franks, 1983). Janis also studied disastrous business decisions, such as the decision to distribute the drug Thalidomide, which led to so many birth deformities, and the Ford Motor Company's record flop with the 'Edsel' car. (Janis might also have been interested in the UK flop of the Sinclair C5 electric car which topped 15 miles per hour.) According to Janis, several features combine to create groupthink:

- group members assume they are invulnerable
- group members assume that their decision is morally correct
- opposition views are disposed of by belittling their holders – as with the co-pilot above
- negative evidence is explained away – see the Challenger example below
- pressure to conform (see Asch, above); open dissent is seen as food for the enemy
- group members suppress their own misgivings, as did the co-pilot eventually
- illusion of unanimity; PLURALISTIC IGNORANCE (Latané and Darley, 1968) may operate where, since others aren't saying anything, it is assumed there is no problem and that they all agree
- 'mind guards' operate – members who hustle for support and keep bad news from their leader; the engineer played this role in the air accident above.

Although Janis, and many other writers *assume* that cohesiveness is a major factor contributing to groupthink phenomena, some research contradicts this and offers *style of leadership* as a crucial variable. Flowers (1977) demonstrated this in a simulation experiment. Groups whose leaders were open and non-directive, permitting all group members to participate, produced more solutions

and studied more information. ECOLOGICAL VALIDITY was provided by Vinokur et al (1985) who analysed real-life expert conferences in which decisions were taken on medical technology. Quality of decisions made was dependent on leadership style but in some cases *positively* correlated with cohesiveness, rather than *negatively* as Janis would predict. What seems important, whether the group is tight-knit or not, is that groups consider information fully and do not rush to embrace the first acceptable solution. This latter tendency was noted by Hoffman and Maier as early as 1961, especially where the problem was complex.

Janis suggested several strategies for the avoidance of groupthink decisions:

- appoint devil's advocates to take contrary positions (as Kennedy did for the Cuban Missile Crisis of 1962)
- permit members to discuss issues with associates outside the meeting (as far as security permits)
- form sub-groups to discuss policy aspects then reconvene
- allow a period of second chance reconsideration of doubts and alternatives
- leader encourages *all* members to speak their mind and encourages criticism.

This last point is important where groups are large because people generally lower their input the larger the group – known as SOCIAL LOAFING (Latané et al, 1979). This effect, however, is probably (Western) culture bound in that Earley (1989) found management trainees from China did not perform in this manner compared with North Americans, possibly because a sense of shared responsibility is paramount in strongly socialist societies.

Brainstorming Further strategies to avoid early and possibly inferior or unwise solutions are contained in the procedure of BRAINSTORMING, where participants in a problem-solving session are instructed to call out any associations once they occur in the mind and not to censor anything just because it *seems* irrelevant. Members make no critical comment on others' productions. This way, it is hoped, inhibited members will feel free to speak, no ideas will be lost and the group will not move too soon down one track to the exclusion of all others.

Communication in groups and organisations

Why do spaceships blow up?

A more recent disaster which appears to have suffered from some features of groupthink was the loss of the US space shuttle Challenger in 1986, seen by millions on television as it blew to pieces soon after launch with a civilian schoolteacher on board. Here, several clear warnings had been given of highly likely dangers connected with 'O' ring seals, yet a series of seemingly irrational group decisions to proceed occurred. Some warning signs, presented by worried engineers, were explained away. For instance, 'burn out' (erosion) of one third of the Challenger 'O' ring on previous launches was taken as a 'safety factor' of three (there's two-thirds left after all!) See Saks and Krupat (1988) and Reason (1990).

To some extent groupthink phenomena were present. Staff did not want to be personally responsible for delaying the launch (especially as President Reagan was organised to talk with the teacher on live television). There was pressure not to dissent and there were 'mind guards' hustling others and filtering information. However, further analysis by the presidential commission investigating the decision-making process revealed that a major problem lay with the system of communication within the NASA (National Aeronautics and Space Administration) organisation. One member of the commission said, 'It's so structured that communication is inhibited. No matter how big a problem is, there ought to be a top dog who is responsible.' (*Newsweek*, March 3, 1986, cited in Saks and Krupat, 1988).

NASA is a huge organisation and the system at that time permitted full discussion and decision-making at various levels with only very serious problems making it to the top. It was thought that, with so many teams involved in a launch, decisions would not be at all possible if they all had to go to the top for confirmation. Even the head of the space shuttle programme admitted that the top level of decision-making (who ought to have heard about the 'O' ring problem) was

Features of groupthink and weaknesses in organisational communication were apparent in the sequence of decisions leading to the fatal launch of Challenger in 1986.

'hard to define' (Saks and Krupat, 1988). Some even argued that this was purposely constructed so that it would be hard to pinpoint responsibility in the event of this kind of disaster.

The communication system or network within organisations, then, is crucial in decision-making and eventual performance. It depends on several of the organisational factors so far considered (leadership style, traditions of formality, cohesiveness, state of conflict, decision-making style) as well as on simple environmental factors, such as layout of offices, telephone links, media used (e-mail, memo, fax, etc.) and so on.

Organisational communication patterns

Consider the difference between hearing, through the informal grapevine, that your office team is to be moved to an inferior building, or that you will have a new, disliked head of department, and being told this at a formal meeting with explana-

tion of more positive compensations, or participating in a group discussion where the outcome
proposed emerges as the only satisfactory one for
everybody's secure future. We have seen already in
several places that where workers are *involved* in
discussion and decisions, morale is usually higher.
Further evidence that group satisfaction can be
affected by the level of participation in problem-
solving is provided by now classic work on communication patterns. Bavelas (1969) gave
examples of several patterns of more CENTRALISED
or more DECENTRALISED structures which exist in
working relationships, some of which are shown
in Figure 7.5.

Arrows represent directions of messages
between members. Note that the 'wheel' is highly
centralised, since only the centre person can communicate with other team members. The 'Y' is
fairly centralised. It is usually drawn the right way
up but it is shown here as it would normally occur
in hierarchical organisations. Messages emanating
from higher management pass through heads of
sections to lower grade staff, whose only route for
effective communication is usually up to heads
and either up further or across to other heads in
other branches of the network. Obviously, different networks support, or create, different systems
of power and control.

The circle *without* the dotted lines represents
the sort of information chain passing around
offices on a corridor, whereas *with* the dotted lines
every member can communicate freely with all
others, as in everyday informal situations and
democratic meetings. The wheel represents a
highly structured meeting where all comments
are directed through the chair, or a strong team
system where the leader communicates with each
member in turn but they can only communicate

with their leader. Experiments conducted using
these structures, where participants solve a problem in one of these formations, have shown several abiding features of different patterns. These are
shown in Table 5, where all terms are relative to
the performance of the other pattern type group.

As expected from the socio-technical systems findings and those concerning participative decision-
making, members of decentralised groups gained
more satisfaction from their task. However, they
were not more efficient with simple tasks, taking
longer to find a solution and making more errors.
On the other hand, they were superior with complex tasks and this is of great interest since real-
life tasks are very often more complex than those
found in laboratory experiments. Decentralised
groups sent more messages. This is not surprising
given their structures in the first place. In the
centralised networks, the central members
enjoyed the task more and were almost invariably
selected as the group leader. Since members were
assigned at random, these selections and performances cannot have depended on personality variables, so we see here a very clear demonstration of
the power of *situations* to determine behaviour
rather than *personality traits* (Appendix 1).

These demonstrations involved highly artificial
tasks and interactions, yet it is easy to see how
they can be generalised, with reservation, to real
organisations. Peters and Waterman (1982), in an
influential book directed at managers attempting
to achieve company excellence, argue that organisations should ensure they have systems permitting everyone to speak to everyone. Reservations
about these generalisations would, of course,
include the fact that there are always *formal* and
informal networks in any organisation, there are

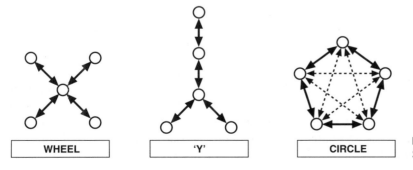

FIGURE 7.5
Simple communication networks

TABLE 5
Features of performance in different communication networks

	Centralised patterns		Decentralised patterns	
	Simple problems	Complex problems	Simple problems	Complex problems
Time to solve	Faster	Slower	Slower	Faster
Number of messages sent	Less	Less	More	More
Errors made	Less	More	More	Less
Satisfaction of group members	Lower	Lower	Higher	Higher

'leaks', and there are personalities who can operate an efficient wheel or 'Y'-type structure yet, exploiting other factors covered in this chapter, still maintain high morale.

Grapevines and rumour

The *informal* network is often known as the 'grapevine' and the effectiveness of this has been investigated by Baird (1977) in real work settings. He suggests that three major factors determine grapevine patterns: *friendship*, *usage* and *efficiency*. Obviously informal communication in organisations is likely to pass easily among friends. A head of department will find it difficult not to let a good but junior friend know who is in line for a promotion interview. Informal communication will occur most between those who are at 'nodes' (joining points) of this network. Whether good friends or not, those working closest together are most likely to pass information along the line. Finally, workers and managers often find it easier to use informal but efficient routes to get messages through, for instance, asking a colleague from another department at lunch, rather than passing a memo through several heads. According to Baird's findings, and contrary to many man-agers' beliefs, over 80 per cent of grapevine information is factually correct. False rumours are fairly rare occurrences and managers who attempt to stifle the grapevine system run the risk of generating serious ill-feeling whilst failing to have much effect on what they perceive to be a source of damage to overall company morale.

Assessing intra-group communication

One system has dominated attempts to code the communication between group members as they discuss an issue or solve a problem – that of Bales (1970) whose system was known as INTERACTION PROCESS ANALYSIS (IPA). Notice from Table 6 the categories come in opposite pairs and can be divided into TASK-ORIENTED GROUPS, asking and giving, or SOCIO-EMOTIONAL GROUPS, positive and negative. Observers are trained in the categorisation of interactions in a group usually set up for specific research processes, though studies have also been conducted in naturalistic situations (see Hare, 1976, for an early review). General findings are that the most active members of groups give out more than they receive back. Those who talk most ('initiate') tend to receive most attention. High initiators are usually popular and seen as having

TABLE 6
Categories for Interactional Process Analysis

Socio-emotional		Task-oriented	
Positive	**Negative**	**Asking**	**Giving**
Seems friendly	Seems unfriendly	Asks for information	Gives information
Dramatises	Shows tension	Asks for opinion	Gives opinion
Agrees	Disagrees	Asks for suggestion	Gives suggestion

from R.F. Bales (1970). *Personality and Interpersonal Behaviour*, New York: Holt, Rinehart and Winston the best ideas, though some studies show the highest initiator being the least liked (Bales, 1953) possibly because others get less time for discussion. In larger groups high initiators tend to take over with others joining in less – supporting the SOCIAL LOAFING concept. In laboratory groups most contributions are task-oriented with around 25 per cent being socio-emotional. Real-life groups tend to behave differently. Union–management negotiations tend to produce more negative socio-emotional behaviour.

Bales did not originally consider the perceptions by group members *themselves* of their intra-group relationships, but rectified this later. Brown (1988) gives a detailed account of SYMLOG (system for the multiple level observation of groups) which allows a more sensitive and sophisticated analysis of group interactions using 27 categories and comparing observers' *interpretations* of behaviour checked against other observers and the participants. Brown argues that a weakness of Bales' system is that it is only relevant to small face-to-face meetings and completely ignores *inter-group* relations.

Organisations as whole units

Organisational culture

Often organisations are said to behave in a similar way to individuals. Just as individual behaviour is determined partly by personality characteristics and partly by external influences, organisational behaviour is determined partly by its own internal characteristics and partly by influences from its external environment. No two organisations are exactly the same. You might notice differences in atmosphere when you shop at two different supermarket chains, possibly a result of the ways in which these different organisations select and train their employees, how they treat and organise their employees generally, and how the employees feel about their organisations. ORGANISATIONAL CULTURE is much talked about but rarely defined and even less often measured. One definition, that of Schein (1988), seems to encompass most of the

characteristics of organisational culture:

'Organisational culture is the pattern of basic assumptions that a group has invented, discovered, or developed in learning to cope with its problems of external adaptation and internal integration, and that have worked well enough to be considered valid, and, therefore, to be taught to new members as the correct way to perceive, think, and feel in relation to those problems.'

One can easily infer from this definition that much of what is done within an organisation, and how it is done, will be determined by its culture. This influence is well expressed by Uttal's (1983) definition of culture as *shared values and beliefs that interact with an organisation's structures and control systems to produce behavioural norms* (in Cooke and Rousseau, 1988). Culture does not only influence how organisation members go about their day-to-day activities, it influences almost all decisions and actions taken by an organisation in its attempts to fulfil its goals.

An organisation will usually have an ESPOUSED CULTURE and an ACTUAL CULTURE. The espoused culture is the positive image that an organisation tries to portray through their public relations officers. It is more often than not quite different from the actual culture which is the 'culture-in-use' – the one which really shapes how organisations manage their internal and external affairs. External affairs include, for instance, the quality of customer service provided, relationships with suppliers, concern about environmental issues and so on. The term ACTION STRATEGIES will be used here to refer to the ways in which an organisation manages its internal and external affairs. Occupational psychologists have developed several forms of analysis which attempt to get at actual culture and have identified the four main types of organisation culture and the features characteristic of each type shown in Box 4.

BOX 4

Types and characteristics of organisational culture

POWER CULTURE

Organisations where this type of culture dominates tend to:

- be authoritarian and hierarchical and have a service based on status differentiation
- have power figures usually concerned with personal benefits
- be highly political as people in them strive to achieve status and power; this is manifested in people endeavouring to develop close relationships with the power figure(s)
- have motivation systems built on fear and dependency
- have middle managers who try to please the boss and tyrannise subordinates whom they expect to be compliant and willing, resulting in a lack of initiative on the part of subordinates
- value leadership based on strength, justice and paternalistic benevolence; leaders should be all-knowing and powerful
- have the ability to respond quickly to changes in their environment because there is very little bureaucracy and decisions are usually made with very little consultation or none
- value honour, responsible authority and paternalism.

ROLE CULTURE

Organisations which operate this type of culture tend to:

- be large and bureaucratic and hierarchical but power is exercised through rules and procedures rather than personal power
- value logic and rationality, efficiency, good administration of systems, justice and fairness in dealing with the different parties of the organisation

- have clear and rigid procedures for roles, e.g. job descriptions, authority definitions etc.
- rely on written as opposed to face-to-face communications and rules for conflict resolution
- associate power with the individual's position in the organisational hierarchy
- encourage behaviour according to formal rules and procedures, in order for employees to be safe and secure and in order for them to succeed
- have long-life products because they are highly bureaucratic and have problems surviving in unstable fast-changing environments.

TASK CULTURE

Organisations which operate this type of culture tend to:

- be job orientated (e.g. universities and high-tech companies)
- have a main concern of getting the job done by bringing together the right people, providing them with appropriate resources and letting them get on with the job
- use neither personal nor positional power; power goes with expertise
- be flexibile and sensitive to changes in the external environment, e.g. market
- value and stress importance of teamwork as most work is project-based and work teams have the power to decide what is the best way to achieve objectives
- provide members with opportunities to use their talents and abilities more than in the previous cultures
- produce people tending to be internally motivated rather than motivated by a system of rewards and punishment
- value professionalism, produce high commitment and make high demands on their members
- possess a top management less concerned with day-to-day control than with resource allocation.

SUPPORT/PERSON CULTURE

Organisations which operate this type of culture tend to:

- be voluntary organisations rather than business organisations
- produce high commitment and have members bonded through close, warm relationships
- exhibit mutual trust and care between members, and between members and the organisation

- respond to and take care of its members' needs; members feel responsible for, and take care of the organisation
- avoid conflicts to preserve the warm climate – this is the main weakness of support culture organisations; warm climate is sometimes achieved at the expense of organisational effectiveness
- be subordinate to the individual and as such the organisation cannot have objectives which go beyond the those of its members
- value mainly compassion and empathy.

Ouchi (1981) has characterised the typical management style in the USA as producing a 'type A' organisation and the Japanese system producing 'type J'. He recommends a fusing of the best of these systems into the ideal 'type Z' organisation shown in Box 5. The systems have their origins in McGregor's (1960) Theory X and Theory Y management styles.

BOX 5

Ouchi's THEORY Z organisation

	Type A	Type J	Type Z
EMPLOYMENT	Short-term	For life	Long-term
DECISION-MAKING	Individual	Consensual	Consensual
RESPONSIBILITY	Individual	Collective	Individual
PROMOTION	Rapid	Slow	Slow
CONTROL	Explicit, formal	Implicit, informal	Implicit, informal but formal measures
CAREER PATH	Specialised	Non-specialised	Moderately specialised
CONCERN FOR PERSON	Only aspects of person	Whole person	Whole person including family

Organisational development

Organisations are dynamic social units operating in an environment which is constantly changing, often forcing them to race against change and attempt to keep their heads above water. Not all of them will be winners but those who do succeed are said to be effective developing organisations. The continuous and rapid social and technological changes outlined at the beginning of this chapter have important implications for organisational culture. Survival in these volatile conditions requires cultures which are highly responsive. Bearing in mind these changes, one can easily see why organisations with a *role culture* find it difficult to cope. Organisations with a *task culture*, on the other hand, have features which make them

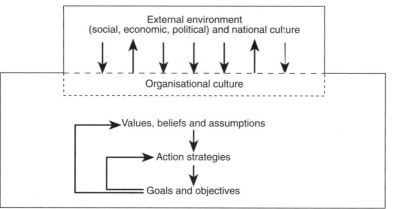

FIGURE 7.6
Organisational systems

more effective in responding to change.

Figure 7.6 depicts organisations as open systems and also shows the process of organisational change and development. Organisations do not exist in a vacuum; they are part of a larger system which is the environment within which they operate. Since organisations are open systems, their cultures are influenced by factors in this wider environment such as social, economic and political conditions. The values, norms, ideas and attitudes which people hold as a result of growing in a given society will influence the culture of an organisation (see Pascale and Athos, 1981; Pascale, 1985). Organisations are themselves systems with sub-units such as the social and the technological sub-systems. Social interaction *within* organisations and the interaction *between* organisations and their wider environment will produce norms, beliefs and assumptions which over time may be shared by organisation members and thus become part of the culture. Newcomers, as we have seen, are initiated into the existing culture through a series of *socialisation methods* of which selection is a part. Schein (1988) defines organisational socialisation as 'the process of teaching the new recruit how to get along with the organisation, what the key norms and rules of conduct are, and how to behave with respect to others in the organisation'. When organisations select new members, they usually assess whether the applicant will fit in. This is a way of trying to reduce external influences and thus maintain culture. The dashed lines in Figure 7.6 show that organisations are open to external influences. The

lower arrows indicate that failure or success in meeting organisation goals feed back to affect further strategies and have effects on the values etc., which make up the culture. A good series of articles on 'organisational culture and change' is provided in Cooper (1991).

Cultural differences in organisational culture

We have argued that shared values, norms, beliefs and assumptions influence the way organisations go about their business. This implies that two organisations may have almost the same goals and objectives yet the action strategies they adopt to achieve them will differ. Each company will have its own 'way we do things around here'. The action strategies are influenced by the differences in organisational culture which exist between the two companies. Japanese motor companies based in Europe employ the same sort of workers and technology as their European counterparts yet often produce more and better quality cars. Lawler (1992) offers the explanation that Japanese companies use a different management style. The management style used in an organisation is determined by the dominant culture within the organisation and the degree to which the norms of this culture are upheld by individual managers. The culture of most Japanese companies can be described as a QUALITY-CENTRED CULTURE which attaches great importance to customer satisfaction. This quality culture translates into a number of action strategies:

■ there is no 'us and them' belief, i.e. no strong division between management and operatives

- the message that quality is the responsibility of everyone from top to bottom is echoed everywhere
- there is open communication and equal access to information for everyone
- individual initiative is encouraged
- there is continuous personal development through training.

The need for change in organisations

Any organisation will have a set of action strategies in use because they are believed to be effective in enabling the achievement of its goals and objectives. These are maintained, reinforced and passed on to new members as long as they carry on producing the desired results. What happens if, for some reason, an organisation is no longer able to achieve its objectives? Here, depending on circumstances, the occupational psychologist may step in to help the organisation diagnose and remedy the problem. Clearly, the question begging an answer is why something which has always worked does not seem to work anymore. The answer to this question can come in several possible forms. The failure may be the result of:

- simple weakness on the part of organisation members (managers or ordinary workers) who have deviated from normal accepted practice
- members rejecting the values and norms of the organisation and thus refusing to conform to them
- external changes such that the old methods are no longer practical or effective.

Organisational development in practice

The involvement of occupational psychologists in organisational change in a business environment is well illustrated through a concrete organisational change intervention carried out in an assembly department of an electronics company (Jackson et al, 1984).

The problem The company required change because of a need to cut costs, to respond more quickly to customer orders and to produce better quality products. It was experiencing problems of unbalanced work flow and many defects in electronic circuit boards usually only detected during final quality tests. Though a variety of changes

were introduced, and the authors stress the need to consider both the social *and* technical aspects of work when introducing change, only the more *social* changes will be described here.

The change The major aim of the change was to create work teams that were highly involved in their work.

1. Rather than organise work *functionally* (i.e. testers and solderers test or solder *all* products), a decision was taken to have just one team for each product. The subsequent work performance of this team was found to be higher.
2. Following this success, product-based teams were introduced throughout the assembly department. The new teams were given broader and more flexible jobs. The acquisition of new skills for the new jobs was supported by continuous training. Management style was altered so that each team had a leader who worked with the rest of the team members, i.e. was one of them. Each team was responsible for measuring its own performance.
3. The JUST-IN-TIME (JIT) technique was introduced. This is Japanese in origin and is intended to increase work and business efficiency. The basic idea is to receive parts at a work point just as they are needed, rather than work with an excess of parts which can be wasteful and tie up resources. The technique also removes bottlenecks and reduces production queues. Since people are usually more committed to decisions in which they participate, the decision on JIT introduction was taken jointly by a group made up of representatives from the work teams, as well as from other related departments. This reinforces the message that 'everyone must be involved and everyone is responsible'. These changes increased on-time production quantity by 16% and quality by 5%.

Evaluation of change The effects of the changes were monitored for three years. During this time four surveys were carried out to discover whether employees' opinions had changed. The employees were assured that (a) the information they provided would be held in strict confidence and that (b) feedback would be provided to everyone taking part in the survey. Employees completed questionnaires during working hours. Overall the programme led to a number of changes which will now be briefly described.

First, employees reported significant improvements to their jobs:

- more opportunity to decide on their work schedules
- more autonomy in deciding how to carry out some of their job tasks
- their job involved a greater variety of tasks which meant they were learning more
- their jobs had become more cognitively demanding; they felt they were thinking more.

Second, the employees reported a number of significant improvements in the social climate at work:

- co-workers had become more supportive of each other than was the case before
- teams were more cohesive and members were working more as a team
- communication between managers and workers increased and workers were involved a lot more in decisions, work planning and change. The workers felt they were valued and listened to more than before
- though changes were not statistically significant, it appeared that workers had also become more trusting of each other; this would need firmer confirmation however.

The social improvements listed above are usually referred to as changes in ORGANISATIONAL CLIMATE. Some argue that *organisational climate* and *organisational culture* are two distinct concepts (e.g. Ashforth, 1985). While differences do exist

between the two concepts, a clear distinction is not possible. Climate is said to be *descriptive*; an idea can be formed about an organisation's climate through collecting the descriptions which its members give of the different characteristics of the organisation. Culture, on the other hand, is *normative*; it is that set of norms which bind together members of an organisation or a unit within an organisation (Cooke and Rousseau, 1988). The opinions related to the social changes stated above are descriptive of the company's *climate*. However, if co-worker support, team cohesiveness, high involvement and trust are reinforced to the extent that they become the *standard* of behaviour within the organisation, then they become part of the organisation's *culture*. If employees were satisfied with the changes and became committed to maintaining the new climate and work procedures, a new normative culture would be borne.

Due to the insight it gives into organisations, culture is becoming increasingly popular as a concept among researchers and practitioners alike. Arnold et al (1995) attribute this upsurge in organisational culture popularity to three main reasons:

- it informs decisions about mergers and acquisitions, i.e. organisations planning to merge, or planning to acquire another organisation, will find it useful to examine differences and similarities between their cultures
- it informs attempts to create a better quality culture (such as that of Total Quality Management)
- it helps create entrepreneurial cultures in newly privatised companies.

THE FUTURE OF OCCUPATIONAL PSYCHOLOGY

As one of the oldest of the applied fields occupational psychology is also probably the most comfortable within and familiar with the private sector in the UK. This familiarity has been important over the last decade and a half which has seen the privatisation of many previously state-owned enterprises. The pace has recently slowed, with an abortive attempt on the Royal Mail and hiccoughs

with railway sell-offs. Occupational psychologists have been busy in consultancy work steering organisations and management through the changes required for adaptation to private ownership. This work is likely to continue for some time as companies fail to adapt, even though the pace is slowing and may even halt with a change of government.

The issue of testing, with all its implications for equal opportunity and bias in selection, has recently been under renewed scrutiny (see, for instance, *The Psychologist*, January, 1994). The BPS now has two levels of test use competence and it is to be hoped that companies, test publishers and academics will move closer together in tackling issues of selection, promotion and equal opportunity employment.

Redundancy and unemployment are set to remain as permanent features of the late 20th century UK world of work. Workers in previously secure job areas are adapting to a climate in which no job is for life and change of occupation, with consequent re-training, is the norm. This provides new roles for occupational psychologists in redundancy counselling and occupational guidance. Ironically, some specialist areas of industry are nevertheless experiencing skill shortages and occupational psychologists will play their role in promoting more long-term, rationalised policies for producing an adequately trained workforce.

A strongly developing field is that of work in stress management where occupational psychologists may often find themselves sharing the applied fieldwork with health and clinical psychologists.

The main areas of occupational psychology interest look likely to remain those of personnel selection, leadership and training. On the academic research side, the cognitive model is thought to be capable of now producing theories specific to occupational psychology, in particular those emanating from studies of selection and appraisal interview situations.

Overall, one of the most refreshing changes appears to be the gradual movement towards realisation that psychology cannot simply focus on individuals at work irrespective of their social context. Thus, the emphasis on the study of organisations, if not simply concerned with a cultural image, looks promising where it takes a 'holistic' approach, incorporates newer qualitative methods and investigates social cognitions and relationships at all levels.

FURTHER RECOMMENDED READING

Arnold, J., Cooper, C. L. and Robertson, I. T. (1995) *Work Psychology: Understanding Work Behaviour in the Workplace*, 2nd edn. London: Pitman Publishing.

Hollway, W. (1991) *Work Psychology and Organizational Behaviour*. London: Sage.

Muchinsky, P. M. (1993) *Psychology Applied to Work: an introduction to industrial and organisational psychology*. Pacific Grove, CA: Brooks/Cole.

Riggio, E. R. (1990) *Introduction to Industrial/Organisational Psychology*. Glenview, ILL: Scott, Foresman.

Schein, E. H. (1988) *Organisational Psychology*, 3rd edn. Englewood Cliffs, NJ: Pretence-Hall.

exercises

1. ON SELECTION: SELECTING A BAR MANAGER

Your local pub has a problem. The friendly staff, whom you know very well since most of them have been there for at least 18 months, tell you that the manager has left yet again. Over the last year no manager has managed to stick with the job for more than three months. Recently, the staff have decided to test the worth of work psychology as a subject of study. Their challenge came in the following form. They gave you one week to ask every question you like about your local and they have promised that they will answer all your questions honestly and to the best of their ability. In return you have to come up with a profile of a manager whom you think is less likely to quit. The profile will be judged by them. They know why the previous managers have left and, therefore, feel they are able to predict the kind of manager who will be able to cope with the job. If you come out with a profile similar to the one they have in their heads, your drinks will be on the house for a week. If they can get the owners to appoint someone fitting the profile, your drinks are free so long as he or she stays.

Write down a profile of a manager you think will cope with the job and stick with it for at least a year and justify your choice of profile.

2. ON WORK ATTITUDES: WHAT CAN YOU DO TO HELP TROUBLES LTD?
Troubles Ltd are very worried. They have recently introduced a computerised information system which enables people to access all the information they need to make job-related decisions without having to leave their offices. A number of problems have emerged which they feel might be connected to these changes:

- more people are arriving late (11% increase)
- more absenteeism (7% increase)
- poorer productivity (low quality and quantity)
- signs of industrial relations difficulties (increased tension between management and workers).

How might the new system be responsible for these problems? What would you do to reduce or eliminate some or all the problems? Write a short proposal, to submit to Troubles Ltd, outlining the different steps you will take to remedy the problems.

3. ORGANISATIONAL CULTURE
Choose a well-known company and collect as much information about it as you can (press cuttings, company reports, recruitment brochures, advertising material, etc. You might even interview friends or acquaintances who work there but pay attention to ethical issues). Then analyse the information carefully and produce a description of the type of culture which dominates within the company.

4. DECISION-MAKING – CAUTIOUS OR RISKY GROUPS?
Get together three friends or acquaintances and ask them to make a decision on the following dilemma firstly on their own with no discussion at all. When they have decided, get them to discuss the dilemma and come to a group decision without revealing what they chose privately.

Mick is bored with his highly secure job as a civil servant. He has the opportunity to go into business with a friend running executive safari trips. This venture, though, carries the risk of failure. On the scale of probabilities below choose the point between 1 and 11 which you think is the highest level of risk you would be prepared to take if you were Mick (20% = only a 20% chance of success).

Odds for the success of Executive Safaris Ltd:

Low risk										High risk
95%	90%	80%	70%	60%	50%	40%	30%	20%	10%	5%
1	2	3	4	5	6	7	8	9	10	11

Do this with as many groups as you can. Perhaps class colleagues could do the test with other groups. Collate your results and decide whether there is a trend for groups to move towards caution, towards risk, or towards the position they were on average before group discussion. You can work out this last value by simply taking the average of the private individual scores (on the 1 to 11 scale) before the group discussion.

5. DECISION-MAKING – A PROMOTION PROBLEM

John and Jane are mechanical engineers who arrived at their positions via different routes. John joined the company as an apprentice mechanical engineer ten years ago. During this time he has demonstrated that he is a fast learner with good problem-solving skills. Jane joined the company three years ago after she graduated with a degree in mechanical engineering. During this period of time she has managed to impress and even change the opinions of most of her colleagues. She demonstrated that, contrary to their beliefs, graduates can be as good in practice as they are in theory.

As a personnel manager you have to decide whether John or Jane should replace the production manager who is retiring in five months. Work on this individually and then in a group. In the group discussion take note of the following:

- the issues raised which you hadn't thought of when deciding alone
- any tendency to close the problem early before all issues had been thoroughly discussed
- if possible, the individual style of each group member's contribution (this would be best performed by a person not taking part in the discussion and using Bales' categories)
- any attempts to weaken another view by irrational means (e.g. by ridicule).

8 SPORT PSYCHOLOGY

WHAT IS SPORT PSYCHOLOGY?

Sport plays a powerful role in modern society. Vast amounts of money, media attention and passion are poured into its many aspects. Kremer and Scully (1994) have argued that, although sport and recreation are integral elements of human experience, there is a 'gaping hole' in our knowledge and understanding of the link between sport and psychology. Recent years have seen a rapid expansion in the recruitment of, and media interest in, the services of sport psychologists. This has led to an interesting debate about whether SPORT PSYCHOLOGY has a sufficiently substantial theoretical base to allow it to deliver with confidence applied techniques aimed at enhancing performance. Putting this debate aside, broadly speaking, sport psychologists are interested in sport both as researchers and practitioners. Research into sport psychology is based on the sci-entific method and sport psychology may be defined as the 'scientific study of human behaviour and experience in sport' (where the term 'sport' is used to cover various levels of recreational activities, competitive sports, and health-oriented exercise programmes).

After the outline of what sport psychologists do, how to qualify as a sport psychologist, and the history and development of sport psychology, this chapter will cover:

- gender and personality issues
- motivation to participate and succeed in sport
- anxiety in sport
- an overview of perceptual-motor skills and mental skills training
- exercise psychology
- aggression in sport.

WHAT DO SPORT PSYCHOLOGISTS DO?

In recent years the role of psychology in sport has become more clearly defined. People have begun to recognise that sport participants do not cease to think, feel or behave when they are playing sport. Indeed many coaches and performers have started to appreciate more fully that the way they think and feel can influence performance very significantly. The 1976 Olympics were the first major games where sport psychologists were appointed to the United States team. However, it took a further eight years before the step was taken by the American team to assign psychologists in a systematic way to both the summer and winter games teams. The most recent development in America has been the use of sport psychology support for teams and individuals throughout their preparation for major sporting events.

Kremer and Scully (1994) discussed the caution shown by the American Psychological Association in accepting sport psychology as a legitimate and credible area of work. This has also been the case in the United Kingdom where the BPS waited until 1992 before acknowledging sport by forming an interest group (see chapter 1). Greater status was achieved in 1993 when a fully fledged Sport and Exercise Psychology Section was established. Well before these significant developments in the professionalisation of sport psychology, sports people at every level of performance were beginning to recognise the importance of sport psychology in terms of performance enhancement and increasing enjoyment of sport and exercise. In addition, many governing bodies of sport require trainee coaches to attend short courses and workshops aimed at increasing awareness of the importance of sport psychology. These courses are co-ordinated by the National Coaching Foundation.

The image that many people have of a sport psychologist is someone who comes in to 'psyche up' players before a game, the purpose being to make them more competitive or even aggressive. This is very misleading. There are three main areas in which sport psychologists work.

Clinical sport psychology

The clinical sport psychologist is a trained clinical psychologist (see the clinical psychology chapter) who deals with sport performers who have emotional and behavioural problems. The experience of sport can be a very intense and stressful one. Several Olympic-level performers from both Great Britain and the United States of America have been successfully treated for a range of psychological problems including acute anxiety, eating disorders, depression and obsessive-compulsive behaviour.

Research sport psychology

This type of sport psychologist is concerned with establishing a theoretical basis for this new and developing area. Many questions concerning people's experiences in sport are currently being addressed by researchers. For example, how does stress affect sport performance? What factors affect people's decision to drop out of sport? How are complex sport skills learned and controlled? A characteristic of much of the research in sport psychology is that it is *applied*. Researchers aim to ensure that their work is concerned with real-life problems confronting coaches and players. They also try to ensure that their results are made available not simply to the academic community, but also to coaches, athletes and teachers – the people dealing regularly with the problems.

Educational sport psychology

The role educational sport psychologists will provide the basis for the remainder of this section. Their main aim is to teach sport participants MENTAL SKILLS which will enhance both their performance in, and their enjoyment of, sport. An educational sport psychologist may be consulted on a wide range of issues.

Mental skills training for sport performers A psychologist can teach performers how to develop skills which will help them with the following:

■ *how to manage the stress of performing* – many performers find themselves being outplayed by inferior opponents because they are unable to control their nervousness prior to performance or at important moments in a game, race or routine

- *how to develop and maintain self-confidence* – research indicates a very strong positive correlation between confidence and the actual level of performance. By learning strategies for developing confidence, players will be able to maintain and develop this most important factor

- *how to increase the player's ability to cope with distractions* – concentration is a very important aspect of sport performance. Many sports require players to respond very quickly to infrequent opportunities, for example, a catch in cricket is as likely to come to a fielder at the end of a day's play as it is at the beginning. By developing concentration skills, a player can exploit the opportunities as they arise. Similarly, there may be many distractions confronting a player in training or performance. Learning how to deal with these can help a player maximise his or her potential

- *how to use mental rehearsal to facilitate learning of skills* – players can learn skills using their imagination. By mentally rehearsing skills, patterns of movement can be learned without making physical demands on the body. This can be very useful in situations when excessive physical training can cause stress or overload on the body in sports such as weightlifting, or when practice time is restricted, such as sky diving or competition rock climbing.

Teambuilding   There are several characteristics of successful sports teams. They tend to be well led, cohesive, and have a clear sense of purpose. Many teams underperform because one or more of these elements is missing. A sport psychologist can be consulted by a coach or manager to work with a team, and can use their knowledge and understanding to build better communication and increase cohesion. The occupational psychology chapter contains some relevant information on cohesion in groups and teambuilding.

Coach education   Sport psychologists are often involved in the training of coaches. The National Coaching Foundation, the body which co-ordi-nates coach education in the United Kingdom, has a programme of short courses and workshops aimed at keeping people who work with perform-ers of all ages and abilities aware of recent devel-opments. Courses cover a range of topics, including skill development, mental preparation for sport, effective coaching and working with children.

Personal and social development   A sport psy-chologist may be consulted on a wide variety of personal development issues, some directly related to sport, others less so. For example, a performer may have problems coping with a long lay-off due to injury or illness. This is often a very distressing time for the athlete. A sport psychologist can encourage a positive attitude to the injury by designing a rehabilitation programme, which might include mental rehearsal, to ensure the ath-lete's hard learned skills are not simply lost through lack of rehearsal. The sport psychologist might recommend to a coach that an injured play-er be given a role within the team. This maintains a player's typical pattern of social interaction with team mates, thereby preventing the distress of injury becoming compounded by the distress of social isolation. The sport psychologist can help with more general lifestyle problems. For exam-ple, élite sport performers are often prominent public figures. It is important that this aspect is regulated and does not have a negative effect on their performance. A sport psychologist can work with a performer to help them cope with the addi-tional stresses which being a public figure might place upon them.

Role of the sport psychologist in the sport performance equation

Figure 8.1 highlights the fact that sport perfor-mance is composed of three major elements: (1) the physical aspects, i.e. developing speed, strength, stamina and flexibility; (2) the technical aspects, i.e. developing skills and techniques; and (3) the psychological aspects, i.e. belief in self

Physical + fitness	Skills and + techniques	Psychological readiness	= Sport performance
Speed	Passing	Concentration	
Stamina	Running	Self-belief	
Strength	Tackling etc.	Confidence	
Flexibility etc.		Positive attitude etc.	

FIGURE 8.1
The performance equation for a rugby player

and/or the team, concentration and ability to deal with the stress of competition.

In most cases, sports people are primarily concerned with the first two aspects, getting fit and getting skilful. The psychological aspects are often severely neglected. It is important to recognise that although developing psychological skills will not turn an unfit or unskilled player into a 'world beater', most players could benefit from systematic mental skills training as an equally systematic part of their training. The role of the sport psychologist is therefore to encourage performers to recognise the importance of the mental aspects of their sport and to consider mental training as they would any other part of their preparation for sport – as something which is done regularly and conscientiously.

How does a sport psychologist work?

The way sport psychologists work has been discussed by Dr Steven Bull (1991), who has been consulted by many successful sport performers and teams. He has identified six characteristic stages in the process of consultation between psychologist and client:

Stage 1: Establish contact   Either a direct personal contact or through the British Association of Sport and Exercise Sciences (BASES) Register of Accredited Sport Psychologists. Sport psychologists are often coaches or athletes themselves. Fellow players or teams might consult them informally.

Stage 2: Get to know the athlete or team   Build

a sense of trust and commitment. This requires time to be spent with a performer or team, watching them in practice and play. The sport psychologist should take care not to try to rush the players into changing their established training patterns. Sports people tend to be rather conservative – they have tried and tested methods. Orlick (1990) argues that simply being available to players is the best way to become accepted.

Stage 3: Develop a profile of the team or player   Through watching training and competitive play a sport psychologist can detect key aspects of a performer's behaviour, possibly using psychometric tests along with observations. The more accurate the profile, the more specific the mental training programme.

Stage 4: Plan an individualised mental training programme   Most performers have several areas of mental skills requiring development and the sport psychologist will aim to provide a package which addresses the most important of these.

Stage 5: Review and monitor the programme   Programmes require regular monitoring for effectiveness. However, unlike physical training, it is hard to check that mental training is regularly performed. Subsequent improvements may be difficult to assess, usually consisting of reports from athletes or their coaches.

Stage 6: Withdraw, but remain available for consultation   Most sport psychologists do not work with performers on a full-time or permanent basis. It is important that a sport psychologist has developed the performer's skills in such a way that dependency is avoided, making the process of withdrawal easier, whilst remaining available for consultation.

Ethical issues in sport psychology

Psychology is a powerful tool in enhancing enjoyment and achievement in sport. However, it takes a great deal of training to develop the skills required to deliver mental training packages effectively. In common with other areas of practice, consideration for the client, the athlete or coach should be paramount. To this end, all sport psychologists who are on the accredited register, and most others who are working outside it, adhere to a code of ethical practice. The code of ethics is available from the BASES office (address below).

BOX 1

How would I become a sport psychologist?

As mentioned earlier in the text there are three main types of sport psychologist. The clinical role has been covered in the chapter dealing with clinical training. This section will deal with how you become either a research sport psychologist or an educational sport psychologist. BASES is the professional organisation concerned with maintaining and enhancing the professional and ethical standards of all sport and exercise sciences including sport psychology. In this capacity, BASES recommends that any client, be it a team or individual, should work only with accredited sport scientists. It is therefore important for anyone wishing to work as a sport psychologist to become accredited. Accreditation may be in either the educational or research role. In order to be accredited as an educational sport psychologist it is expected that you:

- are a full member of BASES
- hold a first degree in sport and exercise science or psychology or a related discipline
- hold a higher degree (or have appropriate postgraduate experience) in either sport and exercise science, if your first degree was in psychology, or in psychology, if your first degree was in sport and exercise science
- have published articles in professional, sport and exercise journals
- have made oral presentations to BASES conferences or workshops
- have undertaken further peer review, either by presenting a portfolio of material demonstrating involvement in research or as an apprenticed sport psychologist.

The apprentice scheme is designed to enable new sport psychologists to work with established supervisors, with a view to observing good practice, working with a wide range of groups, and collaborating in research. Details of the accreditation process can be obtained from the BASES office: British Association of Sport and Exercise Science, 114 Cardingan Road, Headingley, Leeds LS6 3DJ.

THE DEVELOPMENT OF SPORT PSYCHOLOGY

In 1898, Triplett noted that cyclists performed faster with a pacing machine or when competing against other cyclists. He suggested that the presence of others aroused a competitive drive which provoked a better performance. The effect of an audience on social behaviour has since become known as SOCIAL FACILITATION. Whilst Triplett did not identify himself as a sports psychologist or even as a psychologist interested in sport, his work is often referred to as an early experimental investigation in sport psychology.

American sport psychology texts of the 1960s

and 1970s referred to the backwardness of the USA in this field, relative to other countries, principally those in the former Soviet Block. Indeed, since the break-up of communist regimes in Eastern Europe, more has emerged on the systematic use of athletics and other sports, alongside rather questionable practices, as an instrument of political expression. This mantle now appears to adorn China, where youngsters are recruited into intensive and possibly severe training programmes, with a casualty rate reminiscent of East European mass training programmes. The recent astonishing performances of Chinese women athletes have stimulated widespread discussion as have indications of drug usage amongst their world-ranking swimmers.

The first person to pursue sport psychology in the USA was Coleman Griffith in the 1920s and 1930s. Regarded by some as the 'father of sport psychology', in 1923 he taught a course entitled 'Psychology and Athletics' and in 1925 established the *Athletic Research Laboratory* at the University of Illinois. He published *Psychology of Coaching* (1926) and *Psychology of Athletics* (1928).

The Soviet Union was another forerunner in the development of sport psychology. Research into sport psychology began during the period 1945–1967 with the Research Institute of Physical Culture in Leningrad as the focal point. Two leading figures in Soviet sport psychology at that time were Peter Roudik and A. C. Puni.

Sport psychology did not really take off in either North America or Europe until the 1960s. In 1965, the *International Society of Sport Psychology* (ISSP) formed, and continues to hold meetings every four years, normally after Olympic Year. In 1967, the *North American Society for the Psychology of Sport and Physical Activity* (NASPSPA) was formed. Dr Miroslav Vanek, a prominent Czech sport psychologist, summarised the emergence of sport psychology in his 1985 ISSP presidential address:

'The psychology of sport has become an institutionalised discipline within the sports sciences in the latter half of this century ... It is now possible to say that sport psychology has emerged as a distinctive sub-discipline and as a recognised member of the sports sciences. Our membership has grown, we have journals devoted to sport psychology, national and international societies, coursework and textbooks, specific courses for training in sport psychology, increasing research efforts and so on. In fact sport psychology has become a profession in many countries.'

(quoted in Gill, 1986)

A concern for theoretical development and attention to experimental design and control facilitated the recognition and development of sport psychology as a viable academic discipline. Much of the research in the 1960s and 1970s adopted methods and perspectives from experimental social psychology. This emphasis has apparently now waned and sport psychology is focusing more on sport-specific issues and approaches. To date, most applied sport psychology programmes have been limited to élite athletes. One cannot assume, therefore, that such research can be applied to the more general sporting or fitness-oriented population.

Divisions within sport psychology

The struggle for sport and exercise psychology to be recognised as a legitimate branch of the parent discipline has been discussed earlier in the text. The theory–practice debate has also been prominent. Kremer and Scully (1994) highlight a distinction between *pure* or *academic* sport psychology and *applied* sport psychology. Feltz (1992) makes a similar point with respect to American sport psychologists. However, some sport psychologists do combine both roles. Two distinguished researchers, Dishman (1983) and Morgan (1989), have proposed that sport psychology should not be practised until a more substantive knowledge base has been established. Others (e.g. Landers, 1989) have insisted that given the strength of demand for sport psychological services it is necessary to apply whatever appropriate knowledge is available either from mainstream psychology or specific sport research. Whilst caution may be laudable, other professions could ill afford such hesitation. General medical practice comes to mind! Indeed, it may be the attempts to practise sport psychology and the experience thereby gained which can best serve as a springboard for future systematic research and the expansion of theory.

Major themes in sport psychology

Without going into excessive detail, it is possible to discern general trends in the progression of research within sport psychology over the past forty years or so. First there was a focus on the study of the personalities of sportspersons (an area of research initiated by Coleman Griffith in the USA before the Second World War). From the mid-1960s and for about a decade there was an emphasis upon what became known as the *social analysis approach*. It became fashionable to apply a series of theories within mainstream psychology, including *social facilitation, achievement motivation, social reinforcement, arousal and motor skill performance*.

The shift away from the mechanistic approach of (reward/punishment) BEHAVIOURISM towards a cognitive (INFORMATION PROCESSING) perspective within psychology (see Appendix 1) was reflected in the interests of sport psychologists during the late 1970s and early 1980s. For example, Landers (1980) adapted a model which proposed that increased arousal leads to a narrowing of attentional focus and responsiveness to cues. To the sports performer, this means that as individuals become more excited or psyched up they tend to screen out more and more irrelevant information. Anyone who becomes aroused above an optimal level begins to screen out things which might prove important. Examples of this can be regularly seen in competitive contact team games such as rugby league or rugby union. In the dressing room prior to the game, forward players may be seen shouting and hitting themselves in an effort to wind themselves up into a frenzy, believing it will help their performance. However, at the first

tackle, attentional focus might have narrowed so much that the player fails to notice that the ball has already been passed. The player executes the tackle and is penalised for a late or illegal challenge. In Association Football, Paul Gascoigne's famous recklessness which led to serious injury might be seen as another example.

As mainstream psychology became more interested in the *self concept*, further examples could be taken from the application of Duval and Wickland's (1972) work on objective and subjective self-awareness to sport psychology. ATTRIBUTION theory became popular in the 1980s. It attempts to explain the cognitive processes people use to make judgements about what happens to them, such as whether they succeed or fail in sport, and whether this is more the result of skill (ATTRIBUTION, INTERNAL) or luck (ATTRIBUTION, EXTERNAL). It has been applied by Wankel (1975) to understand how motivation may be affected by the presence of an audience, an approach very different to the 1960s work of Zajonc (1965) on social facilitation, also concerned with audience effects.

Current trends in sport psychology

In some ways it may be said that sport psychology has been somewhat sluggish in its development, possibly because it has lacked a clear sense of direction until recently (Feltz, 1992). One leading writer (Dishman, 1983) has suggested that sport psychologists have been overly concerned with linking general theories in psychology to sports behaviour, rather than studying specific features of sport psychology in their own right. This theme has been explored more fully in the recent text by Kremer and Scully (1994), who have attempted to integrate sport psychology into mainstream psychology. However, several researchers (e.g. Alderman, 1980; Dishman, 1983; Martens, 1980; Morgan, 1989) have proposed that direct application from general psychology has its limitations and that a more fruitful line of development would be to consider sport psychology as a sub-discipline within sport science. Also, future progress might involve the further advancement of theories which are specifically appropriate to sport behaviour. Given its present state of evolution, sport psychology has developed its own theoretical frameworks to only a limited extent. For example, in the area of personality research, Morgan and Pollack (1977) have researched the ICEBERG PROFILE of élite athletes, discussed later in this chapter, whilst Vealey (1986) and Scanlan and Lewthwaite (1986) have researched sport confidence and sport enjoyment, respectively.

As we noted earlier, sport psychology is one of a group of sport sciences: *sport sociology*, the social or cultural unit; *sport psychology*, the group or individual unit; and *exercise physiology*, the intra-individual (within the individual) unit. One way forward is to research sport behaviour drawing on general psychology but making links with other areas of sport science. It may be profitable to work on sport research across the sub-disciplines within sport science. A nice example has been included in the discussion by Feltz (1992). Taking the problem of why children drop out of sport she points out that earlier research by sport psychologists considered only psychological explanations (perhaps not surprisingly!) However, by adopting an *interdisciplinary* perspective it has proved possible to study and explain the effects of training, maturation and development. In North America, at the *Institute for the Study of Youth Sports*, Seefeldt and Steig (1986) gave athletes a wide battery of tests ranging from blood samples, video recording, to motor skill performance and psychological testing of young long-distance runners. A research profile was built up annually. It is the combination and interaction of such a wide range of factors, not just purely psychological causes, which may crucially affect athletes' participation. The future for researchers may be that they see themselves less exclusively as sport psychologists and more as sport scientists.

THEORY, RESEARCH AND APPLICATIONS

Gender perspectives in sport

The role of women and girls in sport has changed dramatically over the past twenty-five years. Each new Olympiad has included additional events which are open to females. The marathon, ten thousand metres running and triple jump are all now available to women competitors. The next Olympic Games might also include the women's pole vault. This is a long way from the 1936 Olympiad where it was concluded that women should not run more than 800 metres in the interests of their health! Nowadays, the sight of a middle-aged woman jogging along the roadside will no longer arouse curiosity. The history of women in sport is a fascinating area. Participation by women in sport can be traced back to the time of the ancient Greeks (Le Unes and Nation, 1989), and there are anecdotal reports of female running events in Britain during medieval fairs. A recent issue of a sports magazine reviewed a text devoted to advice for lady athletes at the turn of this century. Hurdling for women (in long dresses) was seemly provided it did not generate too much sweat and certainly no muscle! Perspiration and competition were specifically manly qualities. Interestingly, women were responsible for the introduction of overarm bowling to cricket since underarm bowling was difficult in long dresses. As women's participation in sport has increased, questions have been asked by researcher and lay person alike – do only certain types of women (or men) get involved in sport? Will apparently 'masculine' sport change the personality of women who participate?

Research into gender, within general psychology and sport psychology, gained momentum during the 1970s and accelerated during the 1980s. In her comprehensive review of sport psychological research into gender, Gill (1992) argues that sport psychology research has been narrow and that

1995 Netball World Cup Final between
Australia and South Africa. In Australia and
New Zealand, female netball players have
star celebrity status.

research into psychological sex differences produces ambiguous results. For example, she cites
Jacklin's (1989) view that gender is not a crucial
variable in determining intellectual abilities. Eagly
and Steffin (1986) challenge the stereotype that
males are more aggressive than females. It seems
that the overall context for gender behaviour is
crucial. The situation (see Appendix 1) can make
females as aggressive as males, or males non-
aggressive, in certain circumstances. Gender
behaviour may well not be fixed and is far more
fluid than early research indicated.

Androgyny

One productive line of research has been to assess
female athletes in terms of their adherence to traditional feminine characteristics as measured by
questionnaires such as the BEM *Sex Role
Inventory* (1974) or the *Personal Attributes
Questionnaire* (PAQ) (Spence et al, 1974).

Both these scales attempt to assess an individual's level of orientation towards a masculine or
feminine sex role irrespective of their biological
sex. A person who takes up an ambiguous (or mid-
way) position is termed ANDROGYNOUS. Overall, it
seems that female athletes do not follow a strictly
traditional feminine sex role, though specific studies have found variation across sports and social
groups. It may be premature to draw too many
conclusions at this stage.

However, some women athletes seem to have a
typically masculine sex role orientation, in terms
of how they view themselves. This was characteristic of American college swimmers (Gackenbach,
1982) and of almost 40 per cent of junior college
athletes (Kane, 1982). However, again the picture
is not entirely clear. Henschen et al (1982) found
no differences in sex role orientation when comparing high school female athletes with non-athletes. It is possible that gender role bias may be
related to levels of excellence and time spent in
the sport.

However, given there is at least a trend
amongst female sports players towards an androgynous or masculine sex role bias, it is likely that
these women and girls will not experience the
conflict in gender role felt by more traditional
females. Some researchers feel that the avenues
for self-expression which sport makes available are
therefore denied to 'feminine' females because of
the association of sport with masculinity. For
example, Duquin (1978) laments how ideally sport
should be regarded as an essentially non-sexist or
androgynous activity. This ideal state still seems
far off.

Gill (1992) challenges the value of androgyny
research. For example, if 'competitiveness' is
regarded as a masculine trait, is it helpful to
therefore consider competitive women to be masculine? Gill and colleagues (Gill and Deeter 1988;
Gill and Dzewaltowski, 1988) decided to investigate competitiveness directly, and found that
competitiveness differentiated athletes from non-

athletes, differences which held for both males *and* females. The term 'androgynous' is itself ambiguous. It has been used for people who are neither particularly feminine or masculine in sex role but it has also been reserved for those who are high on only the positive aspects of *both* sex role descriptions.

Achievement motivation

Whilst discussed in more detail in the section on motivation, it is worthwhile exploring the studies on achievement in sport with respect to gender. Female reticence towards achievement in general was reported in early research by McClelland et al (1953). A controversial view of ACHIEVEMENT MOTIVATION in females was proposed by Horner (1972). She felt that many females experience a strong motivation to avoid success (FEAR OF SUCCESS) because aspects of success have some negative consequences for women. Gill (1988) developed the *Sport Orientation Questionnaire* (SOQ), which measured *competitiveness, win orientation* (desire to win/avoid losing), and *goal orientation* (intention to achieve personal goals within competitive sport). Males were found to score consistently higher than females on competitiveness and win orientation, whereas females generally scored a little higher on goal orientation. Gill found females were as likely as males to participate in non-competitive sport and to report non-sport achievements and interests. Again the main gender difference was competitiveness.

Some wider-ranging studies are also of interest. Girls showed more enthusiasm than boys for a co-operative game introduced in Canada (McNally and Orlick, 1975). Weinberg and Jackson (1979) found that males reacted more to success or failure, as compared with females, whilst Weinberg and Ragan's (1979) study suggested that girls had a preference for non-competitive activities, in contrast with boys. Stewart and Corbin (1988) have shown that where a task is gender-neutral and does not involve social comparison with others, females show more confidence.

Cognitive factors – expectations, values and schemas

As explained elsewhere in this book (see educa-

tional psychology), later versions of SOCIAL LEARNING THEORY emphasised the role of *expectations* and *values* in determining our behaviour. Eccles has developed such a model for sport achievement which might help explain gender differences. For instance, Eccles and Harold (1991) found that adolescent boys valued sport more than girls, and also viewed themselves as higher in sporting competence (self-efficacy). This was reflected in how boys and girls spent their free time with respect to sport. Teachers rated boys' sporting ability to be higher than that of girls, and children themselves conformed to gender stereotypes in their ratings of the value of sport. Also, boys gave higher ratings as to how importantly parents valued their success in sport. A wide range of studies (e.g. Eccles, 1987) has found that expectations of success tend to be lower in females, which may of course help to account for gender differences in sport behaviour. Such gender differences in expectation and achievement in sport may well be a product of early gender role socialisation.

Cognitive psychology views gender as a *cognitive* SCHEMA (see GENDER SCHEMA) or *belief system*. Bem's early work on psychological typing and androgyny has evolved into a *gender-schematic* vs *gender-aschematic* approach. *Gender-schematic* persons are high-masculine males and high-feminine females, holding quite clear-cut views on the differences between what is appropriate for either sex. *Gender-aschematic* people tend not to interpret situations in terms of sex-typed perceptions. Some of the results above reflect people's general stereotypes and prejudices about gender. An illuminating study by Brawley et al (1979) found that males were rated higher on a muscular endurance task even though the male and female performances were identical. Whatever the actual biological differences between male and female, it seems that in sport, as elsewhere in psychology, we find evidence that perception can be seriously clouded by what we know before we look. How many men would not argue vehemently that overarm bowling is more 'masculine' than underarm bowling?

Sport and personality

As with gender research, caution in the drawing of firm conclusions applies to personality research. We often hear people talking about 'sports personalities', but what do we actually know about the personality characteristics of sports men and women? For example, are team sports people different from people who play individual sports?

Is there a 'sporting personality'?

It is perhaps somewhat disappointing to report that despite the considerable investment of research effort put into this area, no substantial evidence has emerged which points to the existence of a sporting personality. Also, there seem to be no overall differences in the personality profiles across sports despite a limited number of positive findings.

However, there has been some success in distinguishing the psychological characteristics of successful athletes. Most of the early work was with male athletes, however. In the 1920s and 1930s Coleman Griffith examined the personality profiles of successful athletes. Based upon observations and interviews with top athletes, including participant observation work with the Chicago Cubs football team, Griffith identified the following characteristics of: ruggedness, courage, intelligence, exuberance, buoyancy, emotional adjustment, optimism, conscientiousness, alertness, loyalty, and respect for authority.

A review by Ogilvie (1968) concluded that certain personality characteristics tend to be associated with successful athletes. Ogilvie developed the *Athletic Motivation Inventory* (AMI) to measure such characteristics which include drive, determination, leadership, aggressiveness, proneness to guilt, emotional control, self-confidence, conscientiousness, mental toughness, trust and coachability.

Morgan (1980, 1985) has probably conducted the most systematic work on the relationship between personality and sporting success. He proposed a *Mental Health Model* which would predict success in athletics based on the assumption that mental health and athletic success are positively related. Support for this view has been forthcoming through the analysis of the profiles of Olympic wrestlers, national team rowers, and élite distance runners. Morgan did in fact discover that successful athletes possessed more positive mental health characteristics and fewer negative mental health characteristics in comparison with the general population.

Moods

Using the PROFILE OF MOOD STATES (POMS), successful athletes were found to be above the norm on the one positive state which was measured – vigour, but below the norm on the negative measured states of tension, depression, anger, fatigue and confusion. This became known as the *Iceberg Profile* (see Figure 8.2). However, it is significant that not all successful athletes have this profile. Research by Terry (1993) reported that the mood profile of an athlete can serve as an excellent predictor of performance. In his studies, élite performers completed the POMS directly prior to Olympic- and world-level competition. He also asked participants to rate their expected level of performance. He found that positive mood states could predict performance, but the exact nature of the state was highly subjective. Some performers were energised by high levels of anger or frustration, whilst others were distracted by these. These findings serve to reinforce the view that athletes need to understand how their moods influence their performance. As usual with correlational results however, it should not be assumed that mental health and moods actually *cause* success. Indeed, it may be the sporting success itself which causes or enhances positive mental health and gives rise to positive mood profiles. Also, poor mental health may be associated with lack of success in general life, not just sport. More recent research has developed more sport-specific measures of individual personality characteristics. This has been quite productive. For example, sporting success tends to be related to the management of *competition anxiety* and levels of *self-confidence* and *competitiveness*.

Sporting 'character'

We might ask more general questions such as

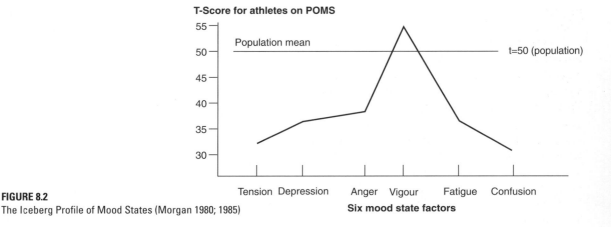

FIGURE 8.2
The Iceberg Profile of Mood States (Morgan 1980; 1985)

does sport participation help to build character or other positive personality traits? The answer from most research to date is 'no'. However, participation in exercise and fitness training does appear to enhance a person's self-esteem and serve as an antidote to negative psychological states such as anxiety and depression. Clearly, the whole question as to the relationship between sport involvement and personality is highly complex.

Motivation in sport

People are motivated to take part in sport for a wide range of reasons. These may include a desire to attain a sense of mastery or competence, a wish for status and achievement, friendship, camaraderie, challenge or excitement (Cratty, 1989). Gross (1992) describes motivation as the 'why' of behaviour, and suggests that trying to define motivation is somewhat like trying to define psychology itself. Gill (1986), in her text on sport psychology, describes motivation as the key construct in psychology. Coaches, teachers or sport enthusiasts are continually involved in motivating others, as well as motivating themselves! Gill (1986) pointed out that motivation has two components:

- *intensity of behaviour* – e.g. levels of arousal; how hard we try
- *direction of behaviour* – e.g. striving to win a game; what we try to do

AROUSAL was a concept central to the early research into motivation. It may be described as the general state of activation or excitation that ranges from deep sleep to intense excitement. Arousal is likely to increase when a person is about to compete in an event and this may be experienced as excitement or stress/anxiety according to various other factors (such as whether an event is perceived as an opportunity or an ordeal!) An important model of stress was that of Selye (1956), covered in the health psychology chapter.

Drive theory

Incorporating the concept of arousal, DRIVE THEORY was one of the most influential theories of motivation in psychology and characterises the BEHAVIOURIST approach to understanding human behaviour. In the early days of sport psychology, drive theory helped to explain the effects of an audience on motor performance. In simple terms, drive theory proposed there was a basic relationship between *arousal* and *performance* (P = f(H x D)). *Performance* (P) is a function of *habit* (H) multiplied by *drive* (D), where *drive* is essentially the same as *arousal*, i.e. a readiness to react. *Habit* refers to the strength of *learned responses* or *behaviours*. The more a response has been *reinforced* (see Appendix 1), the greater the *habit strength* and the more likely it is that the response will occur. Drive theory basically states that as arousal or drive level increases (as in intense competition), the more likely are learned responses to occur.

However, with respect to sport behaviour it is important to note that as arousal/drive level increases, then the performance of the individual's strongest, most *dominant response* increases. Therefore, performance will improve under arousal only if the person's strongest and most likely response is *correct performance*. It is likely, therefore, that until a person becomes proficient at a sport skill, the dominant response is probably *not* the correct performance. With respect to learning complex sports skills, we are more likely to make mistakes than produce a perfect performance (after Gill, 1986).

Drive theory as applied to sports can be summarised as follows:

- raised levels of arousal/drive increase the likelihood of the *dominant response*
- if a skill is relatively simple, or if a skill is very well learned, the dominant response is the *correct* response, and increased arousal will *improve* performance
- if the skill is complex and not well learned, the dominant response is an *incorrect* response, and increased arousal will *impair* performance.

This model might help to explain the mistakes made, say, in junior football as excitement increases. One might compare this to an accomplished international team producing a top performance under pressure, e.g. the Australian Rugby Union team in the 1991 World Cup Final when they overcame an outstanding display from an England XV and played their best rugby of the tournament. South Africa's defeat of the favourites, New Zealand, in the 1995 rugby union world cup final provides a similar example.

The YERKES-DODSON INVERTED-U THEORY OF AROUSAL

This theory proposes that performance is optimal at moderate levels of arousal, and that performance progressively declines as arousal increases or decreases from this optimal moderate level. This is displayed graphically in Figure 8.3.

Zone 1 – the performer is *under aroused* and does not perform as well as he or she could
Zone 2 – the performer is *optimally aroused* and performs up to his or her potential
Zone 3 – the performer is *over aroused* and does not perform as well as he or she could

It seems that the INVERTED-U HYPOTHESIS makes sense in accord with our own observations and experiences. People need some arousal to perform at their best, and overarousal can lead to anxiety, tension and proneness to error. However, these early models have been challenged, for example, by Hardy and Fazey (1987). Martens et al (1990) have presented a *multi-dimensional anxiety* model. Two other challenges – catastrophe theory and reversal theory – are described later.

The cognitive perspective on sport motivation

Vealey (1989) reviewed the literature regarding the types of models adopted to explain behaviour in sport. She found that the majority of the research has adopted a cognitive framework – see Appendix 1. That is, it focuses on the ways people

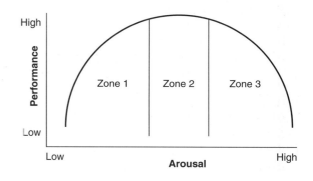

FIGURE 8.3
The Yerkes-Dodson Inverted-U Arousal Hypothesis

The motivation to participate and achieve, essential to team sports, may be encouraged at school.

collect and process information about themselves and their environments. This type of perspective is evident in much of the research regarding motivation.

In recent years motivation in sport has been approached from two main perspectives. One approach has involved the investigation of individual qualities and attributes including aspects of self-perception, such as belief in the strength of one's sport skills. The other approach has involved the exploration of those factors affecting the likelihood that people will participate in sport – i.e. sport participation. Sport motivation may be affected by a range of interacting variables. For example, children low in self-esteem were found to be most affected by coaches who demonstrated frequent encouragement (Smith et al, 1979).

With respect to *participation* and *discontinuation motivation*, the most significant factors found to affect whether people start or stop participating have included sense of competence, affiliation, fitness, being part of a group or team, competition and finally, sheer enjoyment. Most people, children and adults, tend to be affected by *several* motivational factors. Participation also varies across the type of sport, gender, and the sports person's level of appropriate experience. Participation in sport may be influenced by cultural factors. In Israel, Weingarten et al (1984) found greater motivation to participate in sport in city children, as compared to children living in kibbutzim – communal groups. There has been

discussion as to whether a reduction in participation is actually 'negative'. Clearly, there can be some very positive and constructive reasons to reduce one's sporting activity, at least for certain periods. Older children have a wide range of roles to learn and perform. In fact, several studies have pointed toward conflict of interests and commitments as a major reason for discontinuing various sport or exercise activities. On this point it may be constructive to caution against applied psychologists regarding their own areas as relatively isolated from other aspects of human behaviour.

An influential theory of motivation in sport is Harter's (1978, 1981) COMPETENCE MOTIVATION theory. This theory assumes a motivation to demonstrate competence (show that one can do something well) and to achieve mastery in a particular area of sport. The model is outlined in Figure 8.4. Predictions are that individuals who have high levels of perceived competence and internal control will show more effort and persistence.

Achievement motivation

The extensive work on achievement motivation in sport, and its relationship to competition, has derived from the now classic work of McClelland et el (1953) and Atkinson (1964, 1974; see also the educational psychology chapter). Atkinson's theory is a model which emphasises the *interaction* of personality and situational factors in producing

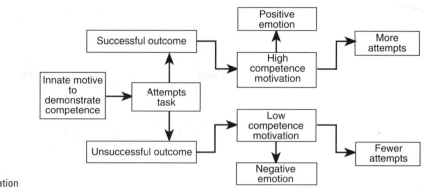

FIGURE 8.4
Harter's model of competence motivation

achievement behaviour (see 'Individual differences – traits or situations?' in Appendix 1). The theory employs precise, formal (i.e. mathematical/logical) terms. However, it is worth bearing in mind that Atkinson's model and techniques of measurement were not specifically designed for sport and as a consequence its value, for example in explaining competitive behaviour, may well be quite limited. As a result, Martens (1977) has applied it specifically to sport psychology and has developed sports-specific constructs and measures of achievement motivation, such as *competitiveness* and *competitive trait anxiety*.

There have also been attempts to develop integrated models of motivation in sport. For example, Weiss and Chaumeton (1992) interrelate achievement behaviour, participation/discontinuation motives and intrinsic/extrinsic motivation – see the educational psychology chapter for an explanation of the latter concept. Cox (1994) and Horne (1992) provide more detailed discussion of these and related theories of sport motivation.

Finally, an entertaining and provocative discussion as to why people *avoid* sport and exercise has been presented by Ellis (1994) in his application of RATIONAL EMOTIVE THERAPY (see the clinical psychology chapter). Ellis suggests that a major factor in sport and exercise avoidance is an irrational fear of failure (e.g. 'I'll never be able to do anything like that') and negative, self-defeating thinking. Ellis then reports how rational emotive therapy may be utilised to remedy the situation.

Anxiety in sport

Sport performers often report the signs and symptoms of anxiety. Before we begin the discussion of anxiety in sport we need to provide a definition. Anxiety has been defined by Levitt (1980) as the subjective feeling of apprehension and heightened physiological arousal (feelings) often associated with fears, worries and doubts (thoughts). An athlete who becomes anxious before or during a performance will show the signs and symptoms of increased arousal and will also be apprehensive and frightened.

It is not unusual for players to be troubled by worries or fears, such as 'I don't want to let myself or my team down'. You might also have fixed in your mind the idea that all the rest of your team are better than you. These thoughts lead you to feel a certain way. They tend to be the types of thoughts which lead to pre-match nervousness or anxiety. In this section we will consider the relationship between the way people feel, before and during a game, race or routine and the actual quality of performance.

Williams (1986) describes the process by which thought interferes with performance as:

Thoughts ⟶ Feelings ⟶ Behaviours

We will work backwards though this model, first of all considering the types of behaviours which we normally associate with anxiety.

Anxiety and behaviour

Extremely anxious and agitated athletes rarely perform very well. Whilst it should be noted that some stimulation is required to motivate an athlete to perform, when this reaches a very high level, the athlete becomes distracted and unable to maintain his or her attention on factors relevant to the task (*task-relevant factors*). This idea was first proposed by Easterbrook (1959). It was his view that increases in anxiety caused attention or concentration to narrow. This can have a positive influence since there may be an optimal level of anxiety associated with attention to vital aspects of athletic performance. However, if anxiety increases beyond this point, attention becomes fixed on *task-irrelevant factors*. The very highly anxious performer becomes so distracted by intrusive doubts, fears and worries that they are often unable to be aware of anything else. If you have any doubts about this, consider the rock climber faced with a difficult sequence of moves. The fears and doubts can, and often do, overwhelm the climber to the extent they cannot either move forward or back. Being 'frozen' with fear is not an experience unique to risk sports. Teams playing in major events such as the FA Cup Final can become so overwhelmed by the occasion they cannot perform at even a moderate level.

Some of the types of behaviour often associated with high levels of anxiety are listed below:

- inability to concentrate
- forgetfulness
- feelings of fatigue
- inability to make decisions
- atypical behaviours (e.g. quietness in usually sociable athletes)
- lethargy
- agitation
- confusion
- apathy
- fearfulness
- irritability

Some of these behaviours can be observed in anxious athletes. However, it should be noted that performers may display these for a whole variety of other reasons. Therefore it is essential for a coach, teacher or parent to have a good rapport with the athlete. If they know what is typical, they will be more sensitive to the atypical.

Anxiety and feelings

Imagine that you are about to begin a 200-foot abseil. You are edging to the start, you have never abseiled before, how do you feel? Why do you feel this way?

Compare this with the feelings you might have when you find you have won the Football Pools or the National Lottery. In the first example, when you feel nervous or excited, your heart rate increases, you begin to sweat, you become agitated and you interpret these signs and symptoms as a threat, 'I am about to abseil and I am frightened'. In the second example, your heart rate increases and you begin to sweat. In fact many of the same physiological responses occur, but you interpret the signs in a different way. This is because the body has a limited repertoire of responses to either positive or negative stimuli. It responds to novel, exciting or frightening situations by increasing its readiness to respond (arousal). This is achieved by the triggering of parts of the AUTONOMIC NERVOUS SYSTEM (ANS). The ANS is divided into two parts, the *sympathetic* and the *parasympathetic* systems. The sympathetic system increases the activity of the vagus nerve and acts to increase heart rate, respiratory activity, and the rate of release of adrenaline into the bloodstream. Increased arousal can be readily observed through these bodily changes. It is the role of the parasympathetic system to counter this state of arousal.

The effect of increased arousal on sport performance

Sport psychologists are often asked whether a person should try to increase his/her level of arousal prior to playing sport, in an effort to enhance performance. The answer depends on several factors: first, the preferred arousal state of the individual; second, the nature of the sport being played; and third, the current or baseline level of arousal.

There has been a great deal of research aimed at identifying the relationship between arousal and performance. The Inverted-U Hypothesis, discussed earlier, has been used to explain the relationship between arousal and performance. This simple model is shown in Figure 8.3 on page 265. However, recent research has indicated that the relationship is more complex than the Inverted-U Hypothesis suggests.

Thought and anxiety

Perhaps the most significant aspect of the arousal–performance relationship is the link between thought and performance. Thoughts associated with anxiety are persistent, intrusive and negative. They tend to be of two types: future-oriented, e.g. 'What happens if . . . ?' or past-orientated, e.g. 'I missed an open goal, I'm an idiot'. When an athlete is focused on performing a skill, he or she is often too absorbed in the activity to allow these negative thoughts to intrude. For example, would you expect a downhill skier to be concentrating on doubts and fears whilst cutting turns at 100 mph? Probably not, and if they were, they would certainly interfere with the skills they were trying to perform.

It should be noted that increased arousal alone is not sufficient to indicate anxiety. As we noted above, there are increases in arousal under a variety of other circumstances.

The stress process in sport

Martens (1982) showed how the anxiety response is part of a process, called the *stress process*. In his model he considers stress to be a process by which the perceived demands of a situation are considered in relation to our perceived coping resources and the current threats, the response being the level of anxiety experienced.

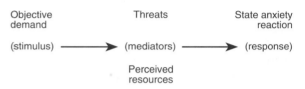

FIGURE 8.5
The stress process in sport (after Martens, 1977)

The stimulus could be a big game or competition. The mediating factor is whether the performer views the situation as being one they can deal with or not, i.e. the level of threat. This mediating step will determine the extent of the anxiety response.

In rock climbing the performer cannot allow fear to undermine skill.

Where a situation is not threatening or easily dealt with, there is a low anxiety response. However, where a situation presents a great threat, or we believe it to exceed our coping resources, a high level of anxiety is experienced. People differ in the way they appraise situations. Some people tend to overestimate threats, or understate their ability to cope with it. This led Spielberger (1971) to suggest that anxiety could be divided into two types:

■ TRAIT ANXIETY – the relatively stable part of our personality, our general anxiety level and our predisposition to interpret situations as stressful

■ STATE ANXIETY – the anxiety experienced in response to events in our immediate environment, such as being at the top of an abseil.

It should be noted that both the thoughts and feelings associated with anxiety have a profound influence on a person's enjoyment of and performance in sport. The early attempts to explain how these factors influence performance have now been dismissed as simplistic and not good at explaining what actually happens in sport. The increasingly scientific research methodologies being applied to sport have begun to develop better explanations.

Conceptual and methodological developments in anxiety in sport research

Above we mentioned that there were major flaws with the Inverted-U Hypothesis. These have been explored by several prominent sport psychologists over the past few years (Jones and Hardy, 1990). The first problem is that the relationship defined by the graph in Figure 8.3 is *uni-dimensional*. The current view of anxiety is that it is *multi-dimensional* – basically, there are different forms of anxiety which may act in combination. A series of studies by Martens et al (1990) identified three major groups of factors which characterised the anxiety responses of sport performers. These were:

■ *cognitive anxiety* – feelings of fear or apprehension, related to the event
■ *somatic anxiety* – the physiological signs and symptoms associated with high levels of arousal

■ *self-confidence* – a sense of confidence in your ability to do the task successfully.

Their research went on to develop the *Competitive State Anxiety Questionnaire*. This is a research tool which has been used to examine pre-competitive anxiety in a whole range of sport settings. It is widely viewed as one of the most significant research developments in the past two decades. It has spawned much research, for example into the ways in which the sub-components of anxiety separate prior to performance.

Catastrophe theory

There are (at least) two further questionable assumptions within the Inverted-U model of anxiety–performance. The first is that small increases in arousal lead to small increases or decreases in performance. This kind of *correlational* relationship between variables is commonly known as a *linear* relationship (see Appendix 2). The second assumption is that people have an optimal level of arousal at which they perform best. CATASTROPHE THEORY questions both these assumptions.

Catastrophe theory researchers acknowledge the often reported phenomenon that once a mistake has been made, and anxiety increases further, the level of performance often does not drop by a small increment. On some occasions there may be, instead, a dramatic or *catastrophic* decrease in performance. For example, after missing an easy putt, a golfer may go on to play several poor shots. In this situation, even if the player lowers his or her anxiety level to pre-error levels they cannot get back to the same performance level. The Inverted-U Hypothesis cannot predict these sudden and extreme changes in performance in response to slightly increased anxiety. The contemporary view of the anxiety–performance relationship is that SOMATIC ANXIETY, COGNITIVE ANXIETY and *self-confidence* interact to influence performance. The work of Hardy and Fazey (1987) demonstrated the complexity of this approach. They developed the work of a French mathematician, Thom (1975), who used a catastrophe model to explain rapid changes ('catastrophes') in systems which are normally linear. Hardy and Fazey presented a three-dimensional model which recognised that the two components of multi-

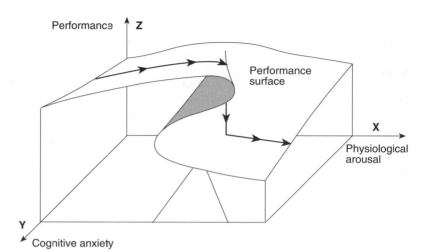

FIGURE 8.6
The catastrophe model of performance
(Hardy and Fazey, 1987)

dimensional anxiety interact to influence performance in different ways.

In the model, performance is represented by the height of the performance surface. Two other factors have a special relationship to this surface: physiological arousal (somatic anxiety) is called the *normal* factor, whilst cognitive anxiety is the *splitting* factor. When cognitive anxiety is low, performance does indeed follow a traditional *Inverted-U* path. However, the decisive factor in the model is the level of cognitive anxiety experienced. When this is increasing it causes a change in the performance surface. This is where catastrophic decreases in performance are seen. The difference between the shape of the performance surface as the splitting factor increases, as opposed to when it is decreasing, is called *hysteresis* (see Fig 8.6). The model represents a considerable conceptual advance since it recognises that the sub-components of anxiety interact to influence performance. It also highlights the cognitive emphasis on the central role of *thought* in affecting performance.

Reversal theory – another way of thinking about anxiety

REVERSAL THEORY (Apter 1989; Kerr 1990) is a way of explaining anxiety, and changes in anxiety, in terms of its *structural phenomenology* or how the experience is perceived and organised by the individual. This model emphasises subjective interpretations of arousal, an important feature being the idea that people differ in their preferred level of arousal.

For example, some people perceive low arousal situations such as sensory deprivation, watching television or lying on a beach as boring, whereas other people view the same situation as relaxing. Similarly, some people perceive high arousal situations such as risk sports or competition as exciting whilst others find them distressing. People who prefer low arousal situations are in a state of TELIC DOMINANCE, and tend to find high arousal situations anxiety-provoking. People who prefer conditions of high arousal are in a state of PARATELIC DOMINANCE and tend to interpret low arousal situations as boring.

Reversal theory, promoted by Kerr (1990), holds that in certain situations we rapidly change or *reverse* from one state to another. For example, in a fairground, people develop a state of anxiety whilst queuing, which rapidly reverses to excitement as the ride progresses. Thus, the HEDONIC TONE goes from the negative state of fear to the positive state of excitement. A novice abseiler might experience high levels of arousal as unpleasant hedonic tone, whilst a more experienced performer will find similar increases in arousal pleasant and exciting.

Introducing skill

How movement is learned and controlled

There has been considerable debate about whether skill acquisition and motor control fall within the boundaries of sport and exercise psychology. The control of movement certainly involves elements of physiology, bio-mechanics and kinesiology (study of muscles). For many sport and exercise psychologists the boundaries between these disciplines and their own leads them to neglect consideration of how movements are learned and controlled. In reality, the boundaries are 'fuzzy'. Movements are sequences of behaviour and therefore the concern of the psychologist. Further weight can be added to this view by noting that, increasingly, skills are viewed as controlled by complex cognitive activity (see Appendix 1). In this section we will consider what we actually mean by *skill* in sport and use a prominent theoretical model to try and explain how novices and experts differ. The second part of the section will consider the major variables influencing skill learning – namely TRANSFER, practice and FEEDBACK.

Can you juggle, play chess, drive a car, ride a bicycle, high jump 1.5 metres?

All these are skills. But what is it about them that makes each a skill? Sharp (1992), in his highly readable discussion, describes skill as 'something which helps the link between intention and action'. He adds that skills are goal-directed, learned, efficient, and are the product of information processing via the nervous system. Motor (physical movement) learning has been defined in a variety of ways by different authors. The following is an early definition, but it very clearly summarises what we mean when we talk about skills:

> 'Skill consists of the ability to bring about some end result with maximum certainty and minimum outlay of energy, or of time and energy.'
>
> (Guthrie, 1952, p.136)

This definition reinforces three elements of skilled behaviour:

- skilled performance has a consistent and highly probable outcome
- it expends the minimum of time
- it expends a minimum of effort.

These elements are emphasised differently depending on the type of skill under discussion.

Schmidt (1988; 1991) has developed the idea of characteristics of skilled behaviour further. He outlined four distinct qualities of MOTOR SKILL:

- skills are learned
- learning occurs as a direct result of practice or experience
- learning, at our current state of knowledge, cannot be observed directly. It must be inferred that learning has occurred on the basis of changes in behaviour that can be observed
- learning is assumed to produce relatively permanent changes in behaviour. Therefore, changes in behaviour caused by easily reversible alterations in mood, motivation, or internal states (e.g. hunger, thirst) are not generally regarded to be the result of learning.

The skills listed at the beginning of this section are similar, in as much as they conform to the criteria for skills. But they are also different, since some are physical skills, some are mental, some involve the whole body, whilst some involve only part of the body. In sport an important distinction which needs to be drawn is between those skills which are executed in a changing or unpredictable environment (OPEN SKILLS), such as passing in soccer, and those which are executed in an essentially predictable environment (CLOSED SKILLS) such as beginning a high board dive. One of the main differences between open and closed skills is the role of FEEDBACK to control movements. A simple diving routine can be executed effectively even when the performer is receiving a minimum of feedback, for example when blindfolded. On the other hand, it would be very difficult to play netball effectively with little feedback – a concept returned to later in this section.

Closed skills		Open skills
predictable ←	Environment →	unpredictable
diving		rugby
gymnastics		netball
archery		martial arts

The information processing model

Martenuik (1975) presented a model which aimed to identify the important steps involved in con-

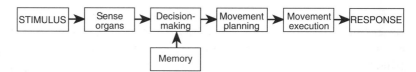

FIGURE 8.7
The information processing model (after Martenuik, 1975)

trolling movement. This model is presented in a simplified form in Figure 8.7.

This type of model (also outlined in Appendix 1) is based on the analogy that people are similar to computers. They take incoming information through their sense organs, they interpret it through a series of operations on it, decide how to respond, and then organise and execute a response. In sport, this type of model can be very useful in describing the sequence of operations that links stimulus to response. For example, in tennis when a player sees the ball coming towards her left-hand side, she has to decide whether to respond by shaping to play a backhand, or running around the trajectory of the ball to play it on her forehand. Memory plays an important part in this process. If the player knows she has a weakness on her backhand she has to respond to that piece of knowledge by organising a different response.

It should be borne in mind that each of the stages in the information processing sequence takes up time. A cricket striker facing a delivery of 90 mph has around 600 milliseconds to process all the following information: the direction of the delivery; its speed; and where the ball will bounce. Once this is done an appropriate response must be decided upon and then executed. The normal range for simple reaction time is between 130 and 250 milliseconds. Therefore there is less than half a second to complete all the steps in the processing sequence. It really isn't a surprise that sometimes cricketers 'mistime' their shots. One of the things that performers do to save time is to anticipate the stimulus, for example, a cricketer might move onto the front foot as the bowler releases the ball. If the anticipation is correct, much time will be saved and the response will usually be positive. On the other hand, if the anticipation is incorrect, a large error results.

Anticipation is a characteristic we normally associate with the experience of expert performance. Several researchers have noticed that

learners appear to pass through relatively distinct stages or phases as they practise a skill and proceed from novice to expert. Fitts (Fitts and Posner, 1967) has discussed the following three phases that are useful for descriptive purposes (similar to Anderson's (1983) model in the occupational psychology chapter).

COGNITIVE PHASE   When the learner is new to the task, the primary concern is to understand what is to be done, how the performance is to be scored, and how best to attempt the first few trials. Naturally, considerable cognitive activity is required, so that the learner can determine appropriate strategies. This is the acquisition of DECLARATIVE KNOWLEDGE in Anderson's model. Good strategies are retained and inappropriate ones are discarded. As a result, the performance gains during this phase are dramatic and generally larger than at any other single period in the learning process.

ASSOCIATIVE PHASE   The second phase of motor learning begins when the individual has determined the most effective way of doing the task (now has PROCEDURAL KNOWLEDGE) and begins to make more subtle adjustments in how the skill is performed. Performance improvements are more gradual and movements become more consistent. This phase can persist for many days or weeks, with the performer gradually producing small changes in the motor patterns that will allow more effective performance.

AUTONOMOUS PHASE   After many months, even years of practice, the learner enters the autonomous phase, so-called because the skill has become largely automatic. That is, the task can now be performed with less interference from many other simultaneous activities. It has been known for a concert pianist to do mental arithmetic whilst sight-reading and piano playing. Such AUTOMACITY is usually only possible with particular kinds of simultaneous tasks, such as verbal–cognitive activities. Other skills could actually interfere with a performance in the autonomous phase. Even so, the performer gives the impression that he or she is performing without having to 'pay attention to' the actions. This stage has the benefit of allowing the person to process information from other aspects of the task, such as the strategy in a game of tennis, or the form or style of movement in ice skating or dance.

Apparently, a major problem for motor behaviour research is that this stage is extremely important for understanding high-level skills yet is almost never studied in experiments on motor learning. Some reasons have been put forward to account for this (Schmidt, 1988). In many experiments, where participants practise on laboratory tasks, such practice would have to continue for weeks or months before even beginning to approximate the levels of skill shown by high-level athletes, musicians, or industrial workers. Understandably, it is very difficult to convince participants to devote this kind of effort to research. Alternatively, we could use other, more natural tasks for which the learners are practising anyway, but it would be very difficult to manipulate and control the many variables that are necessary for a scientific understanding of the learning process.

Old skills combine to form new ones

A reasonable, but apparently untested view about skill learning is that a new skill learned by an adult is not really new at all, but is rather a new combination of (parts of) skills that the individual has learned earlier. An extreme variant of this basic idea is that all motor learning is over by about the age of four, and that all subsequent learning is mainly the recombination of these basic 'building blocks' into other new skills. Researchers who study the learning of skills in children refer to these building blocks as *subroutines*, analogous to computer programs. Examples might include those which have to do with reaching, grasping, releasing, placing objects, tracking, etc. When combined into a larger set of behaviours, these individual sub-routines

can be made to 'look like' a large skill, such as reaching for a biscuit and placing it into the mouth.

Such a general hypothesis about skill learning has considerable potential for understanding certain skills. For example, learning to throw effectively provides the performer with a skill that can be transferred to many playground activities; similarly with running, jumping, catching and so on. However, in other situations, apparently totally new patterns of skills can be learned by adults, patterns that seem to have little if anything to do with previously acquired skills. Examples could be learning gymnastics, or learning to fly an aeroplane. A research point is that this hypothesis is difficult to evaluate scientifically because at present there is no effective method for determining whether or not an earlier skill is 'contained' within the newer skill. However, increasingly the use of digitised images is able to isolate elements of skilled movement.

Theories of motor learning

There are three main variables which underpin how skills are learned: *motivation*, *practice* and *feedback*. As we have discussed motivation earlier in the text, we will now focus attention upon practice and feedback.

Practice makes perfect?

The old saying that 'practice makes perfect' is in many ways inaccurate. We might practice any skill for hours, but, if we do not know how we are actually performing, there is limited value. We might be repeating the same errors over and over again. The saying should be, 'practice with feedback makes perfect'. Some researchers believe that the single most important variable in skills acquisition is *feedback*. Feedback has been defined as:

> *'Sensory information that is contingent on having produced a movement.'*
> *(Schmidt, 1988)*

Feedback is that class of sensory information that is movement-related, and can be divided into two basic categories: *intrinsic feedback* (inherent to the task, e.g. sense or feel of throwing a dart) and *extrinsic feedback* (supplementary to the task, e.g. watching a video recording of skilled performance).

For example, when you are practising badminton you are receiving information from a range of sources: where the shuttle lands; the 'feel' of the shot; the instructions you give yourself; watching other people; instructions from the coach etc. All these are giving you some idea of how you can modify the movement making it more efficient and economical.

There are three main variables which can be controlled in the delivery of feedback. These are the *quality* or detail, the *quantity* and finally the *timing*.

Quality of feedback   We can give information about the outcome of the skill, i.e. where the ball landed, how fast the sprinter ran, where the shuttle landed. This is KNOWLEDGE OF RESULTS (KR). It concentrates on the *outcome* of the skill. We can also give information about how the skill was executed, i.e. position of the body, racket contact, club head position, namely KNOWLEDGE OF PERFORMANCE (KP). It concentrates on the *process* of the skill. Both of these are important. However, for the novice the process of feedback is vital. To develop skill, the learner needs to focus on establishing the basic principles of the movement through KP, before focusing on the outcome, KR.

Quantity of feedback   The coach needs to be aware of the problem of giving learners *too much* feedback. Because coaches are so knowledgeable and enthusiastic about their sport they tend to give novices excess information. It is better to give small amounts of precise information than to give large amounts of information that a learner cannot effectively use.

Timing of feedback   The timing of feedback can be very important in skill learning. Feedback given whilst the skill is being executed is called CONCURRENT FEEDBACK. You can try this by giving yourself an instruction during performance of a skill, for example, 'get set' after a badminton shot etc. Split times for runners, swimmers and cyclists can also be useful forms of concurrent feedback. Feedback given after performance is called TERMINAL FEEDBACK. When giving terminal feedback it should be given as near to the actual completion of the skill as possible.

Practice and the psychology of coaching

It is important the we apply our knowledge of the information processing model and the critical significance of feedback to actual learning situations. The sequence a coach often adopts is summarised in Figure 8.8.

This seems very simple, but every learner learns differently! Recognising and responding to this fact is the true art of coaching.

How much practice?   Practice is a key variable, but how much should we practise and how should practice be organised? In supervising the long-term practice of movement skills, players and coaches have to decide on how much practice to do. In deciding this a coach has to weigh up several factors, such as time available before the

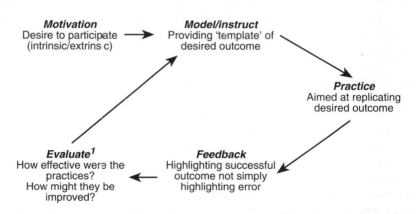

FIGURE 8.8
The Coaching Sequence

1 It might be argued that separating evaluation from feedback is a little contrived as the two steps are closely related. Similarly, feedback plays a part in increasing motivation as well as informing future practice.

skills need to be performed and the level of performance being aimed at. The intuitive coach would suggest that as much practice as possible should be completed. However, a widely cited study by Baddeley and Longman (1978) has shown that this might not be the most appropriate advice. In their study of trainee typists, they found that students who practised for two hours per day did not outperform those who practised less. Baddeley and Longman concluded that practice for long periods on a very regular basis was fatiguing and led to loss of motivation. These two factors reinforced the idea that for practice to be effective it is the *quality* of the practice which is important.

Conflicting goals in practice: learning versus performance   Very often, when people are learning a new skill, coaches encourage learners to 'do their best'. This can provide a problem, in as much as a player experiences conflict between learning and performing. The reason for this conflict lies in the observation that when players are learning new patterns of movement their performance often decreases to start with. When performance is emphasised, players tend to return to old effective patterns of movement rather than persist with the new ones which in the long term will lead to greater performance gains. In addition, GOAL SETTING theory, described in the occupational psychology chapter, argues that learners need *specific* goals not vague 'try harder' ones.

WHOLE PRACTICE versus PART PRACTICE   Some skills are long and complex, for example, gymnastic and trampoline routines. Under such circumstances the coach or instructor cannot expect the performer to learn all the elements at once. Learners trying to do this would be completely overwhelmed with all the information. An often used strategy is to break down the task into parts. For example, a ten bounce trampoline routine can be learned in three 'parts' of three, three and four bounces. However, we must be very careful when we do this. What often happens, particularly in long duration serial skills, is that there is a high degree of interaction across the 'parts'. What that means is that *how* you perform one action influences *how* you perform the next. Any small errors in executing skills in stage one might

become magnified in stage two. Part practice can often result in a performer being able to execute all the elements of a routine quite easily but in not being able to put them together. There are several strategies available to resolve this:

- *progressive part practice* – this type of approach begins with the first element of the skill. When performance has become stable and consistent the second element is added on until progressively the whole performance, including the transitions between the parts, becomes learned. In other words part one is learned, then part two is added. These two parts are learned together, then part three is added and so on
- *reverse chaining* – this is where the final part of the skill is learned first. Once this is mastered the next to last element is then learned. This might be a dismount in a gymnastic routine; learning the hitch kick or sail long jump technique in isolation before linking it with the run-up; or learning the delivery of the bowling action in cricket before learning the bound, which in turn can be learned before the run-up etc.

How can motor learning be tested?

As noted above, we cannot actually measure internal changes responsible for learning. We can only infer that it has occurred through observing behaviour. This is why we should be careful when discussing *learning curves*. We often hear people discussing their improvement in skill in terms of a learning curve. In reality, what they are describing is a *performance curve*. An example is shown in Figure 8.9.

The graph represents an increase in skill – the player's ability to score baskets from the free throw line has become increasingly certain. However, can we infer that the player has learned the skill? There are two main ways in which learning might be tested:

- *recall* – how well can you recall the target skill? For example, if you have spent a long time learning the movement patterns involved in taking free shots, can you recall or repeat that skill consistently? From our graph above we

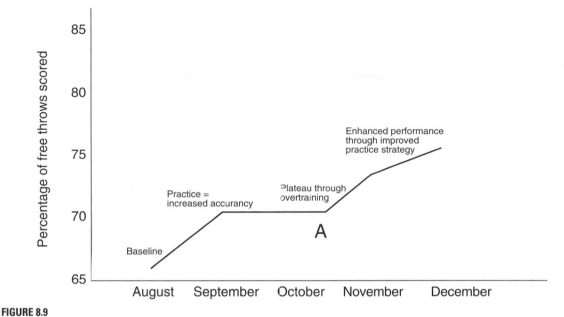

FIGURE 8.9
Performance curve of free shots

would suggest that *yes*, the skill has been learned. Even though at point A there appears to be a drop in performance, this could be explained by fatigue, lack of motivation or some other such temporary state

■ *transfer* – having practised a particular skill, it can be tested by giving a similar task. For example, having learned the strategy of attacking 3 vs 2 in rugby, can the skill transfer to a game setting? Transfer is the reason we practise sports skills. In all training our aim is to develop skills which will be of positive benefit in competition or performance.

Theories of motor control

Closed loop theory

One theory dealing exclusively with motor learning was presented by Adams (1971). He argued that behaviourist stimulus–response theory, whilst possibly explaining the relationship between reward and performance with respect to a skilled action (*why* it is performed), did not explain *how* that skill was acquired in the first place (see Appendix 1, cognitive theory). From this, Adams developed his CLOSED LOOP THEORY/MOTOR CONTROL. He believed that all move-

ments were made by comparing the current feedback from the limbs during movement to a reference of correctness learned during practice – *the perceptual trace*. This reference is assumed to be able to tell us what we *should* be doing or how we *should* be positioned. Movements are initiated by a memory trace which is developed through experience and is based on external knowledge of results as to earlier movements. This memory trace is controlled by the perceptual trace in skill learning which acts as a reference against which current actions can be compared via feedback.

With respect to positioning responses, the perceptual trace represents the feedback qualities of the correct position (e.g. the best position for a golf putt). Therefore, by minimising the difference between the feedback received and the perceptual trace, the limb is brought to the correct position by what are known as *closed loop processes* (i.e. a feedback system whereby a change is detected and then an adjustment made to bring the system back 'on course'). An everyday example of such a 'self-correcting' system is a home central heating system). The perceptual trace is the most important element of all and the accuracy of responding is dependent upon the 'strength' or quality of this trace.

Schema theory

Schmidt (1975) developed this theory as an improvement upon what he considered to be limitations inherent in Adam's theory. Schmidt was concerned that Adam's theory was based on the assumption that there would have to be a separate memory trace for *every* movement, which would make infinite demands on an individual's ability to both remember and recall an action appropriate to every new situation.

Schmidt therefore proposed a *schema theory* of learning, whereby a SCHEMA refers to a rule governing a series of components of an action. In other words, people learn the principles or schema of a movement rather than the movement as such. By acquiring schemas, people store in memory a set of relationships concerning a specific action. For example, practice of catching a ball generates a schema which will generalise to subsequent related instances which involve catching a ball. According to Schmidt, each movement consists of the following four aspects which become stored in memory:

- the initial state of the muscles and the environment prior to the movement
- a MOTOR PROGRAMME of the movement performed
- sensory feedback from the movement
- movement outcome in relation to movement expectation.

Through the continued practice of a sport skill, a person will eventually recall only the overall movement rules or schema which then become available to be activated in future settings. Importantly, the strength or effectiveness of a schema is directly related to the variety of prior experience, which has implications for training and skill education. What this means is that it becomes important for a person to learn schema which refer to the making of errors as well as successful responses.

Since the rules of schemas are acquired when we participate in a sport and receive information (feedback) as to the effects of our actions, the suggestion for coaching and training is that the more varied our practice, the more strongly will the rules of schemas become established. Learning from errors can therefore be considered to be an essential part of sports training. As an example, by

deliberately serving a tennis ball to the outside of a service line, as well as to the inside of the line, the suggestion is that the schemas which govern accurate serving will become more flexible and effective.

This is but a taste of a vast area of theory and applied research, which is increasingly taking a cognitive approach to enhance our understanding.

Exercise psychology

The past decade has seen a great increase in research aimed at understanding the many factors which predispose some people to take up some form of physical activity, and persist with it, whilst many of their peers drop out and return to their sedentary lifestyles. This research has received renewed impetus from the Allied Dunbar National Fitness Survey (1992) and the subsequent government *Health of the Nation* policy document. This research collected data regarding patterns of physical activity from a sample of around 4000 subjects. The data was backed up by fitness tests on a random sample of male and female subjects whose ages ranged from 17 to 65. Results showed that seven out of ten men and eight out of ten women did not exercise sufficiently regularly to gain any discernible health benefits. The *Health of the Nation* policy document aims to reduce by a third the incidence of coronary heart disease by the year 2000. The aim of the exercise psychologist in trying to understand exercise behaviour is twofold: first, to investigate those factors which encourage people to engage in physical activity; and second, to try and find out why so many people drop out of activity after a relatively short period of time.

The psychological benefits of physical activity

Research from a variety of sources has shown that many people participate in exercise simply because it makes them feel better (see final exercise 5). As mentioned earlier, Morgan (1979) proposed a *mental health model* of exercise participation. Using the POMS scale, exercise was shown to reduce negative states and increase one's positive state. Morgan sees the Iceberg Profile (Figure 8.2) as typical of exercise participants.

The physical benefits of exercise have been widely acknowledged. Lack of exercise is regarded by the BMA and the American Heart Association to be the fourth major risk factor in coronary heart disease (CHD), the other three being smoking, high blood pressure and high blood cholesterol (see the health psychology chapter). Research by Blair et al (1992) has suggested that, more important than this, exercise can reduce the negative impact of the three other factors. If a person is an exerciser, despite possessing one, two or even all three additional risk factors, their susceptibility to CHD is reduced.

The psychological benefits of exercise have always been regarded as somewhat less clearly defined. To rectify this point, the *International Society for Sport Psychology* (ISSP) published a position statement (1992) on the psychological benefits of exercise and physical activity. The purpose of this statement has been to reflect areas of consensus within research, which have linked exercise to psychological functioning in the following ways:

- short- and long-term enhancements in psychological function and well-being
- a causal relationship has been demonstrated between activity and self-esteem
- increased incidence of positive mood states
- drug-free lowering of the symptoms of depression
- positive effects appear to be derived from both low- and high-intensity aerobic activities; non-competitive activity is considered most effective
- there appears to be a *dose response* issue, i.e. there is a link between the frequency, intensity and duration of exercise and the psychological benefits
- psychological enhancement through activity can be seen throughout the life cycle
- there are links between physical activity and economic productivity.

How exercise improves psychological functioning

There are many hypotheses aimed at explaining how physical activity improves psychological sta-

tus. Some theories are primarily psychological in nature, whilst others are psycho-physiological. The most prominent psychological theories are the cognitive-behavioural hypothesis, the social interaction hypothesis and the distraction hypothesis.

Psychological theories

Cognitive-behavioural research This approach suggests that exercise encourages the generation of positive thoughts and feelings which serve to displace or counteract negative mood states such as depression, anxiety and confusion. This theory adopts a self-efficacy type of approach – see Appendix 1, social learning theory. When a person completes or achieves in a task which they believe to be difficult, such as exercising, their self-efficacy increases. This leads to greater persistence, effort and reduced anxiety.

Social INTERACTION HYPOTHESIS Based on a meta-analysis (see Appendix 2) by North et al (1990), this suggests that it is the social interaction with colleagues and friends in an exercise context that is pleasurable enough to have the net effect of improving mental health and psychological functioning. Whilst this hypothesis is useful in explaining some aspects of the improvements, it has been shown that exercising by oneself also has positive effects. Indeed, there is some evidence that exercising alone has greater influence on psychological well-being.

The DISTRACTION HYPOTHESIS This argues that exercise provides an opportunity for individuals to be distracted from their worries and frustrations. Support for this view comes from Sachs (1982) and Bahrke and Morgan (1978). The latter study showed that other forms of distraction, such as meditation and quiet rest were as effective as exercise in reducing anxiety. North et al (1990) showed that chronic exercise is more effective in enhancing mood. However, other forms of relaxation, which also provide a distraction, are also considered important.

Physiological theories

CARDIOVASCULAR FITNESS HYPOTHESIS This is based on early work by Morgan (1969). It has not received much support since it has been noted how improvements in psychological functioning often *precede* enhanced cardiovascular fitness, rather than the fitness *causing* psychological well-being.

BIOGENIC AMINE *theory*   This theory states that exercise promotes the secretion of *amine neuro-transmitters* such as adrenalin, noradrenalin, dopamine and serotonin. These are associated with activity in important 'mood' centres in the brain, such as the limbic system.

Endorphin hypothesis   Postulates that exercise induces feelings of well-being through increasing the levels of *endogenous morphine* like substances. These substances have the same effect on a person as morphine from outside the body, i.e. pain-killing and general euphoria. This serves to improve moods and enhance a feeling of well-being. This theory is very appealing, but has received poor support in the research.

We have discussed the arguments surrounding the benefits of exercise. Many people hold a series of attitudes that exercise is beneficial and should have a significant influence in their lifestyles, but they often do no exercise. Why is this? The statistics are of some concern. Around 75% of the population is sedentary and is risking coronary heart disease and other diseases of adaptation. Around one person in four is suffering from mild to moderate depression. Both these could be managed with a programme of physical activity. Yet around half the people who begin an exercise program have dropped out of it within six months. In the next sections we will discuss the research findings into the motives people have to participate in physical activity and also the motives given for non-participation. The final section examines the patterns of participation exhibited.

Motives for participation in physical activity

Do you ever think, 'Why am I doing this?' as you strain to lift a weight or lace up your running shoes for another five-mile slog in the rain? Exercise psychologists are interested in that question. Faced with a major public health problem,

that the sedentary lifestyle adopted by the majority of the population will inevitably lead to a high level of CHD, if psychologists could understand why people don't exercise they might ensure that these factors were de-emphasised or eliminated.

Most people report a whole range of reasons why they do or don't participate in physical activity. Research by Kenyon (1968) found that the main reasons for exercising could be grouped into six factors:

- *Exercise as a social experience.* For many, exercise is an excellent opportunity to meet new people, maintain existing relationships, and generally to express the social aspects of their character. The range of activities available tends to attract different personalities. For example, the social interaction involved in team games such as rugby is very different from the interaction involved in long-distance running. It should be noted that for many people the activity itself can be secondary to the social interaction.
- *Exercise for health and fitness.* As people become more familiar with the positive effects of relatively low levels of exercise, they become more likely to cite health reasons, such as weight loss, a desire to become toned or physically stronger, as motives. Again in some people these can become the primary incentive for exercising.
- *Exercise for stress and excitement.* Some forms of physical activity provide the opportunity for excitement and thrill. For example, skiing and off-road cycling have both become very popular recently. Part of the attraction of these activities is the danger involved in speedy descent.
- *Exercise as an aesthetic experience.* Many forms of exercise involve grace, beauty and artistry. Activities such as dance, yoga, synchronised swimming and gymnastics are aesthetically very satisfying. Many people are drawn to these activities as a form of self-expression.
- *Exercise as catharsis.* Catharsis is a release of pent-up tensions and emotion. Exercise can provide an opportunity for people to release

The combination of athletic achievement, fun and carnival is a feature of modern mass marathon events.

their anger or frustration in a socially acceptable way.

- *Exercise as an ascetic expression*. Every year over 50,000 people apply to run in the London Marathon. Less than 100 people have a real expectation of winning the race. The majority of entrants are expressing ascetic motivation – they are choosing an arduous, painful challenge in an effort to explore their personal limits.

These are the main groupings of PARTICIPATION MOTIVES for physical activity. Alderman and Wood (1976) suggested that several more specific motives might exist for competitive sport, including:

- *excellence* – motive to learn new skills and consolidate existing ones
- *success* – motive to seek status through competition
- *affiliation* – making friends through competing (more prominent in team sport)
- *power* – motive to influence or control other people
- *aggression* – motive to intimidate other people
- *stress* – seeking excitement through competition
- *independence* – motive to become able to do things without the help of other people.

As the research on why people participate in exercise and competitive sport becomes more detailed, it has become more apparent that the key to participation in physical activity is *enjoyment*. People have fun in sport and exercise in many different ways. Some enjoy playing well more than they enjoy winning. The providers of sport and exercise need to be familiar with the theory surrounding participation motives and should ensure that their idea of fun matches very closely with the participants. The other side of the coin is to examine the reasons why people do not exercise. These have been summarised by Willis and Campbell (1992).

- *Lack of time*. This is the most widely cited reason why people do not exercise. When these people examine their lifestyles, they often do find time for other sedentary activities, such as watching television or reading. Very often this reason masks other more profound reasons for not exercising. For example, they endured poor physical education when they were young and cannot even countenance the idea that physical activity can be enjoyable.
- *Fatigue*. The pace of life in the latter part of the 20th century can be very tiring. People often feel too exhausted to even consider exercise, particularly at the end of the day. However, what many people overlook is that light exercise has a restorative and invigorating

effect. Often their exhaustion is more mental than physical. A gentle walk, or swim or game of tennis (all that is necessary to gain health benefits) can relieve tension more effectively than several hours of viewing television.

- *Lack of facilities or resources*. There are few communities totally devoid of recreational facilities. The providers of sport and exercise try to make their facilities as accessible as possible. The physical barriers such as lack of transport or finance can be more significant as barriers to exercise.

- *Lack of knowledge about fitness and exercise*. Many people believe they are fitter than they really are. Modern life is highly automated in an effort to make it easier. People do not have to climb stairs or walk long distances. This leads many people into a false sense of security. They rarely have to stretch themselves, and therefore their health status progressively deteriorates. Health educators co-ordinate local and national advertising campaigns to promote knowledge and understanding of key fitness issues. The evidence is that these messages are hitting the target. People are becoming more informed about health issues. Later in this section we will consider the effect of knowledge on actual exercise behaviour.

- *Lack of motivation*. Willpower is considered an aspect of personality which people can bring to bear in their efforts to change behaviour. This factor is often overstated. As Willis and Campbell noted, many people come to exercise having high levels of motivation from other areas of their lives, but have 'tried and failed' in sport and exercise. Their lack of motivation is often due to their needs not being fully satisfied by the activity.

Exercise adherence – why some people stick at it

The reasons why people adhere or do not adhere to exercise programmes have received a great deal of attention recently. The first area to consider is the process by which people make the transition from sedentary to active lifestyles. A study by Sallis et al (1986) aimed to identify the factors determining adherence in a large sample of adults. They found the following to be important:

- physical exercise/self-efficacy – participants could be discriminated by their belief that they could succeed in an exercise programme
- knowledge about what constitutes a healthy lifestyle
- knowledge of how valuable regular exercise is
- the perception that they have a high level of self control
- positive attitudes about the value and importance of regular exercise
- participants are not initially overweight.

The research also indicates that people tend to pass through specific phases in their adoption of exercise behaviour. These are shown in Figure 8.10.

In particular, the transition from adoption to maintenance or drop out status has received a great deal of research attention. The fact that almost 50% of people drop out of exercise within

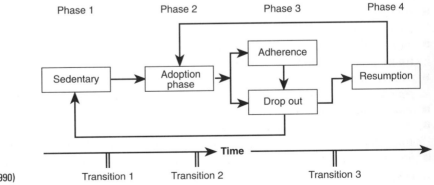

FIGURE 8.10
The four-phase model of exercise participation
(adapted from Sallis and Howell, 1990)

six months is very worrying, since maintenance of the physiological benefits of exercise is very much dependent on regular participation.

Dishman (1987) has conducted a great deal of research in this area. It is his view that the best single predictor of adherence to exercise is *self-motivation*. However, he has identified other factors as being important, including a perception of support from peers, partners or friends, access to facilities, available time, personal perception of positive health status (i.e. a view that exercise is having a positive effect). On the other hand, the following have been identified as factors contributing to *non-adherence*: occupation – low-skilled employees are less likely to adhere to an exercise programme, are more likely to be overweight at the outset and are likely to experience discomfort whilst exercising; smoking – smokers are less likely to exercise; mood – people who already experience mood disturbances are less likely to exercise. This picture is rather gloomy, since it appears that the people who are less likely to adhere to exercise are exactly those people who most need to adhere – the overweight, smokers and those with mood disturbances!

Attitudes and behaviour

The first step in trying to encourage those who need it to adopt an active lifestyle has been to understand the theoretical link between attitudes and behaviour. Human beings are notoriously irrational in their behaviour. A (not too serious!) example could be the National Lottery, whereby the probability of winning makes it almost certain that you are simply giving that pound to Camelot! This irrationality very often makes it impossible to infer even deeply-held attitudes from observing people's behaviour. For instance, a person might have the attitude of wanting good exam grades but behave quite differently.

Several theoretical models to explain the link between health attitude and exercise behaviour have been proposed. These are the HEALTH BELIEF MODEL, the THEORY OF REASONED ACTION and the THEORY OF PLANNED BEHAVIOUR each described in the health psychology chapter. It can be seen, from that chapter, that the theory of planned behaviour assumes that the more *perceived control* a person has over their behaviour, and the factors affecting

it, the more likely they are to behave in a way consistent with their attitudes. For example, a person may have a positive attitude towards exercise, supported by a positive intention to exercise. However, with little time to exercise they may feel the situation is beyond their control. This model has had practical influence on the encouragement of exercise and several high-profile projects have followed it by encouraging people who perceive their level of control to be low to engage in exercise. In Sunderland, a leisure centre offered exercise sessions exclusively to women (who often report not enough time to exercise). The element of control was considered in that the centre offered a facility where washing could be taken for ironing while the women exercised. The scheme won a Sports Council award. Perhaps at colleges and universities the way to persuade students to exercise is to offer an essay writing scheme while they exercise!

In conclusion, the field of exercise psychology is developing rapidly. In response to public health issues, it is becoming increasingly important to understand why people do exercise, and perhaps more importantly why some people are seemingly immune to the message that exercise is good for you.

Aggression in sport

The history of sport is littered with the tragic consequences of aggressive and violent behaviour, both on and off the field. Professional soccer players have had their careers ended by foul play, and amateur rugby union players have been almost blinded by opponents deliberately 'raking' studs over a player's face. AGGRESSION is also seen off the field between rival fans. The Heysel Stadium tragedy in 1985, where 38 Italian soccer fans died after fighting broke out on the terraces, is only one of many serious incidents. Many social psychologists have considered the issue and concluded that there are significant sociological explanations as well as psychological ones. The sociological explanations have been explored by Taylor (1987) and Williams et al (1984) and will not be considered here. In this section we will consider some of the psychological theory which attempts to explain aggression amongst sport participants and spectators.

Within sport there is currently a debate about whether aggression and violence are caused by sport participation or whether sport can help to channel a basic aggressive instinct. There are two opposing views which protagonists of each view believe cannot be reconciled. These are summarised in the following opposing attitudes:

'Sport gives people the opportunity to learn to control their emotions, especially aggression.'

'Competitive sport teaches aggression rather than eliminating or channelling it.'

Defining aggression

A significant issue to confront before we start to discuss aggression is to decide what we actually mean by the word. How many of the following acts could be described as aggressive?

- a rugby player 'driving' his shoulder into a tackle
- a soccer player making a 'professional' foul to save a certain goal
- two boxers fighting for a big money purse
- a tennis player abusing an official after missing an easy shot
- an 800m runner elbowing her way out of a bad position
- a spectator shouting abuse at the opponent's team bus
- a cricketer bowling a 'bouncer' at a batsman he knows to be weak on the back foot
- a sprinter elbowing and cutting directly in front of others in a Tour de France finish.

In many media reports the word 'aggressive' is used to refer to anything from the use of strong but legitimate tactics, for example, a 200m sprinter running a fast 'aggressive' bend, through to the use of illegitimate and potentially life-threatening force, such as aiming to make a tackle in rugby at neck or head level. We need to have a clear basis for defining aggression and also to be able to differentiate between its different manifestations. One of the most widely cited definitions was pre-

sented by Baron (1977), who believed aggression to be:

'any behaviour directed at the goal of harming or injuring another being who is motivated to avoid such treatment.' (p.3)

The key to this definition is the notion of *intent*. But intent alone is not sufficient. Aggression involves the behavioural expression of that intent. Aggressive behaviour has as its aim the intention to harm another person. Since harm can result from both physical and verbal attacks, aggression can be in the form of verbal abuse. This definition excludes unintentional behaviour and behaviour against inanimate objects, such as tennis rackets. To further help clarify the distinction between aggressive acts, Baron also introduced a taxonomy of aggression, which differentiated the aims of the act:

- HOSTILE AGGRESSION – the main goal here is to *harm* and there is the *intention to harm*. The aggressor is usually angry. An example might be retaliation for a clumsy tackle. This is clearly different from the situation where the intention is to do harm in order to weaken an opponent. This is the second form of aggression
- INSTRUMENTAL AGGRESSION – the main goal is to *win*, although there is also the intention to *harm*. In such instances the aggressor is not usually angry, for example, boxing, or bowling a bouncer, to 'soften up' a batsman
- ASSERTIVE BEHAVIOUR – the main goal is to *win* and there is *no intention to harm*. Legitimate force is used. Usually great effort or skill is involved, such as 'tackle like you mean it' in rugby or soccer. Some would argue that this is not really aggression at all.

This classification underscores the key importance of the aggressor's intentions. This makes it sometimes very difficult to tell the difference, with any certainty, between acts which are intended and those which are not. Often the only person who knows the true intent of the act is the player him or herself.

Theories of aggression

Several different theories have been proposed to explain why people are aggressive. These are not theories specific to sport and apply to all forms of aggressive behaviour.

INSTINCT THEORY OF AGGRESSION

Based on the work of Freud (1933), this is a very pessimistic view that aggression is an instinct deeply seated in the human mind. The suggestion is that people have in their subconscious minds a self-destructive death instinct (*thanatos*) which may express itself in various ways. However, some theorists believe that an important function of sport is to provide a socially acceptable expression of the death instinct.

Frustration–aggression theory

Based on the work of Dollard et al (1939), this view suggests that when attempts to satisfy a need or achieve a goal are frustrated, aggression results. This theory suggests that opponents in sporting contests frustrate a desire to win or be successful. This naturally leads to increased aggression. The purpose of the aggression is two-fold, firstly to overcome the frustration; and secondly to release the pent-up emotion that frustration causes.

These two views differ in that aggression in FRUSTRATION–AGGRESSION THEORY is aimed at *removing* the frustrating agent and achieving a goal. In instinct theory, aggressive behaviour itself is the goal.

Social learning theory

This approach is based on the work of Bandura (1969) – see Appendix 1. He found that many social behaviours, including aggressive behaviour, are based on observation, MODELLING and REINFORCEMENT. In experimental studies using Bobo dolls, Bandura found that children who saw adults behaving aggressively towards the doll were more likely to imitate the behaviour. Many subsequent studies have replicated the finding that observation of a high-status model behaving aggressively can encourage or reinforce imitation.

Aggression research in sport

Certain sports tend to be more prone to violence than others. Some researchers have suggested that games which increase players' level of arousal are more likely to be characterised by aggressive behaviour. This view proposes that activation from one source becomes transferred on to another behaviour. This is now considered to be an over-simplification. Le Unes and Nation (1989) summarised several studies which suggested there are a number of sport-specific situational factors which also contribute to aggressive behaviour:

- *the spread of points* – when the score in a game is close, teams tend not to aggress, since penalties can critically influence the final outcome. This has been apparent in international rugby union. Teams are drilled not to commit penalty offences, particularly in their own half of the field, since goal kickers at this level rarely miss
- *playing home or away* – there is some evidence to suggest that soccer teams playing away from home tend to be more aggressive. This has been contradicted by other studies, from North America, showing no difference in the incidence of aggression between ice hockey teams playing home or away
- *time on the clock* – the incidence of aggression increases as the game proceeds, although if the score in the game is close and the result is in the balance, as noted above, the incidence of aggressive acts will decrease
- *the outcome of the game* – as the frustration–aggression hypothesis predicts, aggression is apparently more common amongst losing teams than winning teams. This may also be true amongst spectators
- *perception of victim's intent* – in sport situations, some researchers (e.g. Bredemeier and Shields, 1986) have suggested that people may engage in atypical processes of thinking, for example, by regressing to a lower level of moral or ethical thinking, called GAME REASONING, which can manifest itself in many ways, for example, 'Well she elbowed me, so it's okay for me to elbow her' or 'Get your revenge in first'.

Retaliation is a feature of some sports, but that in itself is not a completely unthinking activity. Players tend to retaliate only when they believe an

Is a tackle assertive or aggressive behaviour?

opponent's intention was to harm them. A batsman will respond differently to a legitimate fast 'bouncer', designed to unsettle, as compared to an illegitimate 'beamer' aimed to incapacitate. Additionally, the fear of retaliation may inhibit acts of aggression. However, if a player believes an aggressive act will be punished or fears counter-retaliation, the initial aggressive act might be inhibited.

Reducing aggression in sport

Many bodies have attempted to identify the causes of aggression amongst sports players and spectators. The British Government suggested in 1984 that an identity card should be carried by all spectators at soccer matches. This scheme was dropped when it became apparent that most of the serious incidents of aggression occurred amongst spectators away from the ground itself.

Goldstein (1983) has proposed that several strategies are available to reduce the incidence of aggressive behaviour in spectators. These include:

- limiting the sale of alcohol to spectators in the ground
- the promotion of spectatorship as a family event

- the presentation of competitors as friendly rivals, rather than hated enemies.

These are easily discussed, but difficult to implement. National governing bodies of sport have implemented schemes which penalise players whose aggressive acts 'bring the game into disrepute'. Leith (1991) suggested a series of recommendations aimed at reducing aggressive behaviour in competitors and performers. These included:

- ensuring young athletes are provided with positive, non-aggressive models of behaviour
- severe, consistent penalties for aggressive behaviour in both players and coaches who encourage such play
- competitors practising strategies aimed at curtailing aggressive behaviour and being rewarded for controlling their aggression.

Again, easy to discuss and recommend but much more difficult to implement.

Anabolic steroid abuse and aggression

Some athletes use ANABOLIC STEROIDS to enhance their ability to recover from heavy bouts of training. These drugs have the effect of increasing the levels of *androgens* (male hormones) in the blood. The effect of this is to increase muscle bulk, and to exaggerate the masculine characteristics in both sexes, for example there is an increase in body hair and the voice deepens. However, prolonged steroid use interferes with reproductive function and can cause sterility in males and females.

The reason we are interested in steroid use in relation to aggression is because, as Lubell (1989) and Choi (1992) among many other writers have reported, use of steroids is associated with the likelihood of aggressive behaviour.

How can steroids increase aggression?

Researchers have tried to explain how increased androgen levels in the central nervous system can lead to aggressive behaviour. Brower et al (1989) have suggested that steroid-type drugs influence certain centres in the central nervous and neuroendocrine systems. Studies have shown that if certain areas in the limbic system of the brain are stimulated using micro-electrodes, laboratory animals respond by becoming aggressive. These areas appear to be highly specific. If other areas of the brain very close by are stimulated, rather than going into a violent frenzy, an animal will coldly stalk and kill a prey. It is believed that these brain centres are also involved in the release of andronergic hormones, the levels of which are influenced by anabolic steroids. This is a biologically based perspective on aggression, which has received wide support.

There is widespread concern about the use of steroids in sport, primarily because athletes are cheating and perhaps harming themselves. It should also be borne in mind that through the use of these drugs perpetrators may be more likely to harm others.

THE FUTURE OF SPORT PSYCHOLOGY

The scientific study of behaviour in sport has evolved rapidly in the past decade. Undoubtedly the next decade will see a similar rate of growth and change. There are many challenges facing this area. Some sport psychologists believe that the most important issue to be faced is the development of a conceptual framework for the science. Several leading sport and exercise psychologists believe that we should be spending more research time understanding techniques such as goal setting, imagery and concentration training work, than we currently spend actually using the techniques with athletes and performers. These psychologists contend that the techniques are working in spite of the fact that we have little understanding of *how* they work. Understanding the theoretical basis of the techniques might lead us to be able to use the various techniques much more effectively. It is very difficult to separate the theoretical from the applied approaches. In the future theoretical work will continue to impact on our applied work with athletes.

Another important challenge facing sport and exercise psychology is in the field of public health and exercise promotion. We are faced with an increasingly inactive population and a demographic problem of increased numbers of older people. The recent government initiative to enhance the health status of the British population has as a central aim a reduction in coronary heart disease. Here sport and exercise psychologists are in the front line promoting healthy lifestyle choices and exercise – one of the main interventions available to prevent heart disease.

The future will certainly see increased opportunity for sport psychologists in the field of performance enhancement. Sport performers at all levels are beginning to become aware of the mind as the final performance hurdle. Exercise physiologists can tell us in very fine detail about how we should train our bodies. But in many sports, especially at the élite level, all participants are as finely tuned as they can possibly be. They are all physically very fit. The factor which discriminates the best from the very good is the mind. Performers want their psychology to be as well tuned as their physiology. It is increasingly likely that sport psychologists will also need counselling skills to help performers handle the stresses of modern competitive sport.

This overview of the current status of, and developments within, sport psychology has we hope demonstrated its vibrant and ebullient nature. Taken in historical context, after a somewhat hesitant beginning, where it drew heavily on existing theory and research from mainstream psychology, sport psychology has now moved forward with confidence both as an applied profession and as a division of psychology with perspectives and research initiatives in its own right.

FURTHER RECOMMENDED READING

Bull, S. J. (ed.) (1991) *Sport Psychology: A Self-Help Guide*. Wiltshire: The Crowood Press.

Cox, R. M. (1994) *Sport Psychology: Concepts and Applications*. Dubuque, IA: W. M. Brown and Benchmark.

Sharp, B. (1992) *Acquiring Skill in Sport*. Eastbourne: Sports Dynamics.

exercises

1. What do sport psychologists do? Outline the sequence of stages of consultation which they might follow when with a client. Which stage in this sequence do you think is most important and why?

2. Try to remember what it felt like before the biggest match or sporting event which you played, supported or participated in. Try to list the feelings. Do you think they had a positive or negative effect on your performance or experience of the event? How does psychological theory help to explain your experiences?

3. What is skill in sport?
(a) How can a coach organise a session so that learning is maximised?
(b) Why is motivation important?
(c) How can practice be organised so as to maximise learning?

4. What types of feedback are available to a person who engages in the following?

- athletics
- rock climbing
- swimming
- soccer

5. For the next few days keep a record of how you feel before and after exercise. Rate your moods on a scale from −5 (not at all tense) to +5 (very tense) for each of the following characteristics:

- tense
- depressed
- angry
- tired
- confused
- vigorous

On a graph, plot your changes in mood before and after exercise over several days. How does psychological theory aim to explain how exercise influences mood?

6. There are many factors which affect people's participation in sport.
(a) List you own motives for exercising or not exercising. Which are the most important?
(b) Ask several people you know who either do or do not take part in sport or exercise. Compare their reasons with your own.

1 THE MAJOR THEORETICAL APPROACHES WITHIN APPLIED PSYCHOLOGY

Approaches are not as clearly outlined as theories. An approach provides a general orientation to a view of humankind. It says, in effect, 'we see people as operating according to these basic principles and we therefore see explanations of human behaviour as needing to be set within these limits and with these or those principles understood'. An approach is a *perspective*. Followers tend to believe that their way is the most useful or productive way to produce explanations. Explanations are usually theories. Rarely does an explanation of human behaviour become *the* factually correct explanation of all similar behaviour.

WHY ARE THERE DIFFERENT APPROACHES?

Levels of explanation

The aim of psychological theorising is to provide the most productive and enlightening explanation of human thought and behaviour. Part of the difference between major approaches to theorising can be attributed to differing *levels of explanation*. Perhaps an example will demonstrate. Suppose we are asked why a certain train disaster occurred. A superficial explanation might run, 'because the signal was at red, but the driver was asleep and didn't see the signal'. A different perspective says, 'This kind of accident has been increasing because management is trying to cut corners. They refuse to update signalling equipment and they demand more work of drivers'. A further perspective might be, 'The driver had been under tremendous domestic pressure; he'd been up all night arguing with his wife about the settlement for their separation'. Notice here that the first explanation sticks close to the immediate facts. The other two speculate about the wider context of causes, all relevant, but in two quite different directions.

Another concrete example might be, 'Why did your car stop?' A nuts and bolts explanation might concentrate on what happens in a car engine when there is no more petrol coming to the carburettor. A completely different level of explanation occurs when the driver explains, 'I'd asked my partner to fill it up. I noticed this wasn't done but I was distracted by the urgency of picking my son up from school and the foul weather'. Notice here that the second explanation is not a wider explanation leading up to the immediate facts of the case. It serves quite a different purpose and the nuts and bolts mechanical explanation is irrelevant here.

Reductionism

The nuts and bolts explanation is an example of REDUCTIONISM – an attempt to reduce an explanation at one level (say psychological) to an explanation at a more basic level. It is not useful to explain why a snooker player won a match in terms of the Newtonian mechanics of every collision of balls in the match. Similarly, within psychological theorising, it is not usually useful to be told what physiological factors or what individual string of thoughts preceded a certain pattern of behaviour. For instance, if we are piloting a programme to increase factory output and decrease errors, an explanation in terms of each worker's arm and leg movements or in terms of their every single thought will not be useful. We shall probably want to consider communication and interaction patterns and possibly the workers' general assessment of the new working conditions. On the other hand, within clinical psychology we may, in some circumstances, be interested in individual thoughts which trigger certain problematic behaviour.

From molar to molecular

Across all the social sciences, as we seek to explain human behaviour at various levels, we are said to move from the MOLAR through the MICRO level and on to the MOLECULAR level of explanation. At each level different kinds of factors are seen as influential and behaviour is analysed at levels of a different complexity. In the train crash example above, the management cutting corners explanation is at a molar level and is somewhat beyond individual level psychology, using organisational and economic analysis. On the other hand, an explanation focusing on the family moves towards the micro level and to say that his hand slipped through a combination of tiredness and alcohol is to use a molecular analysis. Box 1 gives a relative division of various levels of analysis and explanation.

The holistic view

A substantial number of psychologists hold the view that one cannot sensibly isolate *aspects* of an individual (such as their 'intelligence' or a particular, measured attitude). They argue that an individual only makes sense as a *whole individual*. They are therefore opposed to understanding people as the sum of various characteristics or mental processes 'isolated' by psychological research. They are opposed to reductionism in the explanation of human experience and behaviour and are seen as taking a HOLISTIC approach.

Individual differences/differential psychology

Some psychologists make general statements and theories about how humans work *per se*. That is, they are not so much interested in individual differences between people but are keen on explaining how the mind works or in how people acquire behaviour (i.e. learn) in general. Piaget, for instance, developed theories of the pattern in which almost all children's thinking develops, irrespective of any advantages one child has in mathematical or verbal skills. Skinner (1953) developed an overall model of the way in which people's behaviour is shaped irrespective of any particular personality characteristics they might possess. The cognitive psychologists are interested in general features of human thought.

Individual differences – nomothetic and idiographic

On the other hand, DIFFERENTIAL PSYCHOLOGY, or the study of *individual differences*, is an area in which specific differences *between* individuals are the very subject of interest. Some of these differences can be *generalised*, that is, it is thought possible to measure or otherwise assess any individual on the particular characteristic. Examples might be the traits (characteristics) of anxiety, assertiveness or extroversion. Extroversion is seen by some as a dimension on which

BOX 1

Levels of analysis

LEVEL OF ANALYSIS

	Molar	Micro		Molecular
Focus	**Societal/ organisational**	**Group (inter-individual)**	**Individual**	**Intra (within/parts of the) individual**
	Social structures political and economic factors, legal system, social ideology (sociology, politics, economics)	Formal and informal groups work groups, social groups, peer groups, family (sociology, social psychology, communications studies)	External and interpersonal factors (social psychology, differential psychology, humanistic psychology)	Individual responses (behaviourism)

Internal or intrapersonal factors. (biological psychology, cognitive psychology psychodynamics) |
| | Cultural factors: ideology and values of identified culture (anthropology, cross-cultural studies) | | Behavioural goals, large-scale behaviour (behaviourism) | |
| | Organisational factors: authority structures at work | | | |

we all differ, from high extroversion to high introversion. Such measurement and generalising is known as a NOMOTHETIC approach. On the other hand, some psychologists feel it is important to recognise the existence of traits which, though they might seem superficially similar, have a *unique existence* in each individual – an IDIOGRAPHIC position. Aggression may look similar on the outside, for instance, it usually involves hitting and shouting, but its causes, its exact content and its pattern of occurrence vary in important ways from one person to the next. Clinical and educational psychologists, in particular, often express a need to analyse their clients' behaviour at this level.

Individual differences – traits or situations?

A further debate concerns the issue of whether we are justified in assuming that people's behaviour varies largely as result of individual differences at all. In some situations virtually everyone will behave in a similar manner. Most people will stop to help when an elderly person falls down beside them, for instance. Some have argued, from research studies (Hartshorne and May, 1928; Mischel, 1968) that most individual behaviour is not at all consistent across various settings. This position, then, puts more emphasis on *situations* in controlling our behaviour, and argues that individual differences do not account for as much variation in behaviour as most people think. An INTERACTIONIST MODEL accepts that individuals are not consistent across situations – but it also argues that each situation does not produce the same behaviour in each individual. The situation means different things to different individuals and, because of *some* differences in personality traits, different people will behave differently in the *same* situation. Mischel moved towards this position in his later work and for a full account of the angles in this debate see Gross (1995) who cites Krahé (1992) as arguing that, despite the long debate over the existence or nature of personality traits, 'the trait concept presents itself in remarkably good shape at the beginning of the 90s.' Similarly, Deary and Matthews (1993) argue that traits are 'alive and well'.

Mind, body and free will

This is one of two issues underlying all major psychological theories. The MIND–BODY DEBATE is an issue dating back at least to the philosopher Descartes in the 17th century. Suppose I ask you to imagine a purple elephant. With no knowledge of brain physiology or psychology you would nevertheless hasten to agree that, were we to look inside your head we would find no picture or recognisable representation of an elephant. We would find brain cell matter, blood, veins and that sort of thing *only*. The mental image of an elephant is a *mental event* (one could misleadingly call it a 'mental object', as did 17th century philosophers) and it has no defined physical place or shape. In modern thinking it is probably explained as a *state* of our nervous system in the same way as this page of writing appears on my computer monitor but has no particular shape or single physical place within my computer's mechanical insides. The problem for Descartes was how a *non-physical* (mental) event can have a causal effect on a *physical* event. This is still a problem if we continue to view mental and physical things in this way. That is, how can the two meet and one affect the other? As we shall see the early behaviourists had a simple solution to this

dilemma – they simply banished mental events as possible causes of behaviour or as objects worthy of scientific investigation. In clinical psychology they concentrated on what people *do* not on what they *think*. In the health and sport psychology sections of this book we certainly find ourselves switching back and forth between mental and physical concepts and it is worth keeping in mind this 'dualism' and its problems – how can physical events cause mental states and how, in turn can mental states have a physiological effect, as they almost certainly do?

Free will and determinism

This is the other issue running through all psychological perspectives. If one takes an extreme reductionist perspective, one would argue that all behaviour can be explained by past conditioning or underlying physiological processes. A snooker game *can* (theoretically at least) be completely explained by describing all the collisions of balls which took place. Similarly it would be possible (again, theoretically) to explain all behaviour during a job selection interview, including the production of speech sounds, in terms of the underlying physiological events which produced them. If one believes that all these, in turn, were produced in direct causal fashion, by prior stimuli (as when you shout 'watch out!' and I jump) then we are immediately confronted by a problem. This type of explanation assumes that all bodily behaviour is immediately caused by prior bodily events or external physical events. This leaves no room for alternatives. You behaved as you did because your behaviour was caused. What then happens to the concept of responsibility or choice, i.e. *control* over our behaviour? We do not need these concepts since we had no choice, and therefore no responsibility, for what we did. This is precisely the dilemma which prompted Descartes to come up with his mind–body division in the first place, because he saw purely physical explanations of our bodily movements leading to exactly this mechanical and therefore non-moral world where we could dismiss the concept of guilt for our actions. If we couldn't help doing what we did then we can't be blamed for doing it.

This problem is often implicit in the background of any perspective. Major theories present models in which we are always at the mercy of external events (for behaviourists) which condition our responses or (for Freudians) internal unconscious events and 'instincts' over which we have no control. Indeed, it is common for defendants to plead temporary insanity (and lack of control), not as an *excuse* for their criminal behaviour, but as the sole *cause* of it.

THE PSYCHOANALYTIC APPROACH

This perspective, initiated by Freud, generally sees human behaviour as the product of forces within us, many of them largely beyond our conscious control. Athletes' motivation is explained, not in terms of social and financial rewards, not in terms of natural talent, but in terms of what success and winning mean or *symbolise* to the person concerned. The athlete may well be unable to recognise these deeper meanings and may well refer to something handy like 'feeling good' as an explanation. Beneath the surface of consciousness however, in psychoanalytic thought, there is a causally related set of associations, all linked by past and especially emotional experience, which can be investigated with the willing participation of the client. Stressful thoughts and events, buried in our UNCONSCIOUS mind, tend to surface in the form of symbols. Humans make strong use of symbols in their ordinary thinking – a particular car can, for instance, be a symbol of success. One notorious source of symbolic material is our dream life, but there are also our unexplained and out-of-the-ordinary behaviour, slips, accidents, failed memories, outbursts and so on. These give a (rather obscured) 'window' through to our psychological type, our deeper reasons for behaviour and our driving forces. Several of the major principles on which most psychoanalytic thinkers would agree are:

- the very early life of the infant, especially its relationship with its parents, has an all-important effect on later personality and general approach to the world
- development leaves most of us with unresolved strong emotional conflicts which continue to affect our thoughts and behaviour at an unconscious level. Young children cannot reason about their emotions. Consequently, powerful forces are laid down in childhood which are hard to recover in adulthood, yet they may guide our behaviour and we may need to get in touch with them in order to solve a psychological problem and progress with normal life
- a near universal feature of human life is the employment of DEFENCE MECHANISMS in order to deal with and suppress underlying conflicts between thoughts and urges; conflicts too threatening to be consciously admitted to oneself are suppressed
- early psychoanalysts emphasised sexual feelings and emotions but later theorists embrace the full range of emotionality and some de-emphasise the role of sex. Others also put more emphasis on people's ability to be rational and think positively towards change, lessening the pessimistic Freudian focus on unconscious control.

Applications of the psychoanalytic approach

Psychoanalysis and groups

Psychoanalytic explanations tend to concern individuals but there have been attempts, within the world of organisational and work psychology, to apply the principles to whole groups. De Board (1978) is a good reference for the earlier work, in particular that of Bion (1968), working with groups of soldiers in the Second World War, and that related to the 'socio-technical systems' approach to work organisation, associated with the Tavistock Clinic.

Psychoanalysis and motivation

In terms of motivation and conscious life it will be useful to understand Freud's major components of mind – the ID, EGO and SUPER-EGO. These are not Freud's terms but a translator's, since he wrote in the German language. *Id* refers to our basic biological drives, including the important sexual one, and may be seen as Freud's concession to biological determinants in our behaviour, largely overwritten by social and emotional *learned* patterns of behaviour. Only at an early age are we honestly and unambiguously driven by hunger and pain to respond instantly and automatically as we feel at the moment. The *ego* develops, according to Freud, to protect us from the consequences of acting on the spur of the moment. It is not a moral or socialised force but simply our rational sense which tells us that the consequences of acting just as we wish can be uncomfortable and our immediate impulses need to be tempered with caution and forward planning. The ego is what we are mostly aware of when we talk about our self and our reasons for doing things. The *super-ego*, developing from our emotionally charged relationship with our parents, is a mightily powerful 'conscience' in Freud's thinking. It contains the ideal self, possibly an 'introjected' (taken in) image of a parent, and a model of perfection we can never achieve. It also acts as a source of morality, controlling our behaviour even when it will produce no immediate negative consequences. Contravening these moral standards produces guilt and consequent anxiety. This alone will eventually control impulses to act against moral

norms and even impulses to think guilt-provoking thoughts.

The ego has the role of 'protecting' us from the anxiety which follows from serious conflicts, mostly those occurring between id and super-ego. This is achieved with the use of DEFENCE MECHANISMS. For instance, a highly paid executive might *rationalise* that his salary is justified in order to keep him with the company, making good profits for all to benefit from, rather than admit that his salary is excessive and that he is basically greedy. Hence, according to Freud, in general psychology, we might often speculate about the *real* reasons for a person's behaviour rather than accept those *apparent* reasons put forward by the ego and which are accepted even by the individual concerned. The athlete, for instance, may not simply be motivated by financial or social reward. It may be that the father's strict expectations, now part of the athlete's super-ego, can never be satisfied. The athlete may not realise that attempting the near impossible is aimed at damaging the father's image by showing him to be wrong.

Psychoanalysis and therapy

The most prevalent use of psychoanalytic principles is encountered in the clinical psychology chapter. It can be said that the approach is the foundation of all modern individual and group therapy, but much evolution has occurred and the diversity of what is now available can be quite bewildering. It is also important to note here that PSYCHOANALYTIC therapy techniques are not reserved for the clearly psychologically disturbed. They are or have been employed in versions of stress management, in PLAY THERAPY with children, in training sports participants, in the 'treatment' of interpersonal problems at work and in work with offenders.

THE BEHAVIOURIST APPROACH

Let's take another look at the motivation for athletes' behaviour. In normal conversation it is common to hear an explanation in terms of 'her will to achieve' or 'killer instinct'. At the turn of the century, psychologists also used explanatory concepts such as 'instinct' and 'will'. However, we learn nothing new, in fact, when we hear that someone has a 'will to achieve', *after* we have discovered that they do indeed do a lot of succeeding. The explanation is a 'pseudo' one often prompting the reply, 'well, what exactly do you *mean* by a "winning instinct?"' The reply might be 'that which helps athletes to supremacy, to victory over their competitors'. The 'explanation' is now seen for what it really is – a re-description of what we already know and a statement of ignorance about what really drives successful athletes. The speaker says no more than 'successful athletes succeed because they have something which makes them succeed!' Similarly, if a child's survival of horrendous abuse is explained with the child's 'will to survive', the 'explanation' merely re-describes, in retrospect, what actually happened – the child survived. Inventing a 'will to survive' adds no more to the explanation of events, and behaviourists denounced such pseudo-explanatory concepts as 'mystical'. They also dismissed cognitive processes (MENTALISTIC EVENTS) with the same justification. This was partly why so much of their work centred around laboratory experiments with animals. They were concerned not to *assume* what they could not verify directly and began with the investigation of the simplest behaviour patterns. For instance, they were concerned not to *assume* that a dog 'expected' food just because it salivated at the sound of a bell which had accompanied the presentation of food several times. 'Expectancy' was a non-observable, non-physical event which couldn't *cause* behaviour to occur – the issue of the mind–body problem.

Behaviourists believed one should only use as scientific data the facts of observed behaviour. It was argued that some basic principles of learning were similar across species, including humans, and therefore that explanations of learning could not include the power of thought for one species and not the other. Some common threads of fundamental behaviourist belief are:

- almost all human behaviour is learned, that is, developed through experience with and feedback from our environment. It is not the result of biological 'instinct'

- 'mentalistic' events (such as thoughts or ideas), and 'mystical' concepts (such as instinct, will, feeling), which cannot be observed or measured cannot form part of an objective, scientific explanation of human behaviour. 'Problem' behaviour, such as that of a psychiatric patient, 'difficult' worker or disruptive school pupil, is not explained by giving it a label (such as 'mental illness', 'alienation' or 'delinquency'); it is best analysed and modified by treating it as a set of individually observable and modifiable responses to the events in our immediate environment
- behaviour can be investigated scientifically through very careful observation and measurement; the principles of learning, thus derived (many from the study of laboratory animals), can be applied to learning in humans and therefore to the treatment of abnormal or unwanted behaviour patterns
- behaviour is largely influenced by situations, not personality traits (see p. 291)
- behaviour is best analysed as a set of relatively *molecular* (small unit) responses under the control of events in the immediate environment which have been associated with these responses in the past
- a person's 'feelings' may only be assessed by *public* evidence, such as a verbal report from the individual (e.g. 'I feel a level 9 stress on a scale of 1 to 10').

The classical tradition

Few Westerners with even a vague interest in human behaviour in the second half of the 20th century can have remained unaware of Pavlov's (1927) experiments and demonstrations. From these there developed the scientific formulation of a principle which must surely have been known to Roman dog handlers, that dogs, who generally salivate at the sight of food, will also do this at the sound or sight of any stimulus which has regularly accompanied their food in the recent past. However, in the behaviourist model, one must resist the temptation to say that the dog 'expects' or anticipates its food (though the sight of a dog cocking its head on one side, twitching its ears and holding itself like a coiled spring is rather compelling). This notion of 'expectancy' is unobservable – what *can* be observed are the dog's specifically 'conditioned' responses. CONDITIONING is the term used for the experimental demonstration that an animal's behaviour can be systematically altered. However, the term quickly became generalised to any behaviour, including human, where it is assumed that conscious control is irrelevant and the responses are reliably triggered by some environmental stimulus. One is not 'conditioned' *against* one's will. It is simply that 'will' is an irrelevant concept for explaining behaviour patterns. It is easiest to grab hold of the original behaviourist position by accepting the EMPTY ORGANISM MODEL depicted in Figure 1, where the big circle represents the person/organism, whose inner workings we cannot observe, and where the raw data of scientific observation are the stimuli impinging on the individual and that individual's responses and their consequences.

In CLASSICAL CONDITIONING a new stimulus (e.g. a bell), producing no set response, was paired with food, a natural (UNCONDITIONAL) STIMULUS (UCS) making dogs salivate (UNCONDITIONAL RESPONSE –

UCR). Salivation became controlled by the previously neutral CONDITIONAL STIMULUS (CS – bell) which now produced salivation (now a CONDITIONAL RESPONSE – CR).

Initially, the blow naturally caused pain behaviour and fear (UCR), which may include purely physiological reactions, such as sweating and adrenaline secretion. Now, buses alone (CS) produce the fear (*part* of the UCR) and this response (now the CR) is beyond the control of the individual concerned. Similarly, anxiety may become associated with meal times, where trouble has occurred in the past, or with public places where humiliation has occurred (e.g. school) and so on. In this model, from Figure 1, S_1 originally produces R and, after association, S_2 now produces R.

In Pavlov's original model, failure to have the CS and UCS associated over several trials resulted in the dog's salivation response gradually dying away – known as EXTINCTION. A departure from this, and a reason to suspect that the explanation is too rigid and simple, is the fact that people can become phobic about buses or spiders after just one traumatic exposure even though there are no more similar associations. Later adjustments to theory explained the maintenance of fear in terms of 'hidden' REINFORCEMENT (of the 'operant' kind – see below). For instance, whenever the individual

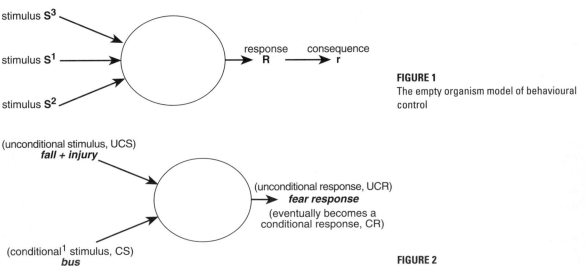

FIGURE 1
The empty organism model of behavioural control

FIGURE 2
The classical conditioning of a phobic response

[1] Pavlov's original term 'conditional' has become better known as 'conditioned'

avoids situations which just might involve buses they would experience a form of reward because their feelings of anxiety would be reduced (an example of NEGATIVE REINFORCEMENT – see below). However, this begs the question of why they should continue to experience anxiety, though this might be because, by avoiding the CS, they never give themselves the chance to *unlearn* their responses to the bus stimulus.

The operant or instrumental model

Classical conditioning offers some sort of an explanation of why we should come to associate a new stimulus with an old feeling or reaction. However, it offers little understanding of how new, and relatively complex patterns of behaviour are developed. INSTRUMENTAL LEARNING is the process by which the *result* of responding *strengthens that response*. If a child is regularly rewarded for crying, by being picked up, it is not surprising that the child should develop a strong and swift crying response, especially on sight of a parent. In the OPERANT model, later developed by Skinner (1953) and following figure 1, the crucial elements are a response (R) and its consequences (or 'reinforcement', denoted by 'r'). A stimulus (e.g. S_3) may permit the animal to *discriminate* the circumstances in which a reward will be likely to occur. If only the baby's mother picks it up when it is crying then mother will become a DIS-CRIMINATIVE STIMULUS for the baby who may learn to cry forcefully when she is around but not (or not so hard) on sight of anyone else. According to this system of explanation, a 'maladaptive' response, for instance, petty shoplifting, may be maintained by the succession of reinforcements (admiration of friends, goods obtained, thrill) in the face of the odd adverse consequence such as being told off and banned from a shop, or being given a warning at a court appearance, especially where this, too, makes one important with peers. Again, 'extinction' occurs where rewards cease to follow responses.

Skinner's work with SCHEDULES OF REINFORCE-MENT or INTERMITTENT REINFORCEMENT demonstrated that animals would work even harder when they were not reinforced for every response but only after several had been produced. For instance, on a *fixed ratio schedule* an animal (or human) is reinforced for every *n* responses produced, for instance, after every tenth response. A *variable ratio schedule* gives reinforcement for every *n*th response *on average. Interval schedules* are based on time elapsed since responding. A two-minute *fixed interval schedule* delivers reinforcement for the first response produced after two minutes from the last response, whilst a two-minute *variable interval schedule* uses an *average* of two minutes. Not surprisingly, animals (and humans in some circumstances) work harder towards the end of a fixed interval but hardest of all with a variable ratio schedule where more responses produce more but somewhat un-predictable reinforcements. This system can explain why a baby may learn to cry very loudly indeed if its parents, trying to withhold re-inforcement in order to 'extinguish' its crying, in fact give in and go to the baby after it has cried for quite some time. Many responses are rewarded only after they have occurred several times – for instance, a boy talking to girls in the hope of a date, a charity collector, a high jump athlete.

A further strength of this model was its appar-ent ability to explain the development of fairly complex patterns of behaviour. A reinforced response will continue to occur for some time without reinforcement. If, during this time (the extinction period), another response is pro-duced with the first, and reinforcement follows this *combination*, the two *together* will now be reliably produced. On this explanation – that of SHAPING – the origin of the excessive rituals of the compulsive or obsessive person become easier to explain. The notion of shaping would also be use-ful, at first glance, in explaining an athlete's grad-ual learning of a skill requiring an intricate combination of well-rehearsed movements. However, as we shall see, the COGNITIVE MODEL argues that simply joining together a set of responses would result in a rather jerky perfor-mance without feedback and constant, controlled refinement.

Negative reinforcement and punishment

A common confusion occurs, even in some text-books, between NEGATIVE REINFORCEMENT and PUN-ISHMENT. The problem can be avoided if the reader always links reinforcement with the *strengthening* of a response. A negative reinforcer strengthens behaviour but in a *negative* manner. The rein-forcement here is the *removal* of an uncomfort-able stimulus. If it is noisy and shutting the window removes the noise, then window shutting is reinforced. If my anxiety reduces because I engage in rapid breathing then I am more likely to breathe rapidly when I next feel anxiety coming on. A further example occurs in the health psy-chology chapter. A person complaining of pain may be reinforced by family members relieving the individual of chores such as the washing up. The washing up is *not* punishment. Its *removal* reinforces the behaviour (pain complaints) which removed it.

Punishment is the delivery of an uncomfortable event to the individual as a *consequence* of their behaviour and it is intended to *weaken*, not strengthen, the response it follows. Punishment, especially physical, has many unwanted side effects, especially those of humiliation and of learning (by the punished) that power is a way to control others. Partly for these reasons, partly because it is often pretty ineffective in reducing behaviour and partly for basic humane reasons, it has not been used much in therapeutic or organi-sational applications.

Applications of behaviourist psychology

We meet behaviouristic approaches everywhere in applied psychology, from the reductionist and reward-oriented TAYLORISM in early psychology work through the revolution in psychotherapy in the 1960s, and on to BEHAVIOUR MODIFICATION for children and adults with learning difficulties which is a very common and powerful approach today. Health psychology mentions methods of BIOFEEDBACK (based on the operant principle) and educational psychology includes the use of shap-ing and reward systems in order to keep 'difficult' children in their seats and on tasks. Wherever we can raise questions like, 'What motivates people to work hard, keep to positive health behaviour pat-terns, keep trying in sport?' there will be a behav-iourist position invoking reinforcement.

COGNITIVE PSYCHOLOGY

The terms 'cognitive psychology' and 'cognitive psychologist' have ambiguous meaning. As a topic, cognitive psychology is the study of mental processes such as memory, attention, perception, language, thinking. As a theoretical position, how-ever, a COGNITIVE APPROACH reflects a radical alter-native to behaviourism, a 'school' which, unlike the approaches above, has no 'great names' famil-iar to the general public. In a nutshell the approach lays great emphasis on the central role of MENTAL EVENTS (or 'cognitive processes') in determining our subsequent behaviour. These were the very events dismissed as mythical and non-explanatory by the original behaviourists. The picture is muddled somewhat by the fact that many researchers of cognitive processes over the last two to three decades have called themselves 'behaviourists'. By this they mean that, although they conduct research designed to verify models of human cognitive processes, the evidence they use is *observable behaviour*. They share the behav-iourists' strong emphasis on the careful definition and analysis of the evidence they use – people's responses to various stimuli, usually controlled in a laboratory setting. However, what we shall con-sider here is the COGNITIVE MODEL – a perspective which considers our behaviour to be guided by internal, structured planning processes. Notice that, above, we skimmed the issue of *how* an animal can discriminate one stimulus from another. This, for the cognitive psychologist, is an extremely interesting and important issue and will involve theories of how we *process information* internally, with no obvious external behaviour being produced.

The shift to cognitive psychology – social learning theory

Although cognitive theories had been around for some time (e.g. Tolman, 1932), the main shift in mainstream research occurred in the early 1960s when the SOCIAL LEARNING theorists, led by Albert Bandura, tried to move the emphasis of pure behaviourism towards the inclusion of mental events as explanatory concepts. Their major principles were as follows:

- operant and classical learning processes are not enough to explain the development and maintenance of complex human behaviour
- other processes, especially MODELLING (imitation), contribute to human development – children spontaneously imitate and then may be reinforced for doing so
- VICARIOUS REINFORCEMENT – observing others being rewarded or punished – may also contribute to the development of our regular patterns of behaviour
- between a *stimulus* and a *response* we must assume that other internal processes occur; social learning theorists called these INTERNAL MEDIATING RESPONSES.

Bandura's studies (e.g. Bandura et al, 1963) demonstrated that children spontaneously imitate specific adult behaviour and adjust their imitation depending on whether the adult 'model' is rewarded or punished. This may be obvious to most parents or workers with children but Bandura's work is important for demonstrating empirically that there need be no reinforcement, however subtle, involved in the emergence of new behaviour. Rewarding it once it has emerged, of course, may well help to maintain it.

Early studies by social learning theorists attempted to bring aspects of Freudian theory into the world of publicly checkable scientific testing. For instance, psychoanalytic theory held that if a child experienced loss of love from a warm, nurturant mother, anxiety would be produced which would motivate the child to 'introject' its mother's behaviour. Social learning theorists recast 'introjection' as modelling – imitating and learning from a significant person. Especially significant would be parents who withdrew affection as part of normal child training. Imitation would supply an *image* of the warmth lost by the child. Research supported this notion but also showed that children copy aggression irrespective of the warmth of the person modelling it (Bandura and Huston, 1961). Here, psychologists were not completely rejecting earlier useful psychoanalytic ideas. They were attempting to support those ideas with empirical evidence. When ideas didn't appear to fit then further explanation and research were attempted.

More recently, Bandura (1989) has emphasised the role of internal expectations in guiding our behaviour, especially those concerning SELF-EFFICACY – our sense of competence in tasks. People with higher self-efficacy (higher levels of belief in their competence) tend to work harder at problems, and tackle them more thoroughly, irrespective of their actual ability. These effects can be seen even when self-efficacy is raised artificially by giving false information to participants (Weinberg et al, 1979).

The cognitive revolution – humans as information processors

The so-called COGNITIVE REVOLUTION in psychology was heralded by the influential work of Miller, Galanter and Pribram (1960). The 'revolution' began in the 1960s partly through Bandura's reintroduction of internal mental processes as valid theoretical ideas, but also through the advent of computers. The computer model was used in two ways.

First, with the use of computers it became possible to show that even an inanimate object could 'act with a purpose', that is have a 'goal' to work towards. Computers were capable of self-adjustment, learning and gradual movement towards a specific goal, using FEEDBACK (data giving information on how the action is progressing). Behaviourists had argued that 'goals' were unmeasurable, unscientific concepts. Changes in behaviour were simply under the control of external, perhaps subtle reinforcement. The cognitivists argued that, as with computers, an internal goal could form part of an explanation of organised sequences of an organism's behaviour.

Second, humans were seen, like computers, as rapid interpreters of large amounts of incoming information. Computers receive stimuli but do not need to respond immediately. They can receive information from a variety of different kinds of source, deal with the information as so many electrical impulses, then act appropriately to the analysis of information. The human information processing system does much the same thing. The physical processes may be different but the important point is that our reactions are not direct, simple responses to incoming stimuli. Information is filtered and analysed, mostly by our cortex, and we can respond both appropriately and flexibly (see below). Our actions are not automatic but the product of *decision-making*. Even the simple act of putting down a tea-cup is under the control of many cycles of incoming information, analysis and consequent fine adjustment of movement.

Operant and cognitive explanations of problem-solving

Tolman (1932) described research in which rats who had learnt to turn right to get food in a cross maze turned *left* when they started from the other side of the maze. Tolman argued that this would not be possible if only their *physical responses* had been acquired in the learning process. The rats, he felt, must be adjusting their behaviour according to an internal map of the maze's turns. This map would now be referred to as a SCHEMA – a

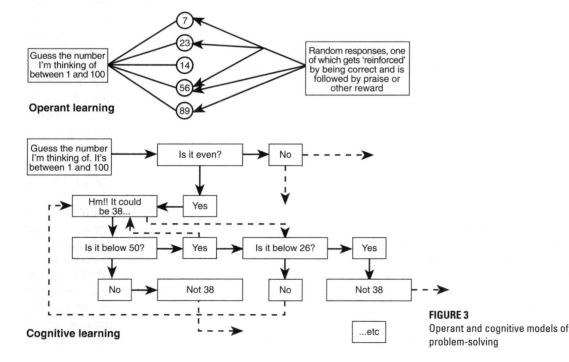

FIGURE 3
Operant and cognitive models of problem-solving

set of rules for understanding aspects of the world and for guiding our behaviour within it. A feel for the working of schemas can be gained by considering how both operant and cognitive theory would account for solving the problem set out in Figure 3. In the pure behaviourist model it is difficult to see how a person would come up with the right answer other than by trying numbers at random until a 'hit' is obtained. It is interesting that, in solving this problem, 'no' sometimes has its usual negative connotation and, at other times, is reinforcing, but one would not know this without a plan. The reinforcement paradigm did not do justice to the reasoning powers which humans possess and use many times each day, very often without consciously realising it. A very young child can work out instantly, and yet for the first time, that if number 13 buses go from one street and number 14s from another, the logical choice is to change streets if a number 13 comes along when a number 14 is required.

Flexibility of planned behaviour

To understand complex human behaviour, then, it seems necessary to work with the concept of a *plan* or *scheme*. Our individual responses are guided by the plan and its goal in a quite flexible manner. For instance, if I want you to pass me the water I can ask for it using a variety of sentences. I can also point urgently at it or do something like hang my tongue out in obvious need of it. I can even lasso it or siphon it out of the jug! Most importantly, *I can produce behaviour which I have never used before* (and for which, therefore, I have never been reinforced). All of these amount to my obtaining a glass of water. Here, the only common factor is the eventual *goal* that I had in mind. Likewise, with no prior reinforcement, when driving to work, I can suddenly change my actions and achieve my goal if I find, one morning, that my way is blocked by road digging or fallen trees. What is important to maintain my guided behaviour is *feedback*. Even observation of very young infants will reveal that they adjust their movements, perhaps not so subtly at first, to

incoming stimuli which inform them of the results of their actions. Infants only a few days old can quickly learn just how hard to suck on a specially made and electronically connected 'pacifier' in order to hear their mother's voice in preference to another woman's voice (deCasper and Fifer, 1980).

Molar and molecular

We have said that behaviour analysed at the level of fine movements, as with sucking or driving movements, or the gradual placement of a teacup, is said to be treated at the *molecular* level. The behaviourists, by contrast, might treat putting down a cup and saucer as a single response under the control of reinforcement – presumably the feeling of success in getting it down right or, as a child, parental responses of 'well done!' and so on. Behaviour can be treated in ever larger units such as 'driving to work', 'riding a bicycle', 'digging the garden', or even 'bringing up a child'. These examples, especially the last, are much more towards the MOLAR end of the molecular-molar continuum described earlier.

In a sense, the behaviourists tended to treat behaviour at a more molar level and to tell us *why* a person produces responses (for reinforcement) whereas cognitive analyses tended to work at a more molecular level and tell us *how* – constant feedback on behavioural adjustment towards a planned goal. In the teaching of maths, for example, a behaviourist orientation might emphasise effective and timely rewards for correct answers. A cognitive approach might concentrate on the most effective structuring of information in order for the child to be able to develop logical schemas for working with numbers. What is essential is that, in the cognitive view, a child is not *passively* responding to rewards but is *actively* seeking information in order to solve the huge number of problems there are in simply understanding how the world works. Most parents will find it hard to deny that their babies are naturally curious. It is very difficult to stop a child learning and the rewards we do employ are often entirely ineffective – for instance, rewarding a young speaker for saying 'went' rather than 'goed'. As adults, we are, unless depressed, still curious when confronted with problems – information not fitting our existing schemas. This is the great attraction of magic, puzzles, speculation about other people ('gossip') and do-it-yourself tasks.

Cognitive psychology and the scientific ('hypothetico-deductive') method

Behaviourists might object that schemas and cognitive models are unmeasurable, internal concepts. Cognitivists would answer that they are doing science much like any other scientist. Physicists can propose a model of what properties a 'quark' has, for instance. They will never directly observe a quark, because this is, in principle and in practice, impossible. What they do is to argue that if their model is correct certain results should follow. If those results occur their model is *supported* (but not 'proven true'). Models survive while evidence supports them. Models may be refined in the light of contrary evidence but if that evidence becomes too great and too unruly the models are jettisoned in favour of alternative ones which deal with all the evidence more effectively and economically. This is the basis of the HYPO-THETICO-DEDUCTIVE METHOD in science.

The scope of cognitive psychology

Since the 1960s cognitive psychology has investigated many areas of human ability and mental operation. In addition, it has had an influence across the whole spectrum of psychological research including the areas of social psychology, abnormal psychology and therapy. Therefore, we find that by far the most popular treatment used by clinical psychologists today is that of cognitive or cognitive-behavioural therapy. This form of therapy is also very often used in work with the rehabilitation of offenders. We shall also find a cognitive approach embedded within all other applied areas. Cognitive psychology has had particular effect within the ERGONOMICS and HUMAN FACTORS areas of work psychology. Ergonomics covers the area of human–machine interaction. Obviously, it is well worth studying the ways in which humans perceive their environment and the limits of their attention and other mental capacities, in order to design human-friendly technology, to organise work efficiently and to set reasonable limits to human work expectations.

THE BIOLOGICAL APPROACH

This book generally concentrates on *psychological* approaches to predicting and altering human behaviour in constructive ways. However, there is certainly a need, at times, to consider biological effects on human behaviour if only to recognise that biological processes, states and constitution may modify or limit any changes which a psychologist may wish to produce or may help us understand why a certain principle does not work in the same way for all people. However, it is important to recognise that a reduction to biological expla-

nation can never be entirely appropriate, as there will always remain a social and psychological context in which to understand behaviour. For instance, just as explaining a snooker game in terms of ball collisions is not appropriate, nor is it useful or productive to understand neurotic behaviour solely in terms of the biological processes underlying anxiety. We shall want to know why *this* neurotic behaviour is directed towards dogs whilst another person's is very much concerned with dinner parties. There will be a social history which may guide us to the reasons for another person being terrified of travel.

We know that chemical and biological events can directly affect human behaviour. The disease of syphilis was eventually found, in the nineteenth century, to be responsible for decaying cognitive faculties. Lithium certainly reduces some extreme reactions in schizophrenics, though it by no means 'cures' them. We also know that human behaviour affects biological bodily events, as when a person's stressful life habits eventually create problems of ulcers and heart deterioration. We know that memory can be affected by physical events (bullets, drugs, nerve decay) and that memory can, in turn, affect behaviour. According to Freud's original findings, a repressed memory or fantasy can manifest itself in pathological behaviour (neurotic symptoms, defensive reactions, accidents and so on).

There is two-way traffic, then, between our behaviour and its effects on our biology and our biology's effects on our behaviour. This is of particular relevance in the health, sport and clinical psychology chapters.

The nature–nurture debate

One important aspect of the biological perspective influences debate on many topics in psychology. This is the question of the extent to which our enduring characteristics or personality are the result of genetic forces (the 'nature' view) or are developed within our lifetime through experience with our environments (the 'nurture' view). If a certain personality feature is largely inherited then this would have implications for employment selection (only select those with/without the fea-

ture) and training. It would presumably be futile to train people in something for which they do not have innate, genetic potential. Similarly, therapists will have little success if certain states of psychological disturbance are largely caused by a natural disposition.

Intelligence and twin studies

One of the first and most illustrious applied psychologists this century, Sir Cyril Burt, Britain's first employed educational psychologist, contributed enormously to the nature–nurture debate concerning intelligence (e.g. 1972). He tested many pairs of identical twins, reared in separate families and correlated their scores (see Appendix 2). In general, twins are very useful subject matter for tests of personality or ability difference, but identical twins, separated near birth, are especially important, since, if they display quite similar characteristics, there is the strong suggestion that these have developed relatively independently of any social influence from the twins' respective families. If they are quite different, given they have identical genes, inheritance theory is undermined and the nurture view is supported. Burt's findings showed very strong IQ correlations (similarities) but his data and methods have since been alleged to be fraudulent. Even if they were not, the intense debate surrounding his work has left these particular data unusable in academic argument. Other researchers used non-separated and non-identical twins, adopted children compared with children of natural parents and many other family comparisons, in order to derive sets of data which *indirectly* support or challenge inheritance theory or which provide more or less support for environmental determinants of our abilities.

THE HUMANISTIC APPROACH

This has often been termed the 'third force' within mainstream psychology. This was intended to mean that it took a new direction away from both

psychoanalysis and behaviourism. It is still true that the HUMANISTIC APPROACH is a uniquely different way, since the cognitive approach shares a concentration on scientific investigation and quantitative assessment of variables. Carl Rogers, one of humanism's founders, did promote a quantitative scientific evaluation of the results of psychotherapy (1957) but, overall, the approach is opposed to the piecemeal investigation of aspects of cognition or behaviour. It concentrates on the *whole* self and is on the other extreme from any reductionism in understanding humans. The approach is PHENOMENOLOGICAL which, in a crude definition, means that priority is given to whatever people *experience*, whether or not we would agree that their experience is actually valid. Objective assessment of 'facts' is a suspect activity in this view since each person's view of the world is unique and no one has a claim to a 'better', more accurate

understanding of reality. Echoes of this original position are very strong today in applied psychology. Many of those researchers who take a QUALITATIVE approach to research methods (see Appendix 2) would largely agree with this analysis of people's view and understanding of their world.

Within the fields of applied psychology covered in this book, the influence of humanism has been largely confined to the practice of therapy, with Rogers' CLIENT-CENTRED THERAPY having great influence on the practice of counselling and on many psychologists in clinical work, even though their preferred approach might not be humanist. Hence, discussion of Rogers' main contribution, his theory of *self*, is to be found in the clinical psychology chapter.

WHAT IS THE VALUE OF DIFFERENT APPROACHES WITHIN APPLIED PSYCHOLOGY?

In the world of BASIC RESEARCH (though the gap between 'basic' and 'applied' is always hazy – see Chapter 1) it is true that these approaches can be quite clearly separated and often hostile to one another. Psychologists defend their favoured approach and conduct research designed to support one view rather than another. In the applied world too it is quite possible to find energetic defence of one approach against another. For instance, psychoanalysts and the original behaviour therapists were completely irreconcilable in their arguments over which technique was the most appropriate, beneficial and effective in treating psychological disturbance. Today, this gulf between proponents of the two views has hardly been bridged and heated debates continue between them, though there are a few meeting points.

Eclecticism

On the other hand, each approach has given rise

to various forms of application not necessarily closely linked to the original theory which produced it. Very many practising psychologists are ECLECTIC in their outlook. Thus, a clinical psychologist might employ aspects of psychoanalysis with some clients, or at certain points in treating one client, yet also find behaviour therapy techniques more effective at other stages of treatment or for different conditions. An occupational psychologist might take a cognitive approach to a problem of organisational communication yet employ the concept of reinforcement when dealing with issues of incentive and disincentive and their effects on production.

One cannot always adopt a 'supermarket' approach to the different schools of thought within psychology. In some areas there are just two rival theories or explanations and both cannot be true at the same time. In other areas, however, one can see the two explanations as operating more at two different levels and hence both can be partly valid at their respective levels. More often than not, though, the various approaches represent quite radically different ways of viewing the human being in the environment. For instance, the child is seen as passively responding to cues and reinforcements by behaviourists, but as an active information processor by cognitivists. For some psychologists working with children the early emotional stages of development are all-important. For others, they are not and the emphasis is on practical change in the here and now. It is very important indeed then, that the student reader, as well as the practising psychologist, is quite clear about the differing implications for behaviour and change which two or more perspectives on the same topic or issue have to offer.

METHODS FOR THE PRODUCTION OF RESEARCH AND PRACTICE DATA

In several applied areas discussed in this book you may find that there is quite a separation between psychologists who carry out a 'hands-on' applied role in their normal working day and those who concentrate on research. Some psychologists manage to balance these two roles but, certainly within clinical and educational psychology, the practitioners tend to report little opportunity to conduct pure research. However, most practitioners also report that, in their everyday work with clients, they are often grateful for their training in investigative methods and fall back on the use of these in tackling some of the practical problems they encounter in their applied working domain. The following section whisks us briefly through some of the major research method procedures and concepts used by psychological researchers and some of the psychological approaches to tackling practical human problems in the field.

PLACES FOR RESEARCH

Field vs laboratory

It is far more likely that applied psychologists will carry out their research in the 'field' than in a laboratory or on research premises. Their research will be conducted with people who are the usual focus of that practitioner – this might be in the hospital, school, factory, office, shopping precinct or clinic. FIELD STUDIES may nevertheless employ conventional experimental designs. An example is given below with Ganster et al's (1982) research on stress. There are times, though, when research may be best carried out in the rarefied but well-controlled environment of a psychological laboratory. If we wish to determine exactly what effect caffeine has on performance levels, it is worth testing selected participants carefully in a well-controlled environment so that any unwanted variables can be ruled out as effects. Using a real athletics environment (assuming permission had been sought all round) would not rule out the effects of weather conditions (affecting all participants differently), audience effects and so on. We shall soon define these unwanted factors as CONFOUNDING VARIABLES. In the laboratory we can be fairly certain that caffeine level is the *only* factor to vary.

General problems with laboratory studies

There are, however, serious problems incurred with the use of laboratory studies in psychological research. We shall consider a few.

Artificiality

Laboratory studies have been much criticised for the artificial environment in which participants perform what is required of them. However, many field studies do not entirely escape this criticism either. The Hawthorne Studies (see below and the occupational psychology chapter) appeared to demonstrate that, even in the everyday work situation, the knowledge of being the object of research can create significantly different behaviour among the participants involved. However, where the claim of 'artificiality' is made, it is always worth pausing to consider exactly what processes are being referred to. These might be, for instance, SOCIAL DESIRABILITY, EXPECTANCY, DEMAND CHARACTERISTICS and *intimidation* by strange, scientific-seeming surroundings and equipment. These will be discussed in the following pages but it is worth noting that only the last is a particular problem for the laboratory study. The others can occur in *any* type of research where participants are aware of being studied.

Expectancy – the participant

A difficulty in comparing groups such as students experiencing different teaching methods or clients receiving different therapies, is that, in applied work, it is often very difficult to keep hidden from participants what the expected outcome of the research is. The effect of participant expectancy gained notoriety through the applied occupational work of the Hawthorne Studies (Roethlisberger and Dickson, 1939). A factory work team of five women increased their productivity over a two-year period no matter what variable (originally illumination) was manipulated. It even increased when conditions were returned to the most adverse ones in operation at the start of that section of the research. History has given us the HAWTHORNE EFFECT now generally interpreted as *the effect that simply being the focus of investigation has on the participants.* It is sometimes more specifically assumed that the workers here raised their output because they *expected* this to be the desired outcome. However, there were several other *confounding variables* present in the study which might have explained the dramatic increase in output (see below and the occupational psychology chapter).

Expectancy has been shown to affect participants' reactions in a wide variety of studies. Bruner (1973) and his colleagues showed that expectancy could affect our perception of the size of objects and content of pictures; participants told that a baby is female or male interpret their characteristics (Luria and Rubin, 1974) and their behaviour (Condry and Condry, 1976) differently and according to sex role stereotype; mental health professionals were affected in their clinical judgement by just the knowledge of a fictitious patient's ethnic background (Lewis et al, 1990 – see the clinical psychology chapter); teachers' grading was affected simply by the attractiveness of pupil names – see the educational psychology chapter.

Placebo groups

It is for this reason that experiments often include a PLACEBO GROUP. The idea is borrowed from medical and pharmacological research where some patients are given an actual drug which is on trial whilst another group is given a substance such as a salt pill with absolutely no effect – the 'placebo'. Should this group show any improvement it will be known that something other than the drug, perhaps the mere thought of having received treatment, can have an effect on the progress of the illness. Similarly, in psychological experiments, we may give one group training – the variable actually under research – whilst we give a placebo group attention or simulated training but nothing we truly believe to be effective. If, in a study of race prejudice reduction for instance, members of a placebo group change attitude to race as much as those in the trained group, we can suspect that the training itself is possibly *confounded* by participant expectancy effects.

Expectancy – the researcher

It has been argued that the expectancy of researchers also has its effect on participants' responses. Rosenthal (1966) showed that students who were told that their experimental rats were either 'dull' or 'bright' obtained results in accordance with the rats' label, although many studies since that time have failed to provide strong evidence for experimenter expectancy effects. However, Eden (1990) demonstrated what is known as the PYGMALION EFFECT – getting people to perform well because you think they can – in an applied (work) psychology context. In defence force platoons where leaders were told their subordinates were above average, the platoon members significantly outperformed control groups where the leader was not so informed. There was no real difference between the two platoon member groups.

Demand characteristics

Closely linked to the concept of expectancy are the 'demand characteristics' of a research situation (Orne, 1962). By this is meant the tendency for human participants, being human enquirers (according to the cognitive model), to attempt to understand what is going on in a study. They may also try to behave according to experimenter expectations – sometimes referred to as 'pleasing the experimenter' though, again, the effect cannot be confined only to true experiments.

TYPES OF RESEARCH

There are three major ways in which psychologists, and social scientists in general, can obtain data from people: they can watch, ask questions or meddle. Watching people behave is better known as *observation* and this may be used in an OBSERVATION STUDY, where observation is the main vehicle for gathering data, or as part of an experiment in which observation is the *method* used to measure one of the variables – for instance, aggression after mild frustration. Questioning comes in the form of the *interview* and the SURVEY, and also as the administration of psychological tests or *scales*, or psychometric measuring instruments. By 'meddling' I meant, facetiously, engaging in an EXPERIMENT. It is generally considered true that, where an experiment *can* be carried out, we have stronger evidence of the direction of a *causal relationship* (i.e. A caused B, not B caused A) than can be obtained by other means. I hope the following will clarify this point.

Correlational studies (or data)

A vast amount of information gathered in applied psychology is not gathered in the laboratory and is not obtained from an experiment (though there are many field experiments). As a result, research designs very often gather FIELD DATA and are CORRELATIONAL. What is meant here can probably be best illustrated with an example. In the fictional Psychology A level study described in chapter 1 it was found that pre-exam confidence *correlated* highly with subsequent exam success. That is, people who scored highly on one measure (confidence) also scored highly on the other measure (exam grade) and vice versa. In general, scores on one measure could be *predicted* fairly well from scores on the other measure. Correlation is the degree of 'agreement' between pairs of scores. For example, in most organisations, salary level will tend to correlate with level of responsibility. The degree of agreement is measured on a scale stretching from -1 through 0 to +1. It is important to note the following:

- the nearer a correlation is to +1, the closer the agreement between pairs of values
- the nearer a correlation is to 0, the closer the association between pairs of values to a random, unpredictable pattern (except in special cases).

NEGATIVE CORRELATION

What is to be made then of a correlation near to −1? In this case there is a strong tendency for *positive* scores on one measure to be associated with *negative* scores on the other. This might occur in the case of anxiety and performance – the higher the anxiety a person experiences the lower may be their performance. In fact, the situation with anxiety and performance is rather more complicated (the relationship is 'U-shaped') and is dealt with in the sport psychology chapter.

Problems with correlational data

A psychologist carrying out research in a factory might notice that people who produce high stress scores on a certain test tend to make more errors in their work. On further investigation a correlation between these two variables is found. The researcher might hold the view that stress increases error and these data would certainly support that view. Trouble is, the data *also* support the view that those making more errors (perhaps because of their inferior working conditions) become more stressed as a *result*. A correlation does not give unambiguous evidence of a *causal link* between variable A and variable B. If we believe that A is a cause of B, and predict a correlation between them, any resulting high correlation will support *both* the A-causes-B *and* the B-causes-A possibility.

A correlation can also be misleading where there is an association for people at the extremes of each variable but little relationship for those with average to moderate scores only. For instance, highly stressed people might do particularly badly on a test and extremely calm people might do particularly well. This might produce a

moderately strong correlation amongst a group where, for the *mid-range* of people there is little association at all between stress and performance. This exemplifies the need to *inspect* any data where an effect is found to see whether it is the product of certain portions of the sample rather than the group as a whole, and then to investigate further.

A related problem is that of RESTRICTION OF RANGE. Usually, we can only correlate the level of work performance and interview test score for those employees who are actually employed by a company. We can't assess those whose low scores caused them to fail the interview (since they are no longer available and haven't produced any work performance). Hence, the *range* of people we assess is restricted and the correlation we obtain may be higher or lower than that which we would obtain if we could include a wider range in our sample. Correlations between maths and English grades at a UK public school would be similarly restricted to a narrow sample range.

The experiment

One way to obtain unambiguous evidence for the stress-creates-errors view is to run a proper *experiment*. Here, one would manipulate the INDEPENDENT VARIABLE of stress (create stress for one group by giving them more work to complete in a shorter time, say) and observe its consequent effect on the DEPENDENT VARIABLE of error. To make this a true experiment we would RANDOMLY ALLOCATE participants to either of the two groups (high stress and low stress). Suppose we didn't do this. We might, for example use the day shift in one condition and the night shift in the other. It could now be argued that initial differences between the two groups (in relevant skills) were in fact responsible for any differences in errors found. In a true experiment, *only the independent variable is varied and all other variables are held constant or balanced* (this includes allocation of participants to groups on a random basis). This way, we can be sure that the independent variable (in this case level of stress) is solely responsible for any changes in the dependent variable.

Control groups

In the stress experiment we might call the group given extra pressure the EXPERIMENTAL GROUP whilst the group working normally is a CONTROL GROUP. We need the latter in order to have a BASE-LINE PERFORMANCE with which to compare the manipulated, higher stress group. In the A level experiment described in chapter 1 you might have noticed the glaring omission of a control group with which to compare the *full notes, discussion* and *both treatments* groups. Here was a typical ethical conflict. Good experimentation requires the use of control groups but could we really expect to select one group of students to whom we gave no special teaching method at all? Many field experiments can only compare two different treat-ments and cannot ethically include a 'not treated' group.

Field experiments

If the stress experiment just described were car-ried out in a laboratory one can appreciate the criticism of artificiality in that workplace stress is a much more varied and unpredictable commodity than the variable manipulated above. An example of a *field experiment* on stress is that of Ganster et al (1982) who allocated 79 public service employ-ees at random to a control group or an experimen-tal group receiving stress management training. The experimental group exhibited less depression, anxiety and adrenaline secretion than the control group (who later also received the training – an

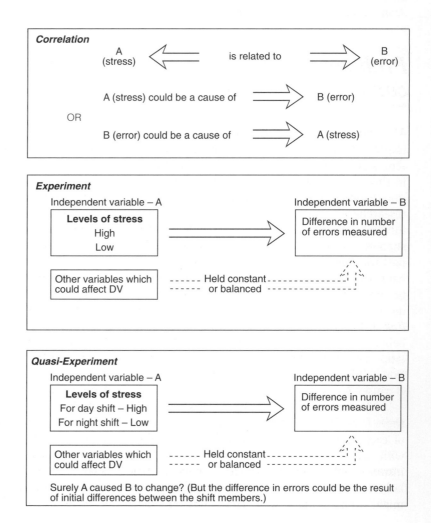

FIGURE 1

Experiments quasi-experiments and correlation

answer to the ethical point just raised). Effects lasted for at least four months.

Quasi-experiments

Where pre-existing groups are used as experimental groups the study is known as a QUASI-EXPERIMENT and these are common in applied psychology. It is often not possible, in applied psychology, to allocate participants to groups at random. In the stress example, above, it may be unreasonable to ask an employer to allocate employees randomly to shifts. We may *have* to use the day and night shifts as our two experimental groups, and maybe a third shift as a control group. Here, it could still be argued that some variation between the shift members, rather than the programmes, is responsible for any group differences found in stress levels. For a thorough review, see Cook and Campbell (1979).

Sampling

We have raised the issue of SAMPLING above. Applied psychologists would obviously like to be able to *generalise* the results of studies from the sample of people used to a wider but similar population. A POPULATION is a tricky concept – it is not just everybody. It could be limited to, for instance, office workers, female bus drivers, violent criminals, truants, javelin throwers or rheumatism sufferers. Suppose we hear of a therapy which has been successful on children with school phobia or a management technique which increases job satisfaction among telephone operators. We would hope that each technique could be generalised to the population of all school-phobic children or all telephone operators. Of course, this is an optimistic notion. The therapy may well be limited in its usefulness to children of a certain age where the phobia is the result of something quite specific such as incidents of bullying.

It is important that any sample used in a study where we wish to generalise is not a specially drawn sample, such as only those children who expressed great interest in the therapy. This would be an example of SAMPLING BIAS. By the very nature

of applied psychology, the sample in many studies *is* biased, because we are working with pre-established groups. What we must know then, in each case, is just how *representative* each sample is of any wider population to which we would wish to generalise.

A large sample drawn on a random basis from a population will normally be fairly representative of the population as a whole. Poll companies attempting to predict election outcomes rely heavily on this principle. The strict meaning of a RANDOM SAMPLE is that *any person within the target population has an equal chance of being selected*. Since this is an unrealistic criterion, many samples in applied studies are made representative not by random sampling but by some form of well-organised *selection strategy* or SAMPLING TECHNIQUE (see Coolican, 1994).

Controlling extraneous and confounding variables

The example of a school-phobic sample given above would be one where the bias in the sample *confounds* the result. We shall obtain, perhaps, very positive results with children who are keen to be studied but this may well be a distortion of the true picture where all types of school-phobic child are included. In the psychology A level experiment described in chapter 1 it was strongly suspected, given the results, that the full notes method was an effective factor in raising exam grades. However, if the experiment were performed in the field it may be that, by chance, we gave the full notes method to a tutor who has other exam grade raising qualities. Technically we should give all groups identical tutors (but how would we know what counted as 'identical'?) or rotate students around the tutors – likely to have a generally confusing effect! In the world of therapy it is a real difficulty, in evaluating treatments, that different treatments are also applied by different therapists.

CONFOUNDING VARIABLES are the heart of research analysis. We are constantly asking the question, 'Ah, but what *else* might be responsible for this difference or trend in results?' Confounding variables are either variables, *other than those intended*, which are producing effects, or they are variables which *obscure* real effects. For instance, people doing a task first without caffeine and then with, may perform at the same level on the second trial because, although caffeine enhances their performance, they are also more tired on the second attempt. Their improvement is obscured by fatigue.

Problems in gathering authentic data in the field

Social desirability

A particular problem in asking people about emotive issues is the tendency to want to 'look good' socially. Few parents will want to admit to a strange interviewer that they sometimes wish they hadn't had their children. Few will easily expose their racist attitudes in a street survey. Few people will easily discuss fears about their relationship or their sexual fantasies and behaviour.

Local pressures

From an ethical point of view the applied researcher must always keep in mind that those interviewed or observed are not acting in a vacuum. Research in organisations invariably raises the ethical issue of *confidentiality*. Even where anonymity is guaranteed for the individual it cannot therefore be assumed that workers will answer truthfully or fully. It will be difficult for the visiting psychologist to appear neutral between management and workforce and, in any case, an individual can often tell when the information they give is precise enough to pinpoint them, with or without anonymity.

OBSERVER AND INTERVIEWER BIAS

Researcher or experimenter expectancy was outlined above. Observers and interviewers can, to some extent, also see or hear what they expect to see or hear, given their prior expectations and social stereotypes. They are trained in the use of

standardised RATING SYSTEMS intended to remove individual bias in perception.

Blinds and double blinds

However, a further safeguard often employed is to have raters give quantitative values to observation or interview data blind to its source. For instance, a SINGLE BLIND occurs where participants do not know whether they received a stimulant or a placebo. Where performance is rated by trained raters also unaware of the substance given to each participant, the study uses a DOUBLE BLIND.

Standardised procedures

Generally, within mainstream experimental psychology research, it has been the norm to use STANDARDISED PROCEDURES with each participant in the interest of controlling all extraneous variables which could affect different participants differently. This concept has usually been carried through into the areas of test administration and, to a lesser extent, interviewing. However, there is a powerful argument against this approach in some areas of applied work. Where what is required are the different accounts and impressions people have of their health or work situation, it would be far more important to conduct what are known as CLINICAL INTERVIEWS, in which the interviewer employs the skills of UNSTRUCTURED or SEMI-STRUCTURED INTERVIEWING (see below) in order to extract the full richness of each person's perspective.

The qualitative-quantitative debate

The last point has brought us to a huge and often hostile debate within psychological research as to whether there should always be an attempt to control variables and *quantify* (that is, measure numerically) psychological phenomena. The alternative extreme argues that the attempt to quantify all psychological variables, and follow a conventional scientific method, has often led to rather arid findings divorced from everyday reality. For instance, it is argued that IQ scores give only an extremely narrow impression of a person's full range of mental capacity. Measuring attitude to authority or the quality of group cohesiveness as a numerical value creates, it is argued, a quite artificial notion that such qualities exist in quantities ranging from one end of a uni-dimensional scale to the other. Incorporated into this debate, on the generally 'qualitative' side, is the argument that the experimental 'scientific' model creates an inappropriate and artificial body of knowledge quite unrelated to the real world of human interaction. Laboratory studies on small, short-lived groups into leadership or team co-operation and performance are seen as quite unlike these phenomena as they operate in the real world of work and recreation.

There is not space here to enter into this now classic debate, though there will no doubt be references to it in parts of this book. The interested reader might refer to Coolican (1994) for a brief account or to the several fuller arguments mentioned in that text. Examples of contemporary qualitative data analysis can be found in Bryman and Burgess (1994). The QUALITATIVE–QUANTITATIVE DEBATE is especially important within applied psychology however, since it is mainly the applied areas which have promoted the debate and developed qualitative methods. The following paragraphs give some flavour of these approaches.

Action research

Initiated by Kurt Lewin in the mid 1940s, this approach calls for psychological research to deal with practical social issues: to enter a situation, attempt to change it and to monitor results – often known as an INTERVENTION STUDY. An important guiding principle is to involve the participants (often members of a work group) in the process of change. The approach sees the researcher–researched (or consultant–client) role as central to any attempted intervention. In contrast, the traditional scientific research model tends to see the researcher or consultant in a neutral position, observing 'the facts', and sees social interaction factors like 'participant expectation' or 'social desirability' as 'nuisance variables' in need of control. For a contemporary discussion of the nature and role of action research, see Zuber-Skerritt (1992). In the UK, especially for work psy-

chology, action research principles are strongly associated with the Tavistock Institute of Human Relations.

PARTICIPATIVE AND COLLABORATIVE RESEARCH

In applied areas of psychology (especially occupational, health and educational) in the 1980s and 1990s, it has become more common for research to include participants as active enquirers in the research process, as Lewin and the Tavistock Institute have recommended. At the extreme, COLLABORATIVE end of this approach, the researcher takes the role of 'consultant' whilst facilitating work group members to conduct their own production of theories, data gathering, analysis and recommendations for change (see Reason, 1994). This is the approach taken by PROCESS CONSULTANCY, described in the educational psychology chapter.

Feminist psychology

Wilkinson (1989) discusses the impact of feminist research and emphasises the extent to which feminist research has concentrated on participative, co-operative and non-hierarchical methods of investigation. Her view is in line with the analysis of the traditional scientific paradigm as largely a product of male emphasis in psychology research and writing – see Ussher (1992) and the clinical psychology chapter.

Qualitative data

Qualitative research generates QUALITATIVE DATA. Some researchers argue that any attempt to quantify the data will destroy much of its richness and meaning. A popular approach is the employment of GROUNDED THEORY (see Strauss and Corbin, 1990) where, it is argued, theory can develop from the data one has gathered. This is to be contrasted with the conventional scientific model in which one sets out to *test* a theory by gathering data. Other researchers gather qualitative data and then, as part of the project, reduce this to some set of categories in order to report on the generalities found during the study. One compromise achieved in dealing with initially non-numeric material is to subject it to some form of CONTENT ANALYSIS. The data may have arrived from:

- open-ended questionnaire items (see below)
- relatively unstructured observation (participant or non-participant)
- relatively unstructured interviews
- projective test responses (all of which are described below)

or from

- already recorded data, such as children's school essays, lavatory graffiti (this *has* been done!), personal advertisements, television advertisements, news items, politicians' speeches and so on.

In content analysis a CODING SYSTEM is devised and raters are trained to use the system to categorise information initially in qualitative form. A rating scale is often then used to apply some quantitative assessment. Raters' level of agreement can then be subjected to RELIABILITY ANALYSIS which is also explained below.

A further use of content analysis has been in work with VERBAL PROTOCOLS where, in the work situation, an operative is asked to state aloud the silent speech they would use to help themselves carry out a task or to mention any thoughts which occur whilst carrying out the task. Martin and Klimoski (1990) used this method to study managers' evaluations of personnel. The managers were asked to speak aloud whilst evaluating their own and their subordinates' performances. It was found that the subordinates' performance was attributed to their relatively permanent personality characteristics, whereas for themselves (the managers) performance was more likely to be seen as a product of the surrounding situation.

HOW DO PSYCHOLOGISTS ASK QUESTIONS?

There are two major approaches to asking questions, first, by *interview*, and second by *questionnaire* or *psychometric test* (or *scale*). Many interviews incorporate the use of a test, scale or questionnaire. Even experiments may involve the use of a questionnaire or scale, often to measure the dependent variable. Patients randomly assigned to two different programmes for dietary control might be assessed on their dietary behaviour, pre- and post-training, using a questionnaire. However, the vast majority of test and questionnaire usage is in non-experimental field studies.

Questionnaires, scales and psychometric tests

Questionnaires, scales and tests are used to obtain information from people and also to assess them. In general, borrowing terminology from the natural sciences and technology, these measures are often known as *instruments*. Those that request information from people about themselves are commonly known as SELF-REPORT MEASURES. Below are listed and defined the general categories of measure which a psychologist might use.

Questionnaire   This is the correct name for a measure which asks several questions, unlike many *attitude* and *personality scales* which are described below. They are often used for survey work in order to obtain current views on a particular issue. They are also used to obtain information (especially with a 'yes/no' answer) about regular behaviour, for instance, modes of child discipline, sexual habits, typical leisure activities, moral principles, voting behaviour.

ATTITUDE SCALES   These are intended to measure a relatively permanent and habitual position of the individual on a particular issue (rather than an opinion). These often employ a set of *statements* (not questions) with which the respondent indicates their level of agreement or disagreement.

PERSONALITY SCALES These are intended to measure a relatively enduring feature of a person's regular behaviour (such as their general anxiety level, extroversion or typical approach to crises). They also mostly use statements with which to agree or disagree. They may use a set of descriptive terms from which the respondent has to select those most closely describing him or her. A few use only 'yes' or 'no' responses.

PSYCHOMETRIC TESTS These are instruments of 'mental measurement' and include personality scales along with measures of mental ability such as intelligence, creative thinking, linguistic ability and so on. It is important here to distinguish between measures of:

- *PERSONALITY TRAIT* – what you are normally like most of the time, e.g. your friendliness
- *PERSONALITY STATE* – what you're like at this moment, e.g. your current state of anxiety
- *ability* – what you are generally able to do, for instance, your numerical ability
- *achievement* – what you have achieved so far, for instance, your performance in a school or college test in psychology
- *aptitude* – your *potential* performance, for instance a general logic test which aims to predict how good you would be at computer programming.

Like interviews, psychological scales and tests can vary along the dimensions of *structure* and *disguise*. Psychometric tests are highly structured since they are viewed as accurately constructed measurement instruments and subject to rigorous testing for RELIABILITY and VALIDITY – see below. However, some questionnaires, often used in an interview or general survey, contain *open-ended* questions, such as, 'Please describe any sexual harassment or disadvantage you feel you have suffered in your employment'. Here results are difficult to quantify but can be subject to content analysis. The specific aim of some scales or questionnaires is sometimes disguised in order to avoid social desirability effects. In other scales there is no disguise, but it would not be clear to the participant what is covered, simply because of the highly theoretical nature of the variables assessed and the complexity of the overall test, especially, for instance, *Cattell's Sixteen Personality Factor Questionnaire* (1970).

PROJECTIVE TESTS These are based on the psychoanalytic notion that, when confronted by ambiguous stimuli, we tend to reveal our inner, normally defended thoughts, by projecting them onto what we perceive in the display. Those who interpret what is reported in projective testing claim to be able to assess such factors as concealed aggression, sexual fantasy, anxiety and so on. Being unstructured and disguised, they are seen as providing rich data with no bias from people guessing the researcher's intentions (except by experienced clients in therapy!) RORSCHACH INK BLOTS are one well-known type of projective test, still often used in clinical psychology. These are symmetrical abstract patterns rather like the 'butterfly' paintings produced in nursery classes. A THEMATIC APERCEPTION TEST (TAT) is a generally ambiguous visual scene. In each case people are asked what they see and, for the TAT, what may happen next.

Why should we trust psychological measures?

Reliability and validity

The description above of projective tests might leave the reader asking two related questions: 'How do we know the Rorschach really *does* measure aspects of personality?' and 'Surely different users will obtain different results?' The first question is one of VALIDITY and the second is a question of RELIABILITY.

We would ask of any measure, for instance our bathroom scales, that it produces the same reading each time the same amount is measured and that it gives us a true measure of what we want. Psychologists expect their measures to be:

- *reliable* – they are consistent and stable
- *valid* – they measure what is intended

■ *standardised* – we can make comparisons with other people measured on the same scale or instrument.

Reliability

An assessment of the reliability of a test or scale is obtained by two means. EXTERNAL RELIABILITY is assessed by comparing results on the measure for the same group of people at two different times. Comparison is conducted using correlation as described earlier. INTERNAL RELIABILITY is assessed either by comparing people's scores on two halves of the test or (using ITEM ANALYSIS) by comparing their scores on each item with their score overall. INTER-RATER RELIABILITY refers to the level of agreement between two raters of, for instance, projective test data or essay content, as in content analysis. The assessments of several observers using a standard assessment schedule might also be correlated in order to test INTER-OBSERVER RELIABILITY.

Validity

The methods above may satisfy us that the test or assessment schedule is consistent in its measurement effects (reliable) but not necessarily that it measures what we want it to measure (it is valid). A test of children's word knowledge, presented in written form, may fail because the children may *know* the words but not be able to *read* them. There are many ways of checking the validity of a psychological measure but a common practice is to check that it predicts what we'd expect. For instance, people scoring highly on an intelligence measure would be expected to do well in academic tests and exams; people scoring highly on a work motivation test would be predicted to be more successful and productive; an anxiety test should discriminate between people with clinical anxiety-related problems and a normal group.

Ecological validity

This special but common use of the term 'validity' refers to the extent to which a measure or an effect observed in one place can be generalised to other settings. It is often used in the process of criticising laboratory findings for their artificiality, but it applies, for instance, when we suspect that a 'local' measure of motivation, developed in one factory, could not be realistically used on a different set of workers.

Standardisation

We would also expect any useful measure to be *transferable* from one test situation to another. A measure of reading ability developed to distinguish between the various years of pupils in a very high-ability school will not be useful for assessing performance in many other ordinary schools. STANDARDISATION is the process of making a test transferable. This is done by taking large enough representative samples from the population with which individual cases are to be compared in future use of the test. Then a good deal of item analysis and adjustment of content and improvement in reliability is carried out until, usually, a NORMAL DISTRIBUTION is obtained. This is a symmetrical spread of scores with most lying near the central point. It is now possible to assess individuals who come from the same population on whom the test was standardised. Scores can be compared with the general distribution, very often in terms of the individual's *deviation* from the mean (average) of the population.

Operational definitions

It is important to recognise that psychologists do not work with a set of measuring instruments that have the universal acceptance that, say, physical measures of electrical current or liquid volume enjoy. For any particular research project it is important to ask, 'what was the measure employed?' If a psychologist is attempting to reduce aggression in disturbed children, and claims to have demonstrated this with a new technique, it is important for that researcher to report the *measure* of aggression employed. An OPERATIONAL DEFINITION is *a description of the steps taken in measuring an entity*. This is true in any science. In the psychological example given, the researcher would need to state how 'aggression' is to be measured, *for the purposes of the present study*. This might be in terms of the specific observations of children's behaviour made (number of hits, number of aggressive verbal responses, and so on) or by means of a questionnaire made

available to anyone interested in the research findings. Many variables mentioned in this book, for
instance, stress, anxiety, personality characteristics, motivation, verbal intelligence and so on, are
measured in terms of an operational definition.

Test factors and factor analysis

With reference to some of the tests mentioned in
this book there may be talk of some 'factors' associated with the test. This is especially true for so-
called general intelligence tests where, upon
analysis, it is argued that the test measures several, at least partially distinct 'factors'. As we said
earlier, a written word knowledge test also partially tests reading ability. Both word knowledge and
reading ability might then be *factors* contributing
to an individual's overall test score. Some would
argue that performance on a general intelligence
test is determined by factors of numerical reasoning, verbal reasoning, verbal knowledge, thinking
speed and so on. Psychologists use the statistical
procedure of FACTOR ANALYSIS to analyse results for
the likely number of factors which contribute to
an individual's test score.

Interviews

An interview is a face-to-face encounter (though
telephone 'interviews' are possible) in which data
are recorded using notes, audio or video tape.
Interview types vary from being pretty unstructured, as is often the case in clinical psychology,
to completely structured as is the case in the
social survey. Box 1 gives some idea of the various
types of interview commonly in use.

Observation

Controlled and naturalistic observation

Although non-experimental studies lack some
control over the independent and extraneous variables, nevertheless, researchers usually *control*
their data gathering as far as is possible. Ways to
exert this control in an observation study are:

- creating a structured assessment system
- creating good INTER-RATER RELIABILITY with

B O X   1

Types of interview

Non-directive – very much used by counsellors
and 'client-centred' therapists where the aim is
not so much to gather data as to help the
client. No direction is given. The interviewer
supports the client in personal growth and in
solving their own problems as far as possible.

Informal – quite unstructured but with an
overall data gathering aim. The interviewee is
prompted to talk while the interviewer listens
patiently and sympathetically, offering useful
comments but no advice or argument. The
interviewer may prompt further expansion on a
point and offer a direction or support in further
exploration by the interviewee.

Informal but guided – the interviewer has a
set of topics to cover and perhaps some specifically worded questions but the interview is conducted as a friendly, natural conversation. The
interviewer 'plays it by ear' and works in the
various questions or topics as the discussion
progresses. The interview is also known as
semi-structured. Piaget used a version of this
in his CLINICAL INTERVIEW/METHOD which follows
up a child's answers to set questions with spontaneous new enquiries which are intended to
do justice to his or her pattern of thought.

Structured but open-ended – there is a fixed
set of questions to ask but replies are 'open-
ended'. Interviewees may answer in any terms
they wish.

Fully structured – there is a fixed set of questions and a fixed set of possible responses for
the interviewee to choose from. This is the type
of interview mostly used in surveys.

further training and practice if necessary

■ controlling, where possible, the environment in which the observation takes place – perhaps an observation room at the research centre.

Most applied psychology observational studies take place in the natural environment of the people observed and are therefore known as NATURALISTIC STUDIES. Bandura's famous research (1969) on the ways children model adult behaviour took place in a controlled laboratory setting but most applied work is not so generalised. Naturalistic observation may occur on the shop-floor, in the office, in the classroom, at the hospital clinic. Because the observed behaviour would have occurred anyway, if the observer is discreet, realism and ecological validity are likely to be high. However, where a researcher or video camera, for instance, follows family members around the house for extended periods, behaviour might still be distorted by the observation.

To avoid this effect of the observer's presence, researchers can become a familiar part of the work, school, leisure or medical environment. Charlesworth and Hartup (1967) made several visits to a nursery school, talked to the children and learnt their names. They found they could also test out the reliability of their proposed observation scheme prior to formal data gathering.

Participant observation

A major method of preference for psychologists who tend to reject the traditionally scientific and experimental model of psychological research has been to get in among the people who are the object of investigation. In action research, described earlier, this means also involving the participants as co-researchers but in classic versions of PARTICIPANT OBSERVATION the people observed were often not aware of the observer's role. This can be queried on ethical grounds since participants therefore do not have the power to censor information which they might not wish to be published. On methodological grounds there have always been doubts about the possible objectivity of the observer under such circumstances, to say nothing of the strain involved in memorising information or somehow recording observations without 'blowing cover'. Very many applied

research projects, however, involve the researcher in working or living with the group studied and attempting to see the world from their point of view.

Case studies

Compared with mainstream psychological research, a good deal of the work within applied psychology involves individual CASE STUDIES. Much of Freud's theory was developed from work with individual patients. Today, in clinical psychology, a great deal of the literature concerns individual clients and their specific problems. An individual case study would generally include several of the following:

■ a case history – notes and evidence concerning the individual's prior history, exam grades, schools attended, medical history and so on
■ detailed observation of the individual, for instance at school or in the hospital ward
■ interviews, perhaps at regular intervals
■ administration of psychometric tests (anxiety, ability, etc. as appropriate)
■ information from diaries written by the person studied
■ reports from those working with the individual – teachers, social workers.

Case studies are of extreme importance in applied psychology (for a full account, see Bromley, 1986). It may be that just one case of a person *not* developing as expected sheds light on a completely new area of thinking or expectation. One seriously deprived child who nevertheless develops well academically and socially is of particular interest. One success with a new therapy used on a case of bulimia will be a good lead. Disasters and serial murders do not occur to order or in enough frequency for generalisations to be easily made, but we can learn from in-depth study of such cases that *do* occur. Many studies in occupational psychology are of one particular organisation in depth.

There is sometimes a form of 'knee jerk' reaction within psychology that investigative work must always be carried out on fairly large groups of people. This is true only where the aim is finally to generalise to at least the population from which the people are drawn. There is no problem whatsoever though in using a statistical significance test (see below) on a set of data drawn from *one* person. For instance, Keith, the custard pie phobic (see clinical psychology chapter) exhibited several forms of behaviour which were the object of attention for his therapist. Suppose we want to assess whether some part of the therapy experience, or the whole of it, had *some* effect on Keith's symptoms. If we start the therapy sessions with 12 aspects of behaviour which we would like to see changed *in a certain direction* and, at the end of the sessions, 11 of these *have* so changed, we can confidently reject the expectation from the NULL HYPOTHESIS (see below) that the changes varied only at chance level. This, in turn, allows us to present evidence *supporting* (but *not* 'proving') our hypothesis that the therapy had some effect on Keith's behaviour.

MEASUREMENT AND STATISTICS

Descriptive vs inferential statistics

Much work in applied psychology involves the gathering of what are known as DESCRIPTIVE STATISTICS. In educational psychology we may wish to know the average reading age of a group of children on a run-down housing estate and we may wish to know the variation within this group. Statistics are summaries of measurements taken of individuals and groups. They simply *describe* those people. Very often though we want to know whether a *difference* exists. For instance, we might want to know whether the average reading age of the housing estate children differs *significantly* (see below) from the general average for children this age. In the development of theory, as we have seen, we deduce a hypothesis, then test it, making use of what are known as INFERENTIAL STATISTICS. These will tell us to what extent we can claim that a difference we have measured, or a correlation, can be taken seriously. We hope to be able to claim with some confidence that the estate children's mean differs markedly from the usual mean for children this age – that their much lower score is not a coincidence. We want to convince others that the difference is not just a 'fluke' variation. We do this by showing how unlikely it is that any two average (randomly selected) groups of children would differ by so much.

The concept of significance

Most quantitative research articles make use of STATISTICAL SIGNIFICANCE *testing* to demonstrate that results are not just random fluctuations. A concrete example should illustrate this. A clinic recently announced that it could help couples to have a baby of the sex they desired. A radio interview produced the claim that 'four out of six couples have left satisfied'. Even the most non-mathematical of readers will probably find this a rather dubious claim for support. The most likely outcome for six couples who have a desire for a baby of a specific sex is that three will be satisfied and three will not, assuming there is no effective intervention. Four out of six is the next most likely outcome *by chance* alone. It is a *likely* outcome in normal (non-treated) conditions.

Suppose an occupational psychologist claims to employ a stress-reducing technique which is really worth its salt. You, as an employer considering purchase of the psychologist's services, will want evidence that the technique is effective. The psychologist might present evidence that 10 out of 12 people in a controlled study, showed a lower stress score (measured by questionnaire) after eight sessions than they had before the sessions began. To understand the logic of significance testing take the sceptical position. Assume that the stress technique does *not* work. If this is so then the results will be at chance level only. What would results obtained by chance look like? Well, if we measure people's scores on a complex test twice there will usually be *some* slight difference. As with the toss of a coin, there is an equal chance that the difference from the first to the second time will be positive or negative. By chance alone then, half the differences in stress level will be an increase and half will be a decrease. In other words, if the technique has no effect *at all*, the most likely effect we could expect would be that six of the 12 people will 'improve' and six will 'worsen'. We must remember that *if* the technique does not work, and there is no confounding variable, these are not 'improvements' at all, just random fluctuations. The assumption that there is absolutely no effect is known as the NULL HYPOTHESIS and the outcome of six 'improvements' and six 'worsenings' is the most likely result *if* the null hypothesis is true.

What the psychologist *actually* obtained was ten improvements and only two not improving. The probability of getting ten results in one direction, when there was an equal chance of each result going either way (the null hypothesis), are around four in 100. That is, for instance, if you tossed 12 coins together very many times you would only get 10 heads or 10 tails about four times in every 100. In other words, 10 out of 12 tails, 10 boys out of 12 babies, or 10 'successes' out of 12 tries (*if each try depends only on luck*) are pretty unlikely events. Having established that, *if the stress results are just chance outcomes*, the likelihood of getting these results is pretty low and the psychologist may legitimately take the step of assuming the null hypothesis *isn't* true and proceed to accept that the therapy works, at least provisionally. It is important to recognise that when researchers obtain significant differences or correlations they do not 'prove that their theory is correct', but simply provide themselves with evidence. This evidence says that if they are *wrong*, then the outcomes they obtained are a remarkable coincidence.

Conventional LEVELS OF SIGNIFICANCE – *p<0.05 and p<0.01*

Probability is not conventionally stated in the way that betting odds are. Probability is written as 'p' and can take any value between zero (absolutely no likelihood whatever) to one (absolutely certain). The probability that the stress results above would occur, *if the technique has no effect*, is 0.04. On a scale of zero to one this is very low indeed. Conventionally researchers make the decision to reject the null hypothesis when the probability (p) of the results occurring, *if the null hypothesis is true*, is less than 0.05. Hence, our result above would be counted as significant. Traditionally it is usual to report results where p<0.05 is 'significant' and results where p<0.01 is 'highly significant', though some dislike this habit. What matters for your understanding of research outcomes reported in this book is that researchers *cannot* claim to have support for their theory or to have an effective technique unless, statistically, their results would be highly unlikely *if* the null hypothesis is true. This is the basis upon which results are reported in this book. If a difference or correlation is reported it can be assumed that the result *has* been tested *and* found to be significant, even if this is not specifically stated.

Combining hypothesis tests – meta-analysis

Some studies support one theory, others do not. META-ANALYSIS is a relatively recent approach to the problem of assessing the *overall* direction of possibly hundreds of tests of the same or very similar hypotheses. It employs a set of statistical techniques in order to use the results of many studies as a new 'data set'. The result of each study is treated rather like an individual participant's result in a single study. Meta-analysis takes account of sample size and various statistical features of the data from each study. Specific examples are encountered in several chapters of this book.

3

CODE OF CONDUCT, ETHICAL PRINCIPLES AND GUIDELINES (BPS, 1991)

CODE OF CONDUCT FOR PSYCHOLOGISTS

The following Code of Conduct has been adopted by the Society following a postal ballot in which all Members were given the opportunity to vote. The code does not supplant earlier statements by the Society on matters of ethics and conduct, it merely supplements them in a more systematic way. Members and Contributors of the Society and Chartered Psychologists, are enjoined also to take account of any further guidelines which may be issued by the Society and its subsystems relating to the specific fields of psychological practice or research in which they are engaged.

1 General

In all their work psychologists shall value integrity, impartiality and respect for persons and evidence and shall seek to establish the highest ethical standards in their work. Because of their concern for valid evidence, they shall ensure that research is carried out in keeping with the highest standards of scientific integrity. Taking account of their obligations under the law, they shall hold the interest and welfare of those in receipt of their services to be paramount at all times and ensure that the interests of participants in research are safeguarded.

2 Competence

Psychologists shall endeavour to maintain and develop their professional competence, to recognise and work within its limits, and to identify and ameliorate factors which restrict it. Specifically they shall:

2.1 refrain from laying claim, directly or indirectly, to psychological qualifications or affiliations they do not possess, from claiming competence in any particular area of psychology in which they have not established their competence, and from claiming characteristics or capabilities for themselves which they do not possess;

2.2 recognize the boundaries of their own competence and not attempt to practise any form of psychology for which they do not have an appropriate preparation or, where applicable, specialist qualification;

2.3 take all reasonable steps to ensure that their qualifications, capabilities or views are not misrepresented by others, and to correct any such misrepresentations;

2.4 if requested to provide psychological services, and where the services they judge to be appropriate are outside their personal competence, give every reasonable assistance towards obtaining those services from others who are appropriately qualified to provide them;

2.5 take all reasonable steps to ensure that those working under their direct supervision comply with each of the foregoing, in particular that they recognize the limits of their competence and do not attempt to practise beyond them.

3 Obtaining consent

Psychologists shall normally carry out investigations or interventions only with the valid consent of participants, having taken all reasonable steps to ensure that they have adequately understood the nature of the investigation or intervention and its anticipated consequences.
Specifically they shall:

3.1 always consult experienced professional colleagues when considering withholding information about an investigatory procedure, and withhold information only when it is necessary in the interests of the objectivity of the investigatory procedure or of future professional practice;

3.2 where it is necessary not to give full information in advance to those participating in an investigation, provide such full information retrospectively about the aims, rationale and outcomes of the procedure as far as it is consistent with a concern for the welfare of the participants;

3.3 refrain from making exaggerated and unjustifiable claims for the effectiveness of their methods, from advertising services in a way likely to encourage unrealistic expectations about the effectiveness of the services offered, or from misleading those to whom services are offered about the nature and likely consequences of any interventions to be undertaken;

3.4 normally obtain the consent of those to whom interventions are offered, taking all reasonable steps to ensure that the consent obtained is valid, except when the intervention is made compulsori-

ly in accordance with the provisions and safeguards of the relevant legislation;

3.5 recognize and uphold the rights of those whose capacity to give valid consent to interventions may be diminished including the young, the mentally handicapped, the elderly, those in the care of an institution or detained under the provisions of the law;

3.6 where interventions are offered to those in no position to give valid consent, after consulting with experienced professional colleagues, establish who has legal authority to give consent and seek consent from that person or those persons;

3.7 recognize and uphold the rights of recipients of services to withdraw consent to interventions or other professional procedures after they have commenced.

4 Confidentiality

Psychologists shall take all reasonable steps to preserve the confidentiality of information acquired through their professional practice or research and to protect the privacy of individuals or organizations about whom information is collected or held. In general, and subject to the requirements of law, they shall take care to prevent the identity of individuals, organizations or participants in research being revealed, deliberately or inadvertently, without their expressed permission.
Specifically they shall:

4.1 endeavour to communicate information obtained through research or practice in ways which do not permit the identification of individuals or organizations;

4.2 convey personally identifiable information obtained in the course of professional work to others, only with the expressed permission of those who would be identified, (subject always to the best interests of recipients of services or participants in research and subject to the requirements of law) except that when working in a team or with collaborators, they shall endeavour to make clear to recipients of services or participants in research, the extent to which personally identifiable information may be shared between colleagues;

4.3 in exceptional circumstances, where there is sufficient evidence to raise serious concern about the safety or interests of recipients of services, or about others who may be threatened by the recipient's behaviour, take such steps as are judged necessary to inform appropriate third parties without prior consent after first consulting an experienced and disinterested colleague, unless the delay caused by seeking this advice would involve a significant risk to life or health;

4.4 take all reasonable steps to ensure that records over which they have control remain personally identifable only as long as is necessary in the interests of those to whom they refer (or, exceptionally, to the general development and provision of psychological services), and to render anonymous any records under their control that no longer need to be personally identifiable for the above purposes;

4.5 only make audio, video, or photographic recordings of recipients of services or participants in research (with the exception of recordings of public behaviour) with the expressed agreement of those being recorded both to the recording being made and to the subsequent conditions of access to it;

4.6 take all reasonable steps to safeguard the security of any records they make, including those held on computer, and, where they have limited control over access to records they make, exercise discretion over the information entered on the records;

4.7 take all reasonable steps to ensure that colleagues, staff and trainees with whom they work understand and respect the need for confidentiality regarding any information obtained.

5 Personal conduct

Psychologists shall conduct themselves in their professional activities in a way that does not damage the interest of the recipients of their services or participants in their research and does not undermine public confidence in their ability to carry out their professional duties.
Specifically they shall:

5.1 refrain from practice when their physical or psychological condition, as a result of for example alcohol, drugs, illness or personal stress, is such that abilities or professional judgement are seriously impaired;

5.2 not exploit the special relationship of trust and confidence that can exist in professional practice to further the gratification of their personal desires;

5.3 refrain from improper conduct in their work as psychologists that would be likely to be detrimental to the interests of recipients of their services or participants in their research;

5.4 neither attempt to secure or to accept from those receiving their service any significant financial or material benefit beyond that which has been contractually agreed, nor to secure directly from them any such benefit for services which are already rewarded by salary;

5.5 take steps to maintain adequate standards of safety in the use of all procedures and equipment used in professional practice or research;

5.6 not allow their professional responsibilities or standards of practice to be diminished by considerations of religion, sex, race, age, nationality, party politics, social standing, class or other extraneous factors;

5.7 where they suspect misconduct by a professional colleague which cannot be resolved or remedied after discussion with the colleague concerned, take steps to bring that misconduct to the attention of those charged with the responsibility to investigate it, doing so without malice and with no breaches of confidentiality other than those necessary to the proper investigatory processes.

ETHICAL PRINCIPLES FOR CONDUCTING RESEARCH WITH HUMAN PARTICIPANTS

1 Introduction

1.1 The principles given below are intended to apply to research with human participants. Principles of conduct in professional practice are to be found in the Society's Code of Conduct and in the advisory documents prepared by the Divisions, Sections and Special Groups of the Society.

1.2 Participants in psychological research should have confidence in the investigators. Good psychological research is possible only if there is mutual respect and confidence between investigators and participants. Psychological investigators are potentially interested in all aspects of human behaviour and conscious experience. However, for ethical reasons, some areas of human experience and behaviour may be beyond the reach of experiment, observation or other form of psychological investigation. Ethical guidelines are necessary to clarify the conditions under which psychological research is acceptable.

1.3 The principles given below supplement for researchers with human participants the general ethical principles of members of the Society as stated in The British Psychological Society's Code of Conduct (q.v.). Members of The British Psychological Society are expected to abide by both the Code of Conduct and the fuller principles expressed here. Members should also draw the principles to the attention of research colleagues who are not members of the Society. Members should encourage colleagues to adopt them and ensure that they are followed by all researchers whom they supervise (e.g. research assistants, postgraduate, undergraduate, A-Level and GCSE students).

1.4 In recent years, there has been an increase in legal actions by members of the general public against professionals for alleged misconduct.

Researchers must recognise the possibility of such legal action if they infringe the rights and dignity of participants in their research.

2 General

2.1 In all circumstances, investigators must consider the ethical implications and psychological consequences for the participants in their research. The essential principle is that the investigation should be considered from the standpoint of all participants; foreseeable threats to their psychological well-being, health, values or dignity should be eliminated. Investigators should recognise that, in our multi-cultural and multi-ethnic society and where investigations involve individuals of different ages, gender and social background, the investigators may not have sufficient knowledge of the implications of any investigation for the participants. It should be borne in mind that the best judge of whether an investigation will cause offence may be members of the population from which the participants in the research are to be drawn.

3 Consent

3.1 Whenever possible, the investigator should inform all participants of the objectives of the investigation. The investigator should inform the participants of all aspects of the research or intervention that might reasonably be expected to influence willingness to participate. The investigator should, normally, explain all other aspects of the research or intervention about which the participants enquire. Failure to make full disclosure prior to obtaining informed consent requires additional safeguards to protect the welfare and dignity of the participants (see Section 4).

3.2 Research with children or with participants who have impairments that will limit understanding and/or communication such that they are unable to give their real consent requires special safe-guarding procedures.

3.3 Where possible, the real consent of children and of adults with impairments in understanding or communication should be obtained. In addition, where research involves all persons under sixteen years of age, consent should be obtained from parents or from those "in loco parentis".

3.4 Where real consent cannot be obtained from adults with impairments in understanding or communication, wherever possible the investigator should consult a person well-placed to appreciate the participant's reaction, such as a member of the person's family, and must obtain the disinterested approval of the research from independent advisors.

3.5 When research is being conducted with detained persons, particular care should be taken over informed consent, paying attention to the special circumstances which may affect the person's ability to give free informed consent.

3.6 Investigators should realise that they are often in a position of authority or influence over participants who may be their students, employees or clients. This relationship must not be allowed to pressurise the participants to take part in, or remain in, an investigation.

3.7 The payment of participants must not be used to induce them to risk harm beyond that which they risk without payment in their normal lifestyle.

3.8 If harm, unusual discomfort, or other negative consequences for the individual's future life might occur, the investigator must obtain the disinterested approval of independent advisors, inform the participants, and obtain informed, real consent from each of them.

3.9 In longitudinal research, consent may need to be obtained on more than one occasion.

4 Deception

4.1 The withholding of information or the misleading of participants is unacceptable if the participants are typically likely to object or show unease once debriefed. Where this is in any doubt, appropriate consultation must precede the investigation. Consultation is best carried out with individuals who share the social and cultural background of the participants in the research, but the advice of ethics committees or experienced and disinterested colleagues may be sufficient.

4.2 Intentional deception of the participants over the purpose and general nature of the investigation should be avoided whenever possible. Participants should never be deliberately misled without extremely strong scientific or medical justification. Even then there should be strict controls and the disinterested approval of independent advisors.

4.3 It may be impossible to study some psychological processes without withholding information about the true object of the study or deliberately misleading the participants. Before conducting such a study, the investigator has a special responsibility to (a) determine that alternative procedures avoiding concealment or deception are not available; (b) ensure that the participants are provided with sufficient information at the earliest stage; and (c) consult appropriately upon the way that the withholding of information or deliberate deception will be received.

5 Debriefing

5.1 In studies where the participants are aware that they have taken part in an investigation, when the data have been collected, the investigator should provide the participants with any necessary information to complete their understanding of the nature of the research. The investigator should discuss with the participants their experience of the research in order to monitor any unforeseen negative effects or misconceptions.

5.2 Debriefing does not provide a justification for unethical aspects of any investigation.

5.3 Some effects which may be produced by an experiment will not be negated by a verbal description following the research. Investigators have a responsibility to ensure that participants receive any necessary debriefing in the form of active intervention before they leave the research setting.

6 Withdrawal from the investigation

6.1 At the onset of the investigation investigators should make plain to participants their right to withdraw from the research at any time, irrespective of whether or not payment or other inducement has been offered. It is recognised that this may be difficult in certain observational or organisational settings, but nevertheless the investigator must attempt to ensure that participants (including children) know of their right to withdraw. When testing children, avoidance of the testing situation may be taken as evidence of failure to consent to the procedure and should be acknowledged.

6.2 In the light of experience of the investigation, or as a result of debriefing, the participant has the right to withdraw retrospectively any consent given, and to require that their own data, including recordings, be destroyed.

7 Confidentiality

7.1 Subject to the requirements of legislation, including the Data Protection Act, information obtained about a participant during an investigation is confidential unless otherwise agreed in advance. Investigators who are put under pressure to disclose confidential information should draw

this point to the attention of those exerting such pressure. Participants in psychological research have a right to expect that information they provide will be treated confidentially and, if published, will not be identifiable as theirs. In the event that confidentiality and/or anonymity cannot be guaranteed, the participant must be warned of this in advance of agreeing to participate.

8 Protection of participants

8.1 Investigators have a primary responsibility to protect participants from physical and mental harm during the investigation. Normally, the risk of harm must be no greater than in ordinary life, i.e. participants should not be exposed to risks greater than or additional to those encountered in their normal lifestyles. Where the risk of harm is greater than in ordinary life the provisions of 3.8 should apply. Participants must be asked about any factors in the procedure that might create a risk, such as pre-existing medical conditions, and must be advised of any special action they should take to avoid risk.

8.2 Participants should be informed of procedures for contacting the investigator within a reasonable time period following participation should stress, potential harm, or related questions or concern arise despite the precautions required by the Principles. Where research procedures might result in undesirable consequences for participants, the investigator has the responsibility to detect and remove or correct these consequences.

8.3 Where research may involve behaviour or experiences that participants may regard as personal and private the participants must be protected from stress by all appropriate measures, including the assurance that answers to personal questions need not be given. There should be no concealment or deception when seeking information that might encroach on privacy.

8.4 In research involving children, great caution should be exercised when discussing the results with parents, teachers or others in loco parentis, since evaluative statements may carry unintended weight.

9 Observational research

9.1 Studies based upon observation must respect the privacy and psychological well-being of the individuals studied. Unless those observed give their consent to being observed, observational research is only acceptable in situations where those observed would expect to be observed by strangers. Additionally, particular account should be taken of local cultural values and of the possibility of intruding upon the privacy of individuals who, even while in a normally public space, may believe they are unobserved.

10 Giving advice

10.1 During research, an investigator may obtain evidence of psychological or physical problems of which a participant is, apparently, unaware. In such a case, the investigator has a responsibility to inform the participant if the investigator believes that by not doing so the participant's future well-being may be endangered.

10.2 If, in the normal course of psychological research, or as a result of problems detected as in 10.1, a participants solicits advice concerning educational, personality, behavioural or health issues, caution should be exercised. If the issue is serious and the investigator is not qualified to offer assistance, the appropriate source of professional advice should be recommended. Further details on the giving of advice will be found in the Society's Code of Conduct.

10.3 In some kinds of investigation the giving of advice is appropriate if this forms an intrinsic part of the research and has been agreed in advance.

11 Colleagues

11.1 Investigators share responsibility for the ethical treatment of research participants with their collaborators, assistants, students and employees. A psychologist who believes that another psychologist or investigator may be conducting research that is not in accordance with the principles above should encourage that investigator to re-evaluate the research.

REFERENCES

Abey-Wickerama, I., a'Brook, M. F., Gattoni, F. E. G. and Herridge, C. F. (1969) Mental hospital admission and aircraft noise. *Lancet*, 2 (7633), 1275–1277.

Abraham, S. C. S., Sheeran, P., Spears, R. and Abrams, D. (1992) Health beliefs and the promotion of HIV preventive intentions among teenagers: a Scottish perspective. *Health Psychology*, 11, 363–370.

Abramson, L. Y., Seligman, M. E. P. and Teasdale, J. D. (1978) Learned helplessness in humans: critique and reformulation. *Journal of Abnormal Psychology*, 87, 49–74.

Adams, J. A. (1971) A closed loop theory of motor learning. *Journal of Motor Behaviour*, 3, 111–149.

Aichorn, A. (1925) *Wayward Youth*. New York: Meridian Books.

Aitkenhead, M. and Liff, S. (1991) The effectiveness of equal opportunity policy. In Firth-Cozens, J. and West, M. A. (eds.), *Women at Work*. Bristol: Open University Press.

Ajzen, I. (1988) *Attitudes, Personality and Behavior*. Chicago, ILL: Dorsey Press.

Ajzen, I. (1991) The theory of planned behavior. *Organizational Behavior and Human Decision Processes*, 50, 179–211.

Ajzen, I. and Fishbein, M. (1980) *Understanding Attitudes and Predicting Social Behaviour*. Englewood Cliffs, NJ: Prentice-Hall.

Alderman, R. B. and Wood, N. L. (1976) An analysis of incentive motivation in young Canadian athletes. *Canadian Journal of Applied Sport Psychology*, 1, 169–176.

Alderman, R. B. (1980) Sport psychology: Past, present and future dilemmas. In Klavora, P. and Wipper, K. A. W. (eds.) *Psychological and Sociological Factors in Sport* (pp. 3–19). Toronto, ON: University of Toronto.

Alexander, F. and French, T. M. (1946) *Psychoanalytic Therapy*. New York: Ronald Press.

Algera, J. A. (1983) Objective and perceived task characteristics as a determinant of reactions by task performers. *Journal of Occupational Psychology*, 56, 95–105.

Allied Dunbar National Fitness Survey (1992) *Health of the Nation: Summary Report*. The Sports Council and The Health Education Authority.

Alloy, L. B. and Abramson, L. Y. (1979) Judgement of contingency in depressed and non-depressed students: Sadder but wiser? *Journal of Experimental Psychology: General*, 108, 441–485, 6.

Altman, I. (1975) *The Environment and Social Behaviour: Privacy, Personal Space, Territoriality and Crowding*. Monterey, CA.: Brooks/Cole.

Altman, I. and Chemers, M. (1980) *Culture and Environment*. Monterey, CA: Brooks/Cole.

American Psychiatric Association (1993) *Diagnostic and Statistical Manual of Mental Disorders*, 4th revision. Washington DC: American Psychiatric Association.

Ames, C. and Archer, J. (1988) Achievement goals in the classroom: Students' learning strategies and motivation processes. *Journal of Educational Psychology*, 80, 260–270.

Anderson, D. B. and Pennebaker, J. W. (1980) Pain and pleasure: alternative interpretations of identical situations. *European Journal of Social Psychology*, 10, 207–212.

Anderson, J. R. (1983) *The Architecture of Cognition*. Cambridge, Mass.: Harvard University Press.

Apter, M. (1989) *Reversal Theory: Motivation, Emotion and Personality*. London: Routledge.

Arnold, J., Cooper, C. L. and Robertson, I. T. (1995) *Work Psychology: Understanding Work Behaviour in the Workplace*, 2nd edn. London: Pitman Publishing.

Aronson, E., Bridgeman, D. L. and Geffner, R. (1978) The effects of a cooperative classroom structure on student behaviour and attitudes. In Bar-tel, D. and Saxe, L. (eds.) *Social Psychology of Education*. New York: Wiley.

Asch, S. (1956) Studies of independence and conformity: a minority of one against a unanimous majority. *Psychological Monographs*, 70.

Ashforth, B. E. (1985) Climate formation: Issue and extensions. *Academy of Management Review*, 4, 837–847.

Association of Educational Psychologists (AEP) *Careers Information Sheet* (1993).

Atkinson, J. W. (1964) *An Introduction to Motivation*. New York: D. van Nostrand Company.

Atkinson, J. W. (1974) The mainsprings of achievement-oriented activity. In Atkinson, J. W. and Raynor, J. O. (eds.) *Motivation and Acheivement* (pp. 13–41). New York: Halstead.

Atkinson, R. C. and Shiffrin, R. M. (1968) Human memory: A proposed system and its control processes. In Spence, K. W. and Spence, J. T. (eds.) *The Psychology of Learning and Motivation*, vol. 2. London: Academic Press.

Austin, J. T. and Bobko, P. (1985) Goal setting theory: unexplained areas and future research needs. *Journal of Occupational Psychology*, 58 (4), 289–308.

Axelrod, D., Hall, R. V. and Tanis, A. (1979) Comparison of two common classroom arrangements. *Academic Therapy*, 15, 29–36.

Baddeley, A. D. and Longman, D. J. A. (1978) The influence of length and frequency of training session on the range of learning to type. *Ergonomics*, 21, 627–635.

Bahrke, M. W. and Morgan, W. P. (1978) Anxiety reduction following exercise and medication. *Cognitive Therapy and Research*, 2, 323–333.

Baird, J. E. (1977) *The Dynamics of Organizational Communication*. New York: Harper and Row.

Bakal, D. A. (1979) *Psychology and Medicine: Psychological Dimensions of Health and Illness*. New York: Springer-Verlag.

Bales, R. F. (1953) The equilibrium problem in small groups. In Parsons, T., Bales, R. F. and Shils, E. A. *Working Papers in the Theory of Action*. Glencoe, ILL: The Free Press.

Bales, R. F. (1970) *Personality and Interpersonal Behaviour*. New York: Holt, Rinehart and Winston.

Bandura, A. (1969) *Principles of Behaviour Modification*. New York: Holt, Rinehart and Winston.

Bandura, A. (1977) Self-efficacy: Towards a unifying theory of behavioral change. *Psychological Review*, 84, 191–215.

Bandura, A. (1986) *Social Foundations of Thought and Action: A Social Cognitive Theory*. Englewood Cliffs, NJ: Prentice-Hall.

Bandura, A. and Huston, A. C. (1961) Identification as a process of incidental learning. *Journal of Abnormal and Social Psychology*, 63, 311–318.

Bandura, A. (1989) Perceived self-efficacy in the exercise of personal agency. *Psychologist*, 2, 411–424.

Bandura, A., Ross, D. and Ross, S. A. (1963) Imitation of film-mediated aggressive models. *Journal of Abnormal and Social Psychology*, 66, 3–11.

Baratz, S. S. and Baratz, J. C. (1970) Early childhood intervention: the social science base of institutional racism. *Harvard Educational Review*, 40, 29–50.

Barefoot, J. C., Dahlstrom, W. G. and Williams, R. B. (1983) Hostility, CHD incidence and total mortality: a 25-year follow-up study of 255 physicians. *Psychosomatic Medicine*, 45, 559–563.

Barefoot, J. C., Williams, R. B., Dahlstrom, W. G. and Dodge, K. A. (1987) Predicting mortality from scores of the Cook-Medley Scale: A follow-up of 118 lawyers. *Psychosomatic Medicine*, 49, 210.

Barker, R. G. (1968) *Ecological Psychology: Concepts and methods for studying the environment of human behaviour*. Stanford, CA: Stanford University Press.

Barker, R. G. and Wright, H. (1955) *Midwest and its children*. New York: Row and Petersen.

Baron, R. A. (1972) Aggression as a function of ambient temperature and prior anger arousal. *Journal of Personality and Social Psychology*, 21, 183–189.

Baron, R. A. (1978) Aggression and heat: The 'long hot summer' revisited. In Baum, A., Valins, S. and Singer, J. E. (eds.) *Advances in Environmental Research*, vol. 1, 186–207. Hillsdale, NJ: Lawrence Erlbaum.

Baron, R. A. (1987) Effects of negative ions on cognitive performance. *Journal of Applied Psychology*, 72(1), 131–137.

Baron, R. A. (1977) *Human Aggression*. New York: Plenum.

Bartlett, F. C. (1932) *Remembering.* Cambridge: Cambridge University Press.

Bartol, C. R. (1980) *Criminal Behaviour: a psychosocial approach.* New York: Prentice-Hall.

Bass, B. M. (1985) *Leadership and Performance: Beyond Expectations.* New York: The Free Press.

Bauer, R. M., Greve, K. W., Besch, E. L. and Schramke, C. J. (1992) The role of psychological factors in the report of building-related symptoms in sick building syndrome. *Journal of Consulting and Clinical Psychology,* 60(2), 213–219.

Bavelas, A. (1969) Communications patterns in task-oriented groups. In Cartwright, D. and Zander, A. (eds.) *Group Dynamics: Research and Theory,* 3rd edn. New York: Harper and Row.

Bayley, N. (1969) *Bayley Scales of Infant Development.* New York: Psychological Corporation, Sidcup, Kent: Harcourt, Brace and Company.

Beck, A. T. (1986) Cognitive therapy: A sign of retrogression or progress. *The Behaviour Therapist,* 9, 2–3.

Beck, A. T., Rush, A. J., Shaw, B. F. and Emery, G. (1979) *Cognitive Therapy of Depression.* New York: Guildford Press.

Beck, A. T., Steer, R. A. and Garbin, M. G. (1988) Psychometric properties of the Beck Depression Inventory: twenty-five years of evaluation. *Clinical Psychology Review,* 8, 77–100.

Beck, A. T., Wards, C. H., Mendelson, M., Mock, J. E. and Erbaugh, J. K. (1961) An inventory for measuring depression. *Archives of General Psychiatry,* 4, 561–571.

Becker, F. D. (1984) Loosely-coupled settings: A strategy for computer-aided work decentralization. In Staw, B. and Cummings, L. L. (eds.) *Research in Organisational Behaviour.* Greenwich, CT: JAI Press.

Becker, F. D. and Poe, D. B. (1980) The effects of user-generated design modifications in a general hospital. *Journal of Nonverbal Behaviour,* 4, 195–218.

Beecher, H. K. (1956) Relationship of significance of wound to pain experienced. *Journal of the American Medical Association,* 161, 1609–1613.

Belloc, N. B. and Breslow, L. (1972) Relationship of physical health status and health practices. *Preventive Medicine,* 1, 409–421.

Beloff, H. (1992) Mother, father and me: Our IQ. *The Psychologist,* July 1992.

Belson, W. (1975) *Juvenile Theft: the causal factors.* New York: Harper and Row.

Bem, S. (1974) The measurement of psychological androgyny. *Journal of Consulting and Clinical Psychology,* 42, 155–162.

Ben-Sira, Z. (1976) The function of the professional's affective behaviour in client satisfaction: A review approach to social interaction. *Journal of Health and Social Behavior,* 17, 3–11.

Ben-Sira, Z. (1980) Affective and instrumental components in the physician patient relationship: An additional dimension of interaction theory. *Journal of Health and Social Behavior,* 21, 170–180.

Bender, M. P. and Richardson, A. (1990) The ethnic composition of clinical psychology in Britain. *The Psychologist,* 3 (6), 250–252.

Benedict, H. (1993) *Virgin or Vamp.* London: Routledge.

Bennett, N. and Dunne, E. (1989) Implementing co-operative groupwork in classrooms. Paper presented At EARLI Conference, Madrid.

Bennett, N. (1979) *Teaching Styles and Pupil Progress.* London: Open Books.

Bergin, A. E. (1971) The evaluation of therapeutic outcomes. In Garfield, S L. and Bergin, A. E. (eds.) *Handbook of Psychotherapy and Behaviour Change: An Empirical Analysis.* New York: Wiley.

Bernstein, B. (1965) A socio-linguistic approach to social learning. In Gould, J. (ed.) *Penguin Survey of the Social Sciences.* Harmondsworth: Penguin.

Berryman-Finck, C. (1985) Male and female managers' views of the communication skills and training needs of women in management. *Public Personnel Management,* 14, 307–313.

Besag, V. (1989) *Bullies and Victims in Schools.* Milton Keynes: Open University Press.

Beutler, L. E. (1991) Have all won and must all have prizes? Revisiting Luborsky et al's verdict. *Journal of Consulting and Clinical Psychology,* 59, 226–232.

Beutler, L. E., Crago, M. and Arizmendi, T. G. (1986) Therapist variables in psychotherapy process and outcome. In Garfield, S. L. and Bergin, A. E. (eds.) *Handbook of Psychotherapy and Behaviour Change,* 3rd edn. New York: Wiley.

Bion, W. R. (1968) *Experiences in Groups.* London: Tavistock Publications.

Blackburn, R. (1993) *The Psychology of Criminal Conduct: Theory, Research and Practice.* Chichester: John Wiley.

Blackler, F. (1982) Organisational psychology. In Canter, S. and Canter, D. (eds.) *Psychology In Practice.* Chichester: John Wiley.

Blair, S. N., Kohl, H. W. and Gordon, N. F. (1992) How much physical activity is good for health? *Annual Review of Public Health,* 13, 99–126.

Blake, R. R. and Mouton, J. S. (1985) *The Managerial Grid III*. Houston: Gulf.

Blinkhorn, S. and Johnson, C. (1990) The insignificance of personality testing. *Nature*, 348, 671–672.

Bonnes, M. and Secchiaroli, G. (1995) *Environmental Psychology: A Psycho-social Introduction*. London: Sage.

Boon, J. and Davies, G. (1992) Fact and Fiction in Offender Profiling. *Issues in Legal and Criminological Psychology*, No. 32, October, pp. 3–9.

Boudewyns, P. A., Fry, T. J. and Nightingale, E. J. (1986) Token economies in VA medical centers: Where are they today? *The Behaviour Therapist*, 9, 126–127.

Bouffard-Bouchard, T. (1990) Influence of self-efficacy on performance in a cognitive task. *Journal of Social Psychology*, 130, 353–363.

Bower, G. H. (1972) Mental imagery and associative learning. In Gregg, L. (ed.) *Cognition in Learning and Memory*. New York: Wiley.

Bower, G. H., Clark, M., Lesgold, A. and Winzenz, D. (1969) Hierarchical retrieval schemes in recall of categorized word lists. *Journal of Verbal Learning and Verbal Behaviour*, 8, 323–343.

Bowlby, J. (1944) Forty-four Juvenile Thieves. *International Journal of Psychoanalysis*, 25, 1–57.

Bowlby, J. (1969) *Attachment and Loss, 1, Attachment*. London: Hogarth Press.

BPS, Scientific Affairs Board (1988) *The Future of the Psychological Sciences: Horizons and Opportunities for British Psychology*. Leicester: British Psychological Society.

BPS (1991) *Code of Conduct, Ethical Principles and Guidelines*. Leicester: British Psychological Society.

BPS, Division of Clinical Psychology (1992) *Core Purpose and Philosophy of the Profession*. Leicester: BPS/DCP.

BPS (1994a) *The Royal Charter, The Statutes, The Rules*. Leicester: British Psychological Society.

BPS (1994b) *Chartered Educational Psychologists* (Information Leaflet). Leicester: British Psychological Society.

BPS (1995) *Report of the Working Party on Recovered Memories*. Leicester: British Psychological Society.

Bransford, J. D., Stein, B. S., Shelton, T. S. and Owings, R. A. (1981) Cognition and adaptation: The importance of learning to learn. In Harvey, J. (ed.) *Cognition, Social Behaviour and the Environment*, pp. 93–110. Hillsdale, NJ: Lawrence Erlbaum.

Branthwaite, A. and Trueman, M. (1989) Explaining the effects of unemployment. In Hartley, J. and Branthwaite, A. (eds.) *The Applied Psychologist*. Milton Keynes: Open University Press.

Brawley, L. R., Landers, D. M., Miller, L. and Kearns, K. M. (1979) Sex bias in evaluating motor performance. *Journal of Sport Psychology*, 1, 15–24.

Bray, R., Struckman-Johnson, C., Osborne, M., McFarlane, J. and Scott, J. (1978) The effects of defendant status on decisions of student and community juries. *Social Psychology*, 41, 256–260.

Bredemeier, B. J. and Shields, D. I. (1986) Athletic aggression: An issue of contextual morality. *Sociology of Sport Journal*, 3, 15–28.

Breslow, L. and Enstrom, J. E. (1980) Persistence of health habits and their relationship to mortality. *Preventive Medicine*, 9, 469–483.

Brewin, C. R. and Bradley, C. (1989) Patient preferences and randomised clinical trials. *British Medical Journal*, 233, 313–315.

Bromley, D. B. (1986) *The Case Study Method in Psychology and Related Disciplines*. Chichester: Wiley.

Brophy, J. E. and Good, T. L. (1970) Teachers' communication of differential expectations for children's classroom performance: some behavioural data. *Journal of Educational Psychology*, 61, 365–374.

Brophy, J. E. and Good, T. L. (1974) *Teacher–Student Relationships: Causes And Consequences*. New York: Holt, Rinehart and Winston.

Broverman, I. K. and Broverman, D. (1970) Sex role stereotypes and clinical judgements of mental health. *Journal of Consulting and Clinical Psychology*, 34, 1–7.

Brower, K. J., Blow, F. C., Beresford, T. P. and Fuelling, C. (1989) Anabolic andronergic steroid dependence. *Journal of Clinical Psychiatry*, 50, 31–32.

Brown, G. W. and Harris, T. O. (1978) *The Bedford College Life Events and Difficulty Schedule: Directory of contextual threat ratings of events*. London: Bedford College, University of London.

Brown, H. (1985) *People, Groups and Society*. Milton Keynes: Open University Press.

Brown, J. M., O'Keefe, J., Sanders, S. H. and Baker, B. (1986) Developmental changes in children's cognition to stressful and painful situations. *Journal of Pediatric Psychology*, 11, 343–357.

Brown, R. (1965) *Social Psychology*. New York: Macmillan.

Brown, R. and Kulik, J. ((1977) Flashbulb memories. *Cognition*, 5, 73–99.

Brown, R. (1988) *Group Processes*. Oxford: Blackwell.

Bruner, J. S. (1966) *Toward a Theory of Instruction*. New York: Norton.

Bruner, J. S. (1973) *Beyond the Information Given*. New York: Norton.

Bryman, A. and Burgess, R. G. (1994) *Analyzing Qualitative Data*. London: Routledge.

Buckhout, R. (1974) Eyewitness Testimony. *Scientific American*, 231, 23–31.

Buckhout, R. (1980) Nearly 2000 witnesses can be wrong. *Bulletin of the Psychonomic Society*, 16, 307–310.

Bull, A. J., Burbage, S. E., Crandall, J. E., Fletcher, C. I., Lloyd, J. T., Ravenberg, R. L. and Rockett, S. L. (1972) Effects of noise and intolerance of ambiguity upon attraction for similar and dissimilar others. *Journal of Social Psychology*, 88, 151–152.

Bull, R. and Rumsey, N. (1988) *The Social Psychology of Facial Appearance*. New York: Springer-Verlag.

Bull, S. J. (ed.) (1991) *Sport Psychology: A Self-Help Guide*. Wiltshire: The Crowood Press.

Bullock Report (1975) *A Language for Life*. London: HMSO, Great Britain/Department of Education and Science.

Burns, J. (1992) Mad or just plain bad? Gender and the work of forensic clinical psychologists. In Ussher, J. M. and Nicolson, P. (eds.) *Gender Issues in Clinical Psychology*. London: Routledge.

Burnstein, E. and Vinokur, A. (1977) Persuasive argumentation and social comparison as determinants of attitude polarisation. *Journal of Experimental Social Psychology*, 13, 315–332.

Burroughs, W. J. (1989) Applied Environmental Psychology. In Gregory, W. L. and Burroughs, W. J. (eds.) *Introduction to Applied Psychology*. London: Scott, Foresman and Company.

Burt, C. (1925) *The Young Delinquent*. London: University of London Press.

Burt, C. (1940) *The Factors of Mind*. London: University of London Press.

Burt, C. (1972) The inheritance of general intelligence. *American Psychologist*, 27, 175–190.

Byerley, W. F., Brown, J. and Lebeque, B. (1987) Treatment of seasonal affective disorder with morning light. *Journal of Clinical Psychiatry*, 48, 447–448.

Byrne, B. (1987) A study of the incidence and nature of bullies and whipping boys in a Dublin City post-primary school for boys. Unpublished M.Ed. thesis: Trinity College, Dublin. Quoted in Besag, V. (1989) *Bullies and Victims in Schools*. Milton Keynes: Open University Press.

Byrne, D. G. (1981) Type A behaviour, life events and myocardial infarction: Independent or related risk factors? *British Journal of Medical Psychology*, 54, 371–377.

Cadbury, E. (1914) Some principles of industrial organisation: the case for and against scientific management. *Sociological Review*, 7(2), 99–117.

Calhoun, J. B. (1962) Population density and social pathology. *Scientific American*, 206, 136–148.

Cameron, P., Robertson, D. and Zaks, J. (1972) Sound pollution, noise pollution and health: Community parameters. *Journal of Applied Psychology*, 56, 67–74.

Cameron, R. J. and Stratford, R. J. (1987) Educational Psychology: a problem-centred approach to service delivery. *Educational Psychology in Practice*, January 1987, pp. 10–20.

Campaign for Racial Equality (1985) *Birmingham Local Education Authority and Schools: referral and suspension of pupils*. London: CRE. In Hicks and Spurgeon (1994) – see below.

Canavan, A. G. M. (1994) Single-case methodology in clinical neuropsychology. In Lindsay, S. J. E. and Powell, G. E. (eds.) *The Handbook of Clinical Adult Psychology*, 2nd edn. London: Routledge.

Cannon, W. B. (1914) The emergency function of the adrenal medulla in pain and the major emotions. *American Journal of Physiology*, 33, 356–372.

Cannon, W. B. (1929) *Bodily changes in pain, hunger, fear and rage*. Boston: Branford.

Cannon, W. B. (1932) *The Wisdom of the Body*. New York: Norton.

Canter, D. (1989) Offender Profiles. *The Psychologist*, 2, 1, 12–16.

Canter, D. (1994) *Criminal Shadows*. London: HarperCollins.

Canter, D. (1968) *The measurement of meaning in architecture*. Unpublished manuscript: Glasgow Building Performance Research Unit.

Canter, D. (1969) An intergroup comparison of connotative dimensions. *Environment and Behaviour*, 1, 37–48.

Canter, D. (1983) The purposive evaluation of places: A facet approach. *Environment and Behaviour*, 15, 659–698.

Canter, D. and Thorne, R. (1972) Attitudes to housing: A cross-cultural comparison. *Environment and Behaviour*, 4, 3–32.

Caplan, G. (1970) *The Theory and Practice of World Mental Health Consultation*. New York: Basic Books.

Caplan, P. J. (1991) Delusional dominating personality disorder (DDPD). *Feminism & Psychology*, 1(1), 171–174.

Carroll, D. (1992) *Health Psychology: Stress Behaviour and Disease*. London: Falmer Press.

Cartridge, S. A. (1851) Report on the diseases and

physical peculiarities of the negro race. *New Orleans Medical and Surgical Journal*, May, 691–715. Reprinted in Caplan, A. C., Engelhardt, H. T. and McCartney, J. J. (eds.) (1981) *Concepts of Health and Disease*. Reading, MASS: Addison-Wesley.

Case, R. (1985) *Intellectual Development: Birth to Adulthood.* New York: Academic Press.

Cassidy, T. (1992) Commuting-related stress: Consequences and Implications. *Employee Counselling Today*, 4(2), 15–21.

Cassidy, T. (1994) Current psychological perspectives on stress: A brief guided tour. *Management Bibliographies and Reviews*, 20(3), 2–12.

Cassidy, T. and Lynn, R. (1989) A multi-dimensional approach to achievement motivation: the development of a comprehensive measure. *Journal of Occupational Psychology*, 62, 301–312.

Cassidy, T. and Lynn, R. (1991) Achievement motivation, educational attainment, cycles of disadvantage and social competence: Some longitudinal data. *British Journal of Educational Psychology*, 61, 1–12.

Cattell, R. B. (1965) *The Scientific Analysis of Personality*. Harmondsworth: Penguin.

Cattell, R. B., Eber, H. W. and Tatsuoka, M. M. (1970) *Handbook for the Sixteen Personality Factor Questionnaire* (16PF). Windsor: NFER.

Charlesworth, R. and Hartup, W. W. (1967) Positive social reinforcement in the nursery school peer group. *Child Development*, 38, 993–1002.

Chesney, M. A., Hecker, M. H. L. and Black, G. W. (1988) Coronary prone components of type A behavior in the WCGS: A new methodology. In Houston, B. and Snyder, C. R. (eds.) *Type A Behavior Pattern, Research, Theory and Intervention*. New York: Wiley.

Children Act (1989). London: HMSO.

Choi, P. (1992) So steroids may work but they also . . . *Coaching Focus: Drugs, Issues, Ideologies and Ideosyncrasies*. Leeds: National Coaching Foundation.

Chomsky, N. (1959) Review of Skinner's Verbal Behaviour. *Language*, 35, 26–58.

Cialdini, R. B. (1980) Full cycle social psychology. In Bickman, L. (ed.) *Applied Social Psychology Annual*, vol. 1. Beverley Hills, CA: Sage.

Clifford, B. and Scott, J. (1978) Individual and situational factors in eyewitness testimony. *Journal of Applied Psychology*, 63, 352–359.

Clinical Psychology Forum, (1989) vol. 22.

Cochrane, R. and Sashidharan, S. (1995) *Mental Health and Ethnic Minorities: A Review of the Literature and Implications for Services*. Birmingham University: Review paper for Northern Birmingham Mental Health Trust.

Cohen, S., Glass, D. C. and Singer, J. E. (1973) Apartment noise, auditory discrimination and reading ability in children. *Journal of Experimental Social Psychology*, 9, 407–422.

Condry, J. and Condry, S. (1976) Sex differences: A study in the eye of the beholder. *Child Development*, 47, 812–819.

Conn, W. (1992) Psychologists, Child Law and the Courts: Contexts and Professional Advice. In Wolfendale, S., Bryans, T., Fox, M., Labram, A. and Sigston, A. (1992) *The Profession and Practice of Educational Psychology: future directions*. London: Cassell Education Limited.

Cook, M. (1978) *Perceiving Others*. London: Routledge.

Cook, T. D. and Campbell, D. T. (1979) *Quasi-experimentation: Design and Analysis Issues for Field Settings*. Chicago: Rand McNally.

Cooke, R. A. and Rousseau, D. M. (1988) Behavioural norms and expectations: a quantitative approach to the assessment of organisational culture, group and organisational studies. In Cooper, C. L. (1991) *Industrial and Organisational Psychology*, vol. 2. Aldershot: Edward Elgar.

Coolican, H. (1994) *Research Methods and Statistics in Psychology*, 2nd edn. London: Hodder and Stoughton.

Coombs, C. H., Dawes, R. M. and Tversky, A. (1970) *Mathematical Psychology: An elementary introduction*. Englewood Cliffs, NJ: Prentice-Hall.

Cooper, C. L. (1991) *Industrial and Organisational Psychology*, vol. 2. Aldershot: Edward Elgar.

Cooper, P., Upton, G. and Smith, C. (1991) Ethnic minority and gender distribution among staff and pupils in facilities for pupils with emotional and behavioural difficulties in England and Wales. *British Journal of Sociology of Education*, 12(1), 77–94.

Cooper, R. (1973) Task characteristics and intrinsic motivation. *Human Relations*, 26, 387–413.

Covington, M. (1984) The self-worth theory of achievement motivation. *Elementary School Journal*, 85, 5–20.

Cowie, H. and Rudduck, J. (1991) *Cooperative Group Work in the Multi-Ethnic Classroom*. London: B P Publications.

Cox, T. (1978) *Stress*. London: Macmillan.

Cox, R. M. (1994) *Sport Psychology: Concepts and Applications*. Dubuque, IA: W. M. Brown.

Craik, F. and Lockhart, R. (1972) Levels of processing. *Journal of Verbal Learning and Verbal Behaviour*, 11, 671–684.

Cratty, B. J. (1989) *Psychology in Contemporary Sport*, 3rd edn. Englewood Cliffs, NJ: Prentice-Hall.

Crombag, H. F. M. (1994) Law as a Branch of Applied Psychology. *Psychology, Crime and Law*, 1, 1–9.

Crouch, A. and Yetton, P. W. (1987) Manager behaviour, leadership style and subordinate performance: An empirical extension of the Vroom–Yetton conflict rule. *Organisational Behaviour and Human Decision Processes*, 39, 384–396.

Crutchfield, R. S. (1955) Conformity and character. *American Psychologist*, 10, 191–198.

Curtis, M. J. and Watson, K. L. (1980) Changes in consultee problem clarification skills following consultation. *Journal of School Psychology*, 18, 210–221.

Dane, F. C. and Wrightsman, L. S. (1982) Effects of defendants' and victims' characteristics on jurors' verdicts. In Kerr, N. L. and Bray, R. M. (eds.) *The Psychology of the Courtroom*. London: Academic Press.

Davenport, G. C. (1994) *An Introduction to Child Development*, 2nd edn. London: Collins Educational.

Davidson, M. J. and Cooper, C. L. (1983) *Stress and the Woman Manager*. London: Martin-Robinson.

Davie, R., Butler, N. and Goldstein, H. (1972) *From Birth to Seven* (Second Report of the National Child Development Study). London: Longman and National Children's Bureau.

Davies, D. R., Lang, L. and Shackleton, V. J. (1973) The effect of music and task difficulty on performance of a visual vigilance task. *British Journal of Psychology*, 64, 383–389.

Davies, G. (1994) Witness error still convicts the innocent. *The Guardian*, September 10.

Davison, G. C. and Neale, J. M. (1994) *Abnormal Psychology*. New York: Wiley.

Dawes, R. M. (1980) Social Dilemmas. *Annual Review of Psychology*, 31, 169–93.

DCLP Training Committee (1994) The Core Knowledge and Skills of the Chartered Forensic Psychologist. In Towl and Lloyd (eds.) *Forensic Update*, Issue 38, Division of Criminological and Legal Psychology, BPS.

de Board, R. (1978) *The Psychoanalysis of Organizations*. London: Tavistock.

Deary, I. J. and Matthews, G. (1993) Personality traits are alive and well. *The Psychologist*, 6(7), 299–311.

deCasper, A. J. and Fifer, W. P. (1980) Of human bonding: Newborns prefer their mothers' voices. *Science*, 208, 1174–1176.

Deci, E. and Ryan, R. M. (1985) *Intrinsic Motivation and Self-determination in Human Behaviour*. New York: Plenum.

DeLongis, A., Coyne, J. C., Dakof, G., Folkman, S. and Lazarus, R. S. (1982) Relationship of daily hassles, uplifts and major life events to health status. *Health Psychology*, 1, 119–136.

Dembroski, T. M., Weiss, S. M., Shields, I. L., Haynes, S. G. and Feinleib, M. (eds.) (1978) *Coronary Prone Behavior*. New York: Springer-Verlag.

Derogatis, L., Lipman, R. and Covi, M. (1973) SCL-90, an out-patient rating scale. *Psychopharmacology Bulletin*, 9, 13–20.

Dessent, T. (1978) The historical development of school psychological services. In Gillham, B. (1978) *Reconstructing Educational Psychology*. London: Croom Helm.

Dessent, T. (1992) Educational Psychologists and 'The Case for Individual Casework'. In Wolfendale, S., Bryans, T., Fox, M., Labram, A. and Sigston, A. (1992) *The Profession and Practice of Educational Psychology: future directions*. London: Cassell Education Limited.

Deutsch, M. (1949) An experimental study of the effects of cooperation and competition upon group process. *Human Relations*, 2, 199–231.

Deutsch, M. and Gerard, H. B. (1955) A study of normative and informational influence upon individual judgement. *Journal of Abnormal and Social Psychology*, 51, 629–636.

Dishman, R. K. (1983) The identity crisis in North American sport psychology: Academic and professional issues. *Journal of Sport Psychology*, 5, 123–134.

Dishman, R. K. (1987) Exercise adherence and habitual physical activity. In Morgan, W. P. and Goldstein, S. E. (eds.) *Exercise and Mental Health* (pp. 57–83). Washington DC: Hemisphere Publishing Corporation.

Dohrenwend, B. S., Dohrenwend, B. P. (eds.) (1974) *Stressful Life Events: Their Nature and Effects*. New York: Wiley.

Dohrenwend, B. S., Dohrenwend, B. P. (eds.) (1981) *Stressful Life Events and their Contexts*. New York: Prodist.

Dohrenwend, B. S., Dohrenwend, B. P., Dodson, M. and Shrout, P. E. (1984) Symptoms, hassles, social supports and life events: Problems of confounded measures. *Journal of Abnormal Psychology*, 93, 222–230.

Dohrenwend, B. S. and Shrout, P. E. (1985) 'Hassles' in the conceptualisation and measurement of life stress variables. *American Psychologist*, 40, 780–785.

Doise, W. and Mugny, G. (1984) *The Social Development of the Intellect.* London: Pergamon Press.

Doll, E. (1965) *Vineland Social Maturity Scale.* American Guidance Service Inc., Publishers' Building, Circle Pines, Minnesota 55014.

Doll, R. and Peto, R. (1981) *The Causes of Cancer.* Oxford: OUP.

Dollard, J., Miller, N., Doob, I., Mourer, O. H. and Sears, R. R. (1939) *Frustration and Aggression.* New Haven, CT: Yale University Press.

Donachy, W. (1976) Parent participation in pre-school education. *British Journal of Educational Psychology*, 46(1), 31–39.

Donaldson, M. (1978) *Childrens' Minds.* London: Fontana.

Dooley, C. (1994) Professional issues in the 1990s and beyond: New demands, new skills. In Lindsay, S. J. E. and Powell, G. E. (eds.) *The Handbook of Clinical Adult Psychology*, 2nd edn. London: Routledge.

Dorn, L. and Matthews, G. (1992) Two further studies of personality correlates of driver stress. *Personality and Individual Differences*, 13(8), 949–951.

Douglas, J. W. B. (1964) *The Home and the School.* London: MacGibbon and Key.

Drennan, D. (1989) How to get your employees committed. *Management Today*, October, 121–131.

Dubos, R. (1965) *Man Adapting.* New Haven: Yale University Press.

Dunn, L. M., Whetton, C. and Pintile, D. (1982) *British Picture Vocabulary Scale (BPVS).* Oxford: NFER-NELSON.

Duquin, M. E. (1978) The androgenous advantage. In Ogilsby, C. A. (ed.) *Women and Sport: From Myth to Reality* (pp. 89–106). Philadelphia, PA: Lea and Febiger.

Duval, S. and Wickland, R. A. (1972) *A Theory of Objective Self-Awareness.* New York, Academic Press.

Dweck, C. S. (1975) The role of expectation and attributions in the alleviation of learned helplessness, *Journal of Personality and Social Psychology*, 31, 674–685.

Eagly, A. H. and Chaiken, S. (1993) *The Psychology of Attitudes.* Fort Worth, TX: Harcourt Brace Janovich.

Eagly, A. H. and Steffin, V. J. (1986) Gender and aggressive behaviour: A meta-analytic review of the social psychological literature. *Psychological Bulletin*, 100, 309–330.

Earley, P. C. (1989) Social loafing and collectivism: a comparison of the United States and the People's Republic of China. *Administrative Science Quarterly*, 34, 565–581.

Earley, P. C., Lee, C. and Hanson, L. A. (1990) Joint moderating effects of job experience and task component complexity: relations among goal setting, task strategies and performance. *Journal of Organizational Behaviour*, 11(1), 3–15.

Easterbrook, J. A. (1959) The effect of emotion on cue utilisation and the organisation of behaviour. *Psychological Review*, 66, 183–201.

Eccles, J. S. (1987) Gender roles and women's achievement-related decisions. *Psychology of Women Quarterly*, 11, 135–172.

Eccles, J. S. and Harold, R. D. (1991) Gender differences in sport involvement: applying the Eccles expectancy-value model. *Journal of Applied Sport Psychology*, 3, 7–35.

Eden, D. (1990) Pygmalion without interpersonal contrast effects: Whole groups gain from raising manager expectations. *Journal of Applied Psychology*, 75(4), 394–398

Education Act (1944). London: HMSO.

Education Act (1981). London: HMSO.

Education Act (1993). London: HMSO.

Education Reform Act (1988). London: HMSO.

Egan, G. (1982) *The Skilled Helper: Model, Skills and Methods for Effective Helping*, 2nd edn. Monterey, CA: Brooks/Cole.

Egglestone, J. (1985) *The Educational and Vocational Experiences of 15–18-year-old Young People of Minority Ethnic Groups.* Department of Education, University of Keele.

Egglestone, J., Dunne, D., Anjali, M. and Wright, C. (1986) *Education for Some: The Educational and Vocational Experiences of 15–18-year-old Members of Minority Ethnic Groups.* Stroke-on-Trent: Trentham Books.

Elashoff, J., Dixon, J. and Snow, R. (1971) *Pygmalion Reconsidered: A Case Study in Statistical Inference.* Belmont, CA: Wadsworth.

Elias, P. and Main, B. (1982) *Women's Working Lives.* Warwick: University of Warwick, Institute for Employment Research.

Elkin, I., Shea, T., Imber, S., Pilkonis, P., Sotsky, S., Glass, D., Watkins, J., Leber, W. and Collins, J. (1986) *NIMH Treatment of Depression Collaborative Research Program: Initial Outcome Findings.* Paper presented to the American Association for the Advancement of Science.

Elliott, C. D. (1992) *BAS Spelling Scale.* London: NFER: NELSON.

Elliott, C. D., Murray, D. J. and Pearson, L. S. (1979, revised 1983) *British Ability Scales.* Slough: National Foundation for Educational Research.

Elliott, M. (1989) Bullying: Harmless Fun or Murder? In

Roland, E. and Munthe, E. (eds.) *Bullying: An International Perspective*. London: David Fulton.

Elliott, M. (ed.) (1991) *Bullying: A Practical Guide to Coping for Schools*. Harlow: Longman/Kidscape.

Ellis, A. (1962) *Reason and Emotion in Psychotherapy*. New York: Lyle Stuart.

Ellis, A. (1994) The sport of avoiding sport and exercise: a rational emotive behavioural therapy perspective. *The Sport Psychologist*, 8, 248–261.

Elton Report (1989) *Discipline in Schools: Report of the Committee of Enquiry*. HMSO: London, Great Britain/Department of Education and Science.

Emery, F. E. (1959) Characteristics of socio-technical systems. *Tavistock Institute Publications*, no. 527.

Engel, G. L. (1977) The need for a new medical model: A challenge for biomedicine. *Science*, 196, 129–136.

Engel, G. L. (1980) The clinical application of the biopsychosocial model. *American Journal of Psychiatry*, 137, 535–544.

Evans, P. D. (1990) Type A behaviour and coronary heart disease: When will the jury return? *British Journal of Psychology*, 81, 147–157.

Eysenck, H. J. (1952) The effects of psychotherapy: An evaluation. *Journal of Consulting Psychology*, 16, 319–324.

Eysenck, H. J. (1964) *Crime and Personality*. London: Routledge Kegan Paul.

Eysenck, H. J. and Eysenck, S. B. G. (1963, reprinted 1973) *Eysenck Personality Inventory*. London: University of London Press.

Eysenck, H. and Gudgonsson, G. (1989) *The Causes and Cures of Criminality*. New York: Plenum Press.

Eysenck, M. W. and Keane, M. T. (1995) Cognitive Psychology: A student's handbook, 3rd edn. Hove: LEA.

Fairbairn, R. (1952) *Object Relations Theory of Personality*. New York: Basic Books.

Farquhar, J. W., Maccoby, N., Wood, P. D., Breitrose, H., Haskell, W. L., Meyer, A. J., Alexander, J. K., Brown, B. W., McAlister, A. L., Nash, J. D. and Stern, M. P. (1977) Communication education for cardiovascular health. *Lancet*, 1192–1195.

Fazey, J. and Hardy, L. (1988). The Inverted-U Hypothesis: A Catastrophe for Sport Psychology? *Monograph*, no. 1, Leeds: British Association for Sport Sciences.

Feldman, D. C. (1976) A practical programme for employee socialization. *Organizational Dynamics*, 57, 64–80.

Feltz, D. L. (1992) The nature of sport psychology. In Horn, T. S. (ed.) *Advances in Sport Psychology*. Champaign, ILL: Human Kinetics Publishers.

Ferenczi, S. (1960) The further development of an active therapy in psychoanalysis. In Richman, J. (ed.), *Further Contributions to the Theory and Technique of Psychoanalysis*. London: Hogarth.

Fernando, S. (1991) *Mental Health, Race and Culture*. London: Mind/Macmillan.

Ferri, G. (1972) *Streaming: Two Years Later*. Windsor: NFER.

Festinger, L. (1957) *A Theory of Cognitive Dissonance*. New York: Harper and Row.

Fiedler, F. E. (1967) *A Theory of Leadership Effectiveness*. New York: McGraw-Hill.

Fiedler, F. E. and Chemers, M. M. (1984) *Improving Leadership Effectiveness: The Leader Match Concept*, 2nd edn. New York: Wiley.

Fiedler, F. E. and Garcia, J. E. (1987) *New Approaches to Effective Leadership: Cognitive Resources and Organisational Performance*. New York: Wiley.

Field, R. G. H. (1982) A critique of the Vroom–Yettom contingency model of leadership behaviour. *Academy of Management Review*, 4, 249–257.

Finkel, C. B., Glass, C. R. and Merluzzi, T. V. (1982) Differential discrimination of self-referent statement by depressives and non-depressives. *Cognitive Therapy and Research*, 6, 173–183.

Fish Report: Inner London Education Authority (1985) *Educational Opportunities for All*. London: ILEA.

Fishbein, M. and Ajzen, I. (1975) *Belief, Attitude, Intention and Behavior: An Introduction to Theory and Research*. Reading, MA: Addison-Wesley.

Fisher, S. and Reason, J. (1988) (eds.) *Handbook of Life Stress, Cognition and Health*. Chichester: Wiley.

Fitts, P. M. and Posner, M. I. (1967) *Human Performance*. Belmont, CA: Brooks/Cole.

Flavell, J. H. (1985) *Cognitive Development*, 2nd edn. Englewood Cliffs, NJ: Prentice-Hall.

Fleishman, E. A. (1967) Performance assessment based on an empirically derived task taxonomy. *Human Factors*, 9, 349–366,

Fleishman, E. A. and Harris, E. F. (1962) Patterns of leadership behaviour related to employee grievances and turnover. *Personnel Psychology*, 15, 43–56.

Flor, H., Kerns, R. D. and Turk, D. C. (1987) The role of spouse reinforcement, perceived pain, and activity levels of chronic pain patients. *Journal of Psychosomatic Research*, 31, 251–259.

Flowers, M. L. (1977) A laboratory test of some implications of Janis' groupthink hypothesis. *Journal of Personality and Social Psychology*, 35, 888–896.

Foot, H. C., Morgan, M. J. and Shute, R. H. (1990) *Children Helping Children*. Chichester: John Wiley.

Fox, M. and Sigston, A. (1992) Connecting Organisational Psychology, Schools and

Educational Psychologists. In Wolfendale, S., Bryans, T., Fox, M., Labram, A. and Sigston, A. (1992) *The Profession and Practice of Educational Psychology: future directions.* London: Cassell Education Limited.

Franks, (Lord) (1983) *Falkland Islands Review, a Report of a Committee of Privy Councillors CMND 8787.* London: HMSO.

Fraser, C., Gouge, C. and Billig, M. (1971) Risky shifts, cautious shifts and group polarisation. *European Journal of Social Psychology*, 1, 7–30.

Freud, S. (1917) The sense of symptoms. In Freud, S. (1971) *The Complete Introductory Lectures on Psychoanalysis.* London: George Allen and Unwin.

Freud, S. (1932) Femininity. In Freud, S. (1971) *The Complete Introductory Lectures on Psychoanalysis.* London: George Allen and Unwin.

Freud, S. (1933) *New Introductory Lectures on Psychoanalysis.* New York: Norton.

Freud, S. (1971) *The Complete Introductory Lectures on Psychoanalysis.* London: George Allen and Unwin.

Furnham, A. and Proctor, D. (1989) Belief in a Just World: review and critique of the individual differences literature. *British Journal of Social Psychology*, 28, 365–384.

Furnham, A. and Thompson, J. (1991) Personality and self-reported delinquency. *Personality and Individual Differences*, **12**, 585–598.

Gackenbach, J. (1982) Collegiate swimmers: sex differences in self-reports and indices of physiological stress. *Perceptual and Motor Skills*, 55, 555–558.

Gale, A. (1994) Futures for Applied Psychology. In Spurgeon, P., Davies, R. and Chapman, T. (eds.) *Elements of Applied Psychology.* Chur, Switzerland: Harwood Academic.

Galle, O. R., Gove, W. R. and McPherson, J. M. (1972) Population density and pathology: What are the relationships for man? *Science*, 176, 23–30.

Ganster, D. C., Mayes, B. T., Sime, W. E. and Tharp, G. D. (1982) Managing organisational stress: a field experiment. *Journal of Applied Psychology*, 67(5), 533–542.

Gardner, H. (1983) *Frames of Mind: The Theory of Multiple Intelligence.* New York: Basic Books.

Garfield, S. L. and Bergin, A. E. (1971) Personal therapy, outcome and some therapist variables. *Psychotherapy: Theory, Research and Practice*, 8, 251–253.

Garland, D. (1994) The Development of British Criminology. In Maguire, Morgan and Reiner (eds.) *The Oxford Handbook of Criminology.* Oxford: Clarendon Press.

Geberth, V. (1983) *Practical Homicide Investigation.* New York: Elsevier.

Geen, R. G. and O'Neal, E. C. (1969) Activation of cue-elicited aggression by general arousal. *Journal of Personality and Social Psychology*, 11, 289–292.

Gibson, J. J. (1979) *The Ecological Approach to Visual Perception.* Boston: Houghton Mifflin.

Gieselman, R., Fisher, R., MacKinnon, D. and Holland, H. (1986) Enhancement of eyewitness memory with the cognitive interview. *American Journal of Psychology*, 99, 385–401.

Gieselman, R. E., Fisher, R. Firstenberg, I., Holton, L., Sullivan, S., Aveztissina, I. and Prosh, A. (1984) Enhancement of eyewitness memory. *Journal of Police Science and Administration*, 12, 74–80.

Gieselman, R. E., Saywitz, K. J. and Bernstein, G. K. (1990) *Cognitive Interviewing Techniques for Child Victims and Witnesses of Crime.* Report to the State Justice Institute, Torrance, California.

Gifford, R. (1987) *Environmental Psychology: Principles and Practice.* Boston: Allyn and Bacon.

Gilbreth, F. B. (1911) *Motion Study.* New York: Van Norstrand.

Gill, D. L. (1986) *Psychological Dynamics of Sport.* Champaign, ILL: Human Kinetics Publishers.

Gill, D. L. (1988) Gender differences in competitive orientation and sport participation. *International Journal of Sport Psychology*, 19, 145–159.

Gill, D. L. (1992) Gender and sport behaviour. In Horn, T. S. (ed.) *Advances in Sport Psychology.* Champaign, ILL: Human Kinetics Publishers.

Gill, D. L. and Deeter, T. E. (1988) Development of the Sport Orientation Questionnaire. *Research Quarterly for Exercise and Sport*, 59, 191–202.

Gill, D. L. and Dzewaltowski, D. A. (1988) Competitive orientations among intercollegiate athletes: is winning the only thing? *The Sport Psychologist*, 2, 212–221.

Gillham, B. (ed.) (1978) *Reconstructing Educational Psychology.* London: Croom Helm.

Gist, R. and Lubin, B. (1989) *Psychosocial Aspects of Disasters.* Chichester: Wiley.

Goldstein, I. L. (1974) *Training: Programme Development and Evolution.* Monterey, CA: Brooks/Cole.

Goldstein, J. H. (1983) *Sports Violence.* New York: Springer-Verlag.

Golin, S., Sweeney, P. D. and Schaeffer, D. E. (1981) The causality of causal attributions in depression: a cross-lagged panel correlational analysis. *Journal of Abnormal Psychology*, 90, 14–22.

Good, T. L. and Brophy, J. E. (1991) *Looking in Classrooms*, 5th edn. New York: Harper Collins.

Goodman, G., Aman, C. and Hirschman, J. (1987) Child sexual abuse: children's testimony. In Ceci, S., Toglia, M. and Ross, D. (eds.) *Children's Eyewitness Memory*. New York: Springer-Verlag.

Gordon, R. A., Bindrim, T., McNicholas, M. and Walden, T. (1988) Perceptions of blue-collar and white-collar crime: The effect of defendant race on simulated juror decisions. *Journal of Social Psychology*, 128(2), 191–197.

Gordon, R. A. (1990) Attributions for blue-collar and white-collar crime: The effects of subject and defendant race on simulated juror decisions. *Journal of Applied Social Psychology*, 20(12), 971–983.

Gould, D., Horn, T. and Spreeman, J. (1983) Sources of stress in junior elite wrestlers. *Journal of Sport Psychology*, 5, 159–171.

Graham, S. and Barker, G. (1990) The downside of help: An attributional-developmental analysis of helping behaviour as a low ability cue. *Journal of Educational Psychology*, 82, 7–14.

Graham, S. (1991) A review of attribution theory in achievement contexts. *Educational Psychology Review*, 3, 5–39.

Green, P. (1985) Multi-ethnic teaching and the pupil's self-concept. In DES *Education for All*. London: HMSO.

Greenberg, R. L. (1989) Panic disorder and agoraphobia. In Scott, J., Williams, J. M. G. and Beck, A. T. (eds.) (1989) *Cognitive Therapy in Clinical Practice*. London: Routledge.

Gregory, R. L. (1966) *Eye and Brain*. New York: McGraw-Hill.

Gregory, R. L. (ed.) (1987) *The Oxford Companion to the Mind*. Oxford: Oxford University Press.

Gregory, W. L. and Burroughs, W. J. (1989) *Introduction to Applied Psychology*. London: Scott, Foresman and Company.

Gresswell, D. and Hollin, C. (1994) Multiple Murder: a review. *British Journal of Criminology*, 34, 1–14.

Griffin, C. (1986) *Black and White Youth in a Declining Job Market*. Leicester: Centre for Mass Communication Research.

Griffith, C. R. (1926) *Psychology of Coaching*. New York: Scribner.

Griffith, C. R. (1928) *Psychology of Athletics*. New York: Scribner.

Griffiths, R. (1970, reprinted 1984) *The Abilities of Young Children: The Griffiths Mental Development Scales*. Association for Research in Infant and Child Development: High Wycombe, Bucks, The Test Agency.

Gross, R. D. (1992) *Psychology: The Science of Mind and Behaviour*, 2nd edn. London: Hodder and Stoughton.

Gross, R. D. (1995) *Themes, Issues and Debates in Psychology*. London: Hodder and Stoughton.

Groth, N., Longo, R. E. and McFadin, J. B. (1982) Undetected recidivism among rapists and child molestors. *Crime and Delinquency*, 28, 450–458.

Guilford, J. P. (1959) Three faces of intellect. *American Psychologist*, 14, 4679.

Guilford, J. P. (1967) *The Nature of Human Intelligence*. New York: McGraw-Hill.

Gulian, E., Glendon, A. I., Matthews, G., Davies, D. R. and Debney, I. M. (1990) The stress of driving: A diary study. *Work and Stress*, 4(1), 7–16.

Guthrie, E. R. (1952) *The Psychology of Learning*. New York: Harper and Row.

Gutkin, T. B. and Curtis, M. J. (1982) School-Based Consultation: Theory and Techniques. In Reynolds, C. R. and Gutkin, T. B. (eds.) *The Handbook of School Psychology*. New York: Wiley.

Hackman, J. R. and Oldham, G. R. (1975) Development of the job diagnostic survey. *Journal of Applied Psychology*, 60, 159–170, 49.

Hackman, J. R. and Oldham, G. R. (1976) Motivation through the design of work: test of a theory. *Organisational Behaviour and Human Performance*, 16, 250–279.

Hackman, J. R. and Oldham, G. R. (1980) *Work Redesign*. Reading, MASS: Addison-Wesley.

Hall, E. T. (1966) *The Hidden Dimension*. Garden City, NY: Doubleday.

Halsey, A. H. (1972) Educational Priority, vol. 1. *EPA Problems and Policies*. London: HMSO.

Harari, H. and McDavid, J. W. (1973) Teachers' expectations and name stereotypes. *Journal of Educational Psychology*, 65, 222–225.

Hardy, L. and Fazey, J. F. (1987) The Inverted-U Hypothesis – a catastrophe for sport psychology. Paper presented at the meeting of the North American Society for the Psychology of Sport and Physical Activity, June 1987, Vancouver, B. C.

Hare, A. P. (1976) *Handbook of Small Group Research*, 2nd edn. New York: The Free Press.

Harris, D. M. and Guten, S. (1979) Health protective behavior: An exploratory study. *Journal of Health and Social Behaviour*, 20, 17–29.

Harter, S. (1978) Effectance motivation reconsidered. *Human Development*, 21, 34–64.

Harter, S. (1981) A model of intrinsic mastery motivation in children. In Collins, W. A. (ed.) *Minnesota Symposium on Child Psychology*, vol. 14, 215–255, Hillsdale, NJ: Erlbaum.

Hartshorne, H. and May, M. A. (1928) *Studies in the Nature of Character, vol. 1, Studies in Deceit.* New York: Macmillan.

Harvey, P. G. (1988) *Health Psychology.* London and New York: Longman.

Hastie, R., Penrod, S. and Pennington, N. (1983) *Inside the Jury.* Cambridge: Harvard University Press.

Hater, J. J. and Bass, B. M. (1986) Supervisors' evaluations of subordinates' perceptions of transformational and transactional leadership. Working paper, State University of New York: Binghampton.

Hawkings, S. (1992) *A Brief History of Time.* Cambridge: CUP.

Hawkins, N. G., Davies, R. and Holmes, T. L. H. (1957) Evidence of psychosocial factors in the development of pulmonary tuberculosis. *American Review of Tuberculosis and Pulmonary Diseases,* 75, 5.

Haynes, S. G., Feinleib, M. and Kannel, W. B. (1980) The relationship of psychosocial factors to coronary heart disease in the Framingham study. III: Eight-year incidence of coronary heart disease. *American Journal of Epidemiology,* III, 37–58.

Haynes, S. G., Levine, S., Scotch, N., Feinleib, M. and Kannel, W. B. (1978) The relationship of psychosocial factors to coronary heart disease in the Framingham study I: Methods and risk factors. *American Journal of Epidemiology,* 107, 362–383.

The Health of the Nation: a strategy for health in England (1992). HMSO.

Health Education Quarterly, 11, 1–47.

Hecker, M. H. L., Chesney, M. A. et al (1988) Coronary prone behaviour in the Western collaborative study. *Psychosomatic Medicine,* 50, 153–164.

Hegarty, S. and Lucas, F. (1979) *Able To Learn: The Pursuit Of Culture-Fair Assessment.* Windsor: NFER.

Heilmann, M. E., Hornstein, H. A., Cage, J. H. and Herschlag, J. K. (1984) Reactions to prescribed leader behaviour as a function of role perspective: The case of the Vroom–Yetton model, *Journal of Applied Psychology,* 69, 50–60.

Henderson, V. L. and Dweck, C. S. (1990) Motivation and achievement. In Feldman, S. S. and Elliott, G. R. (eds.) *At the Threshold: The Developing Adolescent.* Cambridge, MA: Harvard University Press.

Henschen, K., Edwards, S. and Mathinos, L., (1982) Achievement motivation and sex role orientation of high school female track and field athletes versus non-athletes. *Perceptual and Motor Skills,* 55, 183–187.

Herbert, G. (1989) A whole curriculum approach to bullying. In Tattum, D. P. and Lane, D. A. (eds.) *Bullying in Schools.* Stoke-on-Trent: Trentham Books.

Herridge, C. F. (1974) Aircraft noise and mental health. *Journal of Psychomotor Research,* 18, 239–243.

Herzberg, F. (1966) *Work and the Nature of Man.* Cleveland: World Publishing.

Herzberg, F., Mausner, B. and Snydermam, B. (1959) *The Motivation to Work.* New York: Wiley.

Hicks, C. M. and Spurgeon, P. C. (1994) The Child as Learner. In *Elements of Applied Psychology.* Chur, Switzerland: Harwood Academic, pp. 23–54.

Hicks, C. M., Spurgeon, P. C. and Parffrey, V. (1994) The Teacher and the Learning Environment. In *Elements of Applied Psychology.* Chur, Switzerland: Harwood Academic, pp. 55–78.

HMI Report (1990) *Educational Psychology Services in England 1988–1989.* London: Department of Education and Science.

Hobson, R. F. (1985) *Forms of Feeling.* London: Tavistock.

Hoelscher, T. J., Lichstein, K. L. and Rosenthal, T. L. (1986) Home relaxation practice in hypertension treatment: Objective assessment and compliance induction. *Journal of Consulting and Clinical Psychology,* 54, 217–221.

Hoffman, L. R. and Maier, N. R. F. (1961) Quality and acceptance of problem solutions by members of homogeneous and heterogeneous groups. *Journal of Abnormal and Social Psychology,* 62, 401–407.

Hollenbeck, J. R., Williams, C. R. and Klein, H. J. (1989) An empirical examination of the antecedents of commitment to different goals. *Journal of Applied Psychology,* 74(1), 18–23.

Hollin, C. (1992) *Criminal Behaviour: A Psychological Approach to Explanation and Prevention.* London: Falmer Press.

Hollon, S. D., DeRubeis, R. J. and Seligman, M. E. P. (1992) Cognitive therapy and the prevention of depression. *Applied and Preventive Psychology,* 1, 89–95.

Hollon, S. D., DeRubeis, R. J., Tuason, V. B., Weimer, M. J., Evans, M. D. and Garvey, M. J. (1989) *Cognitive Therapy, Pharmacotherapy, and Combined Cognitive-Pharmacotherapy in the Treatment of Depression: 1. Differential Outcome.* Unpublished manuscript, Vanderbilt University, Nashville, TN.

Hollway, W. (1991) *Work Psychology and Organizational Behaviour.* London: Sage.

Holmes, R. M. (1989) *Profiling Violent Crimes.* London: Sage.

Holmes, T. H. and Rahe, R. H. (1967) The social readjustment rating scale. *Journal of Psychosomatic Research*, 11, 213–218.

Horne, T. S. (ed.) (1992) *Advances in Sport Psychology*. Champaign, ILL: Human Kinetics Publishers.

Horner, M. S. (1972) Toward an understanding of achievement-related conflicts in women. *Journal of Social Issues*, 28, 157–186.

House, R. J., Spangler, W. D. and Woycke, J. (1991) Personality and charisma in the US presidency. A psychological theory of leader effectiveness. *Administrative Science Quarterly*, 36, 364–396.

Houston, B. and Snyder, C. R. (eds.) Type A Behaviour Pattern, Research, Theory and Intervention. New York: John Wiley.

Howard, K. I., Kopta, S. M., Krause, M. S. and Orlinsky, D. E. (1986) The dose–effect relationship in psychotherapy. *American Psychologist*, 41, 159–164.

Howard, K. I., Orlinsky, D. E., Saunders, S. M., Bankoff, E., Davidson, C. and O'Mahoney, M. (1991) Northwestern University – University of Chicago Psychotherapy Research Program. In Beutler, L. and Crago, M. (eds.) *Psychotherapy Research*, Washington DC: American Psychological Association.

Hughes, G. (1994) Whatever happened to the Sociology of Deviance? *Social Science Teacher*, 23, no. 2, pp. 9–11.

Hughes, M. (1975) *Egocentricity in Children*. Unpublished PhD thesis: Edinburgh University. Cited in Donaldson, M. (1978) *Childrens' Minds*. London: Fontana.

ILEA (1987) *Ethnic Background and Examination Results 1985 and 1986*. London: ILEA. In Hicks and Spurgeon, 1994 – see above.

Ingham, J. G. and Miller, P. McC. (1986) Self referral to primary care: symptoms and social factors. *Journal of Psychosomatic Research*, 30, 49–56.

ISSP (1992) Physical activity and psychological benefits: a position statement from the International Society of Sport Psychology. *Journal of Applied Sports Psychology*, 4, 94–98.

Jack, S. (1992) Certified to Perform. *Retail Week*, 6 Nov 1992.

Jacklin, C. N. (1989) Female and male: Issues of gender. *American Psychologist*, 44, 127–133.

Jackson, P. R., Mullarkey, S. and Parker, S. (1984) The implementation of high-involvement work teams: a four phase longitudinal study. Paper presented at the BPS Occupational Psychology Conference, January, 1994.

James, W. (1899) *Talks to Teachers on Psychology*. New York: Holt, Rinehart and Winston Inc.

Jamieson, D. W., Lydon, J. E., Stewart, G. and Zanna, M. P. (1987) Pygmalion revisited: New evidence for student expectancy effects in the classroom. *Journal of Educational Psychology*, 79, 461–466.

Janis, I. L. (1958) *Psychological Stress: Psychoanalytic and Behavioral Studies of Surgical Patients*. New York: Wiley.

Janis, I. L. (1972) *Victims of Groupthink: A Psychological Study of Foreign Policy decisions and fiascos*. Boston: Houghton Mifflin.

Janz, N. K. and Becker, M. H. (1984) The health belief model: a decade later. *Health Education Quarterly*, 11, 1–47.

Jeffrey, R. W. (1989) Risk behaviors and health: Contrasting individual and population perspectives. *American Psychology*, 44, 1194–1202.

Jencks, C., Smith, M., Acland, H., Bane, M. J., Cohen, D., Gintis, H., Heyns, B. and Michelson, S. (1975) *Inequality: A Reassessment of the Effects of Family and Schooling in America*. Harmondsworth: Penguin.

Jenkins, C. D. (1978) A comparative review of the interview and questionnaire methods in the assessment of the coronary prone behaviour pattern. In Dembrowski, T. M., Weiss, S. M., Shields, J. L., Haynes, S. and Feinleib, M. (eds.) *Coronary Prone Behaviour*. New York: Springer-Verlag.

Jenkins, C. D., Rosenman, R. H. and Friedman, M. (1967) Development of an objective psychological test for the determination of the coronary prone behaviour pattern in employed men. *Journal of Chronic Diseases*, 20, 371–379.

Jenkins, C. D., Zyanski, S. J. and Rosenman, R. H. (1979) *Jenkins Activity Survey Manual*. New York: Psychological Corporation.

Jepson, C. and Chaiken, S. (1990) Chronic issue-specific fear inhibits systematic processing of persuasive communications. *Journal of Social Behavior and Personality*, 5, 61–84.

Johnson, D. W. and Johnson, R. (1985) Classroom conflict: Controversy over debate in learning groups. *American Educational Research Journal*, 22, 237–256.

Johnson, D. W., Maruyama, G., Johnson, R., Nelson, D. and Skon, L. (1981) Effects of cooperative, competitive and individualistic goal structures on achievement: a meta-analysis. *Psychological Bulletin*, 89, 47–62.

Johnston, M. (1994) Current Trends. *The Psychologist*, 7(3), 114–118.

Jones and Aronson (1973) Attribution of fault to a rape victim as a function of respectability of the victim. *Journal of Personality and Social Psychology*, 26, 415–419.

Jones, E. E., Cumming, J. D. and Horowitz, M. J. (1988) Another look at the non-specific hypothesis of therapeutic effectiveness. *Journal of Consulting and Clinical Psychology*, 56, 48–55.

Jones, J. G. and Hardy, L. (1990) *Stress and Performance in Sport*. Chichester: Wiley.

Jones, M. C. (1924) A laboratory study of fear: The case of Peter. *Pedagogical Seminary*, 31, 308–315.

Jones, N. and Frederickson, N. (eds.) (1990) *Refocusing Educational Psychology*. Lewes: The Falmer Press.

Jung, C. G. (1930) Your Negroid and Indian behaviour. *Forum*, 83(4), 193–199.

Kabanoff, B. (1985) Potential influence structures as sources of interpersonal conflict in groups and organizations. *Organizational Behaviour and Human Decision Processes*, 36, 113–141.

Kahn, J. P., Kornfeld, D. S., Frank, K. A., Heller, S. S. and Hoar, P. F. (1980) Type A behavior and blood pressure during coronary artery by-pass surgery. *Psychosomatic Medicine*, 42, 407–414.

Kalven, H. and Ziesel, H. (1966) *The American Jury*. Boston: Little Brown.

Kane, M. (1982) The influence of level of sport participation and sex role orientation on female professionalization of attitudes toward play. *Journal of Sport Psychology*, 4, 290–294.

Kanner, A. D., Coyne, J. C., Schaefer, C. and Lazarus, R. S. (1981) Comparisons of two modes of stress management: daily hassles and uplifts versus major life events. *Journal of Behavioural Medicine*, 4, 1–39.

Kaplan, M. and Scherching, C. (1981) Juror deliberation: an information integration analysis. In Sales, B. (ed.) *The Trial Process*. New York: Plenum.

Kaplan, S. and Kaplan, R. (1982) *Cognition and Environment: Functioning in an Uncertain World*. New York: Praeger.

Kasl, S. V. and Cobb, S. (1966) Health behavior, illness behavior and sick role behaviour. In health and illness behaviour. *Archives of Environmental Health*, 12, 246–266.

Kehle, T. (1974) Teachers' expectations: ratings of student performance as biased by student characteristics. *Journal of Experimental Education*, 43, 54–60.

Kelly, G. A. (1955) *The Psychology of Personal Constructs*. New York: Norton.

Kenyon, G. S. (1968) Six scales for answering attitudes toward physical activity. *Research Quarterly*, 39, 566–574.

Kerr, J. H. (1990) Stress and sport: reversal theory. In Jones, J. G. and Hardy, L. (eds.) *Stress and Performance in Sport*, pp. 107–131. Chichester: Wiley.

Kerr, N. and Huang, J. W. (1986) Jury verdicts: how much difference does one juror make? *Personality and Social Psychology Bulletin*, 12, 325–343.

Kerr, N. L., Harmon, D. L. and Graves, J. K. (1982) Independence of multiple verdicts by jurors and juries. *Journal of Applied Psychology*, 12, 12–29.

Kirk, S. A., McCarthy, J. J. and Kirk, W. D. (1968) *Illinois Test of Psycholinguistic Abilities*. Chicago: University of Illinois Press.

Kittel, F., Kornitzer, M., Dramaix, M. and Beriot, I. (1993) Health behaviour in Belgian studies. Who is doing best? Paper presented at the European Congress of Psychology, Sept 1–3: Brussels.

Klaus, R. A. and Gray, S. W. (1968) The early training project for disadvantaged children: A report after five years. *Monographs of the Society for Research in Child Development*, 33, 4, serial no. 120.

Klerman, G. L., Weissman, M. M., Rounsaville, B. J. and Chevron, E. S. (1984) *Interpersonal Psychotherapy of Depression*. New York: Basic Books.

Kobasa, S. C. (1979) Stressful life events, personality and health: An inquiry into hardiness. *Journal of Personality and Social Psychology*, 39, 1–11.

Konecni, V. (1975) The mediation of aggressive behaviour: Arousal level vs anger and cognitive labelling. *Journal of Personality and Social Psychology*, 32, 706–712.

Kovrigin, S. D. and Mikheyev, A. P. (1965) The effect of noise level on working efficiency. *Report N65-28297*, Washington DC: Joint Publications Research Service.

Krahé, B. (1992) *Personality and Social Psychology: Towards a Synthesis*. London: Sage.

Kremer, J. M. and Scully, D. M. (1994) *Psychology In Sport*. London: Taylor and Francis.

Kryter, K. D. (1970) *The Effects of Noise on Man*. New York: Academic Press.

Labram, A. (1992) The Educational Psychologist as Consultant. In Wolfendale, S., Bryans, T., Fox, M., Labram, A. and Sigston, A. (1992) *The Profession and Practice of Educational Psychology: future directions*. London: Cassell Education Limited.

LaCrosse, M. B. (1980) Perceived counsellor social influence and counselling outcomes: Validity of the Counsellor Rating Form. *Journal of Counselling Psychology*, 27(4), 320–327, 1.

Lagenspitz, K. M. J., Bjorkquist, K., Berts, M. and King, E. (1992) Group aggression among school children in three schools. *Scandinavian Journal of Psychology*, 23, 45–52.

Lambert, J. F. and Olivereau, J. M. (1980) Single trial passive avoidance learning by rats treated with ionized air. *Psychological Reports*, 47, 1323–1330.

Lambert, M. J., Shapiro, D. A. and Bergin, A. E. (1986)

The effectiveness of psychotherapy. In Garfield, S. L. and Bergin, A. E. (eds.) *Handbook of Psychotherapy and Behaviour Change*, 3rd edn. New York: Wiley.

Landers, D. M. (1980) The arousal performance relationship revisited. *Research Quarterly for Exercise and Sport*, 51, 77–90.

Landers, D. M. (1989) Sport psychology: a commentary. In Skinner, J. S., Corbin, C. B., Landers, D. M., Martin, P. E. and Wells, C. L. (eds.) *Future Directions in Exercise and Sport Science Research*. Champaign, Ill.: Human Kinetics Publishers.

Landy, F. J. (1985) *Psychology of Work Behaviour*. Chicago, Ill.: The Doesey Press.

Langer, W. (1972) *The Mind of Adolph Hitler*. New York: Basic Books.

Last, J. (1963) The iceberg: completing the clinical picture in general practice. *Lancet*, 11, 28–31.

Latané, B. and Darley, J. M. (1968) Group inhibition of bystander intervention in emergencies. *Journal of Personality and Social Psychology*, 10, 215–221.

Latané, B., Williams, K. and Hawkins, S. (1979) Many hands make light work: the causes and consequences of social loafing. *Journal of Personality and Social Psychology*, 37, 822–832.

Latham, G. (1988) Human resource training and development. *Annual Review of Psychology*, 39, 545–582.

Lau, R. R., Kane, R., Berry, S., Ware, J. and Roy, D. (1980) Channelling health: A review of televised health campaigns. *Health Education Quarterly*, 7, 56–89.

Lawler, E. E. (1992) *The Ultimate Advantage*. San Francisco: Jossey-Bas.

Lazar, I. and Darlington, R. (1982) Lasting effects of early education. *Monographs of the Society for Research in Child Development*, 47, nos 2–3.

Lazarus, A. A. (1971) *Behaviour Therapy and Beyond*. New York: McGraw-Hill.

Lazarus, R. S. (1966) *Psychological Stress and the Coping Process*. New York: McGraw-Hill.

Lazarus, R. S. (1976) *Patterns of Adjustment*. New York: McGraw-Hill.

Lazarus, R. S. (1984) Puzzles in the study of daily hassles. *Journal of Behavioral Medicine*, 7, 375–389.

LDA Aston Index (1976) *Materials for Children with Learning Difficulties*. Wisbech, Cambs: LDA.

Le Unes, A. D. and Nation, J. R. (1989) *Sport Psychology: An Introduction*. Chicago, ILL: Nelson Hall.

Leach, D. J. and Siddall, S. W. (1990) Parental involvement in the teaching of reading: a comparison of hearing reading, pause, prompt and praise and direct instruction methods, *British*

Journal of Educational Psychology, 60, 349–355.

Lee, T. (1976) *Psychology and the Environment*. London: Methuen.

Lee, T. (1984) Environmental effects on behaviour. Talk given to the annual congress of psychology students in Ireland; Coleraine, University of Ulster.

Leith, L. (1991) Aggression. In Bull, S. J. (ed.) *Sport Psychology: A Self-Help Guide*. Crowood Press.

Lepper, M. R. and Hodell, M. (1989) Intrinsic motivation in the classroom. In Ames, C. and Ames, R. (eds.) *Research on Motivation in Education*, vol. 3, *Goals and Cognitions*, pp. 73–105.

Lepper, M. R., Greene, D. and Nisbett, R. E. (1973) Undermining children's intrinsic interest with extrinsic rewards: A test of the 'overjustification' hypothesis. *Journal of Personality and Social Psychology*, 28, 129–137. San Diego: Academic Press.

Lerner and Simmons (1966) Observers' reaction to the 'innocent victim': compassion or rejection. *Journal of Personality and Social Psychology*, 4, 203–210.

Leventhal, H. and Cleary, P. D. (1980) The smoking problem: A review of the research and theory in behavioral risk modification. *Psychological Bulletin*, 88, 370–405.

Levitt, E. (1980) *The Psychology of Anxiety*. Hillsdale, NJ: Erlbaum.

Levy-Leboyer, C. (1982) *Psychology and Environment*. London: Sage.

Lewin, K. (1951) *Field Theory in Social Science*. New York: Harper.

Lewin, K., Lippitt, R. and White, R. (1939) Patterns of aggressive behaviour in experimentally created 'social climates'. *Journal of Social Psychology*, 10, 271–299.

Lewinsohn, P. M., Mischef, W., Chapion, W. and Barton, R. (1980) Social competence and depression: The role of illusory self-perceptions. *Journal of Abnormal Psychology*, 89, 203–212.

Lewinsohn, P. M., Steimetz, J. L., Larsen, D. W. and Franklin, J. (1981) Depression-related cognitions: Antecedent or consequences? *Journal of Abnormal Psychology*, 90, 213–219.

Lewis, G., Croft-Jeffreys, C. and David, A. (1990) Are British psychiatrists racist? *British Journal of Psychiatry*, 157, 410–415.

Ley, P. (1988) *Communicating with Patients: Improving Communication, Satisfaction and Compliance*. London: Croom Helm.

Liberman, R. P. and Roberts, J. (1976) Contingency management of neurotic depression and marital disharmony. In Eysenck, H. J. (ed.) *Case Studies in Behaviour Therapy*. London: Routledge and Kegan Paul.

Lindsay, G. and Lunt, I. (1993) The challenge of change. *The Psychologist*, 6(5), 210–213.

Lindsay, S. J. E. and Powell, G. E. (eds.) (1994) *The Handbook of Clinical Adult Psychology*, 2nd edn. London: Routledge.

Linville, P. W. and Jones, E. E. (1980) Polarized appraisals of outgroup members. *Journal of Personality and Social Psychology*, 38, 689–673.

Lipowski, Z. J. (1986) What does the word 'psychosomatic' really mean? A historical and semantic enquiry. In Christie, M. J. and Mellet, P. G. (eds.) *The Psychosomatic Approach: Contemporary Practice and Whole Person Care*. New York: Wiley.

Littlewood, R. (1989) Cannabis psychosis. *Psychiatric Bulletin*, 13, 148–149.

Littlewood, R. and Lipsedge, M. (1982) *Aliens and Alienists: Ethnic Minorities and Psychiatry*. Harmondsworth: Penguin.

Llewelyn, S. P. (1994) Assessment and therapy in clinical psychology. In Spurgeon, P., Davies, R. and Chapman, T. (eds.) (1994) *Elements of Applied Psychology*. Reading: Harwood Academic.

Llewelyn, S. P., Elliott, R. K., Shapiro, D. A., Firth, J. A. and Hardy, G. E. (1988) Client perceptions of significant events in prescriptive and exploratory phases of individual therapy. *British Journal of Clinical Psychology*, 27, 105–114.

Locke, E. A. and Latham, G. P. (1984) *Goal Setting: A motivational technique that works!* Englewood Cliffs, NJ: Prentice-Hall.

Locke, E. A. and Latham, G. P. (1990) *A Theory of Goal Setting and Task Performance*. Englewood Cliffs, NJ: Prentice-Hall.

Loftus, E. (1974) The Incredible Eyewitness. *Psychology Today*, December, 117–119.

Loftus, E. (1979) *Eyewitness Testimony*. Cambridge, MASS: Harvard University Press.

Loftus, E., Loftus, G. and Messo, J. (1987) Some facts about 'weapon focus'. *Law and Human Behaviour*, 11, 55–62.

Loftus, E., Miller, D. and Burns, H. (1978) Semantic integration of verbal information into a visual memory. *Journal of Experimental Psychology: Human Learning and Memory*, 4, 19–31.

Lord, R. G., de Vader, C. L. and Alliger, G. M. (1986) A meta-analysis of the relation between personality traits and leadership perceptions: An application of validity generalisation procedures. *Journal of Applied Psychology*, 71, pp. 402–410.

Lorion, R. P. and Felner, R. D. (1986) Research on psychotherapy with the disadvantaged. In Garfield, S. L. and Bergin, A. E. (eds.) *Handbook of Psychotherapy and Behaviour Change*, 3rd edn.

New York: Wiley.

Lowenstein, L. F. (1978) Who is the Bully? *Bulletin of the British Psychological Society*, 31, 147–149.

Lubell, A. (1989) Does steroid abuse cause or excuse violence? *The Physician and Sports Medicine*, 17, 176–185.

Luborsky, L. (1984) *Principles of Psychoanalytic Psychotherapy: A Manual for Supportive-Expressive Treatment*. New York: Basic Books.

Luria, Z. and Rubin, J. Z. (1974) The eye of the beholder: parents' views on sex of newborns. *American Journal of Orthopsychiatry*, 44, 512–519.

Maass and Kohnken (1989) Eyewitness identification: simulating the weapon effect. *Law and Human Behaviour*, 13, 34–49.

Maas, A., Clark, R. D. III and Haberkorn, G. (1982) The effects of differential ascribed category membership and norm on minority influence. *European Journal of Social Psychology*, 12, 89–104.

Macaskill, N., Geddes, J. and Macaskill, A. (1991) DSM-III in the training of British psychiatrists: A national survey. *International Journal of Social Psychiatry*, 37(3), 182–186.

Macmillan Education Ltd (1989), Macmillan New Reading Analysis. Windsor: NFER NELSON.

Malan, D. (1976) *Toward the Validation of Dynamic Psychotherapy*, New York: Plenum Press.

Malan, D. (1979) *Individual Psychotherapy and the Science of Psychodynamics*. London: Butterworth.

Mann, A. W. and Brennan, P. (1987) Type A behavior and the incidence of cardiovascular disease: A failure to replicate the claimed associations. *Journal of Psychosomatic Research*, 31, 685–692.

Mann, S. (1993) Classifying special needs. In Gabbitas, Truman and Thring (ed. Derek Bingham) *Which School? for Special Needs*. Saxmundham, Suffolk: John Catt Educational Ltd, pp. 10–18.

Manpower Planning Advisory Group (1990) *Clinical Psychology Project: full report*. London: HMSO.

Manuch, S. B., Kaplan, J. R., Adams, M. R. and Clarkson, T. B. (1989) Behaviourally elicited heart rate re-activity and atherosclerosis in female cynomologus monkeys (macaca fascicularis). *Psychosomatic Medicine*, 51, 306–318.

Marks, D. F. (1994) Psychology's role in 'the health of the nation'. *The Psychologist*, 7, 3, 119–121.

Martens, R. (1977) *Sport Competition Anxiety Test*. Champaign, ILL: Human Kinetics Publishers.

Martens, R. (1980) From smocks to jocks: A new adventure for sports psychologists. In Klavora, P. and Wipper, K. A. W. (eds.) *Psychological and Sociological Factors in Sport*, pp. 3–19. Toronto, ON: University of Toronto.

Martens, R. (1982) *Sport Competition Anxiety Test.* Champaign, ILL: Human Kinetics Publishers.

Martens, R., Burton, D., Vealey, R. S., Bump, L. A. and Smith, D. (1990) Development and validation of the competition state anxiety inventory – 2. In Martens, R., Vealey, R. S. and Burton, D. (eds.) *Competitive Anxiety in Sport*, pp. 117–190. Champaign, ILL: Human Kinetics Publishers.

Martenuik, J. G. (1975) Information processing, channel capacity, learning stages and the acquisition of motor skill. In Whiting, H. T. A. (ed.) *Readings in Human Performance.* London: Lepus Books.

Martin, S. L. and Klimoski, R. J. (1990) Use of verbal protocols to trace cognitions associated with self- and supervisor emvaluations of performance. *Organizational Behaviour and Human Decision Processes*, 46(1), 135–154.

Marzillier, J. and Hall, J. (1992) *What is Clinical Psychology?* Oxford: Oxford University Press.

Matarazzo, J. D. (1980) Behavioral health and behavioral medicine: Frontiers for a new health psychology. *American Psychologist*, 35, 807–817.

Matthews, G., Dorn, L. and Glendon, A. I. (1991) Personality correlates of driver stress. *Personality and Individual Differences*, 12(6), 535–549.

Maxwell, R. J. (1984) Quality assessment in health. *British Medical Journal*, 288, 1470–1472.

Mayo, A. (1990) Personnel and the bottom line. *Employment Gazette*, February, 99–105.

Mayo, E. (1933) *The Human Problems of an Industrial Civilisation.* New York: Macmillan.

Mayo, E. (1927) cited in M. Rose (1975) *Industrial behaviour: Theoretical Developments Since Taylor.* Harmondsworth: Penguin.

McCall, I. and Farrell, P. (1993) Methods used by educational psychologists to assess children with emotional and behavioural difficulties. *Educational Psychology in Practice*, 9(3), 164–169.

McClelland, D. C., Atkinson, J., Clark, R. and Lowell, E. (1953) *The Achievement Motive.* New York: Appleton-Century-Croft.

McConnaughty, E. (1987) The person of the therapist in psychotherapeutic practice. *Psychotherapy: Theory, Research, Practice and Training*, 24, 303–314.

McGregor, D. (1960) *The Human Side of Enterprise.* New York: McGraw-Hill.

McGregor, D. (1967) *The Professional Manager.* New York: McGraw-Hill.

McGuire, W. J. (1985) Attitudes and attitude change. In Lindzey, G. and Aronson, E. (eds.) *Handbook of Social Psychology*, 3rd edn., vol. 2, pp. 233–364. New York: Random House.

McKechnie, G. E. (1974) *ERI Manual: Environmental Response Inventory.* Berkeley, CA: Consulting Psychologists Press.

McNally, J. and Orlick, T. (1975) Cooperative sport structures: a preliminary analysis. *Movement*, 7, 267–271.

Meade, R. D. (1967) An experimental study of leadership in India. *Journal of Social Psychology*, 72, 35–43.

Meadows, S. (1988) Piaget's contribution to understanding cognitive development: An assessment for the late 1980s. In Richardson, K. Sheldon, S. (eds.) *Cognitive Development in Adolescence.* Milton Keynes/Hove: Open University Press/Lawrence Erlbaum Associates Ltd.

Mechanic, D. (1978) *Medical Sociology*, 2nd edn. New York: Free Press.

Meichenbaum, D. and Goodman, J. (1971) Training impulsive children to talk to themselves: A means of developing self-control. *Journal of Abnormal Psychology*, 77, 115–126.

Melzack, R. H. (1975) The McGill Pain Questionnaire: Major properties and scoring methods. *Pain*, 1, 277–299.

Melzack, R. H. and Torgerson, W. S. (1971) The language of pain. *Anesthesiology*, 34, 50.

Melzack, R. H. and Wall, P. D. (1965) Pain mechanisms: A new theory. *Science*, 150, 971–979.

Merrett, F. and Wheldall, K. (1978) Playing the game: a behavioural approach to classroom management. *Educational Review*, 30, 41–50.

Meyer, J. P., Allen, N. J. and Smith, C. A. (1993) Commitment to organisations and occupations: extension and test of a three component conceptualisation. *Journal of Applied Psychology*, 78, 538–551.

Middleton, D. and Edwards, D. (1985) Pure and applied psychology: Re-examining the relationship. *Bulletin of the British Psychological Society*, 38, 146–150.

Miller, E. and Morley, S. (1986) *Investigating Abnormal Behaviour.* London: Weidenfeld and Nicolson.

Miller, G. A., Galanter, E. and Pribram, K. H. (1960) *Plans and the Structure of Behaviour.* New York: Holt, Rinehart and Winston.

Miller, N. E. (1978) Biofeedback and visceral learning. *Annual Review of Psychology*, 29, 373–404.

Milne, D., Britton, P. and Wilkinson, I. (1990) The scientist-practitioner in practice. *Clinical Psychology Forum.*

Milne, D. and Souter, K. (1988) A re-evaluation of the clinical psychologist in general practice. *Journal of the Royal College of General Practitioners*, 38, 4560.

Minard, R. D. (1952) Race relationships in the Pocahontas Coal Field. *Journal of Social Issues*, 8, 29–44.

Mischel, W. (1968) *Personality and Assessment*. New York: Wiley.

Mitchel, J. and O'Moore, M. (1988) *Report of the European Teachers' Seminar on Bullying in Schools*. Strasbourg: Council for Cultural Cooperation.

Mitchell, K. M., Bozarth, J. D. and Krauft, C. C. (1977) A reappraisal of the therapeutic effectiveness of accurate empathy, non-possessive warmth and genuineness. In Gurman, A. S. and Razin, A. M. (eds.) *Effective Psychotherapy: A Handbook of Research*. Oxford: Pergamon.

Morgan, P. (1975) *Child Care: Sense and Fable*. London: Temple Smith.

Morgan, W. P. (1969) Physical fitness and emotional health: A review. *American Corrective Therapy Journal*, 23, 124–127.

Morgan, W. P. (1979) Prediction of performance in athletics. In Klavora, P. and Daniel, J. V. (eds.) *Coach, Athlete, and the Sport Psychologist*, pp. 172–186. Champaign, ILL: Human Kinetics Publishers.

Morgan, W. P. (1980) The trait psychology controversy. *Research Quarterly for Exercise and Sport*, 51, 50–76.

Morgan, W. P. (1985) Selected psychological factors limiting performance: A mental health model. In Clarke, D. H. and Eckert, H. M. (eds.) *Limits of Human Performance*, pp. 70–80. Academy Papers no. 18, Champaign, ILL: Human Kinetics Publishers.

Morgan, W. P. (1989) Sport psychology in its own context: A recommendation for the future. Skinner, J. S., Corbin, C. B., Landers, D. M., Martin, P. E. and Wells, C. L. (eds.) *Future Directions in Exercise and Sport Science Research*. Champaign, ILL: Human Kinetics Publishers.

Morgan, W. P. and Pollack, M. (1977) Psychologic characterization of the elite distance runner. *Annals of New York Academy of Science*, 301, 382–403.

Morley, S. (1989) Single case research. In Parry, G. and Watts, F. N. (eds.) *Behavioural and Mental Health Research: A Handbook of Skills and Methods*. Hove and London: Erlbaum.

Mortimore, P., Sammons, P., Stoll, L., Lewis, D. and Ecob, R. (1988) *School Matters – The Junior Years*. London: Open Books.

Moscovici, S. (1985) Social influence and conformity. In Lindzey, G. and Aronson, A. (eds.) *The Handbook of Social Psychology*, 3rd edn. New York: Random House.

Mottaz, C. J. (1988) Determinants of organisational commitment. *Human Relations*, 41, 467–482.

Muchinsky, P. M. (1993) *Psychology Applied to Work: An Introduction to Industrial and Organisational Psychology*. Pacific Grove, CA: Brooks/Cole.

Münsterberg, H. (1908) *On the Witness Stand*. New York: Clark, Boardman.

Münsterberg, H. (1913) *Psychology and Industrial Efficiency*. Boston: Houghton Mifflin.

Murray, H. A. (1938) *Explorations in Personality*. New York: Oxford University Press.

Myers, A. (1962) Team competition, success and the adjustment of group members. *Journal of Abnormal and Social Psychology*, 65, 325–332.

Myers, C. S. (1926) *Industrial Psychology in Great Britain*. London: Jonathan Cape. Cited in Hollway, W. (1991) *Work Psychology and Organizational Behaviour*. London: Sage.

Nash, R. (1976) *Teacher Expectations and Pupil Learning*. London: Routledge and Kegan Paul.

Neale, M. D. (1989) *Neale Analysis of Reading Ability – Revised British Edition*.

Neisser, U. (1976) *Cognition and Reality: Principles and Implications of Cognitive Psychology*. San Francisco: W. H. Freeman.

Nemeth, C. J., Endicott, J. and Wachtler, J. (1976) From the '50s to the '70s: women in jury deliberations. *Sociometry*, 39, 38–56.

Nemeth, C. J. (1977) Interactions between jurors as a function of minority vs. unanimity decision rules. *Journal of Applied Social Psychology*, 7, 38–56.

Nemeth, C. J. (1986) Differential contributions of majority and minority influence. *Psychological Review*, 93, 23–32.

Newman, O. (1972) *Defensible Space*. New York: Macmillan.

Newsom Report (Central Advisory Council for Education) (1963) *Half Our Future*. London: HMSO.

Nicholson, N., Cole, S. G. and Rocklon, T. (1985) Conformity in the Asch situation: a comparison between contemporary British and American university students. *British Journal of Social Psychology*, 24, 91–98.

Nicolson, P. (1992) Gender issues in the organisation of clinical psychology. In Ussher, J. M. and Nicolson, P. (eds.) *Gender Issues in Clinical Psychology*. London: Routledge.

Noone, J. M. and Lewis, J. R. (1992) Therapeutic strategies and outcomes: perspectives from different cultures. *British Journal of Medical Psychology*, 65, 107–118.

Norback, D., Michel, I. and Widstrom, J. (1990) Indoor air quality and personal factors related to the sick building syndrome. *Scandinavian Journal of Work, Environment and Health*, 16(2), 121–128.

North, T. C., McCullagh, P. and Tran, Z. V. (1990) Effect of exercise on depression. In Pandolf, K. B. and Holloszy, J. O. (eds.) *Exercise and Sport Science Reviews*, 18, 379–415. Baltimore: William and Wilkins.

Nottingham NHS Psychologists (1988). Cited in Pilgrim, D. and Treacher, A. (1992) *Clinical Psychology Observed*. London: Routledge.

Novaco, R. W., Stokols, D. and Milanesi, L. (1990) Objective and subjective dimensions of travel impedance as determinants of commuting stress. *American Journal of Community Psychology*, 18(2), 231–257.

O'Sullivan, K. and Dryden, W. (1990) A survey of clinical psychologists in the S.E. Thames Health Region: Activities, role and theoretical orientation. *Clinical Psychology Forum*, 29: 21–26.

Ogilvie, B. C. (1968) Psychological consistencies within the personality of high-level competitors. *Journal of the American Medical Association*, 205, 780–786. Champaign, ILL: Human Kinetics Publishers.

Olweus, D. (1978) *Aggression in the Schools: Bullies and Whipping Boys*. London: Wiley.

Olweus, D. (1989) Bully/victim problems among schoolchildren: basic facts and effects of a school-based intervention program. In Rubin, K. and Pepler, D. (eds.) *The Development and Treatment of Childhood Aggression*. Hillsdale, NJ: Erlbaum.

Orlick, T. (1990) *In pursuit of excellence*, 2nd edn. Champaign, ILL: Human Kinetics Publishers.

Orne, M. T. (1962) On the social psychology of the psychology experiment: with particular reference to demand characteristics and their implications. *American Psychologist*, 17, 776–783.

Ouchi, W. (1981) *Theory Z: How American Business Can Meet the Japanese Challenge*. Reading, MA: Addison-Wesley.

Oyster-Nelson, C. K. and Cohen, L. H. (1981) The extent of sex bias in clinical treatment recommendations. *Professional Psychology*, 12(4), 508–515.

Page, R. A. (1977) Noise and helping behaviour. *Environmental and Behaviour*, 9, 559–572.

Paludi, M. A. (1992) *The Psychology of Women*. Dubuque, IA: W. M. Brown.

Parry, G. (1992) Improving psychotherapy services: Applications of research, audit and evaluation. *British Journal of Psychology*, 31, 3–19.

Pascale, R. T. (1985) The paradox of corporate culture: reconciling ourselves to socialisation. *California Management Review*, Winter.

Pascale, R. T. and Athos, A. G. (1981) The Art of

Japanese Management: Applications for American Executives. New York: Simon and Schuster.

Patrick, J. (1992) *Training: Research and Practice*. London: Academic Press.

Patrick, J. Michael, I. and Moore, A. (1986) *Designing for Learning – Some Guidelines*. Birmingham: Occupational Services Ltd.

Paul, G. L. (1981) Personal communication to. Cited in Davison, G. C. and Neale, J. M. (1994) *Abnormal Psychology*. New York: Wiley.

Paul, G. L. and Lentz, R. J. (1977) *Psychosocial Treatment of Chronic Mental Patients: Milieu Versus Social Learning Programs*. Cambridge, MA: Harvard University Press.

Paul, G. L. and Mendito, A. A. (1992) Effectiveness of inpatient treatment programs for mentally ill adults in public psychiatric facilities. *Applied and Preventive Psychology: Current Scientific Perspectives*, 1, 41–63.

Pavlov, I. P. (1927) *Conditioned Reflexes*. London: Oxford University Press.

Pennebaker, J. (1982) *The Psychology of Physical Symptoms*. New York: Springer-Verlag.

Pennington, N. and Hastie, R. (1986) Evidence evaluation in complex decision-making. *Journal of Personality and Social Psychology*, 51, 2, 242–258.

Pereira, D. (1986) Factors associated with transformational leadership in an Indian engineering firm. Paper given to 21st International Congress of Applied Psychology, Jerusalem.

Peters, L. H., Hartke, D. D. and Pohlmann, J. T. (1985) Fiedler's contingency theory of leadership: An application of the meta-analysis procedures of Schmidt and Hunter. *Psychological Bulletin*, 97, 274–285.

Peters, T. L. and Waterman, R. H. (1982) *In Search of Excellence: Lessons from America's Best-Run Companies*. New York: Harper and Row.

Pettibone, T. J. and Jernigan, H. W. (1989) Applied Psychology in Education. In Gregory, W. L. and Burroughs, W. J. (eds.) *Introduction to Applied Psychology*. Glenview, ILL: Scott Foresman.

Pfeifer, J. E. and Ogloff, J. R. (1991) Ambiguity and guilt determinations: A modern racism perspective. *Journal of Applied Social Psychology*, 21(21), 1713–1725.

Phares, E. J. (1992) *Clinical Psychology: Concepts, Methods and Profession*. Pacific Grove, CA: Brooks/Cole.

Phillips, J. J. (1990) *Handbook of Training Evaluation and Measurement Measures*. London: Kogan Page.

Phillips, R. D. (1985) The adjustment of men and women: Mental health professionals' views today.

Academic Psychology Bulletin, 7(2), 253–260.

Piaget, J. (1954) *The Construction of Reality in the Child*. New York: Basic Books.

Piaget, J. (1963) *Origins of Intelligence in Children*. New York: Norton.

Piaget, J. (1970) Piaget's theory. In Mussen, P. H. (ed.) *Carmichael's Manual of Child Psychology*, 3rd edn., vol. 1, pp. 703–732. New York: John Wiley.

Pilgrim, D. and Treacher, A. (1992) *Clinical Psychology Observed*. London: Routledge.

Pinizzotto, A. and Finkel, N. (1990) Criminal Personality Profiling: an outcome and process study. *Law and Human Behaviour*, 14(3), 215–231.

Platt, J. (1973) Social Traps. *American Psychologist*, 28, 641–651.

Plowden Report (Central Advisory Council for Education) (1967) *Children and their Primary Schools*. London: HMSO.

Plum, A. (1981) Communication as skill: a critique and alternative proposed. *Journal of Human Psychology*, 21, 3–19.

Premack, D. (1965) Reinforcement theory. In Levine, D. (ed.) *Nebraska Symposium on Motivation*. Lincoln, Neb.: University of Nebraska Press.

Pressley, M. and McCormick, C. B. (1995) *Advanced Educational Psychology for Educators, Researchers and Policy Makers*. New York: HarperCollins.

Price, K. P. (1979) Reliability of assessment of coronary-prone behavior with special reference to the Bortner Rating Scale. *Journal of Psychosomatic Research*, 23, 45–47.

Prien, E. P. (1977) The function of job analysis in content validation. *Personnel Psychology*, 30, 167–174.

Proshansky, H. M., Ittelson, W. H. and Rivlin, L. G. (1976) (eds.) *Environmental Psychology*, 2nd edn. New York: Holt, Rinehart and Winston.

Quicke, J. (1982) *The Cautious Expert*. Milton Keynes: Open University Press.

Rabbie, J. M., Benoist, F., Oosterbaan, H. and Visser, L. (1974) Differential power and effects of expected competitive and cooperative intergroup interaction upon intra- and outgroup attitudes. *Journal of Personality and Social Psychology*, 30, 46–56.

Rabbie, J. M. and Horowitz, M. (1969) Arousal of ingroup–outgroup bias by a chance win or loss. *Journal of Personality and Social Psychology*, 13, 269–277.

Rabkin, J. G. and Struening, E. L. (1976) Life events, stress and illness. *Science*, 194, 1013–1020.

Rack, P. (1991) *Race, Culture and Mental Disorder*. London: Routledge.

Rahe, R. (1974) The pathway between subjects' recent life changes and their near-future illness reports:

representative results and methodological issues. In Dohrenwend, B. S. and Dohrenwend, B. P., *Stressful Life Events: their nature and effects*. New York: Wiley.

Raven, J. C. (1965) *Raven's Matrices*. London: H.K. Lewis and Company Ltd.

Reason, J. (1990) *Human Error*. Cambridge: Cambridge University Press.

Reason, P. (ed.) (1994) *Participation in Human Inquiry*. London: Sage.

Ressler, R., Burgess, A. and Douglas, J. (1993) *Sexual Homicide*. London: Simon and Schuster.

Reynell, J. (1977) *Reynell Developmental Language Scales (Revised)*. Windsor: NFER.

Rhodewalt, F. and Zone, J. B. (1989) Approval of life change, depression and illness in hardy and nonhardy women. *Journal of Personality and Social Psychology*, 56, 81–88.

Riggio, E. R. (1990) *Introduction to Industrial Organisational Psychology*. Glenview, ILL: Scott, Foresman.

Rim, Y. (1975) Psychological test performance of different personality types on Sharav days in artificial air ionization. *International Journal of Biometeorology*, 21, 337–340.

Rimm, D. C. and Masters, J. C. (1979) *Behaviour Therapy: Techniques and Empirical Findings*, 2nd edn. New York: Academic Press.

Robertson, I. T. (1990) Behaviour modelling training: its record and potential in training and development. *British Journal of Management*, 1, 117–125.

Robertson, I. T. and Cooper, C. L. (1986) *Human Behaviour in Organisations*. London: Pitman Publishing.

Robinson, J. O. and Granfield, A. (1986) The frequent consulter in primary medical care. *Journal of Psychosomatic Research*, 30, 589–600.

Robson, M. H., France, R. and Bland, M. (1984) Clinical psychologists in primary care: controlled clinical economic evaluation. *British Medical Journal*, 288, 1805–1808.

Roethlisberger, F. J. and Dickson, W. J. (1939) *Management and the Worker*. Cambridge, MASS: Harvard University Press.

Rogers, C. R. (1957) The necessary and sufficient conditions of therapeutic personality change. *Journal of Consulting Psychology*, 21, 95.

Rogers, C. R. (1961) *On Becoming a Person*. Boston: Houghton Mifflin.

Rose, H. S. and Hinds, D. H. (1976) South Dixie contraflow bus and car-pool lane demonstration project. *Transportation Research Record*, 606, 18–22.

Rosen, S. (1985) The weather: Windy and grouchy. *The Catholic Digest*, 94–97.

Rosen, R. C. and Beck, J. G. (1988) *Patterns of Sexual Arousal: Psychophysiological Processes and Clinical Applications*. New York: Guilford.

Rosenhan, D. L. and Seligman, M. E. P. (1989) *Abnormal Psychology*. New York: Norton.

Rosenman, R. H. (1978a) The role of Type A behavior pattern in ischaemic heart disease: modification of its effects by beta-blocking agents. *British Journal of Clinical Practice*, 32, Supplement 1.

Rosenman, R. H. (1978b) The interview method of assessment of the coronary-prone behavior pattern. In Dembroski, T. M., Weiss, S. M., Shields, J. L., Haynes, S. G. and Feinleib, M. (eds.) *Coronary Prone Behavior*. New York: Springer-Verlag.

Rosenman, R. H., Friedman, M., Straus, R., Wurm, M., Kositchek, R., Hahn, W. and Werthessen, N. T. (1964) A predictive study of coronary heart disease: The Western Collaborative Group Study. *Journal of the American Medical Association*, 189, 15–22.

Rosenstock, I. (1974) The health belief model and preventive behavior. *Health Education Monographs*, 2, 354–386.

Rosenthal, R. (1966) *Experimenter effects in behavioural research*. New York: Appleton-Century-Crofts.

Rosenthal, R. and Jacobson, L. (1968) *Pygmalion in the Classroom*. New York: Holt.

Roth, I. (1990) *Introduction to Psychology*, vol. 2. Hove: LEA.

Rothwell-Miller (1968) Interest Blank. Oxford: NFER-Nelson Publishing Company.

Rotton, J. (1990) Stress. In Kimble, C. E. *Social Psychology*. Iowa: W. C. Brown.

Rubin, Z. and Peplau, L. (1975) Who Believes in a Just World? *Journal of Social Issues*, 31, no. 3, 65–89.

Rush, A. J., Beck, A. T., Kovacs, M. and Hollon, S. D. (1977) Comparative efficacy of cognitive therapy and pharmacotherapy in the treatment of depressed outpatients. *Cognitive Therapy and Research*, 1, 17–39.

Rutter, M. (1981) *Maternal Deprivation Reassessed*, 2nd edn. Harmondsworth: Penguin.

Rutter, M. and Madge, N. (1976) *Cycles of Disadvantage: A Review of Research*. London: Heinemann.

Rutter, M., Maughan, B., Mortimore, P., Ouston, J. and Smith, A. (1979) *Fifteen Thousand Hours: Secondary Schools and the Effects on Pupils*. London: Open Books.

Ryan, C. M. and Morrow, L. A. (1992) Dysfunctional buildings or dysfunctional people: an examination

of the sick building syndrome and allied disorders. *Journal of Consulting and Clinical Psychology*, 80(2), 220–224.

Sachs, M. L. (1982) Exercise and running: Effects on anxiety, depression and psychology. *Humanistic Education Development*, 21, 51–57.

Saks, H. (1977) The limits of scientific jury selection: ethical and empirical. *Jurimetrics Journal*, 17, 3–22.

Saks, M. J. and Krupat, E. (1988) *Social Psychology and its Applications*. New York: Harper and Row.

Salame, P. and Baddeley, A. D. (1989) Effects of background music on phonological short-term memory. *Quarterly Journal of Experimental Psychology*, 41, 107–122.

Sallis, J. F., Haskell, W. L., Fortmann, S. P., Vranizan, K. M., Taylor, C. B. and Solomon, D. S. (1986) Predictors of adoption and maintenance of physical activity in a community sample. *Preventive Medicine*, 15, 331–341.

Sallis, J. F. and Howell, M. F. (1990) Determinants of exercise behaviour. In Pandolf, K. B. and Holloszy, J. O. (eds.), *Exercise and Sport Science Reviews*, vol. 18, pp. 307–330. Baltimore: Williams and Williams.

Sarafino, E. P. (1993) *Health Psychology: Biopsychosocial Interactions*. New York: Wiley.

Sattler. J. M. (1982) *Assessment of Children's Intelligence and Special Abilities*, 2nd edn. Boston: Allyn and Bacon.

Saville, P. and Holdsworth, R. (1990) Occupational Personality Questionnaire. SHL Ltd: Surrey.

Sayers, J. (1992) Feminism, Psychoanalysis and Psychotherapy. In Ussher, J. M. and Nicolson, P. (eds.) *Gender Issues in Clinical Psychology*. London: Routledge.

Scambler, G. and Scambler, A. (1984) The illness iceberg and aspects of consulting behaviour. In Fitzpatrick, R., Hinton, J., Newman, S., Scambler, G. and Thompson, J. (eds.) *The Experience of Illness*. London: Tavistock.

Scanlan, T. and Lewthwaite, R. (1986) Social psychological aspects of competition for male youth sport participants: Part 4. Predictors of enjoyment. *Journal of Sport Psychology*, 8, 25–35.

Schein, E. H. (1988) *Organisational Psychology*, 3rd edn. Englewood Cliffs, NJ: Prentice-Hall.

Schmidt, R. A. (1975) A schema theory of discrete motor skill learning. *Psychological Review*, 82, 225–260.

Schmidt, R. A. (1988) *Motor Control and Learning: A Behavioural Emphasis*, 2nd edn. Champaign, ILL: Human Kinetics Publishers.

Schmidt, R. A. (1991) *Motor Learning and*

Performance. Champaign, ILL: Human Kinetics Publishers.

Schmidt, F. L., Hunter, J. E., McKenzie, R. C. and Muldrow, T. W. (1979) Impact of valid selection procedures on workforce productivity. *Journal of Applied Psychology*, 64, 609–626.

Schonell, F. J. and Goodacre, E. (1974) *The Psychology and Teaching of Reading*, 5th edn. Edinburgh: Oliver and Boyd. (Revised norms, 1971).

Schönpflug, W. (1992) Applied psychology: Newcomer with a long tradition? *Applied Psychology: An International Review*, 42, 5–66.

Schulberg, H. C. and Rush, J. (1994) Clinical practice guidelines for managing major depression in primary care practice: implications for psychologists. *American Psychologist*, 49(1), 34–41.

Schunk, D. H. (1991) Self-efficacy and academic motivation. *Educational Psychologist*, 26, 207–232.

Schwarzer, R. and Leppin, A. (1989) Social support and health: A meta-analysis. *Psychology and Health*, 3(1), 1–15.

Scott, J., Williams, J. M. G. and Beck, A. T. (eds.) (1989) *Cognitive Therapy in Clinical Practice: An Illustrative Casebook*. London: Routledge.

Scott, W. D. (1908) *The Psychology of Advertising*. New York: Amo Press.

Seager, M. and Jacobson, R. (1993) Two-plus-one: Misunderstood or incomprehensible? A reply to Davis et al. *Clinical Psychology Forum*, 26, 20–22.

Seamon, J. G. and Kendrick, D. T. (1992) *Psychology*. Englewood Cliffs, NJ: Prentice-Hall.

Seefeldt, V. and Steig, P. (1986) Introduction to an interdisciplinary assessment of competition on elite young distance runners. In Weiss, M. and Gould, D. (eds.) *Sport for Children and Youth*, pp. 213–217. Champaign, ILL: Human Kinetics Publishers.

Seligman, M. E. P. (1975) *Helplessness: On Depression, Development and Death*. San Francisco: W. H. Freeman.

Selye, H. (1950) *Stress*. Montreal: Acta.

Selye, H. (1956) *The Stress of Life*. New York: McGraw-Hill.

Selye, H. (1976) *Stress in Health and Disease*. Reading, MA: Butterworth.

Selye, H. (1985) History and present status of the stress concept. In Monat, A. and Lazarus, R. S. (eds.) *Stress and Coping*, 2nd edn. New York: Columbia University Press.

Shapiro, D. A. and Firth, J. (1987) Prescriptive v. exploratory psychotherapy: Outcomes of the Sheffield psychotherapy project. *British Journal of Psychiatry*, 151, 790–799.

Shapiro, D. A. and Shapiro, D. (1982) Meta-analysis of comparative therapy outcome studies: A replication and refinement. *Psychological Bulletin*, 92, 581–604.

Shapiro, M. B. (1985) A reassessment of clinical psychology as an applied science. *British Journal of Clinical Psychology*, 24, 1–11.

Sharp, B. (1992) *Acquiring Skill in Sport*. Eastbourne: Sports Dynamics.

Sharp, S. and Smith, P. K. (1991) *Bullying in U.K. Schools*. The DES Sheffield Bullying Project, Department of Psychology, University of Sheffield.

Shaw, B. F. (1977) Comparison of cognitive therapy and behaviour therapy in the treatment of depression. *Journal of Consulting and Clinical Psychology*, 45, 543–551.

Shekelle, R. B., Billings, J. H., Borhani, W. O., Gerace, T. A., Hulley, S. B., Jacobs, D. R., Lasser, N. L., Mittelmark, M. B., Neaton, J. D. and Stamler, J. (1985) The MRFIT behavior pattern study: II Type A behavior and incidence of coronary heart disease. *American Journal of Epidemiology*, 122, 559–570.

Sherif, M., Harvey, O. J., White, B. J., Hood, W. R. and Sherif, C. (1961) *Intergroup Cooperation and Competition: The Robbers Cave Experiment*. Norman: University of Oklahoma.

Short, M. (1993) Gifted or cursed? In Gabbitas, Truman and Thring (ed. Derek Bingham) *Which School? for Special Needs*. Saxmundham, Suffolk: John Catt Educational Ltd, pp. 28–29.

Siegler, R. S. (1991) *Childrens' Thinking*, 2nd edn. Englewood Cliffs, NJ: Prentice-Hall.

Sigall, H. and Ostrove, N. (1975) Beautiful but dangerous: effects of offender attractiveness and nature of the crime on juridic judgment. *Journal of Personality and Social Psychology*, 31, pp. 410–414.

Silvern, L. E. and Ryan, V. L. (1983) A re-examination of masculine and feminine sex role ideals and conflicts among ideals for the man, woman, and person. *Sex Roles*, 9(12), 1223–1248.

Singh, B. R. (1991) Teaching methods for reducing prejudice and enhancing academic achievement for all children. *Educational Studies*, 17(2), 157–171.

Skinner, B. F. (1938) *The Behaviour of Organisms: An Experimental Analysis*. New York: Appleton.

Skinner, B. F. (1953) *Science and Human Behaviour*. New York: Macmillan.

Skinner, B. F. (1961) Why we need teaching machines? *Harvard Educational Review*, 31, 377–398.

Skinner, B. F. (1972) *Beyond Freedom and Dignity*. Harmondsworth: Penguin.

Skinner, E. (1995) *Perceived Control, Motivation and Coping*. London: Sage.

Skov, P., Valbjorn, O. and Pedersen, B. V. (1989)

Influence of personal characteristics, job-related factors and psychosocial factors on the sick building syndrome. *Scandinavian Journal of Work, Environment and Health*, 15(4), 288–295.

Skov, P., Valbjorn, O., Pedersen, B. V. and Gravensen, S. (1990) The influence of indoor climate on the sick building syndrome in an office environment. *Scandinavian Journal of Work, Environment and Health*, 16(5), 363–371.

Slavin, R. E. (1994) *Educational Psychology: Theory and Practice*. Boston, MA: Allyn and Bacon.

Sloane, R. B., Staples, F. R., Cristol, A. H., Yorkston, N. J. and Whipple, K. (1975) *Psychoanalysis Versus Behaviour Therapy*. Cambridge, MA: Harvard University Press.

Slobin, D. I. (1975) On the nature of talk to children. In Lenneberg, E. H. and Lenneberg, E. (eds.) *Foundations of Language Development*, vol. 1. New York: Academic Press.

Smith, G. (1975a) Pre-school: the main experiment. In Smith, G. (ed.) *Educational Priority, vol. 4: The West Riding Project*. London: HMSO.

Smith, G. (1975b) Pre-school: the home visiting project. In Smith, G. (ed.) *Educational Priority, vol. 4: The West Riding Project*. London: HMSO.

Smith, M. and Robertson, I. T. (1993) *The Theory and Practice of Systematic Staff Selection*, 2nd edn. London: Macmillan.

Smith, M. L. and Glass, G. V. (1977) Meta-analysis of psychotherapeutic outcome studies. *American Psychologist*, 32, 752–760.

Smith, P. K. and Cowie, H. (1994) *Understanding Children's Development*, 2nd edn. Oxford: Blackwell.

Smith, R. E., Smoll, F. L. and Curtis, B. (1979) Coach effectiveness training: A cognitive-behavioural approach to enhancing relationship skills in youth sport coaches. *Journal of Sport Psychology*, 1, 59–75.

Soyka, F. and Edmonds, A. (1978) *The Ion Effect*. New York: Bantam.

Spearman, C. (1904) General intelligence, objectively determined and measured. *American Journal of Psychology*, 15, 201–293.

Spearman, C. (1927) *The Abilities of Man*. London: Macmillan.

Spence, J. T., Helmreich, R. and Stapp, J. (1974) The Personal Attributes Questionnaire: A measure of sex role stereotypes and masculinity–feminity. *JSAS Catalog of Selected Documents in Psychology*, 4(43), Ms. no. 617.

Spielberger, C. D. (1971) Trait-state anxiety and motor behaviour. *Journal of Motor Behaviour*, 3, 265–279.

Spielberger, C. D., Gorsuch, R. L. and Lushene, R. E. (1983) *Manual for the State-Trait Anxiety inventory*. Palo Alto, Calif: Consulting Psychologist Press.

Stagner, R. and Eflal, B. (1982) Internal union dynamics during a strike: a quasi-experimental study. *Journal of Applied and Social Psychology*, 51, 695–696.

Staley, C. C. and Shockley-Zalabak, S. (1986) Communication proficiency and future training needs of the female professional: self-assessment vs. supervisors' evaluations. *Human Relations*, 39(1), 891–902.

Stanton, A. L. (1987) Determinants of adherence to medical regimens by hypertensive patients. *Journal of Behavioral Medicine*, 10, 377–394.

Stasser, G., Kerr, N. and Bray, R. (1982) The social psychology of jury deliberations. In Kerr, N. and Bray, R. (eds.) *The Psycyhology of the Courtroom*. New York: Academic Press.

Stephenson, G. (1992) *The Psychology of Criminal Justice*. Oxford: Blackwell.

Sternberg, R. J. (1984) Toward a triarchic theory of human intelligence. *Behavioural and Brain Sciences*, 7, 269–287.

Stewart, M. and Corbin, C. (1988) Feedback dependence among low confidence preadolescent boys and girls. *Research Quarterly for Exercise and Sport*, 59, 160–164.

Stimson, G. V. and Webb, B. (1975) *Going to See the Doctor: The Consultation Process in General Practice*. London: Routledge and Kegan Paul.

Stogdill, R. M. (1974) *Handbook of Leadership: A Survey of Theory and Research*. New York: Free Press.

Stogdill, R. M. and Coons, A. E. (1957) *Leader Behaviour: Its Description and Measurement*. Columbus: Ohio State University.

Stokols, D. (1972) On the distinction between density and crowding: Some implications for future research. *Psychological Review*, 79, 275–277.

Stone, G. C., Cohen, F. and Adler, T. E. (eds.) (1979) *Health Psychology: A Handbook*. San Francisco: Jossey Bass.

Stoner, J. A. F. (1961) *A comparison of individual and group decisions involving risk*. Unpublished M.A. dissertation, Cambridge: M.I.T.

Stott, D. H. and Martston, N. C. (1971) *Bristol Social Adjustment Guides*. London: University of London Press.

Strauss, A. and Corbin, J. (1990) *Basics of Qualitative Research*. London: Sage.

Strodtbeck, F., James, R. and Hawkins, C. (1957) Social status injury deliberations. *American Sociological Review*, 22, 713–719.

Stroebe, W. and Stroebe, M. S. (1995) *Social Psychology and Health*. Buckingham: Open University Press.

Strube, M. J. and Garcia, J. E. (1981) A meta-analytic investigation of Fiedler's contingency model of leadership effectiveness. *Psychological Bulletin*, 90, 307–321.

Strupp, H. H. (1986) Psychotherapy – Research, practice and public policy (how to avoid dead ends). *American Psychologist*, 41, 120–130.

Summerfield Report (1968). London: HMSO.

Sundstrom, E., Burt, R. and Kamp, D. (1980) Privacy at work: Architectural correlates of job satisfaction and job performance. *Academy of Management Journal*, 23, 101–117.

Sutton, S. R. (1982) Fear-arousing communications: A critical examination of theory and research. In Eiser, J. R. (ed.) *Social Psychology and Behavioral Medicine*. Chichester: Wiley.

Sutton, S. R. and Hallett, R. (1988) Understanding the effect of fear-arousing communications. The role of cognitive factors and amount of fear aroused. *Journal of Behavioral Medicine*, 11, 353–360.

Swann Report (1985) *Education for All*. London: HMSO.

Sweeney, L. T. and Haney, C. (1992) The influence of race on sentencing: A meta-analytic review of experimental studies. *Behavioral Sciences and the Law*, 10(2), 179–195.

Tajfel, H., Flament, C., Billig, M. G. and Bundy, R. P. (1971) Social categorization and intergroup behaviour. *European Journal of Social Psychology*, 1, 149–178.

Tajfel, H. and Fraser, C. (1978) *Introducing Social Psychology: An Analysis of Individual Reaction and Response*. Harmondsworth: Penguin.

Tang, S.-H. and Hall, V. C. (1993) *Meta-Analytic Review of Overjustification*. Paper presented at the annual convention of the American Psychological Association, Toronto (August).

Tavris, C. (1993) The mismeasure of woman. *Feminism and Psychology*, 3(2), 149–168.

Taylor, D. (1987) Living with unemployment. In Walker, A. and Walker, C. (eds.) *The Growing Divide: A Social Audit 1979–1987*. London: Child Poverty Action Group.

Taylor, F. W. (1911) *The Principles of Scientific Management*. New York: Harper & Row.

Taylor, I. (1987) Putting the boot into a working-class sport: British soccer after Bradford and Brussels. *Sociology of Sport Journal*, 4, 171–191.

Taylor, J. C. (1975) Experiments in work system design: economic and human results. Unpublished paper: University of California, Los Angeles.

Taylor, S. E. (1991) *Health Psychology*. New York: Random House.

Terry, P. (1993) The psychology of the coach–athlete relationship. In Bull, S. J. (ed.) *Sport Psychology: A Self-Help Guide*. Marlborough: The Crowood Press Ltd.

Thom, R. (1975), translated by D. H. Fowler, *Structural Stability and Morphogenesis*. New York: Addison-Wesley.

Thorndike, E. L. (1903) *Educational Psychology*. Bureau of Publications, Teachers' College, Columbia University.

Thomas, K. W. (1976) Conflict and conflict management. In Dunnette, M. (ed.) *Handbook of Industrial and Organizational Psychology*, pp. 889–936. Chicago: Rand-McNally.

Thurstone, L. L. (1938) Primary mental abilities. *Psychometric Monographs*, 1.

Tizard, B. and Hughes, M. (1984) *Young Children Learning*. London: Fontana Paperbacks.

Tizard, B., Hughes, M., Carmichael, H. and Pinkerton, G. (1988) Language and Social Class: Is verbal deprivation a myth? In Woodhead, M. and McGrath, A. *Family, School and Society: A Reader*. Milton Keynes: Open University Press.

Tizard, J. (1973) Maladjusted Children and the Child Guidance Service. *London Educational Review*, 2, 22–37.

Tizard, J. (1978) Nursery needs and choices. In Bruner, J. S. and Garton, A. (eds.) *Human Growth and Development*. Milton Keynes: Open University Press.

Tolman, E. C. (1932) *Purposive Behaviour in Animals and Man*. New York: Century.

Tomlinson, S. (1983) *Ethnic Minorities in British Schools*. London: Heinemann.

Top, B. L. and Osguthorpe, R. T. (1987) Reverse-role tutoring: The effects of handicapped students tutoring regular class students. *Elementary School Journal*, 87, 413–423.

Topping, K. and McKnight, G. (1984) Paired reading – and parent power. *Special Education Forward Trends*, 11(3), 12–14.

Topping, K. (1992) Co-operative learning and peer tutoring: An overview. *The Psychologist*, 5(4), 151–157.

Trasler, G. (1987) Biogenetic factors. In Quay, H. C. *Handbook of Juvenile Delinquency*. New York: Wiley.

Trew, K. (1986) Catholic–Protestant contact in Northern Ireland. In Hewstone, M. R. C. and Brown,

R. J. (eds.) *Contact and Conflict in Inter-group Encounters.* Oxford: Blackwell.

Triplett, N. (1898) The dynamogenic factors in pacemaking and competition. *American Journal of Psychology*, 9, pp. 505–523.

Trist, E. A. and Bamforth, K. W. (1951) Some social and psychological consequences of the longwall method of coal-getting. *Human Relations*, 4, 3–38.

Truax, C. B. (1966) Reinforcement and non-reinforcement in Rogerian psychotherapy. *Journal of Abnormal Psychology*, 71, 1–9.

Truax, C. B. and Mitchell, K. M. (1971) Research on certain therapist skills in relation to process and outcome. In Bergin, A. E. and Garfield, S. L. (eds.) *Handbook of Psychotherapy and Behaviour Change.* New York: Wiley.

Tscheulin, D. (1971) Leader behaviour measurement in German industry. *Journal of Applied Psychology*, 56(1), 28–31.

Tuckman, B. W. (1965) Developmental sequence in small groups. *Psychological Bulletin*, 63, 384–399.

Turco, R. (1993) Psychological Profiling. *International Journal of Offender Therapy and Comparative Criminology*, pp. 147–154.

Turk, D. C., Meichenbaum, D. H. and Berman, W. H. (1979) Application of biofeedback for the regulation of pain: A critical review. *Psychological Bulletin*, 86, 1322–1338.

Turk, D. C., Meichenbaum, D. H. and Genest, M. (1983) *Pain and Behavioral Medicine: A Cognitive Behavioral Perspective.* New York: Guilford.

Turk, D. C., Rudy, T. E. and Salovey, P. (1984) Health protection: Attitudes and behaviors of LPNs, teachers and college students. *Health Psychology*, 3, 189–210.

Turk, D. C. and Rudy, T. E. (1986) Assessment of cognitive factors in chronic pain: A worthwhile enterprise? *Journal of Consulting and Clinical Psychology*, 54, 760–768.

Turk, D. C., Wack, J. T. and Kerns, R. D. (1985) An empirical examination of the 'pain-behavior' construct. *Journal of Behavioral Medicine*, 8, 119–130.

Turnbull, C. (1961) Some observations regarding the experiences of the Bambuti pygmies. *American Journal of Psychology*, 74, 304–308.

Turpin, G. (1995) Practitioner doctorates in clinical psychology. *The Psychologist*, 8(8), 356–358.

Turner, A. N. and Lawrence, P. R. (1965) *Industrial Jobs and the Worker.* Cambridge, Mass.: Harvard University Press.

Tyerman, M. (1993) What is assessment? In Gabbitas, Truman and Thring (ed. Derek Bingham) *Which*

School? for Special Needs. Saxmundham, Suffolk: John Catt Educational Ltd., pp. 5–9.

Ussher, J. M. (1991) *Women and Madness: Mysogyny or Mental Illness?* London: Harvester Wheatsheaf.

Ussher, J. M. (1992) Science sexing psychology: positivistic science and gender bias in clinical psychology. In Ussher, Jane and Nicolson, Paula (eds.) *Gender Issues in Clinical Psychology.* London: Routledge.

Ussher, J. M. and Nicolson, P. (1992) *Gender Issues in Clinical Psychology.* London: Routledge.

Uttal, B. (1983) The corporate culture vultures. *Fortune*, 17 October.

Vealey, R. S. (1986) Conceptualisation of sport confidence and competitive orientation: Preliminary investigation and instrument development. *Journal of Sport Psychology*, 221–246.

Vealey, R. S. (1989) Sport personology: A paradigmatic and methodological analysis. *Journal of Sport and Exercise Psychology*, 11, 216–235.

Veitch, R. and Arkkelin, D. (1995) *Environmental Psychology: An Interdisciplinary Perspective.* Englewood Cliffs, NJ: Prentice-Hall.

Vernimont, P. F. and Campbell, J. P. (1968) Signs, samples and criteria. *Journal of Applied Psychology*, 52, 372–376.

Vernon, P. E. (1961) *The Structure of Human Abilities.* London: Methuen.

Vernon, P. E. (1969) *Intelligence and Cultural Environment.* London: Methuen.

Vinokur, A., Burnstein, E., Sechrest, L. and Wortman, P. M. (1985) Group decision-making by experts: field study of panels evaluating medical technologies. *Journal of Personality and Social Psychology*, 49, 70–84.

Vroom, V. H. and Jago, A. G. (1978) On the validity of the Vroom–Yetton model. *Journal of Applied Psychology*, 63, 151–162.

Vroom, V. H. and Jago, A. G. (1988) *The New Leadership: Managing Participation in Organizations.* Englewood Cliffs, NJ: Prentice-Hall.

Vroom, V. H. and Yetton, P. W. (1973) *Leadership and Decision-making.* Pittsburg: University of Pittsburg.

Vygotsky, L. S. (1978) *Mind in Society: The Development of Higher Psychological Processes.* Cambridge, MA: Harvard University Press.

Vygotsky, L. S. (1986) *Thought and Language.* Cambridge, MA: MIT Press.

Wachs, T. D., Uzgiris, J. C. and McHunt, J. (1971) Cognitive development in infants of different age levels and from different environmental backgrounds. *Merrill-Palmer Quartlery of Behaviour Development*, 17, 288–317.

Wallach, M. A., Kogan, N. and Bem, D. J. (1962) Group influences on individual risk taking. *Journal of Personality and Social Psychology*, 65, 75–86.

Wankel, L. M. (1975) A new energy source for sport psychology research: Toward a conversion from D.C. (drive conceptualisations) to A.C. (attributional cognitions). In Landers, D. M. (ed.) *Psychology of Sport and Motor Behaviour*, vol. 2, pp. 293–314. Champaign, ILL: Human Kinetics Publishers.

Wardle, J. and Jackson, H. (1995) Prescribing priviliges for clinical psychologists. *The Psychologist*, 8(4).

Warnock Report (1978) *Special Educational Needs: Report of the Committee of Enquiry into the Education of Handicapped Children and Young People*. London: HMSO.

Warr, P. (1987) Job characteristics and mental health. In Warr, P. (ed.) *Psychology at Work*. Harmondsworth: Penguin.

Watson, D. and Pennebaker, J. W. (1989) Health complaints, stress and distress: Exploring the central role of negative affectivity. *Psychological Review*, 96, 234–254.

Watson, J. B. and Rayner, R. (1920) Conditioned emotional reactions. *Journal of Experimental Psychology*, 3, 1–4.

Wechsler, D. (1992) *Wechsler Intelligence Scale for Children*, 3rd edn. UK (WISC-111 UK). The Psychological Corporation, Sidcup, Kent: Harcourt Brace and Company.

Wechsler Objective Reading Dimensions (WORD) (1993), Psychological Corporation, Sidcup, Kent: Harcourt Brace and Company.

Wedge, B. (1968) Kruschev at a Distance – a study of public personality. *Transaction*, October, pp. 24–28.

Wedge, P. and Essen, J. (1982) *Children in Adversity*. London: Pan.

Weikart, D. P. and Schweinhart, L. J. (1992) High scope pre-school program outcomes. In McCord, J. and Trembley, R. E. (eds.) *Preventing Anti-Social Behaviour: Interventions from Birth Through Adolescence*. New York: Guilford Press.

Weinberg, R. S., Gould, D. and Jackson, A. (1979) Expectations and performance: an empirical test of Bandura's self-efficacy theory. *Journal of Sport Psychology*, 1, 320–331.

Weinberg, R. S. and Jackson, A. (1979) Competition and extrinsic rewards: Effect on intrinsic motivation. *Research Quarterly*, 50, 494–502.

Weinberg, R. S. and Ragan, J. (1979) Effects of competition, success/failure and sex on intrinsic motivation. *Research Quarterly*, 50, 503–510.

Weinberger, M., Hiner, S. L. and Tierney, W. M. (1987) In support of hassles as measures of stress in predicting health outcomes. *Journal of Behavioral Medicine*, 10, 19–31.

Weiner, B. (1979) A theory of motivation for some classroom experiences. *Journal of Educational Psychology*, 71, 3–25.

Weingarten, G., Furst, D., Tenenbaum, G. and Schaefer, U. (1984) Motives of Israeli youth for participation in sport. In Callaghan, J. L. (ed.) *Proceedings of the International Symposium 'Children to Champions'* (pp. 145–153). LA: University of Southern California.

Weinman, J. (1981) *An Outline of Psychology as Applied to Medicine*. Bristol: John Wright and Sons Ltd.

Weinman, J. (1990) Health psychology in the 1990s. In Drenth, P. J., Sergeant, J. A. and Takens, R. J. *European Perspectives in Psychology*, vol. 2, pp. 169–191. Chichester, New York: Wiley.

Weinstein, N. D. (1987) Unrealistic optimism about susceptibility to health problems: Conclusions from a community wide sample. *Journal of Behavioral Medicine*, 10, 481–500.

Weiss, M. R. and Chaumeton, N. (1992) Motivational orientations in sport. In Horn, T. S. (ed.) *Advances in sport psychology*. Champaign, ILL: Human Kinetics Publishers.

Wells, G. L. and Loftus, E. (1984) *Eyewitness Testimony: Psychological Perspectives*. New York: Cambridge University Press.

Wertheimer, (1944) *Productive Thinking*. New York: Harper.

West, J. and Spinks, P. (1988) *Clinical Psychology in Action*. Sevenoaks: Wright.

Westcott, H. (1992) The cognitive interview: a useful tool for social workers. *British Journal of Social Work*, 22, 519–533.

Wheldall, K. and Merrett, F. (1983) Good behaviour. *The Times Educational Supplement*, 25 November, 1983.

Wheldall, K. and Merrett, F. (1988) *Managing Troublesome Behaviour in Primary and Secondary Classrooms*. Birmingham: Positive Products.

Wheldall, K., Morris, M., Vaughan, P. and Ng, Y. Y. (1981) Rows versus tables: An example of the use of behavioural ecology on two classes of eleven-year-olds. *Educational Psychology*, 1(2), 171–184.

Wicker, A. W. (1969) Attitudes versus actions: the relationship of overt and behavioural responses to attitude objects. *Journal of Social Issues*, 25, 41–78.

Wilkins, W. and Glock, M. (1973) *Teacher Expectations and Student Achievement: A Replication*. Ithoca: Cornwall University Press.

Wilkinson, S. (1986) *Feminist Social Psychology.* Milton Keynes: Open University Press.

Wilkinson, S. (1989) The impact of feminist research: issues of legitimacy. *Philosophical Psychology*, 2(3), 261–269.

Williams, W. O. (1970) A study of general practitioners' workload in South Wales 1965–1966. *Reports from General Practice*, No. 10. Royal College of Practitioners.

Williams, J. M. (ed.) (1986) *Applied Sport Psychology.* Palo Alto, CA: Mayfield.

Williams, J. M., Dunning, E.G. and Murphy, P. J. (1984) *Hooligans Abroad: The Behaviour and Control of English Fans in Continental Europe.* London: Routledge and Kegan Paul.

Willis, J. D. and Campbell, L. F. (1992) *Exercise Psychology.* Champaign: ILL: Human Kinetics Publishers.

Wing, J. K., Cooper, J. E. and Sartorius, N. (1974) *Measurement and Classification of Psychiatric Symptoms.* London: Cambridge University Press.

Winnicott, D. W. (1953) Transitional objects and transitional phenomena. *International Journal of Psychoanalysis*, 34, 1–9.

Wittrock, M. C. and Farley, F. (1989) Toward a blueprint for educational psychology. In Wittrock, M. C. and Farley, F. (eds.) *The Future of Educational Psychology.* Hillsdale, NJ: LEA.

Wolfendale, S., Bryans, T., Fox, M., Labram, A. and Sigston, A. (1992). *The Profession and Practice of Educational Psychology: future directions.* London: Cassell Education Limited.

Wolpe, J. (1958) *Psychotherapy by Reciprocal Inhibition.* Stanford, CA: Stanford University Press.

Wood, D. (1988) *How Children Think and Learn.* Oxford: Blackwell.

Woolfolk, E. (1993) *Educational Psychology*, 5th edn. Needham Heights, MA: Allyn and Bacon.

World Health Organisation (1981) *Global Strategy for Health for All by the Year 2000.* Geneva: WHO.

World Health Organisation (1987) *International Statistical Classification of Diseases, Injuries and Causes of Death*, 10th revision. Geneva: WHO.

Wright, C. (1985) The influences of school processes on the educational opportunities of children of West Indian origin. *Multicultural Teaching*, 4(1), Autumn.

Yarmey, A. D. (1983) Is the psychology of eyewitness identification a matter of common sense? In Lloyd-Bostock, S. and Clifford, B. (eds.) *Evaluating Witness Evidence.* Chichester: Wiley.

Yerkes, R. M. and Dodson, J. D. (1908) The relation of strength of stimulus to rapidity of habit-formation. *Journal of Comparative Neurology and Psychology*, 18, 459–482.

Yetton, P. W. (1984) Leadership and supervision. In Gruneberg, M. and Wall, T. (eds.) *Social Psychology and Organisational Behaviour.* Chichester: Wiley.

Zajonc, R. B. (1965) Social facilitation. *Science*, 149, 269–274.

Zborowski, M. (1958) Cultural components in response to pain. In Jaco, E.G. (ed.) *Patients, Physicians and Illness.* Glencoe, ILL: Free Press.

Zimbardo, P. G. (1969) The human choice: Individuation, reason and order versus deindividuation, impulse and chaos. In Arnold, W. J. and Levine, D. (eds.) *Nebraska Symposium on Motivation, no. 17.* Lincoln, Nebraska: University of Nebraska Press.

Zuber-Skerritt, O. (1992) *Action Research in Higher Education.* London: Kogan Page.

GLOSSARY

ABILITY TEST Test of what a person can do in general, e.g. verbal reasoning

ACCELERATION/ACCELERATED LEARNING Attempt to speed up child's movement through changes in cognitive development using special teaching programmes

ACCOMMODATION Altering SCHEMA as a result of learning or problem-solving

ACHIEVEMENT MOTIVATION Desire to surpass own or others' achievements. Level of drive to succeed in any sphere of activity

ACTION RESEARCH Practical research intervention in everyday situations to produce change and monitor results

ACTION STRATEGIES Carefully thought out and planned ways which an organisation believes will lead it to its goals and objectives

ACTUAL CULTURE The set of values, assumptions and norms which truly determine how an organisation goes about its business; cf. ESPOUSED CULTURE

ACTUAL SELF The way a person thinks they are – relative to IDEAL SELF in the Rogerian approach

ACTUALISATION Motivation to grow and discover new positive experiences

ADDITIONAL DECREMENT Effect of events which are harmful in too small or too great a quantity

ADHERENCE The extent to which patients follow the medical advice of their doctor or other health professional, e.g. diet, drug regime, etc.; synonym – compliance

AFFECTIVE DISORDER Range of psychological problems which involve disruption of mood or affect, e.g. anxiety, depression

AGGRESSION Any action designed to hurt another person, who does not wish to be harmed

AGORAPHOBIA Debilitating NEUROTIC fear of open space or social/ physical contact outside a known and secure base, usually the home

ALARM REACTION The first stage of the GENERAL ADAPTATION SYNDROME as formulated by Hans Selye in which the body's resources are mobilised in its defence

AMBIENT STRESSORS Low/moderate environmental stressors affecting relatively large numbers of people

ANABOLIC STEROIDS Drugs similar in chemical nature to the male hormone testosterone. Increase muscle bulk, but can have serious side-effects

ANDROGYNOUS PERSONALITY Personality type incorporating a near equal balance of both masculine and feminine traditional traits or sex role factors

ANGINA PECTORIS A medical condition comprising the experience of chest pain which results from a reduction in the amount of oxygen supplied to the heart through a narrowing of the coronary arteries.

ANOREXIA NERVOSA Severe weight/appetite loss often through fear of being fat

APPLIED RESEARCH Research aimed at tackling a specific practical problem, not at furthering general theories

APPOINTED LEADERS Leaders who are chosen by some other party rather than by the people they are leading

APPRAISAL The mental processes people use in evaluating the degree to which a demand threatens their well-being.

AROUSAL The state of nervous excitation in organs controlled by the AUTONOMIC NERVOUS SYSTEM

ASSESSMENT CENTRE A method of personnel selection, conducted over a few days, which combines several methods of assessment, e.g. interviews, psychological tests, etc.

ASSESSMENT/ DIAGNOSTICIAN ROLE Early view of appropriate clinical psychologist role – to assess and diagnose but not to engage in therapy or medication

ASSIMILATION Forcing new stimuli/information into existing SCHEMA

ASSOCIATIVE PHASE OF SKILL LEARNING The initial stage of skill learning where instructional, verbal and cognitive components predominate

ATHEROSCLEROSIS A medical condition arising from the narrowing and hardening of the arteries through the development of fatty deposits on the inner walls

ATTAINMENT TEST Assessment of level reached (by child in reading and spelling, for example)

ATTENTION DEFICIT (HYPERACTIVITY) DISORDER An inability to focus and direct attention at an age-appropriate level (related to the child's inability to remain still long enough to focus attention)

ATTENTION DIVERSION STRATEGIES One of several cognitive strategies used to help people cope with pain experience by concentrating on diverting stimuli or activities, e.g. looking at pictures or singing a song

ATTENTIONAL FOCUS A performer's ability to concentrate on what is relevant and ignore what is irrelevant

ATTITUDE SCALE QUANTITATIVE self-report instrument measuring attitudes

ATTRIBUTION, INTERNAL AND EXTERNAL Ways in which we explain people's behaviour including our own; *internal* attributions explain behaviour according to enduring (internal) personality traits and intentions; *external* attributions appeal to causes *outside* the person (environmental and social pressures, accidents, etc.)

ATTRIBUTIONAL STYLE Person's habitual direction of ATTRIBUTION

AUTISM A disorder involving severe social and communication impairments often characterised by inappropriate emotional responses to people and objects

AUTOMACITY/AUTONOMOUS SKILL Stage in skill acquisition where performance is smooth, relatively error-free and learner performs with little direct conscious attention

AUTONOMIC NERVOUS SYSTEM The part of the peripheral nervous system which regulates emotional and hormonal responses

AUTONOMOUS PHASE OF SKILL LEARNING See AUTOMACITY

AVERSIVE THERAPY Association of aversive stimuli with undesired behaviour with the intention of eliminating or reducing that behaviour

BASE RATE OF SUCCESS The proportion of workers who achieve the required standards of work performance when a proposed selection method(s) is not used

BASELINE PERFORMANCE Normal level of performance unaffected by any independent variable; can refer to CONTROL GROUP performance

BASIC RESEARCH See FUNDAMENTAL RESEARCH

BEHAVIOUR MODIFICATION Alteration of behaviour patterns using OPERANT techniques

BEHAVIOUR SETTING Specific place in the environment which holds clues for appropriate roles and tends to produce similar behaviour irrespective of any personality difference

BEHAVIOUR THERAPY Alteration of behaviour using CLASSICAL CONDITIONING techniques, though may also refer generically to operant methods

BEHAVIOURAL ENGINEERING Skinner's term for psychologists' attempts to SHAPE behaviour according to scientific OPERANT methods

BEHAVIOURAL MEDICINE An interdisciplinary field that focuses on the relations between behaviour and health

BEHAVIOURAL RULES Informal learnt norms guiding our behaviour

BEHAVIOURAL SINK Specific physical settings which contain cues that control behaviour in that setting

BEHAVIOURIST APPROACH Belief that behaviour, not cognition, is the proper subject matter for psychology, though many now use cognitive concepts if they are fully OPERATIONALISED

BELIEF IN A JUST WORLD According to Lerner and Simmons (1966) people need to view the world as a fair place where 'we get what we deserve' in order to avoid feelings of vulnerability

BELIEF SYSTEMS Set of linked attitudes about object, e.g. about workers' motives

BIOFEEDBACK A procedure that enables an individual to monitor their own physiological processes, usually via auditory or visual cues, in order to gain voluntary control over such processes, e.g. blood pressure or heart rate

BIOGENIC AMINE Chemical substances which interact with the nervous system, e.g. adrenaline, nor-adrenaline

BIOLOGICAL PSYCHOLOGY Approach concentrating on explanations of human behaviour as caused by electrical and chemical events within the body, especially the brain and central nervous system

BIOMEDICAL MODEL An explanatory model of illness in which physical factors, such as infection or trauma, are considered to be the sole causes of illness

BIOPSYCHOSOCIAL MODEL An explanatory model of health and illness which involves the interplay of biological, psychological and social factors

BLOOD PRESSURE The pressure of the blood against the inner walls of the blood vessels

BOTTOM-UP PROCESSES Hypothetical cognitive processes; environmental objects are recognised by perceptual analysis of specific elements, e.g. lines, comprising what is being perceived – see TOP-DOWN PROCESSES

BRAINSTORMING Group problem-solving method involving production of *any* ideas with no initial criticism, hence all ideas are given an airing

BRIEF PSYCHOANALYTIC/ DYNAMIC PSYCHOTHERAPY Relatively short, economic version of PSYCHOANALYTIC therapy where some reactions are provoked rather than awaited

BUFFERING HYPOTHESIS The view that the positive effect of social support on health arises from its ability to reduce the adverse health consequences of high levels of stress

BULIMIA Episodic binge eating, followed by purging, e.g. vomiting

CARDIOVASCULAR FITNESS HYPOTHESIS Theory that improved mental health through exercising is due to improved functioning of the heart and circulatory systems

CARDIOVASCULAR SYSTEM The system comprising the heart and blood vessels through which blood is circulated around the body providing oxygen and nutrients to the cells and removing waste materials

CARE IN THE COMMUNITY UK government's scheme to release patients from long-term care into the community with professional support/resourcing

CARPENTERED WORLD HYPOTHESIS Theory that susceptibility to many (but not all) geometric visual illusions is made more accute by living in a typically industrialised, built (and hence 'carpentered') environment

CASE STUDIES In-depth study of one individual or group, often QUALITATIVE

CATABOLIC PROCESSES Those physiological processes which are involved in the release of energy from reserves stored in the body

CATACLYSMIC STRESSORS Highly stressful events affecting relatively large numbers and acute in length

CATASTROPHE THEORY A mathematical model which aims to explain the relationship between multi-dimensional anxiety and sport performance

CENTRALISED COMMUNICATION Centralised patterns involve more control by some/a few people at the centre of a communication network, with others dependent on them for information

CENTRED/CENTRING Taking only one aspect of a multi-aspect situation into account, e.g. focusing on height not width of a tumbler

CHARISMATIC LEADERSHIP A leader who inspires pride, confidence and a sense of purpose not because of formal authority but because of a set of personal qualities

CHARTERING System operated by BPS under which psychologists may, under certain conditions of qualification, advertise their 'chartered' status which acts as a guarantee of professional competence and submission to BPS standards

CHRONIC DISEASES Diseases that persist for a long period of time and are usually progressive, e.g. diabetes, multiple sclerosis

CLASS INCLUSION Sorting of items into classes and sub-classes

CLASSICAL CONDITIONING Process in which an UCS is paired systematically with a CS to produce a CR; learning simply by association of stimuli

CLIENT-CENTRED THERAPY Rogerian therapy emphasising client's own active role in self-improvement and growth away from psychological disorder

CLINICAL INTERVIEW/METHOD Interview method with general structure/goals but permitting flexible response to interviewee's replies

CLINICAL PSYCHOLOGY Psychology applied to the assessment and alleviation of personal psychological problems

CLOSED LOOP THEORY/MOTOR CONTROL Movement controlled by the comparison of the desired outcome with feedback. Useful at explaining slow tracking movements such as steering a car or bicycle

CLOSED SKILL A skill executed with little reference to the environment, e.g. diving, target shooting

CO-OPERATIVE LEARNING/WORKING Learning in a group which learns together and/or each team member is essential in the solution of a problem

CODING SYSTEM System to categorise originally QUALITATIVE DATA

COGNITIVE APPROACH/PSYCHOLOGY Psychological perspective emphasising active and interpretive nature of human information processing

COGNITIVE ANXIETY The intrusive negative fears and worries a performer experiences prior to or during a game or event

COGNITIVE (BEHAVIOUR) THERAPY (CT/CBT) Cognitive therapy concentrates almost entirely on 'FAULTY' THOUGHT patterns and assumes these control MALADAPTIVE behaviour; CBT uses a mixture of behavioural and cognitive methods

COGNITIVE CONFLICT Conflict of information which motivates learner to seek solutions and therefore increase their learning

COGNITIVE DELAY A level of reasoning and understanding below that expected at a given chronological age

COGNITIVE-DEVELOPMENTAL PARADIGM A theoretical framework of child development emphasising the relationship between ability to reason and developmental level

COGNITIVE DISSONANCE Theory that attitudes are likely to change where dissonant elements (factors contrary to one's view) and consonant elements (factors in tune with one's view) are badly unbalanced in favour of dissonant elements (dissonance)

COGNITIVE INTERVIEW A technique devised by Gieselman et al (1986) using mnemonics to assist witness recall

COGNITIVE MAPS Tolman's early term for 'schema' implying that the behaviour of intelligent organisms is not randomly emitted but is controlled by the use of previously stored information

COGNITIVE PHASE OF SKILL LEARNING The earliest stage in the learning of a new skill . The 'rules' of the skill are being clarified

COGNITIVE PSYCHOLOGY/MODEL Approach seeing mental events (cognition) as the subject matter of psychology and/or underlying cause of behaviour; 'cognitive psychology' can also refer to study of cognitive performance and this may be performed in a BEHAVIOURISTIC manner – with clearly defined behavioural criteria

COGNITIVE RESOURCE THEORY Later version of Fiedler's (1967) CONTINGENCY theory of leadership which took into account the level of SITUATION FAVOURABILITY, the leader's LPC score and additional features such as the leader's use of intelligence and experience appropriate to specific situations

COGNITIVE REVOLUTION Late 1960s/1970s/1980s switch from BEHAVIOURAL to COGNITIVE emphasis in psychological explanations and research

COGNITIVE STYLES Person's typical way of processing and giving meaning to experience, reflected in typical ways of responding

COMMUNITY PSYCHOLOGY Psychology applied in a HOLISTIC manner to social problems affecting substantial sections of one community

COMMUNITY SCHOOLS Schools offering close community links through parental involvement and community action

COMPENSATORY EDUCATION PROGRAMMES Attempts to compensate for disadvantage by providing increased educational stimulation

COMPETENCE MOTIVATION A motive and desire to become accomplished in an activity

CONCURRENT FEEDBACK Feedback available to the performer whilst the skill is being executed, e.g. split times while racing

CONCURRENT VALIDITY Extent to which PREDICTOR scores CORRELATE with scores of current personnel on a work performance criterion. (Also refers to validation of a new measure by correlation with an existing measure, in general psychological testing)

CONDITIONAL KNOWLEDGE Knowledge of when and where it is appropriate to use previously learned facts and skills

CONDITIONAL POSITIVE REGARD See POSITIVE REGARD

CONDITIONAL RESPONSE (CR) Response to previously neutral stimulus caused by association of that stimulus with UCS which originally triggered the response

CONDITIONAL STIMULUS (CS) Previously neutral stimulus which produces a response (CR) after constant pairing with a stimulus (UCS) which originally produced that response (UCR)

CONDITIONING Process of systematically altering an organism's behaviour using environmental manipulation

CONDITIONS OF WORTH Conditions person feels they must conform to in order to value themselves but which were originally set by others

CONFORMITY The tendency for people to change their opinions and behaviour in ways which are consistent with group norms

CONFOUNDING VARIABLE Variable which is uncontrolled and obscures any effect sought, usually in a systematic manner

CONJOINT THERAPY Therapy with both members of a couple

CONSERVATION Understanding that major attributes of objects (such as weight) do not change after superficial alterations (e.g. to shape)

CONSULTANCY MODELS Model in which 'experts' enable clients to solve their own problems

CONTACT HYPOTHESIS Theory that prejudice and stereotyping can be reduced by increasing contact between stereotypers and stereotyped

CONTENT ANALYSIS Analysis of QUALITATIVE DATA such as media reports, diaries, descriptions, verbal reports, and so on by CODING, categorisation and rating

CONTINGENCY THEORIES View that successful leadership depends on an *interaction* between personality type, behaviour and situation variables

CONTINGENT TEACHING Provision of information when learner requires help but without an overload of passively learnt factual information

CONTROL GROUP 'No-treatment' group compared against EXPERIMENTAL GROUP

CONTROLLED OBSERVATION Observation in which many variables are kept constant

COPING The process by which individuals try to deal with stress

CORONARY HEART DISEASE A class of illnesses which arise as a result of the disease of the heart or blood vessels, e.g. arteriosclerosis; thrombosis

CORRELATION Extent to which two variables statistically vary together

CORRELATIONAL STUDY Study in which two or more non-experimental variables are measured and the strength of the association between them is assessed

COUNSELLING PSYCHOLOGY Growing branch of psychology specialising in counselling – support and therapy for people's problems not counted as illness or of clinical severity

COUNTER-CONDITIONING See SYSTEMATIC DESENSITISATION

CRIMINOLOGICAL PSYCHOLOGY Psychology applied to the criminal justice system, criminal behaviour, its management, and the apprehension of criminals

CRITERION CONTAMINATION Occurs when performance ratings are influenced by the rater's knowledge of how an employee has scored on a set of PREDICTOR(S)

CRITERION SCORE A score which reflects the quality (good/bad) of the work performance of an employee; to be compared with earlier PREDICTORS

CRITERION VALIDITY The extent to which a test measure (PREDICTOR) predicts scores on some measure or criterion of (work) performance

CRITERION-REFERENCED TEST Test of specific tasks child can do, with no peer comparison

CROWDING Substantial invasion of PERSONAL SPACE

CULTURAL DEPRIVATION Idea that apparent lower ability within some identifiable cultural groups is caused by lack of certain experiences within that culture and environment

CULTURE-FREE TESTS Test (e.g. of general intelligence) where attempt is made to avoid contamination/bias from any particular cultural background.

CULTURE-SPECIFIC TESTS Tests designed to apply only to, and therefore only STANDARDISED upon, one specific cultural group

CUMULATIVE EFFECT Effect of events of which we require a minimum but which are not harmful in large quantities

CUT-OFF SCORE Score which is the dividing line between what is considered satisfactory and unsatisfactory performance, i.e. minimum score for a pass

CYCLE OF DISADVANTAGE Assumed cycle in which an environment of poverty and weak education, especially of parents, produces people who cannot improve their position

DEAF NORMS Test norms obtained from a representative sample of deaf or hearing-impaired people and hence relevant to that population

DECENTRALISED COMMUNICATION Networks with less central control and with individuals sharing more information with one another than in CENTRALISED networks

DECENTRE (ABILITY TO) Ability to avoid CENTRING and to take more than one aspect of a situation into account at the same time; facilitates CONSERVATION

DECLARATIVE KNOWLEDGE Knowledge which can be stated, often in the form of the 'rules' of a situation; what goes with what or causes what to happen

DEFENCE MECHANISMS In psychoanalytic thought a strategy employed by the EGO to reduce anxiety caused by conflict (e.g. between SUPER-EGO and ID); distorts reality; can become too dominant and create NEUROSIS

DEFENSIBLE SPACE Area around residential property marked to specify ownership

DEINDIVIDUATION Theoretical state of person who temporarily loses self-identity and takes up the perhaps unacceptable behaviour of a crowd

DEMAND CHARACTERISTICS Cues which convey experimental hypothesis to the participant

DEPENDENT VARIABLE (DV) Variable assumed to be directly affected by changes in the INDEPENDENT VARIABLE

DESCRIPTIVE STATISTICS Methods for numerical summary of sample data

DETERMINISM See FREEWILL

DIAGNOSTIC TEACHING Teaching designed to explore and assess specific areas of learning difficulty for the individual child

DIFFERENCE MODEL Model interpreting (cultural) group differences in terms of environmental variations and not as an internal 'deficit'

DIFFERENTIAL PSYCHOLOGY Study of individual differences between people's personalities and abilities

DIFFUSION OF RESPONSIBILITY Phenomenon where people in a crowd feel that they are less individually responsible since so many others are involved

DISCOVERY LEARNING Process believed by many educationalists to underlie most effective learning; learners 'own' knowledge because they discover rules or systems for themselves

DISCRIMINATIVE STIMULUS Stimulus associated with delivery of REINFORCEMENT

DISEASE An abnormal bodily condition

DISEASES OF ADAPTATION Diseases which arise as a consequence of prolonged activation of the body's stress response, e.g. ulcers, high blood pressure, heart problems

DISTRACTION HYPOTHESIS A theory which suggests that exercise improves mental health because it proves a distraction from everyday worries and concerns

DISTRIBUTIVE PRACTICE Regular memory rehearsal over a period of time

DOUBLE BLIND Experimental procedure where neither participants *nor* data gatherer/assessor know which treatment participants have received

DOUBLE MINORITIES A group with a minority view who are *also* identifiable as a minority (e.g. Asian); this latter minority status is usually irrelevant to the issue

DRIVE THEORY A complex, although rather dated theory, which aimed to show a linear relationship between arousal and sport performance

DYNAMIC PSYCHOTHERAPY See BRIEF PSYCHOANALYTIC THERAPY

DYSCALCULA Inability to deal with mathematical functions at an age appropriate level, relative to other average ability levels

DYSFUNCTIONAL BEHAVIOUR Wide range of problem behaviours seen as having a detrimental effect on human functioning; behaviours as diverse as alcohol and drug abuse, childhood aggression

DYSLEXIA Difficulty in learning to read, often accompanied by spelling/writing difficulty, in children of otherwise average range intellectual ability

DYSPRAXIA Condition affecting body muscle control and consequent co-ordination; may affect muscles involved in speech sounds

ECLECTIC Use of more than one approach or 'school' of treatment

ECOLOGICAL APPROACH (IN EDUCATIONAL PSYCHOLOGY) View that child's development occurs in a network of relationships and is affected at various levels from parent, school, neighbourhood to overall culture

ECOLOGICAL PSYCHOLOGY View that behaviour cannot be separated from physical settings and is more influenced by these than personality factors

ECOLOGICAL VALIDITY Extent to which study and its demonstrated effects may be generalised to other places and conditions

EDUCATIONAL PSYCHOLOGY Psychology applied in the cause of helping children and young people, particularly in the fields of learning and behaviour

EDUCATIONALLY SUB-NORMAL An earlier term for pupils with learning difficulties, considered offensive and limiting

EFFICACY Some measure of the effectiveness of a therapy or treatment

EGO Freud's area of personality dealing with reality, ID/SUPER-EGO conflicts and largely conscious

EGOCENTRICITY Inability to see a situation from any perspective other than one's own

ELABORATED LANGUAGE CODES Language form once assumed to be more likely to be used by the middle class; more objectively exact and generally understandable; relied less on 'local' sense and metaphor

EMERGENT LEADER That group member who is chosen by his/her group to lead them, usually because of his/her personal qualities

EMOTIONAL AND BEHAVIOURAL DIFFICULTIES Emotion handling problems and behaviour patterns interfering with adaptation to the classroom and the learning process

EMPATHY Ability to see/feel emotion from other's point of view; one of three therapist characteristics thought necessary by Rogers for effective NON-DIRECTIVE THERAPY

EMPTY ORGANISM MODEL View that psychology can usefully study stimuli into organism and resultant responses without speculating on internal causes

ENDORPHIN A morphine-like substance produced within the body

ENRICHMENT Adaptation of curriculum for advanced or 'gifted' children

ENTITY VIEW OF INTELLIGENCE View that intelligence is a fixed 'thing' relatively unmodifiable

ENVIRONMENTAL PSYCHOLOGY Psychology applied to the study of transactions between individuals and their physical and social environments

EPISODIC MEMORY Memory for events

EQUILIBRATION Constant attempt to reduce COGNITIVE CONFLICT through problem-solving

ERGONOMICS Psychological study of human behaviour in relation to machines, tools and equipment so as to maximise the person-machine fit

ESPOUSED CULTURE Values, beliefs, norms and assumptions which an organisation would like the outside world to see as guiding the behaviour of its members; cf. ACTUAL CULTURE

ETHNOCENTRIC View of another culture through one's own cultural perspective

EUROCENTRIC View of other cultures through a European perspective only

EXPECTANCY Tendency of experimenter's or participants' knowledge of what is being tested to influence the outcome of research

EXPECTANCY X VALUE THEORY Theory that motivation to achieve a goal is affected by a *combination* of how much the goal is valued and an estimation of how likely the goal is to be achieved

EXPERIMENT Study where INDEPENDENT VARIABLE is manipulated, all variables are controlled and allocation of participants to conditions is RANDOM

EXPERIMENTAL GROUP Group receiving 'treatment' in EXPERIMENT

EXPLANATORY STYLE Distinctive manner in which people tend to explain their world and their experiences, especially success and failure, within it

EXPRESSIVE LANGUAGE Child's ability to communicate

EXTERNAL RELIABILITY Test stability; tendency to produce same results when measures are repeated

EXTINCTION (THERAPY) Reduction of strength of behavioural response consequent upon removal of any REINFORCEMENT (classical or operant) EXTINCTION THERAPY – see OPERANT THERAPY

EXTRINSIC MOTIVATION Motivation from external stimuli – rewards or punishments delivered *to* the person rather than emanating from *within* the person (as would internal task satisfaction)

FACTOR ANALYSIS Statistical location of 'clusters' from patterns of test or sub-test CORRELATIONS, providing support for theoretical constructs

FAILURE ACCEPTERS Stage reached by FAILURE AVOIDERS when their avoidance strategies are leading to eventual failure

FAILURE AVOIDERS Suggested extreme type of learner who does not question, believes intellectual growth is unlikely and uses unhelpful defences in explaining any shortcomings

FAULTY THINKING COGNITIVE THERAPY's assumption that psychological maladjustment is caused by self-destructive thinking

FEAR OF SUCCESS A phenomenon claimed to be common among female athletes, a fear of being successful in a predominantly male activity

FEEDBACK Information passed back to learner/performer giving information on progress (towards goal)

FEMINIST PSYCHOANALYSIS Contemporary version of PSYCHOANALYSIS not accepting original masculine bias but emphasising positive aspects of femininity and seeing causes of psychological problems in masculine bias, aggression and maladjustment

FEMINIST PSYCHOLOGY Emphasis on women's perspective and on methods suitable to research which integrates gender politics

FIELD DATA Data collected in the field, not in laboratory

FIELD EXPERIMENT/STUDY Experiment/study in naturalistic surroundings, not laboratory

FITTING THE JOB TO THE WORKER (FJW) Intervention at the job level meant to change jobs in such ways that they suit the mental and physical characteristics of those doing them

FITTING THE WORKER TO THE JOB (FWJ) Intervention in order to find the best person for a given job, either by changing a person's characteristics, e.g. through training, or by selecting an alternative suitable person

FLASHBULB MEMORY A term used by Brown and Kulik (1977) to describe people's vivid recall of what they were doing at the time of emotionally significant events, e.g. the death of J. F. Kennedy

FLOODING BEHAVIOURAL THERAPY where client tackles most feared situation early on in an attempt to decondition a phobia

FORENSIC PSYCHOLOGY See CRIMINOLOGICAL PSYCHOLOGY

FORMULATION Summary of client's problem with tentative speculations/ hypotheses about causes and appropriate treatment

FREE ASSOCIATION Attempt by client to report any association to therapist's terms or prompts without modification or blocking

FREEWILL AND DETERMINISM Debate concerning the extent to which behaviour is freely produced by choice or caused directly by prior events.

FRUSTRATION-AGGRESSION THEORY A theory which aims to explain the cause of aggression by suggesting that barriers to a goal cause frustration

FULL CYCLE MODEL Cialdini's (1980) research model advocating multiple methods to validate each other. Real-world observations can lead to laboratory experiments and these, in turn, to field studies

FUNCTIONAL ANALYSIS (BEHAVIOURIST) analysis of behaviour into small observable units and their association with triggering events/stimuli

FUNCTIONAL DISORDERS Psychiatric disorders with no known physical root or cause

FUNDAMENTAL RESEARCH Research aimed only at furthering knowledge of the subject in itself, not aimed at solving practical problems

GAME REASONING A type of thinking which legitimises aggression or rule breaking

GATE CONTROL THEORY Explanation of people's experience of pain based on the concept of a 'neural gate' which can be open or closed thereby controlling the degree to which pain signals are sent to the brain

GENDER SCHEMA Collection of general beliefs and attitudes about male or female psychological traits

GENERAL ADAPTATION SYNDROME The physiological reaction to prolonged stress comprising three stages – the alarm reaction, the stage of resistance and the stage of exhaustion. Formulated by Hans Selye

GENUINENESS One of three therapist characteristics thought necessary by Rogers for effective NON-DIRECTIVE THERAPY

GESTALT PSYCHOLOGY Approach emphasising the wholeness and interrelated nature of perception: 'the whole is greater than the sum of its parts'

GOAL SETTING THEORY Theory that people are motivated by clear, specific, moderately challenging goals not by general requests to 'try to do better'

GOOD INFORMATION PROCESSORS Cognitive psychologists' view of good learners possessing several useful problem-solving strategies

GROUNDED THEORY Qualitative research approach stressing the emergence of (relatively local) theory *from* gathered data rather than the idea of obtaining data to test an existing (more general) theory

GROUP COHESIVENESS Extent to which group operates effectively with little conflict

GROUP FORMATION The different stages and processes which a group of strangers go through before they become a well-organised group, with a common goal, and are able to perform harmoniously

GROUP IDENTITY Group members' sense of belonging and loyalty to their group

GROUP POLARISATION Tendency of groups to make decisions more extreme than, but in the same direction as, the average individual member's initial position

GROUP SOCIALISATION The methods used to teach newly recruited group members behaviours that are and are not acceptable within the group

GROUPTHINK Tendency of isolated, close-knit groups to make decisions which seem extremely unwise or irrational from a measured perspective

HARDY PERSONALITY A set of characteristics including a sense of commitment, control and challenge, which enables an individual to view potentially stressful events as less threatening than would those without such characteristics

HASSLES Everyday, low-level problems or unpleasant events which may produce STRESS if they persist over time

HAWTHORNE EFFECT Effect on participants of being the focus of investigation

HAWTHORNE STUDIES Series of studies/experiments conducted by Elton Mayo and his colleagues in the 1920s at the Hawthorne works of the Western Electric Company. These studies led to shift in focus from working conditions to social factors and their influence on performance

HEALTH A positive state of physical, psychological and social well-being

HEALTH BEHAVIOUR Any activity undertaken by individuals in order to enhance or maintain their health

HEALTH BELIEF MODEL Explanation of people's health-related behaviour based on their perception of the threat of the health problem and an analysis of the costs and benefits of taking preventive action

HEALTH PSYCHOLOGY Psychology applied to issues in the maintenance of health and the development, treatment and prevention of illness

HEDONIC TONE Personal interpretation of arousal as pleasant or unpleasant

HIDDEN CURRICULUM The (often unrecognised) influence of school environment, expectations and teaching styles on the child's beliefs and values

HIERARCHICAL TASK ANALYSIS Analysis of task by breaking it into constituent sub-routines and sub-tasks in a 'family tree' pattern

HIGH SCOPE Structured, child-centred teaching approach emphasising the child's own planning and review of learning

HOLISTIC Concentrating on the whole person as opposed to the study of separated aspects such as personality TRAITS or intelligence FACTORS

HOMEOSTASIS Optimal operating state of the individual, deviations from which tend to cause negative effects and motivate the individual to restore the previous balance

HOSTILE AGGRESSION Angry aggression, designed to injure an opponent

HUMAN FACTORS PSYCHOLOGY Sub-area of OCCUPATIONAL PSYCHOLOGY concerned with the study of compatibility between tools/machines/systems and the characteristics of human operators

HUMAN RELATIONS SCHOOL/MOVEMENT A movement which stresses the importance of and influence of social factors (e.g. interpersonal relationships) on work performance

HUMANISTIC APPROACH Theories (especially of Rogers and Maslow) concerned with the 'self'; tend to be HOLISTIC; emphasise personal growth and (SELF-) ACTUALISATION

HYGIENE FACTORS A set of job aspects, identified by Herzberg, which if absent in a job cause dissatisfaction

HYPERTENSION A condition of persistent high BLOOD PRESSURE

HYPOTHESIS Prediction about data relationship made from underlying theory

HYPOTHETICO-DEDUCTIVE METHOD Logical framework underlying the traditional scientific method in which observation promotes theory which in turn promotes HYPOTHESIS; hypothesis is tested and results are taken as support for or refutation of the theory.

ICEBERG PROFILE A healthy mood profile, where vigour is high and tension, depression, fatigue, confusion and anger are low

ID Freud's primary aspect of self – based on instinctive drives

IDEAL SELF (Perfect) self as one would like to be

IDIOGRAPHIC Emphasis on unique characteristics of individual; methods tend to study one case in depth

IMAGERY Strategy to control pain. The individual imagines a scene which is unconnected to or incompatible with the pain

IMPLOSION Desensitisation therapy in which client faces worst fear situation at the outset but only through imagery or with artificial fear objects (e.g. plastic spider)

INCENTIVES Means used to motivate people at work. SCIENTIFIC MANAGEMENT advocates that monetary incentives are the best means to motivate people at work

INCONGRUENCE Rogerian term for distance between aspects of self, especially between IDEAL and ACTUAL SELF; source of anxiety

INCREMENTAL VIEW OF INTELLIGENCE View that intellectual ability can be nurtured; attempt and failure are a natural route to eventual ability and understanding

INDEPENDENT VARIABLE (IV) Variable which experimenter manipulates in an experiment and which is assumed to have a direct affect on the DV

INDIVIDUALISM Cultural emphasis on separate, independent self rather than on one's relationships with others

INDUSTRIAL PSYCHOLOGY This is the old name for OCCUPATIONAL PSYCHOLOGY. It reflected the early focus on work efficiency in the industrial sector

INFERENTIAL STATISTICS Methods used to establish STATISTICAL SIGNIFICANCE

INFORMATION PROCESSING MODEL A model of human behaviour, which draws comparisons between the way in which humans interact with their environment and computers process information

INFORMATIONAL SOCIAL INFLUENCE Occurs when people, wishing to be correct in their judgements, are influenced by others' views to determine accuracy

INSTINCT THEORY OF AGGRESSION A psychodynamic theory suggesting that aggression is a basic characteristic of human behaviour

INSTRUMENTAL AGGRESSION IN SPORT Aggression, where the aggressor is not angry, the motivation for the act is to win, e.g. boxing

INSTRUMENTAL LEARNING/ CONDITIONING MODEL See OPERANT MODEL

INTER-OBSERVER (OR INTER-RATER) RELIABILITY Extent to which observers/raters agree in their use of RATING or CODING scales; assessed by CORRELATION

INTER-ROLE CONFLICT Conflict from the occupation of more than one role by one person

INTERACTION PROCESS ANALYSIS System developed by Bales (1953, 1970) for categorising the contributions of members to a group discussion/problem solution

INTERACTIONIST MODEL (TRAITS VS SITUATION) Theory of personality seeing behaviour as product of interaction between situational factors and enduring individual characteristics

INTERMITTENT REINFORCEMENT REINFORCEMENT for only a certain number of responses or for those occurring after a certain time; increases strength of response

INTERNAL MEDIATING RESPONSES SOCIAL LEARNING THEORY's terminology for internal events (mostly thoughts) which explain the link between stimulus and response in more complex behaviour patterns

INTERNAL RELIABILITY Consistency of a measure; extent to which scale items tend to be measuring the same thing and are not in opposition to one another

INTERVENTION STUDY Research where a major goal is to improve the life situation of participants or people associated with them, often through behaviour change using new resources and training

INTRA-ROLE CONFLICT Conflict between two irreconcilable aspects of a person's specific role

INTRINSIC MOTIVATION Motivation from *within* the person, rather than external rewards or punishments, e.g. internal satisfaction in completing a task

ISCHAEMIA A medical condition in which heart tissues are deprived of oxygen through a reduction in the blood supply to the heart

ITEM ANALYSIS Checking each scale item's contribution to overall INTERNAL RELIABILITY

JIGSAW METHOD Group problem-solving method where each member holds an essential part of the solution, so all members are instrumental

JOB ANALYSIS Well thought-out and carefully conducted study of jobs to determine their requirements and the human qualities required to meet such requirements

JOB CHARACTERISTICS MODEL Those features in a job which are believed to affect work attitudes and work behaviour. (Hackman and Oldham's (1976) model emphasising the effects of task features, autonomy and feedback on psychological states which in turn affect motivation, satisfaction and work performance.)

JOB DESCRIPTION A detailed description of the tasks, duties, responsibilities, procedures, inputs, outputs, working conditions etc. in relation to a given job

JOB DIAGNOSTIC SURVEY Name of questionnaire designed to measure the core job characteristics identified by the JOB CHARACTERISTICS MODEL

JOB ENRICHMENT An intervention aimed at redesigning jobs so as to give job holders greater autonomy in how to do their jobs and greater job responsibility

JOB ROTATION An intervention aimed at enabling workers to work in different job positions to prevent boredom and to enable the acquisition of new knowledge and skills

JOB SPECIFICATION A list of human qualities required for successful job performance as seen in many job advertisements

JUST-IN-TIME Manufacturing production technique in which parts are received at a work-point only when required, with the aim of avoiding bottlenecks

KNOWLEDGE OF PERFORMANCE (KP) Feedback which refers to aspects of the movement performed, e.g. keeping one's eye on the ball

KNOWLEDGE OF RESULTS (KR) Feedback which refers to the effectiveness of a movement in succeeding in its goal, e.g. scoring a goal

LABELLING THEORY View that 'labelling' a child can produce further reaction from others such that the child's behaviour might eventually be seen as fitting the label or actually does fit the label

LANGUAGE (NUMBER, SPELLING, WORD READING) AGE If a child performs at a level equal to that of the average X year old, they are said to have a language (etc.) age of X, irrespective of their actual age

LEADER-MEMBER RELATIONS Factors concerning quality of interpersonal relations between leader and team members, affecting leader effectiveness (Fiedler, 1967)

LEARNED HELPLESSNESS Condition of apathy resulting from experience of no situational control

LEARNING GOALS Goal of learning for its own sake no matter how one may appear to others

LEARNING THEORY Theory of learning based largely on conventional BEHAVIOURIST principles of CONDITIONING and REINFORCEMENT processes

LEAST PREFERRED CO-WORKER (LPC) A measure of a person's attitude to co-workers

LENIENCY BIAS The tendency for jury deliberations to produce a tilt towards acquittal

LEVEL OF PROCESSING Level to which incoming verbal material is analysed

LEVEL OF SIGNIFICANCE Probability value at which it is agreed to reject NULL HYPOTHESIS; probability is of result occurring *if null hypothesis is true*

LEVELS OF ANALYSIS Levels at which causes for behaviour are sought, ranging from intra-individual through groups to the level of society or culture

LIFE EVENTS Occurrences in people's lives which necessitate some degree of adjustment, e.g. marriage, birth of a child

LIFE STRESSORS Severe, individually oriented stressful events, e.g. divorce

LONG-TERM MEMORY (LTM) Relatively permanent storage of material in the cognitive system

MALADAPTIVE Description of behaviour thought to require therapy since it harms others or the individual producing it

MANAGERIAL GRID® Two-dimensional grid on which managers can be placed according to their level of 1) task orientation and 2) person orientation

MASSED PRACTICE Continuous rehearsal of task or verbal material within short period of time

MASTERY-ORIENTED Attribute of effective learners who accept failure as part of the learning process, who independently correct errors and who set themselves achievable but challenging goals

MEDICAL MODEL View of psychiatric conditions as conventional illnesses. Also, in educational psychology, the view that learning difficulties are a specific problem *within* the child, to be 'cured' by experts

MENTAL SKILLS Cognitive strategies developed to enhance enjoyment or performance in sport

MENTAL(ISTIC) EVENTS Cognitive processes, rejected by BEHAVIOURISTS as possible targets of scientific study

META-ANALYSIS Statistical analysis of outcomes of multiple studies of the same or similar hypotheses.

METACOGNITION Extent to which or ways in which learners monitor their own learning and think about thinking and problem-solving

MICRO LEVEL Level of explanation involving individual or small groups

MICROSTRESSORS Low severity daily irritations causing stress

MIND-BODY DEBATE Debate about the nature of the existence of, and relationship between, our minds and our bodies/brains

MINIMAL GROUPS Groups formed on minimum level of purpose or reason for existence; nevertheless research shows some identity is created

MINORITY INFLUENCE Extent to which minority can influence majority in a group

MNEMONICS Cognitive 'tricks' employed to make difficult material simpler to store for future recall

MODELLING Imitation of significant others in SOCIAL LEARNING THEORY

MODERATE LEARNING DIFFICULTIES Difficulty range requiring considerable adaptation and additional support in a mainstream curriculum, *or* special school education

MOLAR LEVEL Level of explanation involving large group or society

MOLECULAR LEVEL Level of explanation involving individual or factors within the individual, such as cognitive or physiological processes

MORBIDITY The occurrence of illness, injury or disability

MORTALITY (RATE) Death (rate) usually given as the number of deaths per unit of population during a particular period of time

MOTIVATORS A set of job aspects, identified by Herzberg, which if present in a job cause job satisfaction

MOTOR PROGRAMME A set of instructions stored in memory which control a specific movement

MOTOR SKILLS Skills which require the production of movement

MULTI-CULTURAL EDUCATION A setting allowing all children to be educated through a perspective recognising the equal, positive value of all cultures

MULTI-METHOD APPROACH Research stressing the use of several methods as the problem requires; a single method does not limit the topics tackled

MULTI-DIMENSIONAL ANXIETY THEORY A theory which acknowledges that state anxiety is made up of more than a single factor

MULTIVARIATE APPROACH Approach emphasising the effect of *combinations* of factors or variables

MYOCARDIAL INFARCTION A medical condition which occurs when the heart is deprived of oxygen and other nutrients and begins to die. It occurs as a result of a blockage in a coronary artery which cuts off the flow of blood to the heart. Otherwise known as a 'heart attack'

NATIONAL VOCATIONAL QUALIFICATIONS/NVQ Not a course but a standard which UK vocational training courses must meet; can be level 1 (basic) to level 5 (advanced/professional); based on demonstration of competence, not abstract knowledge

NATURALISTIC (OBSERVATION) STUDIES Observations, or other data gathering methods, conducted in natural habitat of participants/targets of study

NATURE–NURTURE DEBATE Debate over extent to which behaviour and psychological characteristics are genetically determined or develop as a result of experience

NEGATIVE CORRELATION Relationship between data pairs in which values of one variable tend to increase as values of another decrease

NEGATIVE REINFORCEMENT Process in which a response is strengthened because its performance precedes the removal of an aversive stimulus

NEUROSIS Psychological problem associated with high levels of anxiety; not as severe as PSYCHOSES in terms of loss of cognitive control but producing seemingly irrational behaviour

NOMOTHETIC Emphasis on general laws and measures to explain and describe human behaviour and characteristics

NON-ADHERENCE See ADHERENCE

NON-DIRECTIVE THERAPY Therapy in which client works towards own solution *supported* by therapist

NORM(S) Socially agreed values of attitudes and behaviour

NORM-REFERENCED TEST STANDARDISED test permitting comparison of any child with average scores or norms for his/her age group

NORMAL DISTRIBUTION Bell-shaped distribution typically the shape produced for measures on a variable subject to many random influences, e.g. height

NORMATIVE SOCIAL INFLUENCE Occurs when people conform socially because they fear the negative consequences of appearing deviant

NULL HYPOTHESIS Assumption that real POPULATION difference or CORRELATION is zero

NUMBER AGE See LANGUAGE AGE

OBJECT PERMANENCE Recognition that when objects disappear from view they do not cease to exist

OBJECT RELATIONS Version of PSYCHOANALYTIC thought emphasising infant's early 'objects' – things, especially parents. Interest is in eventual separation from objects to which infant is attached

OBSERVATION STUDY Non-experimental study in which main data gathering procedure is through observation of participants/targets

OBSERVER AND INTERVIEWER BIAS Factors affecting objectivity of observer or interviewer such that they distort or are very selective about recording what occurs

OCCUPATIONAL PSYCHOLOGY Psychology applied to the study and changing of behaviour in work settings and of whole organisations

OFFENDER PROFILING A term coined by the FBI to describe the psychological 'sketch' built up of criminals on the basis of crime scene analysis

OPEN CONFLICT Period when differences of opinion in small groups occur and factions develop

OPEN SKILL A skill performed in an unpredictable or uncontrollable setting, e.g. football, rugby

OPERANT CONDITIONING/MODEL Model developed by Skinner which sees regular behaviour as strengthened and maintained by REINFORCEMENT processes

OPERANT/EXTINCTION THERAPY Based on the OPERANT MODEL; behaviour is strengthened with REINFORCEMENT and/or weakened by its removal

OPERATIONAL DEFINITION Definition of variable as the exact steps taken in its measurement

OPTIMUM LEVEL(S) Person's most comfortable operating state; assumes high and low extremes cause discomfort, e.g. low anxiety leads to boredom and high levels to distress; cf. HOMEOSTASIS

ORGANIC DISORDERS Psychiatric disorders with a known physical root

ORGANISATIONAL CLIMATE Perceptions held by organisational members regarding what the organisation stands for; their view of the principles which guide behaviour within, and between, the organisation and its external environment

ORGANISATIONAL CULTURE The normative set of values, beliefs and assumptions which determine how organisational members think and act within the organisation and towards outsiders

ORGANISATIONAL DEVELOPMENT The process and techniques used within organisations to help them to change and adapt to internal and external requirements

ORGANISATIONAL PSYCHOLOGY Sub-area of OCCUPATIONAL PSYCHOLOGY that focuses on the study of social relationships at work and their effects on individual behaviour and organisational outcomes

ORGANISATIONAL SOCIALISATION The process of teaching new organisational members how to relate to others within the organisation and to best fulfil their roles

ORIENTATION PERIOD The time when small groups set an agenda and raise questions in a relaxed and informal way

OUTCOME STUDIES Studies evaluating the effectiveness of therapies

OVER-JUSTIFICATION EFFECT Tendency to resist doing something once performed with no reward when it is known that the performance *could* now be rewarded, but isn't

OVERLEARNING Rehearsal beyond point where information is correctly recalled

PAIN Sensory and emotional discomfort usually associated with tissue damage

PAIN BEHAVIOURS Characteristic ways in which people behave when they experience pain

PARADIGM Prevailing agreed system of scientific thought and theory construction within which research is generally conducted

PARATELIC DOMINANCE A relatively stable predisposition to emphasise experience of the 'here and now'

PART AND WHOLE LEARNING/PART PRACTICE Breaking information or a complex skill down into simpler parts for easier learning and subsequent linking into a whole pattern

PARTICIPANT OBSERVATION Observation in which observer takes part or plays a role in the group observed

PARTICIPATION MOTIVES The reasons people give for why they are involved in sport or exercise

PARTICIPATIVE AND COLLABORATIVE RESEARCH Research in which participants are fully involved to the extent of organising their own processes of change

PATHOGENIC Used in relation to a factor or substance responsible for the development of disease

PEER TUTORING Use of learners to 'teach' or direct same or lower-level learners

PERFORMANCE GOALS Learning goals set because successful performance may look good (socially) rather than be intrinsically rewarding

PERSON SPECIFICATION Description of qualities required in prospective employees enabling them to perform job to acceptable standard

PERSON-IN-CONTEXT MODEL Lewin's (1951) formula that behaviour is a function of the person, the environment and the interaction between the two

PERSON-JOB FIT Methods by means of which one ensures a best match between a person and his or her job, e.g. through selection, training/retraining and/or job design/redesign

PERSON-SITUATION INTERACTION Theory seeing human behaviour as the result of individual characteristics, situational factors and the interaction between them

PERSONAL GROWTH Progressive positive experience and realisation of what person really wants to achieve in life

PERSONAL SPACE The area around us into which we allow others with varying degrees of discomfort

PERSONALITY SCALE Instrument to quantify personality characteristics or factors

PERSONALITY STATE Current personality orientation/likely responses

PERSONALITY TRAIT Enduring personality orientation/characteristic responses

PERSONNEL PSYCHOLOGY Sub-area of OCCUPATIONAL PSYCHOLOGY concerned with the systematic study of people and job characteristics

PERSONNEL SELECTION The process and methods used to choose from a pool of applicants the person most suited for a particular job position

PERSUASIVE ARGUMENTATION View that GROUP POLARISATION occurs because the majority group view is aired more often and therefore produces more value shift

PHENOMENOLOGICAL Philosophical view that a person's subjective experience, not any objective reality, is primary and these should be the main focus of any attempts to understand or conduct therapy with that person

PLACEBO GROUP/EFFECT Group not receiving the critical 'treatment' but everything else the EXPERIMENTAL GROUP receive; may be led to believe that their treatment will have effect; can show that change in the experimental group is due only to EXPECTANCY

PLAY THERAPY PSYCHOANALYTIC technique with children where their responses to play objects are analysed for SYMBOLIC CONTENT and are seen as clues to hidden pathological trauma and conflict

PLURALISTIC IGNORANCE Circular situation where, since no group member is saying/doing anything, other group members assume no action is appropriate

POPULATION All possible members of group from which a sample is taken

PORTAGE SYSTEM Home programme to facilitate early development of children with various difficulties where parents work with professionals

POSITION POWER The power which certain leaders have in deciding and enforcing decisions simply because they have the formal power to punish or reward particular work behaviours

POSITIVE (SELF-)REGARD Warmth given by others; (self-) regarding oneself with the kind of social warmth others might give; satisfaction in meeting own standards or CONDITIONS OF WORTH. UNCONDITIONAL PR is given on no conditions (as with parental love) whereas CONDITIONAL PR is given only when a person's behaviour conforms to certain conditions set by the giver of warmth

POWER CULTURE A culture where a leader or coalition of leaders has total control over the way an organisation is run. Organisations with a power culture can react very quickly, but not necessarily effectively, to change

PREDICTIVE VALIDITY Validation of test by its prediction of future (work) performance differences

PREDICTOR(S) A test or any measure used to assess job applicants so as to predict whether they are likely to perform successfully if they are hired

PREMACK PRINCIPLE Linking less enjoyable to more enjoyable activities in order to increase involvement in the former

PRIMACY Tendency to learn earlier items of a sequence best

PRIMARY PREVENTION Activity undertaken to prevent the emergence of health problems

PRIMARY TERRITORY Space owned by individual on a relatively permanent basis

PROACTIVE INHIBITION Interference by earlier learning on later learning

PROCEDURAL KNOWLEDGE Knowing *how* to do something where knowledge of 'rules' guiding the skill is not consciously considered during performance

PROCEDURAL MEMORY Ability to recall how to carry out a task

PROCESS CONSULTANCY Method where an 'expert' consults with organisation (e.g. school) managers in order to facilitate the managers in anticipating and solving their own institutional problems

PROFILE OF MOOD STATES (POMS) A psychological test aimed at evaluating changes in emotional responses

PROGRAMMED LEARNING Highly structured tutoring system, promoted by Skinner, in which learner receives feedback or reward on success and further instruction on error; delivered by machine; self-paced and objective; no teacher bias possible; feedback is error-free

PROJECTIVE TEST Open-ended test; person is asked to elaborate on a visual stimulus (e.g. picture); it is assumed that they will 'project' (in PSYCHOANALYTIC terms) their inner feelings onto the stimulus

PROXEMICS Relationship between people and the space surrounding them

PSYCHIATRIST Medical doctor further qualified in the treatment of psychological disorder or 'illness'

PSYCHOANALYSIS Therapy used by PSYCHOANALYTIC/DYNAMIC practitioners involving attempt to reach UNCONSCIOUS feelings and thoughts; relationship with therapist is central to process

PSYCHOANALYTIC/DYNAMIC APPROACH View that much human behaviour is the product of, or driven by, forces in our UNCONSCIOUS mind

PSYCHOMETRIC TESTS Any attempt to measure human characteristics, individual differences or 'factors' in QUANTITATIVE terms

PSYCHOSIS Psychological problem with severe distortion/loss in cognitive processes, hallucination, delusion, loss of contact with reality

PSYCHOSOMATIC MEDICINE A field of medicine which emerged in the 1930s and explored the relations between physical illness and emotion

PUBLIC TERRITORY Unowned space generally accessible to anyone

PUNISHMENT Aversive stimulus occurring after a response is performed and having the potential to reduce the strength of that response – *not* to be confused with NEGATIVE REINFORCEMENT

PYGMALION EFFECT Improved performance assumed to be caused by researcher's or teacher's expectancies

QUALITATIVE DATA Data not reducible to numerical form and/or dealt with as such

QUALITATIVE-QUANTITATIVE DEBATE Argument as to whether it is more useful or valid to treat data QUANTITATIVELY or QUALITATIVELY

QUALITY-CENTERED CULTURE Organisational culture which stresses the importance of continuous improvements in the quality of goods and/or services

QUALITY OF WORKING LIFE (QWL) Movement within OCCUPATIONAL PSYCHOLOGY which aims to evaluate and improve all the work aspects which may affect employee attitudes and their mental and physical health

QUANTITATIVE DATA Data in numerical form; frequencies or measurements

QUASI-EXPERIMENT EXPERIMENT in which experimenter does not have control over the RANDOM ALLOCATION of participants to conditions

QUESTIONNAIRE Set of questions designed to obtain information from respondent *or* measure a psychological TRAIT

RANDOM SAMPLE Sample into which every member of the target POPULATION has an equal chance of being selected

RANDOMLY ALLOCATE Allocate so that each participant has an equal chance of being in any treatment group, e.g. EXPERIMENTAL, CONTROL, PLACEBO

RATING SCALES Scale used to make some QUANTITATIVE assessment of initially QUALITATIVE data – often used in CONTENT ANALYSIS to assess written or graphical material and can be applied by people to assessment of their internal feelings or other subjective judgement of stimuli, e.g. 'beauty' or 'liking'

RATIONAL EMOTIVE THERAPY A therapeutic approach which aims to help people in understanding their irrational beliefs and behaviours and to convert them into rational ones

REACTION FORMATION DEFENCE MECHANISM; person reacts strongly *against* an object by which, it is proposed, they are UNCONSCIOUSLY attracted

READINESS Piagetian idea that child must be ready for stage change and can not be 'accelerated' through major cognitive changes

REALITY TESTING Procedure recommended by COGNITIVE THERAPISTS; client tests their perhaps distorted ideas against others' perceptions

RECENCY Tendency to learn later items of a sequence best

RECEPTIVE LANGUAGE Ability to understand (not necessarily produce) language

RECONCILIATION PERIOD The time when small groups smooth over any conflicts and affirm their satisfaction with the outcome

RECONSTRUCTIONISTS A group of educational psychologists wishing to move to a SYSTEMS APPROACH, placing less emphasis on assessment and 'treating' individual problems and more on overall prevention

RECOVERED MEMORY Alleged memory of early abuse 'recovered' from UNCONSCIOUS during therapy

REDUCED RESPONSIBILITY Explanation of GROUP POLARISATION – group members feel less responsible for risky/safe decisions since responsibility is shared

REDUCTIONISM Attempt to reduce explanations at MOLAR LEVEL to those at a more basic, elementary MICRO or MOLECULAR LEVEL

REINFORCEMENT In Skinner's (OPERANT) terms, any stimulus which strengthens a response when it follows that response

RELIABILITY Stability or consistency of test

RELIABILITY ANALYSIS Statistical testing to establish test's level of RELIABILITY

RESTRICTED LANGUAGE CODE Language form once assumed to be more likely to be used by working class; more reliant on 'local' sense and metaphor; not widely understandable; listener needs to know local context

RESTRICTION OF RANGE Limitation of CORRELATION studies where entire range of values on one variable cannot be obtained, e.g. candidates not selected for employment; students not selected into college

RETROACTIVE INHIBITION Interference by later learning on earlier learning

REVERSAL THEORY A theory aimed at explaining how people interpret changes in their motivation and arousal, in terms of switches between TELIC and PARATELIC states

RISKY SHIFT Early group polarisation view where it was thought groups always veered to a 'riskier' decision than the average group member

ROLE Position within a group, formal or informal, with attached behaviour expectations

ROLE CONFLICT See INTER-ROLE or INTRA-ROLE CONFLICT

ROLE CULTURE Organisational culture tending to be large, bureaucratic, formal and with power based on position; highly rational, logical and rigid

RORSCHACH INK BLOTS PROJECTIVE TEST in the form of abstract, symmetrical pattern

SAMPLE/SAMPLING TECHNIQUE Selection of individuals from a POPULATION/method of selecting participants

SAMPLES APPROACH The approach to PERSONNEL SELECTION which recommends that applicants be given a subset of job activities to perform during assessment, e.g. a typing test for someone applying for a secretarial position

SAMPLING BIAS Over- or under-representation of a sub-group in a SAMPLE

SANCTIONS Socially agreed 'punishment' (negative consequences) to be applied when group members transgress group norms

SCAFFOLDING Teaching approach which focuses on the area where the learner is somewhat, but not hopelessly, challenged, provides learning support adequate for progress, then withdraws ('removes scaffold') as learner gains in competence

SCHEDULES OF REINFORCEMENT The schedules used in the delivery of INTERMITTENT REINFORCEMENT

SCHEMA Set of mental instructions or rules believed by COGNITIVE PSYCHOLOGISTS to guide intelligent and purposive behaviour. May be altered and expanded through new learning experiences

SCIENTIFIC MANAGEMENT A turn-of-20th-century view that work productivity and efficiency can be improved by using systematic measurement methods and principles

SCIENTIFIC ('HYPOTHETICO-DEDUCTIVE') METHOD/MODEL

Traditional method of natural sciences used in mainstream psychology for conducting research and theory generation; subject to heated debate as to relevance for some or all areas of psychology

SCIENTIST-PRACTITIONER ROLE/MODEL Role of clinical psychologist in applying scientific psychological findings to practical problems with clients

SEASONAL AFFECTIVE DISORDER (SAD) Alteration of behaviour according to season, especially relative withdrawal in winter months

SECONDARY REINFORCEMENT Consequence of behaviour which has reinforcing strength but, unlike food, satisfies no basic drive, though it has been *associated* with such 'primary' reinforcers, e.g. token or money

SECONDARY TERRITORY Space owned less exclusively than PRIMARY TERRITORY

SEGREGATION Separate education for children with certain needs

SELECTION RATIO The number of vacant positions compared to the number of applicants. A selection ratio of 0.1 means there are ten applicants for one position

SELECTION UTILITY Measure of financial gains to an organisation as a result of performance improvements with given methods of PERSONNEL SELECTION

SELF-ACTUALISATION Maximum realisation of a good self-image, close to the IDEAL SELF and with little INCONGRUENCE

SELF-EFFICACY Level of confidence in the likelihood of achieving a goal

SELF-INSTRUCTIONAL TRAINING (SIT) Meichenbaum's methods of helping clients to control their inner speech in order to control fears and behaviour

SELF-MANAGEMENT General techniques to control one's own behaviour

SELF-MONITORING Checking one's own behaviour and progress towards goals

SELF-REGULATORY SPEECH Speech made internally and used to control one's own actions or learning and problem-solving strategies

SELF-REPORT MEASURES/STUDY Data gathering instrument with which participants assess or report on their own attributes and behaviour. Study in which this method is used

SELF-SERVING BIAS Normal tendency to ATTRIBUTE success mainly to one's own efforts and failure mainly to external circumstances; often found reversed in depressed clients

SELF-WORTH See POSITIVE SELF-REGARD

SEMANTIC MEMORY Memory for the meaning of words or other material

SEMI-STRUCTURED INTERVIEWING See UNSTRUCTURED INTERVIEWING

SENSORY MEMORY Hypothetical memory area holding purely sensory information, some of which will be processed into SHORT-TERM MEMORY, the rest lost

SERIATION Ability to understand ordering of events (sizes, weights, etc.)

SEVERE LEARNING DIFFICULTIES Difficulties associated with slow learning, the need for a modified environment, and, often, with sensory and neurological impairment. Affected children are usually not integrated into mainstream schools and are unlikely to lead an independent life

SHAPING Gradual changes in behaviour produced by systematic REINFORCEMENT of incremental steps towards final pattern

SHORT-TERM MEMORY (STM) Hypothetical memory area holding information only for several seconds before loss or processing into LONG-TERM MEMORY

SICK BUILDING SYNDROME Idea that aspects of a building itself can be responsible for unusually high employee sickness and absenteeism

SIGNIFICANCE See STATISTICAL SIGNIFICANCE

SIGNS APPROACH The approach to PERSONNEL SELECTION which recommends that future job performance can be predicted by measuring certain human characteristics such as special abilities, personality traits, etc

SINGLE BLIND Experimental procedure where participants do not know which was their treatment or condition

SITTING BY NELLIE Learning about a job by closely observing (sitting with) skilled worker

SITUATION FAVOURABILITY Effect of leader's influence, through three major factors (LEADER-MEMBER RELATIONS, leader's POSITION POWER and TASK STRUCTURE) on the performance of subordinates

SOCIAL COMPARISONS Explanation of GROUP POLARISATION – members will wish to appear to behave in accord with what is socially valued – risk or safety

SOCIAL DESIRABILITY Need to 'look good' and provide socially acceptable responses

SOCIAL FACILITATION A group of theories aimed at explaining the effect of an audience on a performer

SOCIAL LEARNING THEORY Bandura's augmentation of traditional LEARNING THEORY principles with cognitive factors of MODELLING, INTERNAL MEDIATING RESPONSES and VICARIOUS REINFORCEMENT

SOCIAL LOAFING Tendency of larger groups to produce relatively less output

SOCIAL SUPPORT The emotional and material help which an individual obtains from others

SOCIAL TRAP Effect working against attitude/behaviour change since benefits are distant and will not benefit the individual directly, whilst the change itself is uncomfortable in the near future

SOCIALISATION The social influences which impact on a person's development, e.g. parents, siblings, peers, etc.

SOCIO-EMOTIONAL CONTRIBUTIONS Individual contributions in Bales' (1953) analysis which concern the emotional or social atmosphere or interactions within the group

SOCIO-TECHNICAL SYSTEMS APPROACH (TO JOB DESIGN) Theories which stress the importance of match between an organisation's social arrangements and its technological systems

SOMATIC ANXIETY The physical signs and symptoms of anxiety, e.g. butterflies in stomach, clammy hands, etc.

SOMATIZATION One of several cognitive strategies used to help people cope with pain experience. Individual attempts to analyse, rationally and objectively, the sensations associated with pain

SPECIAL EDUCATIONAL NEEDS Needs which have to be provided for (legally, by the LEA) to enable a child to make appropriate academic progress

SPECIFIC LEARNING DIFFICULTIES Difficulty in one/several areas (e.g. literacy, numeracy) in children of average range intellectual ability

SPELLING AGE See LANGUAGE AGE

SPORT PSYCHOLOGY Psychology applied to the study and alteration of human behaviour and experience in sport and exercise

STAGE OF EXHAUSTION The third stage of the GENERAL ADAPTATION SYNDROME in which the body's reserves of energy are used up

STAGE OF RESISTANCE The second stage of the GENERAL ADAPTATION SYNDROME in which the body tries to adapt to the stressor

STANDARD ASSESSMENT TASKS (SATS) Tasks given to school children at particular educational stages in order to assess their knowledge of the (National) curriculum

STANDARDISATION/STANDARDISED TEST Adjusting test until scores on it form a NORMAL DISTRIBUTION. Calculation of population distribution norms for the test

STANDARDISED PROCEDURES Way of testing or acquiring measures from participants which is repeated in exactly the same way each time for all common parts of the method

STANFORD-BINET TEST Well-used (USA-developed) intelligence assessment test

STATE ANXIETY A transient feeling of anxiety, often in anticipation of a performance or event

STATEMENT(ING) Legal document stating a child's identified SPECIAL EDUCATIONAL NEEDS and the LEA's provision for them/making this statement

STATISTICAL SIGNIFICANCE If probability of result occurring, *if the* NULL HYPOTHESIS *is true*, is less than 0.05, it is said to be 'statistically significant'

STEREOTYPE Set of behavioural characteristics generalised to all members of a group identified on a superficial basis, e.g. sex, ethnic group

STRESS A condition which arises when a person experiences a deficit between the demands of the environment and their ability to deal with them

SUPERORDINATE GOAL Goal of value to two groups which might have the effect of reducing existing conflict between them if worked for co-operatively by all members

SUPER-EGO Freud's 'moral conscience'; area into which child internalises social values and norms of appropriate sex role behaviour

SUPERSTITIOUS BEHAVIOUR Effect of random REINFORCEMENT. Animal (or human, according to Skinner) repeats (i.e. *learns*) whatever it happened to be doing when reinforced

SUPPORT/PERSON CULTURE Organisational culture valuing the individual and putting socio-emotional support before the overall organisation and sometimes even before effectiveness

SURVEY Relatively structured questioning of (large) sample

SYMBOLIC CONTENT Can refer to content of dreams, responses to PROJECTIVE TESTS, conscious fantasies, NEUROTIC symptoms and so on; assumed by PSYCHOANALYTIC theorists to have a disguised reference to UNCONSCIOUS desires, conflicts and fantasies

SYSTEMATIC DESENSITISATION Gradual replacement of fear response to aversive object (e.g. dogs) by a relaxation response

SYSTEMS APPROACHES Approach to effective problem-solving emphasising the *whole* system and its organisational structure and communications

SYSTEMS MODEL View that individual behaviour does not occur in isolation; behaviour of people and groups is part of an interrelated process

TASK CULTURE Organisational culture valuing individual expertise and professionalism. Tends to be flexible, encourage teamwork and concentrate on getting the job done

TASK-ORIENTED CONTRIBUTIONS Individual contributions in Bales' (1953) analysis which directly concern solving the problem or completing the task at hand

TASK-ORIENTED JOB ANALYSIS Method of JOB ANALYSIS which focuses on determining the tasks that need to be accomplished as part of performing a job, their associated results and the conditions in which they are carried out

TASK STRUCTURE The extent to which the task which a group is called upon to perform has been clearly defined and its objectives have been clearly specified

TAYLORISM See SCIENTIFIC MANAGEMENT

TELIC DOMINANCE A relatively stable predisposition to emphasise planning and future goals

TERMINAL FEEDBACK Feedback available to a performer at the completion of a skilled performance

TERRITORIALITY Marking of space for individual or, more commonly in animals, for the group. Such stereotypical animal behaviour is often extrapolated, controversially, to human activities

THEMATIC APERCEPTION TEST (TAT) PROJECTIVE TEST based on non-abstract drawings

THEORY OF PLANNED BEHAVIOUR Modification of THEORY OF REASONED ACTION, including perceived control over the behaviour as an additonal predictor of the health-related behaviour. Perceived control is assumed to affect behavioural intentions and thus behaviour but, under certain conditions, may affect behaviour directly

THEORY OF REASONED ACTION Explanation of people's health-related behaviour based on the assumption that intentions are the best predictors of behaviour. Behavioural intentions are determined by the individual's attitudes to the behaviour and by subjective norms

THEORY X AND Y (McGregor, 1960) Two extreme and opposing management BELIEF SYSTEMS: X, that workers need external control and are inherently resistant; Y, that workers enjoy good work and require facilitation and encouragement to achieve most effective performance

THEORY Z Ouchi's (1981) proposal that an optimum management system might fuse the best aspects of western (USA) and far-eastern (Japan) management styles

TIME AND MOTION STUDIES Procedures used in SCIENTIFIC MANAGEMENT by F. W. Taylor to break jobs down into smaller tasks and to study the movement involved in performing each task so as to determine the one best way of doing a job

TIME OUT REINFORCEMENT loss by removing child from reinforcing situation

TOKEN ECONOMIES Systematic programme in institution in which clients are given tokens as REINFORCEMENTS for pre-arranged behaviours; tokens can later be exchanged for desired goods

TOP-DOWN PROCESSES Hypothetical cognitive processes; environmental objects are recognised in perception because we already hold an overall expectation of what is being perceived – see BOTTOM-UP

TOTAL COMMUNICATION APPROACHES System of communication combining aural, signing and gestural methods

TRAINING NEEDS ANALYSIS Procedures/methods used to determine the nature and the extent of training needed within an organisation and who needs it

TRAIT ANXIETY A relatively permanent personal characteristic where a person tends to perceive situations as threatening

TRAIT APPROACH View that behaviour differences are largely the product of differences in enduring personality characteristics

TRANSACTIONAL LEADERSHIP A leadership style in which good/desirable work performance is rewarded and changes are only introduced if goals are not being met

TRANSFER OF LEARNING/TRAINING Effect on task performance as a result of practice or performance of another task, e.g. playing badminton and playing tennis. Transfer of skills and abilities from training to real (or altered) work situation

TRANSFERENCE In PSYCHOANALYSIS, client's transfer of emotion to therapist who represents important other(s) in client's life history

TRANSFORMATIONAL LEADERSHIP Leadership style which respects individual autonomy and encourages initiative once the mission, goals and objectives have been clearly specified and communicated by the leader

TRANSITIVITY Logical inference such as A>B, B>C, therefore A>C

TRIAD OF DEPRESSION Beck's view that depressed people saw as hopeless their personal self, their position in the world and their future

TYPE 'A' BEHAVIOUR Behaviour pattern characterised by high levels of competitiveness, anger or hostility, and time urgency. Such people are considered to be at risk of heart disease

TYPE 'B' BEHAVIOUR Behaviour pattern characterised by lack of Type 'A' behaviours

UNCONDITIONAL POSITIVE REGARD See POSITIVE REGARD

UNCONDITIONAL RESPONSE (UCR) In Pavlovian (CLASSICAL) CONDITIONING the response which initially is triggered by a natural or UNCONDITIONED STIMULUS; it will eventually be triggered by the CS and will become a CR

UNCONDITIONAL STIMULUS (UCS) In Pavlovian (CLASSICAL) CONDITIONING the 'natural' stimulus which initially triggers a response; an originally neutral stimulus is paired with this to eventually trigger the UCR (now a CR) on its own

UNCONSCIOUS Area of mind assumed by Freud to contain conflicts and traumatic thoughts irretrievable except through analysis

UNIVARIATE APPROACH Research strategy studying the effect of just one INDEPENDENT VARIABLE on one DEPENDENT VARIABLE

UNSTRUCTURED/ SEMI-STRUCTURED INTERVIEWING Interview method where question and answer are free-ranging or at least only loosely tied to a predetermined pattern

UPLIFTS Everyday, desirable or pleasant events which may help to reduce the adverse effects of HASSLES on health

UTILITY Overall financial gain to organisation occurring through use of selection tests

VALIDITY Measure of extent to which test measures what was intended

VALIDITY GENERALISATION The extent to which a PREDICTOR, developed in a specific job and/or context, can effectively predict work performance in a different job or context

VERBAL PROTOCOLS Recording of talk of participant who has been asked to talk or think aloud through a problem or regular routine

VICARIOUS LEARNING/ REINFORCEMENT Learning to perform or inhibit an action by observing the consequences (REINFORCEMENTS) to another of performing that action.

VICTIM DEROGATION The tendency for victims to be blamed in order to confirm a BELIEF IN A JUST WORLD

VITAMIN MODEL Warr's (1987) model suggesting stress can act like vitamins with CUMULATIVE EFFECT (stress-reducing effects are unharmful in great amounts) and ADDITIONAL DECREMENT – *some* stress is required but it can be too much

VROOM-YETTON DECISION MODEL A model of decision-making developed to help leaders to choose from five decision-making styles the one which best suits the characteristics of the problem at hand

WARMTH POSITIVE REGARD – positive human emotion towards others; form of non-sexual love; one of the therapist qualities thought necessary by Rogers for effective NON-DIRECTIVE THERAPY

WEAPON FOCUS The tendency for witnesses to focus on weapons, thereby impairing their recall of other details

WHOLE LEARNING/PRACTICE Practice which involves the learner rehearsing complete information or skill

WHOLE SCHOOL APPROACH Unified, systematic programme (e.g. for truancy reduction) involving all members of (teaching and non-teaching) staff

WORD ATTACK SKILL Ability to break down words into component letter sounds

WORD READING AGE See LANGUAGE AGE

WORK ATTITUDES The emotions, beliefs and cognitions that workers hold about their work and their employing organisation; satisfaction, motivation and organisational commitment are examples of work attitudes

WORK PSYCHOLOGY Alternative term for OCCUPATIONAL PSYCHOLOGY focusing on work behaviour, personnel matters and job design rather than the larger-scale focus of ORGANISATIONAL PSYCHOLOGY

WORK SATISFACTION Refers to the feeling of happiness and pleasure that a person may experience as a result of doing some work s/he perceives as having a number of positive and worthwhile aspects

WORKER-ORIENTED JOB ANALYSIS The methods of JOB ANALYSIS which focus on the human behaviours involved in performing the set of tasks which make up a job

WORKING ALLIANCE Strength of client-therapist relationship in BRIEF PSYCHODYNAMIC PSYCHOTHERAPY

WORKING MEMORY Version of SHORT-TERM MEMORY theory where working memory is the information we are currently aware of directly, as in the latest result or number carried whilst doing mental arithmetic

YERKES-DODSON (INVERTED-U) LAW The finding that moderate stress levels impair performance less than high or low levels, i.e. there is a curvilinear relationship between arousal and performance on complex tasks. Highest levels of performance (e.g. in sport) are linked with moderate levels of arousal

ZEITGEIST 'Spirit of the age'; influence of prevailing attitudes, values and norms on the development of theory and practice

ZONE OF PROXIMAL DEVELOPMENT Area where learner can solve problems only with help and is hence particularly ready for further development

INDEX

PICTURE CREDITS

The authors and publishers would like to thank the following for permission to use photographic material:

p. 27, Kurgan-Linset/© 1991 Visages/Colorific!; pp. 32, 53 (bottom), 62, 101, 151 (bottom), 241, Associated Press/Topham Picturepoint; p. 41, © 1995 Comstock, Inc.; p. 46, © L. Oligny/Editing/Impact; p. 53 (top), © Laurie Sparham/Network; pp. 18, 66, 69, 229, 231, 269, Topham Picturepoint; p. 73, © 1995 Todd Bigelow/Black Star/Colorific!; pp. 89, 173, Sally & Richard Greenhill; p. 104, Hulton Deutsch; pp. 111, 121, 147 (both), 151 (top), 184, 193, 195, 204, 220, Telegraph Colour Library; p. 117, © Adam Hinton/Impact; p. 123, © Peter Arkell/Impact; pp. 139, 286, Press Association/Topham Picturepoint; p. 149, © Bill Green/Impact; pp. 177, 236, Steve Benbow/Colorific!; p. 281, © Alexis Wallerstein/Impact.

We would also like to thank the following for their permission to reproduce material for which they hold copyright.

Academic Press for Fig 7.3 (p. 221) from Patrick, J. (1992) *Training: Research and Practice*; **Addison-Wesley** for Fig 7.4 (p. 225) from Hackman and Oldman (1980) *Work Redesign* © 1980 Addison-Wesley Publishing Co Inc; **Dr Irwin Altman** for Fig 5.3 (p. 153); **The American Psychological Association** for extract (pp. 76–78) from *Journal of Personality and Social Psychology* (1986), 51, 248–258, © 1986 American Psychological Association; **Human Kinetics Publishers** for Fig 8.2 (p. 264) reprinted by permission of W. P. Morgan (1985) 'Selected Psychological Factors Limiting Performance: A Mental Health Model' in *The Limits of Human Performance: the Academy Papers, no. 18*, edited by The American Academy of Physical Education (Champaign, ILL: Human Kinetics Publishers), 76 and for Fig 8.5 (p. 269) from *Sport Competition Anxiety Test* (p. 8) by Rainer Martens, © 1977 Rainer Martens; **Lawrence Erlbaum Associates Inc Publishers** for Fig 8.4 (p. 267) from Harter, S. (1981) 'A model of intrinsic mastery motivation in children', from Collins, W. A. (ed) *Minnesota Symposium on Child Psychology*, vol 14, 215–255; **The National Coaching Foundation** and **Professor Lew Hardy** for Fig 8.6 (p. 271) from Hardy, L. and Fazey, J. F. (1988) 'The Inverted-U Hypothesis: a catastrophe for sport psychology?' *Monograph*, no. 1, Leeds: British Association for Sport and Exercise Science; **Routledge** for the Greenberg extract (p. 47) from Scott, J. et al (ed.) *Cognitive Therapy in Clinical Practice*; **Sport Dynamics** for Fig 8.7 (p. 273) after Martenuik (1975), in Sharp, B. (1992) *Acquiring Skill in Sport*, Sports Dynamics: Eastbourne. **Tavistock Publications** for Fig 3.1 (p. 58) from Prins, H. (1982) *Criminal Behaviour*; **Williams & Wilkins** © for Fig 8.10 (p. 282) after Sallis and Howell (1990) in Pandolf, B. and Holloszy, J. O. (eds.) *Exercise and Sport Science Reviews*, vol 18, pp. 307–330; **John Wiley & Sons Inc** for Figs 4.1 and 4.2 (p. 96) from Gutkin and Curtis (1982) 'School-based consultation: theory and techniques', in Reynolds and Gutkin (eds.) *The Handbook of School Psychology*.

The publishers have made every endeavour to contact copyright holders for the materials included in this book. If anything has been omitted, we will be glad to make the necessary arrangements at the earliest opportunity.